Get a FREE eBook

To register this book, scan the code or go to
www.manning.com/freebook/kochakadan

By registering you get

- **FREE eBook copy**
  download in PDF and ePub

- **FREE online access**
  to Manning's liveBook platform

- **FREE audio**
  read and listen online in liveBook

- **FREE AI Assistant**
  it knows the book and what you are reading when it answers

- **FREE in-book testing**
  fun tests to lock in your knowledge

In Manning's liveBook platform you can share discussions and comments with other
readers, add your own bookmarks and highlights, insert personal notes anywhere
on the page, see color versions of all the book's graphics, download source code and
other resources, and more!
To register, scan the code or go to www.manning.com/freebook/kochakadan

Build Python Web Apps with Streamlit

AI AND DATA APPLICATIONS IN MINUTES

ANEEV D. KOCHAKADAN

FOREWORD BY ADRIEN TREUILLE

MANNING

SHELTER ISLAND

For online information and ordering of this and other Manning books, please visit www.manning.com. The publisher offers discounts on this book when ordered in quantity.

For more information, please contact

> Special Sales Department
> Manning Publications Co.
> 20 Baldwin Road
> PO Box 761
> Shelter Island, NY 11964
> Email: orders@manning.com

 Recognizing the importance of preserving what has been written, it is Manning's policy to have the books we publish printed on acid-free paper, and we exert our best efforts to that end. Recognizing also our responsibility to conserve the resources of our planet, Manning books are printed on paper that is at least 15 percent recycled and processed without the use of elemental chlorine.

The author and publisher have made every effort to ensure that the information in this book was correct at press time. The author and publisher do not assume and hereby disclaim any liability to any party for any loss, damage, or disruption caused by errors or omissions, whether such errors or omissions result from negligence, accident, or any other cause, or from any usage of the information herein.

Manning Publications Co.	Development editor:	Rebecca Johnson
20 Baldwin Road	Technical editor:	Jill Cates
PO Box 761	Review editor:	Angelina Lazukić
Shelter Island, NY 11964	Production editor:	Aleksandar Dragosavljević
	Proofreader:	Olga Milanko
	Technical proofreader:	Ninoslav Cerkez
	Typesetter:	Tamara Švelić Sabljić
	Cover designer:	Marija Tudor

ISBN 9781633436015
Printed in the United States of America

For my parents, Davis K. K. and Pushpa Davis—
this is built on your foundation

brief contents

contents

10 RAG and agentic apps with LangGraph and Streamlit 313

foreword

In the beginner's mind, there are many possibilities, but in the expert's mind, there are few.

—Shunryu Suzuki

This Zen insight captures the profound value of learning from a true master. For those seeking to deeply understand Streamlit, Aneev Kochakadan is precisely such a guide.

Learning any web framework can feel daunting. Yet Streamlit has exploded as the go-to tool for data science and machine learning apps—from nimble startups to OpenAI, Anthropic, and Fortune 50 giants. It bridges Python's AI dominance with the web's visual power, enabling everything from data dashboards to LLM-driven experiences.

Streamlit's magic: radical simplicity without sacrificing depth. Its concise API transforms complex data into interactive web apps in minutes. Yet beneath this elegance lies profound richness—even experienced developers become perpetual students of its possibilities.

In *Build Python Web Apps with Streamlit*, Aneev captures this duality perfectly. Like a Zen master offering direct transmission, he shares a deep understanding of Streamlit's strengths, quirks, and hidden powers. Through meticulous examples—from foundational apps to sophisticated LLM tools—he teaches not just mechanics but mindful creation: defining requirements, debugging subtle errors, and delivering intuitive experiences.

Above all, *Build Python Web Apps with Streamlit* embodies joyful creation, transforming hesitant tinkerers into confident builders eager to share their work with the world.

xv

Streamlit becomes enlightenment's vehicle—complex ideas made clear and compelling. Under Aneev's guidance, your journey promises clarity, direct realization, and the satisfaction of mastering a truly Zen-like tool.

—Adrien Treuille,
CO-CREATOR OF STREAMLIT

My first encounter with Streamlit occurred when I was building an internal web app at Stripe, using React and TypeScript to analyze the profitability of deals we were striking with customers—something I had cheerfully assumed would be quick and straightforward. As it turned out, "straightforward" was relative, and "quick" was outright fiction.

After a few weeks spent wrestling with React components, centering divs, and trying to get my app's frontend and backend to talk to each other, I was in a meeting with a coworker who casually suggested, "Couldn't we have built this in Streamlit?" At the time, I thought, "Great, another JavaScript framework—precisely what the world needs."

But the remark lingered. Eventually, curiosity took hold, and I began to investigate Streamlit more closely. To my surprise, it wasn't a JavaScript framework at all—it was Python, my favorite language because it seldom makes me question my life choices.

Conveniently, at the time, I'd been mentally drafting an idea for a personal app: a simple calculator to compare rental property investments. I'd been procrastinating on this for months but figured it would be a good way to tell whether the hype around Streamlit was justified. Indeed, I had a basic functional prototype of the calculator up and running in a little over half an hour—and none of it was spent centering anything!

Since then, Streamlit has become my go-to solution for building stuff quickly. Whether visualizing data, performing calculations, or creating something more advanced, Streamlit keeps it intuitive, fast, and delightfully free of CSS frustrations.

I believe Streamlit is here for the long haul, empowering anyone familiar with Python to develop polished web apps with little effort. So, dive in, explore freely, and don't be surprised if you suddenly find yourself awake at night, eagerly imagining your next Streamlit project—that's how I'll know I've done my job.

acknowledgments

If a fortune teller had foretold a few years ago that I'd embark on the journey of writing my first book a *month* after becoming a parent for the first time, I would have taken it as further justification for my general mistrust of fortune tellers. Yet here we are.

The timing in my personal life for writing this book wasn't ideal. It came with considerable sacrifices—most significantly from my wife, Alma, whose unwavering support, patience, and love provided the anchor I desperately needed. You have been a rock, gracefully handling the extra burdens my writing placed on you, even as we navigated the joys and challenges of early parenthood.

To my son, Aidan—thank you for filling my days with delight and reminding me daily of the joy that exists in life's simplest moments.

I am eternally grateful to my parents, Davis K. K. and Pushpa Davis, for laying the foundation on which my life, education, and career have flourished. Your relentless encouragement, generosity (buying me my first, second, third, and fourth computers!), and invaluable support with childcare have made this book possible.

To my parents-in-law, Molly Paul and Paul George, thank you for always being there to lend support and comfort, particularly in helping care for our little one during this busy season of life, and lending me precious time to write.

To my sister, Veena, thank you for being my original inspiration to venture into computer science. Your influence set the stage for the journey that brought me here. To my nephew, Dhruvin, whose curiosity and enthusiasm gave me a vital burst of motivation— thank you for genuinely wanting to read this book. You made this feel real. Several others from my family provided invaluable moral support throughout this process, including Basil George, Annu Basil, and Prashant Pai, among many others who cheered me on along the way.

At work, colleagues such as Simon Li, Andrew Kirk, and Sunny Kanugo, and a multitude of others, have inspired me with their own apps that they've built on Streamlit. I'd also like to thank my managers and mentors, past and present—Amon Khajekar, Steve Wasik, Akansha Singh, Rahul Jindal, Alok Ramgarhia, and Michael Raheem—whose guidance and encouragement have shaped me into the person, engineer, and writer that I am today, capable of confidently undertaking a project like this. Special thanks as well to Sagnika Halder and Nick Rosener, friends and former colleagues whose moral support, kindness, and camaraderie helped carry me across the finish line.

A special thank you to the incredible team at Manning: Rhonda Mason, my first editor, whose meticulousness shaped the early chapters; Rebecca Johnson, who expertly guided the later chapters to completion; Jill Cates, a senior data engineer at Shopify, who worked as a technical editor on the book; Ninoslav Cerkez, the technical proofer; Jonathan Gennick, the acquisitions editor whose belief set everything in motion; and all the reviewers and MEAP readers whose feedback was invaluable: Alejandro Cuevas Rivero, Aneesh Kochuparambil Sajan, Astha Puri, Benjamin Lis, Gaurav Tendolkar, Dirk Gomez, Prashanth Devireddy, Anshuman Guha, John Williams, Jim Whitfield, Josh McAdams, Jonathan Sharley, Marvin Schwarze, Vamshidhar Morusu, Ankit Virmani, Owen Morris, Pankaj Verma, Felipe Coutinho, Rahul Shirale, Rebecca Jones, Sashank Dara, Shreyam Dutta Gupta, Sofia Shvets, Sunaina Premkumar, Karun Thankachan, Tony Dunsworth, Tony Holdroyd, Venkata Reddy, and Walter Alexander Mata López. Your collective efforts transformed a vision into reality.

Finally, I extend my thanks to you, the reader, for taking this journey with me. I hope you find in this book the joy and utility of Streamlit that first drew me in.

Build Python Web Apps with Streamlit is designed to teach you to build web applications quickly and effectively in pure Python using the Streamlit library, guiding you step by step through your Streamlit journey. You'll start by mastering the foundational concepts needed to create and deploy simple, interactive apps quickly. Next, you'll dive deeper into more advanced techniques, developing dynamic, data-rich dashboards and robust applications. In the third part of the book, you'll integrate Streamlit with cutting-edge AI by building interactive apps powered by large language models (LLMs). Finally, you'll ensure that your apps are reliable and production-ready through comprehensive testing practices and professional deployment.

Who should read this book

Build Python Web Apps with Streamlit is perfect for technical and semi-technical professionals who want to quickly turn their ideas into interactive web applications and dashboards. It is particularly well-suited to

- Data scientists and analysts who need interactivity beyond traditional notebooks and business intelligence dashboards
- Anyone tasked with rapidly building internal tools for their company
- Software engineers seeking quick prototyping capabilities
- Semi-technical professionals (such as product managers, program managers, and operations analysts) who know Python and prefer building functional apps without engineering support
- Python developers interested in swiftly turning LLM-related concepts into fully operational applications

How this book is organized: A roadmap

The book contains four parts spread across 12 chapters. Part 1 focuses on quickly establishing foundational Streamlit skills:

- Chapter 1 explores Streamlit's role within the broader ecosystem of web tools.
- Chapter 2 guides you through setting up your environment and running your first Streamlit app.
- Chapter 3 demonstrates turning an idea into a structured, clean interface, exploring some of the most-used Streamlit widgets.
- Chapter 4 covers essential concepts of Streamlit, including its execution model and state management.
- Chapter 5 teaches deployment strategies, connecting external services, and managing secrets.

Part 2 shows you how to build apps suitable for complex, real-world problems:

- In chapter 6, you develop an executive-level dashboard with data loading, transformation, and visualization.
- Chapter 7 walks through enhancing the dashboard with interactive features such as drilldowns and filters.
- Chapter 8 shows how to construct a CRUD application complete with authentication and persistent storage.

In part 3, you'll learn to integrate Streamlit with LLMs:

- In chapter 9, you create Fact Frenzy, an AI-powered trivia game with dynamic interactions.
- In chapter 10, you build Nibby, an advanced chatbot using LangGraph, retrieval-augmented generation (RAG), and the ReAct agentic model for sophisticated, actionable conversations.

Part 4 focuses on robust testing and professional deployment practices:

- Chapter 11 covers implementing testing with pytest, validating frontend interactions, and ensuring app reliability.
- Chapter 12 explains deploying Streamlit apps to AWS, packaging them with Docker, and securing them with HTTPS and custom domains.

About the code

This book contains many examples of source code, both in numbered listings and in line with normal text. In both cases, source code is formatted in a `fixed-width font` `like this` to separate it from ordinary text. Sometimes code is also **in bold** to highlight code that has changed from previous steps in the chapter, such as when a new feature adds to an existing line of code.

In many cases, the original source code has been reformatted; we've added line breaks and reworked indentation to accommodate the available page space in the book. In rare cases, even this was not enough, and listings include line-continuation markers ( ). Additionally, comments in the source code have often been removed from the listings when the code is described in the text. Code annotations accompany many of the listings, highlighting important concepts.

You can get executable snippets of code from the liveBook (online) version of this book at https://livebook.manning.com/book/build-python-web-apps-with-streamlit. The complete code for the examples in the book is available for download from the Manning website at https://www.manning.com/books/build-python-web-apps-with -streamlit, and from GitHub at https://github.com/aneevdavis/streamlit-in-action.

The repository is organized into chapters, with each chapter containing the following:

- A final subfolder with the completed app for reference
- One or more in_progress_* subfolders to help you incrementally build the app as you follow along

Each chapter's folder includes a requirements.txt file. You can easily install all necessary dependencies for each chapter by downloading this file and running the following command:

```
pip install -r requirements.txt
```

This structure helps you follow along step by step, ensuring that you gain practical experience as you build the apps.

If you find that any of the code examples in the book aren't working, double-check the versions of all the Python libraries used against the requirements.txt file for that chapter.

liveBook discussion forum

Purchase of *Build Python Web Apps with Streamlit* includes free access to liveBook, Manning's online reading platform. Using liveBook's exclusive discussion features, you can attach comments to the book globally or to specific sections or paragraphs. It's a snap to make notes for yourself, ask and answer technical questions, and receive help from the author and other users. To access the forum, go to https://livebook.manning .com/book/build-python-web-apps-with-streamlit/discussion. You can also learn more about Manning's forums and the rules of conduct at https://livebook.manning.com/ discussion.

Manning's commitment to our readers is to provide a venue where a meaningful dialogue between individual readers and between readers and the author can take place. It is not a commitment to any specific amount of participation on the part of the author, whose contribution to the forum remains voluntary (and unpaid). We suggest you try asking the author some challenging questions lest his interest stray! The forum and the archives of previous discussions will be accessible from the publisher's website as long as the book is in print.

about the author

ANEEV KOCHAKADAN is a software engineer who is passionate about creating exceptional user experiences and empowering businesses to use their data effectively. With a diverse background spanning the entire data value chain—from designing online transactional services and developing data pipelines to business intelligence and data interpretation—Aneev has refined his expertise at industry leaders including Google, Stripe, and OpenAI.

In his leisure time, Aneev enjoys solving crossword puzzles, exploring cutting-edge technologies, reading fantasy and science fiction novels, and indulging in desserts from around the globe. Connect with him on LinkedIn: https://www.linkedin.com/in/aneevdavis.

about the cover illustration

The figure on the cover of *Build Python Web Apps with Streamlit*, titled "Le Viveur," or "Man about town," is taken from a book by Louis Curmer published in 1841. Each illustration is finely drawn and colored by hand.

In those days, it was easy to identify where people lived and what their trade or station in life was just by their dress. Manning celebrates the inventiveness and initiative of the computer business with book covers based on the rich diversity of regional culture centuries ago, brought back to life by pictures from collections such as this one.

## Part 1

Hitting the ground running

I

f you've ever wanted to build a web app but felt overwhelmed by the prospect of learning frontend development from scratch, Streamlit offers a refreshing alternative.

This part is about speed: building your Streamlit skills as quickly as possible. Even if you stop reading at the end of this part, you'll be able to build and deploy real Streamlit apps with confidence.

We begin in chapter 1 with a lay of the land—what Streamlit is, what it isn't, and where it fits in the ecosystem of web tools. Chapter 2 walks you through setting up your environment and running your first app. Chapter 3 shows you how to take an idea from concept to interface and turn it into clean, organized code. In chapter 4, you'll tackle some of Streamlit's most critical concepts: its execution model and how state works. Finally, chapter 5 teaches you how to deploy your apps for free, connect to external services, and manage secrets like a pro.

Introduction to Streamlit

This chapter covers

- What you need to build web apps and where Streamlit fits in
- How Streamlit's ease-of-use, LLM-friendliness, and other factors make it popular
- What makes Streamlit different from other similar technologies
- What you can (and can't) build with Streamlit

Welcome to the world of Streamlit! By picking up this book, you've joined the ranks of thousands of developers who have discovered Streamlit in recent years. These developers appreciate what Streamlit enables: web apps built entirely in Python, in just minutes!

Consider why you chose this book. Maybe you have an idea for an app that will save your coworkers hours of repetitive, automatable work, and you want the fastest way to turn it into reality. Perhaps you're aiming for a tech job and want to add front-end development to your skill set. Maybe you're a data analyst or scientist who needs to present findings in interactive dashboards for management. Or you're a software engineer looking for a quick way to prototype apps. You might have heard about the buzz about Streamlit and AI and want to learn more.

Whatever your motivation, this book will guide you step-by-step through creating powerful, interactive web applications. You'll learn to use Python's simplicity to build and deploy apps that can impress your audience, solve real problems, and advance your career.

You'll learn Streamlit by building real-world projects that gradually increase in complexity. Early projects include a password strength checker and a unit converter app to teach the basics. Later, you'll build more advanced apps like a dynamic to-do list, an interactive metrics dashboard, and even an AI-powered trivia game and a customer support agent. Each project covers essential skills such as handling user input, managing app state, calling APIs, and working with LLMs. By the end, you'll have a versatile portfolio of apps you can showcase or extend, all built quickly.

Each chapter will deepen your understanding of Streamlit's capabilities and teach you the overall process of app development, including UI design and code organization for maintainability. Whether you're an experienced developer or a beginner, this book will be valuable.

Eager to dive in? Let's begin with the basics.

NOTE The GitHub repository for this book is https://github.com/aneevdavis/ streamlit-in-action. Code snippets from this chapter are in the chapter_01 folder.

1.1 Building web apps

Streamlit lets you build graphical web apps. Unlike command-line programs, which require users to type text into a terminal, graphical apps let users click, scroll, and interact with a visual interface. These are much more approachable, especially for non-technical users.

Web apps are graphical applications that run in a browser. You've used hundreds: Gmail, Netflix, Google Docs. Unlike desktop or mobile apps, web apps don't require installation or updates—they simply work on any device with a browser. This makes them ideal for sharing.

Suppose you've built a script that saves hours of manual work. If your teammates have to run it from a terminal, most won't bother. Wrap it in a web app, and it becomes much more usable.

1.1.1 What do you need to build a web app?

Generally speaking (and simplifying somewhat), a web app has two main parts:

- The backend, where your app's logic lives (e.g., crunching numbers, querying databases)
- The frontend, which contains the on-screen elements that users interact with, such as buttons, text boxes, and menus.

You can write your backend logic in Python (which this book assumes you're familiar with). But writing the frontend means focusing on the user experience, where there are fewer "right" answers. It has traditionally required learning a completely different skill set. Picking up these new tools often takes at least as much effort as learning Python in the first place.

This challenge has stymied many busy Python developers who lack the time to acquire an entirely new skill set, preventing them from building full-fledged web apps. Fortunately, there's a solution: Streamlit.

1.2 *What is Streamlit?*

Streamlit is a pure-Python frontend development framework for quickly creating web apps called *Streamlit apps*. Traditionally, Python developers either run scripts from the command line or write non-Python code to build web interfaces. Streamlit changes this by letting you build web-based UIs entirely in Python, combining frontend and backend code. I often describe Streamlit apps to newcomers as "Python scripts where you can click buttons and stuff."

Launched in 2019 with a focus on data visualization, Streamlit has rapidly grown in popularity. Its simple syntax, utility in data science, and support for building LLM-based chatbots have fueled its adoption. In 2022, Snowflake Inc. acquired it for $800 million.

Figure 1.1 shows a Google Trends chart illustrating Streamlit's growth.

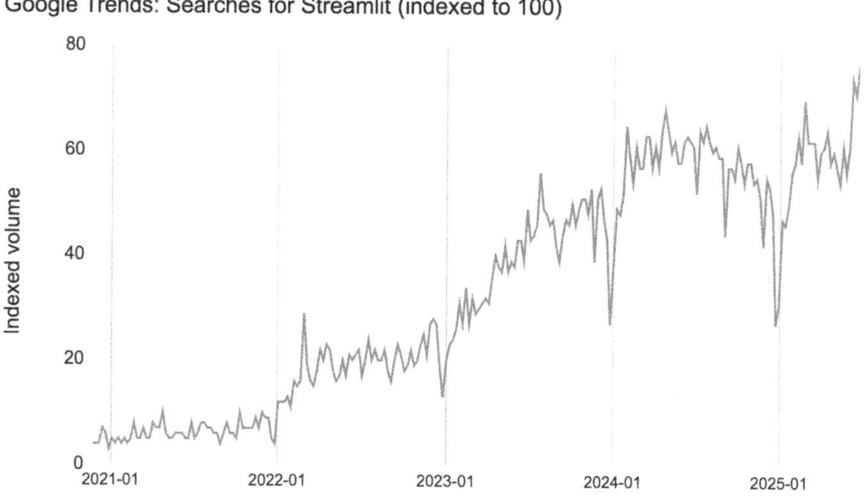

Figure 1.1 A Google Trends chart showing the popularity of Streamlit over time. (Note: the periodic dips near the end of each year correspond to the week between Christmas and New Year's Day, when relatively few people are working.)

1.3   *Ten reasons Streamlit is so popular*

As figure 1.1 shows, Streamlit has seen a steady rise in popularity, especially since 2022. In addition to its vibrant community of individual users, companies like Netflix, Airbnb, Stripe, OpenAI, and Square use Streamlit internally. Streamlit's widespread adoption stems from many factors, chief among them its pure-Python nature and ease of use for data science and AI applications.

1.3.1   *Streamlit is pure Python*

Any code you write with Streamlit is Python. Traditionally, creating a web-based interface has required developers to write HTML, CSS, and JavaScript—the three core web languages. HyperText Markup Language (HTML) is used for page structure, Cascading Style Sheets (CSS) for appearance and layout, and JavaScript adds functionality.

These languages (especially CSS and JavaScript) can be hard to master if you want to build anything complex. Some frameworks built on top of them help, but they often have their own learning curves. In any case, you need to know HTML, CSS, and JavaScript to use them effectively.

Python is popular among data scientists, hobbyists, and even semi-technical professionals because of its rich ecosystem of libraries for data wrangling and analysis (and because it's fun). These groups, illustrated in figure 1.2, may not know the three web languages, or may have only a passing knowledge of them—usually not enough to create complex applications.

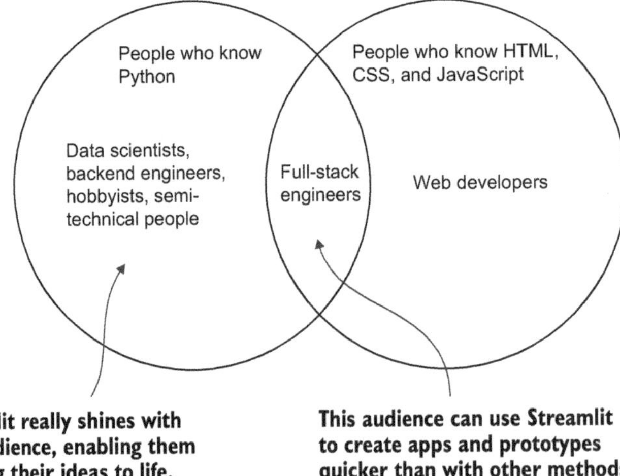

Figure 1.2 Streamlit unlocks web app development for anyone who knows Python and helps even full-stack developers prototype and build faster.

Streamlit is a boon for these users because it removes a major barrier: it lets them create rich web applications without first investing time in learning another stack of languages.

1.3.2 Streamlit lets you go from idea to app in minutes

When you start using Streamlit, you'll be impressed by how quickly you can create a working application. Because of its intuitiveness and sensible defaults (meaning you don't have to customize or configure everything), you can develop Streamlit apps quickly. The time from idea to a fully working app is often measured in minutes, not hours or days.

1.3.3 Streamlit makes beautiful apps

Even if you know some web-based languages, *knowing* them is very different from being skilled at *using* them to create attractive web pages. In Streamlit, your apps look good by default. The elements Streamlit provides (individual parts of an app, such as buttons, checkboxes, or tabs) are pre-designed to look appealing. All you have to do is put them together.

Anyone who has tried to style a webpage by hand with CSS knows how frustrating it can be to get the spacing or effects just right. Even if you manage to implement your vision, you still can't guarantee it will look good because UI design is as much art as science. Streamlit doesn't necessarily solve all those problems, but it *does* make it hard to create something that *doesn't* look nice.

1.3.4 Streamlit lets you focus on your app, not UI details

Using pre-designed elements to build apps has another advantage: it frees you to focus on what you know best—your app's logic. Streamlit intentionally limits your UI choices by making many decisions for you.

For example, consider the snippet of code shown in listing 1.1 (chapter_01/tabs_example.py in the GitHub repo).

Listing 1.1 Using tabs in Streamlit

```python
import streamlit as st

tab1, tab2, tab3 = st.tabs(["Mission", "About us", "Careers"])
with tab1:
    st.header("Our Mission")
    st.write("Our mission is to teach people to make web apps in Python.")

with tab2:
    st.header("About Us")
    st.write("We are a group of Python enthusiasts.")

with tab3:
    st.header("Careers")
    st.write("We are hiring! Apply today!")
```

NOTE The code listings in this chapter give you a sense of what Streamlit code looks like and what it can do before we dive in. If you'd like to run these examples, see the appendix for installation instructions, and section 2.4 for how to run the code. (You can't run python `<filename.py>` as you would with regular Python scripts.)

Listing 1.1 produces the tabbed page shown in figure 1.3.

About Us

Figure 1.3   **Tabs in Streamlit, illustrating how Streamlit makes UI choices for you**

Notice the line beneath the active tab and the highlight on the tab you're hovering over. You can't see it in a screenshot, but the transition between tabs includes a small animation where the orange line moves under the new tab.

The following line produces the tab bar:

```
tab1, tab2, tab3 = st.tabs(["Mission", "About us", "Careers"])
```

Notice that this line doesn't mention styling. We just said tabs, and Streamlit handled the details. Streamlit recognizes that most developers don't want to design UI-related minutiae and would rather focus on business logic.

As a consequence of this approach, Streamlit app developers are highly productive and can create sensible interfaces that complement, rather than detract from, the app's functionality. You face a trade-off between hassle-free UI development and fine-grained control. Streamlit is ideal if you value the former, not the latter. If you want detailed control of your interface, Streamlit may not be the right tool.

For example, as of this writing, if you want to put a shaded box around the current tab instead of a line underneath, you can't do that easily unless you know HTML and CSS.

1.3.5   *Streamlit's syntax is simple, concise, and intuitive*

Like Python itself, Streamlit code is self-documenting and often obvious. For example, suppose you want to simulate rolling a die and plot the results. Listing 1.2 shows a short snippet that does this (chapter_01/line_chart.py in the GitHub repo).

Listing 1.2   **A die roll simulator in Streamlit**

```
import streamlit as st
import random

st.title("Die Roll Simulator")
num_rolls = st.slider('Number of die rolls', min_value=10, max_value=100)
if st.button('Plot Graph'):
```

```python
die_rolls = [random.randint(1, 6) for _ in range(num_rolls)]
st.line_chart(data=die_rolls)
```

Figure 1.4 shows the output.

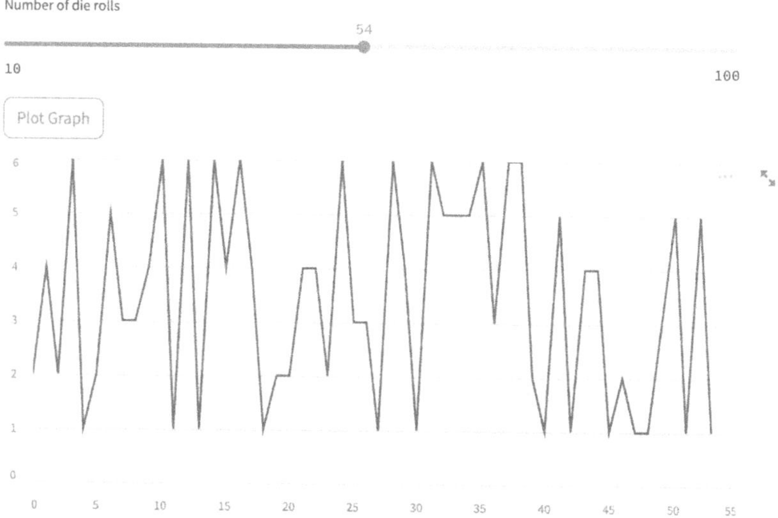

Figure 1.4　Output of a die roll simulator in Streamlit

You can understand the code in listing 1.2 even if you've never seen a single line of Streamlit code before. The app shows a title. It displays a slider so the user can pick the number of die rolls to plot (between 10 and 100). It also shows a Plot Graph button. When the user clicks it, we generate the die rolls (random numbers between 1 and 6) and plot them in a line chart.

There's no setup code—as you'd see with other languages or libraries—such as event handlers or long lists of slider attributes. It's short and simple.

1.3.6　*Streamlit works well with LLMs*

In 2022, technology saw a watershed moment with the launch of OpenAI's generative AI chatbot, ChatGPT. To understand how the rise of generative AI fueled Streamlit's popularity, consider the following:

- AI has captured the world's imagination.
- Python is the most popular language for AI development due to its widespread adoption across the industry and its extensive ecosystem of AI-related libraries, including TensorFlow, PyTorch, scikit-learn, and LangChain.
- Streamlit is the fastest way to write visual apps in Python.

Taken together, these facts mean developers of all kinds are flocking to Streamlit to build AI apps. Streamlit quickly capitalized on the popularity of large language models (LLMs) like GPT. For instance, Streamlit makes writing conversational chatbots a cinch by introducing chat elements.

Listing 1.3 shows a *complete,* working AI chatbot I built with Streamlit chat elements in fewer than 30 lines of code (chapter_01/basic_chatbot.py in the GitHub repo):

Listing 1.3   A working AI chatbot in less than 30 lines of code

```python
import os
import streamlit as st
from openai import OpenAI

os.environ["OPENAI_API_KEY"] = "sk-..." # Replace with your own API key
openai = OpenAI()

human_message = lambda m: {"role": "user", "content": m}
ai_message = lambda m: {"role": "assistant", "content": m}

def talk_to_ai(question, history):
    return openai.chat.completions.create(
        model="gpt-5-mini",
        messages=history + [human_message(question)],
    ).choices[0].message.content

st.session_state.history = st.session_state.get("history", [])
history = st.session_state.history

for message in history:
    st.chat_message(message["role"]).markdown(message["content"])

prompt= st.chat_input("Chat with me!")
if prompt:
    st.chat_message("human").markdown(prompt)
    response = talk_to_ai(prompt, history)
    history.extend([human_message(prompt), ai_message(response)])
    st.chat_message("ai").markdown(response)
```

NOTE   To use this example, create an OpenAI account, buy some credits (unless your account already has them), generate an API key, and plug it into the following line: `os.environ["OPENAI_API_KEY"] = "sk-..."`. You'll also need to install the OpenAI module with `pip install openai`. Importantly, this code is for demonstration purposes only. Never include API keys in any code you share. Later in this book, we'll cover how to handle this securely.

Figure 1.5 shows the output. Streamlit creates a fully functional chat interface, complete with bot and user avatars.

Time will tell if the generative AI hype is justified. In the meantime, if you're building an AI app, Streamlit has you covered.

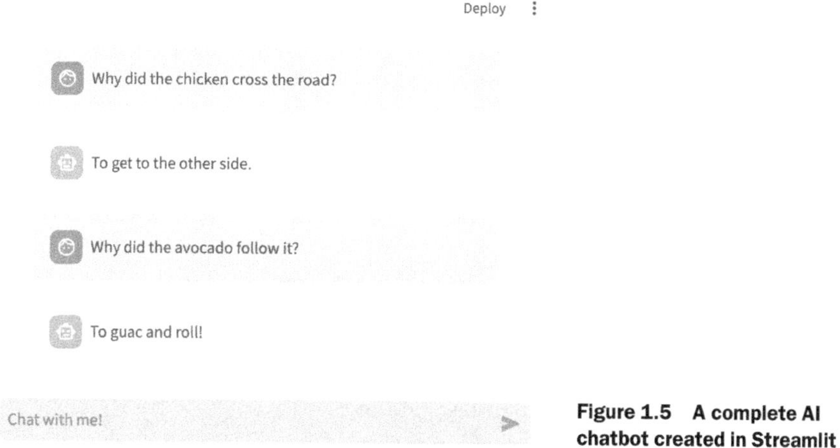

Figure 1.5   A complete AI chatbot created in Streamlit

1.3.7   *Streamlit has excellent support for data science and visualizations*

Streamlit's creators originally designed it for data scientists. It offers excellent support for data visualizations, using Python's rich set of visualization libraries. You can use your favorite library to create charts (Matplotlib, Plotly, Altair, etc.), graphs (Graph-Viz), or 3D renders (PyDeck), and display them in Streamlit.

Figure 1.6 shows a histogram rendered in Streamlit using the Matplotlib library.

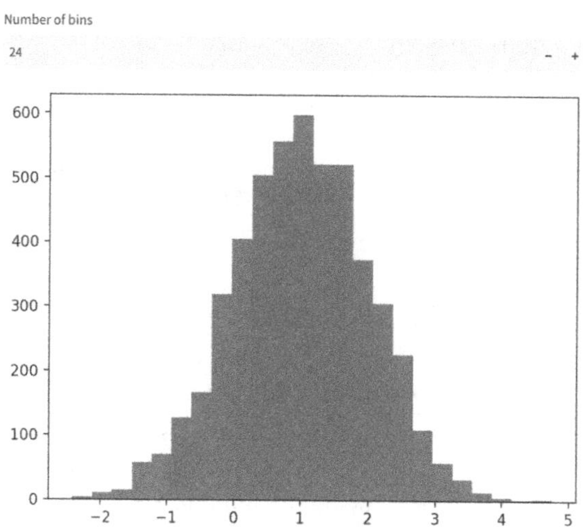

Figure 1.6   A histogram in Streamlit created using the popular Matplotlib library

Listing 1.4 (chapter_01/basic_histogram.py in the GitHub repo) shows the short, sweet code that generates the chart in figure 1.6.

Listing 1.4   Rendering a histogram with dummy data in Streamlit

```python
import streamlit as st
import matplotlib.pyplot as pyplot
import numpy as np


nums = np.random.normal(1, 1, size=5000)
figure, subplot = pyplot.subplots()


bins = st.number_input("Number of bins", min_value=1, max_value=100)
subplot.hist(nums, bins=bins)
st.pyplot(figure)
```

Streamlit also works well with pandas. Pandas is an extremely popular library that makes working with tabular data easy through its core concept of dataframes. A dataframe is a table-based data structure that lets developers ingest, wrangle, and analyze data in various ways. If you're a data scientist, there's a good chance you use it regularly in your work.

Streamlit offers first-class support for dataframes, allowing them to be displayed and edited visually. Figure 1.7 shows an example of enabling the user to edit a pandas dataframe live in the Streamlit app.

We'll explore pandas and dataframes in more detail in a later chapter.

1.3.8   *You can share your Streamlit apps for free, in record time*

Building a web app is one thing; making it available to others is another. For a public-facing web app that doesn't use Streamlit, you usually need hosting—for example, a cloud provider like Amazon Web Service (AWS) or your own servers. That can be intimidating and expensive for time-strapped data scientists or casual hobbyists, especially for a simple app that doesn't need to serve thousands of users.

Streamlit Community Cloud is a free, fast way to deploy public Streamlit apps. You can publish an app by linking it to a GitHub repository, which helps you share code and track changes. Most projects and examples in this book are on GitHub and published to Streamlit Community Cloud, so you can try them out.

Community Cloud has limitations and may not suit everyone, but it's a hassle-free way to share your creations. We'll cover deploying to Community Cloud in chapter 5,

Figure 1.7   An editable pandas dataframe displayed in Streamlit (see chapter_01/ data_editor_example.py in the GitHub repository).

and we'll discuss other options in chapter 12 if Community Cloud doesn't meet your specific needs.

1.3.9 *Streamlit has a huge, friendly community*

Streamlit's user base grows every day, and that growth brings more questions. Luckily, Streamlit's forums—at https://discuss.streamlit.io—are friendly, and the members (including the Streamlit team) respond quickly.

For example, while doing research for this book, I wanted to understand how Streamlit works under the hood. A forum comment from a Streamlit engineer helped me find the right place in the source code. If you've exhausted your Google-fu and still have a question, help is at hand.

1.3.10 *You can extend Streamlit with third-party components or build your own*

As we've seen, Streamlit saves you time by providing pre-built UI elements and reducing customization options. Most of the time, that's good because it lets you focus on the app's logic. At other times, it can feel restrictive if you want to build a specific experience that you can't easily create with Streamlit's built-in elements.

In these cases, Streamlit offers Streamlit Components. Third-party developers can create these modules to extend Streamlit's functionality. Streamlit Components range from features that fill perceived gaps in Streamlit's natively available elements—such as a search box with autocomplete—to entire mini-apps (like an audio recorder) that you can embed in your app.

Streamlit publishes popular components in a gallery (https://streamlit.io/gallery) on its website, where you can see how they look and work. Installing a component is as easy as installing any other Python library.

If you have some frontend development experience, you can even create your own components. This requires knowledge of HTML, CSS, and JavaScript but it can enable you to fine-tune the experience you create for your users.

1.4 *What can you build with Streamlit?*

Streamlit is a versatile platform for building a wide range of interactive applications. I've used Streamlit to build both work projects, such as a tool that lets my colleagues export internal spreadsheets to a data warehouse, and non-work projects, like a simulator that helps me make real estate investment decisions. In this section, we'll explore the variety of projects you can build with Streamlit, showcasing its adaptability and utility.

1.4.1 *Data applications*

Streamlit's creators originally designed it for data scientists, and its value in creating data applications remains one of its greatest strengths. The types of data-related applications you can build with Streamlit include:

- Dashboards that display metrics important to company decision makers.
- Data exploration apps that let you dive into and better understand datasets.

- Interactive visualizations that help users explore data.
- Machine learning model deployments that allow users to upload inputs and receive predictions.

1.4.2   Apps that use Generative AI like LLMs

Building generative AI apps often involves adding a thin layer of business logic to API calls to services like OpenAI's GPT or Anthropic's Claude. Streamlit is well-suited for these tools, allowing you to quickly roll out AI functionality with a UI, thanks to built-in support for common AI form factors, such as chatbots. Python's libraries for interacting with generative AI (LangChain, for example) are second to none, and Streamlit is ideally positioned to take advantage of them.

1.4.3   Internal tools for your workplace

While data apps are the most well-known use case for Streamlit, you can use it just as effectively to develop internal tools for employees. These might include applications such as:

- Project management dashboards
- Time tracking apps
- Shift scheduling tools
- Inventory management systems
- File converter utilities

Several factors make these tools ideal candidates for Streamlit apps:

- They generally only need to support a limited number of concurrent users.
- They are scrappy in nature and may be required within a short timeframe.
- Most companies don't have the budget to hire full-time engineers to build their systems.

Streamlit is simple enough that even semi-technical users with basic Python knowledge can use it to build what they need.

1.4.4   Prototypes for large apps

Streamlit can even help dedicated software engineering teams tasked with building large, ambitious applications. These projects tend to be expensive in terms of developer time and effort, often spanning months or years. Even with an iterative approach to development, it can take a long time to see results, at which point many incorrect and costly assumptions may have been made.

Early design mockups help, but prototypes are even more effective. With Streamlit, you can quickly create lightweight prototypes that mimic the functionality of the larger app. This approach shows stakeholders what to expect and helps you validate basic assumptions about functionality early in the process.

If you're a software engineer, this approach saves the company time and money, generates excitement among your stakeholders, and builds support for your work because people appreciate something they can experience firsthand more than design documents or static mocks.

1.4.5 Anything else you can imagine

Earlier in the chapter, I characterized Streamlit apps as "Python scripts where you can click buttons." That means your Streamlit app can do almost anything Python can. You don't have to use Streamlit in conventional ways—you can find new, creative things to code into an app. Here are some unconventional app ideas for inspiration:

- A personal AI habit-building assistant that lets you record activities and offers advice and encouragement
- A maze generator that creates fun puzzles (see figure 1.8)
- A laundry tracker that reminds you when your clothes need washing

The point is that you should feel free to experiment. Learning a new technology often sparks ideas for new applications that only you can imagine!

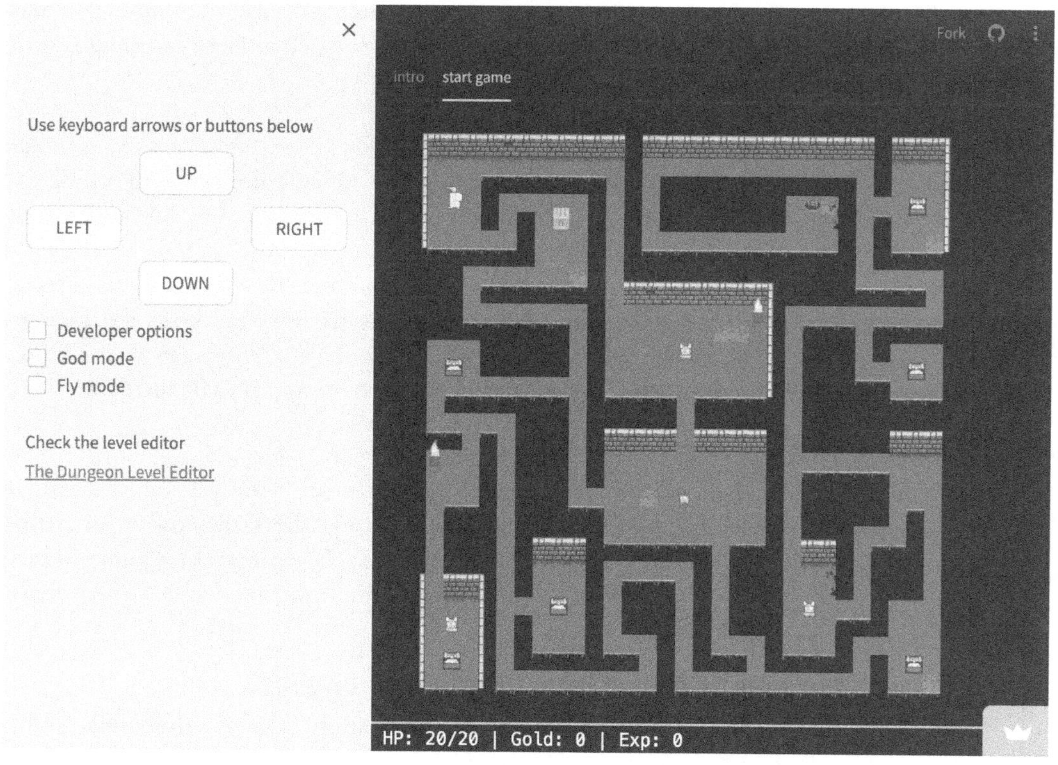

Figure 1.8 Dungeon, a game Tomasz Hasiów built with Streamlit (https://dungeon.streamlit.app/)

1.5   *When not to use Streamlit*

Like any technology, Streamlit has trade-offs. You may encounter these limitations as your app's requirements become more sophisticated and nuanced. For example, I once started a project with Streamlit for rapid prototyping, but switched to a React-based app when UI requirements grew more complex. Let's address this head-on by looking at a few things you can't (or probably shouldn't) develop with Streamlit.

1.5.1   *Complex, large-scale applications*

Streamlit apps are best suited for user bases in the hundreds or thousands, not millions. For concurrent users (those accessing your app simultaneously), performance may degrade as you scale up, depending on your app's resource needs.

Streamlit runs your entire Python script whenever something changes on the app screen. This can hurt performance, especially if your script runs heavy computations or loads large datasets. Streamlit's caching can help, but you can't always use it.

Streamlit may not be suitable for large, production-grade applications, but you can often overcome these limitations by using third-party components. For instance, Streamlit doesn't allow you to resize or drag most UI elements, but other people have created Streamlit components that add this functionality (for example, `streamlit-elements`).

As your app becomes more complex, you may find it difficult to implement in Streamlit. The Streamlit forums can help identify workarounds, but at a certain point you may need to migrate to a different, more flexible framework (such as Flask or Django) with enhanced capabilities.

1.5.2   *Apps that require a high degree of UI customization*

Streamlit simplifies adding common UI elements, but offers limited control over interface behavior. While theming and custom components add some flexibility, Streamlit still restricts customization.

If you need precise control over your app's appearance or specific visual effects, Streamlit may not be the right choice for you. Consider alternatives like React, a framework known for its flexibility and extensive customization capabilities (explored in the following section), or even manual page design with traditional HTML and CSS.

1.5.3   *Native desktop or mobile apps*

Streamlit is a web framework that produces apps that run within a web browser. If you're trying to develop desktop or mobile apps outside the browser, opt for native application frameworks such as PyQt or React Native. While Streamlit apps are accessible on mobile devices, it does not produce standalone Android or iOS apps that run independently of the browser.

1.6   *How is Streamlit different from other technologies?*

If you've researched ways to create interactive applications, chances are you've come across or used technologies similar to Streamlit. In this section, we compare Streamlit to some of them to clarify your understanding.

1.6.1 Jupyter notebooks

A Jupyter notebook is an interactive environment for data exploration, code development, and visualizations. You write Python code or text in Markdown in a "cell," execute it, and see the output directly below. The output can be text, a visualization, or even something interactive. The notebook keeps the output of each cell, so you can see what came before it.

Jupyter notebooks are a mainstay in the data science community. They are useful for explaining your thought process, playing around with data, and sharing your work with colleagues.

Jupyter is similar to Streamlit in a few respects: both are Python-based, support tabular and graphical data, integrate with popular libraries like pandas, and are widely used in data science. Still, they differ in important ways:

- Jupyter is used to create interactive documents rather than actual apps. It is best suited for sharing code and explanations with collaborators rather than having that code executed by actual end users. Streamlit is used to create apps for end users.

- Jupyter's support for engineering practices, such as version control, is limited. This is acceptable because it's intended for exploratory analysis, not shipping production dashboards. Streamlit, on the other hand, fits nicely into a regular engineering workflow.

- Jupyter notebooks are generally intended for technical people, not laypeople. Streamlit doesn't require your app's users to be able to read or understand code.

Jupyter notebooks are excellent for experimenting with code, data, and charts. Streamlit is ideal for building and sharing polished interactive experiences for users, often using the code, data, and charts you refined in your Jupyter notebook.

1.6.2 HTML, CSS, and JavaScript

As we discussed earlier, HTML, CSS, and JavaScript are the web's three core languages. HTML provides the structure and content of a web page, defining elements such as headings, lists, divisions, and links through a tree of "tags" that can contain other tags. CSS manages the appearance, layout, and formatting of multiple web pages in a centralized location. It sets colors, spacing, fonts, borders, and more. JavaScript is a programming language that primarily defines a web page's dynamic behavior. It can also create animations, validate forms, connect to other web pages, and do pretty much anything else a website needs.

Together, these languages enable you to build any web experience you want. Although they aren't difficult per se to learn, it takes a lot of work to use them effectively to create complex apps—so much so that frontend development is its own discipline in software engineering.

Streamlit abstracts away the complexity of using these languages in their raw form. It lets you use a simpler, more concise syntax to write web pages and generates, in the background, the equivalent code that a web browser can understand.

1.6.3   React

React is a popular JavaScript framework for building fast and responsive web pages. Like Streamlit, you can use it instead of writing raw HTML, JavaScript, and CSS to create web applications.

React follows a reusable component-based design. You build up parts of a web page using smaller parts and then combine those parts to build larger parts, working all the way up to a full application. Each such part you create is called a component and can be reused in your app or even shared with other people so they can use it in their own.

React uses a declarative programming approach. You describe the UI you want, and React updates the DOM (the tree of HTML elements that lies under your web page) to match it. While React is incredibly powerful and used by frontend developers to create complex UIs, its architecture and approach can be challenging to understand. It is also not Python-based.

Though Streamlit actually uses React under the hood, from the programmer's perspective Streamlit trades some of React's power and flexibility for simpler semantics, pre-built elements with some customizability, and the ability to use Python to write web pages.

1.6.4   *Flask, Django, and FastAPI*

Flask, Django, and FastAPI are three of the most popular Python web frameworks.

Flask is lightweight and minimalistic. It is straightforward and flexible, allowing developers to choose their preferred libraries and tools. Flask provides essentials like routing and HTTP request handling, leaving most of the design choices to the developer. It's popular with those who want a modular approach or a high degree of control.

Django is a feature-rich, sophisticated framework. It's more opinionated than Flask and follows specific design patterns, such as the MVT (Model-View-Template) architecture. It includes built-in modules for common tasks, such as an admin panel for managing data models. Django is a popular choice for building powerful, enterprise-grade applications.

FastAPI is a newer tool for building fast, efficient web APIs. It simplifies data and request handling and automatically creates helpful documentation for your app.

While Flask, Django, and FastAPI can all be used to build web applications, they are primarily *backend* frameworks to be used in conjunction with your *frontend*, which still consists of HTML/CSS/JavaScript that you have to write or embed within your Python code. Not so with Streamlit, which lets you write frontend code in pure Python.

1.6.5   *Tkinter and PyQt*

Tkinter (pronounced tee-kinter) and PyQt (pie-cute) are Python libraries for creating graphical user interfaces (GUIs). Tkinter comes bundled with Python and provides a set of widgets you can use to create a desktop application. It is popular with beginners and suitable for creating simple apps.

PyQt is similar to Tkinter but more powerful, mature, and complex. It's actually a wrapper around the C++ Qt application framework. With PyQt, you can create sophisticated GUIs and use many built-in features.

The key difference between Tkinter/PyQt and Streamlit is that you use Streamlit to create web applications, not desktop applications. As users have become increasingly comfortable with web-based software that requires no installation or updates, Streamlit is arguably more useful than the other two for most use cases.

Summary

- Streamlit is a framework for building web apps in pure Python without HTML, CSS, or JavaScript.

- Streamlit has been gaining popularity due to its simplicity, development velocity, LLM support, powerful visualizations, and integration with data science libraries, among other features.

- With Streamlit, you can create many types of applications: data apps, internal workplace tools, LLM apps, prototypes for larger apps, and more.

- You shouldn't use Streamlit for large-scale apps meant for millions of users, or apps that require extensive UI customization.

Getting started with Streamlit

Welcome to chapter 2. This is where the rubber hits the road! By the end of this chapter, you'll be interacting with your first very own Streamlit app!

This book is not just about teaching you Streamlit. It's also about helping you stay productive with Streamlit and well positioned to develop real-world apps. Before we jump into writing code, let's take some time to set up your development environment. Specifically, we'll discuss three key workflow considerations: version control with Git, code editing tools, and virtual environments.

Next, we'll examine the workflow you'll follow when coding with Streamlit so you know what to expect as you build apps throughout this book. After that, we'll work through a step-by-step process to create your first app: a password checker.

Excited yet? Let's dive in!

NOTE The GitHub repo for this book is at https://github.com/aneevdavis/streamlit-in-action. The chapter_02 folder contains the code for this chapter.

2.1 Getting Streamlit up and running

Before building any apps, you need to install Streamlit and get it ready to go. This involves two steps:

1. Install the correct version of Python (3.9 and above are currently supported, but I recommend 3.11+), and install `pip` (a tool that ships with Python and makes it easy to install Python packages).
2. Use `pip` to install Streamlit (spoiler alert: type `pip install streamlit`)

For a detailed installation guide, see the appendix.

2.2 Setting up your development environment

The tools you use and the way you set up the environment in which you code your apps are largely a matter of preference. But over time, these choices can significantly affect your productivity as a developer, so it's worth taking the time to consider them.

I'll briefly discuss a few important aspects of your development environment: version control, editing tool, and virtual environments. If you're an experienced Python developer and already have a setup you're comfortable with, skip to the section on running Streamlit for the first time.

2.2.1 Version control with Git

If you've never written code in a professional setting, you might not have used a version control system like Git before, or you might not fully understand what it's for. *Version control* provides a structured way to track, manage, document, and experiment with changes to your programs. Think of it as a time machine for your code. Git is the most popular version control system today, so in this book, we'll use the terms *Git* and *version control* interchangeably.

While working on your apps, you'll sometimes change your mind and decide to design something differently. In those situations, Git lets you "go back in time" to how your code *used* to be and apply changes from that point.

You can also experiment with different versions of your code as you test multiple design options and easily switch between them with Git. Perhaps my favorite aspect of Git is that it lets you document changes to your code and gives you a place to explain your thought process behind the decisions you made. Trust me—you'll thank yourself six months later when you're reading through your code and trying to decipher it.

These situations are extremely common when you're working on a large project or collaborating with others. Even if that *doesn't* currently apply to you, I highly recommend learning and incorporating Git into your development workflow because its benefits are too numerous to ignore. Section 5.2 has a minimal introduction to Git (just enough to deploy your app in production), but if you want to learn Git in some more depth, I recommend Atlassian's Git tutorials at https://www.atlassian.com/git/tutorials (you can ignore the BitBucket Cloud parts).

2.2.2 Code editors

Streamlit apps, like all Python scripts, are just text files, so all you *really* need to write code is a simple text editor (like Notepad in Windows). But an advanced code editor or an Integrated Development Environment (IDE) makes you much more productive, with features like syntax highlighting, easy debugging tools, and code navigation—it's hard not to recommend one. Many tools can fit the bill, but I'd like to mention two of the most popular ones here.

> **NOTE** Since this section was first written, software development has evolved rapidly, with many developers now preferring to use AI-first tools such as Codex, Claude Code, or Cursor to write their code. While these tools are incredibly powerful in day-to-day use, I'd recommend sticking with a regular non-AI-based IDE while you're in the process of learning.

PYCHARM

PyCharm is an IDE that JetBrains developed specifically for Python. It provides comprehensive support for Python, including code completion, error detection, and quick-fix suggestions.

PyCharm is an excellent choice if you're seeking advanced functionality right after installation, without having to tinker too much. The Pro edition costs money, but PyCharm also offers a free Community Edition (see figure 2.1) at https://www.jetbrains .com/pycharm/download (scroll down to where it says Community Edition).

VISUAL STUDIO CODE

Microsoft's Visual Studio Code (or VS Code) is an immensely popular code editor that supports many languages. VS Code offers some essential functionality—such as syntax highlighting—right away, but its true strength lies in its ecosystem of plugins that can extend its capabilities. Indeed, with the correct set of plugins, you can make VS Code do essentially everything a paid version of PyCharm can do. Since VS Code is free, it's an attractive proposition for learners willing to spend time setting everything up.

> **NOTE** Since both of these (and many others, such as Sublime Text and Notepad++) are viable code-editing tools, I won't assume you're using any particular one. As long as you have a terminal you can type commands into and a program to edit text files, you're good to go.

2.2.3 Virtual environments

In most real-world Python projects you will rely on various libraries. These libraries constantly change, with new versions that add and remove features or modify existing ones. As you gain experience and create more complex applications, you'll often find that updating a library for one project breaks another or leads to unpredictable bugs and conflicts.

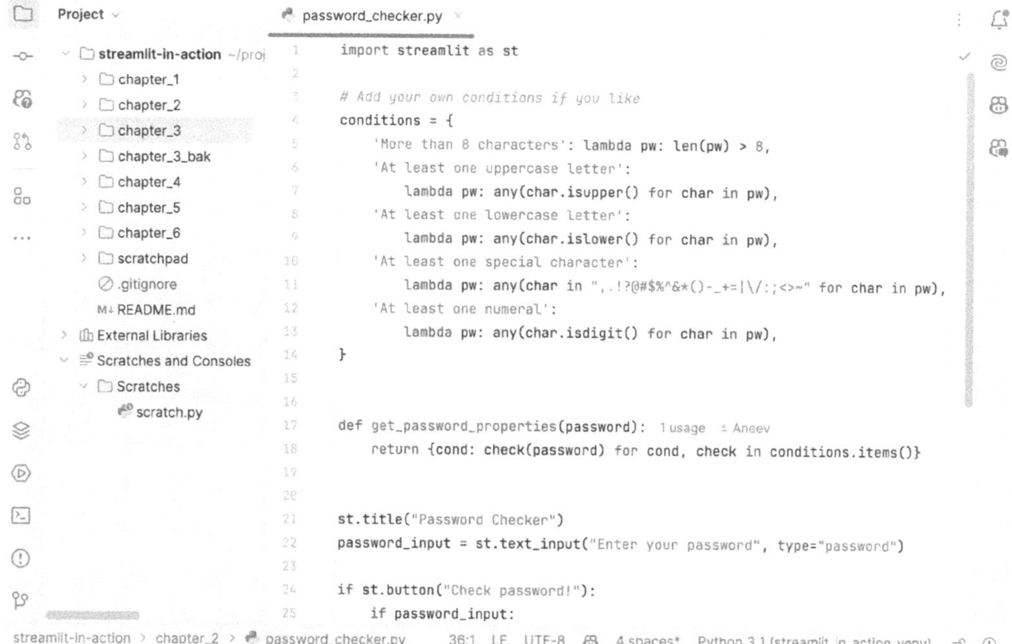

Figure 2.1   The project editor window in PyCharm Community Edition

Virtual environments offer a way out of this dilemma. A virtual environment consists of an isolated instance of Python, along with a set of necessary libraries and dependencies. If you put each project you start in its own virtual environment, you'll be able to modify the dependencies of one project without affecting others.

Even if you're just starting out and haven't run into dependency management problems, it's a great idea to get familiar with virtual environments. You can choose from several virtual environment-related libraries and tools, each with varying levels of sophistication. You may come across `venv`, `pipenv`, `pyenv`, `poetry`, and others.

2.3　Running Streamlit for the first time

This is where the fun begins! We'll run a Streamlit app for the first time and get a first-hand look at the kind of things you can build with Streamlit. If you haven't already done so, please go to the appendix and install Streamlit. If you have installed it, open a terminal window and let's get started!

We'll run the Hello app included with Streamlit. To see it in action, type `streamlit hello` in your terminal. You should see output in the terminal that you can ignore for now. After a few seconds, your web browser should open and display the app.

The Hello app showcases Streamlit's capabilities, including animation, graph plotting, maps, and tables. As shown in figure 2.2, one demo is an animation built from a mathematical visualization. The sidebar on the left lets you navigate to other demos.

As shown in figure 2.3, a more practical demo relates to pandas dataframes. We'll become intimately familiar with these later in the book. I hope these examples inspire you!

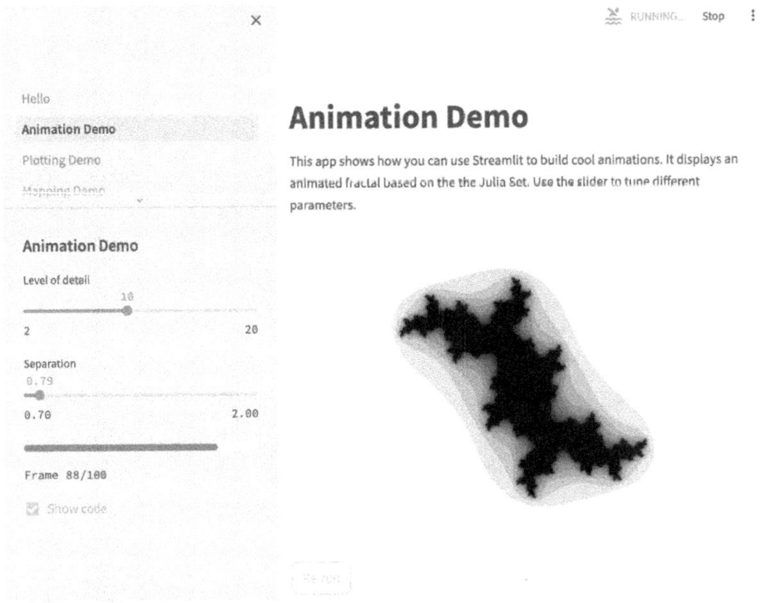

Figure 2.2   Animation Demo from the Hello app

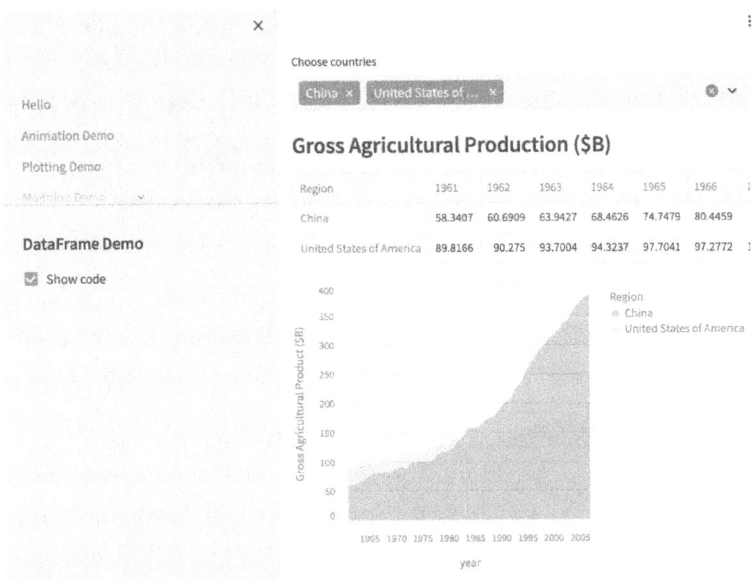

Figure 2.3   DataFrame Demo from the Hello app

The sidebar also includes a Show Code checkbox that displays each app's source code below the app itself. In each instance, you'll find that the code isn't verbose. You don't have to understand how it all works right now, but hopefully you'll gain some appreciation for what Streamlit makes possible.

2.4 *The Streamlit development workflow*

Writing Streamlit apps, or any kind of programming, is an iterative process where you write some code, test if it works, and repeat. If you've never written graphical applications before, you may be curious about what this process looks like.

Figure 2.4 describes the development workflow you'll soon get used to.

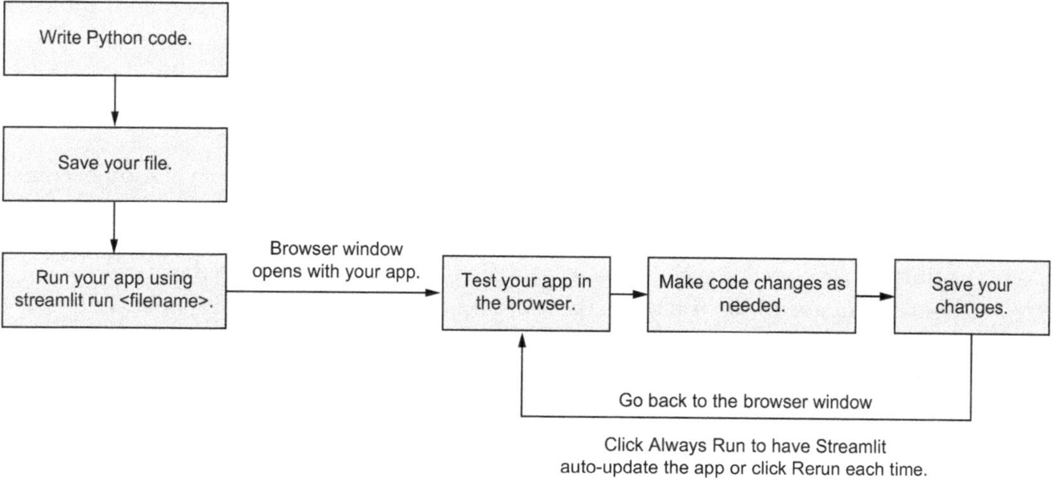

Figure 2.4 The Streamlit development workflow

Let's take a look at each of the workflow steps:

1 *Write your Python code.* Create a first draft of your app in a Python file in your code editor. This can be as basic or as fleshed out as you like. Some people like to run the app from the outset as they shape it and visualize every change, so their first draft might be an empty app with a title.

   I find this distracting because it's tempting to spend time fine-tuning the app's appearance if I see it early on. Instead, I prefer to code a roughly complete version of the app before running it for the first time. This is entirely a matter of preference.

2 *Save your file.* This should be self-explanatory. Save your Python file as you would normally, with a .py extension.

3   *Run your app using* `streamlit run <filename>`. Run this command in your terminal, and replace `<filename>` with the path to your file. This opens a browser window with your app, as you saw when you ran the *hello* app.

4   *Test your app in the browser.* Interact with your app. Play around with it by entering values, clicking buttons, and checking whether the output matches your expectations.

5   *Make code changes as needed.* Based on the test outcomes, return to your Python code and make any needed edits.

6   *Save your changes.* Again, this step is self-explanatory.

7   *Switch back to your browser window.* Remember, you don't need to rerun `streamlit run <filename>` to see the changes in the app.

8   *You have two options here.* If you want Streamlit to rerun your updated app automatically, you can click Always Rerun in your app. Otherwise, you can still click Rerun each time.

9   *Repeat steps 4–7.*

You'll encounter these steps frequently throughout this book, and they'll soon become second nature. But enough theory—let's put this into action!

NOTE   While making changes (especially those outside your Python code—such as in a text file or a database your app depends on), you might occasionally need to shut down and restart your Streamlit app to see them take effect. See section 2.5.6 for details.

2.5   *Building your first app*

Let's craft our first app! I'll start by introducing the concept behind the app and outlining the logic flow. Then I'll walk you through the complete app code, explaining each part step by step. Finally, we'll run the app and modify it.

A word of advice before we dive in: your learning experience will be richer if you take an active role, tinkering and experimenting as you go. Be curious, and don't be afraid to make changes beyond those suggested in the text. You'll often find that the parts of the material which stick in your mind best are the ones where you took the initiative to explore and understand on your own.

That said, it's time to get our hands dirty!

2.5.1   *A password checker*

You've probably seen websites with a long list of password rules—for example, requiring at least one lowercase letter, a special character, an even number of underscores, the names of up to two dwarves from Snow White, and so forth. In this app, the user enters a password and sees which rules pass and which fail.

2.5.2 Logic flow

In figure 2.5, we lay out the flow of our app's logic. It begins when the user enters a password in a text input box and starts the checking process by clicking a button.

Internally, the app keeps a list of rules (a dictionary in the code) in memory and checks each one. The program loops through this list categorizing each rule as either PASSED or FAILED, depending on whether the entered password meets it. Then, it generates a fresh list (or dictionary) of results.

Next, the program iterates through the results and presents the outcomes on the screen. Each condition appears as a box shown in green if it passed or red if it failed.

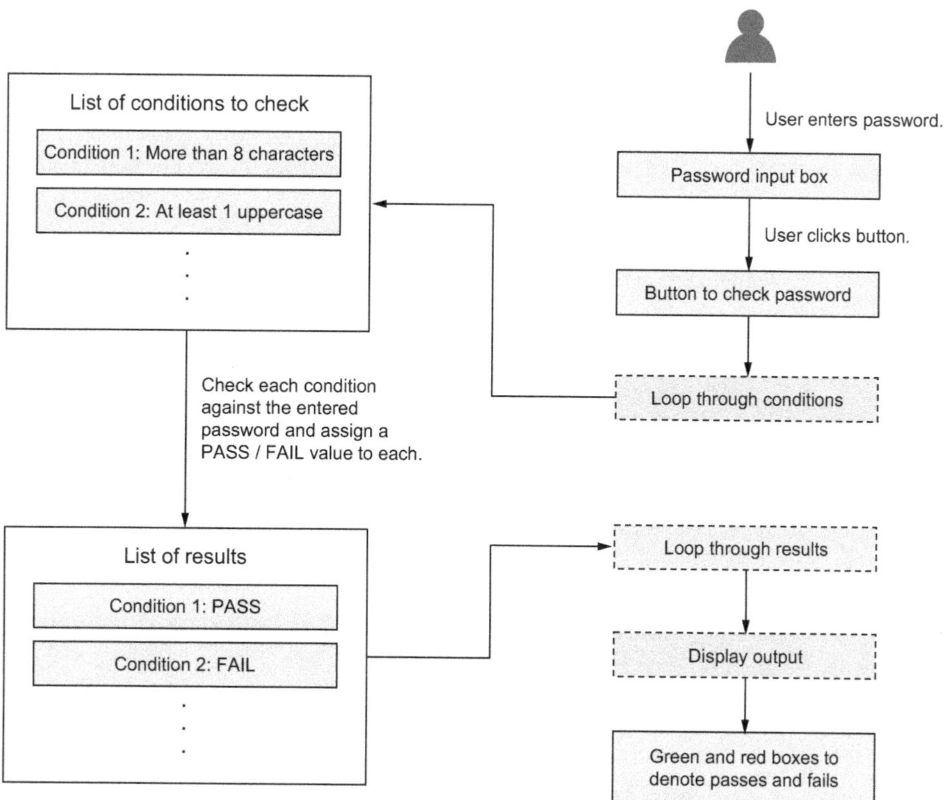

Figure 2.5 The flow of logic in our password checker app

2.5.3 Going through the code

By now, you should have a clear understanding of the logic we want to implement, so let's jump right in and start building. To get started, go to this book's GitHub page, copy the code in listing 2.1 (chapter_02/in_progress/password_checker_in_progress_01.py in the GitHub repo) into a new file, and save it.

Listing 2.1   The code for the password checker app

```python
import streamlit as st

# Add your own conditions if you like
conditions = {
    'More than 8 characters': lambda pw: len(pw) > 8,
    'At least one uppercase letter':
        lambda pw: any(char.isupper() for char in pw),
    'At least one lowercase letter':
        lambda pw: any(char.islower() for char in pw),
    'At least one special character':
        lambda pw: any(char in ",.!?@#$%^&*()-_+=|\\/:;<>~" for char in pw),
}

def get_password_properties(password):
    return {cond: check(password) for cond, check in conditions.items()}

st.title("Password Checker")
password_input = st.text_input("Enter your password", type="password")

if st.button("Check password"):
    if password_input:
        properties = get_password_properties(password_input)

        # Loop through password conditions and show the status for each
        for condition, passes in properties.items():
            if passes:
                st.success(f'✔ Pass: {condition}')
            else:
                st.error(f'✘ Fail: {condition}')
    else:
        st.write("Please enter a password.")
```

Let's go through it part by part.

The first line imports Streamlit itself (you'll need this in every app) and notes that we'll use st to refer to it later:

```python
import streamlit as st
```

You can use whatever you like here, but the st convention is so widely used that you'll often hear people refer to Streamlit elements as st.<whatever>.

Use the following block to define the conditions you want to check:

```python
# Add your own conditions if you like
conditions = {
    'More than 8 characters': lambda pw: len(pw) > 8,
    'At least one uppercase letter':
        lambda pw: any(char.isupper() for char in pw),
    'At least one lowercase letter':
        lambda pw: any(char.islower() for char in pw),
```

```
    'At least one special character':
        lambda pw: any(char in ",.!?@#$%^&*()-_+=|\\/:;<>~" for char in pw),
}
```

The code uses a Python dictionary in which the keys represent the rules and the values correspond to the functions we'll use to check each rule.

In this case, the functions are *lambdas,* or anonymous inline functions. A lambda is a cool way to define a short, one-line function in Python without a name. Each function accepts one parameter—the password, `pw`—and returns `True` if the corresponding rule holds, and `False` otherwise.

The first lambda function checks whether the password length is greater than eight characters. In the others, we loop through the characters in `pw` and apply a test to each character, such as `char.isupper()` or `char.islower()`.

We'll run the following function to evaluate the password against all the rules defined above:

```
def get_password_properties(password):
    return {cond: check(password) for cond, check in conditions.items()}
```

It returns a new Python dictionary where the keys are the conditions and the values are the results of running the lambda function corresponding to each condition we defined above. The syntax we've used here is called a *dictionary comprehension* in Python, and it's shorthand to create a new dictionary from some input.

Next is our first actual Streamlit element. It's a simple one called `title`:

```
st.title("Password Checker")
```

It does what you'd expect: it displays the text you pass in as a title in nice, large type.

The following line displays a password input box to the user:

```
password_input = st.text_input("Enter your password", type="password")
```

Streamlit's implementation also offers a toggle to show or hide the entered text. When the user enters text, Streamlit saves it in the `password_input` variable.

`st.button` is one of the simplest Streamlit elements, and you'll work with it frequently. Unsurprisingly, it displays a button with the text Check Password.

```
if st.button("Check password"):
```

Notice that this goes in an `if` clause. When you click the button, the code nested within the `if` (see below) runs. There are some interesting nuances to this that we'll dive into in chapter 4.

After the user clicks the button, our app checks whether `password_input` has a non-empty value (that is, whether the user entered a password). If so, it calls `get_password_properties` to evaluate the rules we defined:

```
if password_input:
        properties = get_password_properties(password_input)

        # Loop through password conditions and show the status for each
        for condition, passes in properties.items():
            if passes:
                st.success(f'✔ Pass: {condition}')
            else:
                st.error(f'✘ Fail: {condition}')
```

The program then loops through the returned dictionary, where each key is a rule and the corresponding value is a boolean that indicates whether the rule passed. If the rule passes, we use another Streamlit element, st.success, to indicate success; if it doesn't, we use st.error to show failure.

st.success and st.error act as containers for text with semantic styles applied (that is, mostly a green box for st.success and a red one for st.error).

This else corresponds to the if password_input from earlier:

```
else:
        st.write("Please enter a password.")
```

Here, we use another Streamlit element, st.write, to prompt the user to enter a password.

2.5.4   *Running the app*

To run the app, open a terminal, navigate to the directory where you saved the file, and type:

```
streamlit run <filename>
```

For instance, if you saved your code as password_checker.py, you would type:

```
streamlit run password_checker.py
```

As you saw when you ran streamlit hello earlier, this displays some output in your terminal window and opens your web browser, where you can see the app. Feel free to enter various input passwords and play around with the app! If everything has gone according to plan, you should see something similar to figure 2.6 when you click Check Password.

Don't close this page, because we want to see what happens when you change the code. First, turn your attention to the terminal output:

```
You can now view your Streamlit app in your browser.

Local URL: http://localhost:8501
Network URL: http://192.168.50.68:8501
```

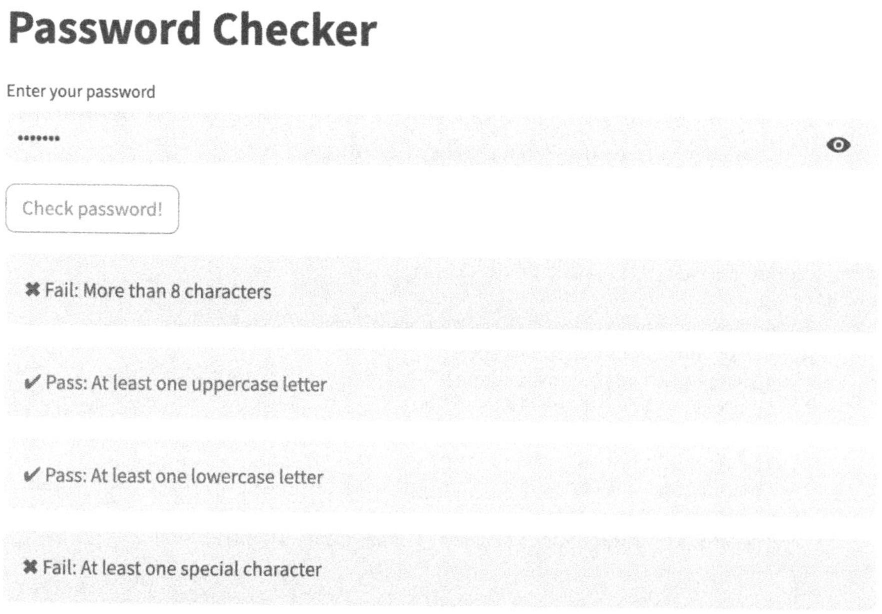

Password Checker

Enter your password

```
•••••••                                                    ◉
```

┌─────────────────────────┐
│ Check password!   │
└─────────────────────────┘

✖ Fail: More than 8 characters

✔ Pass: At least one uppercase letter

✔ Pass: At least one lowercase letter

✖ Fail: At least one special character

Figure 2.6   The Password Checker app

Note the line that reads `Local URL: http://localhost:8501`. This is Streamlit's way of telling you that a Streamlit *server* is running on your computer (that's what `localhost` means) on port 8501. The port in the output you see might be different, like 8502; this is totally fine. We'll explore how this works in more detail in chapter 3, but for now, all you need to know is that you can also access your app by going to the Local URL specified in the output.

If there are other computers on your network, they may be able to use the displayed Network URL to access your app, depending on network and firewall configurations.

Don't close the terminal window or exit it just yet!

Troubleshooting streamlit run

In some cases, your browser window does not open automatically when you enter `streamlit run`, or the browser window opens, but the page is blank. If this is true for you, here are some things to try:

1. In your browser, manually type in the address listed against Local URL in the terminal output, e.g., `http://localhost:8501`
2. Make sure you're running the latest version of your browser.
3. Navigate to http://localhost:8501 in a different browser. I've found that Google Chrome tends to have the fewest problems.

2.5.5   *Making changes to the app*

Now that we know our app works, let's try changing it. For instance, let's say we want to add a check that the entered password contains at least one numeral, as shown in listing 2.2 (chapter_02/in_progress/password_checker_in_progress_02.py in the GitHub repo). Add a new rule to our `conditions` dictionary:

Listing 2.2   Adding a new rule

```python
# Add your own conditions if you like
conditions = {
    'More than 8 characters': lambda pw: len(pw) > 8,
    'At least one uppercase letter':
        lambda pw: any(char.isupper() for char in pw),
    'At least one lowercase letter':
        lambda pw: any(char.islower() for char in pw),
    'At least one special character':
        lambda pw: any(char in ",.!?@#$%^&*()-_+=|\\/:;<>~" for char in pw),
    'At least one numeral':
        lambda pw: any(char.isdigit() for char in pw),
}
```

Our button doesn't sound excited enough, so let's also add an exclamation point to the text:

```python
if st.button("Check password!"):
```

Once you've saved your file, return to the browser window with the app open. In the upper-right corner, you should see a message saying that the source file has changed (figure 2.7), along with options to Rerun or Always Rerun.

i   Source file changed.   <u>R</u>erun   <u>A</u>lways rerun   Deploy   ⋮

Figure 2.7   Streamlit displays a message in your app when the source changes.

This is because Streamlit monitors your app file to see whether you've made any changes. Click Rerun to rerun your app with the latest code. You'll see that our button now says Check Password! with the exclamation point, and if you enter a password and click it, you'll see the new numeral test we added. This updated view is shown in figure 2.8.

You can also choose Always Rerun, which means Streamlit will automatically update your app whenever you change your code. This results in a smoother development experience, where you can edit your code and immediately switch to your browser to see the effect it has.

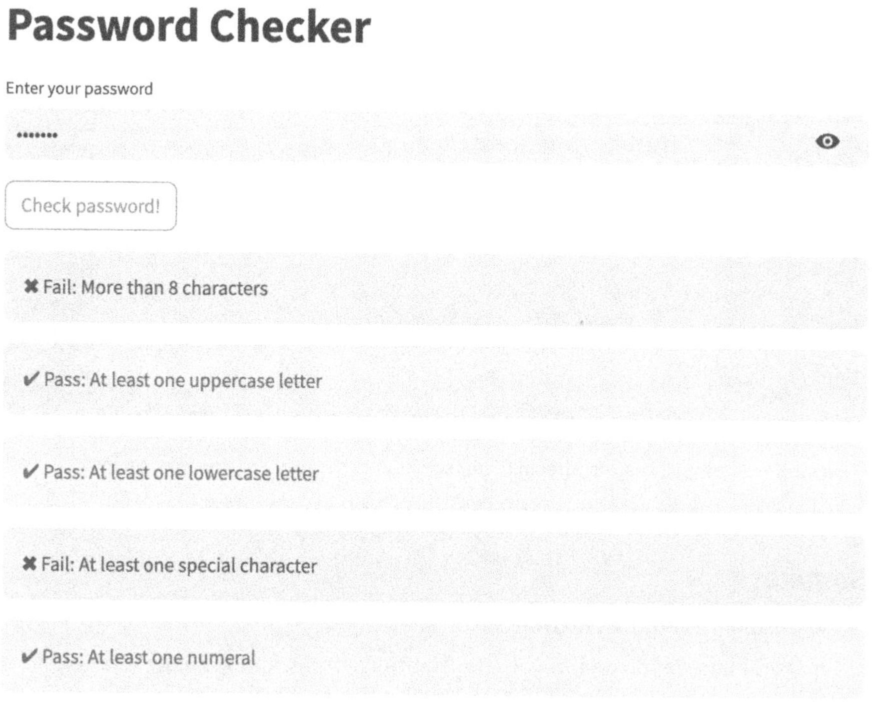

Password Checker

Enter your password

••••••   ◉

Check password!

✖ Fail: More than 8 characters

✔ Pass: At least one uppercase letter

✔ Pass: At least one lowercase letter

✖ Fail: At least one special character

✔ Pass: At least one numeral

Figure 2.8   The Password Checker app with the latest changes

To disable this behavior (it can be hard to spot what changed on a page when it's enabled), click the hamburger menu in the upper-right corner, select Settings, and uncheck Run on Save.

2.5.6   Killing and restarting the server

Remember that you've kept your terminal window (where you typed `streamlit run ...`) open throughout all of this. This window is where the Streamlit server that "serves" your app runs. Once you're done playing with the app, you may want to shut down the server so it doesn't consume resources. To do so, go to the terminal window and either close it or press Ctrl-C.

If you return to the open browser window, you'll find that you can no longer interact with the app. The button is disabled and the app shows "CONNECTING" in the top-right corner as well as a connection error (figure 2.9).

You can bring your app back to life by running `streamlit run <filename>` again, which restarts your server and re-establishes the connection between the frontend and the newly restarted server. This will open a new browser window with a *different* instance of your app. You'll find that the old window is also now alive because it's able to re-establish the connection to the server.

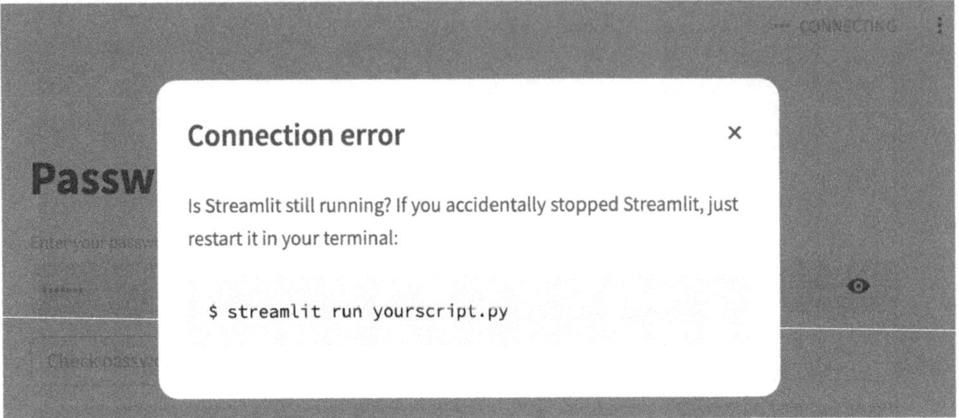

Figure 2.9   Shutting down the Streamlit server prevents the frontend app from running.

Summary

- Streamlit requires Python 3.9 or later.
- Git is a form of version control that helps track and manage changes to code.
- Advanced code editors like VS Code and IDEs like PyCharm make you more productive through syntax highlighting, debugging tools, code navigation, auto-complete, and more.
- Virtual environments allow you to isolate the libraries and dependencies of each project you work on.
- You run Streamlit apps using `streamlit run <filename>`, which opens a web browser window with the app.
- You can configure Streamlit to always rerun the app whenever the source code changes, providing a seamless development experience.

Taking an app from concept to code

This chapter covers

- Defining the scope of an application
- Designing the user interface
- Organizing the code for an app
- Streamlit's workhorse input widgets

In my early days as a software engineer, I was often surprised by how much time I spent on activities other than writing code. I'd spend multiple days, or even weeks, simply understanding the problem I was trying to solve, and even more time on design, all before typing a single line of code.

I felt anxious because I didn't feel *productive*. Scribbled meeting notes and design docs didn't *do* anything. Over time, I realized those days and weeks weren't wasted. Deep thinking about what I was trying to do made the end product better. Likewise, this book is not *just* about teaching Streamlit code. It's about helping readers develop apps in the real world. Planning and design are inescapable parts of the process.

Though we don't have weeks to spend on these topics, this chapter gives a taste of the end-to-end experience of developing an app. We'll start with the app concept and convert it into a set of requirements. Then, we'll develop a design that meets those requirements, working backward from the user experience, and considering code organization. Finally, we'll walk through the code and logic, introducing some of Streamlit's most common widgets along the way. There's a lot to do, so let's get started!

NOTE   The GitHub repo for this book is at https://github.com/aneevdavis/ streamlit-in-action. The chapter_03 folder has all the code for this chapter, including in-progress versions you can use to follow along.

3.1   *Concept to code: A six-step process*

Writing a piece of software can be overwhelming once you get past the initial spark of inspiration. There are so many things to consider! Where do you start? What features will you develop, and how long will it take? How will users interact with the app? Should you start coding right away and figure things out as you go?

Desmond Tutu said, "There is only one way to eat an elephant: a bite at a time." In creating Streamlit apps, as in consuming large land mammals, the optimal approach is to break it down into smaller chunks. Figure 3.1 shows a simple six-step process of developing an app—or just about any piece of software.

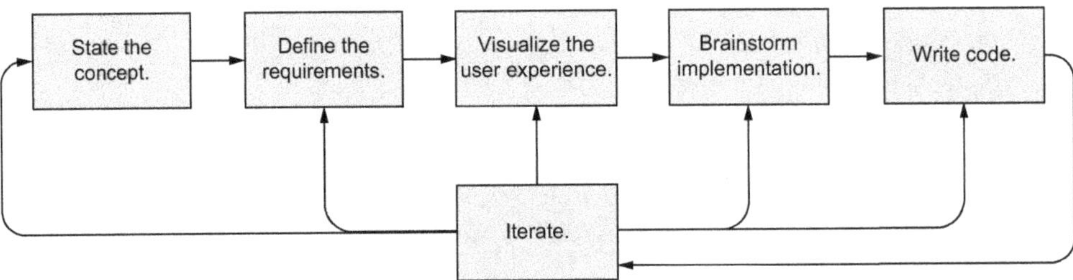

Figure 3.1   The six-step app development workflow

1   *State the concept.* To solve a problem—or describe it to others—you first need to state it succinctly at a high level.

2   *Define the requirements.* In this step you refine the concept and break it down into cold, hard requirements. This step involves defining the scope of what the app will do and—perhaps more importantly—what it *won't* do.

3   *Visualize the user experience.* Draw diagrams and mocks of the experience you envision for users as they use the app.

4   *Brainstorm implementation.* What components will your solution have, how will they integrate, and what trade-offs do you face?

5   *Write code.* Actually implement the app.

6   *Iterate.* Inspect the output and refine steps 1 through 5 as necessary.

This may sound like a lot, and you might think, "Is this all really necessary? I'm not building enterprise software with a large team; I'm making a fairly small app for a handful of users."

The beauty of the above steps is that you can adjust them to suit the project's needs. In large projects, each step may take a considerable amount of time because many people likely need to agree on the overall approach.

But if you're building a small app, you can scale each step down. For instance, you can define the requirements in a quick bullet-point list that takes five minutes to generate, and the visualization of the user experience can be a simple sketch. In the rest of this chapter, we'll go through each of these steps in the context of an example app.

> **NOTE** For the initial parts of this chapter, our attention will be on the end-to-end app development process; we'll cover various Streamlit elements later on when we discuss the implementation of the frontend. This is by design, to reflect the real world, where your primary focus in developing a graphical app will be the app itself, not Streamlit. That explains the success of Streamlit: it *gets out of your way,* allowing you to develop your app without worrying too much about how to implement the UI. So, even though you won't see much discussion about Streamlit itself in the initial sections, hang in there! We'll get to it organically where it fits best.

3.2 Stating our concept: A unit converter

Whether it's while studying physics, cooking a meal from a recipe, or traveling internationally, many of us have had to convert between units of measurement. Often, that means looking up a conversion factor online and using a calculator to do the math. The app we'll build in this chapter makes the task easier and more streamlined.

As discussed in the previous section, the first step in the development process is to state the concept—that is, express the problem we want to solve succinctly, preferably in a single sentence or line.

Here's our concept:

A Streamlit app that lets users convert between different units of measurement.

Stating the concept uncovers the core of what you're trying to do and focuses thinking, preventing it from wandering off in a dozen directions. Of course, this doesn't mean the stated concept is set in stone. If you encounter an idea that significantly enriches the experience, you can offer it to users; however, if it doesn't fit well with the concept, feel free to restate the concept. Stating the concept also provides a concise one-line description to share with others, helping them understand the work. This can be especially valuable for attracting users or finding collaborators.

3.3 Defining the requirements

The concept works well as an app's mission statement, but it's somewhat high level. The next step is to break it down into concrete *requirements* you can build toward. Think of these as a list of things *stakeholders* (users, teams you work with, and so on) would want the app to do.

Requirements should

- express a capability the app should have
- be free of "implementation" language, e.g., it should not refer to any technology

For an app you're building in real life, creating a list of requirements might involve interviewing people to understand their needs. Here's the list of *requirements* we'll use as the foundation for our app:

- Users can enter a numeric quantity and the unit in which the quantity is expressed (the "from" unit).
- The user should be able to select a unit to convert to (the "to-unit"), which must measure the same type of thing as the from-unit. No converting from pounds to yards, for instance.
- The app displays the converted value as output.
- The app handles conversions within both imperial and metric systems (e.g., feet to inches or meters to centimeters), as well as conversions across systems (e.g., feet to meters).
- Adding new units or quantities in the app is straightforward.

Note that the above points are much more concrete than the initial concept. Also, note that requirements don't just come from the user; they can come from other people as well.

To elaborate, the first four requirements listed above are things that the *user* wants, while the last one makes life easier for the developer or maintainer. You'd want to minimize the time spent responding to common requests, such as adding another unit of measurement to the app. In an organizational setting, you can also imagine requirements from other stakeholders, such as the analytics team ("we should be able to monitor and track usage of the app") or the monetization team ("the app should allow the user to subscribe for a monthly fee").

The requirements don't specify the *technology* to accomplish them. For example, they don't say, "the app should display a Streamlit button the user can click to perform the conversion." This is intentional. Requirements describe what stakeholders need; the developer decides how to fulfill them.

3.3.1 Defining what the app won't do

While listing requirements is an important step that provides clear goals, it can sometimes feel like you're stating the obvious. In practice, there's value in doing it anyway, because what seems obvious to you may not be obvious to users or collaborators. People may assume that your app will have a feature you have no intention of building. For that reason, it's vital—and possibly more enlightening—to also define what falls outside the app's scope.

For the unit conversion app in this chapter, we'll keep things as simple as possible. We don't want to spend too much time on it; we're mainly building it to familiarize ourselves with Streamlit.

We'll remove any auxiliary functionality that doesn't directly relate to the goal of unit conversion. We will not build usage logging or fancy visualizations and we will keep the conversion logic simple. Converting from pounds to kilograms is easy enough since you can bake the conversion factor into the app. But how about, say, currencies?

Converting from dollars to euros is hard because the exchange rate changes daily, or even from hour to hour. Incorporating current rates means fetching exchange rates from somewhere, such as from an online API. Later projects in this book will include querying an API, but for now it's best to avoid the additional complexity. So we'll skip the currencies. To state it formally, here is *what's out of scope*:

- Usage tracking, logging, and visualizations that don't directly relate to unit conversion.

- Conversions between units that don't share a simple, constant conversion factor, such as those between currencies.

This list can be a useful tool for prioritization and phasing. Even if you placed something out of scope now, you may want to build it later. Articulating the requirements and scope helps clarify which features are priorities and which to include in a future version. If additional stakeholders are involved, writing these down helps elicit feedback and start a conversation about prioritization.

3.4 Visualizing the user experience

So far, we've spent a fair amount of time thinking about the problem to solve. We've conceptualized what we'll be building, refined what the app needs to do, and even articulated what it *won't* do. Next, we can start designing a solution.

When you start developing an app, you may wonder what to do first. Do you simply start coding your Python app from top to bottom, figuring out your design as you go? Do you figure out what the basic components of your app are and how they'll fit together? Or you could work on what you think will be the hardest part of the problem to get it out of the way.

Those are all valid approaches, and there are arguments to be made in favor of each. One approach I've always found valuable, which we'll follow in this chapter, is to *work backwards from the user experience*.

Starting with the user experience helps ensure end-product quality by putting the user front and center and addressing their needs and preferences. It also helps identify and resolve potential usability problems early in the process.

3.4.1 Creating a mock

What experience do we want app users to have? To answer that, let's create a mock-up of the UI, as shown in figure 3.2. You can use any drawing software you like, or just pen and paper. Looking back at the requirements we listed in section 3.3, at its core, the app needs to:

1 Let users enter a numeric value and the units to convert from and to (both units must measure the same type of quantity).

2 Output the converted value.

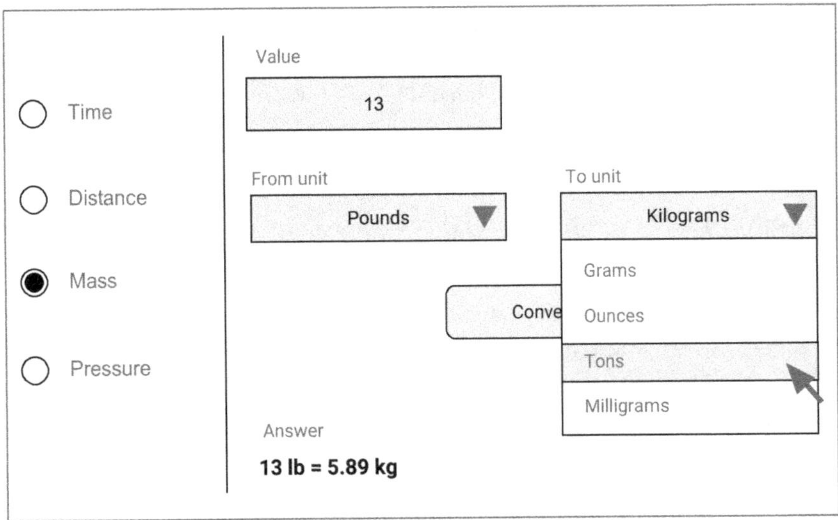

Figure 3.2   A mock-up of the unit conversion app

Figure 3.2 illustrates a preliminary UI design that meets these conditions. It's quite simple: there's a box where you can type in the value to convert and choose the from and to units from a select box. Once you're done, click the Convert button, and the answer appears below.

On the left, a unit category selector limits the units available in the two drop-down menus to the selected category, so the interface shows only units relevant to the current task.

You can make a diagram like this using a pen and paper, a marker and whiteboard, or any graphics program you prefer. It doesn't have to be elaborate or even particularly neat. It should show the end outcome you want to create, forcing you to think about the app from the user's perspective.

At this stage, the UI design isn't necessarily final. As we move into implementation, you may spot optimizations to make. In the following sections, we'll encounter a few and iterate on the design.

> **NOTE** Since you'll implement the UI design using Streamlit, you might wonder, as you visualize the user experience, whether to keep Streamlit's available elements in mind so you don't design something you can't build. In my opinion, that's putting the cart before the horse. In an ideal world, determine the best user experience and then *implement* it using Streamlit. Don't let Streamlit limit thinking about the ideal user experience. Of course, this carries some risk; Streamlit may not have the exact elements you hoped for in the design, and you'll need to adjust the implementation. But that will enrich the learning journey by making Streamlit's deficiencies clearer. It will also keep the user experience from being constrained by preconceptions about Streamlit's feature set, which is constantly expanding.

3.5 Brainstorming the implementation

We now have a rough idea of what the end-user experience in the app will be like. Let's turn our attention to making that experience a reality. In this step of the process, we'll enumerate the various parts of the solution, discuss how they fit together, and map out the flow of thinking.

Most applications have two primary components: a frontend and a backend. The frontend handles how users interact with an app—how it collects inputs and displays outputs. The backend is the app's "brain": it takes input from the frontend, processes it, and returns the output to the frontend for display.

Based on the previous section, we already have a fair idea of what the app's frontend looks like. We just need to translate the UI into the corresponding elements available in Streamlit, which we'll do later in the code walkthrough. Next, we'll turn our attention to the backend, starting with the unit conversion itself.

3.5.1 Converting units

Let's say we want to convert 5 pounds (lb) to ounces (oz). According to an online search (I grew up with the metric system), 1 pound equals 16 ounces. So, to convert 5 pounds to ounces, multiply 16 by 5 to get 80 ounces. We'll refer to 16 here as the *lb-to-oz conversion factor.*

Each pair of units has a similar conversion factor. For instance, 1 yard equals 3 feet, so the yard-to-foot conversion factor is 3. For an imperial-to-metric example, 1 mile equals 1.609344 km, so the mile-to-km conversion factor is 1.609344.

In general, for any pair of units X and Y, you can convert a value expressed in X to Y as follows:

$$\text{Value in unit Y} = \text{Value in unit X} \times \text{X-to-Y conversion factor}$$

To do the reverse conversions (e.g., ounces to pounds), use a conversion factor calculated by dividing 1 by the original conversion factor:

$$\text{1 yard = 3 feet; 1 foot = } \tfrac{1}{3} \text{ yard; foot-to-yard conversion factor = } \tfrac{1}{3}$$

$$\text{1 mile = 1.609344 km; 1 km = 1/1.609344 = 0.621372 miles;}$$
$$\text{km-to-mile conversion factor = 0.621372}$$

With this information, it seems like all we need to do is collect the conversion factor for every pair of possible units within a quantity type and apply the formula given above. But there's a problem: we could end up with a lot of conversion factors to keep track of. If there are 20 different units of length we want to convert between, we'd have to keep track of 190 conversion factors (there are 20 units, and each can be converted into 19 other units—but since we can get the reverse of a conversion factor by dividing 1 by it, we only need to store half of these, which gives us $20 \times 19 / 2 = 190$).

Whew! That's a *lot* of numbers to track in code. Clearly, calculating and storing conversion factors for every single pair of units is not sustainable. Instead, we will designate one unit from each category as the *standard unit* for that category, and keep track only of conversion factors to that unit from all the others. For instance, if we make meters the standard unit for distance, we would only keep track of the conversion factor from each unit to meters, i.e., "what is the value 1 in this unit when converted to meters?"

To convert from unit X to unit Y, convert from unit X to meters and then from meters to unit Y. For example, to convert 5 yards to centimeters:

Yard-to-meter conversion factor equals 0.9144

Centimeter-to-meter conversion factor equals 0.01

We can then follow a two-step conversion process (figure 3.3):

1 5 yards = 5×0.9144 meters = 4.572 meters

2 4.572 meters = $4.572 \times 1 / 0.01$ centimeters = 457.2 centimeters

Notice that since we always store the conversion factor of a unit *to* meters, in step 2, we had to divide 1 by the factor to get the reverse conversion factor, i.e., meter-to-centimeter.

More generally, given a pair of units X and Y and a standard unit S, you can convert a value expressed in X to a value in Y like this:

$$\text{Value in unit S = Value in unit X} \times \text{X-to-S conversion factor}$$

$$\text{Value in unit Y = Value in unit S} \times \text{1 / Y-to-S conversion factor}$$

We now end up with a much more manageable number of conversion factors. Since we only care about how many standard units a given unit is equivalent to, we can get away with storing just one factor per unit.

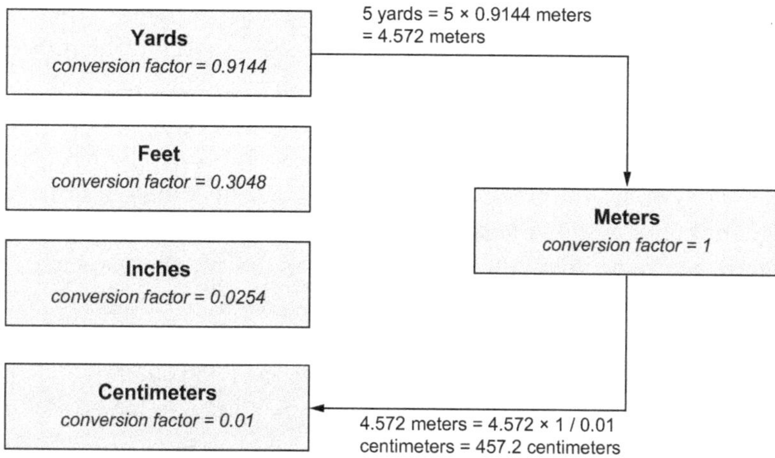

Figure 3.3　Converting yards to centimeters using meters as a standard intermediate unit.

3.5.2　Tracking units and conversion factors

Recall that one of the original requirements is that adding new units to the app must be straightforward. Here, "adding new units" means updating the app to include additional conversion units, not letting users add units dynamically.

This is an example of a *non-user requirement*. Users presumably do not care how easy it is to add new units; they care that the units are available to convert between. So, who *does* care? The developer does.

As a developer, you're rarely done with a piece of software once you've launched it. If enough people use an app, you can count on a steady stream of feedback, bug reports, and feature requests, which can consume the time you planned to spend on other projects. Worse, someone *else* may end up maintaining the code and have no idea how it works.

In this situation, if you haven't designed the app's implementation for ease of maintenance, someone will spend a significant amount of time digging through the code to determine where to make a change and ensure no unintended side effects occur. Even if you're not feeling particularly charitable toward other developers, there's always the likelihood that *the other developer* will be you. Speaking from personal experience, you'd be surprised at how little you'll remember about code you wrote as recently as a month ago.

Returning to the unit converter, one of the most common maintenance tasks is adding new units, so we want to keep that as simple as possible. Ideally, the code should have a single, obvious place to add a unit and its conversion factor.

To achieve this, keep a master list of all quantities, units, and conversion factors in a single *configuration file*. Use an obvious format, and make adding a new unit as easy as appending a few lines to the file.

Critically, this configuration file should be the *only* file that refers to specific quantities. That means no other parts of the app should refer to specific quantities or units. Otherwise, adding a new quantity or unit would require updating that code too, which breaks the requirement that updating the code should be straightforward.

This has an interesting implication: quantities or units can't be hard-coded into the UI code at any point. Information related to specific quantities or units should be pulled from the configuration file, and the rest of the code should be independent of them. We'll see how to do this in the code walkthrough later in the chapter.

3.5.3   Mapping the flow of logic

We now have a good understanding of the app's pieces: the frontend, the conversion logic, and the configuration. Before we code them up, it helps to have a mental model of how they fit together. Figure 3.4 shows the app's overall design.

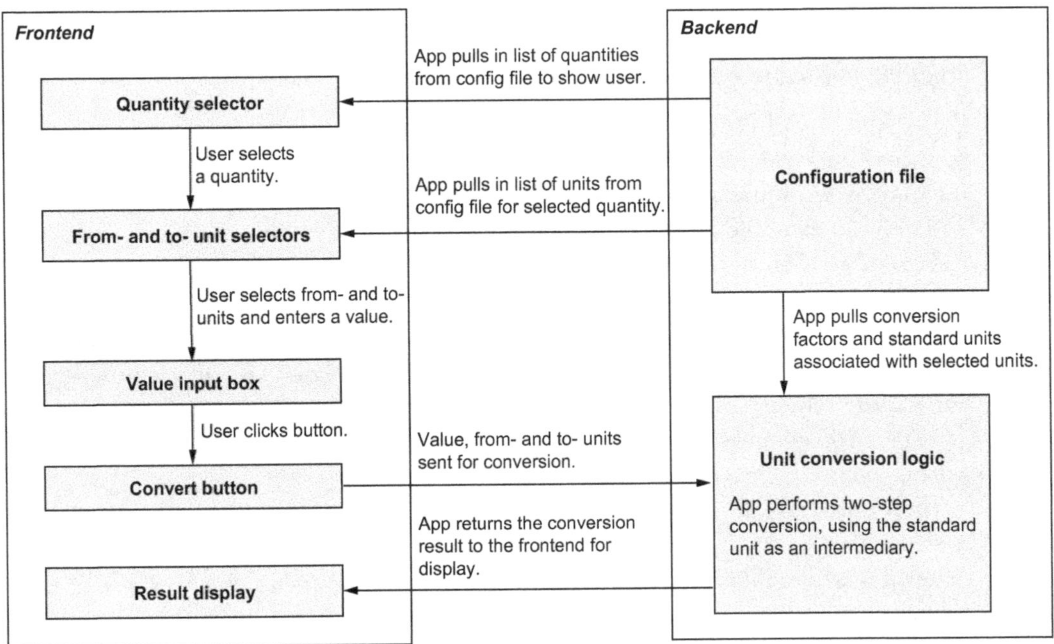

Figure 3.4   Overall design and logic flow for the unit conversion app

The configuration file from the previous section powers the quantity-selector radio buttons in the UI we visualized earlier (figure 3.5). After the user selects a quantity, the From Unit and To Unit drop down menus update based on that selection (again, powered by the configuration file). When the user selects the From and To units and clicks the Convert button, the frontend sends the entries to the backend. The backend uses the conversion factors from the configuration file to perform the two-step conversion outlined in section 3.5.1, and returns the converted value to the frontend for display.

3.6 Writing code

At this point, we've spent enough time thinking about the app design that we're ready to write some code. In this section, we'll create a dummy frontend, learning about the Streamlit widgets that make the UI possible as we do so. We'll then implement the backend and logic flow we've been discussing, starting with the configuration file. We'll define a *contract* or *API* between the frontend and backend, and make the backend fulfill that contract. Finally, we'll wire the frontend to the backend, having it issue calls to the backend through the contract to close the loop.

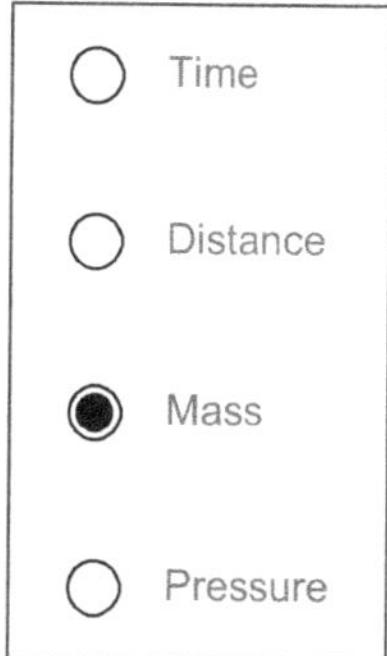

Figure 3.5 Quantity selector radio buttons from the mock

3.6.1 Implementing the frontend

We're now (*finally*) at the part of this chapter where you can actually play with Streamlit! We'll explore each Streamlit feature used in the app (refer back to the UI design reproduced in figure 3.6), and use these pieces to build the frontend incrementally.

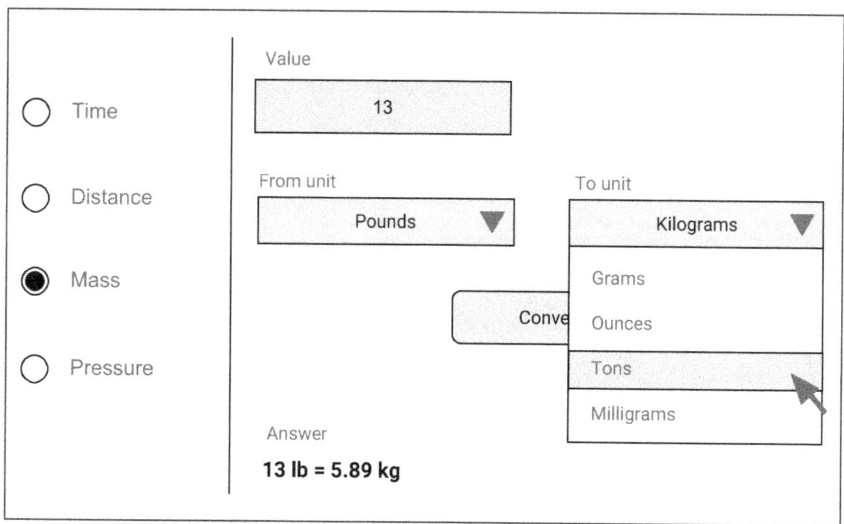

Figure 3.6 UI visualization for our Unit Converter app

To start, create a new Python file called frontend.py and import Streamlit.

```
import streamlit as st
```

Save the file and run the following command in the terminal:

```
streamlit run frontend.py
```

Or run `streamlit run <path to frontend.py>` if the working directory is not the one that contains frontend.py.

This opens a browser window showing the app (currently just a blank screen). Whenever you make a change, switch back to the browser window and click Rerun or Always Rerun to see the results.

ST.RADIO

The first component of the UI we'll focus on is the quantity selector, a panel on the left with a set of radio buttons. Radio buttons are UI elements that let users select a single item from a list. For example, if you append the following to the frontend.py file you just created:

```
quantity = st.radio("Select a quantity", ["Mass", "Length", "Time"])
```

Streamlit will display the question Select a quantity and a list of radio buttons with Mass, Length, and Time as options. Once the user has selected one, the variable `quantity` will contain the option that the user picked (i.e., the string Mass, Length, or Time).

We eventually want to fetch the list of quantity names from the backend, but we're hardcoding it for now since we don't *have* a backend yet. The code we wrote so far produces the output shown in figure 3.7.

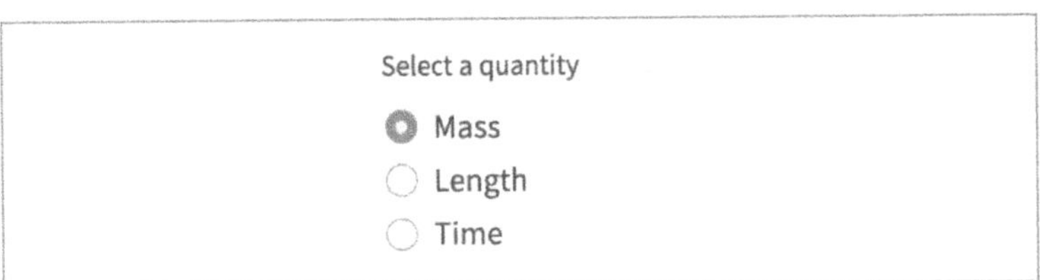

Figure 3.7   An example output for `st.radio`

Streamlit offers plenty of options for customizing `st.radio`. You can arrange the options horizontally instead of vertically, add a caption to each option, disable them altogether, and more. For a complete list of options, see the Streamlit docs at https://docs.streamlit.io/develop/api-reference/widgets/st.radio.

ST.SIDEBAR

We've created the radio buttons, but we need them in a panel on the left, as shown in figure 3.8. In Streamlit terminology, this kind of panel is called a *sidebar*. Sidebars are useful when you want to create links to different pages in the app, provide metainformation about the app, or offer additional content.

To use `st.sidebar`, you need to put content inside it. You can do this using a context manager (i.e., Python with statement) like this:

```
with st.sidebar:
    quantity = st.radio("Select a quantity", ["Mass", "Length", "Time"])
```

Place any Streamlit element inside the `with` statement to show it in the sidebar.

You can also use a dot notation and refer to an element you want to place inside the sidebar as a member of the sidebar, like so:

```
quantity = st.sidebar.radio("Select a quantity", ["Mass", "Length", "Time"])
```

Appending either of the above to frontend.py produces the output shown in figure 3.8.

Figure 3.8 `st.sidebar` **in action with a set of radio buttons inside**

The UI displays a sidebar with an "X" icon that collapses it or a ">" icon that expands a collapsed sidebar.

ST.TITLE

With the sidebar in place, let's focus on the main area of the app. Users need to know what the app is and what it does, so add a title:

```
st.title("Unit Converter")
```

This is pretty self-explanatory, but to say it explicitly, `st.title` writes the string you pass to it as a title—in large, bold text.

ST.TEXT_INPUT

Next, we need the user to enter the value they want to convert. Let's use a text input for this.

`st.text_input` is Streamlit's way of letting users enter single-line values. Write:

```
input_num = st.text_input("Value to convert", value="0")
```

to display a text input with the caption "Value to convert" and an initial value of 0. Note that `st.text_input` returns a string, so `input_num` has the string 0.

To keep this as a number, we'll also cast the value to a float:

```
input_num = float(st.text_input("Value to convert", value="0"))
```

With the title and text input, our app should look like figure 3.9.

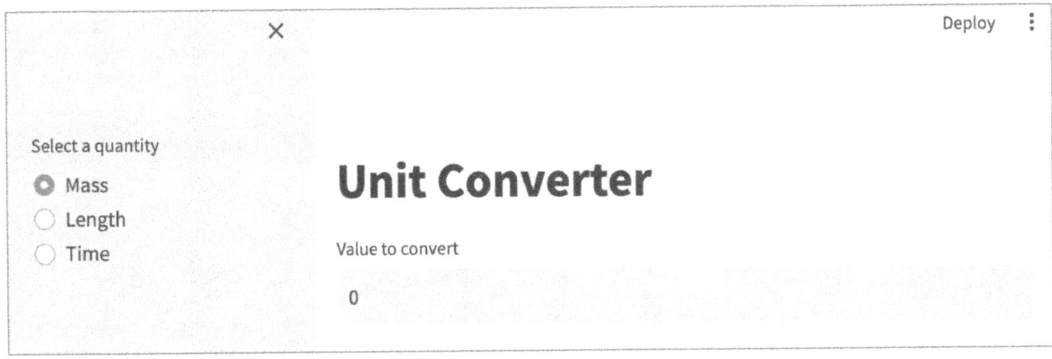

Figure 3.9   Unit Converter app after adding a title and text input

`st.text_input` has many customization options, such as placeholder text displayed when there's no entered value, an optional tooltip, and the ability to enter passwords (we encountered this in our password checker app in chapter 2). Again, https://docs .streamlit.io has more details on what's available.

ST.SELECTBOX

We need dropdowns for the user to select the From and To units, so let's create those next.

`st.selectbox` is what we need here. It displays a basic select widget with a label and a set of options. The arguments are similar to what you would pass to `st.radio`. For example, write

```
unit = st.selectbox("Pick a unit", ["Kilograms", "Grams", "Pounds", "Ounces"])
```

to display a unit dropdown with the variable `unit` containing the selected option. When the dropdown first renders, the first option ("Kilograms" in this case) is selected by default. For our use case, we have two dropdowns to populate, so we'll define the list separately and use it in both:

```
units = ["Kilograms", "Grams", "Pounds", "Ounces"]
from_unit = st.selectbox("From", units)
to_unit = st.selectbox("To", units, index=1)
```

The `index` parameter in the second dropdown sets the option selected by default. A value of 1 selects the second option on the first render. This prevents the From and To dropdowns from defaulting to the same selected value, which would rarely be useful. For now, we're hardcoding the unit names as placeholders to build the frontend, but later we'll pull them from the backend. At this point, the app looks like figure 3.10.

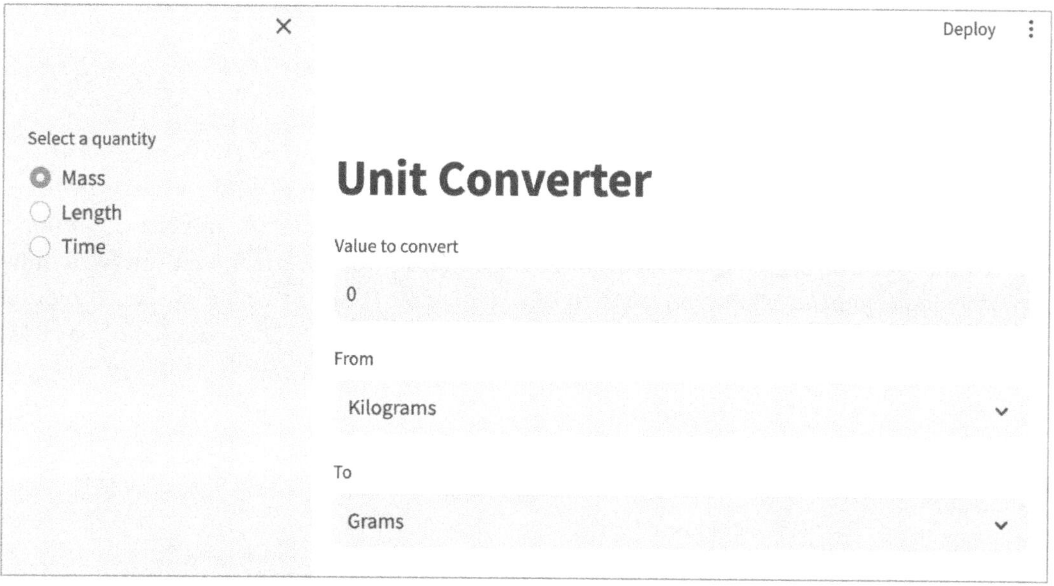

Figure 3.10 **Unit Converter app after adding From and To dropdowns**

This is fine, but our design had the From and To dropdowns side by side, which feels more natural.

ST.COLUMNS

By default, Streamlit displays UI elements from top to bottom in the same order it encounters them in the code. That isn't always ideal; sometimes a side-by-side layout works better. We saw how to do this with `st.sidebar`, but an app can only have one sidebar, and it appears to the left of the overall UI; it can't be inline.

`st.columns` is the answer here. To use it, first create a list of columns, specifying the number of columns you want:

```
from_unit_col, to_unit_col = st.columns(2)
```

Here, the call to `st.columns(2)` returns a list of two columns. This syntax is called *list unpacking*, and it assigns the individual list items to different variables. Here, `from_unit_col` contains the first column and `to_unit_col` contains the second.

As in the case of `st.sidebar`, there are two ways to put something in a column: using the `with` context manager or the dot notation. So we could write:

```
with from_unit_col:
    from_unit = st.selectbox("From", units)
with to_unit_col:
    to_unit = st.selectbox("To", units, index=1)
```

Or more concisely:

```
from_unit = from_unit_col.selectbox("From", units)
to_unit = to_unit_col.selectbox("To", units, index=1)
```

Generally speaking, the `with` context manager makes more sense when you have multiple elements to display within a container (whether it's a sidebar, a column, or something else). At the same time, dot notation works better when you have only a single item or when you want to display elements out of order. We'll see plenty of examples of these cases throughout this book. Figure 3.11 shows the app at this point.

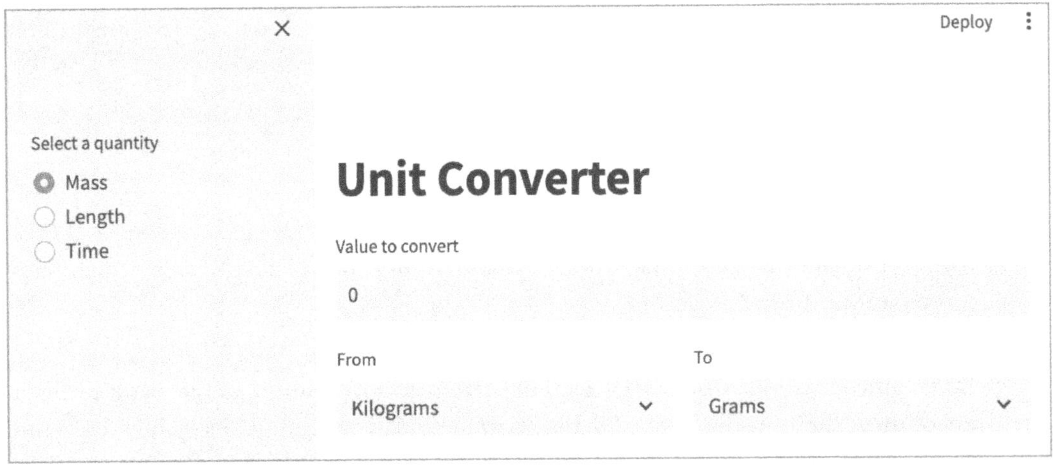

Figure 3.11   Unit Converter app with side-by-side From and To dropdowns

ST.BUTTON

With all inputs captured, we're ready to add the Convert button. Recall `st.button` from chapter 2—Streamlit's ol' faithful make-something-happen element. To add the button, write:

```python
if st.button("Convert"):
    pass # Placeholder for future statements to execute
```

This should be easy enough to understand. It says, "display a button that says 'Convert' and if/when the user clicks it, execute some statements." For the moment, we'll use the keyword `pass` as a placeholder, indicating no action. This will render a barebones Streamlit button that we can later use to trigger the conversion. Listing 3.1 (chapter_03/in_progress/frontend_in_progress_08.py in the GitHub repo) shows our full code so far.

Listing 3.1 Creating the base UI with Streamlit in frontend.py

```python
import streamlit as st

quantity = st.sidebar.radio("Select a quantity", ["Mass", "Length", "Time"])

st.title("Unit Converter")
input_num = float(st.text_input("Value to convert", value="0"))

units = ["Kilograms", "Grams", "Pounds", "Ounces"]
from_unit_col, to_unit_col = st.columns(2)
from_unit = from_unit_col.selectbox("From", units)
to_unit = to_unit_col.selectbox("To", units, index=1)

if st.button("Convert"):
    pass # Placeholder for future statements to execute
```

Run this code using the `streamlit run` command to see the results shown in figure 3.12.

We've come as far as we can with a pretty frontend that doesn't do anything. Next, we'll build the backend to complete the app.

3.6.2 *Implementing the backend*

We now have a dummy frontend with interactive widgets. To make the app useful, we need to define and implement the actions those widgets trigger. We'll start this section by creating a configuration file that lists the quantities and units to support. After that, we'll define a contract between the frontend and backend and write a backend that implements it.

CREATING THE CONFIGURATION FILE

The configuration file holds information about the quantities and units the app understands. Our design requires the app to look up the units for a given quantity. Also, given a unit, it needs to look up its conversion factor relative to the standard unit for that quantity.

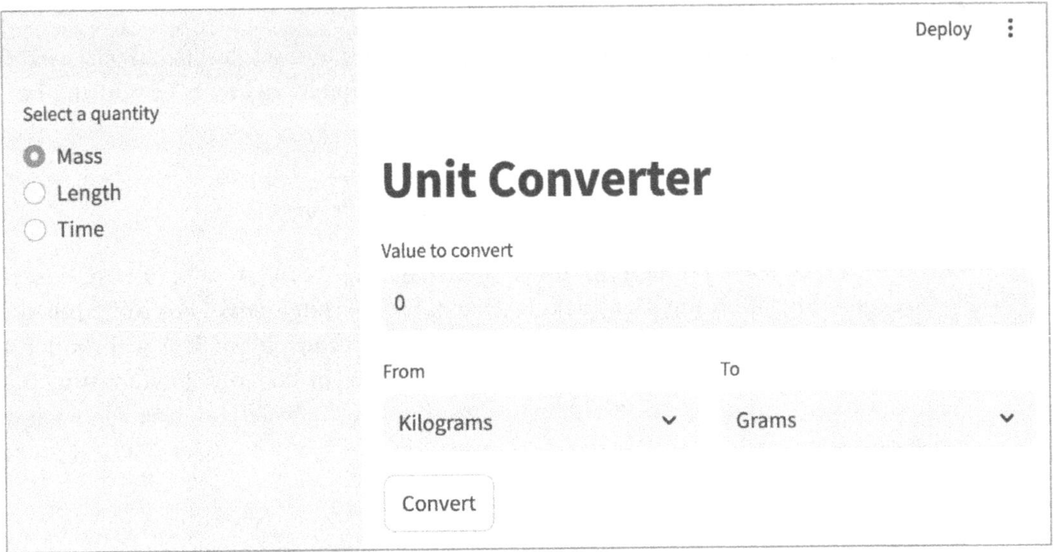

Figure 3.12   Unit Converter app with a dummy frontend

A Python dictionary is ideal for this task. Each key represents a quantity, and the associated values are a list of units—or better yet, *another* dictionary whose keys are units and whose values are the corresponding conversion factors.

One way to write this is as follows:

```
unit_config = {
    "Mass": {
        "Kilograms": 1, # Standard unit
        "Grams": 0.001,
        "Pounds": 0.453592,
        # ...
    },
    "Length": {
        "Meters": 1,  # Standard unit
        "Centimeters": 0.01,
        # ...
    },
}
```

This certainly works, but it would be nice to also display the abbreviation for a unit (e.g., oz for ounces or kg for kilograms) and to store the standard unit for a quantity as well. At this point, units and quantities are well-defined "things" with their own attributes (a unit has an abbreviation and a conversion factor; a quantity has a set of units and one unit designated as the standard). One option is to represent this complexity by expanding the dictionary with more "layers," but defining classes for units and quantities would be better practice.

Open a code editor and create a file called unit.py (listing 3.2) to define the Unit class (chapter_03/in_progress/unit.py in the GitHub repo). Use a dataclass, a special type of class in Python, provided by the `dataclasses` module in the Python standard library.

> **Listing 3.2 The Unit dataclass in unit.py**

```python
from dataclasses import dataclass

@dataclass
class Unit:
    abbrev: str
    value_in_std_units: float
```

A dataclass is an easy way to create a class with some standard basic functionality. For instance, with dataclasses, you don't need to specify a `__init__` method as you would do with a normal class, and once you have an object of the dataclass, you can access its attributes with the dot-notation, like this:

```python
gram = Unit(abbrev="g", value_in_std_units=0.001)
print(gram.abbrev) # Prints 'g'
```

To achieve the same functionality with a regular class, you would have to write:

```python
class Unit:
    def __init__(self, abbrev, value_in_std_units):
        self.abbrev: str = abbrev
        self.value_in_std_units: float = value_in_std_units
```

With dataclasses, you can write the more concise syntax shown in listing 3.2 by adding the `@dataclass` decorator above the class definition. Looking at the class contents, the structure is simple: an `abbrev` string field holds the unit abbreviation, and `value_in_std_units`—a floating-point number—represents the conversion factor discussed in section 3.5.1.

The `: str` and `: float` from listing 3.2 are called *type annotations*. They specify the data type of a field. Type annotations aren't strictly required, but it's a good practice to include them, since (among other things) they make code easier to understand and let code editors or IDEs catch and highlight errors early. Notice that we haven't included a `name` field in the Unit class. We'll discuss the reason when we get to the configuration file.

Let's also define a Quantity class in a new file, quantity.py, as shown in the following listing (chapter_03/in_progress/quantity.py in the GitHub repo).

> **Listing 3.3 The Quantity dataclass in quantity.py**

```python
from dataclasses import dataclass
from typing import Dict
```

```
from unit import Unit

@dataclass
class Quantity:
    std_unit: str
    units: Dict[str, Unit]
```

In listing 3.3, you can see the `Quantity` class with two fields: `units` and `std_unit`. Here, `std_unit` is the name of the standard unit for the quantity.

Notice the more complex type annotation used for the `units` field. `Dict[str, Unit]` means that `units` is a dictionary where each key is a string (the unit's name) and the corresponding value is an object of the `Unit` class. Annotations for some of the more advanced types (such as `Dict` and `List`, which appear later) must be imported from the `typing` module. Also notice the line that imports the `Unit` class we wrote earlier in `unit.py`:

```
from unit import Unit
```

The file unit.py is a *module* and we refer to it without the .py extension. Splitting code into modules is a great way to organize it and avoid putting everything in a single, overwhelming script. Modules promote code *reusability*; functions and classes defined in a module can be imported and used in other Python files.

Now create the final configuration file, as shown in listing 3.4.

Listing 3.4   The unit configuration file, unit_config.py

```
from typing import Dict

from quantity import Quantity
from unit import Unit

unit_config: Dict[str, Quantity] = {
    "Mass": Quantity(
        std_unit="Kilograms",
        units={
            "Kilograms": Unit(abbrev="kg", value_in_std_units=1),
            "Grams": Unit(abbrev="g", value_in_std_units=0.001),
            "Pounds": Unit(abbrev="lb", value_in_std_units=0.453592),
            "Ounces": Unit(abbrev="oz", value_in_std_units=0.0283495),
            # Add more units here
        }
    ),
    "Length": Quantity(
        std_unit="Meters",
        units={
            "Meters": Unit(abbrev="m", value_in_std_units=1),
            "Centimeters": Unit(abbrev="cm", value_in_std_units=0.01),
            "Inches": Unit(abbrev="in", value_in_std_units=0.0254),
            "Feet": Unit(abbrev="ft", value_in_std_units=0.3048),
        }
```

```
    ),
    "Time": Quantity(
        std_unit="Seconds",
        units={
            "Seconds": Unit(abbrev="s", value_in_std_units=1),
            "Minutes": Unit(abbrev="min", value_in_std_units=60),
            "Hours": Unit(abbrev="hr", value_in_std_units=3600),
            "Days": Unit(abbrev="d", value_in_std_units=86400),
        }
    ),
    # Add more quantities here
}
```

The configuration is still a dictionary, but each value is now an object of the `Quantity` class (imported from the quantity.py module). The file includes three quantities: `Mass`, `Length`, and `Time`.

Let's inspect one of these:

```
"Mass": Quantity(
        std_unit="Kilograms",
        units={
            "Kilograms": Unit(abbrev="kg", value_in_std_units=1),
            "Grams": Unit(abbrev="g", value_in_std_units=0.001),
            "Pounds": Unit(abbrev="lb", value_in_std_units=0.453592),
            "Ounces": Unit(abbrev="oz", value_in_std_units=0.0283495),
            # Add more units here
        }
    )
```

This is quite readable. It configures a quantity named `Mass` as a `Quantity` object with a standard unit of kilograms. The `units` dictionary has four entries, one for each unit; each value is a `Unit` object with an abbreviation and conversion factor. Since Kilograms is the standard unit, its `value_in_std_units` is 1.

You may now also realize why neither of the `Unit` and `Quantity` classes have a `name` field. Since the unit and quantity names are already incorporated into the dictionary keys in unit_config.py, including them in the class is unnecessary and would make the configuration file longer and less readable.

Adding more units is easy: add new entries to the `units` dictionary within `Quantity`. Similarly, to add new quantities, append to the `unit_config` dictionary, following the format of the previous entries. This approach keeps the configuration file easy to update. Next, we'll design and build the backend that uses the configurations we've defined.

THE BACKEND API

A key concept in software development is the *separation of concerns*. In essence, each building block in a piece of software should focus on one aspect of the overall system's functionality and remain independent of the other building blocks. When one block interacts with another, it should do so in strictly controlled ways as defined by a contract.

To better understand this concept, consider how a drive-in fast-food restaurant typically operates. A person at the front takes orders from customers, and a kitchen prepares the food according to the menu. The order-taker doesn't care what ingredients the kitchen uses as long as it can prepare the items on the menu, and the kitchen doesn't care what language the order-taker uses to communicate with the customer, as long as the customer orders items from the menu.

If the kitchen wants to hire new cooks or use different ingredients, it can do so without informing the order-taker, as long as the kitchen prepares dishes that match the menu. If the restaurant replaces the in-person order taker with someone on the phone, it can do that too without affecting the kitchen. The menu makes this possible. It serves as a shared contract between the order-taker and the kitchen.

Similarly, it's a good idea to develop an app by separating its components and having them interact exclusively through a contract called an *Application Programming Interface* (API for short). In this app, we'll keep the frontend and backend separate. That means the frontend should interact with the backend only to request a specific set of actions.

What exactly are these actions? Let's revisit the logic flow diagram in figure 3.13. There are four arrows running between the frontend and the backend:

- One where the frontend pulls in the quantities to show users
- One where it pulls in the units for the quantity the user selected
- One where the frontend provides the values for conversion, and
- One where the backend returns the conversion value

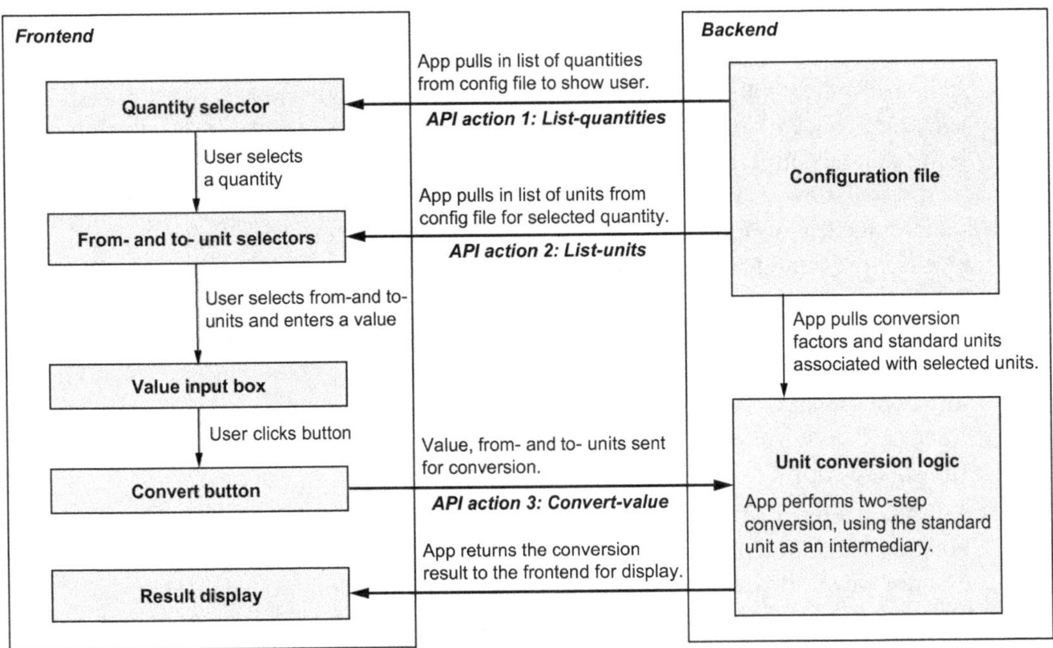

Figure 3.13   Flow diagram for the app, highlighting the API actions

This breaks down into three interactions (the last two arrows are really two parts of the same interaction) that the frontend has with the backend:

- *List-quantities*—The frontend asks the backend to provide the list of quantities it supports.
- *List-units*—The frontend gives the backend a quantity and asks it to list the units it can convert between for that quantity.
- *Convert-value*—The frontend gives the backend the value to convert and the units the user selected, and asks it to convert the value.

The above actions form the menu or API of the backend. As in the fast food example, as long as the backend can fulfill these responsibilities, it's free to implement them however it wants. Perhaps we'll find a more efficient way to perform conversions at some point, or maybe the backend will connect to an external service to perform the conversion. Either way, we can change the backend implementation without touching the frontend code.

Or we might later add a command-line interface to the conversion app alongside the graphical UI. In that case, we can do it without changing the existing frontend code.

As you can see, separating concerns between the frontend and backend gives us a lot of flexibility. Our app is simple enough that the benefits may not be obvious, but this is a good habit to develop as it'll help you in the real world when you develop more complex apps and need to switch out components easily.

Next, we'll look at how to implement this API approach.

NOTE We're using the term "API" here in its simplest sense, which is just a contract that defines how you're allowed to interact with a piece of software (in this case, our backend), even if the thing that does the interacting is another component of the same application (our frontend). Usually, when you hear the word "API" in the wild, it takes on a more specialized meaning, often referring to web APIs—interfaces designed to allow communication with a web service over the internet. We'll encounter this kind of "API" in chapter 5.

IMPLEMENTING THE API

Next, we'll implement the actions the backend needs to support: list-quantities, list-units, and convert-value. Each action will be a function in the backend. For each one, we'll first create the function signature, and then implement it.

Before you start, create a file called backend.py and import the main items you need: `unit_config` from unit_config.py, the `Result` class (which we haven't defined yet, but will shortly), and `List` for type definitions.

```python
from unit_config import unit_config
from result import Result
from typing import List
```

Turning to the API actions themselves, *List-quantities* is pretty simple; it asks the backend for a list of all the quantities it knows. It requires no arguments, and the output is likely a list of strings. Thus:

```
def list_quantities() -> List[str]
```

How do we implement this? We need the quantities that are the keys of the configuration object in unit_config.py (listing 3.4). So we simply write:

```
def list_quantities() -> List[str]:
    return list(unit_config.keys())
```

List-units does take an argument (the quantity to list units for), and it again returns a list of strings. This yields:

```
def list_units(quantity_name) -> List[str]
```

Implementing this is fairly straightforward. The list we need consists of the keys in the `units` dictionary of the `Quantity` object corresponding to the `quantity_name` key in `unit_config`:

```
def list_units(quantity_name) -> List[str]:
    return list(unit_config[quantity_name].units.keys())
```

> **NOTE**   Notice that the code doesn't handle the case where `quantity_name` doesn't exist in `unit_config`. In real-world code, you should add that check, but this chapter leaves out error handling to keep the code relatively concise. Later chapters cover error handling.

Convert-value takes four arguments: a quantity name, the from and to units, and a value to convert. We want to include the quantity name because different quantities may use units with the same name (though the example configuration doesn't).

As for the return type, we *could* simply return the converted value—a floating-point number. But recall that the configuration also includes abbreviations for each unit. On conversion, it would be nice if we could also return the appropriate abbreviations to the frontend so it can display something like 15 ft = 5 yd.

On the other hand, we don't want to be prescriptive about how the frontend *actually* displays the results. That's the frontend's business—remember *separation of concerns*? If the frontend wants to show the converted number with no abbreviation, that's totally fine too.

One approach is to wrap any metadata the frontend might need in a dedicated `Result` class and let the frontend decide what to do with it.

Let's define the `Result` class in a new file called result.py, as shown in listing 3.5 (chapter_03/in_progress/result.py in the GitHub repo).

Listing 3.5 The Result dataclass in result.py

```python
from dataclasses import dataclass
from unit import Unit


@dataclass
class Result:
    from_unit: Unit
    to_unit: Unit
    from_value: float
    to_value: float
```

Note that rather than placing just the abbreviation for each unit in the result, this approach includes the entire `Unit`. If the `Unit` class changes later and gains additional properties, this code won't need to change.

Now, we're ready to define the signature for *Convert-value:*

```python
def convert_value(
        quantity_name: str,
        from_unit_name: str,
        to_unit_name: str,
        value: float) -> Result
```

We already discussed how to implement the conversion; here it is in code form:

```python
def convert_value(
        quantity_name: str,
        from_unit_name: str,
        to_unit_name: str,
        value: float) -> Result:
    quantity = unit_config[quantity_name]
    from_unit = quantity.units[from_unit_name]
    to_unit = quantity.units[to_unit_name]

    # Two-step conversion: from-unit to standard unit, then to to-unit
    value_in_to_units = (value *
                        from_unit.value_in_std_units /
                        to_unit.value_in_std_units)

    return Result(from_unit, to_unit, value, value_in_to_units)
```

Notice the two-step conversion discussed earlier. `value * from_unit.value_in_std_units` gives the value in standard units, and `/ to_unit.value_in_std_units` converts it to the target unit.

Listing 3.6 puts this all together in a single backend.py file (chapter_03/in_progress/backend.py in the GitHub repo).

Listing 3.6   The backend functions in backend.py

```python
from unit_config import unit_config
from result import Result
from typing import List

def list_quantities() -> List[str]:
    return list(unit_config.keys())

def list_units(quantity_name) -> List[str]:
    return list(unit_config[quantity_name].units.keys())

def convert_value(
        quantity_name: str,
        from_unit_name: str,
        to_unit_name: str,
        value: float) -> Result:
    quantity = unit_config[quantity_name]
    from_unit = quantity.units[from_unit_name]
    to_unit = quantity.units[to_unit_name]

    # Two-step conversion: from-unit to standard unit, then to-unit
    value_in_to_units = (value *
                        from_unit.value_in_std_units /
                        to_unit.value_in_std_units)

    return Result(from_unit, to_unit, value, value_in_to_units)
```

3.6.3   *Wiring up the frontend and backend*

We're close to a working app! Our frontend lays out beautiful widgets that collect inputs from the user, and our backend can perform the unit conversion, given those inputs. All that's left to do is to wire the two up. We'll be making changes to frontend. py again, so open it, and—to begin with—add imports at the top for the functions we just defined in backend.py:

```python
from backend import list_quantities, list_units, convert_value
```

It's time to fix all the hard-coded values added earlier, before there was a backend. The first instance is in the quantity selector, where we defined the radio button options like this:

```python
quantity = st.radio("Select a quantity", ["Mass", "Length", "Time"])
```

The `list_quantities` function can now return the list of options directly, so replace the hardcoded list with a function call:

```python
quantity = st.sidebar.radio("Select a quantity", list_quantities())
```

There's another hardcoded list we need to get rid of—the unit list used for the drop-downs, which is currently unresponsive to the actual quantity the user chooses in the sidebar:

```
units = ["Kilograms", "Grams", "Pounds", "Ounces"]
```

We have a `list_units` function that returns the list of units from the configuration file when you pass it a quantity, so let's use it to replace the preceding code with:

```
units = list_units(quantity)
```

Run the app now to see that the list of From and To unit options changes when you click a different quantity, as intended (figure 3.14).

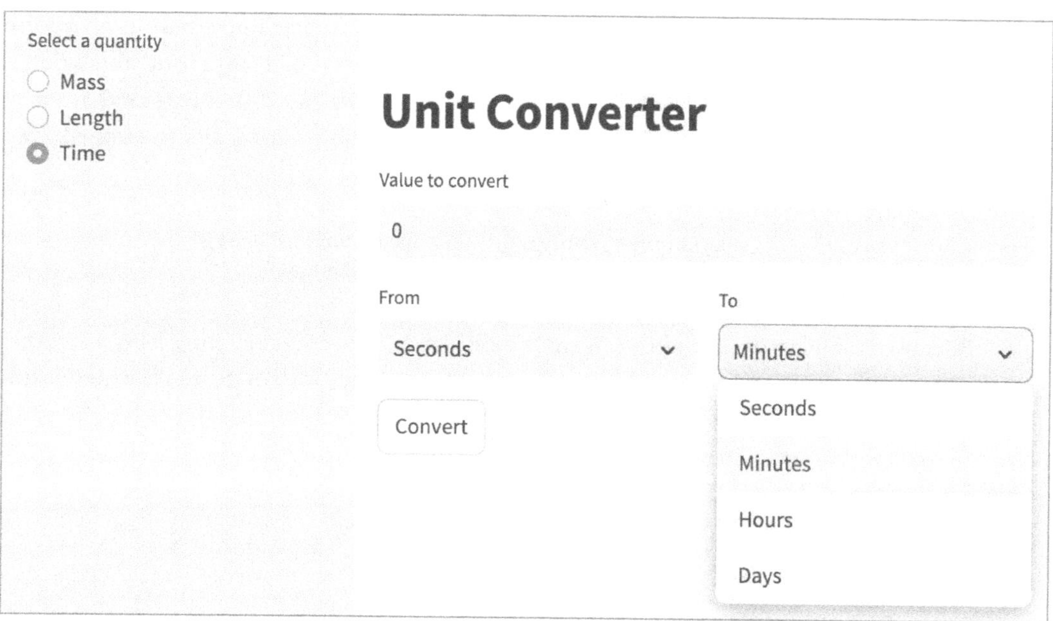

Figure 3.14 **With the backend wired up, choosing a different quantity updates the unit dropdowns.**

Let's pick up where we left off: the Convert button currently doesn't do anything:

```
if st.button("Convert"):
    pass # Placeholder for future statements to execute
```

What should the button do? The backend includes a `convert_value` function that per-forms unit conversion, so start by calling it:

```
if st.button("Convert"):
    result = convert_value(quantity, from_unit, to_unit, input_num)
```

This call passes `convert_value`, the user-selected quantity, the from and to units, and the value to convert. Recall that `convert_value` returns a `Result` object (defined in result.py). The `result` variable now holds the conversion result, complete with the from/to values and abbreviations. All that remains is to display it on the screen.

ST.METRIC

We could have displayed the result as plain old paragraph text, but this is the big outcome of the app—the grand finale. We want something that packs more *punch*.

`st.metric` is a widget commonly used in dashboards to show important numbers—like a company's revenue—and how they're trending compared with a prior period.

A single `st.metric` element represents a measure a user is interested in and consists of three parts: a text label, the number itself displayed in a large font, and a delta indicator, which shows how much the number has increased or decreased from a prior period. Use `st.metric` to display the from and to values along with the unit abbreviations. So, first prepare these:

```
from_display = f"{result.from_value} {result.from_unit.abbrev}"
to_display = f"{result.to_value} {result.to_unit.abbrev}"
```

Because result is a `Result` object, form the display text by concatenating its `from_value` or `to_value` field and taking the abbreviation from `from_unit` or `to_unit`, which is an instance of `Unit`.

To use `st.metric`, write:

```
st.metric("From", from_display, delta=None)
st.metric("To", to_display, delta=None)
```

The delta indicator in `st.metric` doesn't make sense, so set it to `None` to hide it.

This code displays the from and to results vertically, but the layout needs them side by side, so use `st.columns` again:

```
from_value_col, to_value_col = st.columns(2)
from_value_col.metric("From", from_display, delta=None)
to_value_col.metric("To", to_display, delta=None)
```

Figure 3.15 shows the completed app. Listing 3.7 shows the frontend.py file you should have ended up with if you've been following along (chapter_03/in_progress/frontend_in_progress_12.py in the GitHub repo).

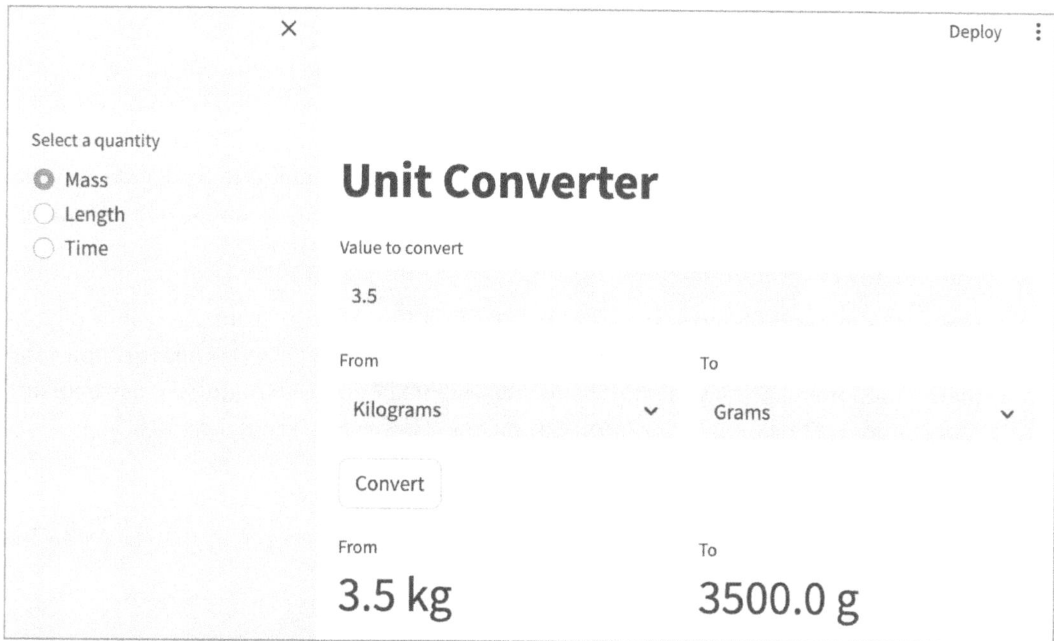

Figure 3.15 Completed Unit Converter app

Listing 3.7 The fleshed-out frontend in frontend.py

```python
import streamlit as st
from backend import list_quantities, list_units, convert_value

quantity = st.sidebar.radio("Select a quantity", list_quantities())

st.title("Unit Converter")
input_num = float(st.text_input("Value to convert", value="0"))

units = list_units(quantity)
from_unit_col, to_unit_col = st.columns(2)
from_unit = from_unit_col.selectbox("From", units)
to_unit = to_unit_col.selectbox("To", units, index=1)

if st.button("Convert"):
    result = convert_value(quantity, from_unit, to_unit, input_num)
    from_display = f"{result.from_value} {result.from_unit.abbrev}"
    to_display = f"{result.to_value} {result.to_unit.abbrev}"

    from_value_col, to_value_col = st.columns(2)
    from_value_col.metric("From", from_display, delta=None)
    to_value_col.metric("To", to_display, delta=None)
```

3.7   *Iterating on the app*

Whew! We did it! We now have a fully functional app. In the real world, this is the *start* of the journey: you'd launch the app and show it to users. Users often provide very opinionated feedback about the experience you've built for them, which can help uncover usability problems and blind spots you may not have encountered in testing. In this section, we'll simulate this process by using the app and identifying potential improvements.

3.7.1   *Rounding conversion results*

Let's take our completed app for a spin. Figure 3.15 shows the example results of converting kilograms to grams. That looks mostly fine, but let's try a metric-to-imperial conversion now. Let's say we want to convert 4,000 kilograms to pounds. We fire up our app, choose "Mass," enter our inputs, and click "Convert" to see figure 3.16.

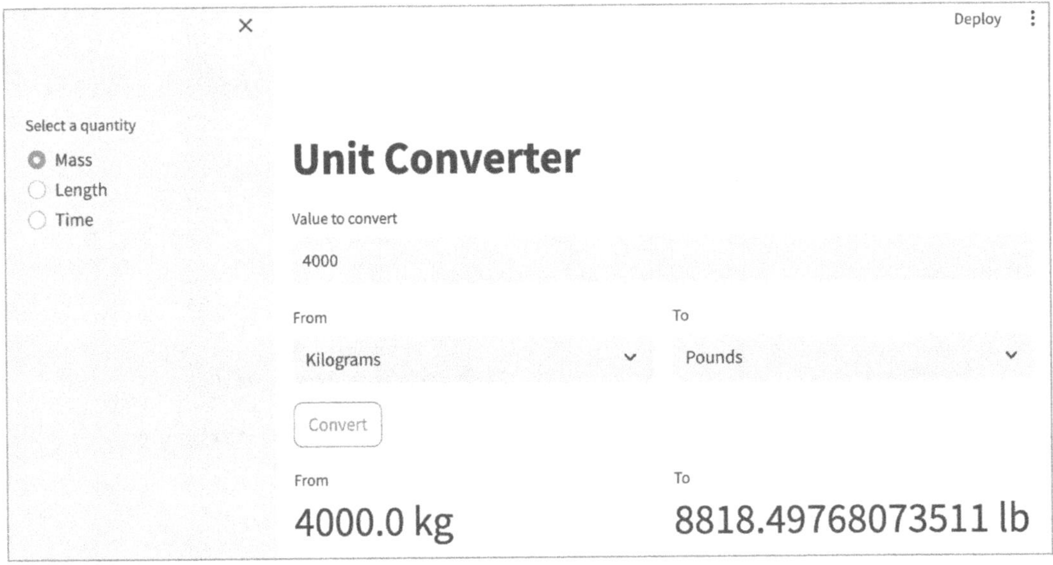

Figure 3.16   Converting metric units to imperial shows why rounding matters.

The answer seems right, but that's a lot of decimal places. Most people probably don't need that level of precision; in fact, it probably detracts from their experience as it takes them a second to figure out why the displayed number is so long. It would be nice if users had the option of rounding the result to the precision they need. And come to think of it, for larger numbers, we should ideally separate the thousands by commas.

To implement this, let's first create a function called `format_value` in frontend.py that will format a number the way we want, i.e., with commas separating the thousands, and optionally rounded to a certain number of decimal points.

`format_value` takes three arguments: the value to format, the abbreviation, and an optional number of `decimal_places` to round the value to. If you omit `decimal_places` (causing `is_rounded` to be `False`), the function does no rounding.

```
def format_value(
        value: float,
        unit_abbrev: str,
        decimal_places: int = None) -> str:
    is_rounded = decimal_places is not None
    rounded = round(value, decimal_places) if is_rounded else value
    formatted = format(rounded, ",")
    return f"{formatted} {unit_abbrev}"
```

This code uses the `round` function to perform rounding when necessary and Python's built-in `format` function to add commas, using "," as the *format spec*. You can hard-code the number of decimal places to round to, but it's better to let users decide, which means adding a new input widget.

ST.NUMBER_INPUT

`st.number_input` is Streamlit's numeric input widget. It's similar to `st.text_input`, but adds features such as minimum and maximum values and step buttons for increasing or decreasing the value with a click. We'll use it to collect a user's preferred number of decimal places. Add this line to frontend.py right after the From and To dropdowns:

```
places = st.number_input("Decimal places to round to", value=3, min_value=0)
```

We specify a default value of 3 and a minimum value of 0 because we can't have a negative number of decimal places (trying to enter a lower value shows an error). `places` holds the number entered. This should produce the widget shown in figure 3.17.

Figure 3.17 **The numeric input widget produced by** `st.number_input`.

Notice the - and + buttons. They increase or decrease the value by 1. You can change the step interval by specifying the `step` parameter in `st.number_input`.

You may wonder why we used `st.text_input` to collect the value to convert and then convert it to a float instead of using `st.number_input`. At the time of writing, Streamlit doesn't provide an easy way to remove the - and + buttons from `st.number_input`. Those buttons make sense when collecting the number of decimal places (an integer in a tight range), but the value to convert is virtually unbounded, and no predefined step interval makes sense.

With the decimal places set, you can apply formatting to the results. Update the `from_display` and `to_display` variables to use the `format_value` function we defined earlier:

```
from_display = format_value(input_num, result.from_unit.abbrev)
to_display = format_value(result.to_value, result.to_unit.abbrev, places)
```

We pass `places` (which we collect from the user) to round the `to_display` variable. We could have done this for `from_display` as well, but it's likely the user entered the precision they want to see in the from-value, so we don't want to mess with that. This gives us figure 3.18.

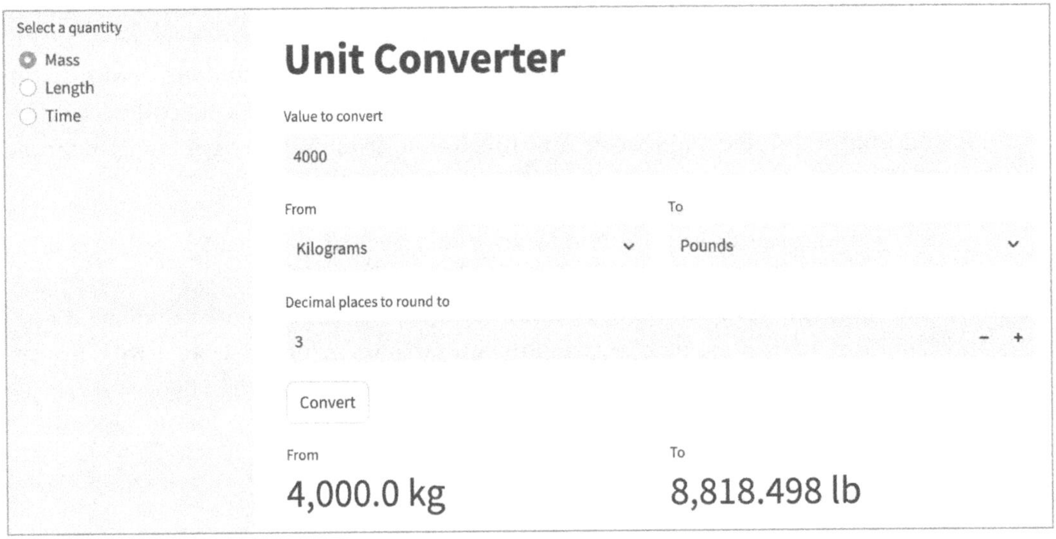

Figure 3.18 **Unit Converter app with a decimal places input**

> **NOTE** This won't pad to-values with extra trailing zeroes. For instance, if the to-value is a whole number, say 600, it will be displayed as "600.0" with just one trailing zero.

The formatted result looks much nicer, but we've added an extra numeric input that increases the user's cognitive load. Let's only introduce the decimal-places input if the user requests it.

ST.CHECKBOX

st.checkbox is a Streamlit checkbox, i.e., a box that you can, well, check. Please try to contain your shock, we have an app to ship.

Like st.button, st.checkbox is a *conditional* element. You can use an if statement to branch the logic based on whether it's checked.

Our use case is to let the user decide if they want to round the conversion result, which we can do by modifying how we obtain the value of the places variable in frontend.py:

```
places = None
if st.checkbox("Round result?", value=False):
    places = st.number_input(
        "Decimal places to round to", value=2, min_value=0)
```

The checkbox is unchecked by default because you pass False to the value parameter.

Notice that the code sets places = None above the st.checkbox call. Later, the code refers to places outside the scope of the if st.checkbox block, so places needs an initial value in case the user leaves the box unchecked. The app should now match figure 3.19.

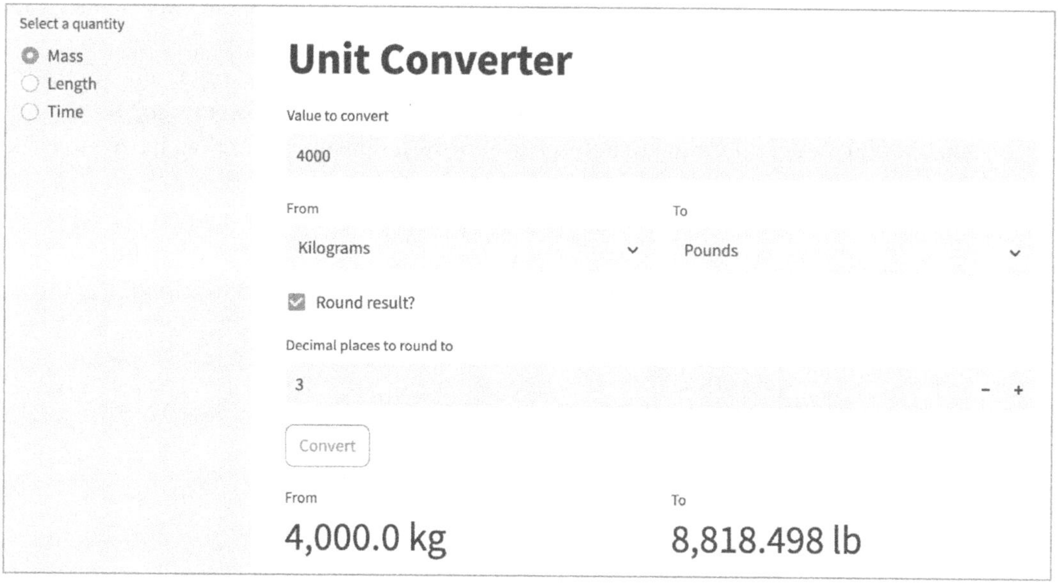

Select a quantity

- Mass
- Length
- Time

Unit Converter

Value to convert

4000

From   To

Kilograms   Pounds

☑ Round result?

Decimal places to round to

3   − +

Convert

From   To

4,000.0 kg   8,818.498 lb

Figure 3.19   Unit Converter app with rounding enabled

Or if the user leaves Round Results? unchecked, we get the full-precision treatment in figure 3.20.

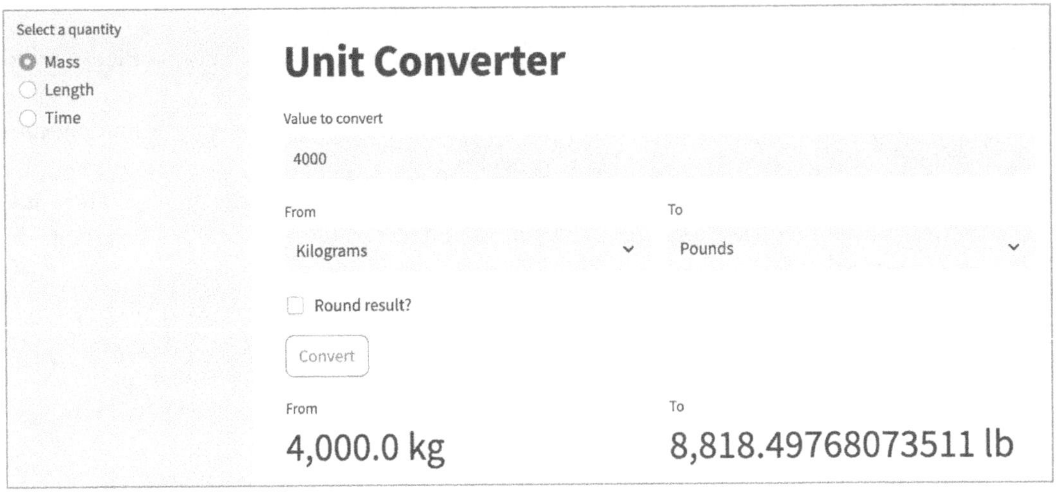

Select a quantity
Mass
Length
Time
Unit Converter
Value to convert
4000
From
Kilograms
To
Pounds
Round result?
Convert
From
4,000.0 kg
To
8,818.49768073511 lb

Figure 3.20   Unit Converter app with rounding disabled

3.7.2   *Getting rid of the button*

The app works great now; it displays rounded output, but only when desired. But adding a click and a numeric input to enable rounding complicates the experience. Can we simplify it? Let's turn to the Convert button. Do we even need it?

The button only triggers the conversion, but an explicit trigger isn't really necessary. Why not have the app always show the result based on the inputs entered? If the user changes the value, they immediately see the converted result rather than having to click the button.

That seems like a more intuitive experience, so let's make it happen. This is easy to do. Simply remove the line `if st.button("Convert"):` and move everything in that block outside. Listing 3.8 shows the final version of frontend.py (chapter_03/final/frontend.py in the GitHub repo).

Listing 3.8   Final version of frontend.py

```python
import streamlit as st
from backend import list_quantities, list_units, convert_value

def format_value(
        value: float,
        unit_abbrev: str,
        decimal_places: int = None) -> str:
    is_rounded = decimal_places is not None
    rounded = round(value, decimal_places) if is_rounded else value
    formatted = format(rounded, ",")
    return f"{formatted} {unit_abbrev}"

quantity = st.sidebar.radio("Select a quantity", list_quantities())
```

```
st.title("Unit Converter")
input_num = float(st.text_input("Value to convert", value="0"))

units = list_units(quantity)
from_unit_col, to_unit_col = st.columns(2)
from_unit = from_unit_col.selectbox("From", units)
to_unit = to_unit_col.selectbox("To", units, index=1)

places = None
if st.checkbox("Round result?", value=False):
    places = st.number_input(
        "Decimal places to round to", value=2, min_value=0)

result = convert_value(quantity, from_unit, to_unit, input_num)
from_display = format_value(input_num, result.from_unit.abbrev)
to_display = format_value(
    result.to_value, result.to_unit.abbrev, places)

from_value_col, to_value_col = st.columns(2)
from_value_col.metric("From", from_display, delta=None)
to_value_col.metric("To", to_display, delta=None)
```

Figure 3.21 shows a final screenshot of the app.

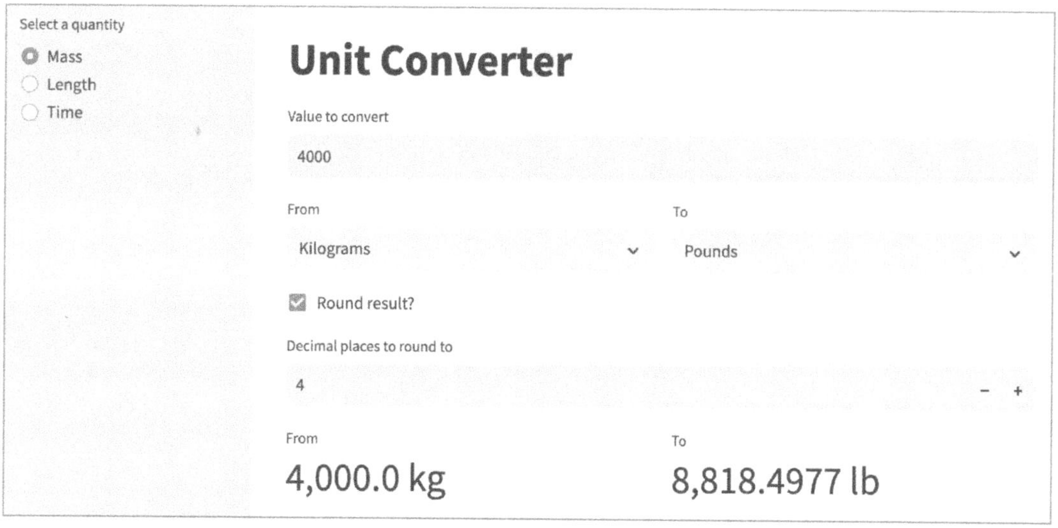

Figure 3.21 Unit Converter app without the Convert button

Removing the button makes the app *flow* a lot better. For instance, changing the decimal places or the value updates the results instantly.

I hope this chapter has been a lot of fun! I wanted to give a sense of what it's like to develop Streamlit apps in the real world while working with real stakeholders. As this chapter has hopefully shown, there's a lot more to the process than writing code; nailing the requirements and designing (and refining) the user experience are equally important.

Summary

- Building an app from a concept involves much more than writing code.
- To create a Streamlit app in practice, follow these steps: state the concept, define the requirements, visualize the user experience, brainstorm the implementation, write the code, and iterate.
- Requirements can come from users or non-user stakeholders.
- It's a good idea to visualize the user experience early by sketching mocks to create a concrete target. Brainstorming the implementation means analyzing trade-offs and mapping the logic flow.
- Separating frontend and backend code and defining an API for them to interact is a great way to organize an app.
- `st.text_input` and `st.number_input` let users enter text and numeric values.
- `st.radio` and `st.selectbox` let users select a value from a list.
- `st.sidebar` and `st.columns` are layout elements that let developers break the natural top-to-bottom way that Streamlit renders UI elements.
- Both `st.button` and `st.checkbox` are conditional elements.

Streamlit's execution model

4

This chapter covers

- Building apps that maintain state between page updates
- Troubleshooting apps
- The all-important `st.session_state` and `st.rerun`
- Streamlit's execution model

In the last two chapters, you got your feet wet with Streamlit by building two fully functional apps: a password checker and a unit converter. You learned the basics of Streamlit syntax and how to create interactive elements. But what happens behind the scenes when a Streamlit app runs? Understanding this is key to building more complex applications. In this chapter, we explore Streamlit's execution model and how to manage an app's state.

This chapter also takes a slightly different approach than the previous ones. While we'll still build a practical application—a daily to-do list app—the primary focus is on building troubleshooting skills. We'll intentionally introduce bugs into the app to simulate real-world situations where things don't go according to plan. By following along and fixing these problems, you'll gain a deeper understanding of Streamlit's inner workings and how to debug your apps effectively.

NOTE   The GitHub repo for the book is at https://github.com/aneevdavis/streamlit-in-action. The chapter_04 folder contains all the code for this chapter, including "in progress" versions you can use to follow along.

4.1   A more complex app: Daily to-dos

Ever juggled multiple deadlines at work while mentally planning a family vacation, while *also* trying to remember to buy bread on the way home? Regardless of the specifics, the frenzy of modern life can get you in its grip, pulling you into a whirlwind of endless activity and demands. Hopefully, this chapter's Streamlit app helps manage the chaos even if it can't actually deliver the bread to the doorstep.

In this chapter, we'll create a to-do list app that lets users track the tasks they need to complete in a day. The primary goal is to familiarize readers with Streamlit's execution model, so we won't walk through the entire six-step development process in detail as we did in the last chapter. Instead, we'll breeze through the concept, requirements, and a mock design, and then jump straight to implementation.

4.1.1   Stating the concept

As we discussed in the last chapter, the concept is a succinct statement of what the app is. Here it is:

> *A Streamlit app for adding tasks to a daily to-do list and tracking their status.*

That seems pretty crisp and clear, so let's dive into the detailed requirements.

4.1.2   Defining the requirements and what is out of scope

To recap from chapter 3, while the concept provides a general idea of the app, requirements make it concrete by outlining what users need from it. What follows are the requirements for the to-do list app we're building. The user should be able to:

- View their daily to-do list, made up of tasks
- Add a task to their to-do list
- Remove a task from their list
- Mark a task as done
- Undo marking a task as done
- See their overall task-completion status (that is, the total number of tasks and the number they've completed)

It's just as important—if not more so—to clarify what the app *won't* do, so we'll also specify what's out of scope:

- Retrieving a to-do list when users refresh or reopen the page
- Exporting a to-do list to an external file or format
- Saving the history of added and completed to-dos

The two lists above give a sense of what we're building in this chapter: a fairly basic daily to-do list that lives entirely within a single browser session. Essentially, we expect the user to interact with the app by opening it in a browser window at the beginning of the day, adding tasks, and marking them as done or not done as the day progresses. The user keeps the window open until the end of the day and never refreshes *it*. Rinse and repeat the next day.

NOTE　We won't add support for *persisting* (saving) tasks outside the browser session. Refreshing the page clears the data.

"Doesn't that limit the usefulness of the app somewhat?" you might ask. Absolutely. We don't want to introduce the complexity of external storage just yet. We'll explore that later in the book, especially in part two.

However, one could argue that giving users a blank slate at the start of each day makes them *more* productive. So you see, being unable to save your tasks is a *feature*, not a bug!

It's mostly about the complexity. Still, spinning the limitations of your product into positives is practically a survival skill in the industry! I bet your other frontend tech manuals don't also give you free life advice.

4.1.3　*Visualizing the user experience*

We now have a clear understanding of what the app needs to do. Following the principle from the last chapter of putting the user experience front and center, let's turn to the mock UI design shown in figure 4.1.

Our design has two sections: a sidebar where you can enter new tasks, and a "main" area where you can view the tasks you've added and update their status. Once you add a task by entering the task text and clicking the button on the left, it appears on the right. Each task is rendered as a checkbox. You mark a task as "done" by checking the box, which also satisfyingly strikes through the task. You can delete a task entirely by clicking the button to its right. A tracker at the top also tells you how many tasks you've completed out of the total.

4.1.4　*Brainstorming the implementation*

You may have realized that the to-do list app is more complex than the password checker we built in chapter 2 or even the unit conversion app in chapter 3. In both cases, the user could ultimately take a single primary action—to evaluate the entered password in the former case and to perform the conversion in the latter.

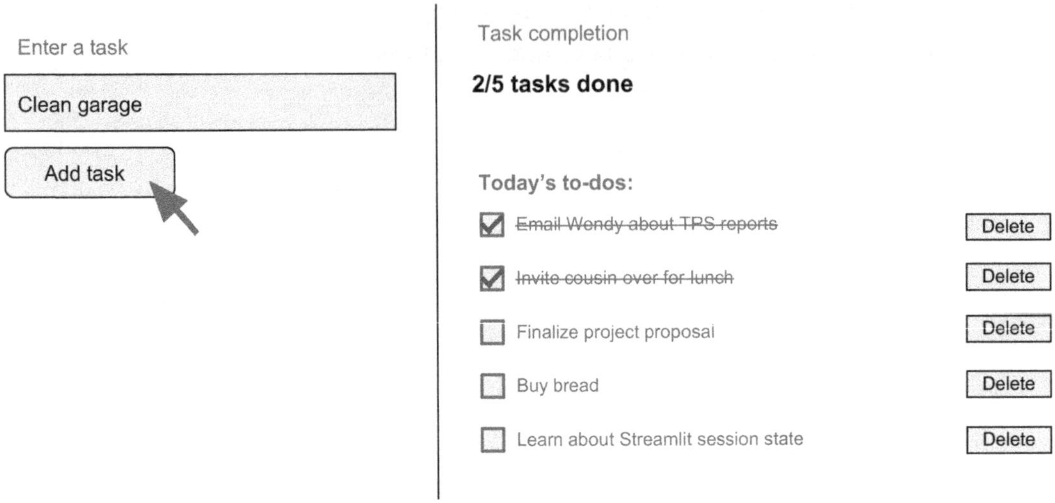

Figure 4.1   The mock UI design for the daily to-do list app

The to-do list includes *four* different actions a user can take:

- Add a task
- Mark the task as done
- Mark the task as not done
- Delete the task

Let's take a moment to brainstorm how to make this happen.

Central to our implementation is the notion of a *task* and, by extension, a *task list*. In this app, a task is an object with two properties: a name and a status that can be "done" or "not done." A task list is simply an ordered list of tasks. The four actions mentioned above are simply different ways to modify the task list. Adding a task adds an item to the list, marking it as done or not done updates the item's status, and deleting a task removes it from the list. The app should always show the latest state of the task list.

Therefore, we can divide the app into three parts:

- The task list
- Actions, which are wired up to buttons and checkboxes, and modify the task list
- Display logic, which renders the task list on the screen

Whenever an action occurs, it updates the task list, and the display logic automatically updates what appears on the screen. As shown in figure 4.2, when you add a new task, the app appends it to the task list, and the display logic loops through all the tasks again and renders them on the screen based on several rules, such as "strikethrough if done."

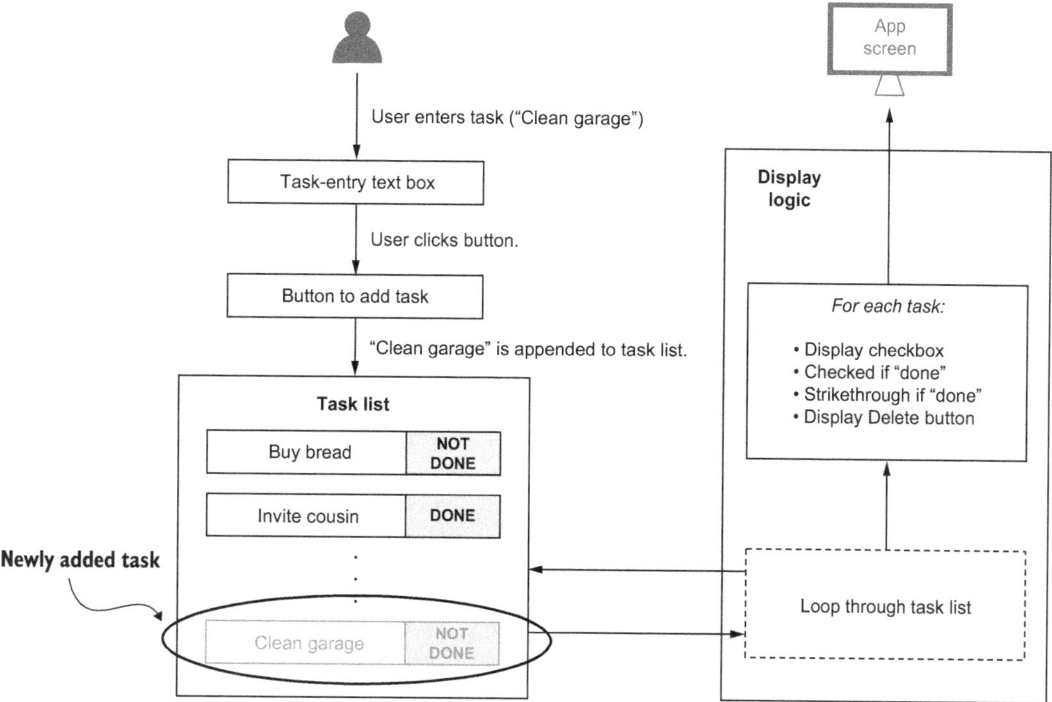

Figure 4.2 Adding a task appends an item to the task list, and the display logic renders the updated task list.

Something similar happens when a task is checked off, as shown in figure 4.3. This time, the task status is updated in the task list. Everything else proceeds in the same manner; the display logic loops through every task again. The "checked if done" and "strikethrough if done" rules are picked up to give the completed Buy bread task the appearance we want.

Deleting or unchecking a task works the same way; the display logic updates and re-renders the task list stored in memory. At this point, we've identified how we'll represent the key entities in the app and what effect each user action will have. It's now time to implement the logic.

4.2 Implementing and troubleshooting the app

When we built the unit conversion app in chapter 3, we took the scenic route, walking through each step of the app development process in detail. But we didn't dwell on what happens when things go wrong or how to troubleshoot the problem.

This time, we'll take a bumpier path—one that's more representative of the real world. As we build the to-do list app, we'll run into problems and errors. Those errors will push us to learn about Streamlit in more depth, and that deeper understanding will help us work through and fix the problems.

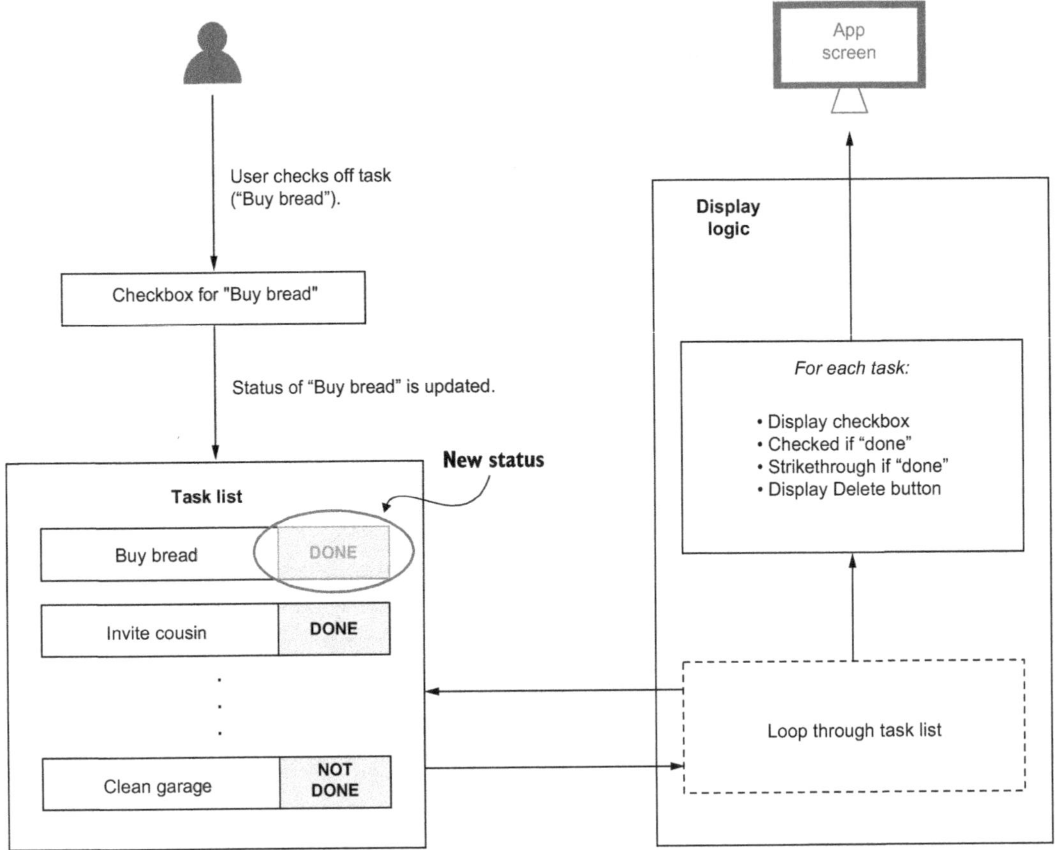

Figure 4.3   Checking off a task updates the item's status in the task list, and the same display logic re-renders the task list.

NOTE   Since this chapter focuses on giving hands-on experience troubleshooting app problems, we'll eschew some of the best practices we learned in chapter 3 (such as maintaining a strict separation between backend and frontend or defining a clear API), in favor of more concise code.

To begin, spin up a new file in your code editor and name it todo_list.py.

4.2.1 Displaying the task list

While we've done our planning upfront in one shot, when it comes to writing the actual code, we're going to build our app iteratively, as we did in chapter 3, going part by part and viewing the results in Streamlit along the way. So, where do we start? What's the first iteration?

As discussed in the previous section, a task list is central to the app's implementation. The display logic component always needs to show the latest state of the task list. Our first step can be as simple as creating the heading for the task list.

ST.HEADER

Streamlit provides several elements for displaying text in different sizes and formats. Earlier, we used `st.title` to render large titles. `st.header` is similar, but it displays text slightly smaller than `st.title`. Use it by putting the code in listing 4.1 (chapter_04/ in_progress/todo_list_in_progress_01.py in the GitHub repo) into todo_list.py.

Listing 4.1 todo_list.py with just a header

```python
import streamlit as st

st.header("Today's to-dos:", divider="gray")
```

Notice that we've included a `divider` argument, which simply displays a gray line beneath the header. Neat, huh?

To see the app in action, save the file and run `streamlit run todo_list.py` or `streamlit run <path to todo_list.py>`, if you're in a different working directory.

Figure 4.4 `st.header` with a divider

If your app has multiple headers, you can even cycle between divider colors by setting `divider` to `True` instead of to a specific color.

CREATING A TASK LIST

Next, let's turn to our notion of a task: it has a name and a status indicating whether it is done or not. We can therefore use a dataclass to represent a task with exactly those two fields: a string `name` and a boolean `is_done` to represent the task status. Listing 4.2 shows the `Task` class (chapter_04/in_progress/task.py in the GitHub repo). Save this into a new file called task.py in the same directory as todo_list.py.

Listing 4.2 Task class in the task.py

```python
from dataclasses import dataclass

@dataclass
class Task:
    name: str
    is_done: bool = False
```

Notice the line `is_done: bool = False`. This sets `is_done` to `False` by default in case it's not specified when creating an instance of `Task`. This will come in handy momentarily.

Now that we have a task, the task list is a Python list of `Task` objects. Create this in todo_list.py with a couple of dummy tasks to test it out, like this:

```
task_list = [Task("Buy milk"), Task("Walk the dog")]
```

Because `is_done` defaults to `False`, there's no need to set it for each `Task` instance.

Don't forget to import your `Task` class at the top of the file:

```
from task import Task
```

CHECKBOXES FOR TASKS

The display logic can be simple. Let's display a checkbox for each task. We know how to create a static checkbox with a string label; recall that we used `st.checkbox` to make a checkbox that enables rounding the results of a unit conversion in chapter 3.

But here, we don't know each checkbox's label ahead of time. Instead, we have to infer it from `task_list`. How do we do that? The answer, of course, is a loop. When a Streamlit element is placed in a loop, a new element is rendered whenever the loop runs. We've already encountered this in our initial password checker example in chapter 2, where we used `st.success` and `st.error` in a loop to display the green and red boxes indicating each condition's pass/fail status.

Create checkboxes from the task list like this:

```
for task in task_list:
    st.checkbox(task.name, task.is_done)
```

Recall that the first argument passed to `st.checkbox` is the label (the task's name in this case) and the second is a boolean indicating whether the checkbox should be rendered as checked. We want each checkbox to be checked if the task is done, so it makes sense to pass the task's `is_done` field here directly.

Listing 4.3 shows what todo_list.py looks like at this point (chapter_04/in_progress/todo_list_in_progress_02.py in the GitHub repo).

> **Listing 4.3   todo_list.py with checkboxes for each task**

```
import streamlit as st
from task import Task

task_list = [Task("Buy milk"), Task("Walk the dog")]

st.header("Today's to-dos:", divider="gray")
for task in task_list:
    st.checkbox(task.name, task.is_done)
```

Save the file and run it to see the output shown in figure 4.5.

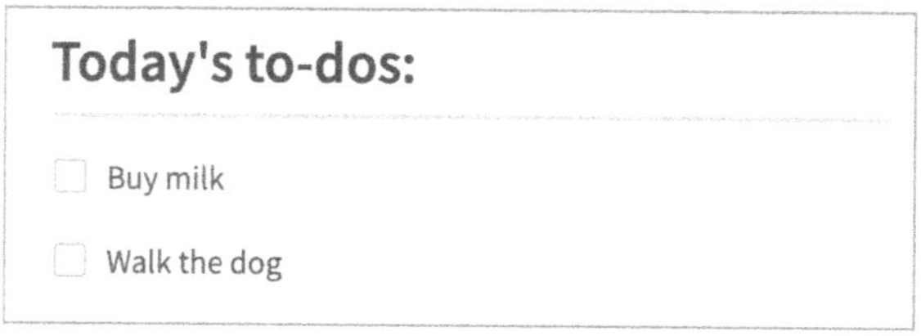

> **Today's to-dos:**
>
> ☐ Buy milk
>
> ☐ Walk the dog

Figure 4.5 Using `st.checkbox` in a loop to display one checkbox for each task

The checkboxes don't do anything yet. We'll fix that in a minute, but first let's add a Delete button to each task.

ADDING DELETE BUTTONS

We want a button to delete each task in the list, situated to its right. Like the checkboxes, we will generate these buttons dynamically, so they should go into the loop we wrote earlier. But if we simply add the button inside the loop, Streamlit will put it *under* the checkbox for the task, not to the *right* of the task, because Streamlit renders elements vertically by default as we saw in chapter 3.

As before, use `st.columns` to work around this. Create two columns—one for the checkbox and task text, and another for the button. Replace the existing `for task in task_list` loop with this:

```
for task in task_list:
    task_col, delete_col = st.columns([0.8, 0.2])
    task_col.checkbox(task.name, task.is_done)
    if delete_col.button("Delete"):
        pass
```

Notice that this code calls `st.columns` in a slightly different way than in the previous chapter: `st.columns([0.8, 0.2])`. Instead of passing the number of columns, it passes a list of numbers. This list specifies the *relative widths* of each column. The column with the task description takes up 80% of the horizontal space, and the column with the button takes up 20%. If only the number of columns is passed (for example, `st.columns(2)`), Streamlit makes the two columns equally wide, which doesn't make sense because the task text can be arbitrarily long, while the button can't.

We're not making the button do anything yet, so we wrote `pass`, a Python keyword that means "do nothing."

WIDGET KEYS

Run the app again to see how it looks. Figure 4.6 shows the result.

There's a button to the right of the first task, but not the second. Most importantly, a big red box underneath shows an error message. Streamlit complains because we created multiple `st.button` widgets with the same *key*. A key is text Streamlit uses to identify a *widget*—what we've been calling a Streamlit element, such as `st.button`, `st.checkbox`, and so on. Widget keys need to be unique so that Streamlit can distinguish one widget from another.

Today's to-dos:

☐ Buy milk   Delete

☐ Walk the dog

DuplicateWidgetID: There are multiple identical `st.button` widgets with the same generated key.

When a widget is created, it's assigned an internal key based on its structure. Multiple widgets with an identical structure will result in the same internal key, which causes this error.

To fix this error, please pass a unique `key` argument to `st.button`.

Traceback:

```
File "/Users/aneevdavis/projects/streamlit_book/streamlit-in-action/chapter_4/
    if delete_col.button("Delete"):
       ^^^^^^^^^^^^^^^^^^^^^^^^^^^^^^^
```

Figure 4.6   Streamlit throws an error when there are multiple identical widgets.

Most of the time, there's no need to manually specify a widget key because Streamlit generates keys internally based on the widget's characteristics. For a button, Streamlit bases its internal key on the button text. So with two Delete buttons Streamlit assigns identical keys, breaking the uniqueness constraint.

As the error description suggests, the way around this problem is to manually specify a unique key for each button you create. Since you need a unique key for every Delete button, one way to ensure uniqueness is to include the task's index in the key. For instance, the key for the first task's Delete button could be `delete_0`, the key for the second could be `delete_1`, and so on:

```
for idx, task in enumerate(task_list):
    task_col, delete_col = st.columns([0.8, 0.2])
    task_col.checkbox(task.name, task.is_done)
    if delete_col.button("Delete", key=f"delete_{idx}"):
        pass
```

To get both the task index and the task itself, change the for-loop header to `for idx, task in enumerate(task_list)`.

On enumerate

`enumerate` is a handy little Python function that lets you iterate through a list elegantly, getting both the index and the element in one shot. The less elegant alternative is to write:

```
for idx in range(len(task_list)):
    task = task_list[idx]
    ...
```

You may now wonder "Why didn't we need to pass a key to the checkboxes then?" Well, the checkboxes already had unique internal keys because their labels (the task names) were different. You'll hit the same problem if you try to put two identical tasks in the list. For instance, if you change the task list to `task_list = [Task("Buy milk"), Task("Buy milk")]`, you'll see an error message similar to the one shown for the buttons.

It's probably a good idea to let users enter the same task twice if they want to, so we'll fix the problem by passing a unique key to each checkbox:

```
task_col.checkbox(task.name, task.is_done, key=f"task_{idx}")
```

This lets you have two tasks with the same name without problems, as shown in figure 4.7.

Today's to-dos:

Buy milk — Delete

Walk the dog — Delete

Figure 4.7 Passing a unique key to each button lets Streamlit distinguish between otherwise identical buttons.

4.2.2 Enabling actions

So far, we've set up the app to display tasks roughly as they should appear, using dummy tasks for testing. But we still need to let users interact with the tasks and modify them. In this section, we'll do that. We'll start by defining functions that update the task list, and then hook them up to Streamlit UI elements.

ADDING A TASK

To add a task to the task list, we need a task name. Once we have one, we can add it by creating a `Task` object and appending it to the list.

Write this as a simple add_task function in todo_list.py:

```
def add_task(task_name: str):
    task_list.append(Task(task_name))
```

MARKING A TASK DONE OR NOT DONE

The is_done field of a Task instance denotes the task's status. To mark it done or not done, update this field. Let's create two functions for this:

```
def mark_done(task: Task):
    task.is_done = True

def mark_not_done(task: Task):
    task.is_done = False
```

The argument to these functions is the Task instance itself, not the task name string.

DELETING A TASK

Deleting a task is straightforward. This function needs the task index in the list so you can remove it.

```
def delete_task(idx: int):
    del task_list[idx]
```

ENABLING USERS TO ADD TASKS

We now have an add_task function, so we no longer have to seed the task list with dummy tasks. Let's replace the line task_list = [Task("Buy milk"), Task("Walk the dog")] with an empty list:

```
task_list = []
```

Next, we'll add Streamlit elements so users can call the add_task function. We'll need an st.text_input for entering the task name and an st.button to trigger the addition. We'll wrap both in st.sidebar so they appear in a left-hand panel in the app. Again, if any of this sounds unfamiliar, review chapter 3.

```
with st.sidebar:
    task = st.text_input("Enter a task")
    if st.button("Add task", type="primary"):
        add_task(task)
```

Note the type="primary" in st.button. The type parameter lets you emphasize a button (with a different color) to denote that it is linked to a "primary action". In UI design, it helps to draw users' attention to the actions they commonly perform. Here, adding a task is something users will do often, so using a primary button makes sense. If you don't specify this parameter (as in the earlier examples), it defaults to "secondary," which results in a white button. Note also that no widget key is needed for the button because there is only one Add Task button, and Streamlit can distinguish it from other buttons. At this point, the todo_list.py file should look like what's shown in listing 4.4 (chapter_04/in_progress/todo_list_in_progress_06.py in the GitHub repo).

Listing 4.4 todo_list.py so far

```python
import streamlit as st
from task import Task

task_list = []

def add_task(task_name: str):
    task_list.append(Task(task_name))

def delete_task(idx: int):
    del task_list[idx]

def mark_done(task: Task):
    task.is_done = True

def mark_not_done(task: Task):
    task.is_done = False

with st.sidebar:
    task = st.text_input("Enter a task")
    if st.button("Add task", type="primary"):
        add_task(task)

st.header("Today's to-dos:", divider="gray")
for idx, task in enumerate(task_list):
    task_col, delete_col = st.columns([0.8, 0.2])
    task_col.checkbox(task.name, task.is_done, key=f"task_{idx}")
    if delete_col.button("Delete", key=f"delete_{idx}"):
        pass
```

Save and run the code. To check the result, enter a new task called Clean garage and click Add Task (see figure 4.8.)

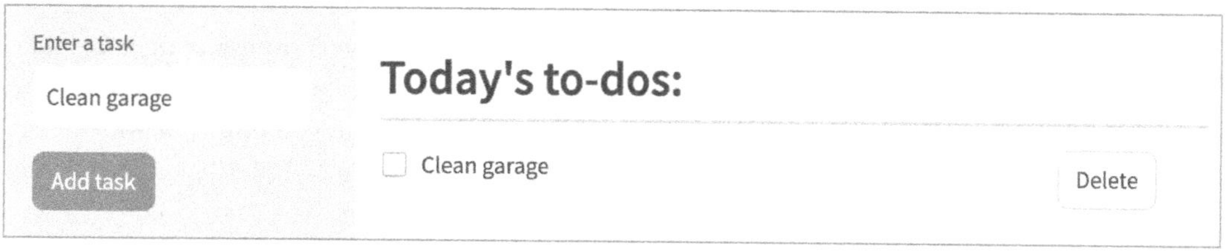

Figure 4.8 To-do list app with a task added

So far, so good, but adding another task, say Finalize project proposal, reveals the problematic output shown in figure 4.9.

Enter a task
Finalize project proposal
Add task
Today's to-dos:
Finalize project proposal
Delete

Figure 4.9   When a new task is added, the old one disappears.

The new task appears, but the old one, Clean garage, is gone. Something seems wrong, but no error appears as it did with the widget key problem. Oddly, clicking Delete removes the remaining task (figure 4.10) even though the code doesn't wire it up to anything; remember that the code uses pass to make the button do nothing—something commonly referred to as a *no-op*.

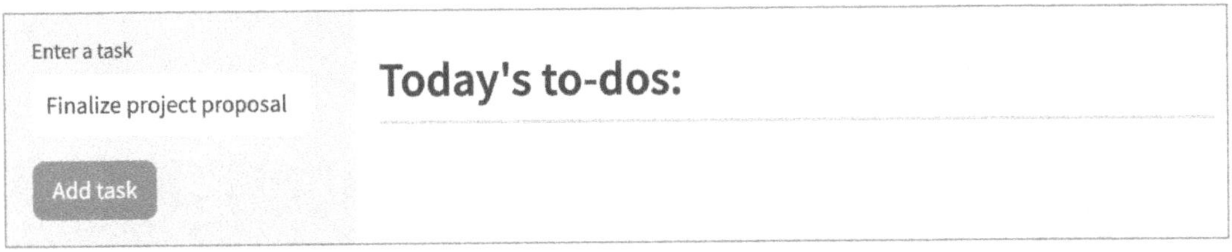

Enter a task
Finalize project proposal
Add task
Today's to-dos:

Figure 4.10   Clicking Delete removes the task even though we didn't connect the button to anything.

If you add the task again and click the checkbox, the task disappears. Try that out, too.

WHAT'S GONE WRONG?

Clearly, the app isn't working as intended. Streamlit doesn't show an error, so we need to figure out what's happening. Is the display logic showing only the most recently added task? Or is something wrong with the task list itself?

Let's find out. One of the most important parts of troubleshooting code is inspecting variable values while a program is running. In a normal Python script (that is, one you run from the command line rather than using Streamlit), you might include `print` statements to display a variable's value. You could also use an IDE debugger or the `pdb` module.

`print` statements don't appear in the Streamlit app's browser window. Instead, use an appropriate Streamlit element. To inspect the `task_list` variable, add the following code right under the line `st.header("Today's to-dos:", divider="gray")`, before the display-logic for loop:

```
st.info(f"task_list: {task_list}")
```

`st.info` displays text in a colored box. It belongs to a family of elements introduced in chapter 2 along with `st.success`, `st.error`, and `st.warning`, which also display text in colored boxes. For `st.info`, the box is blue.

After you save and run the app (or refresh the page), a box with the text `task_list: []` appears, since there are no tasks yet. Add a task as before to see the output in figure 4.11.

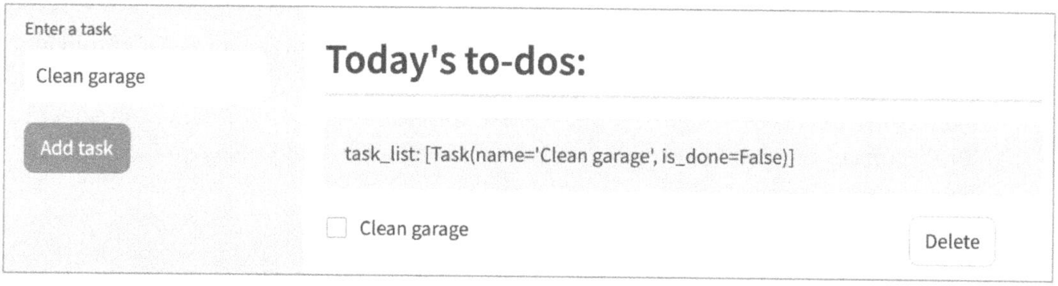

Figure 4.11 `task_list` **contains a single** `Task` **instance.**

As you can see, `task_list` now contains a single instance of `Task`, corresponding to Clean garage. After adding a second task, `task_list` contains only the new task. This shows that the display logic is not faulty; `task_list` itself has lost the Clean garage task. Checking the box next to the task or clicking Delete empties `task_list` again, so no tasks are displayed.

Okay, so here's what we know: adding a task seems to add a task to `task_list` correctly, but whenever you do *anything* else afterward—adding another task, clicking a checkbox, or clicking the Delete button—it removes the previously added task from `task_list`. To fix this, we need to understand why it happens. Let's review how a Streamlit app actually works.

4.3 *How Streamlit executes an app*

The last two chapters covered using Streamlit and developing some non-trivial apps. But the focus was mostly on syntax and a surface-level understanding of how apps work. Writing more complex Streamlit apps requires going deeper. That starts with something fundamental to Streamlit: its execution model.

4.3.1 *Frontend and server*

A Streamlit app has two parts: a backend *Streamlit server* and a *frontend*. Here, a server is a software program that runs on a computer and waits for requests. In technical terms, a server *listens* on a *port*.

A port is a virtual designation that identifies a particular communication channel, like an extension number in a large office. Just as an extension lets callers reach a specific person within a company, a port lets network communication reach a specific program running on a computer. When you enter `streamlit run <filename.py>` in a terminal, Streamlit prints output similar to the following:

```
Local URL: http://localhost:8502
```

A Streamlit server starts up and listens for requests on port 8502 (the exact port number may differ). When you open a browser and navigate to the address (for example, http://localhost:8502)—or when the server opens it automatically—the browser sends a request to the Streamlit server on port 8502.

In response, the Streamlit server executes the Python script from top to bottom and sends a message back to the browser, telling it what to display (that is, the frontend). The frontend is the front-facing part of the app that users can see and interact with, and it runs in the web browser. It consists of HTML, CSS, and JavaScript code that the browser understands.

4.3.2   App reruns

Now, here's the important part: the Streamlit server runs the Python script in its entirety *whenever* the page changes, including when a user interacts with a widget in the app. For example, figure 4.12 shows what happens when a user clicks a button.

Once the frontend detects the button click, it sends a message to the server to report it. The server responds by rerunning the Python code and setting the button to evaluate

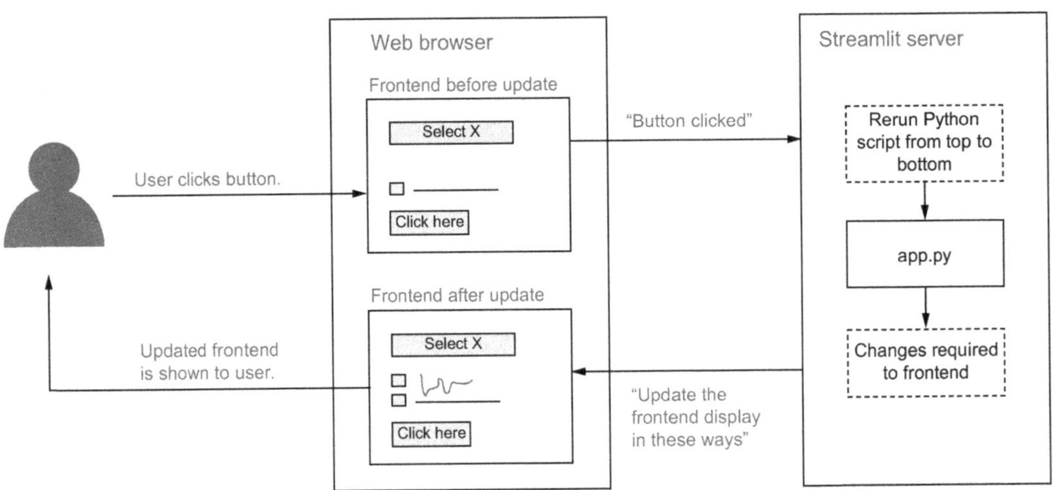

Figure 4.12   Whenever the user interacts with the app, the app reruns the Python script.

to True. After that, the server sends the frontend a message describing the required display updates. The frontend applies them, and the user sees the updated display.

Note that such behavior isn't unique to button clicks. It applies to *any* interaction or *any* time Streamlit determines the display needs to change. This means that whenever the user clicks a button, selects a different item from a dropdown, or moves a slider, the cycle repeats, and the server reruns the whole Python script.

4.3.3 *Applying reruns to the app*

With this knowledge of app reruns, let's figure out what's happening in the to-do list app. Listing 4.5 shows the code as it exists now (chapter_04/in_progress/todo_list_in_progress_07.py in the GitHub repo).

Listing 4.5 todo_list.py

```python
import streamlit as st
from task import Task

task_list = []

def add_task(task_name: str):
    task_list.append(Task(task_name))

def delete_task(idx: int):
    del task_list[idx]

def mark_done(task: Task):
    task.is_done = True

def mark_not_done(task: Task):
    task.is_done = False

with st.sidebar:
    task = st.text_input("Enter a task")
    if st.button("Add task", type="primary"):
        add_task(task)

st.header("Today's to-dos:", divider="gray")
st.info(f"task_list: {task_list}")
for idx, task in enumerate(task_list):
    task_col, delete_col = st.columns([0.8, 0.2])
    task_col.checkbox(task.name, task.is_done, key=f"task_{idx}")
    if delete_col.button("Delete", key=f"delete_{idx}"):
        pass
```

Next, we'll walk through how this code runs at various points in the app.

FIRST RUN

The first time the app runs (that is, when the user loads it), it initializes task_list to an empty list.

Now consider this line in the `st.sidebar` context manager:

```
if st.button("Add task", type="primary"):
```

This is an `if` statement, so the line under it—add_task(task)—runs only if the `st.button` expression evaluates to `True`. Since the button hasn't been clicked yet, it evaluates to `False`. The code doesn't call `add_task` and the `task_list` is still an empty list. The code proceeds to the `st.info` box and display logic. Because no tasks exist, `st.info` displays an empty list and the loop never runs, so no checkboxes appear.

USER ADDS A TASK

Suppose the user enters a Clean garage task and clicks the Add Task button. As mentioned earlier, this action reruns the entire Python code.

> **NOTE** Technically, a rerun may already have occurred at this point, even *before* the user clicks the button. After they finish entering Clean garage, if they shift focus out of the textbox (for example, by clicking outside it), that counts as an interaction because the textbox value changed, and triggers a rerun of the code. This doesn't lead to any interesting changes, so we can ignore it for now.

Starting from the top of the script again, the code sets `task_list` to an empty list. The line `task = st.text_input("Enter a task")` assigns the text-box value to `task`, so `task` now holds the string Clean garage.

Because the user just clicked the button, `st.button` evaluates to `True`. The `if` statement then runs and calls `add_task`. `add_task` creates a `Task` instance for Clean garage and appends it to `task_list`, so `task_list` is no longer empty. This is what `st.info` shows.

Thus, the display logic loop runs once and renders a checkbox and the Delete button. This concludes the rerun, producing the results visible in figure 4.13.

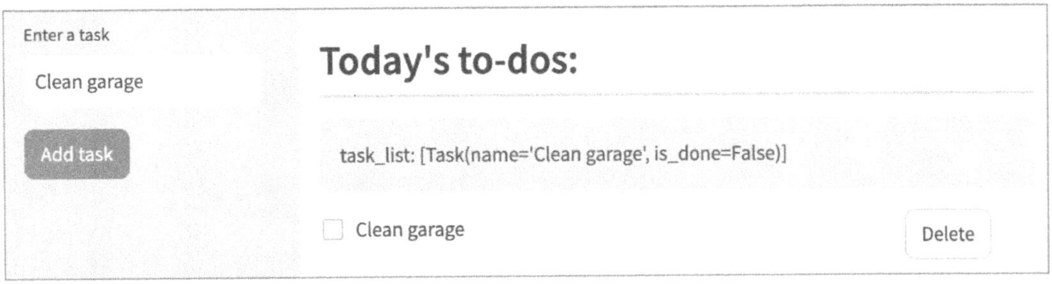

Figure 4.13 When the user clicks Add Task, `st.button` evaluates to `True` and `task_list` contains a task.

USER CLICKS THE TASK CHECKBOX

So far, everything seems to be working. But when the user clicks the Clean Garage checkbox, it triggers another rerun. Execution starts again from the top at `task_list = []`, which resets the list to empty list and discards the Clean garage task that was added before.

But assume the *textbox* hasn't been cleared yet and still says, "Clean garage." That means that once the line `task = st.text_input("Enter a task")` runs, the variable `task` still contains the string Clean garage.

What happens when we get to the `st.button` line? The button has been clicked before, so does that mean it evaluates to `True`? If so, `add_task` would run again, appending "Clean garage" to `task_list`, restoring its earlier state, and everything would be fine.

But that's not how `st.button` works. It evaluates to `True` only in the rerun that happens *immediately* after a click. In all later reruns, it reverts to its original `False` value. In this case, clicking the checkbox triggered a new rerun, so `st.button` now evaluates to `False`. As a result, the app never calls `add_task` and never updates `task_list`. It remains an empty list, so the for loop never runs, and no tasks are displayed.

THE USER ADDS ANOTHER TASK INSTEAD OF CLICKING THE TASK CHECKBOX

To close this discussion, consider the scenario in which, instead of clicking the task checkbox, the user adds another task by entering "Finalize project proposal" in the textbox and clicking Add Task.

Execution proceeds similarly. At the top, `task_list` is set to an empty list, which clears the previous Clean garage task. After you enter a new task, the textbox holds Finalize project proposal, so that's what the `task` variable contains.

This time, `st.button` evaluates to `True` because of the latest button click. The code calls `add_task` with Finalize project proposal as the argument value. That call adds a new `Task` to an otherwise empty list. By the end, `task_list` contains just one element: Finalize project proposal, which `st.info` and the display logic loop show, as seen in figure 4.14.

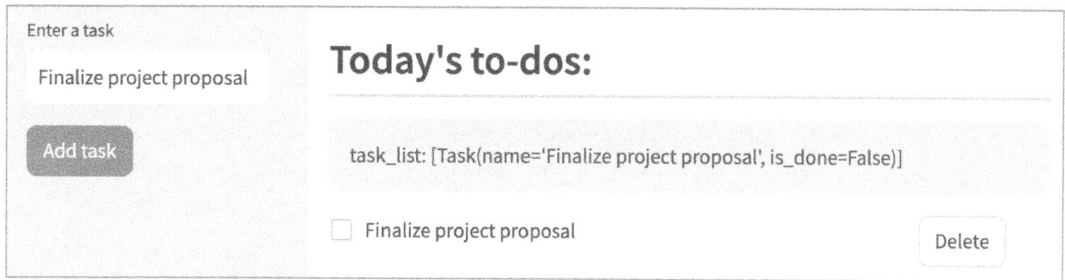

Figure 4.14 **When the user adds a different task,** `st.button` **evaluates to** `True` **again and adds "Finalize project proposal" to** `task_list`, **which was empty at the start.**

Now we can explain the weird results we were seeing: the script resets `task_list` each time it reruns.

4.4 *Persisting variables across reruns*

In the previous section, we explained the unexpected output we got by reviewing Streamlit's execution model and stepping through the app's execution at various stages. In this section, we'll identify an approach to solving the problem.

To recap, the dilemma is that the app behaves like a goldfish: it has no memory of anything that happened in any previous run. Since Streamlit reruns the entire code every chance it gets, it repeatedly wipes the app's memory, resetting the `task_list` variable used to hold the user's tasks.

4.4.1 *st.session_state*

Streamlit offers a solution to the dilemma in the form of `st.session_state`. In a nutshell, `st.session_state` stores variables that persist across reruns. *Session* refers to an app session—the time between opening an app and refreshing the page or closing it. If the same app is open in multiple browser tabs, each tab counts as a separate session.

To remember a value, save it in `st.session_state` and retrieve it on the next run. This approach is illustrated in figure 4.15.

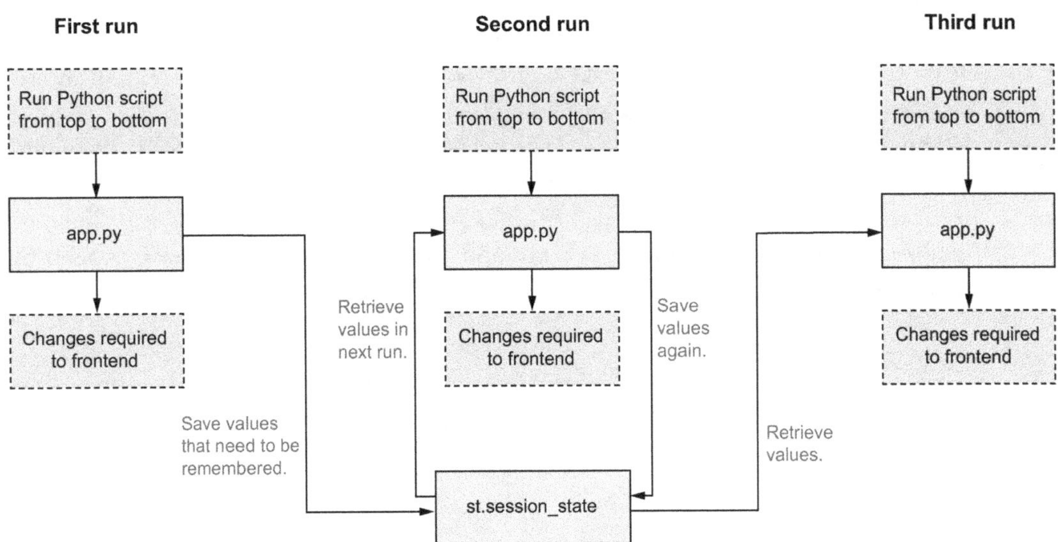

Figure 4.15 Use `st.session_state` to save and retrieve values between reruns.

`st.session_state` acts almost exactly like a Python dictionary, though it technically isn't one. As with a dictionary, you can add key-value pairs, check whether a key exists, look up a value, or remove a key altogether. For the most part, it uses the same syntax as a dictionary.

For example, to store a variable x with a value of 5 in `st.session_state`, write `st.session_state["x"] = 5`, and then retrieve the value with `st.session_state["x"]`. To check whether x exists in the session state, write `if "x" in st.session_state`. Iterate through the items in `st.session_state` with `for key, value in st.session_state.items()`, and delete the "x" key with `del st.session_state["x"]`.

Unlike a dictionary, you can also use dot notation to refer to the value of a key x, like this: `st.session_state.x`. Listing 4.6 shows a toy Streamlit app that uses `st.session_state` to track and increment a number (chapter_04/session_state_example.py in the GitHub repo).

Listing 4.6   A simple number-incrementing app

```python
import streamlit as st

if "number" not in st.session_state:
    st.session_state.number = 0

if st.button("Increment"):
    st.session_state.number += 1

st.info(f"Number: {st.session_state.number}")
```

We start by checking whether the `"number"` key exists in the session state. If it doesn't, we add it with a value of zero.

Next, there is a button that increments the value of a number whenever you click it and `st.info` box that retrieves and displays the value of `number`. Figure 4.16 shows the output after pressing the Increment button five times.

Figure 4.16   A toy Streamlit app using `st.session_state` to keep track of and increment a number

Without `st.session_state`, storing `number` in its own variable or in a regular dictionary wouldn't work because the app would reset the value or the dictionary itself each time it re-ran. Only `st.session_state` retains state across app reruns.

Why do we need to do an initial check to see whether number already exists in the session state before adding it? Without this check, we'd run into the same problem as before. Each time the app runs, it sets `st.session_state.number` to zero, overriding whatever value it reached in earlier runs, and we'd never see the number change.

Checking whether number exists ensures that the line `st.session_state.number = 0` runs only once—in the first run, before `"number"` is added.

4.5   *Completing the app*

We now know how to give the app a memory. When you start writing Streamlit apps, you'll quickly realize this knowledge is crucial—to the point that you can write only the simplest apps without it. Armed with the powerful `st.session_state`, we're ready to take another crack at getting the to-do list app to work!

4.5.1   *Adding session state*

When you last ran the app, the main problem was that the `task_list` variable, which holds all tasks, reset on every rerun. We will fix this by adding `task_list` to `st.session_state`. Replace the earlier line `task_list = []` with the following code:

```
if "task_list" not in st.session_state:
    st.session_state.task_list = []
```

This mirrors the toy example from the previous section. The only difference is that the code stores `task_list` in `st.session_state` rather than a single number.

We could modify the rest of the code to reference `st.session_state.task_list` wherever it currently references `task_list`, but that seems tedious and clunky. Instead, point the variable `task_list` to the version in `st.session_state` like this:

```
task_list = st.session_state.task_list
```

The rest of the code should work fine since the functions refer to `task_list`. Listing 4.7 shows the updated code (chapter_04/in_progress/todo_list_in_progress_08.py in the GitHub repo).

Listing 4.7   todo_list.py with st.session_state

```
import streamlit as st
from task import Task

if "task_list" not in st.session_state:
    st.session_state.task_list = []
task_list = st.session_state.task_list

def add_task(task_name: str):
    task_list.append(Task(task_name))

def delete_task(idx: int):
    del task_list[idx]
```

```python
def mark_done(task: Task):
    task.is_done = True

def mark_not_done(task: Task):
    task.is_done = False

with st.sidebar:
    task = st.text_input("Enter a task")
    if st.button("Add task", type="primary"):
        add_task(task)

st.header("Today's to-dos:", divider="gray")
st.info(f"task_list: {task_list}")
for idx, task in enumerate(task_list):
    task_col, delete_col = st.columns([0.8, 0.2])
    task_col.checkbox(task.name, task.is_done, key=f"task_{idx}")
    if delete_col.button("Delete", key=f"delete_{idx}"):
        pass
```

Save, rerun, and add multiple tasks. Figure 4.17 shows the result.

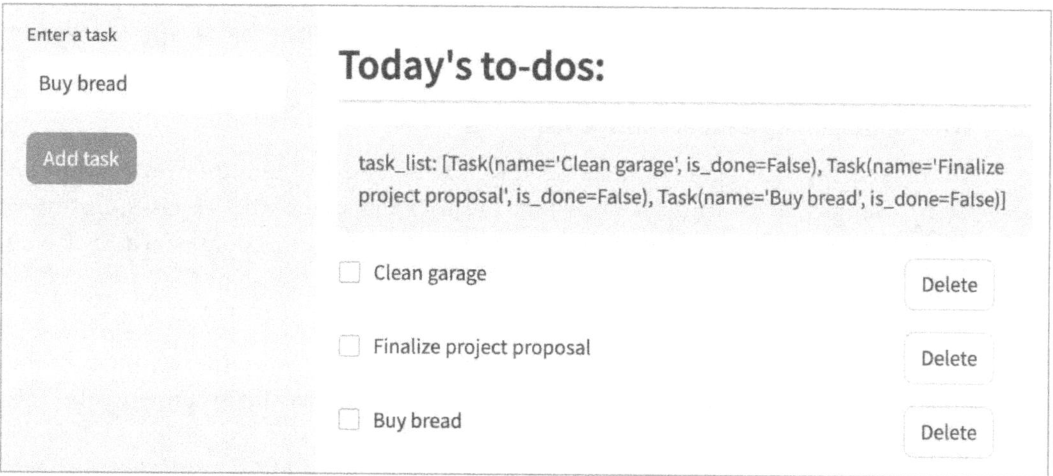

Figure 4.17 With `st.session_state`, Streamlit remembers previous tasks.

And voila! You can finally update `task_list` with multiple tasks, and the display logic shows everything.

4.5.2 *Wiring up the Delete buttons*

Now let's get the Delete buttons working. Earlier, we made them do nothing by placing `pass` under the button code in the display loop.

```python
if delete_col.button("Delete", key=f"delete_{idx}"):
    pass
```

We've since created a `delete_task` function, so let's call it here instead:

```
if delete_col.button("Delete", key=f"delete_{idx}"):
    delete_task(idx)
```

If we now click Delete next to Buy bread after saving and rerunning (and adding the three tasks back in order if you refreshed the page), we see … no change! But if we click the button a second time, the app removes the task. Something still isn't right.

I won't detail all of it with screenshots, but if you experiment with the app at this point, more odd behavior shows up. The first time you click the Delete button next to the last task in the list, nothing happens. But the task disappears if you immediately click any checkbox.

Or if you delete a task from the middle of the list, the *next* one disappears, not the one you deleted! But if you *then* do something else, like clicking a checkbox or adding another task, that task comes back, and the app correctly removes the one you intentionally deleted, and everything is the way it should be.

All in all, there seems to be a *lag* between clicking the Delete button and removing the task. You need to do something else (anything else, like clicking one of the checkboxes or editing the text in the task entry textbox and clicking outside) *after* clicking the button for the correct results to be displayed.

4.5.3   *What's happening behind the scenes*

To understand what's going on, we need to take a deep dive into the app's execution again. Assume we're at the point where the user has entered three tasks, in order: Clean garage, Finalize project proposal, and Buy bread. At this point, `task_list` contains these three tasks.

STEPPING THROUGH THE APP'S EXECUTION

Let's say the user tries to delete the third task. Figure 4.18 shows what happens in the app. The Streamlit widget keys identify the Delete buttons (for example, `delete_0`, `delete_1`, and so on).

The first run happens before you click the button. Streamlit simply loops through the task list, displaying each task along with its checkbox and Delete button. As discussed earlier in the chapter, each `st.button` evaluates to `False`, since you haven't clicked any yet.

When the user clicks the Delete button for Buy bread, the app reruns. Everything remains the same until the app displays the third task's `st.button`. This time, the button evaluates to `True` because it was just clicked. The condition is now true, the app enters the code nested under `st.button` and calls `delete_task(idx)`. Since `idx` is 2 in this iteration of the loop, the app calls `delete_task(2)` and removes Buy bread from `task_list`. Execution stops at this point.

See the problem? The app displayed all three buttons *before* `delete_task` ran and updated `task_list`. And because no other user actions trigger reruns, nothing runs

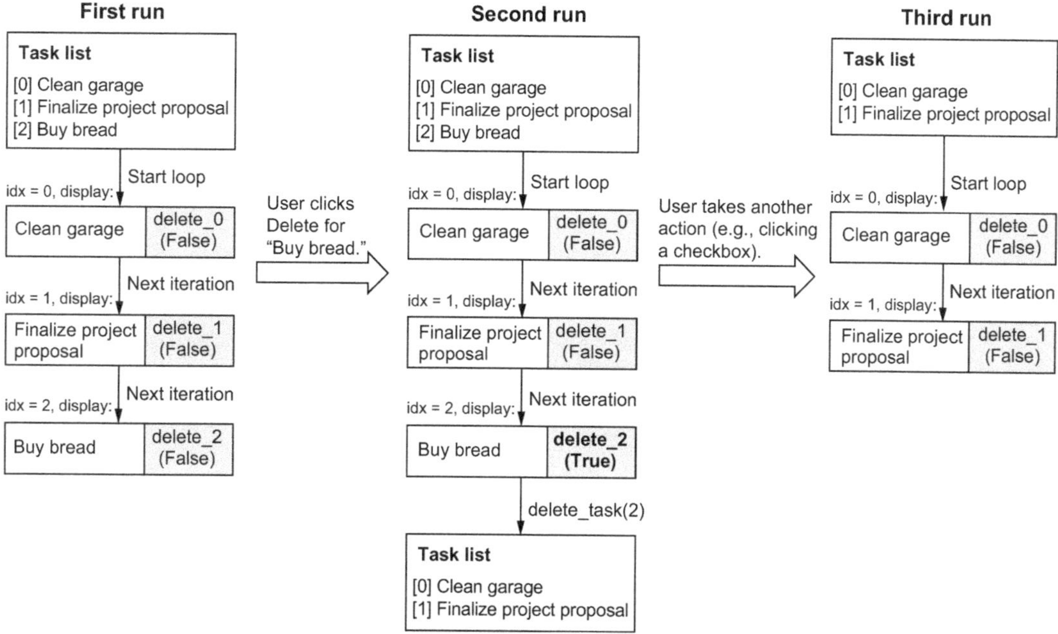

Figure 4.18 **Step-by-step app execution: the Delete button evaluates to** `True` **in the second run, but the app displays the task and button** *before* **it calls** `delete_task`**.**

again. So `delete_task` updates `task_list`, but the display logic has already executed against the old version of `task_list`. That's why the UI still shows the three tasks after you click Delete.

But if the user does something else, like clicking a checkbox or clicking the Delete button again, that triggers another rerun. This time, the display logic runs over the latest version of `task_list`, so the UI finally shows the third task, and the app removes its checkbox and Delete button.

NOTE Stepping through the execution like this can also explain the other odd behavior we noticed: when you click the Delete button for a task in the middle of the list, the *next* task disappears. This happens because `delete_task` moves the list indices up by one, and the next display loop iteration skips a task because its index changed.

4.5.4 *Triggering reruns automatically*

As we've seen, although the Delete button doesn't work correctly right away, Streamlit eventually gets the results right, provided the user takes an extra action to trigger a rerun. We can use this behavior to our advantage. To do that, we need a way to trigger a rerun of the app in code rather than through a user action. Streamlit provides this functionality through st.rerun, and you can call it at any time without arguments, like here:

```
st.rerun()
```

When you call st.rerun, you tell Streamlit, "Quit the current run and start again from the top." In our case, trigger the rerun after deleting a task:

```
if delete_col.button("Delete", key=f"delete_{idx}"):
    delete_task(idx)
    st.rerun()
```

After making this change, rerun and recreate the tasks, and try deleting Buy bread again. The output appears in figure 4.19.

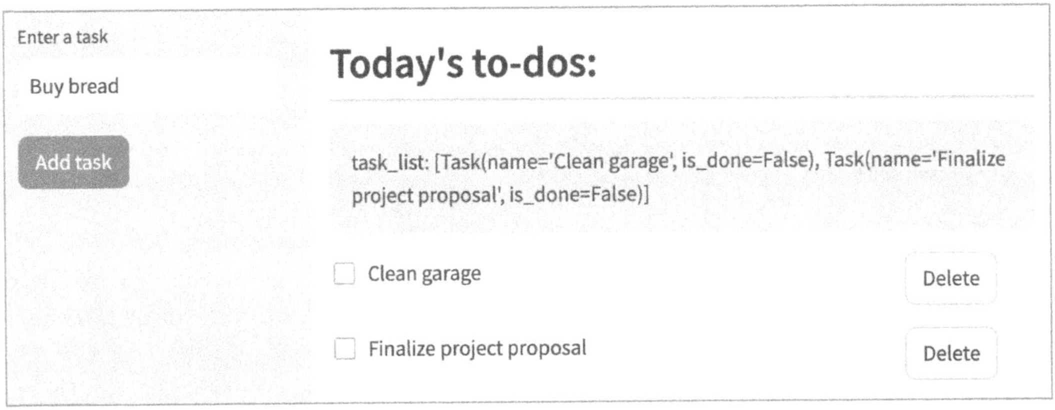

Enter a task

Buy bread

Add task

Today's to-dos:

task_list: [Task(name='Clean garage', is_done=False), Task(name='Finalize project proposal', is_done=False)]

Clean garage

Finalize project proposal

Delete

Delete

Figure 4.19   With st.rerun, clicking Delete works as expected.

It worked! Buy bread is gone, and it's also missing from task_list, as the st.info box in the screenshot shows.

4.5.5   *Wiring up the checkboxes*

Let's move on to the next part of the app: the checkboxes. We've added them to the display, and you can check them, but they don't do anything. Next, we'll hook them up to the functionality we've defined for changing a task's status.

The current checkbox code is a single line:

```
task_col.checkbox(task.name, task.is_done, key=f"task_{idx}")
```

When the user checks a task checkbox, we want to accomplish two things:

- Mark the task as done, and
- Strike it through

We also want to reverse the above changes if the user unchecks a box. To change a task's status, we can use the functions created earlier, `mark_done` and `mark_not_done`.

How do we achieve the strikethrough? Streamlit supports a language called *markdown* for this formatting effect (and several others). Markdown is a text-based notation that lets you apply various kinds of formatting to the text. It can display text in bold or italics, create links, lists, headings, and much more. Later chapters cover these features and for now we'll focus on the strikethrough effect.

To strike through a piece of text in Markdown, surround it with two pairs of tildes, like this:

```
~~Text to be struck through~~
```

This plugs into the checkbox through the `label` parameter, which supports Markdown. We'll define a variable that contains just the task name when it's not done, and the name with a Markdown strikethrough when it is done:

```
label = f"~~{task.name}~~" if task.is_done else task.name
```

We can then feed it into the checkbox:

```
task_col.checkbox(label, task.is_done, key=f"task_{idx}")
```

Finally, wire the checkboxes to the `mark_*` functions. Call `mark_done` when the checkbox is checked; otherwise, call `mark_not_done`. The code should now match listing 4.8 (chapter_04/in_progress/todo_list_in_progress_11.py in the GitHub repo).


```python
import streamlit as st
from task import Task

if "task_list" not in st.session_state:
    st.session_state.task_list = []
task_list = st.session_state.task_list

def add_task(task_name: str):
    task_list.append(Task(task_name))

def delete_task(idx: int):
    del task_list[idx]

def mark_done(task: Task):
    task.is_done = True

def mark_not_done(task: Task):
    task.is_done = False
```

```python
with st.sidebar:
    task = st.text_input("Enter a task")
    if st.button("Add task", type="primary"):
        add_task(task)

st.header("Today's to-dos:", divider="gray")
st.info(f"task_list: {task_list}")
for idx, task in enumerate(task_list):
    task_col, delete_col = st.columns([0.8, 0.2])
    label = f"~~{task.name}~~" if task.is_done else task.name
    if task_col.checkbox(label, task.is_done, key=f"task_{idx}"):
        mark_done(task)
    else:
        mark_not_done(task)
    if delete_col.button("Delete", key=f"delete_{idx}"):
        delete_task(idx)
        st.rerun()
```

Add a strikethrough effect to the label if the task is done.

Call mark_done if the checkbox happens to be checked and therefore evaluates to True.

Call mark_not_done if the checkbox is not checked.

Save, rerun, and add the tasks back. Then check one task to get result similar to figure 4.20.

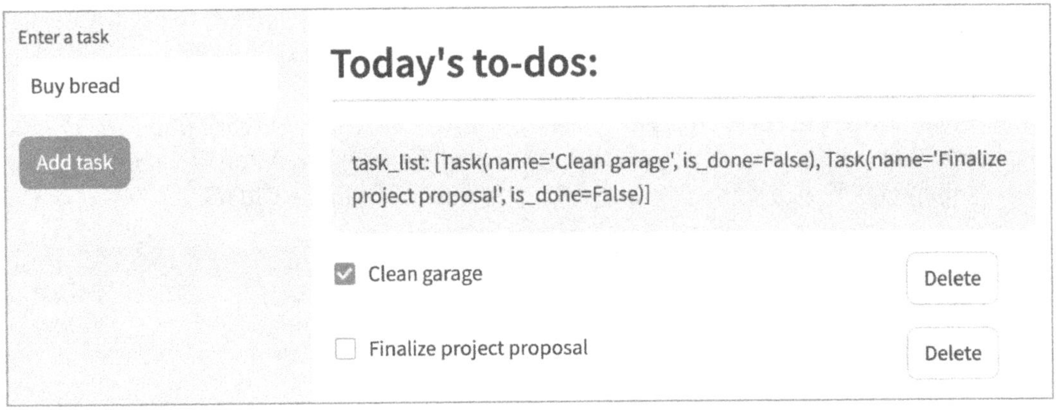

Enter a task

Buy bread

Add task

Today's to-dos:

task_list: [Task(name='Clean garage', is_done=False), Task(name='Finalize project proposal', is_done=False)]

Clean garage   Delete

Finalize project proposal   Delete

Figure 4.20   **Checking a task doesn't work immediately as expected**

Once again, we didn't get the results we expected. Clean garage still isn't struck through, and the info box shows that task_list hasn't changed. Before you throw the computer out the window and dedicate the rest of your existence to sheep-farming, try checking off another task. Now the original task has a strikethrough, and the st.info box shows its is_done field is True.

Does this sound familiar? There's a lag of one user action between clicking a checkbox and seeing the result. What's going on here is very similar to what we saw in the case of the Delete button. Clicking the checkbox triggers the function and sets `is_done` to `True`, but by that point, the app has already displayed the task and its label. Only the *next* rerun updates the *actual display*, and that rerun happens only when the user takes a further action. The solution is the same as before: trigger a manual rerun whenever one of the `mark_*` functions runs:

```
if task_col.checkbox(label, task.is_done, key=f"task_{idx}"):
    mark_done(task)
    st.rerun()
else:
    mark_not_done(task)
    st.rerun()
```

Save the output, refresh the page, and try again. Figure 4.21 shows the result.

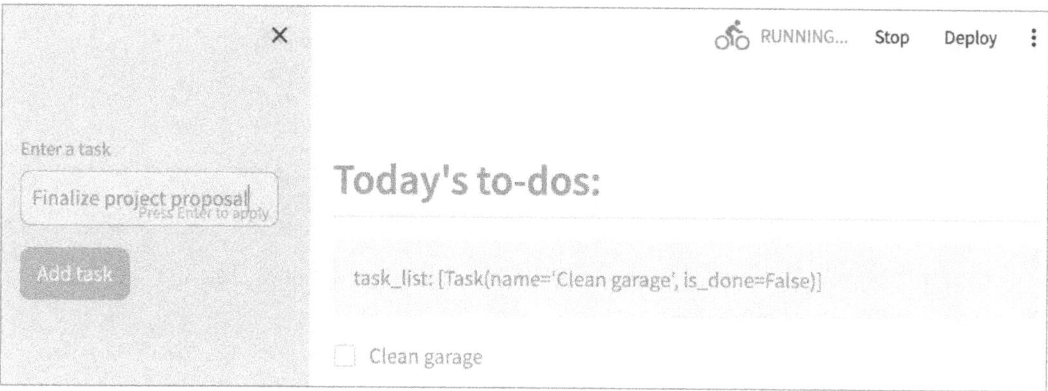

Figure 4.21　The app hangs and never stops loading

Something's very wrong here. The app seems to stop responding entirely once we add the first task. The screen's grayed out, and the RUNNING... indicator appears at the top.

4.5.6　*An infinite rerun loop*

You've just encountered your first Streamlit infinite rerun loop. Let's try to understand what went wrong by stepping through the execution one more time. Figure 4.22 shows this in a diagram.

After adding the Clean garage task, `task_list` contains a single `Task` instance and stores `False` in its `is_done` field. Since `task_list` is non-empty, the code enters the display loop, which displays the Clean garage checkbox.

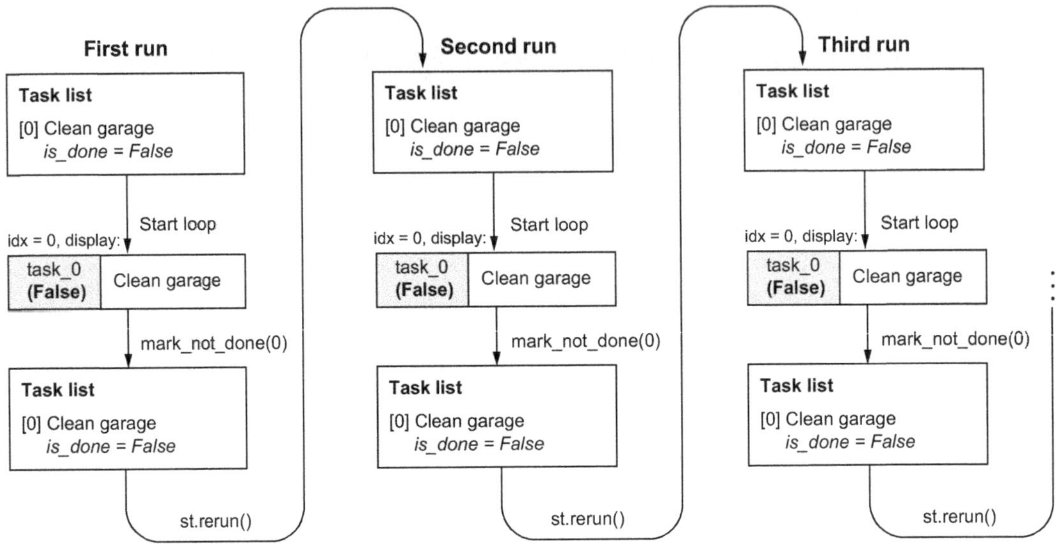

Figure 4.22   Step-by-step app execution: a chain of `st.reruns` leads to an infinite loop.

Now, the task has branching logic:

```
if task_col.checkbox(label, task.is_done, key=f"task_{idx}"):
    mark_done(task)
    st.rerun()
else:
    mark_not_done(task)
    st.rerun()
```

The checkbox evaluates to `False` since it is not checked, and the app enters the `else` clause. The code calls `mark_not_done` to set `is_done` to `False` (even though it's already `False`), and then calls `st.rerun()` to force Streamlit to stop the current run and start again from the top. The code enters the loop once again, in the second run. The checkbox is still not checked, so the code calls `mark_not_done` again, then `st.rerun()`, which starts a third run, and so on. Since this chain of calls never ends, Streamlit chokes and stops responding.

4.5.7   *Preventing the infinite rerun*

The trouble here is that `mark_not_done` gets called even when it isn't needed. Review the execution steps shown earlier, and you'll notice that the Clean garage task's `is_done` field was already set to `False`, so there was no need to call `mark_not_done` again.

The code is set up so that, once you enter the display `for` loop, you can't exit it. If the checkbox evaluates to `True`, `st.rerun()` runs after the `mark_done` function. If it evaluates to `False`, `st.rerun()` runs after the `mark_not_done` function.

Ensure that the call happens only when it needs to. Call `mark_done` (and the associated `st.rerun`) only when the checkbox is checked and the task isn't already marked as done. Similarly, call `mark_not_done` and its `st.rerun` only when the checkbox isn't checked and the task is currently marked as done.

You can do this by editing the code as follows:

```
checked = task_col.checkbox(label, task.is_done, key=f"task_{idx}")
if checked and not task.is_done:
    mark_done(task)
    st.rerun()
elif not checked and task.is_done:
    mark_not_done(task)
    st.rerun()
```

Save the checkbox's value in a new variable called checked, for readability.

Only call mark_done if the checkbox is checked AND the task is not yet marked as done.

Only call mark_not_done if the checkbox is not checked AND the task is still marked as done.

This way, when the checkbox is checked, the code sets the task's status to done, but on the next rerun, both the `if` and `elif` clauses evaluate to `False`, and `st.rerun` never executes.

Go ahead and try it out. The checkboxes should now work correctly, as shown in figure 4.23.

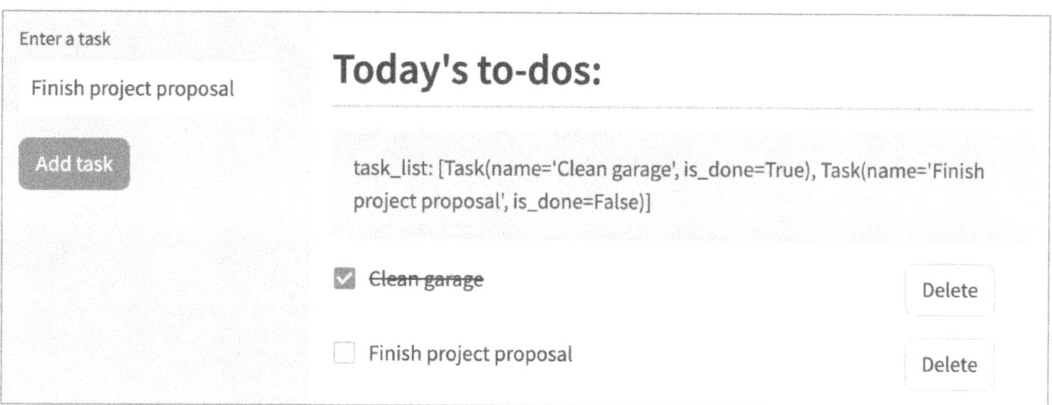

Figure 4.23 Checkboxes now work as expected

4.5.8 Adding the completion progress indicator

We're *almost* done with the app. The only functionality remaining from the earlier mock design is a progress indicator to give the user an extra sense of accomplishment.

Adding a progress indicator is relatively straightforward. To make the indicator large, the `st.metric`, first introduced in chapter 3, seems ideal.

To display the progress, get two values from `task_list`: the total number of tasks and the number of completed tasks. The code for `st.metric` could look like this:

```python
total_tasks = len(task_list)
completed_tasks = sum(1 for task in task_list if task.is_done)
metric_display = f"{completed_tasks}/{total_tasks} done"
st.metric("Task completion", metric_display, delta=None)
```

To get `completed_tasks`, use a list comprehension (the square brackets can be omitted when the expression is wrapped in a function) for conciseness. We can remove the info box (`st.info`) since we're no longer in troubleshooting mode. The final code should look like in listing 4.9 (chapter_04/final/todo_list.py in the GitHub repo).

Listing 4.9   The final version of todo_list.py

```python
import streamlit as st
from task import Task

if "task_list" not in st.session_state:
    st.session_state.task_list = []
task_list = st.session_state.task_list

def add_task(task_name: str):
    task_list.append(Task(task_name))

def delete_task(idx: int):
    del task_list[idx]

def mark_done(task: Task):
    task.is_done = True

def mark_not_done(task: Task):
    task.is_done = False

with st.sidebar:
    task = st.text_input("Enter a task")
    if st.button("Add task", type="primary"):
        add_task(task)

total_tasks = len(task_list)
completed_tasks = sum(1 for task in task_list if task.is_done)
metric_display = f"{completed_tasks}/{total_tasks} done"
st.metric("Task completion", metric_display, delta=None)

st.header("Today's to-dos:", divider="gray")
for idx, task in enumerate(task_list):
    task_col, delete_col = st.columns([0.8, 0.2])
    label = f"~~{task.name}~~" if task.is_done else task.name
    checked = task_col.checkbox(label, task.is_done, key=f"task_{idx}")
    if checked and not task.is_done:
        mark_done(task)
        st.rerun()
```

```
elif not checked and task.is_done:
    mark_not_done(task)
    st.rerun()
if delete_col.button("Delete", key=f"delete_{idx}"):
    delete_task(idx)
    st.rerun()
```

Figure 4.24 provides a final glance at our app in all its glory.

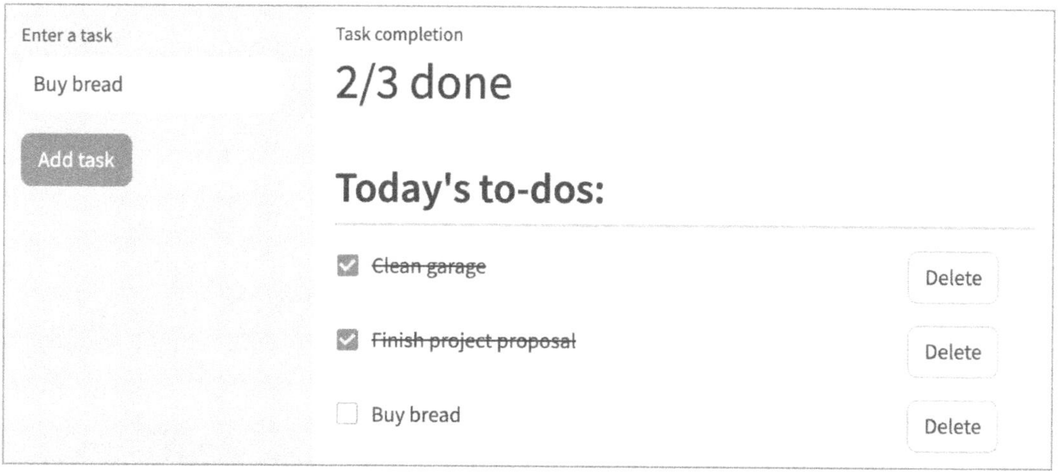

Figure 4.24 The final to-do list app

That's another full app under your belt and a tool you can use daily to stay productive. You're ready to use Streamlit in projects of your own. In the next chapter, you'll learn how to publish apps for others to use.

Summary

- The development process is not smooth. Expect to spend much of the time troubleshooting things that don't work as expected.
- `st.header` displays headings in a large font.
- Streamlit identifies UI widgets using a unique key based on widget's characteristics.
- When two widgets are identical in every respect, you need to specify a widget key yourself so Streamlit can tell them apart.
- To keep track of variable values as the app executes, display them on the app screen using `st.info`.
- Whenever the page needs to change, the Streamlit server reruns the Python code from top to bottom.

- Reruns reset all the regular variables in the app.
- `st.session_state` stores variables that you want Streamlit to remember between reruns.
- It's a good idea to step through the app's execution when unexpected results appear.
- You can trigger a rerun of the app using `st.rerun`.
- If you don't provide an exit path while using `st.rerun`, the app may end up in an infinite rerun loop.

Sharing your apps with the world

This chapter covers

- Options to share your app with users
- Deploying an app to Streamlit Community Cloud for free
- Connecting an app to an external service like an API
- Safeguarding your API keys and other secrets in production
- Managing your app's dependencies

The moment you first successfully run an app built from scratch is magical—it's when all the hours spent designing, developing, and refining finally pay off. After multiple iterations, bug fixes, and feature tweaks, the work comes together.

But what's next? Do you keep it hidden away on a local machine? Unless you've built something solely for personal use, the answer is probably no. To make the app truly useful, you need to get it into the hands of its intended audience.

This chapter is about making the leap from local development to global deployment. We'll briefly discuss the various paths available for sharing apps. We'll then settle on one of them and walk through putting an app into production for the world to experience. Along the way, we'll cover key considerations in making an app public, such as safeguarding confidential information like API keys and managing code dependencies. As always, we'll take a practical approach, with direct, hands-on experience for everything we discuss.

> **NOTE**   The GitHub repo for this book is at https://github.com/aneevdavis/streamlit-in-action. The chapter_05 folder contains this chapter's code and a requirements.txt file with exact versions of the required Python libraries. Install them all at once by downloading the file and running `pip install -r requirements.txt` in a terminal window.

5.1   Deploying apps

We've come a long way since we began using Streamlit. Over the last three chapters, you've created three fully functional—dare I even say, *useful*—applications. But the light has been hidden under the proverbial bushel. No one else has experienced the craft. It's time to change that!

5.1.1   What is deployment?

Deploying an app loosely means making it available for other people to use. More specifically, it means hosting the application at a place intended users can readily access.

Recall from chapter 4 that a Streamlit app consists of a backend server and a frontend that runs in a web browser. The frontend makes requests to the server and displays the results, but the server ultimately runs the show.

To set up the connection between the frontend and the server and thus load an app, the user navigates to the URL and port where the server is running. You may have seen this before: when you start an app with the `streamlit run` command, the command opens a web browser and navigates to a URL like https://localhost:8501.

You could have done this manually, too. In fact, as long as the Streamlit server is running, opening the URL in a new browser tab or window creates a new connection to the server and a new instance of the app.

Deploying an app involves starting and keeping a Streamlit server running, ready to accept new connections. Instead of accessing the app through the `localhost` URL, other people will access it through a different URL. There are several approaches for deploying an app.

5.1.2   Options for deployment

Depending on the requirements, budget, and effort involved, you can choose from multiple deployment options. Let's look at a few.

RUNNING A SERVER OVER YOUR LOCAL NETWORK

The simplest way to deploy an app is something you've already done each time you've run Streamlit. Recall that, when you run the `streamlit run` command, Streamlit starts a server, and you'll see output similar to the following in the terminal:

```
You can now view your Streamlit app in your browser.

  Local URL: http://localhost:8501
  Network URL: http://192.168.50.68:8501
```

As we've seen several times by now, the local URL lets you access the app from the computer running it. But if the computer is connected to a local network or even a home Wi-Fi network, other devices on the network can access it through the *network URL*.

Go ahead and try it out! If you're on Wi-Fi (or a LAN) and have another device—like a smartphone or another computer—connected to the same Wi-Fi/LAN, run one of the apps you've created, note the network URL, and open it in the second device's web browser.

For instance, figure 5.1 shows the to-do list app running on my phone, connected to the same Wi-Fi network as the laptop where I ran the `streamlit run` command:

> **NOTE** Getting this sharing approach to work depends on how the network is set up. For instance, a firewall may block incoming traffic from other devices, preventing it from reaching the Streamlit server, or other similar rules may be in place. This book doesn't cover fixing these problems, but you can often resolve them with online research or help from a network administrator.

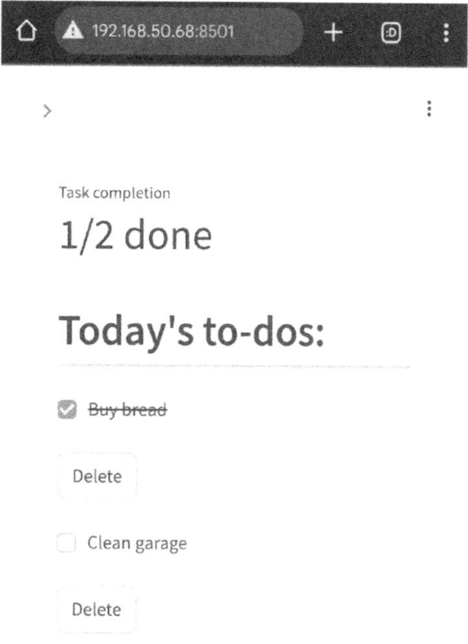

Figure 5.1   Using the network URL of a Streamlit app to access it from a different device connected to the same network

One advantage of this deployment method is that you can make changes in the app, and users will see them as soon as you edit the code—no extra steps are needed!

- It only works while the computer running the Streamlit server is on and connected to the network.
- It allows devices connected to your local network to access the app, not the general public.

Still, it can come in handy in a bunch of places. For example, you could create apps for a household and share the link with family. You could even use this type of deployment for basic, non-business-critical apps at work, depending on how lenient the networking and security policies are.

SETTING UP A DEDICATED SERVER

If you're looking to make a Streamlit app available to a broader audience, setting up a dedicated server *may* be a logical step beyond local deployment. This involves using a separate physical or virtual machine that runs independently of a personal computer. This setup helps ensure the app is available around the clock and accessible to users outside the local network.

In this setup, start by selecting a suitable server—either a repurposed extra computer or a new machine set up specifically for this purpose. After selecting a server computer and installing Python and Streamlit, launch the Streamlit server for the app and expose the correct port to external traffic. Also configure the network to allow access, such as setting up port forwarding on the router if the server sits behind a firewall.

Operating a dedicated server can be a daunting undertaking that comes with many responsibilities, especially around security. You'll need to configure firewalls and regularly maintain and update the server's operating system and software.

The advantage of this route is that it gives you complete control over deployment. On the other hand, it requires significant technical expertise and, more importantly, a substantial time commitment. If you want the general public to use the app you've developed, I recommend one of the remaining options discussed next.

DEPLOYING TO THE CLOUD

If you need better scalability, reliability, and ease of access, deploy the app on a cloud-based platform. This approach uses the infrastructure of public cloud service providers—such as Amazon Web Services (AWS), Microsoft Azure, or Google Cloud—and lets you host the app without physical hardware. It offers benefits such as automatic scaling to handle varying traffic levels, robust security measures to protect data, and high availability to keep the app accessible at all times.

A key benefit of cloud deployment is that the cloud provider handles many infrastructure responsibilities involved in maintaining an application. This includes server maintenance and security updates, so you can focus on developing and improving the app.

Many companies have already migrated, or are in the process of migrating, internal applications to the cloud. If you're considering making an app available to users within an organization or to a broader audience, cloud deployment can be an efficient and effective solution. Work with the cloud administrator or IT team to ensure a smooth setup and integration process.

But it's important to note that using a cloud provider can become expensive as an app gains popularity. Cloud providers usually base costs on the resources the app uses, which increase as more users access it. Chapter 12 discusses how to deploy an app to public cloud platforms such as AWS.

STREAMLIT COMMUNITY CLOUD

That leaves us with the option we'll use for most of this book—Streamlit Community Cloud, a way to publish apps *completely free of charge.*

Snowflake, the company that owns Streamlit, runs Streamlit Community Cloud. It prioritizes ease of use and, as the name suggests, is custom-built for Streamlit apps.

Community Cloud comes with resource limitations, such as how much computational power, memory, and storage an app can use. If the app exceeds those limits—say, if it suddenly gains popularity—it may make sense to consider a different option, such as deploying to a paid cloud provider (see chapter 12).

But since we're learning Streamlit, Community Cloud is ideal for this purpose. In the rest of this chapter, we'll deploy an app to it.

5.2 Deploying the to-do list app to Streamlit Community Cloud

As discussed in the previous section, Streamlit Community Cloud serves deployment needs well. It's free, custom-built for Streamlit, and easy to use. In this section, we'll deploy one of the apps built earlier—the to-do list app from chapter 4—to Community Cloud so anyone with an internet connection can access it.

5.2.1 Prerequisites

Besides Python and Streamlit itself, you'll need the following to deploy an app to Streamlit Community Cloud:

- `git`, the popular version control tool we briefly discussed in chapter 2
- A GitHub account
- A Streamlit Community Cloud account
- Connecting your GitHub account to Community Cloud

CREATING A GITHUB ACCOUNT AND SETTING IT UP

GitHub is a web-based platform for version control and collaborative software development. It relies on `git`, a distributed version control system, to help developers track code changes, collaborate on projects, and manage software versions.

> **NOTE** Don't confuse GitHub with Git. Git is the version control system, and Git*Hub* is the most popular platform for hosting Git repositories. You can also host Git repositories on other platforms, such as Bitbucket, but Streamlit Community Cloud requires GitHub.

A link to a GitHub account is a standard fixture on most developers' resumes these days. Streamlit Community Cloud expects you to store the app's code in a GitHub *repository*, which is a collection of files and directories along with their revision history.

Start by visiting `github.com` and signing up for a new account. The sign-up process is similar to most websites: enter an email address and verify it, create a username, and choose a strong password.

After creating an account, configure your command line to authenticate and push code to any repositories you create. There are several ways to do this, but here we'll use personal access tokens (PATs), which are password alternatives for accessing GitHub from the command line or an API.

At the time of writing, follow these steps to get to the PAT creation screen:

1 Click the profile picture, then select Settings
2 Find Developer Settings in the side panel and click it
3 Select Personal Access Tokens > Tokens (Classic)
4 Select Generate New Token

Figure 5.2 illustrates this path, although, of course, GitHub may change its configuration

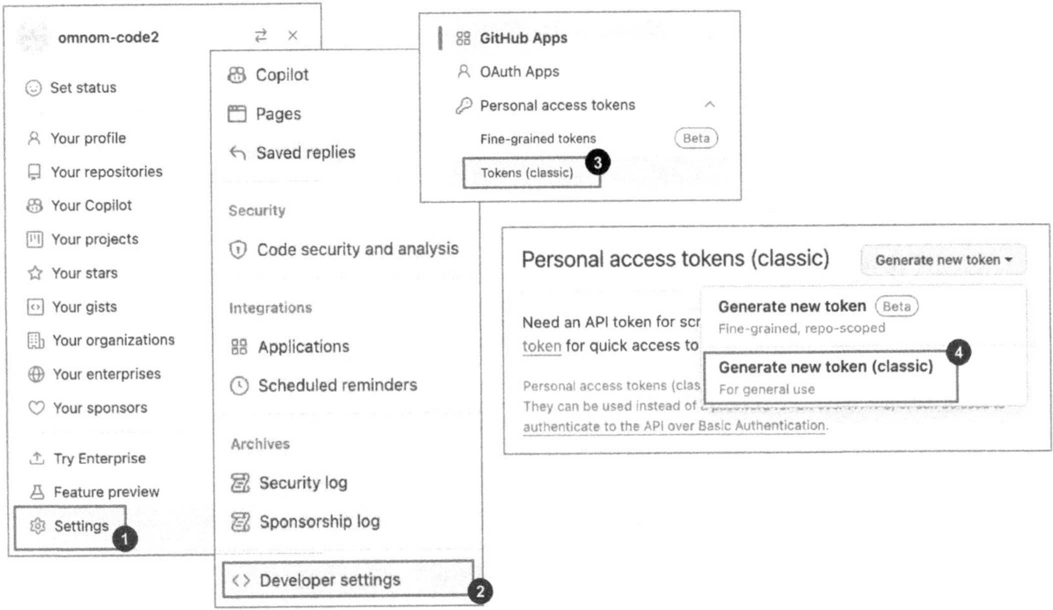

Figure 5.2   Getting to the personal access token generation page on GitHub

On the screen that opens select the Repo scope to grant full control over repositories. Then enter a note describing the token's purpose (for example, "Token to push Streamlit code") and set an expiration date.

When a PAT expires, it can no longer be used, and you'll need to create a new one, so choose the expiration date accordingly. A shorter expiry is more secure—if someone compromises the token, it remains valid for less time—but it also means you'll need to rotate it more frequently.

Figure 5.3 shows the selections you can make.

New personal access token (classic)

Personal access tokens (classic) function like ordinary OAuth access tokens. They can be used instead of a password for Git over HTTPS, or can be used to authenticate to the API over Basic Authentication.

Note

Token to push Streamlit code

What's this token for?

Expiration *

60 days ⇕   The token will expire on Fri, Oct 4 2024

Select scopes

Scopes define the access for personal tokens. Read more about OAuth scopes.

☑ **repo**	Full control of private repositories
☐ repo:status	Access commit status
☐ repo_deployment	Access deployment status
☐ public_repo	Access public repositories
☐ repo:invite	Access repository invitations
☐ security_events	Read and write security events

Figure 5.3   The PAT creation screen on GitHub. Make sure you select the Repo scope.

Click Generate Token to create it. GitHub will now show you the token you created. Copy it and store it somewhere safe, because you'll never be able to see it again. You'll use the PAT later when pushing code.

CREATING A STREAMLIT COMMUNITY CLOUD ACCOUNT

To create a Community Cloud account, go to https://streamlit.io/cloud and sign up with the GitHub account you just created. After signing up, Streamlit opens the My Apps page, which lists any apps you create.

If you haven't signed up with GitHub credentials, connect the GitHub account to Community Cloud separately. At the time of writing, you can do this by selecting Workspaces and then Connect GitHub Account.

If you're already logged into GitHub, you don't need to do anything else. Otherwise, enter your GitHub account credentials.

5.2.2   Deployment steps

Now that you've set up your accounts, deploying the app is a three-step process:

1. Creating a GitHub repo
2. Pushing code to GitHub
3. Telling Community Cloud where to find the code

If an app needs to connect to an external service or requires specialized libraries, we'll explore a couple of additional steps later in this chapter. But the preceding steps work for the to-do list app built in the previous chapter.

If `git` is already part of your regular development workflow (as recommended in chapter 2), you may have created a repo and pushed code to it. If so, skip ahead to the section "Telling Community Cloud where to find your app." If not, continue with the following sections.

CREATING A GITHUB REPO

To start, sign in to your GitHub account. The button to create a new repo should be fairly obvious. If you've never created one in this account, you should see a Create Repository button on the left (figure 5.4.) If the account already has repositories, GitHub displays a list of top repositories. Click New to create a new one.

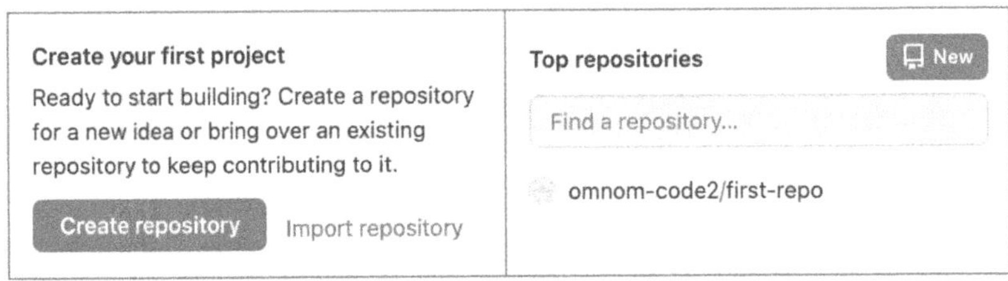

Figure 5.4   Buttons for creating a new repository on GitHub

This should direct you to a page for entering details about the new repository (figure 5.5). You can ignore most settings here. Give the repository a memorable name and select Public for visibility. When you're done, click Create Repository. GitHub then shows a screen with instructions and, importantly, the URL of the repo, as shown in figure 5.6. Make a note of this URL—you'll need it in the next section. If needed, you can find it again later by navigating to the repo. The repo is now ready for code!

PUSHING THE CODE TO GITHUB

At this point, you have a *remote* GitHub repo, but the Streamlit app code is stored *locally* on your computer. Next, push the code to the remote repo.

Open a terminal window and navigate to the directory that contains the to-do list app from chapter 4. You'll see two files: todo_list.py and task.py.

Enter the following command to initialize this directory as a *local* Git repository (as opposed to the remote one on GitHub):

```
git init
```

The `git init` command creates an empty Git repo and sets up all the required files in a hidden subdirectory called .git.

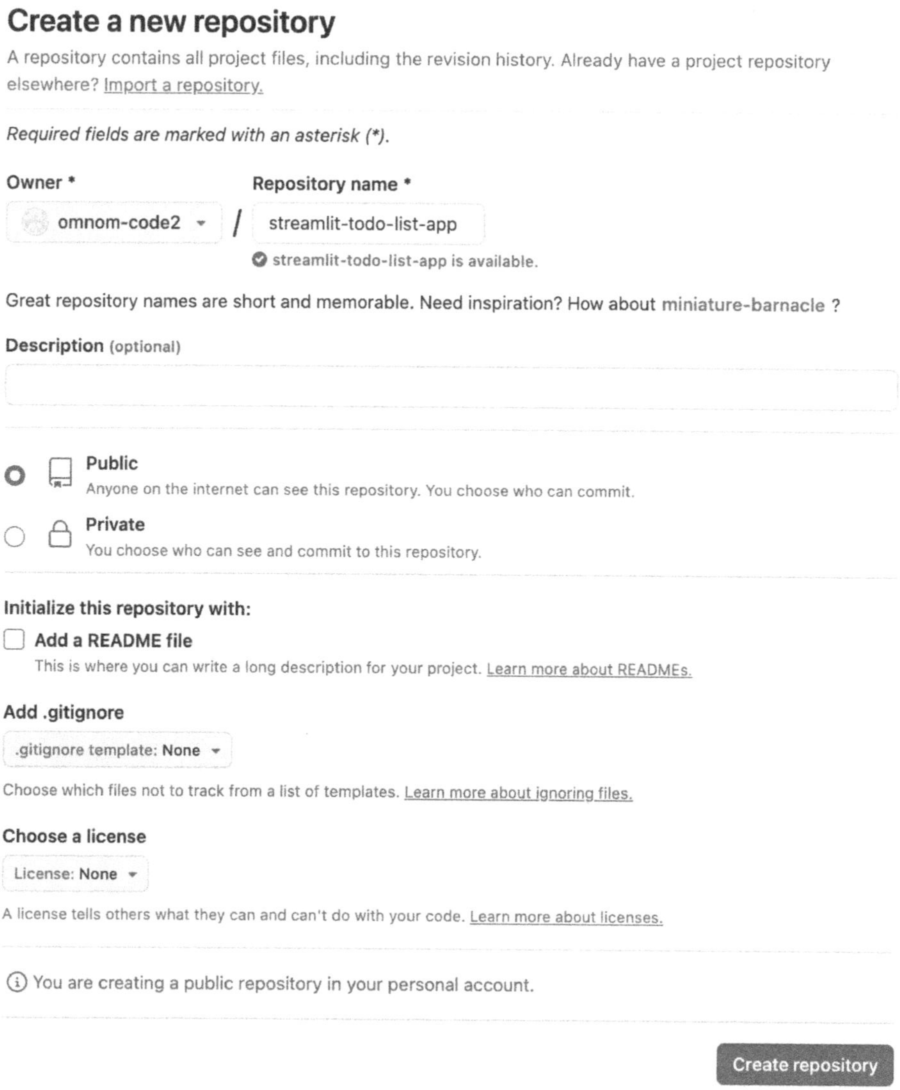

Figure 5.5 The repository creation screen on GitHub

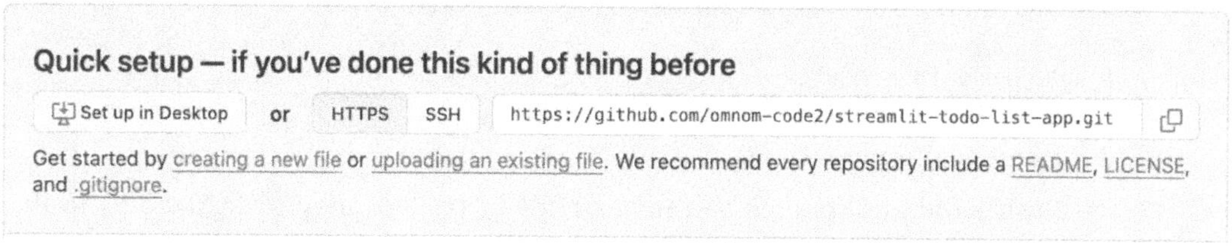

Figure 5.6 Repo URL

Next, type:

```
git add .
```

This command adds the contents of the current directory to Git's *staging area,* a temporary holding place for changes to the code. Use the staging area to prepare an exact snapshot of the code to save.

It's time to *commit* the changes, so type:

```
git commit -m "Commit Streamlit to-do list app"
```

This command captures a snapshot of the code's current state and saves it in the local repository with a descriptive message about the changes.

The final step is to copy the code to GitHub. First, make the local Git repo aware of the remote repo on GitHub:

```
https://<Your PAT>@<Repo URL without the https://>
```

For example, if the PAT is `ghp_fLbbSwjMlw3gUs7fgRux8Ha3PIlG9w3ZY3zY` (not a real one) and the repo is https://github.com/omnom-code2/streamlit-todo-list-app.git, the PAT-embedded URL is:

```
https://ghp_fLbbSwjMlw3gUs7fgRux8Ha3PIlG9w3ZY3zY@github.com/omnom-code2/
streamlit-todo-list-app.git
```

You can now add this URL as a *remote* to the local repo by typing:

```
git remote add origin <PAT-embedded URL>
```

Or in our example:

```
git remote add origin https://ghp_fLbbSwjMlw3gUs7fgRux8Ha3PIlG9w3ZY3zY@
github.com/omnom-code2/streamlit-todo-list-app.git
```

This command tells Git to add a remote repository with the alias "origin" to the local Git configuration and associate it with the specified PAT-embedded URL. This lets you interact with the remote repository using that alias in Git commands, and the PAT for authentication.

Finally, run the following command to push the code:

```
git push -u origin master
```

This command does two things:

- Pushes the local branch you're currently in (called "master" by default) to the remote repo you designated as "origin," thus making your code available in the "master" branch of the remote repo.

- Sets the default *upstream branch* (`-u` is shorthand for `--set-upstream`) of the local repo to the remote `master` branch, so in the future you can push code with just `git push`, without `-u origin master`.

> **NOTE** Here, we assume the default branch Git creates in the repo is called "master." Some versions of Git use "main" instead. If you get an error using "master," try replacing it with "main." The command then becomes `git push -u origin main`. Alternatively, type `git branch` (Git highlights the current branch) and use that branch name.

Navigate to the repo you created on GitHub to see the code, as shown in figure 5.7.

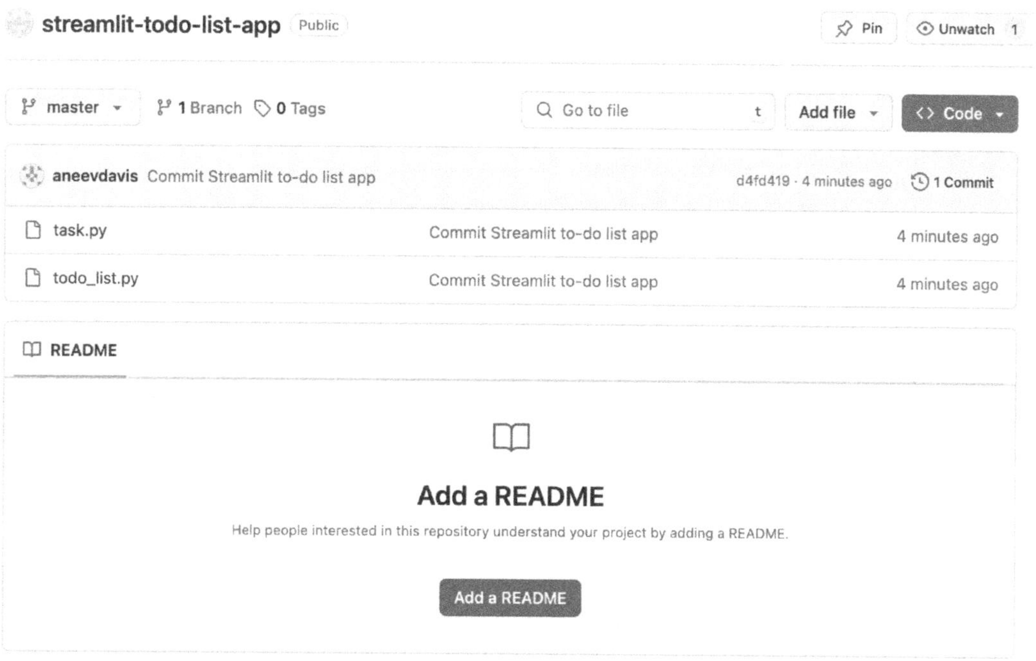

Figure 5.7 Repo in GitHub after pushing the code

> **NOTE** Git can be a complex tool to work with. This section covers only the bare minimum you need to deploy code to Streamlit Community Cloud. But ideally, you should use Git as part of a regular development workflow, committing code whenever you complete a meaningful piece of work.

TELLING COMMUNITY CLOUD WHERE TO FIND YOUR CODE

We've set up the Streamlit code on GitHub. Next, tell Streamlit Community Cloud where to find it.

Log in to a Community Cloud account at https:// streamlit.io and click the Create an App button in the upper-right corner. If prompted to confirm that you already have an app, select the option that says you do. This link opens the Deploy an App page shown in figure 5.8.

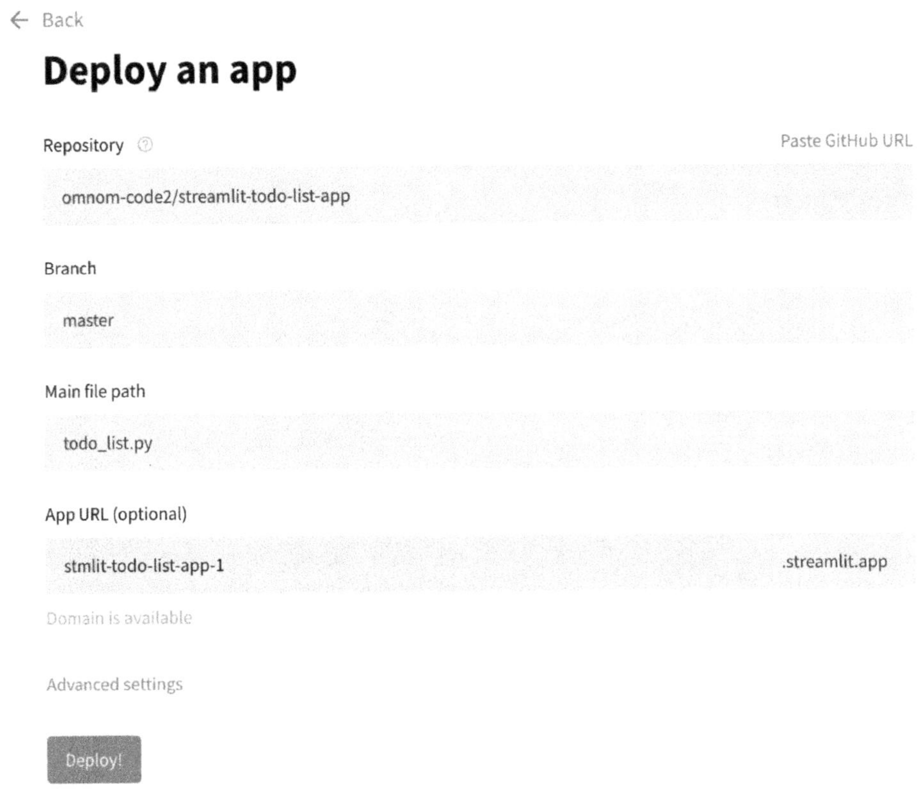

← Back

Deploy an app

Repository ⑦   Paste GitHub URL

omnom-code2/streamlit-todo-list-app

Branch

master

Main file path

todo_list.py

App URL (optional)

stmlit-todo-list-app-1   .streamlit.app

Domain is available

Advanced settings

Deploy!

Figure 5.8   The app deployment screen on Streamlit Community Cloud

Enter the details of where you pushed the code, including:

- The GitHub repository you created
- The branch you pushed your code to (e.g., `master` from `git push -u origin master`)
- The path to the app (this would be todo_list.py, since that's the file used in the `streamlit run` command, and it's located in the repo's root directory)

In the App URL field, choose the address people will use to access the app. Streamlit suggests a default URL, but you can override it with a more meaningful one. In figure 5.8, I chose `stmlit-todo-list-app-1.streamlit.app`.

Some advanced settings are available that we'll look at later in the chapter. Ignore them for now. That's it! Click the Deploy! button.

After a minute or so, the app should be ready! Anyone with an internet connection can now visit the address you chose (https://stmlit-todo-list-app-1.streamlit.app/ in this case) to run the to-do list app and get their life in order. You difference-maker, you!

NOTE Streamlit Community Cloud shuts down apps that no one has accessed in approximately 12 hours. If you visit the URL above, you might see a message saying the app is waking up and will take some time to load. This is one of the caveats of using a free hosting service. In chapter 12, we explore alternatives to Streamlit Community Cloud if this is a deal-breaker.

5.3 Deploying an app that uses an external service

In the last section, we saw that deploying a simple app to Streamlit Community Cloud follows a straightforward logical path. The to-do list app is simple in the sense that it's fairly self-contained.

For one thing, apart from Streamlit and Python itself, the app relies on no other libraries or software. For another, it does not interact with any external service or API. That won't be true for most practical apps. In the real world, developers build software on top of software built by other people. Therefore, business logic will likely need third-party libraries that don't come pre-installed with Python.

You will also find that, often, an app needs to connect to internet services to perform a useful task. In fact, it's almost inevitable. At some point, an app will need access to an English dictionary to check whether a user-entered word is valid, currency exchange rates to show a price in a different currency, or news headlines from around the globe. In these cases, you typically sign up for and connect to an application programming interface (API) that provides the specific service you need.

In this section, we'll add some of this complexity to the existing to-do list app and deploy the changes correctly.

5.3.1 A joke of the day to entertain users

Imagine a user of a to-do list app starting their day. The sky is clear, the birds are chirping, and they have a clean slate in front of them. The *diem* is theirs to *carpe*. So, humming the spring portion of Vivaldi's *Four Seasons*, they begin adding tasks.

Fast forward five minutes, and they've added the eighteenth thing they just remembered has to be done *today*. As their shoulders sag, the user vaguely hums the *Imperial March* from *Star Wars*, slowly realizing what an uphill climb the day will be.

Well, we can't have that! What if the app could lighten their mood? Might we find a tidbit of humor to share—something like *"Why don't skeletons fight each other? They don't have the guts"*—to inspire a smile before they dive into the madness? Of course, some more jaded users will just throw their coffee mugs at the screen, but hey, you can't please everyone.

Regardless, let's think about what adding a joke of the day to the app means. We could hardcode a bunch of jokes in the code, but that seems wasteful and not very scalable. Instead, we'll use a public API to obtain the jokes.

APIs AND HOW TO CALL THEM

An API is just a fancy term for a set of instructions that lets different pieces of software talk to each other. You might remember that in chapter 3, we defined an API for the backend of the unit conversion app—a *contract* that defined how the frontend could interact with it.

In general parlance, API means much the same thing, except that instead of a contract between two parts of the same application, it refers to the contract which defines how software can interact with a particular external service.

An API can be structured however its developer wants, and the only reliable way to understand how to use it is to read its documentation. Still, APIs often follow common *conventional* patterns. In general, you can *call* this type of API by sending an HTTP (or web) request to a URL in the following form:

```
https://<base address>/<endpoint>
```

The base address is a common address that every request to the API includes, whereas the endpoint is specific to the type of request you make. For instance, a weather-related API might have `api.weathersite.com` (not a real website) as its base address, with `forecast` and `history` as endpoints for weather predictions and past weather data, respectively.

Often, you can customize an API request by passing key-value parameters either in the URL (for a GET request) or as a request payload (for a POST request). You might also need to include additional information, such as an API key, in HTTP headers. See the next sidebar to learn more about how HTTP works.

In our made-up weather example, you might pass a date as a URL parameter to the API to get the forecast for that date, so the URL becomes:

```
https://api.weathersite.com/forecast?date=2024-08-01
```

The API then returns a response, often in a format called JSON (JavaScript Object Notation), which you can parse in code to interpret.

In this example, the response might look like:

```
{
  "high_temp": 72,
  "low_temp": 60,
  "forecast_text": "Nice and sunny, a good day for the park"
}
```

How HTTP requests work

HTTP, which stands for Hypertext Transfer Protocol, is the set of rules that define how messages travel across the web. Think of it as the grammatical structure computers use to communicate over the web.

To communicate using HTTP (for example, when a web browser talks to a web server to retrieve a web page), an HTTP *client*—such as a browser—sends well-formed HTTP *requests* to a web server. The server then returns an HTTP *response*, which may consist of an HTML file, an image, text, or almost anything else.

HTTP requests consist of:

- A request line (for our purposes, think of it as a URL)
- Some HTTP headers are key-value pairs that provide additional information about how to handle the request
- An optional body that contains data the client sends to the server

There are several types of HTTP requests, but the two most common are GET and POST.

Loosely speaking, GET requests are lightweight requests that don't have a body. The URL contains all the request information. To send data to the server, encode it as key-value pairs and append it to the end of the URL like this:

```
?param1=value1&param2=value2...
```

Entering a query in a search engine usually sends a GET request. For example, typing a URL in the browser address bar and pressing return sends a GET request to that URL.

POST requests *can* include a body with additional information. This body is often called a *payload* and might include data from a web form or an uploaded file.

THE API NINJAS DAD JOKES API

We'll use an API from the API Ninjas website (https://api-ninjas.com/). API Ninjas offers free APIs for various services, including real-time commodity prices, exchange rates, URL information lookups, face detection in images, and more.

They make money from the paid version of their APIs. As of the time of writing, if an app issues more than 10,000 calls a month, it needs the paid version. For learning, the free version is enough. Specifically, this chapter uses their Dad Jokes API, which, according to their documentation, "provides thousands of hilarious dad jokes for your entertainment apps."

To access it, you'll need to create an account. Go to https://api-ninjas.com/ and sign up. As usual, you'll need to provide and verify an email address and create a password. Once signed in, find the API key (one key can access all of their APIs). This key is a set of characters that identifies you when you connect to the API. As I write this, a Show API Key button appears under My Account. Make a note of the key.

Check the documentation at https://api-ninjas.com/api/dadjokes to get a sense of how to connect to the Dad Jokes API. The base URL is `api.api-ninjas.com`, which all of their APIs share. The endpoint for the Dad Jokes API is `/v1/dadjokes`, which returns one (or more) random jokes.

The documentation also mentions a limit parameter for setting the number of jokes returned, but it's a paid feature, so this book doesn't use it. By default, the API returns one joke, which is all this example needs. To get a random joke, send a GET request to the following URL:

```
https://api.api-ninjas.com/v1/dadjokes
```

As an experiment, try going to this URL in a browser (which, as the sidebar on HTTP requests mentions, sends a GET request). If everything works as intended, you should get an authentication error message:

```
{"error": "Missing API Key."}
```

That's because the request also needs the API key noted earlier. The documentation says to pass this value as an HTTP header named `X-Api-Key`. To do this, we'll use a Python library called `requests`.

5.3.2   *Using the requests library to connect to an API*

As we've seen, the API used to generate jokes is web-based, which requires the code to send and receive messages via HTTP. This is possible with vanilla Python, but this book uses `requests`, the Python world's go-to library for HTTP communication. `requests` provides built-in functionality for handling HTTP requests and offers a more user-friendly set of tools than the alternatives.

First, install `requests` by running the following command in a terminal:

```
pip install requests
```

Once that's done, verify that it's installed by running `pip show requests`. This command should display the version of the `requests` library, along with some other information.

Sending an HTTP request with the `requests` module is quite easy using simple `get` and `post` methods. To try this, open a Python shell (type `python` or `python3` at the command line) and run the following:

```
>>> import requests
>>> response = requests.get("https://api.api-ninjas.com/v1/dadjokes")
>>> response
<Response [400]>
>>> response.text
'{"error": "Missing API Key."}'
```

Here, we use the `requests.get` method to send the same request sent through the browser earlier. The method returns an instance of the `Response` class, which encapsulates the HTTP server's response to the request.

Then, we access the `text` property of `response`, which gets the response body as a string. As you can see, the string is exactly what we got before in the browser.

As we learned from the documentation, we can pass an API key using the `X-Api-Key` header. The `requests.get` method accepts an argument called `headers` in the form of a regular Python dictionary, so set that up:

```
>>> headers={"X-Api-Key": "+4VJR..."}
>>> response = requests.get("https://api.api-ninjas.com/v1/dadjokes",
        headers=headers)
>>> response.text
'[{"joke": "I want to name my puppies Rolex and Timex so I can have watch dogs."}]'
```


Looks like it's working now! Include the API key from API Ninjas in the `X-Api-Key` header, and the API returns an actual joke!

There's a lot more to the `requests` library than this. This book uses the module several times later on, but for more details, see the documentation at https://requests .readthedocs.io/.

5.3.3 *Incorporating jokes in the app*

We now have everything we need to add a joke of the day feature to the to-do list app. Since this is quite different from the core functionality of managing to-dos, it makes sense to create a new file, jokes.py, for it.

Specifically, we need a function, such as `generate_joke`, that takes an API key and pulls a joke from the Dad Jokes API. Listing 5.1 shows what jokes.py might look like (chapter_05/jokes.py in the GitHub repo).

Listing 5.1 The jokes.py file

```
import requests

API_URL = "https://api.api-ninjas.com/v1/dadjokes"

def generate_joke(api_key):
    headers = {"X-Api-Key": api_key}
    response = requests.get(API_URL, headers=headers)
    if response.status_code == requests.codes.ok:
        joke_obj = response.json()[0]
        return joke_obj['joke']
    # Fall back to a default joke if the API fails
    return f"Time flies like an arrow. Fruit flies like a banana."
```

We put `API_URL` at the top of the file as an easily configurable constant so later changes don't require modifying the function itself.

In the function, the first couple of lines prepare the headers dictionary, as we did in the Python shell, and call `requests.get`.

The next section checks whether the request went through:

```
if response.status_code == requests.codes.ok:
```

Every HTTP response comes with a status code that classifies the result of the request. These codes may be familiar—a status code of 200 means OK, code 404 means Not Found, and so on.

In the preceding snippet, the `if` statement checks whether the status code indicates success—in this case, whether the request returned a joke. `requests.codes` provides a more readable way to refer to specific HTTP status codes. `requests.codes.ok` means status code 200.

If everything is fine, we can move on to parsing the response:

```
joke_obj = response.json()[0]
```

Here, instead of using `response.text` as before, we use `response.json()`. From an earlier experiment in shell we know that the API response is in JSON format:

```
>>> response.text
'[{"joke": "I want to name my puppies Rolex and Timex so I can have watch dogs."}]'
```

JSON is a format that lets you create arbitrary hierarchies of data using text. Python developers can usually read a blob of JSON data easily, because the way you store data in JSON is almost identical to the way you encode the same data in a Python literal.

From the `response.text` value above, you can see that the data is encoded as a list (square brackets) with one element: a dictionary with a single key, "joke". `response.text` is a string, but parsing it into a Python object makes the data easier to work with. The `response.json()` method does that by parsing the response body into a Python object, assuming the text is JSON.

After calling `response.json()`, treat the result as a normal Python object. Here, the data is a single-element list, so use `response.json()[0]` to get its only element—a single-key dictionary:

```
return joke_obj['joke']
```

Then, we return the joke text by extracting it from the `joke_obj` dictionary with `joke_obj['joke']`, which we parsed from the JSON result:

```
return f"Time flies like an arrow. Fruit flies like a banana."
```

Finally, if the API call goes wrong and returns a status code other than 200, the function responds gracefully by returning an evergreen dad joke about the nature of time and the dietary preferences of insects.

Once jokes.py is complete, creating a joke to display in the main app is simple. In todo_list.py, import the `generate_joke` function at the top:

```
from jokes import generate_joke
```

To display the joke, call `generate_joke` with an API key right above where you show the task completion metric, and put the result in an `st.info` box:

```
st.info(generate_joke("+4VJR..."))
```

As before, don't forget to replace the argument to `generate_joke` with the actual API key. If you run `streamlit run` now, you should see the joke of the day (figure 5.9.)

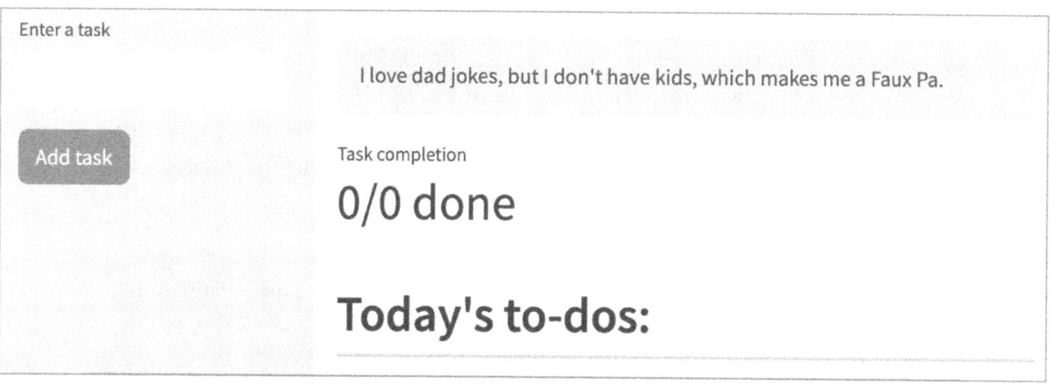

Figure 5.9   Joke of the day in the to-do list app

Great! That seems like the API call is working exactly as intended. We can rest assured that if a user feels like giving up in the middle of organizing their day, they'll get a daily joke to inspire them to stay strong.

But wait! Recall that Streamlit reruns the *entire* script whenever an interaction takes place. That includes calling the API through `generate_joke`. Basically, each time a user adds a task, marks something done, or does anything in the app, the app makes an API call and generates a new joke. Forget joke of the day—we're dealing with joke of the click here.

Normally, you might be forgiven for wanting to chalk that up as a feature, not a bug. But remember: the plan includes only 10,000 free API calls per month. If the app pulls a joke every time a user clicks anything, it will burn through even that hefty quota pretty quickly.

Instead, let's use `st.session_state` from chapter 4. Just as we saved the task list so it doesn't get reset with every run, we'll also save the joke to avoid unnecessary API calls:

```
if "joke" not in st.session_state:
    st.session_state.joke = generate_joke("+4VJR...")
```

Again, replace the "+4VJR..." with
the API key you noted down earlier.

Now replace the earlier st.info line with this:

```
st.info(st.session_state.joke)
```

Try the app now and you'll see that the joke doesn't change when you add a task or do anything else in the app. It changes only when you refresh the page. So, is that it? Not quite...

5.3.4 *Accessing an API key safely with st.secrets*

The app works just fine now, but it has a glaring security flaw: the code embeds the API key directly. If we commit this code to a public GitHub repository, anyone can see it and find the API key. With a free API, the stakes are low, but could be high if you pay for the API. Anyone who accesses a GitHub repo might—unwittingly or with malicious intent—set themselves loose on an API account, costing hundreds or even thousands of dollars.

> **NOTE** It's worth internalizing this rule right now: never store any secret information—an API key, password, or other credential—in code, especially if the code will be publicly accessible.

What's the alternative, then? How do we grant an app access to the API key if we can't include it in the code? Generally speaking, there are a few ways to do this: put the key in an environment variable and store it securely on the server where the app runs. Another option is to use a secrets management service, such as AWS Secrets Manager or HashiCorp Vault, which lets the app retrieve confidential information securely.

Streamlit provides an easy way to keep secrets safe: `st.secrets`. Like `st.session_state`, it is a dictionary-like structure for storing secret information.

To make a value available to `st.secrets`, store it in a special file called secrets.toml. During local development, Streamlit will read the values from it. When pushing code, be careful not to commit secrets.toml. Later in the chapter we'll discuss the .gitignore file which helps prevent that.

Instead, configure the information directly in Streamlit Community Cloud so the deployed app can access it in production.

THE SECRETS.TOML FILE

In the root folder of the local repository (where you ran `git init` earlier), create an empty directory called .streamlit, and inside it, create an empty text file called secrets .toml. Next, enter the API key in the file as shown in listing 5.2.

Listing 5.2   The secrets.toml file

```
[jokes_api]
api_key = "+4VJR..."
```

As before, use the actual API key here.

The .toml format may be new to you. TOML stands for Tom's Obvious Minimal Language. It's a format for configuration files designed to be concise and easily readable by humans, and was initially created by a guy named—Tom.

.toml files mostly consist of key-value pairs and support a range of simple and complex data types, including arrays and tables. Square brackets denote sections that divide the file.

The file shown in listing 5.2 has a single section, `jokes_api`, with a single key-value pair, where the key is `api_key`. Reading it in Python (outside Streamlit, you would usually use the `toml` module) maps it to the following nested dictionary:

```
{'jokes_api': {'api_key': '+4VJR...'}}
```

In Streamlit, `st.secrets` contains something similar. Now replace the call to `generate_joke` in todo_list.py with the following:

```
if "joke" not in st.session_state:
    api_key = st.secrets["jokes_api"]["api_key"]
    st.session_state.joke = generate_joke(api_key)
```

At runtime, Streamlit reads the secrets.toml file to populate `st.secrets`, as shown above. The code uses `st.secrets["jokes_api"]["api_key"]` to refer to the API key. Try it out—you'll see that the app can still fetch a joke from the API.

> **NOTE**   Technically, the .streamlit directory should be located in the directory from which you run `streamlit run <file_path>`. For instance, if you're currently in a directory called apps, the code is located in a folder called todo_list_app, and the command to run the app is `streamlit run todo_list_app/todo_list.py`, then the .streamlit folder should be located in the apps folder, not in the todo_list_app folder. When you deploy the code to Streamlit Community Cloud, Streamlit effectively runs `streamlit run` from the repo root, which is why I suggested placing .streamlit there. While developing locally, if the local repo root is different from the folder you usually run `streamlit run` from, you'll probably need to change the directory to the repo root to get this to work.

The todo_list.py file should now look like listing 5.3 (chapter_05/todo_list.py in the GitHub repo).

Listing 5.3   The final state of todo_list.py

```
import streamlit as st
from task import Task
from jokes import generate_joke
```

```python
if "task_list" not in st.session_state:
    st.session_state.task_list = []
task_list = st.session_state.task_list

if "joke" not in st.session_state:
    api_key = st.secrets["jokes_api"]["api_key"]
    st.session_state.joke = generate_joke(api_key)

def add_task(task_name: str):
    task_list.append(Task(task_name))

def delete_task(idx: int):
    del task_list[idx]

def mark_done(task: Task):
    task.is_done = True

def mark_not_done(task: Task):
    task.is_done = False

with st.sidebar:
    task = st.text_input("Enter a task")
    if st.button("Add task", type="primary"):
        add_task(task)

st.info(st.session_state.joke)

total_tasks = len(task_list)
completed_tasks = sum(1 for task in task_list if task.is_done)
metric_display = f"{completed_tasks}/{total_tasks} done"
st.metric("Task completion", metric_display, delta=None)

st.header("Today's to-dos:", divider="gray")
for idx, task in enumerate(task_list):
    task_col, delete_col = st.columns([0.8, 0.2])
    label = f"~~{task.name}~~" if task.is_done else task.name
    checked = task_col.checkbox(label, task.is_done, key=f"task_{idx}")
    if checked and not task.is_done:
        mark_done(task)
        st.rerun()
    elif not checked and task.is_done:
        mark_not_done(task)
        st.rerun()
    if delete_col.button("Delete", key=f"delete_{idx}"):
        delete_task(idx)
        st.rerun()
```

5.4   Deploying changes to Streamlit Community Cloud

Generally speaking, making changes to an already deployed Streamlit app is simple.
Commit the changes and run `git push` to update the GitHub repo. Streamlit Community Cloud picks them up automatically.

However, recent changes to the app make this process slightly more complicated. Three factors complicate it:

- The project now uses an additional third-party library, `requests`, so you must ensure the correct version is installed in production
- We should never push secrets.toml to GitHub, even by accident
- Because the API key won't be stored in the GitHub repo, we should configure it directly in Community Cloud

5.4.1 Using a requirements.txt file to manage Python dependencies

When you first publish apps, you must manage two *environments*: a development environment (often simply called *dev*) on a laptop or other computer used to code the app, and a production environment (called *prod*) in Streamlit Community Cloud. To ensure the app you coded in dev works as expected in prod, configure the two environments the same way, or verify that *any differences between dev and prod don't affect the app.*

This means the Python code that runs in prod should match what runs on a development machine. But the code may rely on third-party software such as the `requests` module (as in the to-do list app) or Streamlit itself. Keep these *dependencies* consistent between prod and dev, or at least ensure any differences don't affect the app's functionality.

For instance, if a feature in the `requests` library was introduced in version 2.1.1 but prod uses `requests` version 2.0.5, the app will run into an error in prod. To avoid breakage, install `requests` version 2.1.1 or higher in prod. To be completely sure the code won't break, install exactly version 2.1.1, because a future release could deprecate or remove the feature in use.

In the Python world, it's conventional to use a file called requirements.txt to prevent discrepancies between prod and dev environments. The premise of requirements .txt is simple: each line represents a Python module and a string that specifies a version or a range of versions of that module that is compatible with the codebase.

Pass the file to the `pip install` command (for example, `pip install -r requirements .txt`), and `pip` will automatically read it and install the specified version of each module. Streamlit Community Cloud recognizes a requirements.txt file, so adding one to a GitHub repository triggers automatic installation of the libraries needed to run the app.

CREATING A REQUIREMENTS.TXT FILE

The app has only two external dependencies—`streamlit` and `requests` (you can confirm this by examining the import statements across the .py files). Therefore, the requirements.txt file can be quite simple, as shown in listing 5.4.

> **Listing 5.4 A simple requirements.txt file**

```
requests
streamlit
```

While this is a valid requirements.txt file, it doesn't say anything about which versions to install. A safe approach is to identify the versions of these libraries installed in dev and list those exact versions in requirements.txt. This can be done in a couple of ways:

- To see (among other information) the installed versions of each library, type `pip show streamlit` and `pip show requests`
- Another option is to run `pip freeze > requirements.txt` to generate a requirements.txt file from the packages installed in the dev environment. This command includes *every* installed package, even ones the code doesn't import. If you choose this approach, delete all lines except those for `streamlit` or `requests`.

Either way, after determining the correct versions with `pip show` or creating the file with `pip freeze`, the requirements.txt file should look like listing 5.5.

Listing 5.5 A strict requirements.txt file

```
requests==2.31.0
streamlit==1.34.0
```

We don't *have* to be this strict with versions. Instead, allow any version of these libraries that matches or exceeds the versions installed. This approach lets the app benefit from future under-the-hood improvements in these libraries while still being *reasonably* sure it won't break. In that case, the file may look like listing 5.6.

Listing 5.6 A this-version-or-higher requirements.txt

```
requests>=2.31.0
streamlit>=1.34.0
```

Once the file is ready, save it to the root of the local Git repo.

> **NOTE** An app can still work in production even if you *don't* create a requirements.txt file. Streamlit Community Cloud preinstalls the two libraries used here: streamlit and requests. The streamlit library is required for any Streamlit app to run. Because Streamlit depends on requests internally, Community Cloud preinstalls requests as well. In most projects, additional libraries are needed, and requirements.txt tells the platform what to install. Even in this example, include the file to pin the exact module versions used in production.

5.4.2   *Using .gitignore to protect secrets.toml*

You may wonder how a secrets.toml file protects an API key from prying eyes—the key may no longer appear in the Python code, but it still sits in a file next to the code. The solution is to keep secrets.toml locally and never commit it to the Git repo.

To avoid accidentally committing secrets.toml, use a .gitignore file. A .gitignore file in the repository root tells Git which files to ignore and keep out of commits. If the file doesn't already exist, create an empty text file called .gitignore in the repo root. Then append the path to the .streamlit folder. Since the .streamlit folder should also be in the repo root, add the following to .gitignore:

```
.streamlit/
```

If you now run `git add` or `git commit`, Git won't commit secrets.toml (or any file in the .streamlit directory).

> **NOTE** Git may already be tracking the .streamlit folder from before it was added to .gitignore. If so, remove it from Git's index with this command: `git rm -r --cached .streamlit/`

At this point, the directory structure should look like the following:

```
Root of your Git repo
├── .streamlit (folder)
│   └── secrets.toml
├── .gitignore
├── requirements.txt
├── jokes.py
├── task.py
└── todo_list.py
```

Add changes to Git, commit them with a message, and then push them to GitHub. Run the following commands:

```
git add .
git commit -m "Add joke-of-the-day functionality"
git push
```

Use the simple `git push` command above because `git push -u` set the branch upstream to the remote repo earlier. You should now see the changes in the production Streamlit app. Or should you? Open the public URL for the app to see what's shown in figure 5.10.

One final configuration step remains before the app works properly.

5.4.3   *Configuring secrets in Community Cloud*

We keep the API key secret, but the app still needs it in production. Configure the key in Streamlit Community Cloud, which hosts the deployed app.

You can configure the key on the *App Settings* screen in Community Cloud. Access this screen in one of the following two ways:

KeyError: This app has encountered an error. The original error message is redacted to prevent data leaks. Full error details have been recorded in the logs (if you're on Streamlit Cloud, click on 'Manage app' in the lower right of your app).

Traceback:

```
File "/mount/src/streamlit-todo-list-app/todo_list.py", line 10, in <module>
    api_key = st.secrets["jokes_api"]["api_key"]
              ~~~~~~~~~~~^^^^^^^^^^^^^
File "/home/adminuser/venv/lib/python3.12/site-packages/streamlit/runtime/secr
    raise KeyError(_missing_key_error_message(key))
```

Figure 5.10   The app throws an error because it can't access an API key.

- On the deployed app's public URL, click Manage App at the bottom right. Then click the three vertical dots and choose Settings.
- Log in to Community Cloud on streamlit.io, click the three vertical dots next to the app in the app list, then select Settings.

Either way, after you open the App Settings page, click Secrets on the side panel to see the screen shown in figure 5.11.

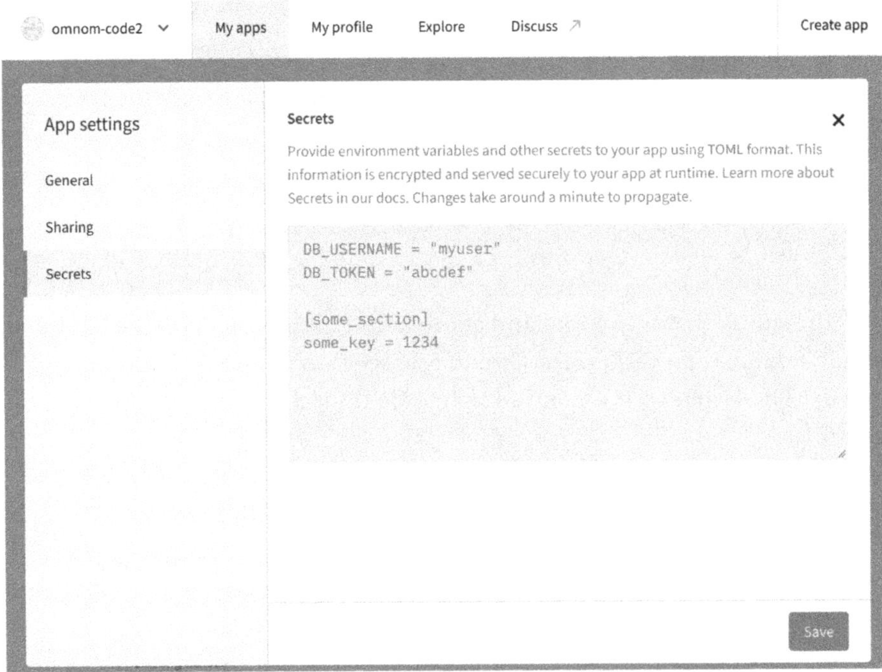

Figure 5.11   The secrets configuration screen on Streamlit Community Cloud

In the Secrets textbox, copy the contents of secrets.toml from the development machine, and then click Save.

That's it! Return to the app's public URL. The app should now be fully functional (figure 5.12).

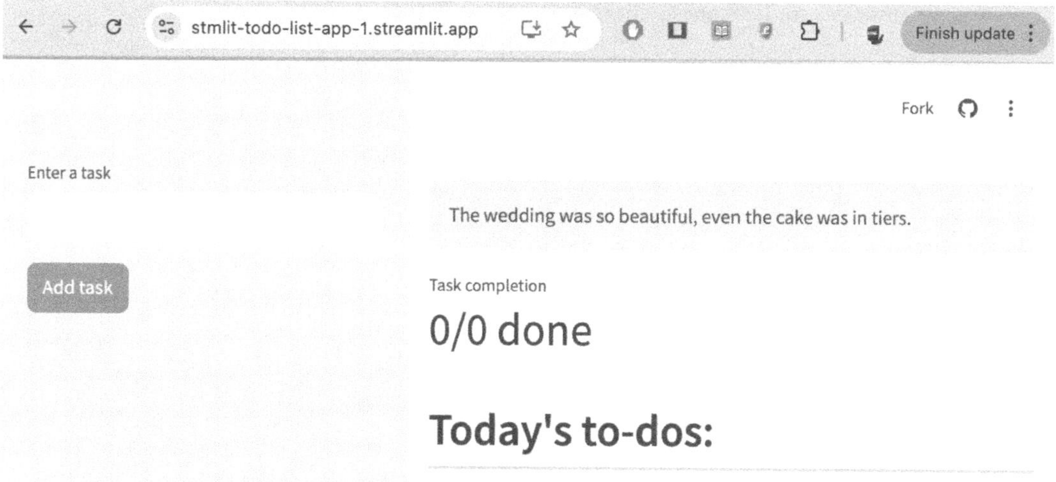

Figure 5.12   Fully functional app deployed to production

By now, you can build and share useful Streamlit apps with a public audience. In the next chapter, we explore a more advanced app focused on working with data.

Summary

- Deployment is the process of hosting and setting up an app so intended users can access it.
- There are multiple ways to deploy an app—you could simply run a server over your local network, set up a dedicated server, or use a cloud provider.
- Streamlit Community Cloud lets developers deploy an unlimited number of apps for free, subject to resource usage limits.
- Deploying to Community Cloud involves creating a GitHub account, pushing local code to a remote GitHub repo, and telling Community Cloud where to find the code.
- You can connect to external services over HTTP using a library called `requests`.
- Use `st.secrets` with a secrets.toml file in the .streamlit folder to keep credentials safe.

- Never commit the secrets.toml file—prevent accidents by adding it to .gitignore. Instead, use the App Settings page on Streamlit Community Cloud to store in production the information you keep in secrets.toml locally.
- You can use a requirements.txt file to specify the versions of various Python libraries the app depends on.
- To deploy changes to an app already running on Community Cloud, push the updates to the remote GitHub repo.

## Part 2

Diving into more complex apps

Now that you've got the basics down, it's time to push Streamlit further, into the kinds of apps that solve real problems. This part explores what it means to build Streamlit apps that are dynamic, data-driven, and capable of supporting complex use cases.

In chapter 6, you'll build an executive-level dashboard from scratch, learning how to load, transform, and visualize data using pandas and Plotly. In chapter 7, you'll evolve that dashboard in response to user feedback—adding drilldowns, interdependent filters, and deep links to create a polished, interactive experience. Chapter 8 shifts gears into app architecture: you'll build a full-featured CRUD app, complete with user authentication, persistent storage in a relational database, and a multi-page interface.

Together, these chapters show how Streamlit isn't just for demos—it's a serious tool for building powerful internal apps and prototypes quickly.

A dashboard fit
for a CEO

This chapter covers

- Building an interactive metrics dashboard
- Wrangling data using the pandas library
- Caching the results of functions to improve Streamlit app performance
- Creating filters, panels, and other widgets in a dashboard
- Developing data visualizations and charts using Plotly

Ever wondered how executives at large companies manage to stay on top of the businesses they run? Imagine the complexity and the sheer *number* of products and services offered by a company like Amazon, 3M, or Google. How can one person make sense of it all? How do they know if their business is meeting expectations and what areas need their focus?

In well-run companies, the answer—or part of it—is *metrics*. Executives rely on a carefully curated set of metrics, or numbers, that provide a high-level overview of the company's performance. Metrics help leaders make informed decisions, identify potential obstacles before they become major problems, and pinpoint areas where the company can improve or innovate.

However, metrics alone are not enough—teams must present them clearly and in a digestible way. That's where dashboards come into play. A good dashboard lets users explore various cuts of data, transforming raw data into a story, highlighting what's important, and helping leaders stay focused on the bigger picture.

In this chapter, we'll develop such a dashboard designed for a CEO to monitor key performance indicators (KPIs) for their business. By the end, you'll know not only how to build a robust, interactive metrics dashboard using Streamlit, but also understand how to present data in a way that empowers decision-makers to focus on what truly matters.

> **NOTE** The GitHub repo for this book is https://github.com/aneevdavis/ streamlit-in-action. The chapter_06 folder has this chapter's code and a requirements.txt file with exact versions of the required Python libraries. You can install all of them in one shot by downloading this file and running `pip install -r requirements.txt` in a terminal window.

6.1 A metrics dashboard

Change is afoot at Note n' Nib Inc., everyone's favorite fictional online shopping site for stationery! The founder-CEO has retired to enjoy his millions in Ibiza, and his successor, a data-obsessed bigwig from Silicon Valley, has big plans for the company.

His enthusiasm is punctured a little when, in his first staff meeting, he asks the VP of Sales where he can look up the latest sales numbers, and the VP fishes into his suitcase and retrieves a *paper* report from two months ago.

"Don't we have a dashboard where we keep track of daily sales data?" the CEO asks, dreading the answer. His fears are confirmed when the VP mutters something about the *old* CEO having possessed a marvelous *intuition* that he frequently relied upon to make decisions, and that pen-and-paper was, after all, the core of the business.

An hour later, the VP of Sales summons you, a rising star in the department (and his go-to for stuff he doesn't want to deal with himself), and tasks you with building "one of those fancy metrics pages with line charts" for his boss.

You know Engineering is busy with a major overhaul of the website, so you don't want to add this to their already full plate. Luckily, you've been experimenting with the cool new Python framework called Streamlit, and you're eager to use it at work.

6.1.1 Stating the concept

The VP didn't give you a lot to work with, but you've been around long enough to have a pretty good idea of what the boss wants. As always, let's start by spelling this out:

> *A dashboard that lets executives view various cuts of sales data and track key metrics to make decisions.*

6.1.2 Defining the requirements

We have our work cut out for us to translate the concept into concrete requirements. Specifically, the phrases "sales data", "various cuts", and "key metrics" need to be expanded upon.

EXPLORING THE DATA

You've managed to get Engineering to export key data fields from their systems that you think will be relevant to your project into a Comma-Separated Values (CSV) file. You can download this file from the GitHub repo for this book (the file is called sales_data.csv and is in the chapter_06 directory).

> **NOTE** In the real world, we wouldn't typically use a CSV file as the main data source for a dashboard because it's static and not particularly efficient. However, in this chapter, we want to focus on what to do *with* the data once it's in your app, rather than *how* you get the data in the first place—and using a CSV is the easiest way to do that. In chapter 7, we'll modify our app to source data from a data warehouse instead.

Once you've downloaded it, open it up in a spreadsheet program like Microsoft Excel or Numbers on macOS, and inspect the first few rows (shown in figure 6.1)

date	product_name	segment	category	gender	age_group	state	sales	gross_margin	transactions
2019-01-01	InkStream	Fountain pens	Writing tools	M	18-25	CA	134.91	83.61	8
2019-01-01	InkStream	Fountain pens	Writing tools	M	18-25	TX	149.9	92.9	9

Figure 6.1 First two rows of the CSV data used in this example.

The data represents the sales of various products sold by Note n' Nib, broken out by various *dimensions* such as segment and category. It also has demographic information about the kind of people who bought these products, specifically their gender and age group, as well as the state they hailed from. The file has data from January 2019 to August 2024, and contains *measures* such as sales (how much revenue Note n' Nib made), gross margin (how much of the sales was profit, accounting for the cost), and the number of transactions covered by each row.

For instance, here's how we would interpret the first row: on Jan 1 2019, men aged 18-25 from California buying Inkstream fountain pens (classified as Writing tools) made eight transactions on the Note n' Nib website, bringing in $134.91 in sales to the company, of which $83.91 remained after subtracting costs.

In this table, the *primary key* (the set of columns that uniquely identify a row) consists of date, product_name, segment, category, gender, age_group, and state.

After speaking with the CEO, you also determine that he primarily cares about the following numbers: total sales, gross margin, margin percentage, and average transaction value. We'll dive into these and how they're calculated later in the chapter, but these are the key metrics from our stated concept.

The CEO wants to be able to see how these numbers differ across different products, categories, age groups, genders, and states—the various cuts from the concept—as well as across time. You also consider how the data should be represented and ultimately come up with an initial set of requirements.

REQUIREMENTS

The dashboard user should be able to:

- View total sales, gross margin, margin percentage, and average transaction value for products sold on Note n' Nib
- See how the numbers vary by year, product, category, age group, gender, and state
- Filter the data by these dimensions to explore data cross-sections
- Visualize metric trends over time, with breakdowns by each dimension

To deliver an initial version of the dashboard quickly without getting bogged down in additional feature requests, you need to clearly define what's out of scope, too.

WHAT'S OUT OF SCOPE

At first launch, the dashboard will *not* support:

- Drilling down into the data to view specific rows
- Forecasting future values for any metric
- Providing explanations about why a metric has changed over time

Some of these can be future expansions to the dashboard, but for now, we'll try to limit its functionality to *observing* data as opposed to actively *analyzing* or *predicting* it.

6.1.3   *Visualizing the user experience*

The next step in the app development flow, which we explored in chapter 3, is to visualize the user experience. From the requirements, it's evident that the four key metrics are of vital importance, so we should display them prominently, ideally in a way that immediately draws the user's eye to them. The requirements also mention filtering the data based on the dimensions and cuts we discussed. It seems reasonable to include a panel where users can do this.

A picture speaks a thousand words, so we want to provide clear visualizations of the data; the trends and breakdowns indicated in the requirements could be realized through *time series charts,* which show the progression of a number over time, and *pie charts,* which tell you how a whole quantity breaks down into its components. Figure 6.2 shows a mock interface designed based on the above.

As you can see, this design incorporates everything we discussed: the four key metrics are shown in a large, unmissable font, and their values correspond to a slice of the data that is controlled by the filters at the top and a date range selector on the left. There's

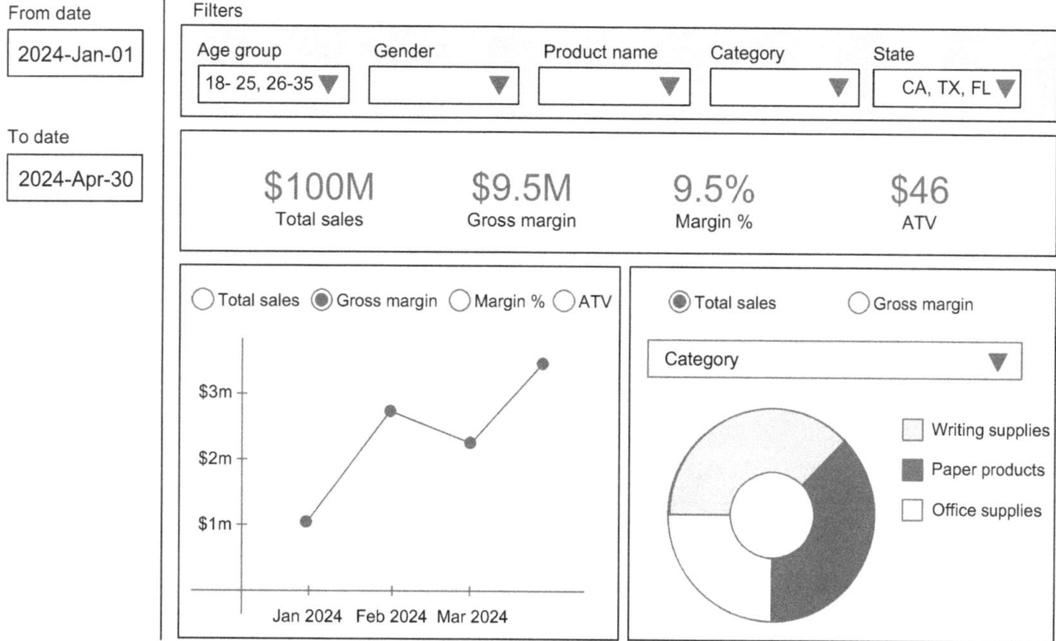

Figure 6.2   A UI mock for the dashboard

a line chart that shows how any selected metric has changed over time, and a pie chart that breaks down the total sales or gross margin by a selected dimension, like the product category.

6.1.4   Brainstorming the implementation

Before we begin writing code, let's outline the high-level flow of logic and data in our dashboard. Figure 6.3 illustrates one possible approach to structuring this.

The first step is to read the raw data from our CSV file and to load it into memory. There may be some basic data preparation or cleaning we want to perform next, such as renaming columns for convenience.

In our mock UI in figure 6.2, the filter bar at the top and the date range selectors to the side are meant to be *global*, i.e., they affect all of the widgets in the dashboard. So it stands to reason that we should apply the filters and select just the range we need before we pass the data around to the other parts of the dashboard.

There are three sections in the dashboard where we'll display data in some form: the metric bar with the overall metric values, the change-over-time line chart, and the pie chart. To display the content in each of these, we need to apply transformations to the filtered data, which involves grouping, aggregating, and otherwise transforming it.

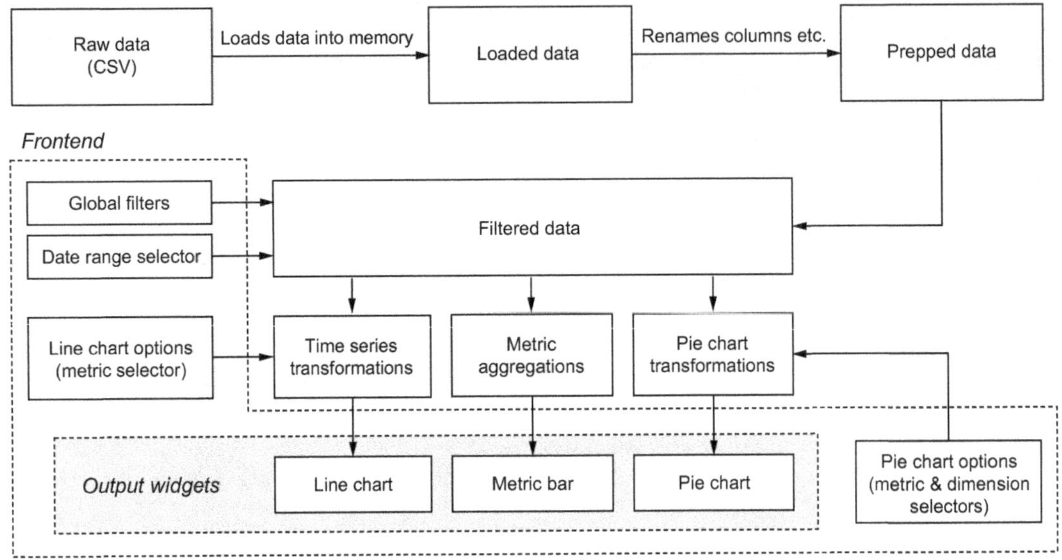

Figure 6.3 Flow of logic and data in the dashboard

The line and pie charts have additional options (you need to choose a metric to display in both charts, and a breakdown dimension—like the product category or gender—in the pie chart), which will serve as inputs to the transformations we'll apply.

This hopefully gave you an overview of the design we'll be implementing in the rest of the chapter. Don't worry if some of these parts aren't quite clear to you yet; we're about to explore each part in a lot more detail.

6.2 Loading the data

In any application that presents or visualizes data, the first step involves obtaining data from some source. Sometimes this source is simply information entered by the user, but often it's an external source such as a database or a file. We'll talk about connecting to databases in later chapters, but for now, we'll use the CSV file we reviewed earlier.

In this section, we'll walk you through the process of loading data into your app from an external file, storing it in memory, and displaying it in Streamlit. Along the way, we'll introduce pandas, the quintessential Python library for data manipulation. We'll also discuss how to improve your app's performance through caching when the data you need to load is very large.

6.2.1 The pandas library

I mentioned pandas briefly in chapter 1 as a popular library for working with tabular data. In practice, pandas is so integral to the data ecosystem that it's hard to imagine working with data in Python without it.

INSTALLING PANDAS

Install pandas like any other Python library using `pip`. Run the following command to set it up:

```
pip install pandas
```

Once that finishes running, verify that everything is set up correctly by running `pip show pandas`, which should display information about the library.

EXPLORING OUR SALES DATA IN PANDAS

Pandas revolves around the concept of the dataframe, which is a two-dimensional, tabular data structure similar to a table in a spreadsheet. It consists of rows and columns, where each column holds data of a specific type (eg, integer, float, string). Dataframes allow for efficient data manipulation and analysis, making them a versatile tool for handling structured data.

To see dataframes in action, let's load our sales data CSV into a pandas dataframe. Navigate to the local directory where you downloaded sales_data.csv, open a Python shell, and type the following commands:

```
>>> import pandas as pd
>>> df = pd.read_csv('sales_data.csv')
```

The `import pandas as pd` is a regular Python import statement. It's conventional to refer to the pandas module as `pd` (just as we use `st` for Streamlit).

```
>>> df = pd.read_csv('sales_data.csv')
```

This is where we actually load the CSV file. Pandas makes this incredibly easy using the `read_csv` method. `read_csv` has a ton of parameters you can pass to it (such as whether the file contains a header, what column names and types to use, and so on), but since all of these have sensible default values, you can also just pass it the path to the file and nothing else.

At the end of this, we have a variable `df` that holds a pandas dataframe. Let's verify this using Python's built-in `type` function, which returns the type of the object that a particular variable holds:

```
>>> type(df)
<class 'pandas.core.frame.DataFrame'>
```

Use the `info()` method to get more information about the dataframe:

```
>>> df.info()
<class 'pandas.core.frame.DataFrame'>
RangeIndex: 1035000 entries, 0 to 1034999
Data columns (total 10 columns):
```

```
 #    Column         Non-Null Count      Dtype
---   ------         --------------      -----
 0    date           1035000 non-null    object
 1    product_name   1035000 non-null    object
 2    segment        1035000 non-null    object
 3    category       1035000 non-null    object
 4    gender         1035000 non-null    object
 5    age_group      1035000 non-null    object
 6    state          1035000 non-null    object
 7    sales          1035000 non-null    float64
 8    gross_margin   1035000 non-null    float64
 9    transactions   1035000 non-null    float64
dtypes: float64(3), object(7)
memory usage: 79.0+ MB
```

The output reveals several things. The dataframe has more than a million rows, numbered from 0 to 1,034,999. It has 10 columns: the first seven are `object` type (essentially strings), and the last three are `float64` type (floating-point numbers).

Python and pandas types

The names `object` and `float64` may be confusing to you since they're not the regular Python types (`str`, `float`, etc.) that you're likely used to. This is because pandas uses its own data types (or dtypes), derived from a related Python library called numpy, for efficient computations. You also have the option of having pandas use the Apache Arrow format, which can be more performant for large datasets. To do so, while reading the CSV, add a `dtype_backend` parameter like so:

```python
pd.read_csv('sales_data.csv', dtype_backend='pyarrow')
```

If you do this, you'll notice that the data types shown by `.info()` are `string[pyarrow]` and `double[pyarrow]` rather than `object` and `float64`. Note that you *may* have to first install pyarrow with `pip install pyarrow` to get this to work.

Let's look at some of the content in the dataframe next. Since we don't have enough space on this page to print all the columns, we first select a subset of them:

```python
>>> only_some_cols = df[['date', 'product_name', 'segment', 'state']]
```

You can create a new pandas dataframe by performing an operation on another dataframe. That's essentially what happened here. When we pass a list of columns to a dataframe using pandas' user-friendly square-bracket notation (`df[<list of column names>]`), we get a new dataframe containing only the columns we passed, which we can then assign to another variable (`only_some_cols` in this case).

Finally, to see the first few rows, we use the `.head()` method on our smaller dataframe, which shows us the values in the first five rows.

```
>>> only_some_cols.head()
          date product_name        segment state
0   2019-01-01    InkStream  Fountain pens    CA
1   2019-01-01    InkStream  Fountain pens    TX
2   2019-01-01    InkStream  Fountain pens    FL
3   2019-01-01    InkStream  Fountain pens    UT
4   2019-01-01    InkStream  Fountain pens    RI
```

We'll learn more about pandas as we go along, so let's stop here for now and get back to building our dashboard.

6.2.2 Reading and displaying a dataframe

Our dashboard app will involve more code than some of the previous apps we've written, so it is a good idea to spread it across multiple modules or .py files.

LOADING DATA FROM THE RIGHT FILE PATH

We'll start with a dedicated Python script file to read in the data from our CSV. Copy sales_data.csv to the folder where you intend to keep your code files, and then create data_loader.py with the content shown in listing 6.1 (chapter_06/in_progress_01/data_loader.py in the GitHub repo).

> **Listing 6.1 Loading data using data_loader.py**

```python
import pandas as pd
from pathlib import Path

BASE_DIR = Path(__file__).resolve().parent
SALES_DATA_PATH = BASE_DIR / "sales_data.csv"

def load_data():
    return pd.read_csv(SALES_DATA_PATH)
```

The `load_data` function simply uses pandas to read in the CSV as we saw in the last section, but there seems to be more going on here. How are we populating the SALES_DATA_PATH variable? Why couldn't we just set it to `"sales_data.csv"` directly, given that data_loader.py is in the same directory as sales_data.csv?

The trouble here is that file paths in Python are considered to be relative to the *working directory you're executing a script from,* not the directory in which the file containing the line currently being executed is located.

For instance, if you're currently in /Users/alice/, your .py file and CSV are in the folder /Users/alice/streamlit_project/ and you write `pd.read_csv('sales_data .csv')`, Python will look for the path /Users/alice/sales_data.csv, which doesn't exist.

You could hardcode the absolute path to the CSV and pass /Users/alice/streamlit_ project/sales_data.csv, but that will obviously create problems when your app is deployed on a different computer where it won't be in that exact path.

What we need is a way to refer to the current .py file and construct a path relative to that file's path. This is what the two lines near the top do:

```
BASE_DIR = Path(__file__).resolve().parent
SALES_DATA_PATH = BASE_DIR / "sales_data.csv"
```

`__file__` is a special variable in Python that contains the path of the file currently being executed. Path is a class from the `pathlib` module (which comes built-in with Python) that lets you work with file paths in a user-friendly, object-oriented way. `Path(__file__)` creates a `Path` object corresponding to the current Python script, data_loader.py, and `.resolve()` dynamically generates the absolute path to data_loader.py (regardless of whether it's in your local machine or a production deployment). The `.parent` then refers to the directory data_loader.py is in.

Finally, we use the `'/'` operator, which works with `Path` objects (and is *not* the mathematical divided-by operator in this context) to generate the final path to our CSV, stored in `SALES_DATA_PATH`. If you're on Windows, don't worry—using `'/'` with `Path` objects joins paths correctly on any OS, even though it's not the usual backslash you might expect.

It's worth noting that `SALES_DATA_PATH` is not a string, it's still a `Path` object. Fortunately, pandas' `read_csv` knows how to handle those, so we can pass it directly to that function.

USING ST.WRITE TO DISPLAY THE DATAFRAME

Let's now use the `load_data` function we just created in our Streamlit app. Create an entry point (the file we'll use with `streamlit run`) to the app called dashboard .py, shown in listing 6.2 (chapter_06/in_progress_01/dashboard.py in the GitHub repo).

> **Listing 6.2   Using `st.write`**

```
import streamlit as st
from data_loader import load_data

data = load_data()
st.write(data.head(5))
```

This part is fairly straightforward. `data` is a pandas dataframe with data from our CSV (since that's what `load_data` returns).

The last line, `st.write(data.head(5))`, is interesting. We've briefly encountered `st.write` before, in chapter 2. Streamlit's docs describe `st.write` as "the Swiss Army knife of Streamlit commands," and that's fairly accurate.

You can pass almost any object to `st.write`, and it'll display the passed object in a graceful and sensible way. This means you can pass it a string and it'll write the string to the screen, but you can also pass it a dictionary and it'll print out the contents of the dictionary in a well-formatted way (try it out!). You can even pass it internal Python objects like classes or functions, and it'll display information about them.

`st.write` works well for our purposes because we can pass it a pandas dataframe, and it'll show the data on the screen. `data.head(5)` returns a dataframe with only the first five rows of the data, and using `st.write` on it helps us verify that the data was loaded correctly, as shown in figure 6.4, which is what you'll get if you execute `streamlit run dashboard.py`.

Deploy

	date	product_name	segment	category	gender	age_group	state	sales	gr
0	2019-01-01	InkStream	Fountain pens	Writing tools	M	18-25	CA	134.91	
1	2019-01-01	InkStream	Fountain pens	Writing tools	M	18-25	TX	149.9	
2	2019-01-01	InkStream	Fountain pens	Writing tools	M	18-25	FL	74.95	
3	2019-01-01	InkStream	Fountain pens	Writing tools	M	18-25	UT	29.98	
4	2019-01-01	InkStream	Fountain pens	Writing tools	M	18-25	RI	0	

Figure 6.4   Streamlit can display pandas dataframes natively.

You may notice that it takes a few seconds for the app to load. This is because our CSV file is quite large (over 90 megabytes) and reading it takes time. At first glance, this might not sound like a huge deal, but recall once again that Streamlit reruns your *entire* script whenever anything needs to change on the screen.

That means that each time the user changes a selection or clicks out of a text box, your app will re-read the CSV, slowing down the entire app. Besides being incredibly wasteful, that would degrade your dashboard's user experience, so let's address that next.

6.2.3   Caching data

One of the effects of Streamlit's execution model is that, without intervention, expensive operations such as reading a file or performing a complex computation are executed repeatedly to obtain the same results every time. This can be problematic for data apps like the one we're building now, since they frequently rely upon such operations.

In prior chapters, we've seen one way to deal with the problem: we could save the data into `st.session_state`. That way, the data would only have to be read once per user session, and the app wouldn't slow down during user interactions. This is an *okay* solution, but it doesn't solve a couple of problemss:

- The data would still need to be loaded whenever the web page is refreshed. If the user opens the dashboard in multiple tabs—and given the number of browser tabs the average person has open at any point, they probably will—it would take a while to load each time.

- The dashboard would have to read the data from scratch for *each* user, even though it's the same data.

Streamlit offers a better way to deal with this situation, in the form of `st.cache_data`.

ST.CACHE_DATA

`st.cache_data` is Streamlit's way of *caching* or storing the results of a slow function call so that the next time the function is called with the same parameters, it can simply look up the stored result of the *last* call rather than actually executing the function again.

For our use case, we can cache the result of the `load_data` function we wrote earlier. Streamlit would then store the pandas dataframe it returns, and subsequent app reruns or even page refreshes wouldn't cause the function to be executed again.

`st.cache_data` uses a different Python construct from the Streamlit elements we've seen so far: it's a *decorator*, which you can think of as something that takes a function or a class and adds some new feature to it without you having to rewrite the function or class.

To apply `st.cache_data` on the `load_data` function (in data_loader.py), simply write `@st.cache_data` above it, like this:

```
@st.cache_data
def load_data():
  return pd.read_csv(SALES_DATA_PATH)
```

Here, `st.cache_data` is *decorating* the `load_data` function, transforming it with the caching feature so that when it's called again, it'll return the previous cached result rather than executing its logic.

Since we're now referring to a Streamlit element within data_loader.py, we also need to include the Streamlit import at the top:

```
import streamlit as st
```

If you run the app now, you'll briefly see a spinning icon with the text "Running `load_data()`." (see figure 6.5) before your dataframe is displayed, but if you reload the page, your data should now load instantly.

Figure 6.5   By default, `st.cache_data` shows a spinner with a function name when running the function.

Looks like the caching is working! Here's a question, though: what happens when the data changes? The CEO wants a dashboard with *up-to-date* sales data, so we can assume the source data will change periodically, at least daily if not more frequently than that. For our example, let's assume that Engineering will overwrite the existing CSV with a version with newer data every day.

If the data is cached the way we've set it up, Streamlit won't pull in the updated CSV when it changes. Instead, it sees that the return value of `load_data` is cached from the first run (perhaps several days ago) and uses it.

We need a way to set an *expiry date* for the cache, essentially telling it that if the cached data is older than a certain threshold, the function needs to be executed and the results re-cached.

We achieve this using the `ttl` argument of `st.cache_data`. `ttl` stands for "time-to-live" and sets the amount of time that the cached data is valid for before Streamlit will re-execute the function during a rerun. If we assume that our CSV data will change every day, we could set a `ttl` of 1 day like so:

```
@st.cache_data(ttl="1d")
```

This way, the loaded data will be pulled once every day when a user runs the app. That run will take a while, but all subsequent runs in the following 24 hours will use the newly cached data and therefore be quick. Figure 6.6 illustrates how this works.

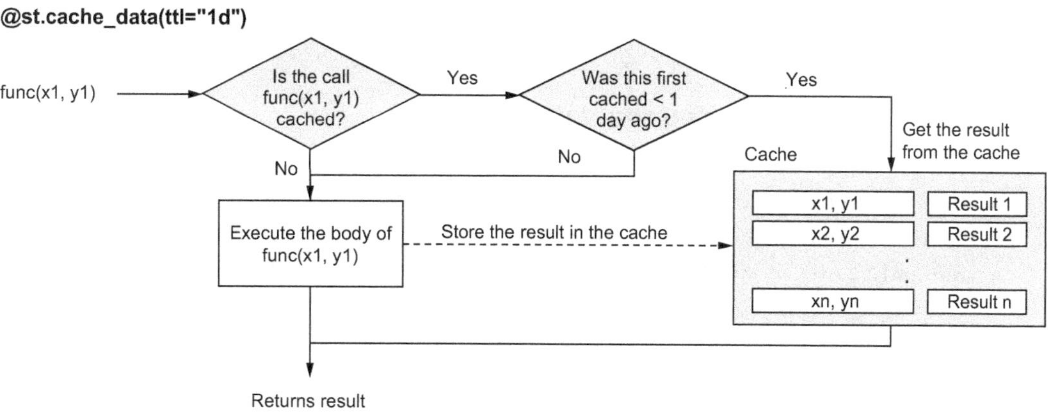

Figure 6.6 A diagram showing how `st.cache_data` works

Another thing we want to change is the message displayed with the spinning icon. The name `load_data` is internal to our code, and we don't want it exposed to users. We can change this message using the `show_spinner` argument of `st.cache_data`, so our code becomes (chapter_06/in_progress_02/data_loader.py in the GitHub repo):

```
@st.cache_data(show_spinner="Reading sales data...", ttl="1d")
def load_data():
    return pd.read_csv(SALES_DATA_PATH)
```

Run the app again, and you'll notice the loading indicator has changed (figure 6.7).

Figure 6.7   Setting the show_spinner parameter in st.cache_data displays a user-friendly message while the data is loading.

It's valuable to realize that when a user runs the app and the data is cached, the cached values are available to *all* users of the app, not just the current one. There are times when this can lead to unexpected results (we'll probably encounter some of these in later chapters), but in this case, since we want to show all users the same data, it's desirable behavior.

> **NOTE**   Due to the caching, whenever you make changes to load_data and want to see the results, you'll need to do a "hard reset" of the app by stopping the running Streamlit server and rerunning the streamlit run command, instead of merely refreshing the page. Otherwise, you'll simply see the cached results of when load_data was executed initially, unless you're past the TTL and the cache has expired.

With the data loaded and available within our app, let's move on to constructing the dashboard itself.

6.3   Prepping and filtering the data

A key requirement for our dashboard is the ability to inspect various *slices* of the data, as opposed to its entirety. This is quite logical; our source data spans over 5 years. Today, a user is probably more interested in the most recent year of data than in older years. Similarly, a user may only be interested in sales related to the "Paper products" category.

Filtering a table of data involves considering only the rows of data that are relevant and excluding all others. Our envisioned dashboard features two key components that enable this functionality: a *filter panel*, which allows users to select the values of each field they wish to consider, and a *date range selector*.

In this section, we'll build both of these components visually and perform the pandas data wrangling that enables their functionality.

6.3.1   Creating a filter panel

Let's revisit our UI mock, focusing on the filter panel at the top, reproduced in figure 6.8. The panel is a collection of dropdown menus, one for each field that we want to filter by.

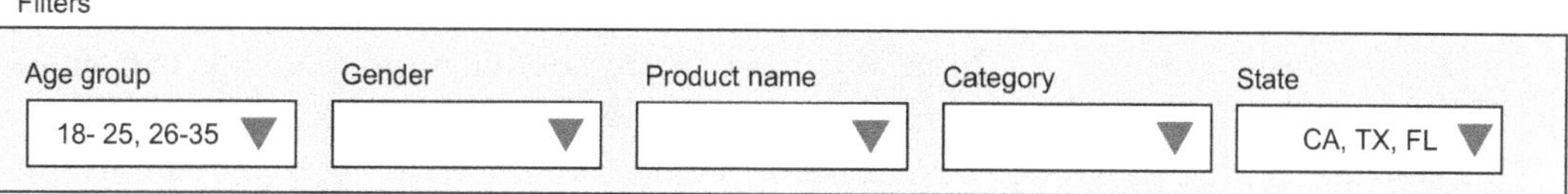

Figure 6.8 The filter panel from the UI mock

Each menu presumably contains the unique values corresponding to each field as options, and the user can choose multiple options (eg, in figure 6.8, the State filter has CA, TX, and FL all selected). Additionally, the user can choose not to select *any* option (e.g., Gender in figure 6.8), which we should probably treat as if there is no filter on that field.

The selections shown in figure 6.8 should cut the data down to rows corresponding to the 18-25 and 26-35 age groups for customers in CA, TX, or FL. Since there's no filter on, say, Product name, the data should include all products sold by Note n' Nib.

OBTAINING THE LIST OF UNIQUE VALUES FOR A FIELD

Clearly, we need a way to populate the options in the drop-downs when they are created. A plausible way to do this might be to hardcode the list of possible values for each field, but this presents some glaring issues: we would need to change our code every time there's a new product or category, or if the way we're grouping ages changes, or for plenty of other reasons.

A better approach is to get the list of options dynamically, from the data *itself*. Start a new Python file called data_wrangling.py and add a function to do this, as shown in listing 6.3 (chapter_06/in_progress_03/data_wrangling.py in the GitHub repo).

Listing 6.3 A simple function to get unique values in a column

```
def get_unique_values(df, column):
    return list(df[column].unique())
```

The `get_unique_values` function accepts a pandas dataframe `df` and a column name `column`. It returns a list of unique values for that column in the dataframe.

When you pass a column name to a pandas dataframe within square brackets (an operation named *column selection*), you get a pandas *series*, which is a one-dimensional array-like object (you could think of it as a single-column dataframe).

For instance, `df['age_group']` would return a series with the same number of elements as there are rows in `df`, with each element being the `age_group` corresponding to a row.

Calling `.unique()` on it dedupes the elements and gives you a new series with just the five or six distinct age groups in the data. We finally convert it into a regular Python list with the `list` function.

ADDING THE DROP-DOWN MENUS WITH ST.MULTISELECT

As we've seen, the user should be able to select any combination of options in each filter. Streamlit provides this functionality through `st.multiselect`, which is quite similar to `st.selectbox`, which we've come across before. As in the case of `st.selectbox`, the first two parameters (the only required ones) that you pass to `st.multiselect` are the label and the list of options.

For example, you could write `st.multiselect('Color', ['blue', 'green', 'red'])` to display a dropdown labeled "Color" from which you can select one or more colors. Keeping with our approach of spreading our code into several modules, we'll create a new one for the filter panel and call it filter_panel.py. Listing 6.4 shows a starting draft of filter_panel.py (chapter_06/in_progress_03/filter_panel.py in the GitHub repo).

Listing 6.4   A starting draft of filter_panel.py

```python
import streamlit as st
from data_wrangling import get_unique_values

filter_dims = ["age_group", "gender", "category", "segment",
               "product_name", "state"]

def filter_panel(df):
  with st.expander("Filters"):
    filter_cols = st.columns(len(filter_dims))
    for idx, dim in enumerate(filter_dims):
      with filter_cols[idx]:
        unique_vals = get_unique_values(df, dim)
        st.multiselect(dim, unique_vals)
```

`filter_dims` holds the list of fields from the dataframe that we want to filter on. The `filter_panel` function is what displays the dropdowns. It takes a dataframe as input and renders the dropdowns using the unique values for each field.

Some of this code should be familiar by now. We want to display the dropdowns side by side, so we use `st.columns(len(filter_dims))` to create as many display columns as there are fields we want to filter on. For each field, we obtain the unique values with the `get_unique_values` function from data_wrangling.py and use them to populate the dropdown:

```python
with filter_cols[idx]:
    unique_vals = get_unique_values(df, dim)
    st.multiselect(dim, unique_vals)
```

Listing 6.4 also shows a new Streamlit widget called `st.expander`, a collapsible box that users can expand or collapse as needed. This choice makes sense because most users probably don't want to see the filters all the time. The option to hide them helps users focus on the displayed data.

Include the `filter_panel` in the main dashboard by editing dashboard.py (chapter_06/in_progress_03/dashboard.py in the GitHub repo):

```
...
from filter_panel import filter_panel

data = load_data()
filter_panel(data)
st.write(data.head(5))
```

This yields the output shown in figure 6.9.

Figure 6.9 By default, the Streamlit app centers the layout, which can be problematic when the app needs to display a lot of content horizontally.

With six fields to filter on, the filters get squished against each other. Additionally, the filter field names are currently the raw column names from the CSV, including underscores. A more polished design would present these as user-friendly labels, such as Age group, instead of technical identifiers like `age_group`.

FIXING THE WIDTH ISSUE

Notice in figure 6.9 that there's a lot of unused whitespace to the sides of the filter panel. By default, Streamlit apps have a centered layout where the body of the app is rendered horizontally at the center of the window, and the sides are blank.

This is usually fine, but with a UI as dense as what we're building, screen real estate comes at a premium. Thankfully, Streamlit allows us to change this and use more of the screen. We can do this using the `st.set_page_config` method in dashboard.py.

```
st.set_page_config(layout='wide')
```

Importantly, this only works if it's the very first Streamlit command executed in an app, so make sure it's at the top of `dashboard.py`, right after the imports.

DISPLAYING USER-FRIENDLY LABELS FOR FIELDS

To swap out the raw field names for labels, we could retain a mapping between the raw names and their associated labels in a dictionary, and look up the label whenever we needed to display the name of a field. That sounds tedious though, so instead let's just rename the fields in the data frame to be user-friendly ones.

We'll probably need to make several similar cleaning-up modifications to the data. Bundle them into a `prep_data` function in data_wrangling.py (chapter_06/in_progress_04/data_wrangling.py in the GitHub repo):

```
...
from data_loader import load_data          ◄──   Don't forget to import the functions
                                                  we need from other modules.
...
def clean_column_names(df):
  df.columns = df.columns.str.replace('_', ' ').str.capitalize()
  return df

@st.cache_data(show_spinner="Reading sales data...", ttl="1d")   ◄──
def prep_data():
  return clean_column_names(load_data())
```

Move the st.cache_data decorator so it applies to prep_data instead of to load_data.

Here we define a function called `clean_column_names` that replaces the underscores in each column name of a dataframe with spaces and capitalizes it. `df.columns` returns the dataframe column names, and `.str.replace()` and `.str.capitalize()` are the respective string operations. We use `.str` to apply the replace and capitalize operations to each element in `df.columns` in one go, which is something which you'll see quite frequently in pandas. For now, the `prep_data` function calls `load_data` internally and returns the result of applying `clean_column_names` to the returned dataframe, but we'll add more logic later.

We've also moved `st.cache_data` decorator to the `prep_data` function (you should remove it from `load_data` in data_loader.py) because `prep_data` is supposed to contain basic operations we always want done on the data. After this, Streamlit will cache the result only after prepping the data, not immediately after loading it.

To close the loop, open dashboard.py and replace `data = load_data()` with `data = prep_data()`:

```
import streamlit as st
from data_wrangling import prep_data...

st.set_page_config(layout='wide')

data = prep_data()
filter_panel(data)
...
```

Finally, in `filter_panel.py`, update `filter_dims` to use the newly polished field names:

```
filter_dims = ["Age group", "Gender", "Category", "Segment",
               "Product name", "State"]
```

Save the file and rerun the app. The result appears as in figure 6.10.

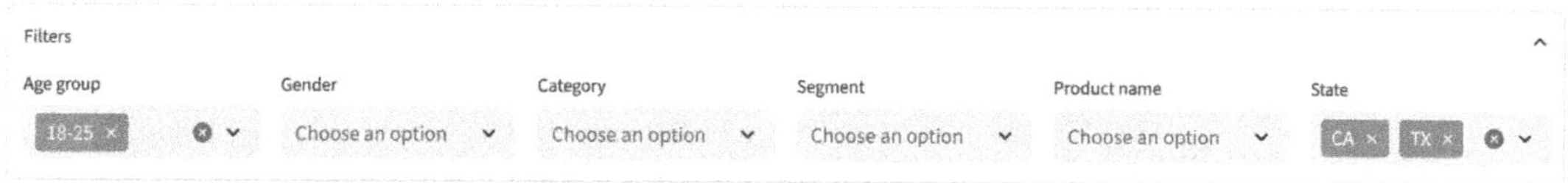

Figure 6.10   Filter panel with user-friendly field names and a wide layout

The dashboard now uses the full width of the screen and uses labels for the filters.

> **NOTE**   Due to the amount of code in this chapter and the limited space available on the printed page, while providing code snippets here, we'll focus primarily on how the code in a particular file has *changed* rather than reproducing the entire file as we did in previous chapters.

APPLYING THE FILTERS TO THE DATA

So far, we've created the UI elements corresponding to the filters, but we've not yet applied them to the data. To do this, let's first consider how we should represent the output from the filter panel.

To apply the filters, we need to look up the values the user has selected for each dimension. This is a good use case for a dictionary where each field name serves as a key and the list of selected options is the corresponding value for that key.

Our current `filter_panel` function (from filter_panel.py) simply displays the filter bar, but we want to modify it so that it returns such a dictionary that we can use for further processing.

```
def filter_panel(df):
    filters = {}
    with st.expander("Filters"):
        filter_cols = st.columns(len(filter_dims))
        for idx, dim in enumerate(filter_dims):
            with filter_cols[idx]:
                unique_vals = get_unique_values(df, dim)
                filters[dim] = st.multiselect(dim, unique_vals)
    return filters
```

Though we weren't making use of this earlier, `st.multiselect` returns the list of options a user has selected in the UI. As the highlighted lines show, we're now storing the returned value in the `filters` dictionary, using `dim` (the field name) as the key, and returning the filters at the end.

Next, we need to use the dictionary to produce the slice of the data the user wants. Since this involves data manipulation operations, let's put this functionality in `data_wrangling.py`, in a function called `apply_filters`.

```
def apply_filters(df, filters):
  for col, values in filters.items():
    if values:
      df = df[df[col].isin(values)]
  return df
```

`apply_filters` takes `df`—a pandas dataframe—and the filters dictionary that `filter_panel` returns. It goes through each key-value pair in filters and iteratively modifies the dataframe by filtering it using the statement:

```
df = df[df[col].isin(values)]
```

This is worth breaking down. The square brackets are quite versatile in pandas. When you pass a column name in the brackets following a dataframe variable (like `df['Age group']`), it returns that column as a pandas series, as shown earlier.

If you pass a pandas boolean series (a series where each item is a boolean) instead, pandas matches the numbered elements of the series against the ordered rows of the dataframe and returns only the rows where the corresponding boolean value is `True`. This approach is called *boolean indexing*. Both usages appear in the previous line—`df[col]` selects the `col` column (the column to filter) from `df`.

The `.isin(values)` applies an element-wise operation on the column, checking whether each value in it is present in values, the list of dropdown options selected by the user. This returns another series with a `True/False` value for every corresponding item in `df[col]`. This is an example of a *vectorized* calculation, which is responsible for much of pandas' performance.

Finally, we perform boolean indexing, using the boolean series obtained in the previous step to produce a new filtered dataframe and assign *that* to `df`. Effectively, whenever it executes, the line `df = df[df[col].isin(values)]` filters the dataframe to include only rows where the column we're currently looking at contains one of the values the user selected.

The `if values` part ensures that we don't filter if the user hasn't selected any values for a field, thus correctly implementing the requirement. To see this in action, make the required modifications to dashboard.py (chapter_06/in_progress_05/dashboard.py in the GitHub repo):

```
...
from data_wrangling import apply_filters, prep_data
...
```

```
data = prep_data()
filters = filter_panel(data)

main_df = apply_filters(data, filters)
st.write(main_df.head(5))
```

We now put the dictionary returned
by filter_panel(data) in a variable.

We're now capturing the dictionary of filters, using `apply_filters` to create a new dataframe called `main_df`, and displaying that instead of the data. This should give us the result in figure 6.11.

Filters

Age group		Gender		Category	Segment		Product name	State
18-25 ×	⊗ ⌄	M ×	⊗ ⌄	Choose an option ⌄	Staples ×	⊗ ⌄	Choose an option ⌄	CA ×

	Date	Product name	Segment	Category	Gender	Age group	State	Sales	Gross margin	Transactions
328,000	2019-01-01	SecureStitch	Staples	Office supplies	M	18-25	CA	12.4	10.04	2
328,050	2019-01-02	SecureStitch	Staples	Office supplies	M	18-25	CA	49.6	40.16	7
328,100	2019-01-03	SecureStitch	Staples	Office supplies	M	18-25	CA	37.2	30.12	5
328,150	2019-01-04	SecureStitch	Staples	Office supplies	M	18-25	CA	37.2	30.12	5
328,200	2019-01-05	SecureStitch	Staples	Office supplies	M	18-25	CA	43.4	35.14	6

Figure 6.11 Selections in the filter panel correctly filter the displayed rows (see chapter_06/in_progress_05 in the GitHub repo for the full code).

As you can see, the displayed dataframe only shows rows corresponding to the user's selections in the filter panel (18-25, M, Staples, CA). There's still one more kind of filter to apply: the date range! Let's deal with that next.

6.3.2 Creating a date range selector

As usual, Streamlit provides an easy way for users to select a date range. In its typical intuitive naming fashion, the widget we want is called `st.date_input`. It accepts a label, a default value, minimum and maximum values and more. You can have the user select a single date or a range of dates. For instance, to allow the user to select a single date with today's date as the default:

```
date = st.date_input("Select a date", value=datetime.date.today())
```

To enable a date range selection between a default start and end date, write:

```
range = st.date_input("Select a date range", value=(datetime.date(2023, 1, 1),
datetime.date(2023, 12, 31)))
```

Create the date range selector in a new file called date_range_panel.py, as shown in listing 6.5 (chapter_06/in_progress_06/date_range_panel.py in the GitHub repo).


```python
import streamlit as st
from datetime import date, timedelta

# Hardcode this to the last date in dataset to ensure reproducibility
LATEST_DATE = date.fromisoformat("2024-08-31")
THIRTY_DAYS_AGO = LATEST_DATE - timedelta(days=30)

def date_range_panel():
    start = st.date_input("Start date", value=THIRTY_DAYS_AGO)
    end = st.date_input("End date", value=LATEST_DATE)
    return start, end
```

The `date_range_panel` function displays two date selector widgets—one for the start and one for the end of the range—and returns the dates selected by the user.

For the default date range values, we show a start date of one month ago and an end date of today, using the variables `THIRTY_DAYS_AGO` and `LATEST_DATE`. Since we're dealing with a static dataset, we hardcode `LATEST_DATE` to a particular date that's available in the CSV. If we were working with real-time or regularly updated data, we would have replaced this with `LATEST_DATE = date.today()`. `THIRTY_DAYS_AGO` is obtained by subtracting 30 days from `LATEST_DATE` using the `timedelta` class from the `datetime` module.

The values `LATEST_DATE` and `THIRTY_DAYS_AGO` are of the type `date`, from the built-in `datetime` module. `st.date_input` understands this type and even returns it. The variables `start` and `end` returned by `date_range_panel` are thus both also of type `date`.

Now use these values by editing data_wrangling.py this way:

```python
import pandas as pd
import streamlit as st

...

@st.cache_data(show_spinner="Reading sales data...", ttl="1d")
def prep_data() -> pd.DataFrame:
    df = clean_column_names(load_data())
    df['Day'] = pd.to_datetime(df['Date'])
    return df

def get_data_within_date_range(df, start, end):
    if start is not None and end is not None:
        dt_start, dt_end = pd.to_datetime(start), pd.to_datetime(end)
        return df[(df['Day'] >= dt_start) & (df['Day'] <= dt_end)]
    return df

def get_filtered_data_within_date_range(df, start, end, filters):
    df_within_range = get_data_within_date_range(df.copy(), start, end)
    return apply_filters(df_within_range, filters)
```

This section includes a few changes. In addition to cleaning up the column names, `prep_data` adds a new column called Day, the result of applying `pd.to_datetime()` to the existing Date column. Recall that the Date column is currently an opaque object type. `pd.to_datetime()` converts it to `datetime[ns]` which can be optimized by pandas.

We've wrapped a call to `apply_filters` within the `get_filtered_data_within_date_range` function, which first accepts the start and end dates of the date range and uses them to call `get_data_within_date_range`.

`get_data_within_date_range` is the function that applies the date range filter on our dataframe. The first line in this function does a date format conversion:

```
dt_start, dt_end = pd.to_datetime(start), pd.to_datetime(end)
```

This happens because pandas uses a `datetime[ns]` type to represent dates. Unlike Python's `date` type, used for `start` and `end`, `datetime[ns]` works more efficiently in dataframe operations.

```
return df[(df['Day'] >= dt_start) & (df['Day'] <= dt_end)]
```

This is boolean indexing again, similar to what we encountered in the `apply_filters` function, but we're using a combination of two conditions (`df['Day'] >= dt_start` and `df['Day'] <= dt_end`) to filter the dataframe, joining them with `&`, which is pandas' element-wise logical AND operator.

We need to update dashboard.py again:

```
import streamlit as st
from data_wrangling import get_filtered_data_within_date_range, prep_data
from filter_panel import filter_panel
from date_range_panel import date_range_panel

st.set_page_config(layout='wide')

with st.sidebar:
  start, end = date_range_panel()

data = prep_data()
filters = filter_panel(data)

main_df = get_filtered_data_within_date_range(data, start, end, filters)
st.write(main_df.head(5))
```

We place the date range panel in a sidebar (which you should be quite comfortable with by now). And since `apply_data` is now contained within `get_filtered_data_within_date_range`, we assign the result of this wrapping function to `main_df`.

Figure 6.12 shows the new date range panel.

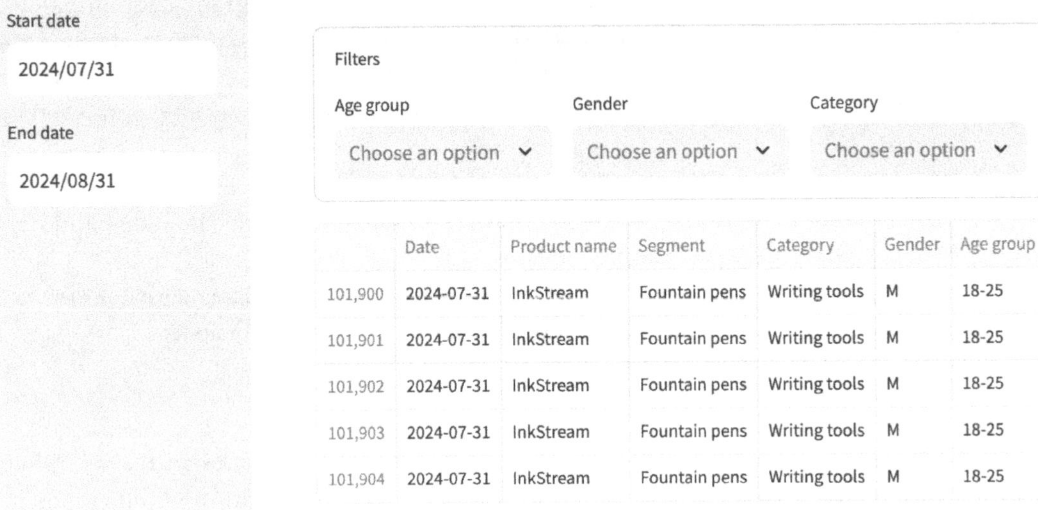

	Date	Product name	Segment	Category	Gender	Age group
101,900	2024-07-31	InkStream	Fountain pens	Writing tools	M	18-25
101,901	2024-07-31	InkStream	Fountain pens	Writing tools	M	18-25
101,902	2024-07-31	InkStream	Fountain pens	Writing tools	M	18-25
101,903	2024-07-31	InkStream	Fountain pens	Writing tools	M	18-25
101,904	2024-07-31	InkStream	Fountain pens	Writing tools	M	18-25

Figure 6.12   Date range inputs displayed in a sidebar (see chapter_06/in_progress_06 in the GitHub repo for the full code).

The dashboard is slowly taking shape. However, it isn't very useful to the CEO yet because it shows no summary information or metrics. That's up next!

6.4   Calculating and displaying metrics

Imagine you're running a business. How do you know if it's thriving or struggling, whether it's about to go through the roof or come crashing down? One obvious answer is to examine how much the company is earning and the amount of profit it's generating. You'll likely also want to know the rate at which your revenue is growing. If you're a fan of Shark Tank's Mr. Wonderful, you probably also keep track of more esoteric numbers, such as how much it costs you to acquire a customer.

All of these numbers are called *metrics*. Metrics are useful because they help you boil down all the complexity of a vast business (or any project, really) into a few figures. If a positive metric (such as profit) is increasing or a negative metric (like cost) is decreasing, that means things are going well. If the opposite is happening, something likely needs to change.

In this section, we'll calculate and display the metrics that Note n' Nib's CEO cares about. To do this, we'll first understand what the metrics mean and how to calculate them. We'll then set up a scalable way to define new metrics and display them prominently in the dashboard.

6.4.1   Calculating the metrics

Referring back to our requirements, there are four metrics we care about: total sales, gross margin, margin percentage, and average transaction value. Let's try and understand these in reference to our data. Recall that our source CSV has one row for every combination of date, product (and its associated segment and category), gender, age group, and state. For each row, it gives us three numeric fields: sales, gross margin, and transactions.

A transaction refers to a single purchase of some number of items, and the figure "transactions" refers to the number of them represented by a row. Sales are relatively easy to understand: it's the amount in dollars that Note' n' Nib collects from those transactions. Gross margin is the profit, or sales minus the cost that the company paid to acquire the items it sold.

Given this, let's calculate the metrics for any slice of the CSV:

- *Total sales*—Sum of the sales column
- *Gross margin*—Sum of the gross margin column
- *Margin percentage*—Gross margin expressed as a percentage of total sales, so it's calculated as total gross margin / total sales × 100
- *Average transaction value*—What Note n' Nib earned per transaction, so that we can calculate it as total sales/sum of the transactions column

Consider a quick example to crystallize these terms. Imagine the following rows:

Date	Product	State	Sales	Gross Margin	Transactions
2024-01-01	Fountain Pen	CA	500	200	10
2024-01-01	Notebook	TX	300	120	5
2024-01-01	Pencil	NY	200	80	8

- *Total sales* is $500 + $300 + $200 = $1000
- *Gross margin* is $200 + $120 + $80 = $400
- *Margin percentage* is $400 / $1000 = 0.4 = 40\%
- *Average transaction value* is $1000 / (10 + 5 + 8) = $1000 / 23 = $43.48

6.4.2 Setting up the metrics configuration

A recurring theme you'll come across in software development is that it's a good idea to keep your design reasonably *general*. By this, I mean that if you have a choice between coding something in a very specific way (hardcoding a list of values, for instance) and coding it in a flexible way (populating the list from a configuration file), it's often better practice to do the latter.

A more general design makes your code more adaptable to future changes and easier to maintain. We saw this when we developed a unit converter app in chapter 3, where rather than putting the conversion factors directly in our code, we opted to use a configuration file.

This is exactly what we'll do to set up the metrics in our dashboard—define a configuration file that defines how to calculate them.

As we did in chapter 3, we'll start by creating a dataclass—Metric—to hold the object we want to configure. Let's put this in a new file called metric.py, as in listing 6.6 (chapter_06/in_progress_07/metric.py in the GitHub repo).

Listing 6.6   A `Metric` dataclass

```python
from dataclasses import dataclass
@dataclass
class Metric:
  title: str
  func: callable
  type: str
```

The `Metric` class contains a title, which is the label displayed on the interface, and a type, which indicates how it should be formatted (eg, dollars as the type would instruct our app to prefix a $ sign before the number).

It also has a member called `func`, which is apparently a *callable*. Callables are essentially just functions, and `func` is meant to be a function that accepts a pandas dataframe object and calculates the value of the metric.

To truly understand this, let's see how objects of the `Metric` class are defined in our configuration file, metric_config.py, shown in listing 6.7 (chapter_06/in_progress_07/metric_config.py in the GitHub repo).

Listing 6.7   Configuring metrics

```python
from metric import Metric

def margin_percent(df):
  total_sales = df["Sales"].sum()
  return df["Gross margin"].sum() / total_sales if total_sales > 0 else 0

def average_transaction_value(df):
  total_sales = df["Sales"].sum()
  return total_sales / df["Transactions"].sum() if total_sales > 0 else 0

metrics = {
  "Total sales": Metric(
    title="Total sales",
    func=lambda df: df["Sales"].sum(),
    type="dollars"
  ),
  "Gross margin": Metric(
    title="Gross margin",
    func=lambda df: df["Gross margin"].sum(),
    type="dollars"
  ),
  "Margin %": Metric(
    title="Margin %",
    func=margin_percent,
    type="percent"
  ),
```

```
  "ATV": Metric(
    title="Average transaction value",
    func=average_transaction_value,
    type="dollars"
  )
}

display_metrics = ["Total sales", "Gross margin", "Margin %", "ATV"]
```

Turn your attention to the variable `metrics`, a dictionary with the names of each of our metrics as keys, and their corresponding `Metric` objects as values. Again, this is reminiscent of unit_config.py from chapter 3, where we did essentially the same thing.

Let's inspect the first item in the dictionary:

```
metrics = {
  "Total sales": Metric(
    title="Total sales",
    func=lambda df: df["Sales"].sum(),
    type="dollars"
  ),
  ...
```

This is the "total sales" metric, which has a sensible display label as its `title`, and "dollars" as its `type`. `func` here is a lambda (which, you might remember from chapter 2, is an anonymous one-line function). It accepts a single argument—df, a pandas dataframe—and calculates total sales using the expression:

```
df["Sales"].sum()
```

`df["Sales"]`, as we've discussed before, selects just the Sales column from `df`, and `.sum()` adds up all the values in it to obtain the final value of the metric. The other metrics defined in the dictionary are fairly similar, and their calculations should make sense after the discussion in the previous section. The Margin % and ATV metrics *don't* use a lambda for their funcs.

Rather, in each of these cases, `func` points to a regular function (`margin_percent` and `average_transaction_value`) defined above. Since these metrics are both ratios, we need to handle the possibility that the denominator is zero, preventing a division-by-zero error:

```
def margin_percent(df):
    total_sales = df["Sales"].sum()
    return df["Gross margin"].sum() / total_sales if total_sales > 0 else 0
```

At the bottom of the configuration file is the following line:

```
display_metrics = ["Total sales", "Gross margin", "Margin %", "ATV"]
```

The variable is meant to hold the metrics we'll display in our metric bar. This may seem somewhat pointless, as we're simply listing all the keys in the `metrics` dictionary.

However, this might come in handy if we ever decide to include more metrics and don't want to display all of them, or want to display them in a specific order. We'll see in a bit how `display_metrics` is used.

6.4.3   *Formatting the metrics*

One of the pieces of information we capture in the `Metric` class is the type of the metric, used primarily for formatting. In our configuration file, three of our metrics are of the dollars type, while Margin% is of the percent type.

Let's now define the formatting logic in its module, formatting.py (see listing 6.8). For this, we'll be using a third-party library called `humanize` (install it the usual way, i.e., by running `pip install humanize`), which provides some nice formatting features (chapter_06/in_progress_07/formatting.py in the GitHub repo).

Listing 6.8   Formatting metrics

```python
import humanize

def format_metric(value, metric_type):
  if metric_type == "dollars":
    return f'${humanize.metric(value)}'
  elif metric_type == "percent":
    return f'{round(value * 100, 1)}%'
  return f'{value}'
```

The `format_metric` function takes a numeric value and a metric type, and returns a formatted display string.

The `humanize` library we just installed comes into play while formatting a dollar-type metric. Since Note n' Nib is such a popular retailer, its sales figures are in the millions. If the raw revenue number we're tasked with displaying is $25,125,367, we'd rather not show the precise value to the CEO. An abbreviated version like $25.1m will do the trick while reducing cognitive load for the user.

This is exactly what the `humanize.metric` method does. Given a raw number, it returns a rounded number with a sensible lower precision and a suffix (k for thousands, m for millions, etc.). We add the $ sign manually to get the f-string `f'${humanize.metric(value)}'`.

For percent metrics, we multiply the actual value by 100 to convert it from a fraction to a percentage and then round it to a single decimal point before adding the % sign. For anything else, we don't perform any formatting and simply print the value as is.

6.4.4   *Displaying the metrics*

With all the building blocks in place, we can now create the metric bar in Streamlit. To do this, create yet another Python module, called metric_bar.py, with the code from listing 6.9 (chapter_06/in_progress_07/metric_bar.py in the GitHub repo).

Listing 6.9   A metric bar

```python
import streamlit as st
from metric_config import metrics, display_metrics
from formatting import format_metric

def get_metric(df, metric):
  return metric.func(df)

def metric_bar(main_df):
  with st.container(border=True):
    metric_cols = st.columns(len(display_metrics))
    for idx, metric_name in enumerate(display_metrics):
      metric = metrics[metric_name]
      with metric_cols[idx]:
        value = get_metric(main_df, metric)
        formatted_value = format_metric(value, metric.type)
        c1, c2, c3 = st.columns([1, 3, 1])
        with c2:
          st.metric(metric.title, formatted_value)
```

The `metric_bar` function iterates through the list of metrics we flagged for display (`display_metrics` from metric_config.py), adding an `st.metric` element within a display column for each of them.

That's the gist of it, but there are a few interesting bits here. The first is the use of `st.container`, a new Streamlit element. Here we're just using it to put the metric bar within a box with a border:

```python
with st.container(border=True):
```

There is more to `st.container`, however. One use case for it is when we want to display elements "out of order", or in a different order than they are written in the code. We'll come across this later in the book.

We use the `get_metric` function to extract the value of a metric, given a dataframe and a Metric object. Since each Metric object already has a `func` member that defines how to do this, the body of `get_metric` is as simple as calling it:

```python
def get_metric(df, metric):
  return metric.func(df)
```

The last interesting part is:

```python
c1, c2, c3 = st.columns([1, 3, 1])
    with c2:
        st.metric(metric.title, formatted_value)
```

You may find this rather strange. We've already defined a column for the metric (`metric_cols[idx]`), but it seems like we're splitting that column into three *sub*-columns, and then putting the `st.metric` widget in only the second one! What's the point of this?

Well, this is actually a layout hack. Unfortunately, as of the time of writing, Streamlit doesn't offer a great way of horizontally centering items within a column without HTML. So instead, here we're creating three columns within the main column, with the first and third being equal-width blank ones and the second holding the actual content. The overall effect is that the content of the second sub-column appears centered within the main column.

With that, all we need is a quick update to dashboard.py, and we should be good to move on:

```
...
from metric_bar import metric_bar

...
main_df = get_filtered_data_within_date_range(data, start, end, filters)
if main_df.empty:
  st.warning("No data to display")
else:
  metric_bar(main_df)
```

We've removed the sample dataframe rows from the display and replaced them with the metric bar. Rerun the dashboard to see the metric bar shown in figure 6.13.

Total sales	Gross margin	Margin %	Average transacti...
$3.77 M	$2.91 M	77.1%	$28.0

Figure 6.13   Metrics bar showing key metrics in aggregate for a selected date range (see chapter_06/in_progress_07 in the GitHub repo for the full code).

Let's tackle some of the visualization components of the dashboard next.

6.5   *Constructing visualizations*

Humans are intuitively visual beings. When you're trying to convey a message through data, it's usually more memorable and *clicks* much faster when you use a graph rather than a table of numbers. This is especially important for busy executives who may have to deal with a wide range of matters and need to develop a comprehensive understanding of the business so they can make informed decisions quickly.

In this section, we'll add visualizations to our dashboard in the form of a line chart to illustrate how the tracked metrics have changed over time, and a pie chart to display the breakdown of those metrics across a chosen dimension. In each case, we'll use pandas to wrangle the data into a form we can visualize easily, whip up the actual images using a library called Plotly, and display them using Streamlit.

6.5.1 *Creating a time series chart*

A time series is simply a sequence of data points recorded at regular time intervals, showing how a particular metric or variable changes over time. This is crucial for spotting trends, seasonality, and outliers, which can inform decision-making.

You can think of a simple time series as a series of data with two variables—one representing a date or time, and another representing the measure we're tracking. For instance, this is a time series:

```
+------------+-------+
|   Date     | Sales |
+------------+-------+
| 2024-01-01 |  120  |
| 2024-01-02 |  135  |
| 2024-01-03 |  142  |
| 2024-01-04 |  130  |
| 2024-01-05 |  155  |
+------------+-------+
```

OBTAINING A TIME SERIES FROM A DATAFRAME

Recall that the data we're dealing with has many different fields, including date, product name, gender, sales, and so on. We'll have to transform it into the specific shape of a time series before we can pass it to the visualization we'll build.

We have a Day field in our data, but one particular row in our dataframe represents the value for a particular combination of gender, age group, product name, etc. What we need is something that, given any particular slice of our full dataframe (which is what our filters give us), *aggregates* the data up to the Day level.

For example, a user may have applied the filters State = CA, giving us the following slice of data (simplified for clarity, excluding the other fields):

```
+------------+-------+--------+-----------+-----------+
|    Day     | State | Gender | Product   |   Sales   |
+------------+-------+--------+-----------+-----------+
| 2024-08-01 |  CA   |   M    | RoyalQuill|   1500    |
| 2024-08-01 |  CA   |   M    | GripLink  |   1300    |
| 2024-08-02 |  CA   |   M    | RoyalQuill|   1600    |
| 2024-08-02 |  CA   |   M    | GripLink  |   1200    |
+------------+-------+--------+-----------+-----------+
```

Our time series should contain only Day and Total sales, so we need to add up the sales for each date across state, gender, and product:

```
+------------+-------+
|    Day     | Sales |
+------------+-------+
| 2024-08-01 | 2800  |
| 2024-08-02 | 2800  |
+------------+-------+
```

To do this in pandas, assuming the dataframe is called `df`, write the following:

```
grouped = df.groupby('Day')
data = grouped.apply(lambda df: df['Sales'].sum(), include_groups=False).
reset_index()
```

Let's break this down. `df.groupby('Day')` gives a grouped dataframe, which you can think of as being represented internally like this:

```
+-------------+----------------------------------------------------------+
|    Day      |                     Grouped Rows                         |
+-------------+----------------------------------------------------------+
| 2024-08-01  | (2024-08-01, CA, M, RoyalQuill, 1500)                    |
|             | (2024-08-01, CA, M, GripLink, 1300)                      |
| 2024-08-02  | (2024-08-02, CA, M, RoyalQuill, 1600)                    |
|             | (2024-08-02, CA, M, GripLink, 1200)                      |
+-------------+----------------------------------------------------------+
```

Next, consider the line `grouped.apply(lambda df: df['Sales'].sum(), include_groups=False)`. The `apply` method is an extremely powerful pandas construct that lets you apply a function to each row or column of a dataframe or to the values of a series. When you use it on a grouped dataframe like the one above, you can perform operations on each group separately.

In this case, the lambda function `lambda df: df['Sales'].sum()` takes each group (which corresponds to a specific day) and calculates the total sales for that day by summing the `Sales` values. In the example above, the day 2024-08-01 would have a total `Sales` value of 2800, adding up the sales for the RoyalQuill and GripLink rows.

The `include_groups = False` bit indicates that we don't want the function to also operate on group labels (the `Day` values). It's kind of redundant here as our lambda function specifically refers to the `Sales` column, but if you don't include this, pandas will whine about it.

Finally, the `reset_index()` method converts the results back to a standard dataframe format. An *index* is a pandas concept referring to a unique identifier column for each row, enabling efficient data retrieval and alignment; after summing, the `Day` column becomes the index. By calling reset_index(), we restore `Day` as a regular column and create a new index that ranges from 0 to n-1, where n is the number of unique days.

We need a slightly more generalized version of the above code for our dashboard, as our line chart may need to show any of our four key metrics, not just sales (see figure 6.14 from our UI mock).

So, rather than passing in `df["Sales"].sum()` as the function to apply, we'll obtain this function from the `func` attribute of the `Metric` class we defined in metric.py and instantiated in metric_config.py.

Let's add such a function to the bottom of data_wrangling.py:

```
def get_metric_time_series(df, metric):
  grouped = df.groupby('Day')
  data = grouped.apply(metric.func, include_groups=False).reset_index()
  data.columns = ['Day', 'Value']
  return data
```

Our function accepts a dataframe `df` and `metric`, one of the `Metric` objects from metric_config.py. As you can see, we pass `metric.func` to `grouped` `.apply` to make it general. The line `data` `.columns = ['Day', 'Value']` resets the column names of the resultant dataframe to new ones. Now that we have our time series, let's build our line chart.

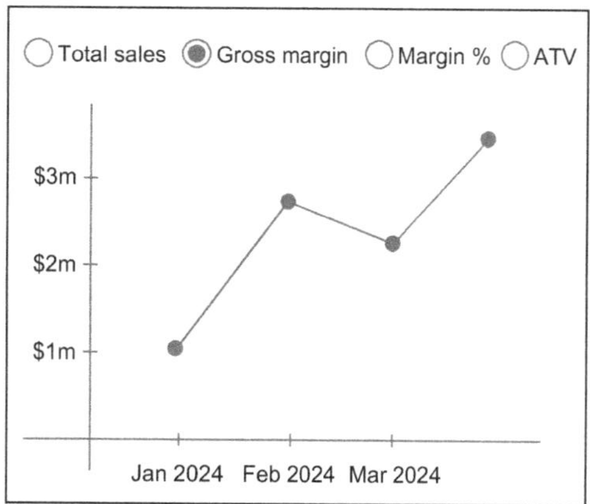

Figure 6.14   The time series chart from our UI mock

USING PLOTLY TO BUILD A LINE CHART WITH A TIME SERIES

As we briefly touched upon in chapter 1, Streamlit supports various data visualization libraries. Plotly is one such library that is fairly easy to use and offers a range of engaging interactive visualizations. To use it, install it with `pip install plotly`.

The flavor of Plotly we'll use is called Plotly Graph Objects (GO for short). GO allows you to construct plots with a high degree of control and customization, making it ideal for interactive charts where you can define every detail.

Create a new Python module named time_series_chart.py containing the code in listing 6.10 (chapter_06/in_progress_08/time_series_chart.py in the GitHub repo).

Listing 6.10   A time series chart

```
import plotly.graph_objs as go
from data_wrangling import import get_metric_time_series

def get_time_series_chart(df, metric):
  data = get_metric_time_series(df, metric)
  fig = go.Figure()
  fig.add_trace(
    go.Scatter(x=data['Day'], y=data['Value'], mode='lines+markers')
  )

  fig.update_layout(
    title=f"{metric.title}",
    xaxis_title='Day',
    yaxis_title=metric.title
  )
  return fig
```

The import statement at the top makes Plotly Graph Objects available; the abbreviation `go` is conventionally used to refer to it.

The `get_time_series_chart` metric takes our dataframe as well as an object of type `Metric` and returns the line chart (a Plotly `Figure` object) that we can pass later to a Streamlit widget for display.

We first obtain our time series data by calling the `get_metric_time_series` function we defined earlier.

Plotly charts are constructed incrementally. We start with an empty chart and add the components we need bit by bit. Here, the line `fig = go.Figure()` initializes the chart and assigns it to `fig`.

The next part adds the line to the chart:

```python
fig.add_trace(
    go.Scatter(x=data['Day'], y=data['Value'], mode='lines+markers')
)
```

We're creating a `go.Scatter` object here, which represents a scatterplot. A scatterplot simply plots points on a graph with two axes (the x-axis and the y-axis). Each point has a pair of coordinates. In this case, the x-coordinates are supplied by `data['Day']`, or the dates we want to show in the chart, and the y-coordinates are in `data['Value']`, which will be the values of one of our key metrics (depending on which one the variable `metric` contains).

We also pass `mode='lines+markers'`, which makes it so that in addition to plotting the points (using "markers"), Plotly also puts lines between them. The effect is that every (`Day`, `Value`) pair in our dataframe has a marker, and all the markers are connected by lines, forming the line chart we need. We then add the plot we just created to our `Figure` object by passing it to `fig.add_trace()`.

```python
fig.update_layout(
    title=f"{metric.title}",
    xaxis_title='Day',
    yaxis_title=metric.title
)
```

The last part, shown above, simply adds some text to our graph, such as a title (which we get from our `Metric` object's `title` attribute, defined in metric_config.py), and the titles of the x- and y-axes.

We now know how to create the chart we require. We still need to actually display it, though, so go ahead and update time_series_chart.py, adding a `time_series_chart` function at the bottom and the corresponding imports at the top:

```python
import plotly.graph_objs as go
import streamlit as st
from data_wrangling import get_metric_time_series
from metric_config import metrics, display_metrics
```

```
...
def time_series_chart(df):
  with st.container(border=True):
    chart_tabs = st.tabs(display_metrics)
    for idx, met in enumerate(display_metrics):
      with chart_tabs[idx]:
        chart = get_time_series_chart(df, metrics[met])
        st.plotly_chart(chart, use_container_width=True)
```

Once again, we use `st.container(border=True)` to make a box to put our line chart in.

The next bit, `chart_tabs = st.tabs(display_metrics)`, introduces a new Streamlit UI widget: `st.tabs`. As the name suggests, `st.tabs` creates a tabbed area in your app that lets users switch between pieces of content by clicking tabs at the top. The argument to `st.tabs` is the list of tab titles to use. For instance, `st.tabs(["Home", "About us", "Careers"])` would create three tabs with the titles Home, About us, and Careers.

We're trying to create one tab for each metric with its respective line chart, so we can pass the variable `display_metrics` from metric_config.py—which, you may recall, is a list of the metrics we care about that we can use as tab titles.

We define the content within a tab in the same way that we would do it for `st.column`: using the with context manager. Since `chart_tabs` now contains the list of tabs (returned by `st.tabs`), we can iterate through each list index/metric name pair (`idx`, `met`) in `display_metrics` and use `chart_tabs[idx]` to refer to the corresponding tab, calling `get_time_series_chart` to create the Plotly line chart for that metric. Finally, we pass the created chart to the `st.plotly_chart` element to render it on the screen:

```
st.plotly_chart(chart, use_container_width=True)
```

The `use_container_width=True` ensures that the line chart expands to fill the width of the box that contains it. This prevents weird layout problems where the chart ends up being larger than the container or leaves a lot of whitespace around it.

Let's now include the line chart in our main app by updating dashboard.py:

```
...
from time_series_chart import time_series_chart


...
if main_df.empty:
  st.warning("No data to display")
else:
  metric_bar(main_df)
  time_series_chart(main_df)
```

If you save and rerun the app now, you'll see your first Streamlit visualization (figure 6.15).

Figure 6.15   Time series chart created using Plotly (chapter_06/in_progress_08 in the GitHub repo has the full code).

Pretty, n'est-ce pas? You can see the tabs and switch between them to see how each metric has changed over the given data range. Visualizations created using `st.plotly_chart` throw in a lot of useful functionality for free, such as the ability to zoom in to specific points in the chart, tooltips when you hover over specific data points, a full-screen mode, and a download button to save the image.

> **NOTE** We could have used radio buttons as our metric selection widget, as our UI mock indicates, but I didn't want to pass up the chance to introduce `st.tabs`. Also, there is one important difference in how selection via `st.radio` and that via `st.tabs` works: switching between tabs does not trigger an app rerun, while changing between radio button options does. This makes using tabs faster and more efficient, with the trade-off that charts for all the metrics need to be created at once, during the initial load.

6.5.2   Creating a pie chart

The time series chart we just created allows us to identify trends over time, but we also need to be able to break down a particular data point and see what contributes to it.

For instance, if we know that the total sales for the Fountain pens segment are $500k, it would be helpful to know that 70% of that was driven by the RoyalQuill brand, while Inkstream only accounted for 30%, or that 45% of stapler sales are from the 56+ age group. Pie charts, which illustrate the percentage breakdown of a whole into its component parts, are a good way to instantly form a picture of the data.

> **NOTE** Pie charts are a controversial choice in the data analysis world, mostly because they make it hard to compare slice sizes accurately—bar charts are better at that. Still, for all their sins, pie charts *do* make it visually obvious that we're looking at parts of a whole, and I don't have the heart to condemn them entirely. So we're going with a pie chart. You can always replace it with a bar chart if it keeps you up at night.

Figure 6.16 shows the pie chart from our UI mock again. There are two selections you can make here: a metric for the pie chart to display, and a breakdown dimension. The metric can only be Total sales or Gross margin, not Margin % or ATV. This is because the latter two metrics are ratios, and the corresponding dimension-wise ratios won't add up to 100%, so a pie chart does not apply.

For instance, let's say the average transaction value (sales divided by the number of transactions) for fountain pens is $50. We can't break this down by gender and say that 60% ($30) of that comes from males and 40% ($20) comes from females. To get the ATV for males, we have to calculate the ratio by dividing the total sales for males by the corresponding transaction count.

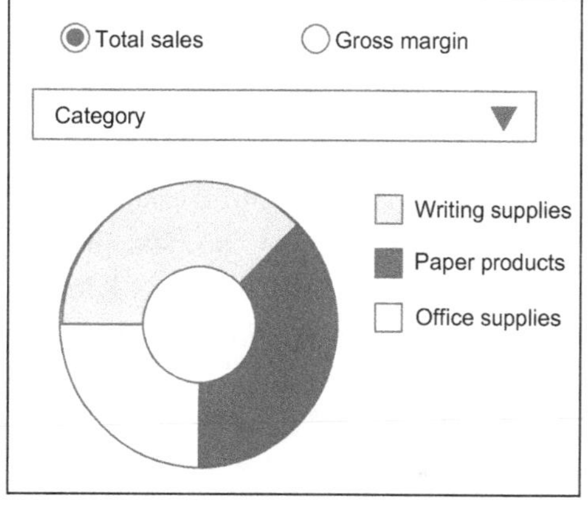

Figure 6.16   The pie chart from our UI mock

Record this smaller list of pie-chart-applicable metrics in a new variable at the bottom of metric_config.py:

```
pie_chart_display_metrics = ["Total sales", "Gross margin"]
```

GETTING DATA INTO THE RIGHT SHAPE

Just as we wrangled our data into a date/value time series to feed it to the time series chart, we also need to prepare our data for the pie chart. The pie chart requires the value of our metric corresponding to each dimension value; it will perform the conversion to percentages on its own.

For example, consider the sample data we processed into a time series earlier:

```
+-------------+-------+--------+-----------+-----------+
|    Day      | State | Gender | Product   |   Sales   |
+-------------+-------+--------+-----------+-----------+
| 2024-08-01  |  CA   |   M    | RoyalQuill|   1500    |
| 2024-08-01  |  CA   |   M    | GripLink  |   1300    |
| 2024-08-02  |  CA   |   M    | RoyalQuill|   1600    |
| 2024-08-02  |  CA   |   M    | GripLink  |   1200    |
+-------------+-------+--------+-----------+-----------+
```

If we want to show a breakdown of the total sales by product, we would group by product and add up the sales:

```
+-----------+------------+
|  Product  |   Sales    |
+-----------+------------+
| RoyalQuill|    3100    |
| GripLink  |    2500    |
+-----------+------------+
```

This is remarkably similar to what we did earlier; the only difference is that instead of grouping by the date field, we're grouping by a particular dimension (Product) instead. The function we'll include at the bottom of data_wrangling.py is thus also very similar to `get_metric_time_series`:

```python
...

def get_metric_time_series(df, metric):
  grouped = df.groupby('Day')
  data = grouped.apply(metric.func, include_groups=False).reset_index()
  data.columns = ['Day', 'Value']
  return data

def get_metric_grouped_by_dimension(df, metric, dimension):
  grouped = df.groupby(dimension)
  data = grouped.apply(metric.func, include_groups=False).reset_index()
  data.columns = [dimension, 'Value']
  return data
```

The sole distinction between the newly added `get_metric_grouped_by_dimension` and `get_metric_time_series` is that in the former, we're accepting the dimension as an input and grouping by that instead of by Day.

A PLOTLY PIE CHART

The ever-versatile Plotly Graph Objects can also be used to create the pie chart we want. In fact, the code you'll put in a new file pie_chart.py—shown in listing 6.11 (chapter_06/in_progress_09/pie_chart.py in the GitHub repo)—is closely related to that in time_series_chart.py.

Listing 6.11　Displaying a pie chart

```python
import plotly.graph_objects as go
from data_wrangling import get_metric_grouped_by_dimension

def get_pie_chart(df, metric, dimension):
  data = get_metric_grouped_by_dimension(df, metric, dimension)
  fig = go.Figure()
  fig.add_trace(
    go.Pie(labels=data[dimension], values=data['Value'], hole=0.4)
  )
  return fig
```

The differences should be fairly obvious: we use `get_metric_grouped_by_dimension` in place of `get_metric_time_series`, and `go.Pie` instead of `go.Scatter`.

`go.Pie` accepts `labels`, that will be displayed in a color legend, `values`, and `hole`, which indicates how large the "donut hole" in the pie chart should be.

We're not using `fig.update_layout()` here to set any text in the chart, since the title will simply be the tab header (which we'll get to in a second), and there are no x- or y-axes.

As we did previously, we also need to write another function in pie_chart.py to render the image:

```python
import plotly.graph_objects as go
import streamlit as st
from data_wrangling import get_metric_grouped_by_dimension
from metric_config import metrics, pie_chart_display_metrics


...
def pie_chart(df):
  with st.container(border=True):
    split_dimension = st.selectbox(
      "Group by",
      ["Age group", "Gender", "State", "Category",
        "Segment", "Product name"]
    )
    metric_tabs = st.tabs(pie_chart_display_metrics)
    for idx, met in enumerate(pie_chart_display_metrics):
      with metric_tabs[idx]:
        chart = get_pie_chart(df, metrics[met], split_dimension)
        st.plotly_chart(chart, use_container_width=True)
```

The `pie_chart` function, too, is similar to its counterpart—`time_series_chart`—from time_series_chart.py. The key difference is the added `split_dimension` variable (the dimension to break down the metric for) that we need to collect from users using `st.selectbox`. Everything else stays more or less analogous; we create a tab for each metric in `pie_chart_display_metrics` (which we defined in metric_config.py), iterate through those metrics, create the Plotly object with `get_pie_chart`, and display it using `st.plotly_chart`.

In dashboard.py, we want to display the line and pie charts side-by-side, so we use `st.columns`:

```
...
from pie_chart import pie_chart

...
if main_df.empty:
  st.warning("No data to display")
else:
  metric_bar(main_df)
  time_series_col, pie_chart_col = st.columns(2)
  with time_series_col:
    time_series_chart(main_df)
  with pie_chart_col:
    pie_chart(main_df)
```

With this, our dashboard's UI is complete! Rerun to see figure 6.17.

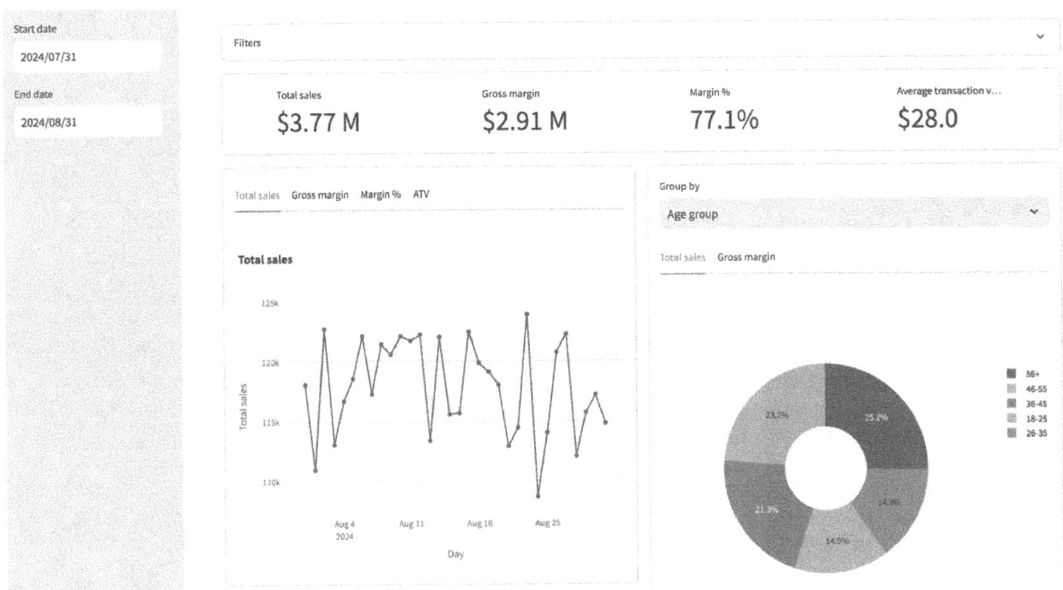

Figure 6.17   **Completed app, with the newly added pie chart at the bottom right**

We've covered a lot of ground in this chapter, and we're ready to launch our dashboard. We're not quite done with Note n' Nib, though. In the next chapter, we'll explore several ways to improve our app, including usability enhancements and transitioning from a static CSV file to a data warehouse.

Summary

- A metrics dashboard is an essential decision-making tool for executives.
- Pandas is a popular Python library for manipulating tabular data in dataframes. Streamlit can display pandas dataframes natively.
- Use pandas `read_csv` function to load data from a comma-separated values (CSV) file.
- The `st.cache_data` decorator can be used to cache the results of functions, improving performance. Its `ttl` parameter sets the time period for which a cached result is valid.
- The dataframe's square-bracket notation is quite versatile in pandas. It lets you select columns, filter rows, and more.
- `st.container` holds other Streamlit widgets, letting you display them out of order or add a border around them.
- `st.multiselect` creates a drop-down menu that lets you select multiple options.
- `st.set_page_config` sets Streamlit app configuration options, including switching from a centered layout to a maximized one.
- `st.date_input` displays date selectors in an app.
- The `humanize` library is useful for formatting numbers in a user-friendly way.
- A time series is a sequence of data points, each with a date and a corresponding value.
- The `groupby` method on pandas dataframes can aggregate data across dimensions.
- Plotly Graph Objects (abbreviated to `go`) is a Python library for creating visualizations that Streamlit can display directly.
- Use `go.Scatter` to create scatterplots and line charts, and `go.Pie` to create pie charts.

The CEO strikes back: Supercharging the dashboard

7

This chapter covers

- Critically evaluating an app and addressing user feedback
- Adding flexibility to Streamlit visualizations
- Improving usability by making frequently used features easy to access
- Creating modal dialogs in Streamlit
- Using query parameters to enable deeplinks in a Streamlit app

No software is perfect at launch. Instead, developers refine it over time, fixing bugs and adding new features incrementally. The projects in this book are no exception.

In the previous chapter, we created a metrics dashboard for a company called Note n' Nib. Now, we'll review user feedback, critically assess the app, and make targeted improvements. Along the way, we'll explore advanced Streamlit visualizations, introduce modal dialogs and query parameters, and learn how to build an advanced, flexible dashboard.

If chapter 6 was about *launching* a dashboard based on user requirements, chapter 7 is about *landing* it, addressing users' concerns, and iterating on the app to ensure quality and satisfaction.

NOTE The GitHub repository for this book is at https://github.com/aneevdavis/streamlit-in-action. In the chapter_07 folder, you'll find the code for this chapter and a requirements.txt file listing the exact versions of the required Python libraries.

7.1 Feedback on the dashboard

The dashboard you built in the last chapter has made waves at Note n' Nib. For the first time, the company's executives can access up-to-date sales numbers, compare product performance, and analyze trends independently, without relying on engineering assistance. The CEO has requested that all staff meetings begin with a review of key sales metrics, which means the top brass is now intimately familiar with the dashboard. With this attention comes increased scrutiny, so it's no surprise when, a few weeks after launch, you found an email from the CEO in your inbox.

The email contains consolidated feedback from the higher-ups—essentially a wishlist of additional features to implement. There goes the rest of the week. Still, you're excited about the opportunity to work with Streamlit again! In this chapter, we'll review and address each item of feedback.

NOTE This chapter has a substantial amount of code, as it builds on the final state from the previous chapter. To make things easier, I recommend opening the GitHub repo in a browser tab as you follow along, so you can reference the complete code.

7.2 Granularity in the time series chart

The first bullet point in the email says, "The time chart is useful for reviewing a few days of data, but it's hard to make sense of for longer periods."

Recall that the dashboard features a line chart showing the evolution of a selected metric over time. For smaller date ranges (about a month), it works reasonably well (see the left side of figure 7.1), but for longer ones (such as a year or more), it resembles the right side.

All the data is present, but there's so much of it that it's overwhelming. When considering *years* of data, we don't need to plot a single point for every date in the range. Plotting every date increases the number of individual markers in the chart; for a two-year range, that's $365 \times 2 = 730$ points—far too many to interpret.

How do we address this? A daily granularity is too fine for longer time horizons, but for shorter ranges, like a week or a month, it's reasonable. For longer ranges, we likely want one marker per week, a month, or even year. The simplest solution is to let the user pick the granularity they want. Let's tackle this now.

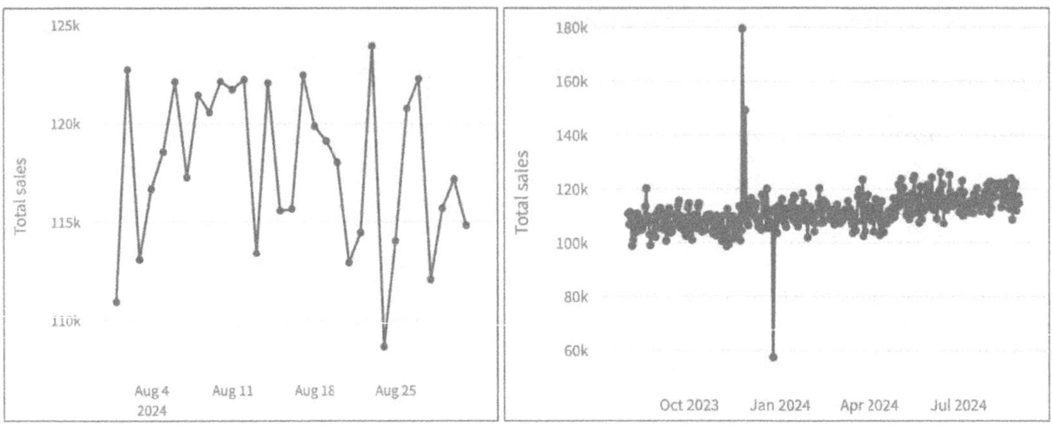

Figure 7.1   The day-level granularity in the existing time chart works for short time frames like a month (left), but not for longer time frames (right).

7.2.1   *Enabling different time granularities*

To enable weekly, monthly, and yearly granularities, we first need to ensure our data includes those fields, which it currently doesn't. Once added, we can aggregate each metric to the appropriate grain.

Recall that the flow of data in our app starts with the `load_data` function in data_loader.py, which obtains the data from an external source, currently a CSV file. This is followed by `prep_data` in data_wrangling.py where we rename the columns and add the Day field. This is also where we need to make changes to incorporate the other grains. Edit `prep_data` so it now looks like this:

```python
@st.cache_data(show_spinner="Reading sales data...", ttl="1d")
def prep_data() -> pd.DataFrame:
    df = clean_column_names(load_data())
    df['Day'] = pd.to_datetime(df['Date'])
    df['Week'] = df['Day'].dt.to_period('W').dt.to_timestamp()
    df['Month'] = df['Day'].dt.to_period('M').dt.to_timestamp()
    df['Year'] = df['Day'].dt.to_period('Y').dt.to_timestamp()
    return df
```

We're adding three new columns to the pandas dataframe: `Week`, `Month`, and `Year`. To populate each field, we start with the `Day` column (`df['Day']`), convert it to a period, and then convert the result to a timestamp. Consider one such statement:

```python
df['Month'] = df['Day'].dt.to_period('M').dt.to_timestamp()
```

`.dt` here is used to access the date/time-related properties of the column in an element-wise manner. `to_period('M')` converts the Day column into a monthly "period" type internal to pandas, representing a whole month rather than a specific point in time. We then use a second `.dt` accessor to get the date/time properties of the transformed column, and finally `.to_timestamp()` to convert each monthly period into a date representing the start of the month. For instance, if an element in `df['Day']` is the date 2024-07-12, we get the date 2024-07-01, the start of the corresponding month. The statements creating the `Week` and `Year` columns are analogous, adding dates representing the start of the week and the year, respectively.

Elsewhere in the code—specifically within (other) functions in data_wrangling .py and time_series_chart.py—we've been treating `Day` as a hardcoded column name. Once we have these other columns, all we need to do in the backend is introduce a variable to represent the grain.

The `get_metric_time_series` function in data_wrangling.py now looks like this:

```python
def get_metric_time_series(df, metric, grain):
  grouped = df.groupby(grain)
  data = grouped.apply(metric.func, include_groups=False).reset_index()
  data.columns = [grain, 'Value']
  return data
def get_time_series_chart(df, metric, grain):
  data = get_metric_time_series(df, metric, grain)
  fig = go.Figure()
  fig.add_trace(
    go.Scatter(x=data[grain], y=data['Value'], mode='lines+markers')
  )

  fig.update_layout(
    title=f"{metric.title}",
    xaxis_title=grain,
    yaxis_title=metric.title
  )
  return fig
```

In both cases, we're making the same change: adding `grain` as a new parameter to the function, and replacing `'Day'` wherever it occurs with `grain`.

7.2.2 *Creating a time grain selector*

Now that we've updated the functions that ultimately generate the time series chart to handle `grain` as a variable, we need to provide the user with a way to select what grain they want.

ST.SELECT_SLIDER

Let's use a new Streamlit widget for this: `st.select_slider`, another selection element. `st.select_slider` is a cross between `st.selectbox`, which lets you pick a single value from a dropdown, and `st.slider`, which lets you choose a numeric value.

Use it when you have a list of text options for users to pick from, but also want to impose an order. For instance, in a survey, options like Strongly Agree, Agree, Neutral,

Disagree, and Strongly Disagree are strings, but have a specific order—from most to least agreement.

In our case, the time grain options we want the user to see—Day, Week, Month, and Year—also have an order, from smallest to largest unit of time. We can use `st.select_slider` like this within the `time_series_chart` function in time_series_chart.py:

```python
def time_series_chart(df):
  with st.container(border=True):
    grain_options = ["Day", "Week", "Month", "Year"]
    grain = st.select_slider("Time grain", grain_options)
    chart_tabs = st.tabs(display_metrics)
    for idx, met in enumerate(display_metrics):
      with chart_tabs[idx]:
        chart = get_time_series_chart(df, metrics[met], grain)
        st.plotly_chart(chart, use_container_width=True)
```

`grain_options` holds the ordered list of options, which is passed as the second parameter to `st.select_slider`, the first being the label to display. These parameters are similar to those of `st.selectbox` and `st.radio`. `st.select_slider` returns the user's selection, which we store in `grain`, and pass as the new parameter we recently added to `get_time_series_chart`. Save and run your app with `streamlit run <path to dashboard .py>` to see figure 7.2.

Play around with the grain selector. Using the month grain makes the chart much more readable when viewing a long date range spanning multiple years.

7.3 *Interdependent filters*

"If I've already selected the 'Writing tools' category, why does it still ask me if I want to see staples and calendars?" reads a comment in the email, reportedly from the CFO, one of the dashboard's most engaged users.

It's a valid question. She's referring to the filter bar in figure 7.3, which doesn't consider existing selections when displaying options in the filter dropdowns. This leads to nonsensical combinations, such as "Writing tools" paired with "Paper clips."

The filter bar isn't "intelligent." Filtering by product category doesn't update the options available to the user in the segment and product name filters, even if those segments and products don't belong to the selected category.

If a user filters the data for "Writing tools," it's frustrating to still see all the other product lines (like "Paper clips") in the segment dropdown. The example data we've used only has ten products, so it isn't a dealbreaker per se, but imagine a scenario with hundreds. At that scale, using the higher levels in the product hierarchy (like "Category") to filter out irrelevant products from the other dropdowns becomes essential. Let's consider how to fix this.

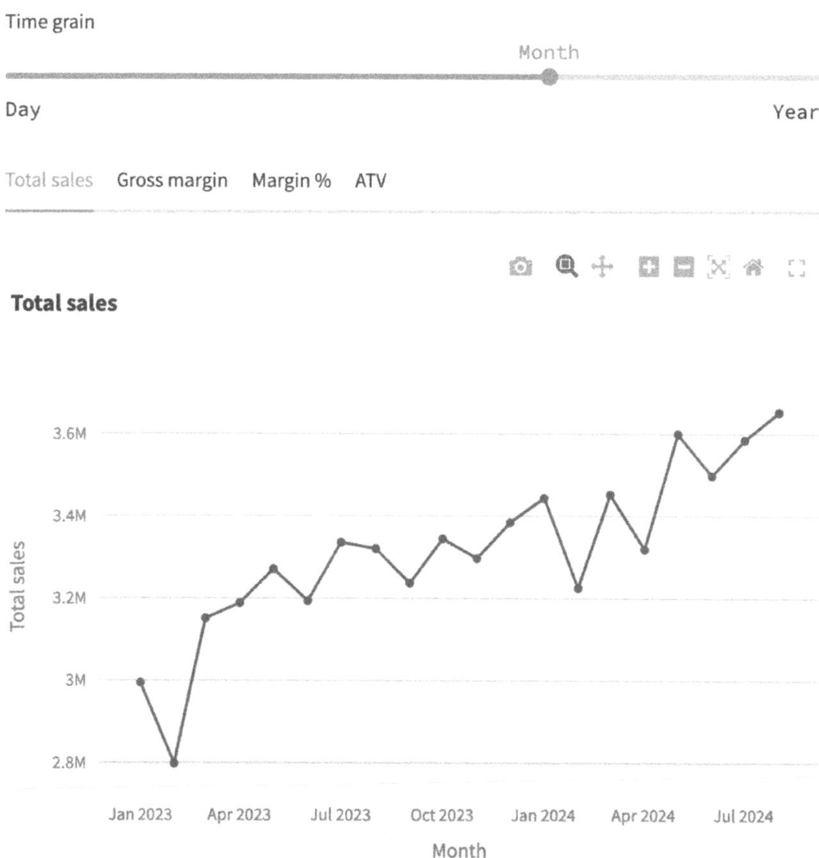

Figure 7.2 The line chart now has a time grain selector (see chapter_07/in_progress_01 in the GitHub repo for the full code at this point).

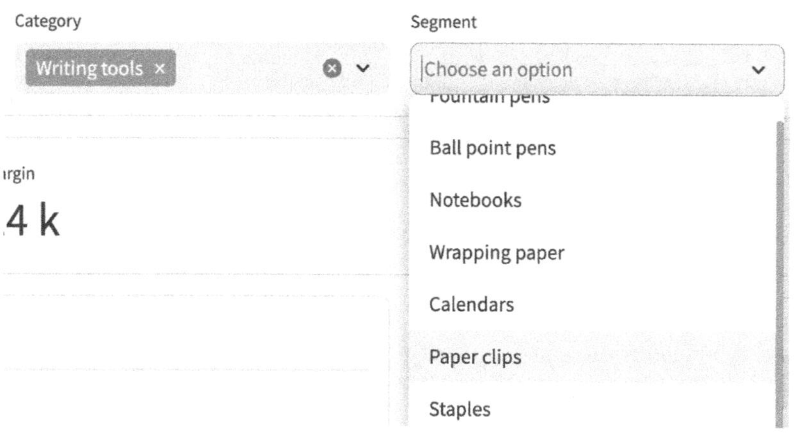

Figure 7.3 The filter bar options can have mismatching combinations.

One approach is to record the interdependencies between dimensions, then resolve those dependencies when obtaining unique values for each field. For example, since `Product name` should depend on the selections for `Category` and `Segment`, we could record that dependency. However, this requires maintaining a new configuration, and the logic can become fairly involved.

There's an easier alternative: rather than obtaining all unique filter values first and *then* filtering the dataframe (see figure 7.4), we can get the unique values for the first filter, apply the filter to get a new dataframe, get the unique values for the second filter, apply that, and so on.

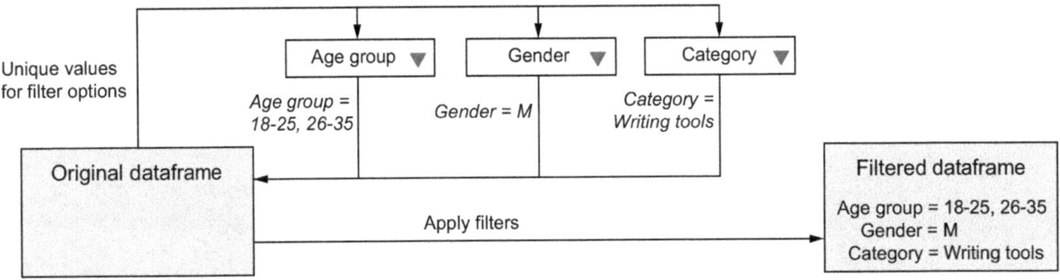

Figure 7.4   Old filtering approach: get unique values for all filters first, then filter based on selections.

In the new approach (figure 7.5), since we filter the data frame before getting the unique values for the next filter, we only show available values.

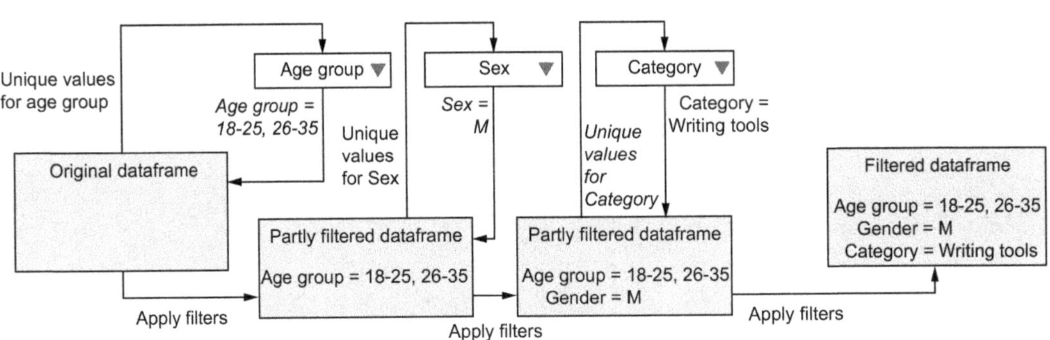

Figure 7.5   New filtering approach: get unique values for each filter, apply filter based on selection, then repeat for other filters.

So, when a user selects the category Writing tools the dataframe is filtered to include only those rows, and the unique values for the segment filter are drawn from this filtered set, which won't include staplers and the like.

To implement this, modify filter_panel.py like this:

```python
import streamlit as st
from data_wrangling import get_unique_values, apply_filters

filter_dims = ["Age group", "Gender", "Category", "Segment",
               "Product name", "State"]

def filter_panel(df):
  filters = {}
  with st.expander("Filters"):
    filter_cols = st.columns(len(filter_dims))
    effective_df = df
    for idx, dim in enumerate(filter_dims):
      with filter_cols[idx]:
        effective_df = apply_filters(effective_df, filters)
        unique_vals = get_unique_values(effective_df, dim)
        filters[dim] = st.multiselect(dim, unique_vals)
  return filters
```

The changes are straightforward. In each iteration through the filter fields, instead of passing `df` directly to `get_unique_values` to get the set of dropdown options, we use a variable called `effective_df` and pass that. As described above, `effective_df` is recomputed in each loop iteration by applying the filters selected so far (we import `apply_filters` at the top for this purpose).

Rerun your app. Figure 7.6 shows what happens when you select Writing tools as the only category of interest.

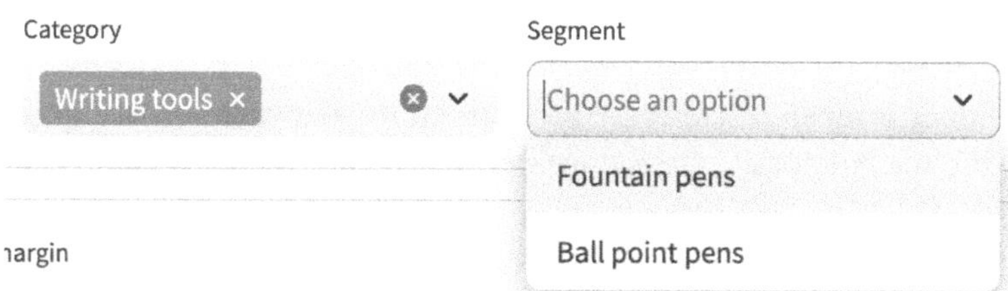

Figure 7.6   **The filter bar only shows valid option combinations (see chapter_07/in_progress_02 in the GitHub repo for the full code).**

As expected, the Segment filter now only shows writing instruments.

NOTE   The *order* of the filters is now important. If the Category filter is placed *after* Segment, choosing a category will not affect Segment, because the unique values for Segment will already have been computed before the selected Category values are evaluated.

7.4   *Date range comparisons*

A product line chief posted a screenshot (figure 7.7) with this feedback: "I can see that sales for RoyalQuill were \$1.32M for July. But is that good or bad? How did we do last year?"

Start date
2024/07/01

End date
2024/07/31

Filters

Age group | Gender | Category | Segment | Product name | State
Choose an option | Choose an option | Choose an option | Choose an option | RoyalQuill × | Choose an option

Total sales | Gross margin | Margin % | Average transaction value
\$1.32 M | \$1.10 M | 83.0% | \$62.8

Figure 7.7   Sales for RoyalQuill were \$1.32M, but there's no indication of whether that's good or what the sales were in a previous comparable period.

Often, the challenging part about analyzing data is not obtaining or transforming it, but rather *contextualizing* it. A metric alone means little. To make it useful, you must *compare* it to something. For example, if sales for a product are \$1M per year, the decisions you'd make if last year's sales were \$10M are very different from those you'd make if last year's sales were only \$100K.

Our dashboard doesn't currently offer an easy way to make this comparison. Ideally, when we see a metric for a certain time period, we should also be able to see how it *changed* compared to the past. In this section, we'll explore this requirement more deeply and incorporate it into our dashboard.

7.4.1   *Adding another date range selector*

What exactly does it mean to compare a metric to its past value? What start and end dates do we use for "the past"? Let's consider some common comparisons users may want.

For instance, if the user is viewing total sales for August 1 to August 15, 2024, they might want to compare that to the same dates in the previous month, i.e., July 1 to July 15, 2024. This is referred to as a month-over-month (MoM) comparison.

Other comparisons users might want to make are QoQ (quarter-over-quarter) and YoY (year-over-year). QoQ means comparing to analogous dates in the same quarter of the previous year. For example, August 1 to August 15 is the first 15 days of the second month of Q3, so QoQ would compare this to the first 15 days of the second month of *Q2*, or exactly three months earlier: May 1 to May 15. YoY is the date range exactly a year earlier, so August 1 to August 15, *2023*, in our example.

Executives might also want to compare to the immediately prior X days, where X is the number of days in the currently selected main date range. So, if the main range is

August 1 to August 15, the "previous period" would be the 15 days immediately preceding August 1, i.e., July 17 to July 31.

Let's implement these common comparisons. We'll start by updating our `date_range_panel` function in date_range_panel.py to add a comparison selector and return two more dates to the caller (dashboard.py, which we'll edit later):

```
...
def date_range_panel():
  start = st.date_input("Start date", value=THIRTY_DAYS_AGO)
  end = st.date_input("End date", value=LATEST_DATE)
  comparison = st.selectbox(
    "Compare to", ["MoM", "QoQ", "YoY", "Previous period"])
  compare_start, compare_end = get_compare_range(start, end, comparison)
  st.info(f"Comparing with:  \n{compare_start} - {compare_end}")
```

Since the comparison options are discrete values, we use `st.selectbox` to let users choose, and call a new function, `get_compare_range`, to get the actual start and end dates of the comparison range. We also show these comparison dates in an `st.info` box so users don't have to do calendar math themselves.

Let's also define the `get_compare_range` function we referenced above (in the same file, date_range_panel.py):

```
import pandas as pd...

def get_compare_range(start, end, comparison):
  offsets = {
    "MoM": pd.DateOffset(months=1),
    "QoQ": pd.DateOffset(months=3),
    "YoY": pd.DateOffset(years=1),
    "Previous period": pd.DateOffset((end - start).days + 1)
  }
  offset = offsets[comparison]
  return (start - offset).date(), (end - offset).date()

...
def date_range_panel():
  ...
```

This function takes three parameters: the start and end dates of the main date range, and `comparison`, a string indicating the type of comparison—MoM, QoQ, YoY, or Previous period. Calculating the comparison date range means subtracting the right *offset* from both the start and end dates. For MoM, subtract one month from both dates. For QoQ, subtract three months, and for YoY, subtract one year.

For the Previous period comparison, find the number of days in the main date range using (end - start).days + 1, and use that as the offset.

We store these offsets in a dictionary (called `offsets` in the code above) with the comparison name as the key and a pandas `DateOffset` object as the value. We then get the new start and end dates by subtracting the offset from each:

```
return (start - offset).date(), (end - offset).date()
```

> **NOTE** Why are the `.date()`s necessary? If you've been paying close attention, you'll notice that `start` and `end` are `datetime.date` objects, not pandas timestamp objects. Pandas ensures that `pd.DateOffset` is compatible with `datetime.date` and that the former can be subtracted from the latter, but the result is a pandas timestamp object. Since we've been trying to keep our date ranges `datetime.date` objects elsewhere, we use the `.date()` method of the pandas timestamp class to convert `start - offset` and `end - offset` to `datetime.dates`—thus ensuring consistency.

Since the function `date_range_panel` now returns four values (`start`, `end`, `compare_start`, and `compare_end`) instead of just two, we need to update the code that calls it to reflect this. This code happens to be in dashboard.py, within the sidebar. Change it from:

```
with st.sidebar:
    start, end = date_range_panel()
```

to:

```
with st.sidebar:
    start, end, compare_start, compare_end = date_range_panel()
```

The app's sidebar should now look like figure 7.8.

Although we're not actually using the comparison date range, you can see the new selectors.

7.4.2   Showing the comparison in the metric bar

Now that we've collected the comparison date range, how do we use it to address the feedback?

Let's look at an example. Say we have two date ranges: August 1 to August 31, 2024 (the main date range) and July 1 to July 31, 2024 (the comparison date range). To compare total sales, we calculate them separately for both date ranges and then display the *delta* (difference between them).

If the August sales are $5M and July sales are $4M, the delta (relative to August) is $1M. Expressing the difference as a percentage of the past value is more useful, so the delta is 20% ($1M / $5M x 100). We would show this number alongside the August sales to provide a complete picture: sales in August were $5M, up 20% from the previous period.

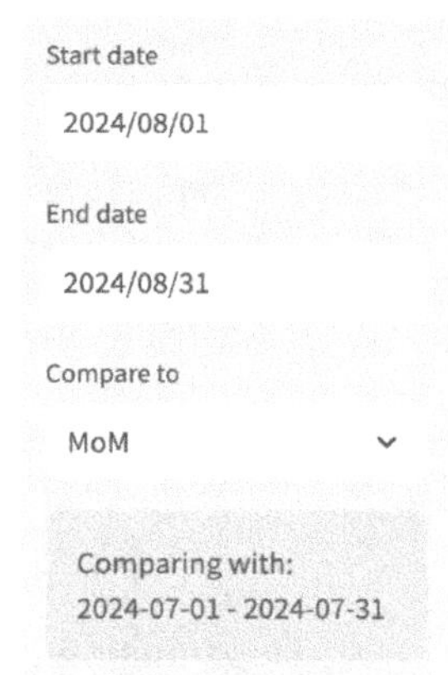

Figure 7.8   Sidebar showing a start/end date selector for the main date range as well as a Compare To input (see chapter_07/in_progress_03 in the GitHub repo for the full code).

This approach requires two steps:

1 Calculate the metric separately for the comparison date range, keeping all other filters the same.

2 Compute the percentage delta and display it with the main metric.

For the first step, let's modify dashboard.py:

```python
import streamlit as st
...


with st.sidebar:
  start, end, compare_start, compare_end = date_range_panel()


...
main_df = get_filtered_data_within_date_range(data, start, end, filters)
if main_df.empty:
  st.warning("No data to display")
else:
  compare_df = get_filtered_data_within_date_range(
                  data, compare_start, compare_end, filters)
  metric_bar(main_df, compare_df)
  ...
```

Here, we obtain a new pandas dataframe, compare_df, in much the same way that we get main_df—by passing the raw prepped data to get_filtered_data_within_date_range with the appropriate start and end dates and filters. The filters are the same as those used for main_df. This is important: if a user has filtered for a particular category or gender, the comparison should use the same filters, just for a different date range.

We also pass compare_df as a second argument to metric_bar, which we'll update to support this.

To compute and display the percentage delta, we need to update metric_bar.py. Let's start by modifying metric_bar to accept the extra argument we passed in:

```python
def metric_bar(main_df, compare_df):
  with st.container(border=True):
    metric_cols = st.columns(len(display_metrics))
    for idx, metric_name in enumerate(display_metrics):
      metric = metrics[metric_name]
      with metric_cols[idx]:
        value = get_metric(main_df, metric)
        formatted_value = format_metric(value, metric.type)
        formatted_delta = get_formatted_delta(value, compare_df, metric)
        c1, c2, c3 = st.columns([1, 3, 1])
        with c2:
          st.metric(
            metric.title, formatted_value, formatted_delta, "normal")
```

Previously, for each metric, we got the formatted value using `format_metric` and passed it, along with a title, to `st.metric` for display like this:

```
st.metric(metric.title, formatted_value)
```

However, `st.metric` supports showing a delta as well, through its third and fourth arguments (internally named `delta` and `delta_color`).

The third argument is the formatted number to show as the change (the percentage difference), while the fourth argument, `delta_color`, controls the color scheme.

`delta_color` can be `"normal,"` `"inverse,"` or `"off."` If it's set to `"normal,"` positive deltas are green, and negative are red. If it's `"inverse,"` the reverse is true: increases are red, and decreases are green (useful for metrics where a lower value is better, like cost). If it's `"off,"` Streamlit just shows everything in gray. In this case, we call `st.metric` like this:

```
st.metric(metric.title, formatted_value, formatted_delta, "normal")
```

`"normal"` is appropriate for all of our metrics since a higher value is better for all of them (you'd want higher sales, a higher gross margin, a higher margin percentage, and a higher average transaction value). For the third argument, we pass in `formatted_delta`, which we get by calling a function we'll define next:

```
formatted_delta = get_formatted_delta(value, compare_df, metric)
```

Let's now create `get_formatted_delta` and any associated functions:

```python
def get_delta(value, compare_df, metric):
  delta = None
  if compare_df is not None:
    compare_value = get_metric(compare_df, metric)
    if compare_value != 0:
      delta = (value - compare_value) / compare_value
  return delta

def get_formatted_delta(value, compare_df, metric):
  delta = get_delta(value, compare_df, metric)
  formatted_delta = None
  if delta is not None:
    formatted_delta = format_metric(delta, "percent")
  return formatted_delta
```

We've defined two functions: `get_delta` calculates the actual delta, while `get_formatted_delta` calls it and formats the result.

`get_delta` accepts the value of the main metric, `compare_df`—the comparison dataframe we computed in dashboard.py—and `metric`, which is the `Metric` object that represents the measure we're trying to show the change in.

The body of `get_delta` is simple. We use the `get_metric` function on `compare_df` to calculate the metric for the comparison date range, and get the percentage delta as follows:

```
delta = (value - compare_value) / compare_value
```

If a delta can't be displayed (because `compare_df` contains no data or because trying to calculate it would cause a divide-by-zero error since the comparison value is zero), we return `None`.

In `get_formatted_delta`, we format the returned value by calling `format_metric`:

```
formatted_delta = format_metric(delta, "percent")
```

Recall from chapter 6 that `format_metric` (in formatting.py) converts a numeric value into a user-friendly string depending on its type. In this case, the metric type is a percent, so format_metric will add a % sign at the end. If there's no delta to format (which happens when `get_delta` returns None), `get_formatted_delta` returns None as well.

When this is passed to `st.metric`, Streamlit handles the None value correctly by not displaying anything.

You can now rerun the dashboard to view your updated metric bar (remember to choose a comparison date range for which we have data), as shown in figure 7.9.

As you can see, the metric bar now shows how each metric has changed as compared to its value in the comparison date range. Boom! We've addressed another key piece of feedback and are well on our way to version 2.0 of our dashboard! Let's see what else the email says.

Figure 7.9 Metric bar showing how each metric has changed from the comparison date range (see chapter_07/in_progress_04 in the GitHub repo for the full code).

7.5 A drilldown view

Note n' Nib's CEO prides himself on being a "details guy," so when he sees a number on the dashboard, he wants to investigate *why*. For instance, if he notices that the average transaction value (ATV) on ball pens is lower than that on fountain pens, he wants to dig deeper to understand if a specific demographic is driving the ATV down. Our dashboard currently only displays data in the metrics bar, line, and pie charts; however, there's clearly a need for a more flexible, detailed view that shows individual rows from the source data.

So far, our dashboard design has aimed to shield users from unnecessary complexity. We've relied on visualizations to make data easy to grasp and used a clear, friendly metrics bar to display key aggregate numbers. Abstracting away complexity is usually beneficial for most users. Now and then, however, you'll encounter a power user who wants to delve deeper and interact with your software in more advanced ways.

In our case, Note n' Nib's CEO fits this description—he's comfortable with data and has expressed frustration at not being able to drill down for more detailed insights. Addressing this feedback will likely be the most complex task in this chapter, as we'll need to create a completely new view rather than just improve upon the existing features.

7.5.1 *Inserting a modal dialog*

Before considering what a drilldown view might contain, let's ponder where to place this functionality. Since we're classifying it as an advanced feature, it shouldn't be in the main dashboard window. Casual users should be able to ignore the new, more detailed view, while advanced users should be able to find it easily.

Let's use this opportunity to introduce a new UI construct: a modal dialog. A *modal dialog* is an overlay displayed on top of the main content, temporarily blocking interaction with the underlying interface until it has been dismissed. This overlay remains focused on a particular task, making it ideal for presenting advanced functionality, such as drill-downs.

ST.DIALOG

Streamlit offers modal dialogs out of the box with `st.dialog`. Let's see this in action now.

For our first iteration on the drilldown view, to keep things simple, when a user wants to drill down into the data, we'll just show them the entire pandas dataframe. Of course, since users are likely to want to also dive into the comparison date range we recently added, we'll need to show both the main and the comparison dataframes.

Listing 7.1 shows a new file, drilldown.py, set up to achieve this (chapter_07/in_progress_05/drilldown.py in the GitHub repo).

Listing 7.1   A drilldown dialog

```python
import streamlit as st

@st.dialog("Drilldown", width="large")
def drilldown(main_df, compare_df):
    main_tab, compare_tab = st.tabs(["Main", "Compare"])
    with main_tab:
        st.dataframe(main_df, use_container_width=True)
    with compare_tab:
        st.dataframe(compare_df, use_container_width=True)
```

It may surprise you to learn that `st.dialog` is *not* structured like `st.columns`, `st.tabs`, or `st.container` (i.e., as a widget that holds other widgets). Instead, it's similar to `st.cache_data` from chapter 6 in that it's a *decorator*. A function decorated with `st.dialog` runs and has its content rendered inside a popup dialog.

```python
@st.dialog("Drilldown", width="large")
```

The `width` parameter sets the dialog size, which may be `small` (500 pixels wide) or `large` (750 pixels wide). The function being decorated is called `drilldown`, and it accepts `main_df` and `compare_df` from dashboard.py as arguments. It renders two tabs, Main and Compare, and uses a new widget, `st.dataframe`, to display the passed pandas dataframes in their respective tabs.

Using `st.dataframe` like this simply displays the dataframe, just as `st.write` did in chapter 6. We'll encounter it again later. To see the dialog, we need to *trigger* it, so let's focus on that next.

USING ST.CONTAINER TO DISPLAY UI ELEMENTS OUT OF ORDER

As mentioned earlier, the drilldown view should be unobtrusive for casual users, but fairly obvious for power users. One way to achieve this is to add a Drilldown button to the sidebar that triggers the dialog when clicked.

Let's examine the existing code in dashboard.py (chapter_07/in_progress_04/dashboard.py in the GitHub repo).

```
...
with st.sidebar:
  start, end, compare_start, compare_end = date_range_panel()

...
main_df = get_filtered_data_within_date_range(data, start, end, filters)
if main_df.empty:
  st.warning("No data to display")
else:
  compare_df = get_filtered_data_within_date_range(
              data, compare_start, compare_end, filters)
  ...
```

The sidebar already contains the date range panel, with four widgets (two date inputs for the main range, a comparison selectbox, and an info box showing the comparison range), all lined up vertically. Since we want the drilldown trigger to be easily visible, we don't want it to be *below* the date range panel. Cool, so we put it above the panel instead, right?

Except, there's a bit of an ordering issue here. To trigger the drilldown view, we need to call the `drilldown` function we just decorated with `st.dialog`. The parameters to this function are `main_df` and `compare_df`.

If you inspect the dashboard.py code, you'll realize that obtaining `main_df` and `compare_df` requires that we already *have* the `start`, `end`, `compare_start`, and `compare_end` values so we can pass them in like this (for `main_df`):

```
main_df = get_filtered_data_within_date_range(data, start, end, filters)
```

But where do we get these values? Why, in the sidebar!

```
with st.sidebar:
  start, end, compare_start, compare_end = date_range_panel()
```

Do you see the dilemma? To place the drilldown button above the date range panel, we'd need to write its code *before* this line, but that code requires values that are available only *after* this line!

This is a perfect example of the need to display elements out of order. We need a way to separate the order in which Streamlit renders widgets on the screen from the order in which it computes them.

We'll use st.container for this. In chapter 6, we used it to display a border around the metrics bar and visualizations. This time, we'll use a different property—st.container can put a *placeholder* widget on the screen that we can populate with other widgets later.

For our use case, the placeholder will be positioned above the date range panel within the sidebar, and we'll only populate it with the actual drilldown button once we have main_df and compare_df later in the code. Let's lay this out in dashboard.py:

```
...
from drilldown import drilldown

...
with st.sidebar:
  dd_button_container = st.container()        ◄——  This is the placeholder
  start, end, compare_start, compare_end = date_range_panel()    defined within st.sidebar.

...
main_df = get_filtered_data_within_date_range(data, start, end, filters)
if main_df.empty:
  st.warning("No data to display")
else:
  compare_df = get_filtered_data_within_date_range(
                data, compare_start, compare_end, filters)
  if dd_button_container.button("Drilldown", use_container_width=True):
    drilldown(main_df, compare_df)...
```

As promised, we use st.container above the date range panel to put a placeholder and refer to it by the name dd_button_container. Then, once we have main_df and compare_df, the code creates the button that calls the drilldown function when clicked. Notice that we're using the syntax dd_button_container.button instead of the with/ st.button structure, just as with columns or tabs.

It's finally time to see the dialog come to life! Rerun dashboard.py and click the drilldown button to see the modal dialog as shown on figure 7.10.

You may have noticed that the drilldown button took a second to appear before you can click it. That's because we delayed its rendering until other processing was complete. How? Upon reviewing the code from top to bottom, Streamlit first encounters the line dd_button_container = st.container(), which inserts a placeholder in the sidebar. It then executes the remaining code (displaying the date range panel, getting the filtered data, etc.) until it gets to this line: if dd_button_container.button("Drilldown", ..., which inserts the actual drilldown button into the placeholder it added earlier.

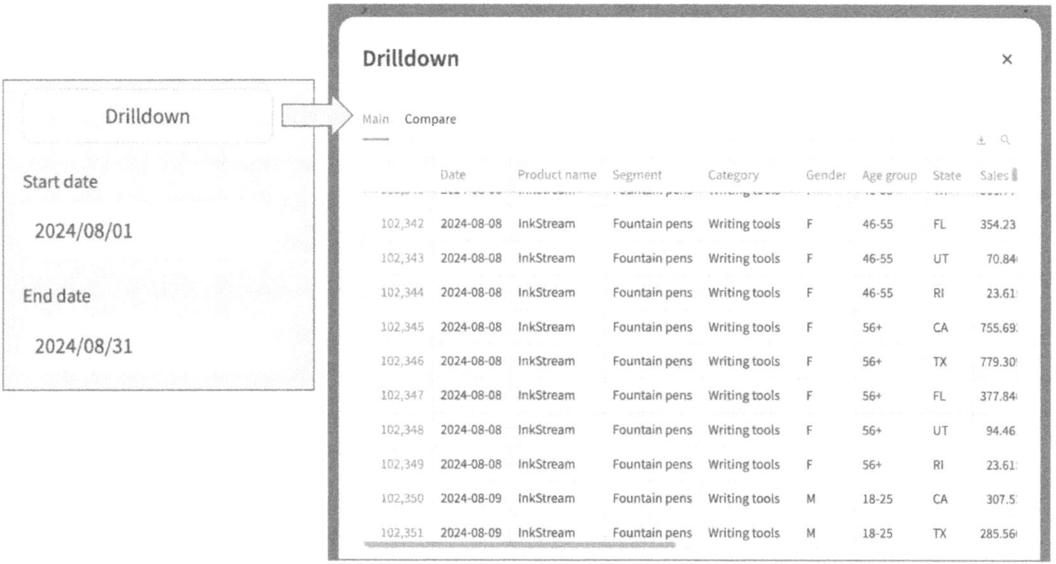

Figure 7.10 A basic raw dataframe view rendered in a dialog using `st.dialog` (see chapter_07/in_progress_05 in the GitHub repo for the full code).

7.5.2 Designing the content of the drilldown

Turn your attention to the dialog in figure 7.10. We're currently just displaying `main_df` and `compare_df` as-is. It's rather ugly, with the horizontal *and* vertical scrollbars indicating that we only see a tiny portion of the data. More importantly, we can't easily use this view to look for specific data points or view a specific subset. The boss would not be pleased if he had to use this. We need to think carefully to get the experience right.

WHAT DO USERS NEED FROM A DRILLDOWN VIEW?

It's clear that the content of the drilldown page needs to change, but how? What do users need from this view? The best way to find out is to talk to a user. So, you book a slot on the CEO's calendar—it's a sign of his enthusiasm for the dashboard that he readily accepts. In your interview, he outlines the original motivation behind his feedback about the drilldown view.

Note n' Nib has two separate products in its best-selling line of fountain pens: Inkstream and RoyalQuill. Inkstream is a chic, modern take on the fountain pen, while RoyalQuill—reminiscent of the classic elegance of vintage pens—targets older customers.

Recently, the company ran an advertising campaign for RoyalQuill, specifically targeting women in the 46–55 and 56+ age groups. The CEO wanted data about the assumptions and results of this campaign. Specifically, he wanted to know how sales for InkStream and RoyalQuill broke down by age *and* gender. The current dashboard shows a breakdown of a metric by age *or* gender, but not by both, so users can't easily access this information.

This feedback can be generalized to any combination of dimensions in the data, not just age group and gender. Also, it would be tricky to present this kind of detail in a coherent, repeatable visualization.

What we need is a highly flexible tabular form to show the data, similar to pivot tables that you may be familiar with from spreadsheet programs like Microsoft Excel. This table should:

- Enable viewing numbers for any combination of dimensions
- Allow focusing on just the fields we care about, hiding irrelevant rows and columns
- Show aggregate numbers for a full breakdown

A mock UI created with these requirements in mind is shown in figure 7.11.

Drilldown fields

Age group, Gender, Category	▼

Main	Compare

Age group %	Gender ATV		Category	Total sales	Gross margin	Margin
Total			$1.7M	$1.3M	79%	$36
18-25	F	Writing tools	———	———	———	———
26-35	F	Writing tools	———	———	———	———
36-45	F	Writing tools	———	———	———	———
…	…	…	…	…	…	…

Figure 7.11   A mock UI for the drilldown view

The mock shows us a fairly flexible table that's similar to a pivot table. The Drilldown Fields box is a multi-select option that allows users to choose the dimensions they care about. Below that is a table showing the dimensions we've selected. It *aggregates* the data over those dimensions, showing the metrics for every combination of the selected dimensions. There's also a total row that sums everything.

We've also retained the main and comparison tabs, allowing users to switch between them to view past and present metrics. This format is quite flexible and meets our requirements, so it's time to build it!

7.5.3 *Implementing the drilldown view*

The drilldown view shown in figure 7.11 is fairly complex, so we'll assemble it piece by piece, starting with the drilldown field selector and ending with some formatting and styling.

AGGREGATING BY A FEW CHOSEN DIMENSIONS

Building the dimension selector (the top widget in figure 7.11) is just a matter of passing the possible dimension options in an `st.multiselect`. Add a new function to drilldown.py that does this and returns the list of the user's selections:

```
def drilldown_dimensions():
  return st.multiselect(
    "Drilldown fields",
    ["Age group", "Gender", "Category", "Segment", "Product name", "State"]
  )
```

As our mock in figure 7.11 shows, we want to display all key metrics simultaneously. Let's add another function (also in drilldown.py) that takes in a dataframe (or a slice), calculates all the metrics by aggregating it, and returns the results. Remember to import all modules!

```
import pandas as pd
import streamlit as st
from metric_config import metrics


...
def get_metric_cols(df):
  metrics_dict = {met: metric.func(df) for met, metric in metrics.items()}
  return pd.Series(metrics_dict)


...
```

The expression `{met: metric.func(df) for met, metric in metrics.items()}` is a dictionary comprehension. We encountered one before in chapter 2, but to recap: a dictionary comprehension is shorthand for creating a dictionary by iterating through something. Here it means "iterate through the metrics dictionary (from metric_config.py) and return a new dictionary where each key is the name of the metric, and the corresponding value is the result of applying the metric function `metric.func` on `df`, i.e. the value of that metric". We use a pandas series here because, as you'll see, it's a versatile data type that integrates seamlessly with various dataframe operations.

To prepare the aggregated table given a dataframe and a list of dimensions, add a new function called `get_aggregate_metrics` to the same file:

```
def get_aggregate_metrics(df, dimensions):
  if dimensions:
    grouped = df.groupby(dimensions)
```

```
    return grouped.apply(get_metric_cols).reset_index()
  metric_cols = get_metric_cols(df)
  return pd.DataFrame(metric_cols).T
```

If `dimensions` is not empty, i.e., if the user has indeed selected some drilldown dimensions, `get_aggregate_metrics` groups `df` by those fields, and applies `get_metric_cols` to each of the groups (using `grouped.apply`, which you should recall from chapter 6), thus obtaining metric values for each group.

If no dimensions are selected, we call `get_metric_cols` directly on `df` to get a pandas `Series` object with the aggregated metrics for the entire dataframe. We then convert this series into a dataframe and return its *transpose*.

```
return pd.DataFrame(metric_cols).T
```

The transpose (referenced using a pandas dataframe's `.T` property) of a dataframe is another dataframe whose rows and columns are interchanged. In this case, `metric_cols` is a `pd.Series` object, and calling `pd.DataFrame` on it would return a one-column dataframe where each metric is a row. The `.T` turns this into a one-*row* dataframe where each metric is a column—a more useful format.

Next, we write a function that returns our full drilldown table. For now, it's pretty thin since we're only doing some aggregations:

```
def get_drilldown_table(df, dimensions):
  aggregated = get_aggregate_metrics(df, dimensions)
  return aggregated
```

We'll add more logic to `get_drilldown_table` later. To wrap up, we also need a function that displays the drilldown table (currently a pandas dataframe):

```
def display_drilldown_table(df):
  if df is None:
    st.warning("No data available for selected filters and date range")
  else:
    st.dataframe(df, use_container_width=True, hide_index=True)
```

This is simple; we display a warning if there's no data, or use `st.dataframe` to display the aggregated table otherwise. Note the use of `hide_index=True`. By default, Streamlit displays the index field (which, as you may recall from chapter 6, is a unique identifier for the row, defaulting to a simple serial number) alongside each row. You can see this in figure 7.10 (they're the numbers to the far left in the dataframe). We don't want the index displayed, so we hide it.

With these changes made, we can update the `drilldown` function too:

```
@st.dialog("Drilldown", width="large")
def drilldown(main_df, compare_df):
  dimensions = drilldown_dimensions()
```

```
main_data = get_drilldown_table(main_df, dimensions)
compare_data = get_drilldown_table(compare_df, dimensions)

main_tab, compare_tab = st.tabs(["Main", "Compare"])
with main_tab:
  display_drilldown_table(main_data)
with compare_tab:
  display_drilldown_table(compare_data)
```

The order of operations is logical: first, we get the drilldown dimensions from the user
(`dimensions = drilldown_dimensions()`), then we compute the aggregated dataframes
(`main_data` and `compare_data`) using `get_drilldown_table`, and finally display them in
separate tabs using `display_drilldown_table`.

If you rerun the dashboard now, you should see a much more palatable version of
the drilldown view, as shown in figure 7.12.

Drilldown

Drilldown fields

Gender × Category ×

Main Compare

Gender	Category	Total sales	Gross margin	Margin %	ATV
F	Office supplies	45,492.9304	35,777.5738	0.7864	10.1253
F	Paper products	310,673.1373	222,725.9512	0.7169	18.2181
F	Writing tools	1,696,765.754	1,333,765.6899	0.7861	36.4449
M	Office supplies	50,145.1769	39,111.8811	0.78	9.9712
M	Paper products	358,841.4117	260,572.6291	0.7261	18.2682
M	Writing tools	1,190,424.4791	923,964.7547	0.7762	31.7091

Figure 7.12 Drilldown view with a dimension selector, aggregated by the selected dimensions (see chapter_07/ in_progress_06 in the GitHub repo for the full code).

The user can now select any combination of dimensions they want and view the metrics
for each. This effectively lets the user drill into the required level of detail, but perhaps
a summary "total" row would help to understand the whole that's being broken down.

ADDING A TOTAL ROW

Adding a summary row to the drilldown table is relatively complex for a couple of reasons:

- Pandas dataframes do not natively support designating a row as a summary of all others. When we want totals, we have to assemble them using various operations.
- The dimension values are meaningless in a total row and should be blank.

As an example, let's say we have the following drilldown dataframe (after the filtering and aggregation):

```
+--------+---------------+--------------+-------------+--------------+----------+------+
| Gender |    Segment    | Product name | Total sales | Gross margin | Margin % | ATV  |
+--------+---------------+--------------+-------------+--------------+----------+------+
|   M    | Fountain pens | InkStream    |  $100,000   |   $60,000    |   60%    | $10  |
|   M    | Fountain pens | RoyalQuill   |  $200,000   |   $150,000   |   75%    | $40  |
+--------+---------------+--------------+-------------+--------------+----------+------+
```

With the total row added to the top, we would have a dataframe that looks like this:

```
+--------+---------------+--------------+-------------+--------------+----------+------+
| Gender |    Segment    | Product name | Total sales | Gross margin | Margin % | ATV  |
+--------+---------------+--------------+-------------+--------------+----------+------+
| Total  |               |              |  $300,000   |   $210,000   |   70%    | $20  |
|   M    | Fountain pens | InkStream    |  $100,000   |   $60,000    |   60%    | $10  |
|   M    | Fountain pens | RoyalQuill   |  $200,000   |   $150,000   |   75%    | $40  |
+--------+---------------+--------------+-------------+--------------+----------+------+
```

Let's implement this with a new function, `add_total_row`, in drilldown.py:

```python
def add_total_row(df, all_df, dimensions):
  total_metrics = get_metric_cols(all_df)
  if dimensions:
    dim_vals = {dim: '' for dim in dimensions}
    dim_vals[dimensions[0]] = 'Total'
    total_row = pd.DataFrame({**dim_vals, **total_metrics}, index=[0])
    return pd.concat([total_row, df], ignore_index=True)
  total_row = pd.DataFrame({'': 'Total', **total_metrics}, index=[0])
  return total_row
```

`add_total_rows` takes three arguments: `df`, `all_df`, and `dimensions` (the same list of dimension names we've been passing around). `df` is the drilldown dataframe we have so far (e.g., the first table above), while `all_df` is the dataframe with the original granular columns *before* aggregation.

Why do we need both `df` *and* `all_df` here? Recall that we have a `get_metric_cols` function that can calculate all the metrics we need for a given dataframe—in other words, the numeric values for the "total" row we're building. `get_metric_cols` expects a raw, non-aggregated dataframe, not the aggregated version. This means we need to pass it `all_df`, not `df`. That is indeed what the first statement in the function does, storing the results in `total_metrics`.

The next part builds the total row if the dimensions list is non-empty (`if dimensions:`), i.e., if the user has selected some drilldown dimensions. The following two lines are associated with populating the dimension values:

```
dim_vals = {dim: '' for dim in dimensions}
dim_vals[dimensions[0]] = 'Total'
```

The first line is a dictionary comprehension that assigns a blank value for every dimension key. We then set the value for the first dimension to `Total`. This effectively creates the text display values for our total row, as shown in the example above—Total in the first field and blanks for all other fields.

We have the dimension values for the total row in `dim_vals` (a dictionary) and the metric values in `total_metrics` (a `pd.Series`). All we need to do is put them together! That's what the next line does:

```
total_row = pd.DataFrame({**dim_vals, **total_metrics}, index=[0])
```

There's some interesting syntax here, so let's break it down.

The character sequence `**` is called a *dictionary unpacking operator*. It unpacks the items from a dictionary so they can be combined with other items to form a new dictionary, or even passed as function arguments.

That's what's happening here. For instance, if `dim_vals` is something like `{'Gender': 'Total', 'Segment': '', ...}` and `total_metrics` is `{'Total sales': 300000, ...}`, `{**dim_vals, **total_metrics}` produces a *combined* dictionary: `{'Gender': 'Total', 'Segment': '', ..., 'Total sales': 300000, ...}`. The `index=[0]` sets the index of the only row in this single-row data frame to 0.

You might notice one problem: didn't we just say that `total_metrics` is a `pd.Series` and *not* a dictionary? Well, though that's true, a pandas series has many of the properties of a regular Python dictionary—among them support for the `**` operator.

The next line concatenates this total row to the rest of the drilldown dataframe and returns it:

```
return pd.concat([total_row, df], ignore_index=True)
```

Now, if the user has *not* selected any dimensions and `dimensions` is empty, getting the dataframe with a total row becomes easier; we just need to add a blank column that says `'Total'` to `total_metrics`, and there's nothing to concatenate the row to—the dataframe consists of only the total row:

```
total_row = pd.DataFrame({'': 'Total', **total_metrics}, index=[0])
```

We can now add the act of obtaining the total row to the transformations in `get_drilldown_table` like so:

```
def get_drilldown_table(df, dimensions):
    aggregated = get_aggregate_metrics(df, dimensions)
    with_total = add_total_row(aggregated, df, dimensions)
    return with_total
```

Rerun the dashboard to see what your total row looks like (figure 7.13):

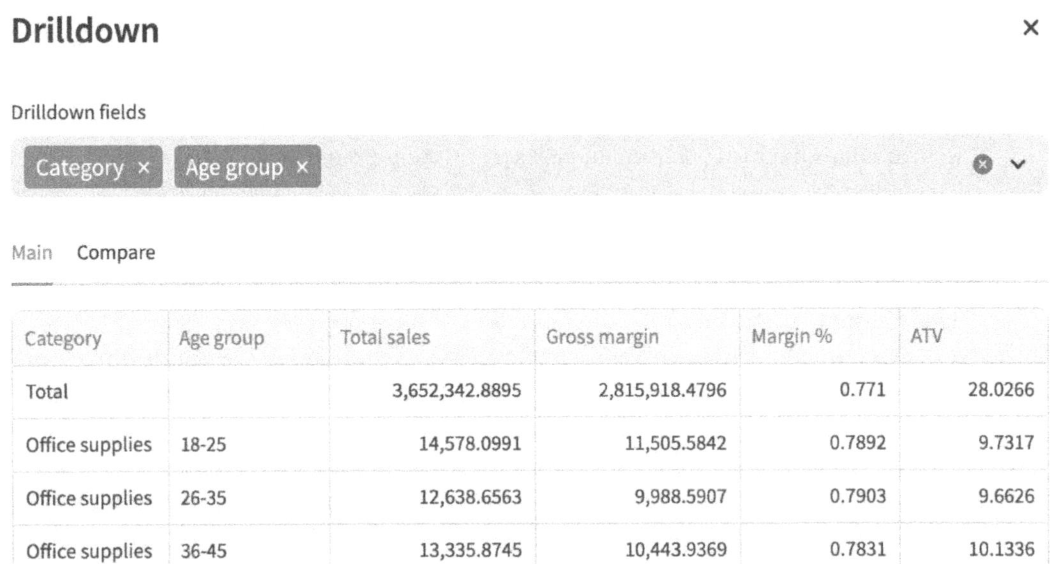

Category	Age group	Total sales	Gross margin	Margin %	ATV
Total		3,652,342.8895	2,815,918.4796	0.771	28.0266
Office supplies	18-25	14,578.0991	11,505.5842	0.7892	9.7317
Office supplies	26-35	12,638.6563	9,988.5907	0.7903	9.6626
Office supplies	36-45	13,335.8745	10,443.9369	0.7831	10.1336

Figure 7.13 Drilldown dataframe view with a total row (see chapter_07/in_progress_07 in the GitHub repo for the full code).

This is *almost* perfect, but wouldn't it be nice if the total row were highlighted or shaded to make it stand out?

FORMATTING AND STYLING THE DRILLDOWN TABLE

While the content of our drilldown table is ready, the presentation leaves a couple of things to be desired:

- As figure 7.13 shows, the numbers in the table are user-unfriendly and raw, with hardly any formatting. Ideally, we'd want these to be shown in the same way as in the metrics bar (e.g., $1.2M instead of 1200000).
- No shading distinguishes the total row from the rest of the table.

Let's tackle the first issue. Formatting the numbers in the table should be straightforward because we've already defined the actual formatting rules in the formatting.py file from chapter 6.

All we need is a function to apply the formatting to an entire pandas dataframe rather than the individual numbers displayed in the metrics bar. Spin up a new function for this in formatting.py:

```python
import humanize

def format_metric(value, metric_type):
  ...

def format_dataframe(df, metrics):
  cols = df.columns
  for col in cols:
    if col in metrics:
      df[col] = df[col].apply(format_metric, metric_type=metrics[col].type)
  return df
```

The `format_dataframe` function is straightforward. After accepting two parameters (`df`, the dataframe to format, and the `metrics` dictionary from metrics.py), we simply iterate through the columns in `df`, and apply `format_metric` (from chapter 6) element-wise to each column. Notice how we're passing `metric_type` to `format_metric` as *another* parameter to `.apply()`. Essentially, the following expression:

```python
df[col] = df[col].apply(format_metric, metric_type=metrics[col].type)
```

is saying: "issue the function call `format_metric(element, metric_type=metrics[col].type)`" for every element in `df[col]`, and save the result, which should be our formatted dataframe.

We'll turn to the shading problem next: let's say we want to give the total row a gray background so it stands out. The key is the `style` property of a pandas dataframe, which enables us to apply *conditional formatting* (i.e., formatting based on certain rules) to the dataframe. To achieve this, we would use the `.apply` method of the `style` property, along with a custom function that defines the conditional style.

Let's create a new function in drilldown.py to implement this logic:

```python
def style_total_row(df):
  def get_style(row):
    first_col = row.index[0]
    return [
      'background-color: #d9d9d9' if row[first_col] == 'Total' else ''
      for _ in row
    ]
  return df.style.apply(get_style, axis=1)
```

The `style_total_row` function accepts the drilldown dataframe `df`, and applies the shading we need. To achieve this, it does something interesting: it defines *another* function called `get_style` within its body!

In Python, a function defined within another is called a *nested function* or an *inner function*. Python considers a nested function to be local to the enclosing function's scope. Code outside of `style_total_row` cannot call `get_style`.

The `get_style` function operates on an individual row of a pandas dataframe, so it takes a row as a parameter. It identifies the name of the first column using `first_col = row.index[0]`. The `index` property of a dataframe row is a list-like object containing the column names, so `index[0]` returns the name of the first column.

The next line defines (and returns) the conditional style to apply:

```
return [
  'background-color: lightgray' if row[first_col] == 'Total' else ''
  for _ in row
]
```

The expression returned is a *list comprehension,* which builds a new list by iterating through something (similar to how the dictionary comprehensions we've seen build new dictionaries). In this case, we're iterating through the fields in the dataframe row, using `for _ in row`. We don't need to refer to the fields themselves, which is why we use `_`—a perfectly valid Python identifier, by the way—as the loop index here.

For each field, if the passed row is the total row (which we verify by checking if the value of the first column is `Total`), we add a peculiar string, `'background-color: lightgray'`, to the list we're constructing. This notation comes from CSS, the language used to style web pages. We're telling pandas to give a light gray background to every field in a total row. We've defined the conditional style, but we still need to apply it. The last line in `style_total_row` does this:

```
return df.style.apply(get_style, axis=1)
```

`.apply` here expects a function that accepts a dataframe row, so it can call it on every row (as we've seen before). To complete our drilldown view, the final step is to add the formatting and styling to `get_drilldown_table`:

```
...
from formatting import format_dataframe


...
def get_drilldown_table(df, dimensions):
  aggregated = get_aggregate_metrics(df, dimensions)
  with_total = add_total_row(aggregated, df, dimensions)
  formatted = format_dataframe(with_total, metrics)
```

```
styled = style_total_row(formatted)
return styled
```

And that's it! Our drilldown view is now fully formed. Check it out in figure 7.14.

Drilldown   ✕

Drilldown fields

Age group ✕   Category ✕   ⊗ ⌄

Main   Compare

Age group	Category	Total sales	Gross margin	Margin %	ATV
Total		$3.65 M	$2.82 M	77.1%	$28.0
18-25	Office supplies	$14.6 k	$11.5 k	78.9%	$9.73
18-25	Paper products	$128 k	$92.7 k	72.6%	$18.3
18-25	Writing tools	$401 k	$311 k	77.4%	$30.8

Figure 7.14   Completed drilldown view with shaded total row and formatted values (see chapter_07/in_progress_08 in the GitHub repo for the full code).

Whew! That was a lot of work! However, we have more feature requests to address before we're done.

The fragment-like behavior of st.dialog

If you paid close attention in chapter 4, where we learned about Streamlit's execution model, there's one aspect of how we implemented the drilldown view that may be puzzling.

To show the dialog, we nested it under a button like this (in dashboard.py):

```
if dd_button_container.button("Drilldown", use_container_width=True):
    drilldown(main_df, compare_df)
```

with `drilldown` being a function decorated with `st.dialog`. Within drilldown, we can perform many interactions, such as selecting a dimension or setting a filter.

(continued)

But in previous projects, we've seen that the clicked state of `st.button` only holds for a single rerun, and that whenever we interact with something nested under a button, the app gets rerun again, and the button click gets cleared. We had to use `st.session_state` in chapter 4 to achieve the desired behavior.

However, we didn't need to do any of that here. Shouldn't interacting with the drilldown have caused a rerun with the button-click getting reset and the drilldown disappearing?

This doesn't happen because of special behavior in `st.dialog`. When a user interacts with a widget within an `st.dialog`-decorated function, only the decorated function gets rerun, *not* the entire app!

In the above case, when someone selects a drilldown dimension, only the drilldown function gets rerun, and the button remains in the clicked state. `st.dialog` gets this behavior from a more general decorator called `st.fragment`.

7.6 *Enabling deeplinks*

A common complaint is the inability to share dashboard views with others. The CEO frequently emails his subordinates about the data he sees after applying various filters and selections. Recipients then waste time trying to recreate what their boss saw on the dashboard, often by trial and error. "This," the CEO writes, "amounts to a collaboration tax."

Data-driven decision-making should be collaborative. Currently, the dashboard makes this difficult. Users who spot a key trend or data point must send a screenshot or provide step-by-step instructions to recreate the view.

Neither approach is ideal. Screenshots prevent interaction, and manual instructions are error-prone and inefficient (imagine: "Set the date range to last year, filter for the 18–25 age group, and select monthly granularity!").

Wouldn't it be better if users could simply copy and paste the current URL, allowing others to see exactly the same dashboard state? This is standard on many websites. For instance, search engines like Google or DuckDuckGo let you share search results via the URL. This is called *deeplinking*, in the sense of linking someone deep into your website.

How do deeplinks work? Let's take an example from the search engine Duck-DuckGo. If you search for `streamlit` on duckduckgo.com, the URL of the search results page will be something like:

```
https://duckduckgo.com/?t=h_&q=streamlit&ia=web
```

Copy and paste this URL in your browser, and it'll take you directly to the search results page for the query streamlit. The part of the URL where it says `q=streamlit` is what makes this possible. The URL has embedded information about the inputs entered by the first user, and DuckDuckGo uses this information to direct the second user to the right page. If we apply this logic to our app, we need two things to implement deeplinks:

- A way to embed user inputs in the app's URL
- A way to repopulate these inputs in the app automatically from such a URL

7.6.1 Using st.query_params

The part of the URL that contains the extra information after the actual address is called a *query string*. It is separated from the rest of the URL by a question mark (?) character. The query string is made up of several key-value pairs called *query parameters*, separated in turn by the ampersand (&) character.

For example, in the URL https://duckduckgo.com/?t=h_&q=streamlit&ia=web:

- The query string is `t=h_&q=streamlit&ia=web`
- The query parameters are: `t=h_` (key `t` and value `h_`), `q=streamlit` (key `q` and value `streamlit`), and `ia=web` (key `ia` and value `web`).

If our app were to have query parameters, what would they look like? Well, since the query string needs to capture the inputs entered by the user, it might be something like the following:

```
start_date=2024-08-01&end_date=2024-08-31&product_name=RoyalQuill
```

Essentially, the user's selections need to be part of the query string (and, therefore, the URL). Streamlit lets you manage query parameters through `st.query_params`, a dictionary-like object similar to `st.session_state`. At any time, `st.query_params` contains the key-value pairs from the app's URL query string. You can also update the query string in the browser by modifying `st.query_params`.

Getting and setting parameters in `st.query_params` works like a dictionary. For example, the code `st.query_params["pie_chart_dimension"] = "Gender"` sets the `pie_chart_dimension` parameter and updates the URL to include `pie_chart_dimension=Gender`.

You can also read the parameter value like this:

```
dimension = st.query_params["pie_chart_dimension"]
```

Figure 7.15 illustrates the solution.

When a user first navigates to the app, extract any query parameters from the URL and set widget values accordingly. For instance, if `start_date=2024-08-01` is present, set the start date in the date range selector widget to 2024-08-01. If there are no query parameters or no value is specified for a particular widget, we don't set the value of the widget; instead, we let the default behavior take over.

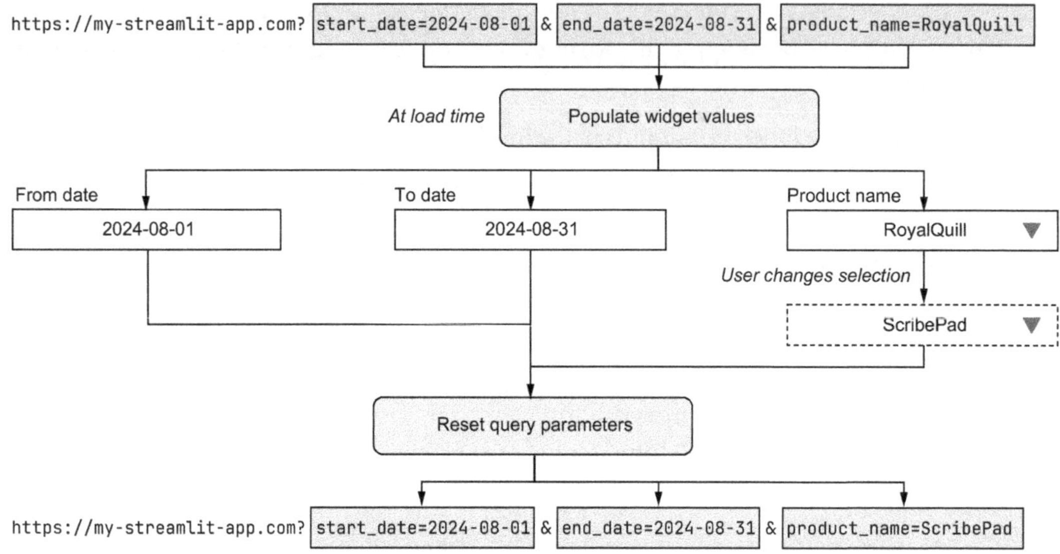

Figure 7.15   Approach to implementing deeplinking

When a user changes a widget selection, we *update* the query parameters to reflect that change, thus also changing the URL in the address bar. This ensures the URL always reflects the current app state.

7.6.2   *Setting widget defaults through st.session_state*

One aspect remains: how do we programmatically set the value of an input widget?

Recall from chapter 4: every Streamlit widget (or UI element) has a unique key. The key is usually created automatically by Streamlit; however, if you have two identical widgets, you must manually assign a key to each one so that Streamlit can distinguish them. When you provide a key, the widget's value is accessible in `st.session_state`. So if you have a dropdown input coded like this:

```
st.selectbox("Pick a field", ["Gender", "Product name"], key="select_dim")
```

you can access its value using `st.session_state["select_dim"]`. Importantly, you can also *set* its value, simulating a user selection:

```
st.session_state["select_dim"] = "Product name"
```

One caveat is that you can only do this *before* the widget code is run. In other words, you can set the value of the widget key in `st.session_state` *first* and have the widget take on that value when it renders later, but you can't render the widget with a key *first* and *then* overwrite its value by setting the value of the key in `st.session_state`.

7.6.3 *Implementing deeplinks*

We now have all the information needed to build the deeplink functionality. Create a new file called query_params.py with the content shown in listing 7.2 (chapter_07/ in_progress_09/query_params.py in the GitHub repo).

Listing 7.2 Getting and setting query params

```python
import streamlit as st

def get_param(key):
  return st.query_params.get(key, None)

def set_widget_defaults():
  for key in st.query_params:
    if key.startswith('w:') and key not in st.session_state:
      st.session_state[key] = get_param(key)

def set_params():
  query_params_dict = {}
  for key in st.session_state:
    if key.startswith('w:'):
      value = st.session_state[key]
      query_params_dict[key] = value
  st.query_params.from_dict(query_params_dict)
```

The get_param function gets the value of a query parameter given its name. It does so by using the .get() method of st.query_params, which—identically to that of a regular dictionary—returns a default value of None if the key does not exist.

set_widget_defaults populates the values of various widgets in the app from the query parameters by iterating through them and setting the value of each widget key in st.session_state.

Why do we have the following condition?:

```python
if key.startswith('w:') and key not in st.session_state:
```

We don't necessarily want *every* key stored in st.session_state to appear in the URL, just those representing widgets. To ensure this, later on, we'll prefix the string 'w:' to every widget key we want in the query parameters. This gives us the flexibility of using st.session_state for other purposes should we need to, while still being able to auto-populate widget values with it.

We also don't want Streamlit to try to set the widget value from st.query_params in every rerun of the app, because then *users* wouldn't be able to change the value. Instead, we only want to set each widget value once, when the app is being loaded for the first time from the parameter-embedded URL. That's why we have the subcondition key not in st.session_state.

set_widget_defaults fulfills the first part of what we need for deep links—the ability to populate widget inputs from the URL. However, we still need to change the query parameters whenever a user makes a selection.

That's what the `set_params` function does. It loops through `st.session_state`, gets the value of every widget key and stores them in a dictionary, `query_params_dict`. It then populates all of `st.query_params` directly from this dictionary using the `from_dict` method. As I illustrated earlier, we could also have set each value in `st.query_params`, but I wanted to show you this way too.

For this to work, all widgets we want in the query parameters must have keys defined, starting with `'w:'`. We'll need to go through all of our code and add widget keys to each widget. Not a lot of fun, I'm afraid, but it has to be done.

Here are the changes we'll need to make, if you're following along.

CHANGES TO DATE_RANGE_PANEL.PY

In date_range_panel.py, there are three date selection widgets that we show the user. We need to add keys to each of them. These would become:

```python
start = st.date_input("Start date", value=THIRTY_DAYS_AGO, key="w:start")
end = st.date_input("End date", value=LATEST_DATE, key="w:end")
comparison = st.selectbox(
    "Compare to", ["MoM", "QoQ", "YoY", "Previous period"], key="w:compare")
```

The exact names for the keys don't matter as long as they start with `w:`. There's an additional wrinkle here: currently, we assign default values `THIRTY_DAYS_AGO` and `LATEST_DATE` to the start and end date selectors, respectively, through the `value` parameter in `st.date_input`.

When using `st.session_state` to set widget values (as in `set_widget_defaults`), Streamlit will throw an error if we *also* set the value using the `value` parameter. We can't use both methods; we have to choose one. So instead, we'll modify our code to:

```python
if 'w:start' not in st.session_state:
  st.session_state['w:start'] = THIRTY_DAYS_AGO
if 'w:end' not in st.session_state:
  st.session_state['w:end'] = LATEST_DATE
start = st.date_input("Start date", key="w:start")
end = st.date_input("End date", key="w:end")
```

Here, we've removed the `value` parameter from both widgets and added some logic at the beginning to set the same values using `st.session_state`. These lines must come before the widgets are defined. Here's the updated `date_range_panel` function:

```python
...
def date_range_panel():
  if 'w:start' not in st.session_state:
    st.session_state['w:start'] = THIRTY_DAYS_AGO
  if 'w:end' not in st.session_state:
    st.session_state['w:end'] = LATEST_DATE
  start = st.date_input("Start date", key="w:start")
  end = st.date_input("End date", key="w:end")
```

```python
comparison = st.selectbox(
  "Compare to", ["MoM", "QoQ", "YoY", "Previous period"], key="w:compare")
compare_start, compare_end = get_compare_range(start, end, comparison)
st.info(f"Comparing with:  \n{compare_start} - {compare_end}")
return start, end, compare_start, compare_end
```

CHANGES TO FILTER_PANEL.PY

filter_panel.py has multiselects we need to add a key to:

```python
...
def filter_panel(df):
  ...
  with st.expander("Filters"):
    ...
    for idx, dim in enumerate(filter_dims):
      with filter_cols[idx]:
        ...
        filters[dim] = st.multiselect(
            dim, unique_vals, key=f'w:filter|{dim}')
  return filters
```

In this case, since multiple widgets are populated through a loop, we use the f-string `f'w:filter|{dim}'` as the key, using the dimension name `dim` to differentiate between the keys.

CHANGES TO PIE_CHART.PY AND TIME_SERIES_CHART.PY

In pie_chart.py, add a key to the `st.selectbox` assigned to `split_dimension`:

```python
...
    split_dimension = st.selectbox(
      "Group by",
      ["Age group", "Gender", "State", "Category",
       "Segment", "Product name"],
      key="w:pie_split"
    )
```

Similarly, in time_series_chart.py, add keys to `grain` and `split_dimension` in the `time_series_chart` function:

```python
...
def time_series_chart(df):
  with st.container(border=True):
    grain_options = ["Day", "Week", "Month", "Year"]
    grain = st.select_slider("Time grain", grain_options, key="w:ts_grain")
    ...
```

With the widget keys in place, we can now call the relevant functionality we defined earlier in query_params.py from dashboard.py:

```
...
from query_params import set_widget_defaults, set_params

st.set_page_config(layout='wide')
set_widget_defaults()


...


set_params()
```

Pay attention to exactly where we've placed the calls to `set_widget_defaults` and `set_params`. As mentioned earlier, we can only use `st.session_state` to set widget key values *before* any of the widgets are created, so the call to `set_widget_defaults()` needs to go right at the top (just after `st.set_page_config(layout='wide')`, which needs to be the first command).

On the other hand, the query parameters need to capture changes to *any* widget that the user has changed, so the call to `set_params` has to go at the very *end* of dashboard.py, after all the widgets have been created.

Let's test out our deeplinks! Save everything and rerun the app. Then try making the following selections in the app:

- Set Start Date to 2024/07/01, and Compare To to YoY.
- Set the Time Grain slider in the line chart to Week.

If you now check the URL in your browser's address bar, it should look something like: http://localhost:8501/?w%3Ats_grain=Week&w%3Acompare=YoY&w%3Aend=2024 -08-31&w%3Astart=2024-07-01&w%3Apie_split=Age+group.

When a URL contains certain special characters, such as a colon (`:`) or a space, it is converted into *percent-encoded* characters to ensure that browsers and web servers interpret them correctly. Each special character is typically replaced by a % sign followed by a two-digit hexadecimal code that represents the original character in the ASCII standard. One exception is the space character, which, when it appears in the query parameters part of the URL, is encoded as a + sign.

In our case, the following substitutions have occurred:

- The colon character has become `%3A`, so `w:ts_grain` becomes `w%3Ats_grain`
- The space character has become `+`, so `Age group` becomes `Age+group`

Reverse those substitutions and the URL becomes: http://localhost:8501/?w:ts_grain= Week&w:compare=YoY&w:end=2024-08-31&w:start=2024-07-01&w:pie_split=Age group.

This is as expected—the selections are reflected in the URL (including the pie chart dimension selectbox, which gets a non-blank value—`Age group`—by default, which is automatically captured in the URL).

> **NOTE** The URL starts with http://localhost: because we're developing locally. When deployed, the localhost part will be replaced by the app's address. For

instance, on Streamlit Community Cloud under https://ceo-dashboard.streamlit .app, our URL with query parameters would look something like https://ceo -dashboard.streamlit.app?query_param1=value1&query_param2=...

Next, paste the original URL you copied into another browser tab and navigate to it. Unfortunately, the app throws an error (see figure 7.16).

```
StreamlitAPIException: DateInput value should either be an date/datetime or a list/tuple of 0 - 2 date/datetime values

Traceback:

File "/Users/aneevdavis/projects/streamlit_book/streamlit-in-action/chapter_7/in_progress_09/dashboard.py"
    start, end, compare_start, compare_end = date_range_panel()
                                             ^^^^^^^^^^^^^^^^^^^^

File "/Users/aneevdavis/projects/streamlit_book/streamlit-in-action/chapter_7/in_progress_09/date_range_pa
    start = st.date_input("Start date", key="w:start")
            ^^^^^^^^^^^^^^^^^^^^^^^^^^^^^^^^^^^^^^^^^^^^
```

Figure 7.16 **We get an error when we inadvertently pass a string to an** `st.date_input` **(see chapter_07/in_ progress_09 in the GitHub repo for the full code).**

The error says we passed the wrong kind of value to a DateInput, presumably the Start date and/or End date widgets. In the (parsed) URL above, the value given to the start date widget (with the key `w:start`) is the string `2024-07-01`:

```
w:start=2024-07-01
```

When Streamlit attempts to assign this value to the date input widget, it errors because `st.date_input` expects a date object, not a string. There's a similar problem with our filter inputs: these widgets expect lists (as you can select multiple values), but we're passing strings. We need logic to handle lists and dates, not just strings.

To fix this, when setting a widget value in `st.query_params`, add a prefix to denote lists or dates—say `L#` for a list and `D#` for a date. Here's the `set_params` function in query_ params.py with this modification:

```python
import streamlit as st
from datetime import date

...
def set_params():
  query_params_dict = {}
  for key in st.session_state:
    if key.startswith('w:'):
      value = st.session_state[key]
```

```
    if value:
      if isinstance(value, list):
        value = f'L#{",".join(value)}'
      elif isinstance(value, date):
        value = f'D#{value.isoformat()}'
      query_params_dict[key] = value
  st.query_params.from_dict(query_params_dict)
```

See https://github.com/aneevdavis/streamlit-in-action/blob/main/chapter_07/in_
progress_10/query_params.py for the exact file.

Before adding a value to `query_params_dict`, we check its type using `isinstance`. If
it's a list, we convert it to a string in a specific format (e.g., `['M', 'F']` becomes `L#M,F`).
If it's a date, we convert it into a different format (e.g,. `2024-08-01` becomes `D#2024-08
-01`). We also need the reverse logic to decode these string formats and convert them
into the original values. This part goes in the `get_param` function, which we'll rewrite
entirely:

```
def get_param(key):
  if key not in st.query_params:
    return None
  value = st.query_params[key]
  if value.startswith('L#'):
    return value[2:].split(',')
  if value.startswith('D#'):
    return date.fromisoformat(value[2:])
  return value
```

For each key, if the value starts with `L#` or `D#`—we convert it back to a list or date,
respectively. When used in `set_widget_defaults`, the returned value will be the correct type which removes the error. You can see for yourself by retrying the earlier
steps. You should now see figure 7.17, which demonstrates that you can copy and
paste the current URL of your dashboard to share with others exactly what you're
seeing.

Explore the deeplinks some more. Note n' Nib's execs can now spend less time fid-
dling with the dashboard and more time making decisions!

7.7 Sourcing data from a data warehouse

We've addressed all user feedback on the dashboard, but there's one glaring practical
problem with it that we've yet to discuss: the data displayed in the dashboard is sourced
from a static CSV file.

I chose this approach to keep our focus on data processing rather than data ingestion. Reading from a static CSV file is the easiest way to ingest data in our app. However,
this method has several drawbacks:

- While a CSV is manageable when dealing with a small amount of data, it quickly
  becomes inefficient when handling large datasets.

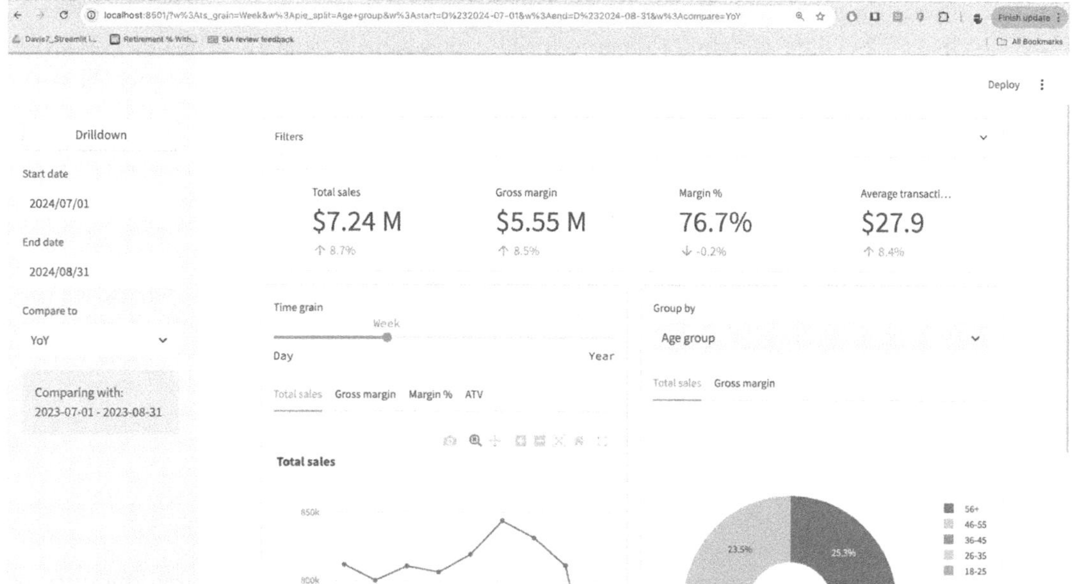

Figure 7.17 The URL values populate the dashboard widgets (see chapter_07/in_progress_10 in the GitHub repo for the full code).

- We can't query the data flexibly at the source and instead have to load it into memory to perform operations such as filtering, aggregations, and joins.

In the real world, data is typically stored in a *data warehouse,* a specialized system designed to manage large volumes of structured data. In this section, we'll replace our CSV file with a table in a data warehouse—specifically, Google BigQuery.

7.7.1 Getting data into BigQuery

Google BigQuery is a cloud-based data warehouse service that's part of the Google Cloud Platform (GCP). It lets you efficiently store and analyze massive datasets using *Structured Query Language* (SQL), without needing to manage infrastructure or worrying about scaling.

To get started, set up a GCP account at cloud.google.com. You'll need to provide a payment method, but you won't be charged since we're only using free resources for this exercise.

When you create a new account, Google also creates a *GCP project* for you. In GCP, a project is a container for organizing and managing your Google Cloud resources. You need one to use BigQuery; you can use the default or create a new one. A project has a unique ID; you can choose what this is when you create a project, but the default one is a randomly generated string. For instance, my default project ID was `dauntless-brace-436702-q0`.

Next, navigate to BigQuery. Google Cloud offers many products and services, which can make its UI intimidating to beginners. The most reliable way to find BigQuery is probably to enter the search string "bigquery" in the search box at the top (see figure 7.18)

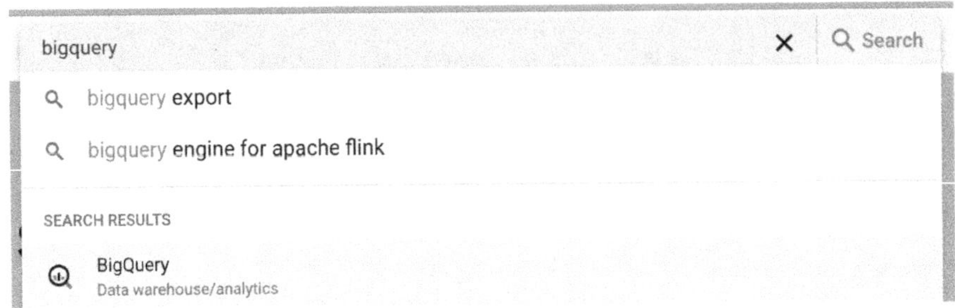

Figure 7.18   The most reliable way to find something on GCP is to use the search bar.

Once on the BigQuery page, you'll see your BigQuery resources organized under your GCP projects in an Explorer side panel to the left (see figure 7.19). "Resources" here means things like "queries", "notebooks", "workflows", etc., all of which you may ignore.

We're going to create a BigQuery table by uploading our CSV file. Before we can do this, we need to create a *dataset*. A BigQuery dataset organizes your tables within a project.

Create your first dataset by clicking the three dots next to your project ID in the Explorer panel and then Create Dataset (figure 7.19).

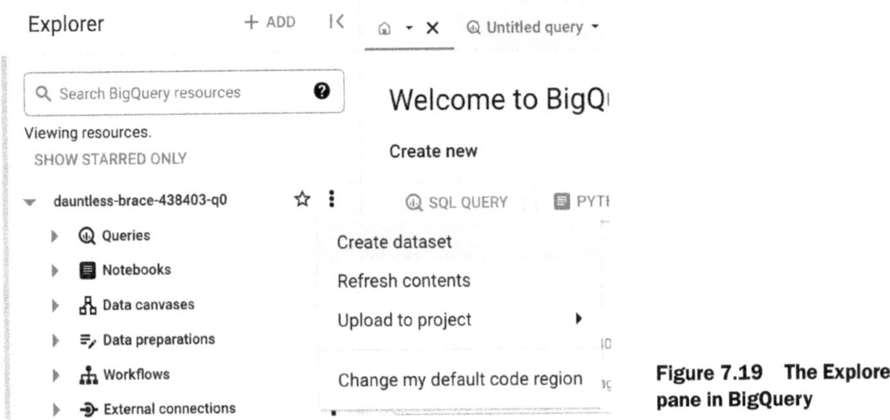

Figure 7.19   The Explorer pane in BigQuery

This opens a screen where you can configure the dataset. Enter a name (I chose `sia_ceo_dashboard`); you can use the defaults for the remaining options.

Once created, your dataset should appear in the Explorer panel. Click the three dots next to it and select Create Table to access the table creation screen, where you can upload your file. Select Upload under the Create Table From options, and CSV as the file format. You can then select the `sales_data.csv` file from your local disk. Pick a name for the table (`sales_data` works). The remaining options should be straightforward and will likely be auto-populated: your project ID and the name of the dataset you just created. Figure 7.20 shows this screen.

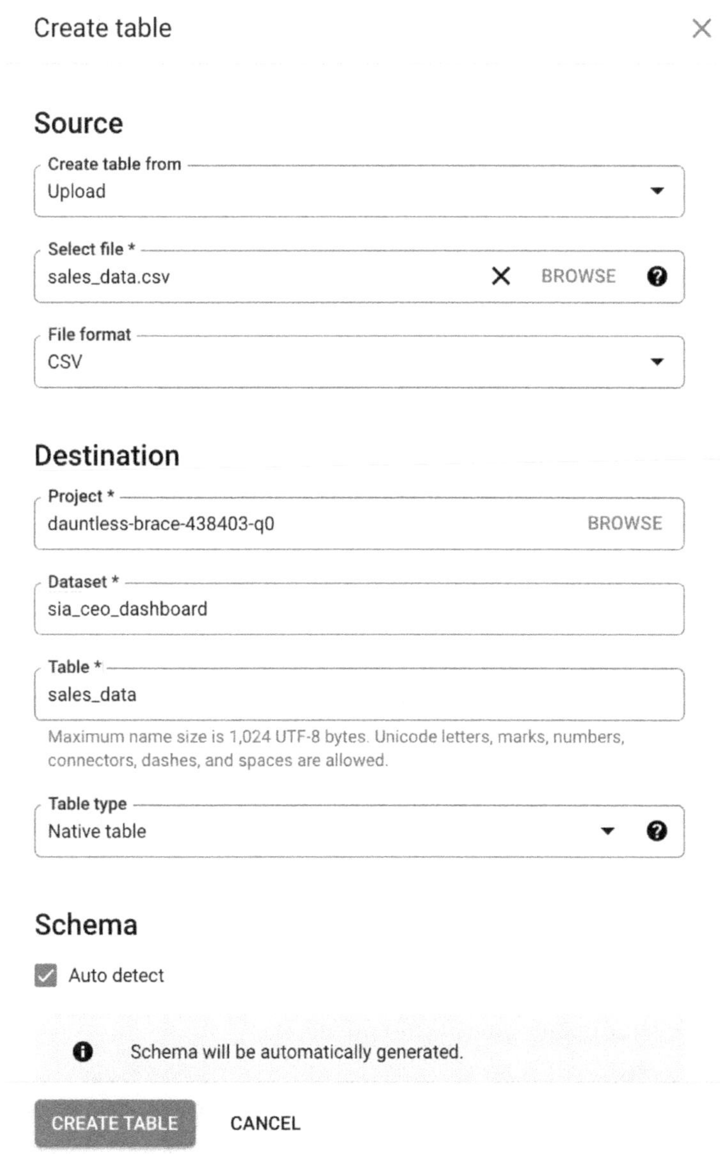

Create table   ✕

Source

Create table from
Upload ▼

Select file *
sales_data.csv   ✕   BROWSE   ❓

File format
CSV ▼

Destination

Project *
dauntless-brace-438403-q0   BROWSE

Dataset *
sia_ceo_dashboard

Table *
sales_data

Maximum name size is 1,024 UTF-8 bytes. Unicode letters, marks, numbers, connectors, dashes, and spaces are allowed.

Table type
Native table ▼ ❓

Schema

☑ Auto detect

ℹ Schema will be automatically generated.

CREATE TABLE   CANCEL

Figure 7.20 The table creation screen in BigQuery

Check the Auto Detect box under Schema so you don't have to enter it manually. Then click the button at the bottom to create your table. Your data is now in BigQuery, and the table should appear under your dataset in Explorer. You can click on it and navigate to the "Preview" tab to view the data.

7.7.2   *Setting up the Python-BigQuery connection*

We can now access our data in the BigQuery interface, but we also need to be able to connect to it from our Python code.

ENABLING THE BIGQUERY AND BIGQUERY STORAGE APIS

First, enable a couple of BigQuery-related APIs in our GCP project: the BigQuery and BigQuery Storage APIs. The BigQuery API enables us to connect to BigQuery in the first place, while the Storage API enables faster ingestion of data into a Pandas dataframe.

These APIs may already be enabled, but if not, you can enable them manually by searching for "BigQuery API" and then for "BigQuery Storage API." In each case, the corresponding result should lead you to a page where you can enable the API.

CREATING A SERVICE ACCOUNT

Since our app will connect to BigQuery programmatically, we need a *GCP service account* to handle authentication. A service account is a special type of account that belongs to your application, rather than to an individual user. It enables your app to authenticate and interact with Google Cloud services, including BigQuery.

To create a service account, first navigate to "IAM & Admin" and then select "Service accounts" in the Google Cloud navigation menu (or search for "service accounts" and click the first result).

On the Service Accounts page, click the option to create one. This screen will ask you for a service account name (I used `sia_service_account`) and description. Once you've created the account, you'll also need to grant it access to your project on the same screen. Choose the role Viewer when you do this. Your service account should now appear in the Service Accounts page.

CREATING A SERVICE ACCOUNT KEY

We have a service account that can access our BigQuery resources, but we still need to obtain the credentials that will let our Streamlit app act *as* the service account. For this, we require a service account key. Find the account you just created on the Service Accounts page, click the three dots under Actions next to it, and then click Manage Keys.

Click ADD KEY > Create New Key and select JSON as the key type. When you click Create, your computer should automatically download a JSON file. Inspect this file in a text editor. It should contain the credentials you need to access BigQuery from your app, as well as additional details such as your project ID.

GENERATING SECRETS.TOML

The credentials we've obtained must be kept secret, as they allow anyone who has them to read your BigQuery data. Recall from chapter 5 that the best way to store confidential info in Streamlit is to use a secrets.toml file in conjunction with `st.se-crets`. Unfortunately, the credential file we have is in JSON, so we need to convert it to TOML. You can do this manually, but let's use Python instead.

First, create a .streamlit folder to hold your secrets.toml. Rename your JSON file to sia-service-account.json, then open a Python shell from the same folder and enter the following commands:

```
>>> import json
>>> import toml
>>> with open('sia-service-account.json') as json_file:
...     config = json.load(json_file)
...
>>> obj_to_write = {'bigquery': config}
>>> with open('.streamlit/secrets.toml', 'a') as toml_file:
...     toml.dump(obj_to_write, toml_file)
...
'[bigquery]\ntype = "service_account"\nproject_id = "dauntless-...'
<Rest excluded for brevity>
```

> **NOTE** If it doesn't work, run `pip install toml` first.

Here, we open the JSON file from GCP, load it into a Python dictionary, and write it back to secrets.toml under the key "bigquery". If you now open secrets.toml, you should be able to see the credentials in TOML format.

```
[bigquery]
type = "service_account"
project_id = "dauntless-brace-436702-q0"
private_key_id = ...
...
```

7.7.3 *Updating the dashboard to load data from BigQuery*

It's time to update our code to source data from BigQuery instead of a static CSV file. We need to install three new Python modules, so enter the following commands into a terminal window:

```
pip install google-cloud-bigquery
pip install google-cloud-bigquery-storage
pip install db-dtypes
```

The first two packages are needed to access the BigQuery and BigQuery Storage APIs. `db-dtypes` is required to enable converting the data returned by BigQuery to a Pandas dataframe.

Since our code is modular, we only need to update the `load_data` function in data_loader.py, and the rest of our app should work as before. This is an advantage of the "separation of concerns" principle we discussed in chapter 3. Listing 7.3 shows the new data_loader.py with `load_data` re-implemented to use BigQuery (chapter_07/in_progress_11/data_loader.py in the GitHub repo).

Listing 7.3   data_loader.py reimplemented to use BigQuery

```python
import streamlit as st
from google.cloud import bigquery, bigquery_storage

DATASET = "sia_ceo_dashboard"
TABLE = "sales_data"

def load_data():
  service_account_info = st.secrets["bigquery"]
  client = bigquery.Client.from_service_account_info(service_account_info)
  creds = client._credentials
  storage_client = bigquery_storage.BigQueryReadClient(credentials=creds)
  project_id = service_account_info["project_id"]
  query = f"SELECT * from `{project_id}.{DATASET}.{TABLE}`"
  query_job = client.query(query)
  result = query_job.result()
  return result.to_dataframe(bqstorage_client=storage_client)
```

We keep a couple of constants at the top (`DATASET` and `TABLE`) to hold the names of the dataset and table we created in BigQuery. Within `load_data`, we first save the credentials from the `bigquery` key in `st.secrets` to `service_account_info`. We then pass in these credentials to create a BigQuery client (essentially an object that contains the methods and abstractions needed to interact with BigQuery):

```python
client = bigquery.Client.from_service_account_info(service_account_info)
```

We want to use the same credentials in the BigQuery Storage API client, so we extract the credentials from the BigQuery client and use them to initialize `storage_client`:

```python
creds = client._credentials
storage_client = bigquery_storage.BigQueryReadClient(credentials=creds)
```

The connection is now established.

Tables in BigQuery are referred to using a dot-separated combination of the project ID, dataset name, and table name. For instance, the table I created would be referenced as:

```python
dauntless-brace-436702-q0.sia_ceo_dashboard.sales_data
```

We obtain the project ID from the credentials (`project_id = service_account_info["project_id"]`) and the dataset and table names from the constants defined earlier.

We use the table reference to construct a SQL query like this:

```python
query = f"SELECT * from `{project_id}.{DATASET}.{TABLE}`"
```

We'll encounter more SQL in chapter 8, but for the moment, all you need to understand is that "SELECT * from <table>" means "get me all the columns from <table>". Essentially, we're telling BigQuery to return all the data in the table.

Though we're not doing it here, we could have used a different SQL query to obtain some *subset* of the data; we couldn't have done this if we were still using a CSV file. Often, the data you're trying to access may be very large, in which case filtering it within the data warehouse using SQL would be more efficient than trying to load all of it in memory first. The next two lines execute the query itself, wait for it to finish, and save the results to result:

```
query_job = client.query(query)
result = query_job.result()
```

Lastly, we convert the result to a pandas dataframe, utilizing the BigQuery Storage client for better performance, and return it.

If you execute streamlit run dashboard.py again (you can't just rerun the app in the browser since we're using st.cache_data and simply rerunning would return a previously cached version), the app will now pull data from BigQuery!

7.7.4 *Notes on deployment to Streamlit Community Cloud*

In chapter 5, we explored how to deploy our apps to Streamlit Community Cloud. The process is the same for our metrics dashboard, but there are a few key points to note. First, consider where the data is stored. When deploying, if you're using the static CSV approach to source the data, you need to commit the CSV file to Git, essentially storing it in your GitHub repository.

If you're using BigQuery, the CSV is not required, and you don't have to check it into your repository. However, you do need to configure your GCP credentials in Streamlit Community Cloud using the same process we used in chapter 5.

You'll also need to create a requirements.txt file with all the modules we're using and need Community Cloud to install. As discussed in chapter 5, you can use the pip freeze command to identify the specific versions of the libraries we're using.

Listing 7.4 provides an example requirements.txt for the dashboard.


```
streamlit==1.40.2
pandas==2.2.2
plotly==5.23.0
humanize==4.10.0
toml==0.10.2
google-cloud-bigquery==3.25.0
google-cloud-bigquery-storage==2.26.0
db-dtypes==1.3.0
```

We're finally ready to release version 2.0 of our dashboard! Without a doubt, there will be more feedback later, and each iteration will further refine our dashboard.

For now, it's time to bid farewell to Note n' Nib and its data needs. In the next chapter, we're shifting gears from data insights to interactive tools, as we dive into a web app for creating, storing, and sharing haikus.

Summary

- *Launching* an app is only the first step to making it successful. You also have to *land* it, ensuring that it meets your users' needs. For this, it is critical to hear from users directly.

- `st.select_slider` is a cross between `st.selectbox` and `st.slider`. Use it to impose a logical order of the options.

- `st.metric` can show the delta associated with a metric, i.e. how a value has changed over time.

- `st.dialog` is a decorator that lets you create a modal dialog—an overlay that blocks interaction with the rest of the app.

- You can use `st.container` to create placeholders in an app, rendering only the content to show once it's available.

- In pandas, dataframes have a style property you can use to set conditional rules that control how they display on screen.

- `st.query_params` is a dictionary-like object that lets you read and update URL query parameters, enabling deep links in an app.

- A data warehouse is a specialized system that stores and retrieves large amounts of data.

- Google BigQuery, part of GCP, is an example of a data warehouse. To enable an app to connect to it, create a service account key and record the credentials in `st.secrets`.

Building a CRUD app
with Streamlit

This chapter covers

- Setting up a relational database for persistent
  storage
- Performing CRUD operations using SQL
- Developing a multi-page Streamlit app
- Creating shared database connections
  in a Streamlit app
- Authenticating users

In 1957, science fiction author Theodore Sturgeon famously said, "Ninety percent of *everything* is crud." While this was originally a cynical defense of the science fiction genre—the point being that it was no different from anything else in that regard— the adage has since taken on a different meaning, becoming the worst-kept secret in software engineering: ninety percent of everything is CRUD.

By CRUD, I'm referring to Create, Read, Update, and Delete, the four mundane operations that appear repeatedly in almost any notable piece of software.

Think about it. Social media platforms like Facebook revolve around creating posts, reading feeds, updating profiles, and deleting content. E-commerce sites manage products, orders, customer accounts, and reviews with similar operations. Even something as simple as Notepad on Windows centers on creating, reading, updating, and deleting text files.

Mastering CRUD operations is essential for building a strong foundation in software design, as their implementation often involves tackling non-trivial challenges. In this chapter, we'll create a CRUD application with Streamlit, implementing these operations from scratch while covering related topics such as user authentication.

> **NOTE** The book's GitHub repository is at https://github.com/aneevdavis/ streamlit-in-action. The chapter_08 folder contains the code for chapter 8 and a requirements.txt file that lists the exact versions of all required Python libraries.

8.1 *Haiku Haven: A CRUD app in Streamlit*

For our excursion into CRUD, we're drawing inspiration from the Japanese art of *haiku*—specifically, we will create a website that allows users to write and share their own haikus. For those not intimately familiar with Japanese literature, a haiku is a short three-line poem conforming to certain rules: the first and the third lines must have five syllables, while the second must have seven. For instance, here's one I wrote about Streamlit:

> *So many web apps!*
> *With Python can I make one?*
> *Then I tried Streamlit.*

I know, right? I sometimes wonder if I missed my calling, too. Regardless, you'll notice that the poem adheres to the 5-7-5 syllable rule I mentioned above, and is therefore a valid haiku.

Haiku Haven will be a place where budding poets can author, refine, and manage haikus. It will enable users to *create* haikus from scratch, *read* what they've created, *update* a haiku once created, and *delete* it if they decide it doesn't pass muster.

8.1.1 *Stating the concept and requirements*

As usual, we'll start by stating the concept of our app succinctly:

> *Haiku Haven—a website that allows users to create, edit, and manage haikus.*

This concept, along with our earlier discussion about CRUD, should provide a basic idea of what we want. However, let's outline the concrete requirements so we're on the same page regarding the Haiku Haven vision.

REQUIREMENTS

Users of Haiku Haven should be able to:

- Create and log in to an account with a username and password
- Create haikus under their username
- View the haikus they created
- Update haikus
- Delete their haikus

Hopefully, you'll realize how frequently you encounter this kind of app. If you replace the word "haiku" in the requirements with "image", you get a barebones version of Instagram. Substitute "task" to get a productivity tool like Asana or "post" to get Twitter or WordPress.

The point is that these requirements aren't just about haikus—they represent a universal pattern in software design. Almost every app revolves around managing some kind of data, founded on CRUD operations. By building Haiku Haven, you're not just creating a playful app for poetry lovers; you're learning how to construct the essential workflows of modern software. You'll tackle user authentication, data storage, and retrieval—skills that apply to nearly any app or system you might create in the future.

WHAT'S OUT OF SCOPE

We could fit a lot of functionality into Haiku Haven (think of everything you can do on Twitter), but since we only have one chapter, we'll focus on the absolute core essentials. That means we *won't* concern ourselves with:

- Making haikus visible and searchable to other users. Haikus will remain private to the author.
- Social features such as liking, commenting, and sharing.
- Auxiliary functionality such as pagination.
- Advanced security features (once the basics are in place).

8.1.2   *Visualizing the user experience*

Haiku Haven will be our first multi-page app. We'll need to craft multiple experiences or flows—the account creation flow, login and logout, and the actual CRUD part (creating, reading, updating, and deleting haikus).

Figure 8.1 attempts to sketch out what the different portions of our app might look like. Because of how common these flows are in various common apps, I won't take too much space here to explain them in detail, but here are a few highlights:

- The login page uses a password for authentication, which you can set in the signup page.

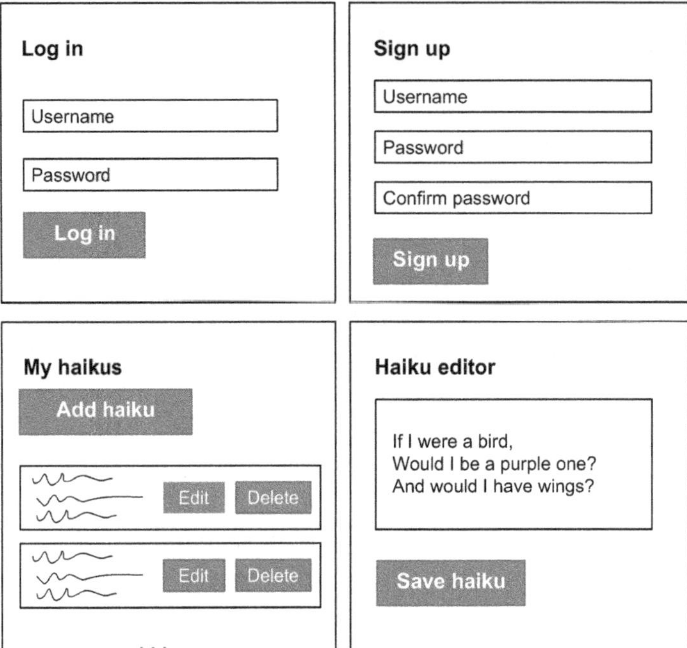

Figure 8.1   Rough sketches of the pages we want in Haiku Haven

- The My haikus page represents the logged-in experience within the app, allowing users to create, view, edit, or delete their haikus.
- There's also a haiku editor page where haikus are authored.

8.1.3   *Brainstorming the implementation*

Given that Haiku Haven represents CRUD web apps—and thus, by Sturgeon's law, 90% of *all* web apps—it stands to reason that its implementation should involve some very common patterns. Indeed, the design we'll use consists of three components that are seen in most live online applications: a frontend, a backend, and a *database*. Figure 8.2 lays out this approach.

The frontend, as we've seen in prior apps, consists of the widgets that the user interacts with. Each major action, such as creating an account or updating a haiku, calls a corresponding function in the backend.

We'll divide the functions available in the backend into two groups: one that includes actions related to users, like creating an account or authenticating a user, and another that includes haiku-related actions—creating, reading, updating, or deleting haikus.

The interesting section here—one that's new to us—is the database, which is used to permanently store information related to users and haikus in *tables*. As we'll soon see, the database also makes it easy to retrieve the information we've stored.

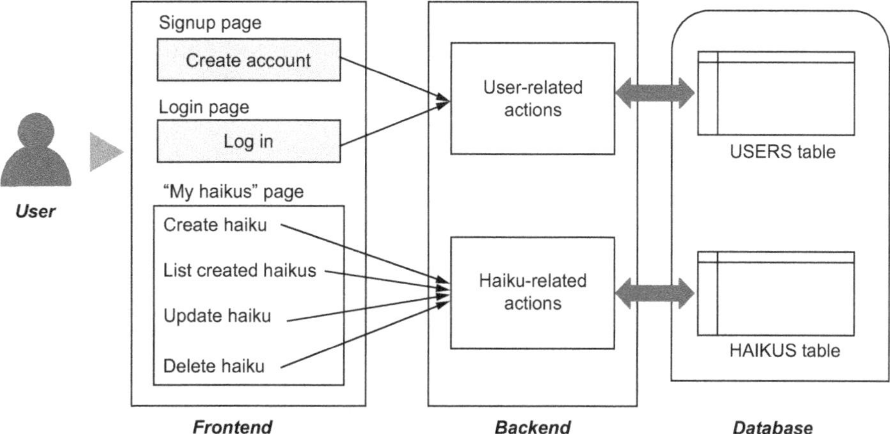

Figure 8.2 Design for the app showing a frontend, backend, and database

While our app is intentionally simple, it captures the core elements of most web applications: a frontend for user interaction, a backend for handling requests, and a database for storing and retrieving data. These three pillars work together seamlessly, forming the foundation of countless applications, whether simple or complex.

8.2 Setting up persistent storage

One of the most important deficiencies in the apps we've created thus far is the lack of persistent storage. Essentially, in all of our apps so far, if the user closes their browser window, they lose their data and progress. This won't do at all for Haiku Haven; we need users to be able to save and access their haikus after they log out and log back in again at some point in the future—we need to store data *outside* of the app itself.

There are several approaches to solving the problem of data storage, but we'll use a fairly common technique: a relational database.

8.2.1 Relational database concepts

A *relational database* is a type of data storage system that organizes data into structured *tables*, where each table consists of *rows* (also called *records*) and *columns* (also called *fields*). A row represents some kind of entry or entity, and a column is an attribute of the entity. A *schema* defines the structure of these tables, including the *data types* of each column and the *relationships* between different tables.

Relational databases rely on a language called Structured Query Language (SQL) to create, manage, and *query* tables. If some of this rings a bell, it's likely because we've been dealing with this kind of thing for a while now. In chapters 6 and 7, we worked with pandas dataframes, which also handle tabular data. However, dataframes are stored in memory while a program is running, whereas a database is used for *persistent* storage, i.e., storage that exists even when a program finishes running.

We also briefly encountered SQL in chapter 7, where we used it to fetch the rows of the sales data stored in Google BigQuery. Indeed, BigQuery is often considered a relational database, albeit of a different kind than the one we'll use in this chapter.

8.2.2   *Haiku Haven's data model*

To understand this better, let's try to figure out how we can *model* Haiku Haven's data in a relational database. Broadly speaking, modeling data for an app consists of the following steps:

1. Identifying the *entities* involved in the app
2. Defining the *relationship* between those entities
3. Listing the *attributes* of each entity
4. Converting the entities, attributes, and relationships into a relational database schema

IDENTIFYING THE ENTITIES

Generally speaking, a good way to identify the entities involved in an app is to list all the *nouns* that represent core concepts in the app. For instance, on Twitter, the following might all be considered entities: users, tweets, retweets, direct messages, mentions, followers, hashtags, and so on.

Haiku Haven is way simpler, of course. We can easily identify the two key entities our app will need to handle: *haikus* and *users*.

DEFINING THE RELATIONSHIP BETWEEN THE ENTITIES

The relationship between any two entities should be defined in terms of the *nature* and *cardinality* of the possible interaction between them. In English, that means you should lay out *how* one entity is related to the other, and *how many* of each entity can be on each side of this relationship.

For instance, haikus and users are related because a user *can write* a haiku (the "nature" we spoke of above). Also, one user can write many haikus, while a particular haiku can only be written by one user. So the relationship between a user and a haiku is *one-to-many* or 1:n (the cardinality).

LISTING THE ATTRIBUTES OF EACH ENTITY

The attributes of an entity are the fields that describe it. In this case:

- A user has a *username* and a *password*. In real life, we'd want to capture the name of the user or the time a user's account is created, but let's keep things simple.
- A haiku has its *text* and an *author* (who happens to be a user). We should also give each haiku a *numeric ID* for easy reference. The *creation time* for a haiku may be important to display in the app, so let's consider that too.

An entity-relationship diagram (ER diagram) can represent all of these attributes, as shown in figure 8.3.

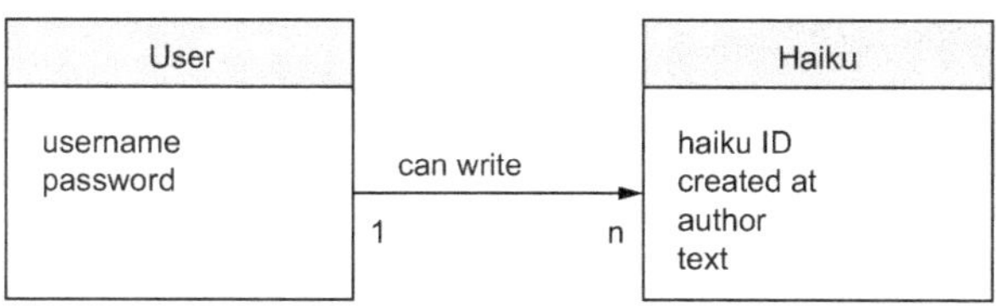

Figure 8.3 **Entity-relationship (ER) diagram showing User and Haiku entities with their attributes**

Of course, ER diagrams for real-world apps are *much* more complex than this, but I hope this serves to illustrate the concept.

CONVERTING ENTITIES, ATTRIBUTES, AND RELATIONSHIPS INTO A DATABASE SCHEMA

Creating an ER diagram helps visualize the data model, but the ultimate goal is to produce a schema that can be used in our relational database. There's no hard-and-fast rule for converting entities, attributes, and relationships into tables in a database, but *generally* speaking, entities become tables, attributes become columns, one-to-many relationships become *foreign keys* (more on this later), and many-to-many relationships become their own tables.

In our case, as figure 8.4 shows, we'll have two tables, users and haikus, with the attributes we discussed earlier as columns. Each row in users represents a single user, and each row in haikus is a single haiku. Additionally, each table has a *primary key*, which is a field that uniquely identifies any row in the table. For users, the primary key is the username field (which makes sense since every user has a username and no two users can have the same username). For haikus, it's haiku_id.

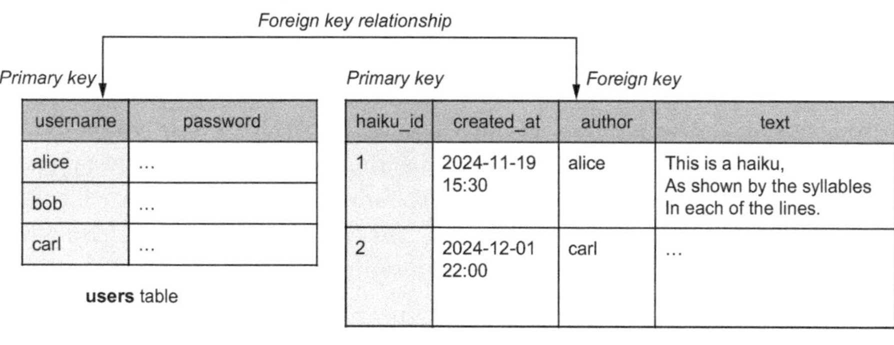

Figure 8.4 **Database schema with a foreign key relationship between the users and haikus tables**

The relationship between users and haikus is reflected in the author column of the haikus table, which contains a username that must appear in the users table. Such a column (author) is called a *foreign key* as it points to the primary key (username) of another ("foreign") table.

8.2.3 *PostgreSQL: A real relational database*

Enough theorizing! Let's now get our hands dirty with a real relational database. The one we'll use in this chapter is PostgreSQL (pronounced "post-gress-cue-ell"), one of the oldest, most robust, and most popular databases in the industry.

> **NOTE** Google BigQuery, which we encountered in chapter 7, can also be considered a relational database (though it's better described as a cloud-based data warehouse). While BigQuery is optimized for analytical use cases (like querying a large amount of data to generate reports or uncover trends), PostgreSQL is better suited for transactional use cases, such as handling frequent small updates to individual records and maintaining data consistency across concurrent operations.

INSTALLING POSTGRESQL

Towards the end of this chapter, when we deploy Haiku Haven to production, we'll use a free cloud service to set up PostgreSQL. However, for local development, we first need a local installation. To install PostgreSQL, download the installer for your operating system from https://www.postgresql.org/download/ and run it, following the on-screen instructions. For most options, you can accept the defaults. During the installation, you'll be prompted to set a password for the database superuser. Make sure to note this password—you'll need it in the next section.

Once installation is complete, you should have access to the PostgreSQL shell, called `psql`, which is located in the bin/ directory of your installation folder. If you kept the default options, this would typically be:

- /Library/PostgreSQL/17/bin/psql on macOS
- C:\Program Files\PostgreSQL\17\bin\psql on Windows

To simplify access, configure your system to run the `psql` command directly from your terminal. This requires adding the bin/ directory to your system's environment variables. You may already have done something similar for the `streamlit` command, which you can find detailed steps for in the appendix (section A.4).

If adding the path to environment variables isn't feasible for any reason, you can still use `psql` by typing its full path instead of just the command. For example:

- macOS: `/Library/PostgreSQL/17/bin/psql`
- Windows: `"C:\Program Files\PostgreSQL\17\bin\psql"` (include quotes)

Throughout the rest of this chapter, substitute the full path whenever you see `psql`, if necessary.

CREATING A DATABASE FOR HAIKU HAVEN

Once you've set up the `psql` command, log in to your local PostgreSQL instance by running the following command:

```
psql -U postgres -d postgres
```

When prompted for a password, enter the one you configured during installation. This command logs you into PostgreSQL as the default user (`-U`) `postgres`, which is an administrative user allowed to do whatever they want. The `-d` specifies that you want to connect to the default database, which is—rather confusingly, if you ask me—also called `postgres`. You should see the `psql` prompt that looks like this:

```
postgres=#
```

When your app talks to PostgreSQL, you don't want it to be running with broad administrative privileges—that would be a security nightmare. Instead, let's create a more narrowly-scoped user. Enter this into the `psql` prompt, replacing the quoted string with a password of your choice:

```
CREATE USER haiku_lord WITH PASSWORD '<Pick a password you like>';
```

Obviously, you can use whatever username you like, but I'll assume we're going with `haiku_lord`. If that works (don't forget the ending semicolon!), you should get an output line that just says `CREATE ROLE`.

Before you can create tables in PostgreSQL, you need to first make a *database* (which you can think of here as a container for tables). The `haiku_lord` user you just created can't do that yet, so enter this command to let it:

```
ALTER USER haiku_lord CREATEDB;
```

Now that we have an appropriately privileged Haiku Haven-specific user, we're done with the default `postgres` user, so exit out of the `psql` shell by typing `exit`, and then rerun it like so:

```
psql -U haiku_lord -d postgres
```

Assuming you entered the password you selected for `haiku_db` when prompted, you're again connected to the `postgres` database, but now you're acting under the capacity of `haiku_lord` (if you like, you can verify this by typing `SELECT current_user;`).

To create a database called `haikudb` to hold the tables for Haiku Haven, enter:

```
CREATE DATABASE haikudb;
```

You can list all the databases available in your local PostgreSQL instance by typing `\l`. You should now be able to see `haikudb`, along with `postgres` and a couple of others.

To start using our database, we need to connect to it. To do this, type:

```
\c haikudb;
```

A confirmation message—You are now connected to database "haikudb" as user "haiku_lord"—should let you know that this worked.

Keep this terminal window with the `psql` shell open. We're going to keep coming back to it throughout this chapter. If you do end up closing it, you can get back to this state by typing:

```
psql -U haiku_lord -d haikudb
```

8.2.4   *A crash course in SQL*

The SQL in PostgreSQL stands for Structured Query Language. Variously pronounced as "sequel" and "ess-cue-ell", SQL is the language of databases, used to create and update tables, and most importantly, to *query* them to get exactly the data we need. It's also one of the most popular and useful languages to know if you're a developer or work in the field of data in any capacity. If you don't know SQL, today's your lucky day because we're going to breeze through the basics in this section.

CREATING TABLES

Previously in this chapter, we developed Haiku Haven's database schema, which contains two tables: `users` and `haikus`. We will create these tables in PostgreSQL. Go back to the `psql` shell where you're connected to the `haikudb` database (or rerun `psql` as indicated earlier), and enter the following SQL command:

```
CREATE TABLE users (
  username VARCHAR(100) PRIMARY KEY,
  password_hash VARCHAR(128)
);
```

The `CREATE TABLE` command creates a table with a specific schema. In the above, the name of the table is `users`, and it has two columns: `username` and `password_hash`, which, if you recall, are the two fields we settled on earlier as being important attributes of a user.

Why does it say `password_hash` instead of just `password`? Bear with me, please— I'll explain this a little later in the chapter. For now, let's just think of it as the user's password.

Turn your attention to the lines where we've defined the columns:

```
username VARCHAR(100) PRIMARY KEY,
password_hash VARCHAR(128)
```

These sequences, separated by commas, are *column specifications* that let you configure each column, including specifying the data type. `VARCHAR` is one such data type in PostgreSQL; it's a string type that can have a varying number of characters. `VARCHAR(100)` means that the column can have any number of characters up to 100. If you try to store more than 100 characters, PostgreSQL will throw an error.

You'll also notice `PRIMARY KEY` against the `username` column. This denotes that the `username` column will be used to uniquely identify a row in the users table. Among other things, this means that every row in users must have a username, and that only one user can have a particular username.

To check that this worked, you can use the psql command \dt, which lists all the tables in the current database. Doing so now should give you:

```
          List of relations
 Schema | Name  | Type  |   Owner
--------+-------+-------+------------
 public | users | table | haiku_lord
(1 row)
```

Next, let's create our second table, haikus, with another CREATE TABLE command:

```
CREATE TABLE haikus (
  haiku_id SERIAL PRIMARY KEY,
  created_at TIMESTAMPTZ DEFAULT CURRENT_TIMESTAMP,
  author VARCHAR(100),
  text TEXT,
  FOREIGN KEY (author) REFERENCES users(username)
);
```

There are a few new things here:

- haiku_id, the primary key, has a data type of SERIAL. This means that PostgreSQL will automatically provide the value for this column as an auto-incrementing integer. The first row inserted will have 1 as its haiku_id, the second will have 2, and so on.

- created_at has the data type TIMESTAMPTZ, which is a timestamp with time zone information. The DEFAULT keyword specifies the value to put in this column if one is not explicitly provided while inserting a row in the table. In this case, we want the current timestamp (CURRENT_TIMESTAMP) to be provided as this default value.

- text has a data type of TEXT, which is like VARCHAR but with no maximum character length. This makes sense for the actual content of the haiku.

- The last line, FOREIGN KEY (author) REFERENCES users(username), says that the author column must have a value that exists in the username column of some row in the users table. This is called a *foreign key constraint*.

INSERTING ROWS INTO TABLES

Next, let's populate these tables with rows using SQL's INSERT INTO statement. We'll first create a new user by adding a row to the users table:

```
INSERT INTO users (username, password_hash) VALUES ('alice', 'Pass_word&34');
```

The INSERT INTO command inserts a row into the table by specifying the column values. The (username, password_hash) after the table name users says that the column values we're about to specify correspond to the columns username and password_hash, in that order.

The part after VALUES gives the actual values to enter. The effect here is that users now has one row—with a username of alice and password_hash set to Pass_word&34.

Now that we have a row in the users table, we can create one in haikus too:

```
INSERT INTO haikus (author, text) VALUES
('alice', E'Two foxes leap high\nOne lands safely on the earth\nWhere is the
other?');
```

Note here that though haikus has four columns, we're only specifying the values for two of them—author and text. PostgreSQL automatically provides the haiku_id as well as a default value for created_at. Also notice the E before the starting quote of the haiku. This marks the value as an *escape string*, correctly translating the \n escape sequence into a newline character.

Before we query these tables, let's add another unsettling haiku under alice for good measure:

```
INSERT INTO haikus (author, text) VALUES
('alice', E'Five frogs are jumping\nFour come down as expected\nBut one goes
missing.');
```

QUERYING TABLES

The real strength of SQL lies in the versatile ways in which we can *query* tables (read data from them) once they have been populated with rows.

To retrieve data, we use the SELECT statement. This command allows us to specify the columns we want to see and filter rows based on certain criteria. Let's start with a simple query to fetch all the rows and columns from the users table:

```
SELECT * FROM users;
```

The * indicates that we want to retrieve all columns from the table. As a result of this, we'll see a list of all users along with their associated user_id and password_hash. We only currently have one user, so we get:

```
 username | password_hash
----------+---------------
 alice    | Pass_word&34
(1 row)
```

> **NOTE** If you're horrified to see passwords so easily queried, don't worry! As we'll soon see, we're not actually going to be storing passwords like this.

We could also choose to only retrieve certain columns from the table. For example, if we only want the haiku_id, created_at, and author fields from the haikus table, we could write:

```
SELECT haiku_id, created_at, author FROM haikus;
```

This yields:

```
 haiku_id |           created_at          | author
----------+-------------------------------+--------
        1 | 2024-12-10 16:12:11.71654-08  | alice
        2 | 2024-12-10 16:12:16.364669-08 | alice
(2 rows)
```

We can also filter the rows we want to see based on a condition (or set of conditions) using a `WHERE` clause. For example, if we want to see the `haiku_id` and `text` for only haikus that are written by `alice` and contain `"fox"`, we could use the following:

```
SELECT haiku_id, text FROM haikus WHERE author = 'alice' AND text LIKE '%fox%';
```

to get:

```
 haiku_id |               text
----------+-------------------------------
        1 | Two foxes leap high          +
          | One lands safely on the earth+
          | Where is the other?
(1 row)
```

We've filtered the `haikus` table using two conditions separated by the keyword `AND` here: `author = 'alice'`, and `text LIKE '%fox%'`.

The `LIKE` keyword is used to perform text-matching. The % symbol means "zero or more characters," making `%fox%` a pattern that matches any text containing the substring 'fox' anywhere within it.

The `SELECT` statement can do a *lot* more than this, such as calculating summary statistics, aggregating rows, fetching data from multiple tables by joining them and more, but these are out of the scope of this chapter.

UPDATING TABLES

You can update rows in a table after you've inserted them, using the `UPDATE` statement. For example, let's say you want to add the string [By Alice] to the start of the haiku with `haiku_id` 1:

```
UPDATE haikus SET text = '[By Alice] ' || text WHERE haiku_id = 1;
```

Here we're setting the column `text` in the `haikus` table for rows where the `haiku_id` is 1. The The || operator is used in SQL to concatenate strings, so `SET text = '[By Alice] ' || text` adds [By Alice] to the beginning. If we now `SELECT` the text for that haiku with:

```
SELECT text FROM haikus WHERE haiku_id = 1;
```

we'll get:

```
            text
--------------------------------
 [By Alice] Two foxes leap high+
 One lands safely on the earth +
 Where is the other?
(1 row)
```

Though we've only updated one row here, `UPDATE` will update all the rows that match the `WHERE` clause. If we omit the `WHERE` clause, the `UPDATE` will apply to every single row in the table.

DELETING ROWS (AND TABLES)

To delete rows from a table, we use the `DELETE FROM` command. Just as in the case of `UPDATE`, it uses a `WHERE` condition to determine the rows to delete. So we could delete the haiku with ID 2 by running:

```
DELETE FROM haikus WHERE haiku_id = 2;
```

Be careful with this command! If you omit the `WHERE` clause, `DELETE FROM` will delete *every single* row!

Finally, we can delete a table itself (as opposed to just the rows in the table), by using the `DROP TABLE` command. For instance, if we wanted to remove the `haikus` table (which we don't, for now), we could have entered:

```
DROP TABLE haikus;
```

Of course, there's much more to SQL than what we've learned—indeed, entire careers can be forged by knowing it well enough—but this is all we'll need for this chapter.

8.2.5   *Connecting PostgreSQL to the app*

We've now set up the database for Haiku Haven. We've also learned to insert rows and query our database *manually*. What's left is to enable our app to query and make changes to the database *programmatically*, through Python.

For this, we'll employ a built-in feature of Streamlit called `st.connection`. This makes it easy to work with a variety of databases—including PostgreSQL—while handling much of the complexity behind the scenes. To get this to work, we'll need to install two additional modules:

- *SQLAlchemy*—A powerful database toolkit Streamlit uses under the hood to manage connections and execute queries. To install it, run `pip install sqlalchemy` in a new terminal window.

- *psycopg2*—The PostgreSQL adapter that SQLAlchemy uses to connect to PostgreSQL. Run `pip install psycopg2-binary` to install it.

After installation, both tools work quietly behind the scenes when you call `st.connection`.

CREATING A DATABASE CLASS

With the right modules installed, we're ready to begin writing the code for the app.

In this chapter, we're going to organize our code in two folders: backend and frontend, and a main entrypoint script (the one we'll use with `streamlit run`) that lies outside of either.

There are several places in the app where we'll need to access the database—while setting up users, creating haikus, etc.—and we'd rather not have to rewrite the connection logic each time. It would be nice if we had a database object that we could just ask to execute the queries we need, without having to worry about how the connection happens under the hood. Whenever we want to run a particular query, we should be able to write `database.execute_query(query, params)`, passing in the query we want to execute and the parameters we want to give it.

To set this up, let's create a `Database` *class*. Create a new Python file called database.py within the backend folder and copy the code in listing 8.1 (chapter_08/in_progress_01/backend/database.py in the GitHub repo).

> **Listing 8.1   The Database class**

```python
import streamlit as st
from sqlalchemy import text

class Database:
  def __init__(self):
    self.conn = st.connection("haikuconn", type="sql")

  def execute_query(self, query, params={}, write=False):
    with self.conn.session as session:
      try:
        result = session.execute(text(query), params)
        if write:
          session.commit()
        return result.fetchall()
      except Exception:
        if write:
          session.rollback()
        raise
```

By this point, you should be used to the simple dataclasses we've used in prior chapters. Dataclasses simplify the syntax used to create classes in Python, but for more complex use cases, we need to peel back that layer and write a traditional class definition.

A class is essentially a blueprint that can be turned into a concrete Python object, which can have attributes—the object's properties or data associated with the object—and methods—or functions that define the object's behavior and can interact with its attributes.

INITIALIZING THE CONNECTION

Let's study the class definition for the `Database` class, shown in listing 8.1. We'll start with the `__init__` method:

```
class Database:
  def __init__(self):
    self.conn = st.connection("haikuconn", type="sql")
```

`__init__` (pronounced "dunder init") is a special method in Python. When an object is first created from a class, the `__init__` method is executed automatically. The only argument our `__init__` takes is `self`.

You'll see `self` extremely often in Python class definitions. The first argument to a method within a class is a special one that's not explicitly passed while calling it (as we'll see in a bit). It always refers to the object on which the method is being called. By convention, this argument is named `self`—though you can technically call it whatever you like.

The line `self.conn = st.connection("haikuconn", type="sql")` uses Streamlit's `st.connection` function to create a connection object to the database. The string `"haikuconn"` refers to a section in the secrets.toml file (we'll set that up shortly), and `type="sql"` tells Streamlit this is a SQL database.

We store the result in `self.conn`—making it an attribute of the object created from the class—so that other methods in the class can reuse it.

THE EXECUTE_QUERY METHOD

Recall that what we really want is a simple `execute_query` method that'll take care of all the underlying database connection logic. Let's turn our attention to that method:

```
def execute_query(self, query, params={}, write=False):
  with self.conn.session as session:
    try:
      result = session.execute(text(query), params)
      if write:
        session.commit()
      return result.fetchall()
    except Exception:
      if write:
        session.rollback()
      raise
```

`execute_query` accepts three arguments:

- `query` is the SQL query string you want to run
- `params` is a dictionary (defaulting to an empty one) that maps any *parameters* (variables) in the query text to the value we want to substitute them with
- `write` is a Boolean flag that tells the method whether this is a write operation (like `INSERT`, `UPDATE`, or `DELETE`) or not (`SELECT`).

For example, if we wanted to obtain all of the haikus created by `alice`, we would pass these values:

- `query="SELECT haiku_id, text FROM haikus WHERE author = :authorname"`
- `params={"authorname": "alice"}`
- `write=False`

Note how the variable in the query—`:authorname`—starts with a colon, and how the corresponding key in the `params` dictionary doesn't have one.

EXECUTING A QUERY

Inside the method, a `with` block opens a *session*:

```
with self.conn.session as session:
```

This line creates a new database session using SQLAlchemy. A session represents a "conversation" with the database; we can use it to send queries, fetch results, and (if needed) commit changes.

Next, we encounter a `try-except` block:

```
try:
  result = session.execute(text(query), params)
  if write:
    session.commit()
  return result.fetchall()
except Exception:
  if write:
    session.rollback()
  raise
```

In Python, `try-except` is a construct that's used for error handling. The idea is to write your regular code in the `try` block. If an exception occurs while running the `try` code, Python stops execution and jumps to an except block that catches the exception, allowing you to log a sensible error message, for example, or use some other kind of handling logic.

The code in the `try` block starts by executing the query:

```
result = session.execute(text(query), params)
```

The `text()` function (imported from `sqlalchemy` near the top of the file) wraps the raw SQL query string so SQLAlchemy can parse and run it correctly. The `params` argument carries the parameter values, enabling safe insertion into the query.

> **NOTE** The safety aspect here relates to preventing *SQL injection*, which is a way attackers try to trick your app into running harmful commands on your database—often by entering sneaky input. If we were building our queries by simply concatenating the user input to the rest of our query, we might accidentally run those commands. Instead, by using SQLAlchemy's `text()` function along

with the `params` dictionary, we keep the query structure and the user input separate, enabling the user input to be scrutinized.

If this is a write query (`write=True`), we commit the results:

```
if write:
  session.commit()
```

Let's take a moment to unpack what that means. When a SQL command modifies the database—like `INSERT`, `UPDATE`, or `DELETE`—those changes don't become permanent right away. Instead, they happen inside something called a *transaction.*

A transaction is like a temporary workspace. You can make changes inside it, but those changes are invisible to other users until you say, "Yes, I'm happy with this—go ahead and save it." That's what calling `session.commit()` does: it makes the changes permanent.

We then return all the results (if any) with `return result.fetchall()`. The results are in the form of a list of tuples, where each tuple represents a single row in the database. For instance, if we ran the query `SELECT haiku_id, author FROM haikus WHERE author = 'alice'` on our database, `result.fetchall()` might produce something like:

```
[(2, 'alice'), (1, 'alice')]
```

The first element in each tuple represents the `haiku_id`, and the second element represents the `author`, matching the order in which they are specified in the query.

HANDLING ERRORS

What we just described in the `try` block is the happy path, but what if some kind of error occurs (for instance, the given query might have incorrect SQL syntax) while Python is trying to execute this code? We then enter the except block marked by `except Exception`, which contains these lines:

```
if write:
  session.rollback()
raise
```

If we were trying to perform a write operation, `session.rollback()` undoes any temporary changes made so that the database is left in a pristine state.

Once that's done, we also re-raise the exception with the one-word line `raise`, letting the regular exception flow take over, such as printing the exception message to the screen. What we've achieved with the `try-except` construct is to inject ourselves into the flow when an exception occurs and make sure any partial changes are rolled back.

We now have an `execute_query` method that's flexible enough to handle both read and write queries while keeping the code clean and concise.

> **NOTE** For read queries, we don't technically need to use a session. `st.connection` objects have a direct `.query` method that can run `SELECT` queries more easily, so

we could also have written `results_df = self.conn.query("SELECT ...")` to run the query and put the output in a pandas dataframe. However, this does not support `UPDATE` or `DELETE` statements.

CONFIGURING OUR DATABASE CONNECTION

You'll notice that our `Database` class does not currently include any information about how to actually connect to our running PostgreSQL database—it has neither the name of our database nor the credentials we created in `psql`.

To complete our implementation of a database connection, we need to supply these details. As this is sensitive information, we'll make use of the secrets.toml file as we've done in the past. Without further ado, create a .streamlit folder in your app's root folder (the parent folder where you created the backend directory), and create a secrets.toml within it, with contents similar to what's shown in listing 8.2.

Listing 8.2 The .streamlit/secrets.toml file

```
[connections.haikuconn]
url = "postgresql://haiku_lord:password@localhost:5432/haikudb"
```


Let's break down what we're seeing here. Our secrets.toml has a single section called `connections.haikuconn`. The `connections` bit signals to Streamlit that this represents the configuration for `st.connection`, while `haikuconn` is the name we passed to our connection object earlier:

```
self.conn = st.connection("haikuconn", type="sql")
```

Within the section is a single key—`url`—with a value that starts with postgresql://.

We learned in prior chapters that a Streamlit app is served by a Streamlit server process which listens to a particular port (usually 8501 or something near that) on a machine. Similarly, a PostgreSQL database runs on a PostgreSQL server that listens to a different port—5432 by default, unless you set a different port number when you installed it.

To connect to this server, we need the address where it's running, the port number it's running on, the username and password of the PostgreSQL user we created, and the name of our database. We can combine all of these into a *connection string* that takes the form:

```
postgresql://<PostgreSQL username>:<Password>@<Address of server>:<Port
number>/<Database name>
```

The value we see in listing 8.2 is this connection string filled in with the right values—don't forget to replace `password` with your actual password. As we learned before, you shouldn't check secrets.toml into Git.

USING THE DATABASE CLASS IN THE APP

With a `Database` class set up, all that's left to do to enable persistent storage and retrieval in our app is to actually use the class in our Streamlit app. To do this, create our app's entrypoint file—say, main.py—in the app's root directory, with the code in listing 8.3 (chapter_08/in_progress_01/main.py in the GitHub repo).

> **Listing 8.3   An initial draft of main.py**

```
import streamlit as st
from backend.database import Database

st.title('Haiku Haven')

database = Database()
query_results = database.execute_query('SELECT * FROM haikus')
st.write(query_results)
```

This is where it all comes together! Firstly, we import the `Database` class we just created using:

```
from backend.database import Database
```

This line means "import the `Database` class from backend/database.py". Notice how, in module import paths, the path separator becomes a dot. For this line to work, Python needs to recognize the parent folder of backend as a starting point from which it can look for modules. We can do this by adding the path to the parent folder of `backend` to `sys`
`.path`, which is the list of paths that determines this in Python.

Fortunately, when you run the `streamlit run <script.py>` command, the parent folder of `<script.py>` is automatically added to `sys.path`. In this case, since the parent folder of main.py is also the parent folder of the backend directory, we don't need to do anything extra.

Next, after displaying a title, create an instance of the `Database` class:

```
database = Database()
```

You'll probably recognize this syntax from when we've used dataclasses before, but this is the first time in this book that we've instantiated a traditional class we wrote, so a deeper explanation is warranted.

What's going on here is that by calling `Database` as though it were a function, we're actually calling `Database`'s `__init__` method, which has the signature line `def __init__` `(self)`. As I mentioned earlier, `self` is automatically set to the object that's being created, so we don't need to pass it explicitly.

This lets `__init__` set up the database connection for us through `st.connection`, and gets the resulting `Database` instance in the `database` variable (note that `__init__` will return the instance even though we didn't write an explicit `return` statement).

Once we have the instance `database`, we use it to execute a simple `SELECT` query:

```
query_results = database.execute_query('SELECT * FROM haikus')
```

Again, even though `execute_query` takes `self` as its first (and only) argument, we don't need to pass it explicitly. Instead `database` itself is passed to `self`. This query has no parameters, so we let the `params` argument have the default value (an empty dictionary) by not specifying it.

Finally, we call `st.write` to display the results of the query:

```
st.write(query_results)
```

Take a look at the page now by typing `streamlit run main.py` (make sure you're in main.py's containing folder first so that Streamlit can find the .streamlit folder). You should see something similar to figure 8.5.

Haiku Haven

```
▼ [
  0 :
  "(2, datetime.datetime(2024, 12, 10, 16, 12, 16, 364669,
  tzinfo=datetime.timezone(datetime.timedelta(days=-1, seconds=57600))), 'alice',
  'Five frogs are jumping\nFour come down as expected\nBut one goes missing.')"
  1 :
  "(1, datetime.datetime(2024, 12, 10, 16, 12, 11, 716540,
  tzinfo=datetime.timezone(datetime.timedelta(days=-1, seconds=57600))), 'alice',
  '[By Alice] Two foxes leap high\nOne lands safely on the earth\nWhere is the
  other?')"
  2 :
  "(3, datetime.datetime(2024, 12, 18, 16, 28, 21, 992101,
```

Figure 8.5 **The contents of the haiku table as read by executing a** `SELECT` **query using the** `Database` **class and displayed using** `st.write` **(see chapter_08/in_progress_01 in the GitHub repo for the full code).**

One interesting thing here is how `st.write` formats the list of tuples within `query_results` in an easy-to-read form. In any case, our app is now connected to a database! Next, let's use this to enable users to create accounts.

Sharing the database between users

Let's consider how a Streamlit app works when there are multiple users accessing it simultaneously. While there's a single Streamlit server that serves the app, each time a user accesses it, a new instance of the app is created, with all of the objects

(continued)

required to run the app created anew for that user. Most of the time, this is what we want; it makes sure different user sessions don't interfere with each other. However, there are some things we don't want to create anew whenever someone loads the app in a new browser tab.

A key example is the object returned by `st.connection` in the `Database` class. We don't want to create a new connection for each user (or each tab opened by a single user). For situations like this, Streamlit offers a solution: `st.cache_resource`.

Like `st.cache_data`—which we used in chapter 6 to make loading the data in our metric dashboard faster—`st.cache_resource` is a way to make sure that only one instance of something exists across all users of an app.

While `st.cache_data` is used for caching things like pandas dataframes or the results of API calls, `st.cache_resource` (also a decorator) is used for resources like database connections.

Fortunately, we don't need to modify our `Database` class to incorporate `st.cache_resource`, as Streamlit applies it internally to the return value of `st.connection`. Our database connection is therefore shared between all of our users and sessions.

8.3 Creating user accounts

Since our users can create their own haikus, there needs to be a way for them to create Haiku Haven accounts to hold their haikus. In this section, we'll wire up our app to enable this, taking care to store passwords securely. Before we get to that, though, let's take a minute to talk about code organization.

8.3.1 Splitting the app into services

In chapter 3, we discussed the principle of *separation of concerns*—the idea that each component of our app should focus on a specific thing and be independent of the other components, interacting with them only in ways specified by a contract or API.

We'll do something similar here, separating the frontend and backend as we did in that chapter. Since we're using classes and object-oriented programming this time, we could define a backend class—let's call this `Hub`—that can be the single point of contact for frontend code to call backend code. Any function that the frontend can call should be a method in the `Hub` class. This is analogous to backend.py in chapter 3, where every backend function called from the frontend code was defined in backend.py.

We might expect the `Hub` class to have methods that fulfill actions a frontend user might want to take, such as `create_user`, `create_haiku`, `update_haiku`, etc. Over time, though, as our app grows more complex, the `Hub` class will have an increasing number of methods, slowly making it unwieldy and difficult to manage.

Rather than taking this monolithic approach, it might be a better idea to divide the actions offered by `Hub` into individual service classes, each pertaining to a specific type of action, and use the `Hub` class as merely a coordinator. For instance, we could have a `UserService` class that offers methods pertaining to users, such as `create_user`, and a `HaikuService` class that offers those related to haikus, such as `create_haiku` and `update_haiku`.

This would make our app more modular and easier to extend and maintain. We can add more user-related functionality to `UserService` independently of the haiku-related actions in `HaikuService`. If we wanted to add limericks to our app later, we could introduce a `LimerickService` without touching either of the two existing services.

With our overall code organization strategy in mind, let's turn our attention towards building one of the components—the user service.

8.3.2 Creating the user service

Just as in prior chapters, we'll use a dataclass to represent the fundamental objects we're concerned with. In chapters 3, 4, and 6, we had `Unit`, `Task`, and `Metric` classes. Here, we'll start with a `User` class.

Create a new Python file called user.py in the backend folder, with the text shown in listing 8.4 (chapter_08/in_progress_02/backend/user.py in the GitHub repo).

Listing 8.4 The `User` dataclass

```python
from dataclasses import dataclass

@dataclass
class User:
    username: str
    password_hash: str
```

You'll see that this directly mirrors the `users` table in the database, with fields for `username` and `password_hash`. Let's now discuss the latter field and why we called it `password_hash` instead of `password`.

STORING PASSWORDS SECURELY

Passwords are naturally some of the most sensitive pieces of information software developers need to deal with, and much of the field of cybersecurity focuses on keeping them secret. We know that we shouldn't store passwords in our code, resorting to the construct of `st.secrets` to avoid this. But what about storing them in a database?

Obviously, our app needs to be able to compare a user-entered password with the one associated with the user, so passwords need to be stored in some form. However, storing them directly as plain text in a database introduces a security vulnerability, because anyone who gains access to our database—through a security breach—will be able to view passwords in their raw form. How do we avoid this, though?

The answer is: with *one-way cryptographic hash functions*, or in other words, a bit of fancy math. There are certain mathematical operations that are easy to perform normally but extremely difficult to perform in reverse. As a trivial example, consider multiplying two prime numbers a and b to get c. Multiplying a and b to get c is easy, but if you're only given c, identifying a and b is difficult, especially when c is very, very large (think hundreds of digits long).

Similarly, you can think of a cryptographic hash function as an operation performed on a password that's very difficult to reverse. Let's say someone's password is `Some-Password123`. If you apply a hash function `H` to it, you might get a password hash that looks like a random sequence of characters:

```
H(SomePassword123) = g53jkdlgfee09ded8d33rr45t5y5y43f2eff
```

Rather than store the string `SomePassword123` directly in the database, we store `g53jkdlgfee09ded8d33rr45t5y5y43f2eff`. Then, when someone enters a password in our app, we apply the hash function to *that* password and compare the result to `g53jkdlgfee09ded8d33rr45t5y5y43f2eff`. If the two are the same, the user is authenticated.

How does this help with security? Well, if a hacker now manages to get into our database, they don't have the actual password, only the password hash. As stated, it's very difficult to obtain the password from the password hash.

The password hash itself is useless to the hacker, as there's no point entering it in the app—if you did, the app would simply apply the hash function to it and generate a completely different hash that would be compared against the real one.

How do we implement this in our app? Fortunately, we don't have to do it from scratch. There are third-party libraries that do it for us. We'll use `bcrypt`, which you should install now with `pip install bcrypt`.

Let's add two more methods to our `User` class so it now looks like this:

```python
from dataclasses import dataclass
import bcrypt

@dataclass
class User:
    username: str
    password_hash: str

    @staticmethod
    def hash_password(password):
        return bcrypt.hashpw(password.encode(), bcrypt.gensalt()).decode()

    def authenticate(self, password):
        return bcrypt.checkpw(password.encode(), self.password_hash.encode())
```

We've decorated the `hash_password` method with `@staticmethod`. This makes it belong to the class itself rather than to any specific instance of the class. We generally use `@staticmethod` for utility functions that are logically related to a class but don't need to access anything from a particular instance.

`hash_password` is a good fit for this since it doesn't need to access any of the instance's attributes or methods (note the absence of a `self` parameter). Rather, it simply accepts a password entered by a user, converts it into a hash using `bcrypt`, and returns it.

```python
return bcrypt.hashpw(password.encode(), bcrypt.gensalt()).decode()
```

I won't go into the details of how this works, but at a high level, we're taking an extra measure of security here by adding a random "salt" to the password (`bcrypt.gensalt()`) before hashing it. This salt helps protect the password against hackers simply looking up the password associated with a password hash from a huge pre-computed table of such hashes (called a *rainbow table*).

We also have an `authenticate` method that we'll use when a user enters a password. `bcrypt.checkpw` compares the entered password (`password.encode()`) and the password hash stored in the `User` object (`self.password_hash.encode()`), returning `True` if they match.

THE USERSERVICE CLASS

We're now ready to create the `UserService` class, which we determined would have methods for user-related operations. Create a user_service.py file under backend/ with the content in listing 8.5 (chapter_08/in_progress_02/backend/user_service.py in the GitHub repo).

Listing 8.5 The `UserService` class

```python
from backend.user import User

class UserService:
  def __init__(self, database):
    self.database = database

  def get_user(self, username):
    query = "SELECT * FROM users WHERE username = :username"
    params = {'username': username}
    results = self.database.execute_query(query, params)
    return User(*results[0]) if results else None

  def create_user(self, username, password):
    existing_user = self.get_user(username)
    if not existing_user:
      query = '''
        INSERT INTO users (username, password_hash)
          VALUES (:username, :password_hash)
          RETURNING username, password_hash
      '''
      password_hash = User.hash_password(password)
      params = {'username': username, 'password_hash': password_hash}
      results = self.database.execute_query(query, params, write=True)
      return User(*results[0]) if results else None
    return None
```

UserService has a `__init__` method that accepts an instance of the `Database` class we created earlier and assigns it to a `database` attribute (`self.database`) of the object. When a user enters a username and password to create an account, we first need to check if a user with that username already exists. To do this, we have a `get_user` method that returns the user if one exists, or `None` if it doesn't. The `get_user` method executes a parameterized SQL query (`SELECT * FROM users WHERE username = :username`) on the database, passing the given username as the only parameter (`{'username': username}`).

As we've seen before, this returns a list of tuples. Due to the `SELECT *`, all the columns in the table will be returned, and the tuples will be of the form (`<username>, <password_hash>`). Consider the last line in `get_user`:

```
return User(*results[0]) if results else None
```

If there's no user with the given username, results will be an empty list, so it'll evaluate to `False`, causing `get_user` to return `None`.

If there *is* such a user, `results[0]` will be a tuple of the form (`<username>, <password_hash>`). In Python, the `*` operator, when applied to a tuple (or a list), *destructures* it for use in things like function calls.

So `User(*results[0])` is equivalent to `User(<username>, <password_hash>)`, which creates a new instance of the `User` dataclass (which you'll recall has two corresponding members: `username` and `password_hash`).

The `create_user` method first uses `self.get_user(username)` to see if a user already exists with the given username. If it does, it simply returns `None`. If it doesn't, it issues the following query to the database:

```
INSERT INTO users (username, password_hash)
  VALUES (:username, :password_hash)
  RETURNING username, password_hash
```

This is an `INSERT` query, which we've seen previously. The only new thing here is the line `RETURNING username, password_hash`. An `INSERT` query doesn't generally need to return any results, as it's a modify operation, not a read operation.

Adding the `RETURNING` clause makes it return the specified fields in the same way that a `SELECT` query would. In this case, the `username` and `password_hash` of the newly created row are returned.

Once again, `create_user` uses the same approach as `get_user` (`User(*results[0])`) to create and return a `User` object if everything is successful.

THE HUB CLASS

When we discussed code organization earlier, we mentioned the `Hub` class, which would serve as the single point of access for our frontend code. Let's write that class now. Create backend/hub.py with the code from listing 8.6 (chapter_08/in_progress_02/backend/hub.py in the GitHub repo).

Listing 8.6 The initial Hub class

```python
from backend.database import Database
from backend.user_service import UserService


class Hub:
  def __init__(self):
    database = Database()
    self.user_service = UserService(database)
```

The Hub class's `__init__` is quite simple: it just creates a Database object and passes it to UserService to create an instance of that class.

Hub has no other methods. This makes sense because, as we've emphasized, Hub is simply a coordinator class that our frontend can use to access the various service class objects (of which user_service, an instance of UserService, is the only one we've created so far).

THE SIGNUP PAGE

Working our way from the bottom up, we've created a User class, a UserService class that accesses the User class, and a Hub class that accesses the UserService class, which currently only has a create_user method.

The part of the Streamlit app that accesses create_user will be the signup page, which we'll define—for now—in main.py.

Our previous main.py initialized the Database object directly and executed a sample query. Since the database is now initialized in the Hub class, we'll rewrite main.py entirely, as shown in listing 8.7 (chapter_08/in_progress_02/main.py in the GitHub repo).

Listing 8.7 main.py, revised

```python
import streamlit as st
from backend.hub import Hub

hub = Hub()

with st.container(border=True):
  st.title("Sign up")
  username = st.text_input("Username")
  password = st.text_input("Password", type="password")
  confirm_password = st.text_input("Confirm password", type="password")

  if st.button("Create account", type="primary"):
    if password != confirm_password:
      st.error("Passwords do not match")
    else:
      user = hub.user_service.create_user(username, password)
      if user:
        st.success("Account created successfully")
      else:
        st.error("Username already exists")
```

By this point in the book, you should be able to read the code in listing 8.7 fairly easily. It starts by creating an instance of Hub. It then displays the usual username-password-confirm password set of inputs, which you've likely seen on various websites before. When the Create Account button is clicked, if the passwords in the two input fields don't match, an error message is displayed. If they do match, we call the create_user method defined in the UserService class to create the user in the database:

```
user = hub.user_service.create_user(username, password)
```

We then show a success or error message based on the return value. At this point, you should be able to see figure 8.6 if you rerun the app and finish the sign-up.

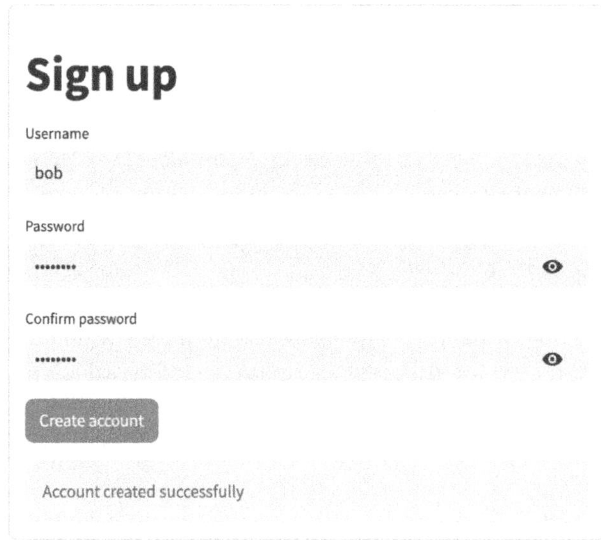

Figure 8.6   Haiku Haven's signup page (see chapter_08/in_progress_02 in the GitHub repo for the full code).

Try creating an account with the username bob. To verify that it worked and that a user has indeed been created, you can issue the query SELECT * from users where username = 'bob' in your psql prompt (which you've hopefully kept open). This should give you something like:

```
username  |                      password_hash
----------+-----------------------------------------------------------------
bob       | $2b$12$hVzjZJN7QMTM94H7ZL.ZJe3PFfgyAPgDOH1F2b38IovcuvKrNAu3G
(1 row)
```

As you can see, due to the hashing, bob's password is no longer directly visible. But can bob log in? Not until we've completed the next part!

8.4 Setting up a multi-page login flow

When we sketched out the user experience, Haiku Haven was intended to be a multi-page app with separate pages for signup, login, and haiku-related functionality, which is something we haven't encountered before.

8.4.1 Multi-page apps in Streamlit

Streamlit has built-in support for multi-page apps. In this scheme, you define your individual pages separately, and let your entrypoint file (the one you run with `streamlit run`) act as a "router" that identifies the page to load and runs it.

The entrypoint file is quite crucial here; it's loaded as usual in every rerun, and it's the one that picks the "current page" to load. Let's see an example. So far in our app, we've created a signup page for users to create their accounts, but not a login page. Once we do create the login page, there needs to be a way to tie the two together, making them part of the same app.

We'll do that by revising the main.py file one more time, using the multi-page approach discussed above. The signup flow included in main.py will need to be moved to a separate file (frontend/signup.py). The new main.py is shown in listing 8.8 (chapter_08/in_progress_03/main.py in the GitHub repo).

Listing 8.8　main.py, revised yet again

```python
import streamlit as st
from backend.hub import Hub

pages = {
  "login": st.Page("frontend/login.py", title="Log in",
                   icon=":material/login:"),
  "signup": st.Page("frontend/signup.py", title="Sign up",
                    icon=":material/person_add:"),
}

if 'hub' not in st.session_state:
  st.session_state.hub = Hub()

page = st.navigation([pages['login'], pages['signup']])
page.run()
```

The first new thing you'll notice here is the `pages` dictionary. The keys in `pages` are `"login"` and `"signup"`, which are the names of the pages we want in our app. The values are `st.Page` objects. Let's inspect the first one:

```python
st.Page("frontend/login.py", title="Log in", icon=":material/login:")
```

`st.Page` is Streamlit's way of defining a single page in a multi-page app. The first argument you pass is the path to the Python script for that page—in this case, frontend/login.py, which doesn't exist yet. We've also given it a sensible title.

The last argument is an icon for the page. It has a curious value: `:material/login:`. This demonstrates a neat way to display icons in Streamlit. The syntax `:material/<icon_name>:` is accepted by most widgets that accept displayable text, and is converted to an image when rendered to the screen.

You can see the supported icons in Google's Material Symbols library at https://fonts.google.com/icons?icon.set=Material+Symbols. In this case, we've chosen the Login icon. Whenever you need to show an icon, you can go to that URL, click the icon you want, identify its icon name from the sidebar that opens to the right, and substitute it within the text `:material/<icon_name>:`.

Now turn your focus to the following lines:

```
page = st.navigation([pages['login'], pages['signup']])
page.run()
```

Here, we pass the two `st.Page` objects in the `pages` dictionary (`pages['login']` and `pages['signup']`) to `st.navigation`, a new Streamlit widget. `st.navigation` is used to configure the available pages in a multi-page Streamlit app, displaying a navigation bar that users can use to select the page they want to go to. It accepts a list of `Page` objects that form the navigation options, and returns a single `Page` object from the list. This returned item is the page selected by the user, or the first item in the list if nothing has been selected yet. Once a page has been returned, it can be loaded using its `.run()` method.

You'll also see that we're saving the `Hub` instance (`hub`) to `st.session_state`, but not doing anything else with it. This is because the session state is shared between the pages in a multi-page app. So if you save something to `st.session_state` in any page, it will be accessible in the other pages too. In this case, we will use the saved `hub` object in the other pages.

What about the signup flow we had earlier? Well, now that our app is multi-page, we'll move it to its own page, signup.py, within a new folder called frontend. As you'll see from listing 8.9, the content has been copied directly from our earlier main.py with no changes (chapter_08/in_progress_03/frontend/signup.py in the GitHub repo).

> **Listing 8.9   The signup page**

```
import streamlit as st

hub = st.session_state.hub

with st.container(border=True):
    st.title("Sign up")
    username = st.text_input("Username")
    password = st.text_input("Password", type="password")
    confirm_password = st.text_input("Confirm password", type="password")

    if st.button("Create account", type="primary"):
        if password != confirm_password:
            st.error("Passwords do not match")
```

```
else:
  user = hub.user_service.create_user(username, password)
  if user:
    st.success("Account created successfully")
  else:
    st.error("Username already exists")
```

The only change we've made (as compared to listing 8.7) is that we obtain the value of the hub variable from st.session_state where we saved it in the new main.py.

8.4.2 Implementing login

With our multi-page app infrastructure in place, it's time to build out the login feature. Before setting up the login page, let's ensure our backend has the necessary functionality.

AUTHENTICATING A USER IN USERSERVICE

As we've discussed, all user-related functionality needs to live in UserService. Currently, that class has create_user and get_user methods. We'll implement a new get_authenticated_user method:

```
from backend.user import User

class UserService:
  ...

  def get_user(self, username):
    ...


  ...
  def get_authenticated_user(self, username, password):
    user = self.get_user(username)
    if user and user.authenticate(password):
        return user
    return None
```

get_authenticated_user accepts a username and password as arguments. It first calls the get_user method we defined earlier to see if a user with that username exists. If it does, this method calls the authenticate method on the returned User object. Recall that the authenticate method in the User class compares the hash of the given password with that of the actual password.

If the authentication succeeds, the User object is returned. If it doesn't, the method returns None, which the calling code can interpret in two ways: either no such user exists or the password is incorrect. To keep things simple, we won't distinguish between these in the return value, though the difference is often significant.

CREATING THE LOGIN PAGE

That's all we need in UserService. We can now proceed with creating a login page to complement the signup page we created earlier.

Create a new file in frontend/ called login.py, with the content shown in listing 8.10 (chapter_08/in_progress_03/frontend/login.py in the GitHub repo).

Listing 8.10 The login page

```python
import streamlit as st

hub = st.session_state.hub

with st.container(border=True):
  st.title("Log in")
  username = st.text_input("Username", key="login_username")
  password = st.text_input("Password", type="password")

  if st.button("Log in", type="primary"):
    user = hub.user_service.get_authenticated_user(username, password)
    if user:
      st.session_state.logged_in = True
      st.session_state.user = user
      st.success("Logged in successfully")
    else:
      st.error("Invalid username or password")
```

This page is similar to signup.py, and should be straightforward to follow with your current understanding of Streamlit. The part to focus on here is what happens when the Log In button is clicked. We first call the authentication method we defined in UserService:

```python
user = hub.user_service.get_authenticated_user(username, password)
```

As we saw, if the method returns a User object, authentication has succeeded; if it returns None, authentication has failed. We write this condition as if user:. For the actual logging in, we'll use a very simple approach—storing a boolean variable called logged_in under st.session_state, along with the User object for the logged-in user (named simply as user). We also display a success or error message depending on whether the login succeeds.

At this point, you should rerun your app using streamlit run main.py. Try logging in with the account you created previously. You should see something similar to figure 8.7.

Note the navigation panel created by st.navigation, which takes up the sidebar and contains links to navigate to either page (along with the icons we added!).

8.4.3 *Navigating between pages*

While we currently have the bare minimum required for a signup/login flow, there's definitely room for improvement. For instance, if the user is on the login page but doesn't have an account, there should be a helpful link right there to sign up; or, if they're on the signup page, there should be a link to log in.

Also, when the user logs in, we should direct them to a logged-in page and give them the ability to log out. Figure 8.8 lays out the ideal signup/login/logout flow we want to design.

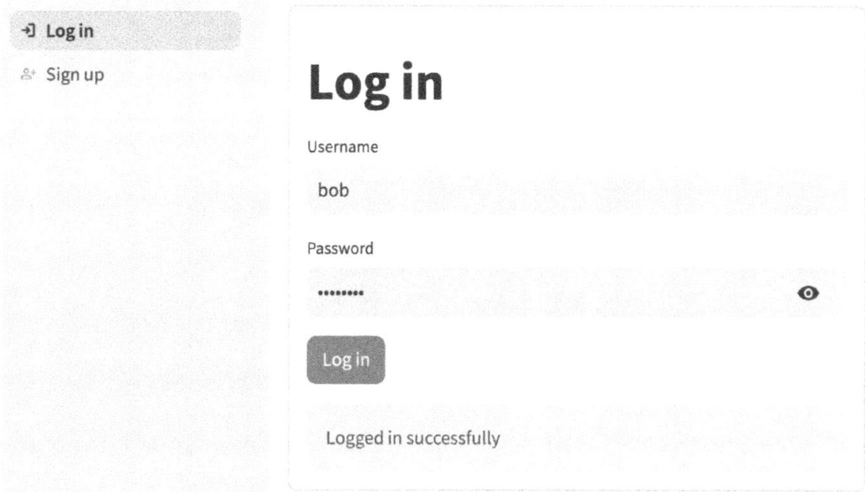

Figure 8.7　Haiku Haven's login page (see chapter_08/in_progress_03 in the GitHub repo for the full code).

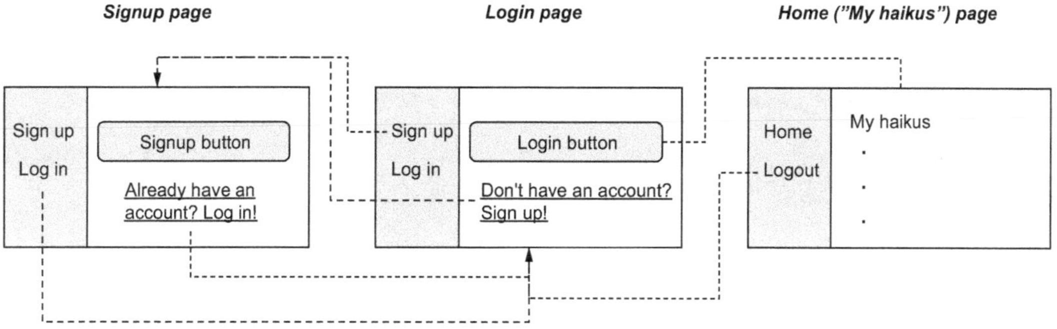

Figure 8.8　Diagram showing the connections between pages via redirection and page links

Besides being able to go back and forth between the signup and login pages and redirect to a home page when logged in, we also want the navigation panel to display different options based on whether the user is logged in or not. If the user is logged in, they should see the home page and have the ability to log out, which shows them the login page again. If they're not, they should see the options to sign up or log in instead.

MOVING THE PAGES DICTIONARY TO ITS OWN FILE

Since we will now be navigating between individual pages, it would be cleaner to put the pages dictionary (the one in main.py that defines the available pages) in its own separate file, so let's move that part of the code to frontend/pages.py, shown in listing 8.11 (chapter_08/in_progress_04/frontend/pages.py in the GitHub repo).

Listing 8.11   The pages dictionary in frontend/pages.py

```python
import streamlit as st

pages = {
  "login": st.Page("frontend/login.py", title="Log in",
                   icon=":material/login:"),
  "signup": st.Page("frontend/signup.py", title="Sign up",
                    icon=":material/person_add:"),
  "home": st.Page("frontend/home.py", title="Home",
                  icon=":material/home:"),
  "logout": st.Page("frontend/logout.py", title="Log out",
                    icon=":material/logout:")
}
```

You'll notice that we've added two new pages: home, which is supposed to represent the logged-in home page, and logout, which will log the user out.

LINKS BETWEEN PAGES

Streamlit allows you to create links between pages in a multi-page app through a widget that is, appropriately enough, named st.page_link. Let's use it to link between the login and signup pages. login.py should look like this, with the page link added to the very bottom:

```python
import streamlit as st
from frontend.pages import pages


...
with st.container(border=True):
    ...
    else:
      st.error("Invalid username or password")

st.page_link(pages["signup"], label="Don't have an account? Sign up!")
```

st.page_link is quite easy to understand; the first argument is the st.Page object (from pages, imported from pages.py) we want to link to, and the second is the label text.

You can also pass a regular URL as the first argument, in case you want to link to an external page. signup.py has very similar changes:

```python
import streamlit as st
from frontend.pages import pages


...
with st.container(border=True):
    ...
    else:
      st.error("Username already exists")

st.page_link(pages["login"], label="Already have an account? Log in!")
```

DYNAMICALLY CHANGING ST.NAVIGATION

The next feature we'll implement is showing the user the right pages for their context in the navigation bar, i.e., signup and login when they're logged out, or home and logout when they're logged in.

Edit main.py so it looks like this:

```
import streamlit as st

from backend.hub import Hub
from frontend.pages import pages

if 'hub' not in st.session_state:
  st.session_state.hub = Hub()

if 'logged_in' in st.session_state and st.session_state.logged_in:
  page = st.navigation([pages['home'], pages['logout']])
else:
  page = st.navigation([pages['login'], pages['signup']])

page.run()
```

Obviously, the pages dictionary is now defined in pages.py and imported into main.py.

As shown above, to dynamically change what's in the navigation panel, we use the logged_in session state variable that we save when the user logs in, and vary the st.navigation object that's assigned to page accordingly. If the user is logged in, the navigation bar will show the home and logout options. Since pages['home'] is the first item in the list passed to st.navigation, that's the page that will be loaded by default when the user logs in.

Let's now set up a placeholder page in frontend/home.py (listing 8.12), so that there's something for a logged-in user to see.

> **Listing 8.12   A placeholder in frontend/home.py**

```
import streamlit as st

user = st.session_state.user
st.title(f"Welcome, {user.username}!")
```

Nothing earth-shattering here for now; we just display a greeting that includes the logged-in user's username. Recall that we save the logged-in User object in st.session_state.user in login.py.

AUTOMATIC REDIRECTION FOR LOGIN AND LOGOUT

Our proposed ideal login flow requires the user to be redirected automatically on login and logout. How does this work exactly?

Remember that when a user clicks the Log In button, the logged_in session state variable is set to True. This means that in the next rerun, main.py will pick up the changed value of logged_in, display the new navigation panel, and load home.py.

To make this truly seamless, we have to trigger the rerun, though. So add an `st.rerun()` to login.py:

```
...
with st.container(border=True):
  ...
  if st.button("Log in", type="primary"):
    ...
    if user:
      st.session_state.logged_in = True
      st.session_state.user = user
      st.rerun()
```

And logging out? Well, that's going to reverse everything that happens at login. Create a logout.py with content shown in listing 8.13 (chapter_08/in_progress_04/frontend/logout.py in the GitHub repo).


```
import streamlit as st

st.session_state.user = None
st.session_state.logged_in = False
st.rerun()
```

That completes our signup/login/logout flow! Rerun the app and try it all out! When you log in, you should now see a different navigation panel and the loaded home page (see figure 8.9).

Figure 8.9   The logged-in page with different options in the navigation bar (see chapter_08/in_progress_04 in the GitHub repo for the full code).

Clicking Log Out in the navigation bar will reload the login and signup pages, which have page links to each other at the bottom.

Using st.login and st.logout

The most recent versions of Streamlit provide native support for authentication, so you don't need to maintain a database table of users or store password hashes yourself. Instead, you would rely on a third-party service to verify a user's identity through an authentication protocol known as OpenID Connect (OIDC).

To set this up, you need to create an account with an *identity provider* that supports OIDC—Google, Microsoft, Okta, or Auth0—and obtain a client ID and secret, which you would then include in `st.secrets`, along with some more metadata.

Within your app, you could then trigger a login action by calling `st.login`, which would take the user to your chosen identity provider's page where they can create an account with your app or log in. For instance, you could give users the option of logging in with their Google account—something you've probably already encountered with plenty of websites before.

Your app can access information about users through an object called `st.user`. For instance, you can check to see if a user is logged in with `st.user.is_logged_in`, or see their email address with `st.user.email`. If you're using Streamlit 1.44.0 or earlier, this object may be called `st.experimental_user`. The `experimental_` is Streamlit's way of marking a feature as unstable and likely to change in the future.

You can end a user's logged-in session by triggering `st.logout`, which takes them back to the app's main page.

This authentication flow has several advantages—it's highly secure, and you never have to deal with passwords or hashes yourself. That said, implementing the password-hashing and login flow ourselves—as we do in this chapter—has plenty of educational value.

8.5 Creating, reading, updating, and deleting haikus

Now that user authentication is taken care of, it's finally time to work on the crux of our app: the ability to create, read, update, and delete haikus. We'll start with haiku creation, encapsulating this behavior in a `HaikuService` class, and then making the appropriate changes to the frontend.

8.5.1 Defining a HaikuService class

The code structure we'll follow in the haiku service is analogous to what we already have in `UserService`.

Let's begin with a `Haiku` dataclass to represent a haiku. Create it as haiku.py in the backend/ folder, as shown in listing 8.14 (chapter_08/in_progress_05/backend/ haiku.py in the GitHub repo).

Listing 8.14 The `Haiku` dataclass

```
from dataclasses import dataclass

@dataclass
class Haiku:
    haiku_id: int
```

```
created_at: str
author: str
text: str
```

As in the User class, the fields mirror those in the corresponding database table (haikus). Listing 8.15 shows HaikuService (chapter_08/in_progress_05/backend/haiku_service .py in the GitHub repo).

Listing 8.15   The HaikuService class

```
from backend.haiku import Haiku

class HaikuService:
  def __init__(self, database):
    self.database = database

  def create_haiku(self, author, haiku_text):
    query = '''
      INSERT INTO haikus (author, text)
      VALUES (:author, :text)
      RETURNING haiku_id, created_at, author, text
    '''
    params = {'author': author, 'text': haiku_text}
    results = self.database.execute_query(query, params, write=True)
    return Haiku(*results[0]) if results else None
```

Again, the code is fairly analogous to that of UserService, so a detailed explanation isn't warranted.

As we've seen, we only need to supply the author and text fields in our SQL query in create_haiku; the database automatically provides haiku_id and created_at, and all of the fields are returned as per the RETURNING clause. To wrap up the backend changes, add an instance of HaikuService to hub.py:

```
...
from backend.haiku_service import HaikuService

class Hub:
  def __init__(self):
    database = Database()
    self.user_service = UserService(database)
    self.haiku_service = HaikuService(database)
```

This will enable the haiku creation function to be accessed from the frontend, as we'll see presently.

8.5.2   *Enabling users to create haikus*

Our earlier home.py was, of course, just a placeholder. Our actual logged-in home page should ideally have a way to create haikus and display them. For creating haikus, let's create a modal dialog similar to the one we created in chapter 7.

Create a new file, frontend/haiku_editor.py, as shown in listing 8.16 (chapter_08/in_progress_05/frontend/haiku_editor.py in the GitHub repo).

Listing 8.16　The Haiku editor dialog

```python
import streamlit as st

@st.dialog("Haiku editor", width="large")
def haiku_editor(hub, user):
  haiku_text = st.text_area('Enter a haiku')
  if st.button('Save haiku', type='primary'):
    haiku = hub.haiku_service.create_haiku(user.username, haiku_text)
    if haiku:
      st.success('Haiku saved successfully!')
      st.rerun()
    else:
      st.error('Failed to save haiku')
```

The `haiku_editor` function is decorated with `st.dialog`—which, as we saw in this previous chapter, executes its body in a modal screen.

The body of `haiku_editor` is not very complicated. We first accept the haiku text entered by the user in an `st.text_area` widget:

```python
haiku_text = st.text_area('Enter a haiku')
```

`st.text_area` is precisely what you'd expect it to be—an area for entering several lines of text. On clicking Save Haiku, we call the `create_haiku` method under `HaikuService` to save it to the database, and show the appropriate success/failure message.

If the operation is successful, we issue an `st.rerun()`. This reruns the entire app, closing the dialog in the process, because the button that triggered it in the first place is now in the unclicked state. Close the loop by including—in home.py—an Add Haiku button that triggers the `haiku_editor` dialog we just defined:

```python
import streamlit as st
from frontend.haiku_editor import haiku_editor

hub = st.session_state.hub
user = st.session_state.user
st.title(f"Welcome, {user.username}!")

if st.button(':material/add_circle: Haiku', type='primary'):
    haiku_editor(hub, user)
```

As you can see, we're using a Material icon again, this time replacing the word Add within the button label. Let's see everything working so far! Rerun your Streamlit app, log in, and add a haiku (see figure 8.10).

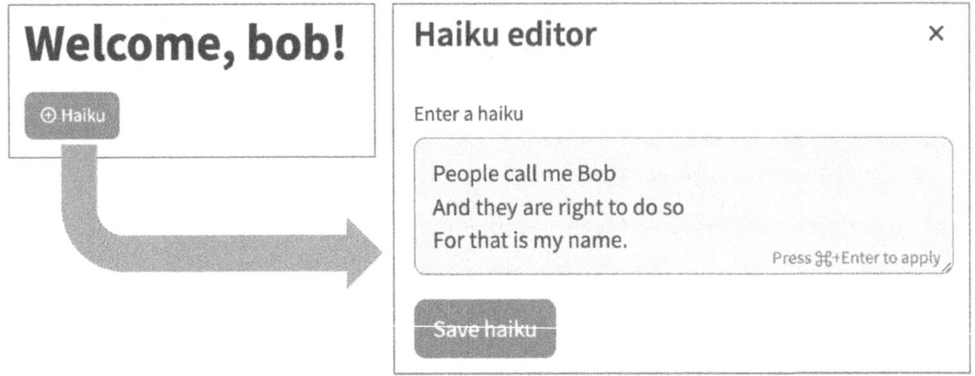

Figure 8.10 Creating a haiku (see chapter_08/in_progress_05 in the GitHub repo for the full code).

Though you can't see the new haiku yet after you click Save Haiku (that's coming up next), you can convince yourself that one has indeed been added to the database by querying your haikus table.

8.5.3 *The other CRUD operations: Read, Update, Delete*

To make our CRUD app feature complete, there are three more operations we need to implement:

- *Reading* the current users' haikus from the database and listing them in the app
- *Updating* a given haiku
- *Deleting* a haiku altogether

DEFINING THE OPERATIONS IN HAIKUSERVICE

As before, define these operations in the backend first by editing the HaikuService class in haiku_service.py:

```
from backend.haiku import Haiku

class HaikuService:
    ...
    def create_haiku(self, author, haiku_text):
        ...

  def get_haikus_by_author(self, author):
      query = 'SELECT * FROM haikus WHERE author = :author'
      params = {'author': author}
      results = self.database.execute_query(query, params)
      return [Haiku(*row) for row in results]

  def update_haiku(self, haiku_id, haiku_text):
      query = '''
        UPDATE haikus SET text = :text WHERE haiku_id = :id RETURNING *
      '''
```

```python
    params = {'text': haiku_text, 'id': haiku_id}
    results = self.database.execute_query(query, params, write=True)
    return Haiku(*results[0]) if results else None

def delete_haiku(self, haiku_id):
    query = 'DELETE FROM haikus WHERE haiku_id = :id RETURNING *'
    params = {'id': haiku_id}
    results = self.database.execute_query(query, params, write=True)
    return Haiku(*results[0]) if results else None
```

We define one method for each operation: `get_haikus_by_author` for reading haikus, `update_haiku` for updating, and `delete_haiku` for deleting a haiku. In each case, we use the same pattern we've seen before: run a SQL command, convert the results into Haiku objects, and return them. In both `update_haiku` and `delete_haiku`, we accept `haiku_id`—the unique identifier of a haiku—as an argument, using `UPDATE..SET` and `DELETE FROM` SQL commands respectively to achieve the desired result.

CREATING THE UI

Our backend methods return instances of the `Haiku` class, but how do we display these in the frontend? We should create a `display_haiku` function that accepts a `Haiku` object and displays it on the screen. The next natural question is: what do we display? What is the user likely to be interested in seeing?

The `Haiku` class has four attributes: `haiku_id`, `created_at`, `author`, and `text`. Of these, `haiku_id` is an internal identifier that holds no meaning for the end user, so we can exclude that. `created_at` might be useful to jog the user's memory of when a haiku was originally created. It would be redundant to show the `author` field since we're only going to be displaying haikus by the current logged-in user. And `text` is the content of the haiku, so we want to display that. That gives us: `created_at` and `text`. Anything else? Well, we also want to give the user the option to edit or delete a particular haiku, so let's pop in a couple of buttons as well.

With this in mind, let's create a new haiku_display.py file under frontend/, as in listing 8.17 (chapter_08/in_progress_06/frontend/haiku_display.py in the GitHub repo).

Listing 8.17　Displaying haikus

```python
import streamlit as st

hub = st.session_state.hub
user = st.session_state.user

def get_haiku_created_display(haiku):
    day = haiku.created_at.strftime('%Y-%m-%d')
    time = haiku.created_at.strftime('%H:%M')
    return f':gray[:material/calendar_month: {day}  \n :material/schedule: {time}]'

def get_haiku_text_display(haiku):
    display_text = haiku.text.replace('\n', '  \n')
    return f':green[{display_text}]'
```

```python
def edit_button(haiku):
  if st.button(':material/edit:', key=f"edit_{haiku.haiku_id}"):
    pass

def delete_button(haiku):
  if st.button(':material/delete:', key=f"delete_{haiku.haiku_id}"):
    pass

def display_haiku(haiku):
  with st.container(border=True):
    cols = st.columns([2, 5, 1, 1])
    created_col, text_col, edit_col, delete_col = cols

    created_col.markdown(get_haiku_created_display(haiku))
    text_col.markdown(get_haiku_text_display(haiku))
    with edit_col:
      edit_button(haiku)
    with delete_col:
      delete_button(haiku)
```

The key function to focus on here is the last one: `display_haiku`. Given `haiku`, an instance of the `Haiku` class, it makes four columns for the four things we want to display: `created_at`, `text`, the edit button, and the delete button. The actual rendering of each of these takes place in its own function.

`get_haiku_created_display` takes haiku's `created_at` property—a timestamp— and breaks it down into a day and a time using a method called `strftime`, which is used to format a timestamp in any given format based on a *format string*. In this case, `%Y-%m-%d` formats it as just a date, whereas `%H:%M` extracts the time in hours and minutes.

We then return this peculiar f-string:

```python
f':gray[:material/calendar_month: {day}  \n :material/schedule: {time}]'
```

A few things are going on here. The `:<color>[<text>]` syntax is used in Streamlit to display text in various colors. For instance, the string `:red[Hello]` would be interpreted by widgets like `st.write` or `st.markdown` as the word `Hello` in red text.

We also see the icon syntax we saw earlier. Here we're using a calendar icon for the date and a clock icon (`schedule`) for the time, creating a user-friendly display for the date and time.

`get_haiku_text_display` is meant to display the content of the haiku. Why do we have the following replace method? Why not just display the content directly?

```python
haiku.text.replace('\n', '  \n')
```

This is something of a workaround. Streamlit handles line breaks in text rather strangely. To get text widgets like `st.markdown` to display the newline character `\n` properly, we have to precede it with two spaces, i.e. `'  \n'` instead of just `'\n'`.

The `edit_button` and `delete_button` functions simply display `st.button` widgets. You'll notice that we use icons as their labels, and give them widget keys—which is required for Streamlit to distinguish between them when we have many haikus displayed on a page. We've given them placeholder bodies with `pass` for now; we'll come back to them later.

Since we're using icons so much throughout the app, our code would actually be a lot more readable if we gave them better names (e.g. `CLOCK` instead of `:material/schedule:`) and put them in a more central location.

Let's put all the icons in their own file, frontend/icons.py (listing 8.18), and *import* them instead (chapter_08/in_progress_07/frontend/icons.py in the GitHub repo).


```
LOGIN = ":material/login:"
SIGNUP = ":material/person_add:"
HOME = ":material/home:"
LOGOUT = ":material/logout:"
ADD = ":material/add_circle:"
CALENDAR = ":material/calendar_month:"
CLOCK = ":material/schedule:"
EDIT = ":material/edit:"
DELETE = ":material/delete:"
```

We can now change haiku_display.py:

```
import streamlit as st
from frontend.icons import CALENDAR, CLOCK, EDIT, DELETE

...
def get_haiku_created_display(haiku):
  ...
  return f':gray[{CALENDAR} {day}  \n {CLOCK} {time}]'

...
def edit_button(haiku):
  if st.button(f'{EDIT}', key=f"edit_{haiku.haiku_id}"):
    pass

def delete_button(haiku):
  if st.button(f'{DELETE}', key=f"delete_{haiku.haiku_id}"):
    pass
...
```

There—that's much more readable! Let's now call `display_haiku` to show the user their list of created haikus! We'll edit home.py to do this:

```
import streamlit as st
from frontend.haiku_editor import haiku_editor
from frontend.haiku_display import display_haiku
from frontend.icons import ADD

...
if st.button(f'{ADD} Haiku', type='primary'):
```

```python
haiku_editor(hub, user)

haikus = hub.haiku_service.get_haikus_by_author(user.username)
if len(haikus) == 0:
  st.info("You haven't written any haikus yet.")
else:
  for haiku in haikus:
    display_haiku(haiku)
```

The changes here are quite simple. After the add button we created earlier—which we've now changed to use an icon imported from icons.py—we display a header that says <username>'s haikus along with a divider (just a horizontal line underneath, controlled by divider="gray").

We then call the get_haikus_by_author method we defined in HaikuService, and loop through the results, calling display_haiku on each. If there are no haikus, we display an st.info message that says so.

Rerun your app now to see the changes in figure 8.11 (after adding one more haiku)!

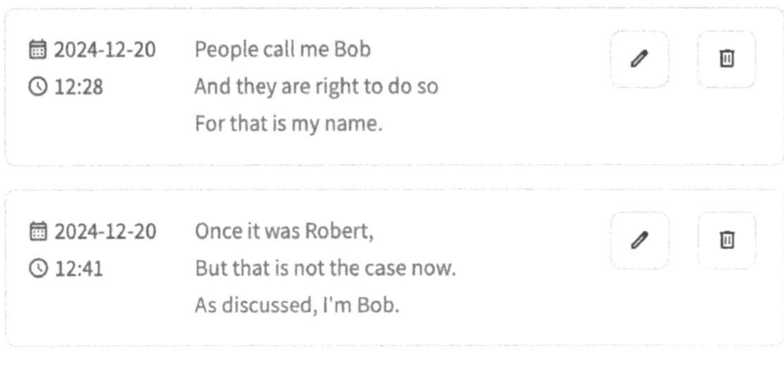

Figure 8.11 Listing created haikus (see chapter_08/ in_progress_07 in the GitHub repo for the full code).

Note that there's one more place we've been using icons: pages.py, where we've defined the pages for the multi-page app. Go ahead and update that file too:

```python
import streamlit as st
from frontend.icons import LOGIN, LOGOUT, SIGNUP, HOME

pages = {
```

```python
    "login": st.Page("frontend/login.py", title="Log in", icon=LOGIN),
    "signup": st.Page("frontend/signup.py", title="Sign up", icon=SIGNUP),
    "home": st.Page("frontend/home.py", title="Home", icon=HOME),
    "logout": st.Page("frontend/logout.py", title="Log out", icon=LOGOUT)
}
```

ADDING THE UPDATE AND DELETE FUNCTIONALITY

Let's get back to the edit and delete buttons, which currently have placeholders under them. The edit button should let a user edit one of their existing haikus. We can repurpose the haiku editor dialog we've already created to work with the Add Haiku button for this:

```python
import streamlit as st

@st.dialog("Haiku editor", width="large")
def haiku_editor(hub, user, haiku=None):
  default_text = haiku.text if haiku else ''
  haiku_text = st.text_area('Enter a haiku', value=default_text)
  if st.button('Save haiku', type='primary'):
    if haiku:
      new_haiku = hub.haiku_service.update_haiku(haiku.haiku_id, haiku_text)
    else:
      new_haiku = hub.haiku_service.create_haiku(user.username, haiku_text)
    if new_haiku:
      st.success('Haiku saved successfully!')
      st.rerun()
    else:
      st.error('Failed to save haiku')
```

The `haiku_editor` function now accepts a `haiku` argument, which is `None` by default. If we're calling the editor to edit an existing haiku, we can pass the corresponding `Haiku` instance to `haiku`. Otherwise, we're calling the dialog to add a haiku, so we pass `None`.

In the rest of the function, we'll use the condition `if haiku` to check if we're performing the edit action or the add action. In the next two lines, we pre-populate the existing haiku's text in the text area as a default value using the `value` parameter of `st.text_area` if we're in the edit action.

```python
default_text = haiku.text if haiku else ''
haiku_text = st.text_area('Enter a haiku', value=default_text)
```

Then, once the Save button is clicked, we pick either the `update_haiku` or the `create_haiku` method from `HaikuService` to execute. In the former case, we pass the existing haiku's `haiku_id` to identify the haiku we want to edit. As before, if the query succeeds—which we determine by checking the return value, `new_haiku`—we rerun the app.

We can now replace the placeholder under the Edit button in haiku_display.py:

```python
import streamlit as st
from frontend.haiku_editor import haiku_editor...


...
def edit_button(haiku):
  if st.button(f'{EDIT}', key=f"edit_{haiku.haiku_id}"):
    haiku_editor(hub, user, haiku)
```

In the same page, let's also make the Delete button trigger a deletion:

```python
def delete_button(haiku):
  if st.button(f'{DELETE}', key=f"delete_{haiku.haiku_id}"):
    deleted_haiku = hub.haiku_service.delete_haiku(haiku.haiku_id)
    if deleted_haiku:
      st.rerun()
    else:
      st.error("Failed to delete haiku.")
```

Here we call the `delete_haiku` method in `HaikuService`. If the deletion is successful, we perform an `st.rerun()` so that the list of haikus can update and no longer show the deleted haiku. If the deletion fails for any reason, an error is displayed. Rerun the app now and try editing or deleting a haiku (figure 8.12)!

Figure 8.12   Deleting a haiku (see chapter_08/in_progress_08 in the GitHub repo for the full code).

Haiku Haven has now been fully built—or at least we have a version that's fit to deploy to production.

8.6   *Deploying Haiku Haven*

Since we have Haiku Haven working locally, it's time to productionize our app on Community Cloud. The process to do so is the same as what we've been following since chapter 5, but there's an additional wrinkle here: our app requires a running PostgreSQL server to host our database.

8.6.1 Setting up a managed PostgreSQL server in production

While we were developing locally, it was a simple matter to install PostgreSQL on the same machine, but Streamlit Community Cloud doesn't provide an option to do that. Instead, we need to set up an external PostgreSQL server somewhere.

We'll use a cloud-based managed PostgreSQL service called Neon, which makes this process super easy and has a significant free quota. Create an account with Neon now at https://neon.tech/. The signup process is quite painless; you can choose to sign up with your GitHub or Google account if you like.

You'll be asked for a project name and a database name. The project name can be whatever you like (Haiku Haven, maybe?), while the database name should be whatever you named your database in your local Postgres—haikudb if you've been following along faithfully.

You may also be asked to select a cloud provider and location—these can be whatever you prefer, although I chose AWS as the provider.

Once your account is set up, navigate to the Quick Start page to see a connection string that looks something like this:

```
postgresql://haikudb_owner:Dxg2HFXreSZ3@ep-flower-dust-a63e8evn.us-west-2
.aws.neon.tech/haikudb?sslmode=require
```

This is the connection string we'll use in production. Neon has taken the liberty of setting up a username (haikudb_owner) and password for you. Store this string somewhere safe.

Next, you'll need to set up the users and haikus tables once again in Neon. To do this, go to the SQL Editor tab. This is where you can enter SQL commands as though you were in the psql prompt. To create the tables, refer back to section 8.2.4 and grab the CREATE TABLE commands we executed locally. You can execute these commands in Neon's SQL Editor without any changes.

8.6.2 Deploying to Community Cloud

The rest of the deployment process should be straightforward and is pretty much identical to what we did in chapter 5. Make sure to create a requirements.txt so that Community Cloud knows to install the third-party modules needed, primarily psycopg2-binary and bcrypt.

For reference, listing 8.19 shows the requirements.txt that I used.

Listing 8.19   requirements.txt file for the Community Cloud deployment

```
streamlit==1.40.2
psycopg2-binary==2.9.10
sqlalchemy==2.0.40
bcrypt==4.3.0
```

Once you've completed deployment, you'll need to copy the contents of secrets.toml and paste it in Community Cloud's Secrets setting (refer to chapter 5 for a refresher), replacing the connection string with the one you copied from Neon.

That's all, folks! Haiku Haven is now live! Tell all your friends they can unleash their seventeen-syllable creativity on your brand-new web app!

As for us, let's turn the page on CRUD and try our hand at building AI apps next.

Summary

- CRUD stands for Create-Read-Update-Delete, the four fundamental operations that most apps perform.
- Relational databases like PostgreSQL organize data in tables with rows and columns, according to a schema.
- Designing the data model for an application involves identifying the entities, defining their relationships, listing their attributes, and converting these into a schema, often assisted by an Entity-Relationship (ER) diagram.
- SQL (Structured Query Language) supports commands for creating tables (`CREATE TABLE`), inserting rows (`INSERT INTO`), reading data (`SELECT..FROM`), updating rows (`UPDATE..SET`), deleting rows (`DELETE FROM`), and dropping tables (`DROP TABLE`).
- `st.connection` is a Streamlit feature that makes it easy to establish a connection to a data source like PostgreSQL.
- Never store passwords in plain text; instead, hash them using a library like `bcrypt` and store the resulting hash. To authenticate, hash the provided password and compare it to the stored hash.
- `st.Page` objects correspond to individual pages in multi-page apps in Streamlit.
- `st.navigation` is used to create a navigation bar and specify the pages in an app.
- `st.page_link` creates links between pages in a multi-page app.
- When deploying to production, you need to set up your database server separately, potentially using a managed service like Neon for PostgreSQL.

Part 3

Streamlit and LLMs

This part is where Streamlit meets AI. Large Language Models (LLMs) are redefining what you can do with a little programming knowledge, and Streamlit is one of the easiest ways to bring them to life.

In chapter 9, you'll build Fact Frenzy, an AI-powered trivia game that generates questions, judges answers, and keeps score, all in real time. You'll learn to prompt LLMs effectively, manage app state across turns, and even inject AI personalities. In chapter 10, you'll level up with Nibby, a customer support chatbot that combines LangGraph, Retrieval-Augmented Generation (RAG), and the ReAct agentic model, to simulate deep, domain-aware conversations—and even take actions in the real world.

These chapters are fast-paced, creative, and packed with hands-on code to help you build AI-native experiences that feel surprisingly polished.

Creating an AI-powered application

Creating software is very different from what it was just a few years ago. This shift comes from major developments in AI (artificial intelligence), which, unless you've been living under a rock, you've probably heard of.

I'm talking, of course, about breakthroughs in LLMs, or large language models, and the exciting possibilities they open up. By processing and generating natural language, LLMs can understand context, answer complex questions, and even write software on their own, all with astonishing fluency. A few well-crafted prompts can now accomplish tasks that once required domain-specific expertise or painstaking programming.

In this chapter, we'll dive into how to harness the power of LLMs in applications, using AI prompts and responses to implement product features that would have required highly advanced techniques half a decade ago. Along the way, we'll also discuss how to tune LLM interactions to get the results you're after, without burning a hole in your pocket.

NOTE   The GitHub repo for this book is at https://github.com/aneevdavis/streamlit-in-action. The chapter_09 folder has this chapter's code and a requirements.txt file with exact versions of all the required Python libraries.

9.1 Fact Frenzy: An AI trivia game

If you watched the game show *Jeopardy!* as a kid—or as an adult, for that matter—you're going to love this chapter. Having grown up outside the US, I was in my thirties before I watched my first episode of the show, but I suffered no dearth of trivia shows to obsess over when I was a boy—*Mastermind, Bournvita Quiz Contest,* and *Kaun Banega Crorepati?* (an Indian take on the original British show *Who Wants to Be a Millionaire?*) were all staples of my youth.

Fifteen-year-old me would never forgive adult me if I didn't include at least one trivia app in this book. Fortunately, trivia is a great fit for our first AI-powered Streamlit app, which will generate questions, evaluate answers, and even mix it up with a variety of quizmaster styles, all using artificial intelligence.

9.1.1 Stating the concept and requirements

Once again, the first step we'll take is to state the concept of the app we want to build.

> *Fact Frenzy is a trivia game that asks players a set of trivia questions and uses AI to evaluate their answers.*

As we've done several times earlier in the book, the requirements flesh out this simple idea further.

REQUIREMENTS

Fact Frenzy will:

- Use an AI model to generate trivia questions
- Ask a player these questions
- Allow the user to enter a free-text response to each question
- Use AI to evaluate whether an answer is correct and provide the correct answer
- Keep track of a player's score
- Allow the player to set a difficulty level for questions
- Offer a variety of quizmaster speaking styles

While we *generally* want our requirements to be free of "implementation" language (as discussed in chapter 3), in this case, the entire point of our app is to demonstrate the use of AI, so we definitely need it to use AI models to perform its functions.

We've also added a fun element in the form of quizmaster speaking styles—or in other words, mimicking the style of various people while asking questions, something we'd only be able to achieve using AI.

WHAT'S OUT OF SCOPE

What are we leaving out? While a professional trivia game could be arbitrarily complex, Fact Frenzy is intentionally a minimal app for hands-on practice with topics not covered yet. For that reason, it won't focus on any of the following:

- Persistent storage and retrieval of questions, answers, and scores
- Creating and managing users
- Letting users choose particular categories of questions

Placing the above items out of scope will let us concentrate on things like interacting with LLMs, state management, and, of course, new Streamlit elements.

9.1.2 *Visualizing the user experience*

To get a concrete sense of what Fact Frenzy is, take a look at the sketch of the proposed UI in figure 9.1.

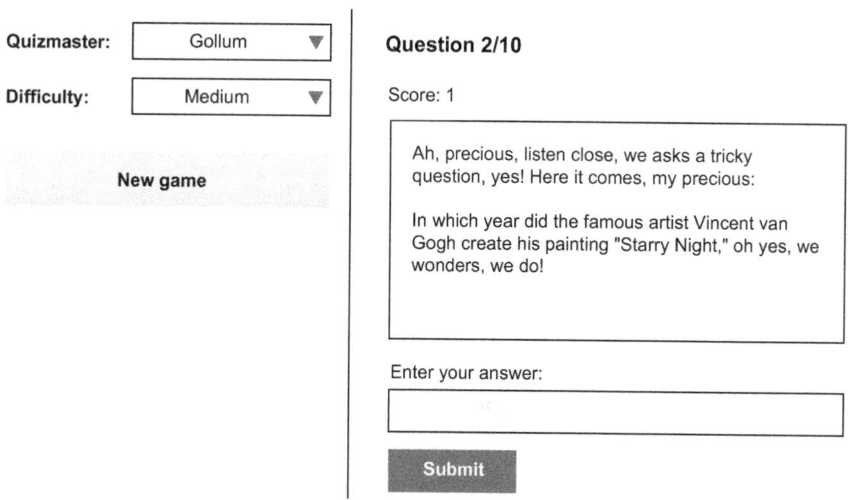

Figure 9.1 A sketch of the UI for the Fact Frenzy game

The game window shown in the sketch has a two-column layout. The left column has a New Game button, as well as a couple of settings: Quizmaster and Difficulty.

Referring to the last requirement identified in the previous section, the Quizmaster setting is supposed to use AI to mimic the speaking styles of various characters. In figure 9.1, the selected value is Gollum, a character from *The Lord of the Rings* who speaks in a distinctive, hissing manner using phrases like "my precious."

The column on the right shows an AI-generated question "spoken" in Gollum's voice, along with the player's score and a box to enter the answer. Gimmicks aside, it's a fairly standard question-and-answer trivia game that allows players to enter free-form text as answers.

9.1.3 *Brainstorming the implementation*

While we'll "outsource" large parts of our logic to an LLM, we'll still need to own the overall game flow. Figure 9.2 illustrates the design we'll implement in the remainder of the chapter.

Unlike some of the other apps we've written, where users could take a variety of actions at any point, Fact Frenzy is quite linear. As the diagram shows, the basic logic runs in a loop—using an LLM to retrieve a trivia question, posing it to the player, getting the LLM to evaluate the answer, stating whether the provided answer was right or not, and doing it all over again for the next question, until the game is done.

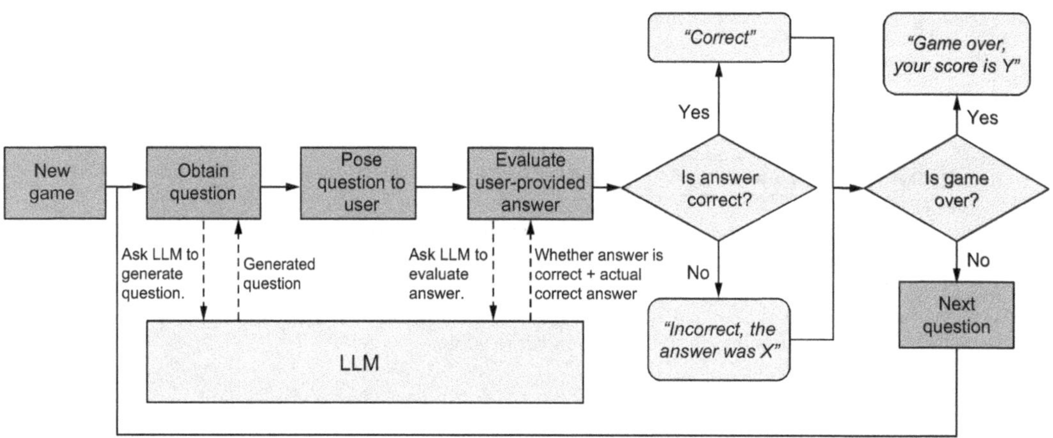

Figure 9.2 **The flow of logic in our AI-based trivia game**

Later on, we'll add a few bells and whistles, such as allowing the player to set the difficulty level and quizmaster, but figure 9.2 is a pretty good representation of the core flow.

9.2 *Using AI to generate trivia questions*

At the heart of Fact Frenzy is an AI model that powers the trivia experience. This model generates questions, evaluates player responses, and even adds personality to the quizmaster. To achieve all this, we use a Large Language Model—a powerful AI system designed to process and generate human-like text.

LLMs are trained on vast amounts of textual data, making them incredibly versatile. They can perform a wide range of tasks from answering factual questions to generating poetry, coding, or—importantly for our purposes—role-playing as a quizmaster. Popular examples of LLMs include OpenAI's GPT series, Anthropic's Claude, and Google's Gemini, all of which use cutting-edge machine learning techniques to generate coherent, contextually appropriate text.

9.2.1 Why use an LLM in Fact Frenzy?

What makes LLMs suitable for use in our trivia game? To answer this, let's take a minute to consider some possible components of such a game and how an LLM can support building each one.

A GIANT LIST OF QUESTIONS

Without an LLM, we would need to maintain a set of trivia questions that are both large and diverse enough to keep our app engaging. Since the major LLMs of today are all trained on text and data pertaining to history, culture, geography, astronomy, and every other category of trivia you can think of, they're able to generate questions on the fly.

THE ABILITY TO EVALUATE ANSWERS

If we took the traditional non-LLM route, we'd only be able to ask multiple-choice questions, as we'd need to accurately match the answer a player gives to the actual one. LLMs, on the other hand, can interpret and respond to free-text user inputs. This allows us to ask open-ended trivia questions and still evaluate player responses correctly.

ENTERTAINMENT VALUE

In addition to handling factual information, LLMs can also be creative and provide humor to enhance engagement. Later in the chapter, we'll ask one to mimic the style of various characters as quizmasters, giving the game a personality, so to speak.

Thus, in Fact Frenzy, the LLM will play the triple role of question generator, answer evaluator, and comic relief provider. In the next section, we'll set up an account with a top-tier LLM provider—OpenAI—enabling us to start interacting with LLMs for the first time.

> **NOTE** While LLMs are undeniably powerful, they are not omniscient. They rely on patterns in their training data to generate responses and may occasionally make mistakes, especially when evaluating highly nuanced or ambiguous answers. Still, for this trivia app, these models strike a balance between intelligence, versatility, and entertainment.

9.2.2 Setting up an OpenAI API key

For this chapter, we'll use an LLM provided by OpenAI, perhaps the best-known among the set of AI firms that have been dominating tech news lately. As we've done many times in this book so far, we'll need to open an account with an external service and wire our Python code to it. If you don't already have an OpenAI account (a ChatGPT account counts), go to https://platform.openai.com/ and sign up for one.

> **NOTE** If you created your OpenAI account recently or just now, you *may* have some free credits applied to your account. However, the free tier currently comes with relatively severe usage limits, such as only being able to call some models three times per minute. While you could *technically* get away with using the free tier for this chapter (assuming your account has the free credits in the first place), if you plan to do any amount of serious AI development, I recommend upgrading to a paid tier. As you'll see, you can get a lot of LLM usage for fairly low prices. Though you'll likely need to *buy* $5 in usage credits to get to the lowest paid tier, you won't need to *spend* much of that in this chapter. For reference, I spent less than 15 cents in credits for all the testing I did while developing this lesson. You can learn more about cost optimization in the sidebar named "Cost considerations," later in this chapter.

Once you're in, go to the Settings page—at the time of writing, you can do this by clicking the gear icon at the top right corner of the page—and then click API Keys in the panel to the left. Create a new secret key and write it down. Leave the defaults unchanged (figure 9.3).

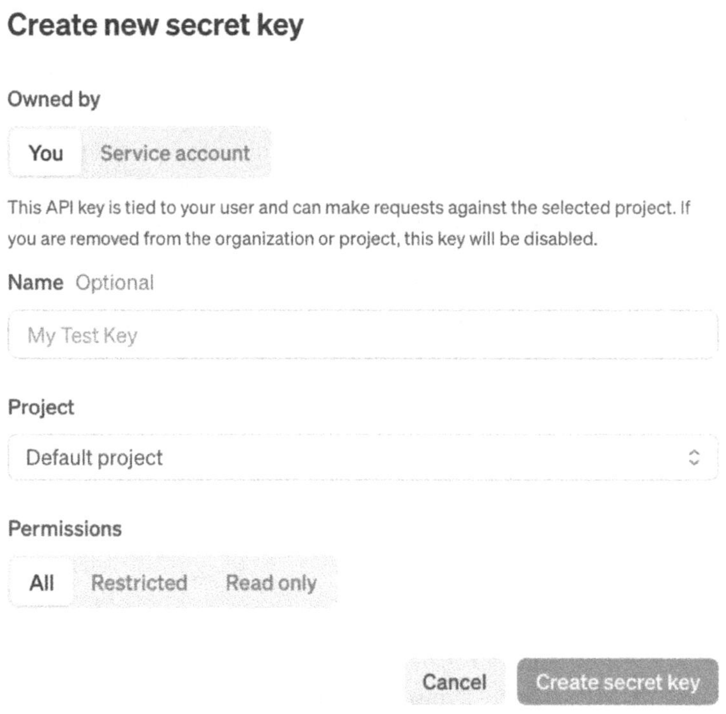

Create new secret key

Owned by

| You | Service account |

This API key is tied to your user and can make requests against the selected project. If you are removed from the organization or project, this key will be disabled.

Name Optional

My Test Key

Project

Default project

Permissions

| All | Restricted | Read only |

Cancel   Create secret key

Figure 9.3 Creating a secret key in an OpenAI account

You'll only be able to see your key once, so be sure to copy and paste it somewhere. This goes without saying, but keep it safe!

9.2.3 *Calling the OpenAI API in Python*

Before we start any development on the app, let's make sure we can call the OpenAI API in Python without any problems. To begin, install OpenAI's Python library with `pip install openai`. You could technically call the API via HTTP calls using the `requests` module (as we did in chapter 5), but this library is more convenient to use.

After that, open a Python shell and import the `OpenAI` class:

```
>>> from openai import OpenAI
```

The `OpenAI` class lets you instantiate a client using an API key to make calls to the OpenAI API:

```
>>> client = OpenAI(api_key='sk-proj-...')
```

Replace `sk-proj-...` with the actual API key copied in the previous step. After creating a `client` object, prepare an instruction to send to the LLM:

```
>>> messages = [
...     {'role': 'system', 'content': 'You are a helpful programming assistant'},
...     {'role': 'user', 'content': 'Explain what Streamlit is in 10 words or fewer'}
... ]
```

Each request to the LLM is called a *prompt*. A prompt (or at least the type we'll use here) consists of *messages*. In the code above, we assemble these into a list. Each message takes the form of a dictionary with two keys: `role` and `content`.

`role` can be one of `user`, `system`, or `assistant`. We'll look at more examples later, but the value of `role` signifies the speaker's perspective in the conversation:

- `system` represents instructions or context-setting for the model, such as rules for how it should behave.
- `user` represents the person interacting with the model
- `assistant` represents the model's responses—we'll discuss this in the next chapter.

The prompt we're creating here tells the LLM (in the system message) to behave like a helpful programming assistant. The actual instruction we want the LLM to respond to is in the user message: `Explain what Streamlit is in 10 words or fewer`.

We can now make an actual request to the API:

```
completion = client.chat.completions.create(model='gpt-5.1', messages=messages)
```

The OpenAI API has several different endpoints—one for turning audio to text, one for creating images, and so on. The one we'll be using is the *chat completions* endpoint, and it's used for text generation.

Given a list of messages in a conversation, this endpoint is supposed to return what comes next—hence the term *completion*. OpenAI has a plethora of models we could use, but here we've picked `gpt-5.1`, mainly because we want a fast model in the GPT-5 family (the latest one at the time of writing) where "reasoning" (a feature that improves quality but slows down responses) can be turned off.

> **NOTE** While we've chosen gpt-5.1 here, it's worth noting that this isn't OpenAI's cheapest model. Given the speed of developments in the AI space, by the time this book goes to print, we may have newer models that are smarter *and* cheaper. Keep an eye on OpenAI's pricing page at https://openai.com/api/pricing to ensure you're using the model that fits best.

The above statement should take a few seconds to execute and will return a `Chat-Completion` object. If you like, you can inspect this object by typing just `completion` into the shell, but you can access the actual text response we want like so:

```
>>> completion.choices[0].message.content
'Streamlit is a framework for building interactive web applications easily.'
```

I couldn't have said it better myself! That concludes this first programmatic interaction with an LLM. Next, let's build this into the trivia game's code.

9.2.4 *Writing an LLM class*

In chapter 8, we created a `Database` class that encapsulated the interaction that our app could have with an external database. We'll follow the same model in this chapter with an `Llm` class that handles all communication with the external LLM. This allows us to separate the logistics of interacting with the LLM from the rest of our app, making it easier to maintain, test, or even swap it out entirely without affecting the remaining code. We've covered the basics of calling the LLM in the prior section, so all that's left is to put the logic in a class.

Create a new file, llm.py, with the content shown in listing 9.1 (chapter_09/in_progress_01/llm.py in the GitHub repo).

Listing 9.1 Creating the `Llm` class in llm.py

```python
from openai import OpenAI

class Llm:
  def __init__(self, api_key):
    self.client = OpenAI(api_key=api_key)

  @staticmethod
  def construct_messages(user_msg, sys_msg=None):
    messages = []
    if sys_msg:
      messages.append({"role": "system", "content": sys_msg})
    messages.append({"role": "user", "content": user_msg})
    return messages
```

```python
    def ask(self, user_msg, sys_msg=None):
        messages = self.construct_messages(user_msg, sys_msg)
        completion = self.client.chat.completions.create(
            model="gpt-5.1",
            messages=messages
        )
        return completion.choices[0].message.content
```

The `Llm` class' `__init__` simply creates a new OpenAI client object using an API key that's passed to it, assigning this to `self.client`.

The `ask` method is what logic outside the `Llm` class will interact with, and returns the LLM's response to our prompt. Its code is essentially the same as what we ran in the Python shell earlier, except that we take in `user_msg` and `sys_msg` as arguments and put the creation of the `messages` list in its own method, called `construct_messages`.

Since we don't *have* to pass a system role message—the LLM will try to be helpful anyway—we give `sys_msg` a default value of `None`. `construct_messages` takes this fact into account while generating the `messages` list. Since this is a utility function that doesn't depend on anything else in the object, we make it a static method by decorating it with `@staticmethod`.

We'll refine the `Llm` class further along in the chapter, but for now, let's move on to writing the code that calls it.

9.2.5   *The Game class*

As in chapter 8, we'll have a single class—appropriately named `Game`—that contains all the backend logic that our app's frontend will call directly. This is somewhat analogous to the `Hub` class from Chapter 8, though we'll structure `Game` differently. This class is going to be critical for keeping track of the state of the game without getting confused.

For the moment, we'll keep it quite simple, as all it needs to do is pass a prompt to our `Llm` class. The initial version of the `Game` class which we'll place in game.py is shown in listing 9.2 (chapter_09/in_progress_01/game.py in the GitHub repo).

Listing 9.2   An initial `Game` class in game.py

```python
from llm import Llm

class Game:
    def __init__(self, llm_api_key):
        self.llm = Llm(llm_api_key)

    def ask_llm_for_question(self):
        return self.llm.ask(
            'Ask a trivia question. Do not provide choices or the answer.',
            'You are a quizmaster.'
        )
```

The initialization of a `Game` instance (through `__init__`) involves creating an `Llm` object by passing it the API key that we'll presumably get from the calling code.

The `ask_llm_for_question` method passes a simple prompt to the LLM, asking it to generate a trivia question. Notice that the system message now tells the LLM to behave like a quizmaster.

The user message instructs the LLM to ask a question, warning it not to provide any choices or reveal the answer.

9.2.6 Calling the Game class in the app

We can now write a minimal version of our frontend code to test out everything we've done. As usual, our API key needs to be kept secret and safe, so we'll put it in a secrets .toml file in a new .streamlit directory, as seen in listing 9.3.

Listing 9.3   Placing your LLM API key in .streamlit/secrets.toml

```
llm_api_key = "sk-proj-..."
```

Replace sk-proj-... with your actual API key.

We've kept secrets.toml quite simple this time around with a non-nested structure—notice the absence of a section like `[config]`. The O in TOML does stand for "obvious" after all.

Go ahead and create main.py as shown in listing 9.4 (chapter_09/in_progress_01/main.py in the GitHub repo).

Listing 9.4   A minimal main.py

```
import streamlit as st
from game import Game

game = Game(st.secrets['llm_api_key'])

question = game.ask_llm_for_question()
st.container(border=True).write(question)
```

There's nothing fancy here yet; we simply create a `Game` instance called `game`, call its `ask_llm_for_question` method to generate a trivia question, and write it to the screen.

Notice how we've combined `st.container` with a border and `st.write` into a single statement:

```
st.container(border=True).write(question)
```

Concise and pretty, much like Streamlit itself. Run the app using `streamlit run main .py` (as in prior chapters, make sure you first `cd` into the directory that contains main .py so Streamlit can find the .streamlit directory) to see something like figure 9.4.

Figure 9.4   The app can now call the OpenAI API to obtain a trivia question (see chapter_09/in_progress_01 in the GitHub repo for the full code).

Excellent—our AI quizmaster can now ask the player a question! Next, we'll have it evaluate the player's answer.

9.3 Using AI to evaluate answers

The prompt we fed GPT-5.1 is a simple one. Vitally, we didn't have to do anything particularly complicated with the output—just display it on the screen as-is. As such, we didn't really care about the *format* in which the LLM responded.

However, evaluating answers presents a slightly different challenge. When a player enters an answer into the app, we need the LLM to tell us two things:

- Whether the answer is correct
- If not, what the correct answer actually is

If you've interacted with AI assistants before, this sounds well within their capabilities. But let's examine a practical challenge: how do you reliably parse the LLM's response?

For instance, let's say we tell the LLM, "Hey, you asked this question: <question>, and the player said the answer was <answer>. Tell me if that's right, or if not, what the correct answer is". The LLM does its thing and responds with: "Incorrect, the answer is actually <correct answer>."

What do we do with this reply? Sure, we could display it on the screen, but we also need to perform additional actions, like deciding whether or not to increment the player's score. This means that we need to *parse* the response to understand whether the answer was right.

But what if the LLM's answer is actually "Nope, that's not right, the answer is <correct answer>" or even "Hah! It *would* have been correct if they'd said <correct answer>. But they didn't, so tough luck."

The point is that there are tons of creative ways the LLM could answer, and while we would be able to understand them as humans, we need a simple way to determine their meaning in a machine-friendly way. We could request the LLM in our prompt to include the words "correct" or "incorrect" somewhere, but it might still occasionally mess it up. Luckily, there's a better approach.

9.3.1 Structured Outputs

Being able to parse LLM outputs reliably is a natural concern for developers, so OpenAI has a solution for this called *Structured Outputs*. Structured Outputs is a feature that ensures the model generates a response adhering to a schema *you* provide, making it simple to parse programmatically.

For our use case, we can request the LLM to provide two structured fields in its response: a boolean field that says whether the provided answer is correct, and the actual correct answer. Let's create this schema as a class named `AnswerEvaluation` (listing 9.5). We'll need the third-party `pydantic` module to get this working, so install that first with `pip install pydantic` (chapter_09/in_progress_02/answer_evaluation.py in the GitHub repo).

Listing 9.5   The `AnswerEvaluation` class in answer_evaluation.py

```python
from pydantic import BaseModel

class AnswerEvaluation(BaseModel):
  is_correct: bool
  correct_answer: str
```

`pydantic` is a data validation library which uses type hints to ensure that data conforms to a specified type. `BaseModel`, which we import from `pydantic`, is a class that allows you to define a schema and perform data validation. It works well with OpenAI's Structured Outputs.

The class we're defining, `AnswerEvaluation`, is a *subclass* of `BaseModel`. *Subclasses* and *superclasses* are related to the concept of *inheritance* in object-oriented programming. Explaining inheritance in detail is beyond the scope of this book, but just know that a subclass can *inherit* functionality and attributes from its superclass, allowing you to reuse code and build on existing functionality without starting from scratch.

In this case, `AnswerEvaluation` (subclass) inherits the features of `BaseModel` (superclass), such as data validation, serialization, and type checking, making it easy to define and work with structured data.

The body of `AnswerEvaluation` is identical to what you might expect if it were a dataclass instead. Indeed, dataclasses are similar to `pydantic`'s `BaseModel` except that dataclasses do not provide the complex validations and related functionality that `BaseModel` does.

Fortunately, we don't need to worry about the internals of how this works—just note that `AnswerEvaluation` has the two fields we spoke of: a boolean `is_correct` and a string, `correct_answer`.

Next, let's modify our `ask` function in the `Llm` class (llm.py) to support Structured Outputs:

```python
from openai import OpenAI

class Llm:
  ...
  def ask(self, user_message, sys_message=None, schema=None):
    messages = self.construct_messages(user_message, sys_message)

    if schema:
      completion = self.client.beta.chat.completions.parse(
        model="gpt-5.1",
        messages=messages,
        response_format=schema
      )
      return completion.choices[0].message.parsed
    else:
      completion = self.client.chat.completions.create(
        model="gpt-5.1",
```

```
        messages=messages
    )
    return completion.choices[0].message.content
```

Here, we've added an argument called `schema` that's `None` by default. If a value is provided (`if schema`), we call a different method in our OpenAI client (`beta.chat.completions.parse`, as opposed to `chat.completions.create` from earlier).

The first two parameters we pass to this new method are the same as before, but we've added a third one: `response_format`, to which we provide the value of `schema`. The final value we return is also different: `completion.choices[0].message.parsed` rather than `completion.choices[0].message.content`. If `schema` is not provided, we simply default to the earlier behavior, thereby ensuring that the `ask` method can handle both Structured Outputs and regular text.

The value we need to pass to `schema` is a *class*—not an instance of the class, but the class *itself*. The value *returned* will then be an *instance* of that class, and will therefore follow the schema. As you may already have guessed, for our use case, we'll pass the `AnswerEvaluation` class to `schema`.

We'll create this calling code in a bit, but first, let's create a new LLM prompt asking the model to evaluate a player's answer. During development, you should expect to have to tweak your prompt many times to get better results—in fact, there's a whole field called *prompt engineering* that has sprung up in recent years.

Since our prompts are meaningfully different from our code, let's put them in a different file where we can edit them without touching the rest of the code. We'll name this prompts.py and give it the contents in listing 9.6 (chapter_09/in_progress_02/prompts.py in the GitHub repo).

> **Listing 9.6 Separating our prompts into prompts.py**

```python
QUESTION_PROMPT = {
    'system': 'You are a quizmaster.',
    'user': 'Ask a trivia question. Do not provide choices or the answer.'
}

ANSWER_PROMPT = {
    'system': 'You are an expert quizmaster.',
    'user': '''
    You have asked the following question: {question}
    The player answered the following: {answer}

    Evaluate if the answer provided by the player is close enough
    to be correct.

    Also, provide the correct answer.
    '''
}
```

Each prompt is structured as a dictionary with keys `system` and `user`, corresponding to the system and user messages.

QUESTION_PROMPT is our prompt from earlier, while ANSWER_PROMPT is new. Notice that its user message (a Python *multi-line string* bounded by ''''s if you're wondering about the syntax) contains these lines:

```
You have asked the following question: {question}
The player answered the following: {answer}
```

We're treating {question} and {answer} here as variables that we can replace with real values when we send the prompt to the LLM later. Also note the last two lines in this message, where we're telling the LLM to evaluate the answer for correctness and *also* to provide the correct answer. The model is smart enough to interpret this instruction and provide the results in our AnswerEvaluation schema.

Speaking of which, let's actually write the code that passes this schema along with the prompt to fulfill our answer evaluation use case. We'll do this by modifying game.py (chapter_09/in_progress_02/game.py in the GitHub repo):

```python
from llm import Llm
from prompts import QUESTION_PROMPT, ANSWER_PROMPT
from answer_evaluation import AnswerEvaluation

class Game:
  def __init__(self, llm_api_key):
    self.llm = Llm(llm_api_key)

  def ask_llm_for_question(self):
    usr_msg, sys_msg = QUESTION_PROMPT['user'], QUESTION_PROMPT['system']
    return self.llm.ask(usr_msg, sys_msg)

  def ask_llm_to_evaluate_answer(self, question, answer):
    sys_msg = ANSWER_PROMPT['system']
    user_msg = (
      ANSWER_PROMPT['user']
      .replace('{question}', question)
      .replace('{answer}', answer)
    )
    return self.llm.ask(user_msg, sys_msg, AnswerEvaluation)
```

We've refactored the ask_llms_for_question method to use our new prompts.py module. But the main change here is the new function, ask_llm_to_evaluate_answer, which takes in the originally asked question, and the answer provided by the user, plugging these values into the {question} and {answer} slots in the user message we discussed a minute ago. This time, we pass in AnswerEvaluation (imported from answer_evaluation.py) as a third argument to self.llm's ask method—schema, as I hope you recall. One interesting aspect to this is that we're passing in AnswerEvaluation *itself* here—not an *instance* of AnswerEvaluation, but the class. In Python, most of the constructs in your code are *objects* you can pass around like this, including classes—something that enables powerful and flexible programming patterns.

But I digress. Let's get back to enabling our game to accept and evaluate answers from a player. The last step is to make the requisite changes to the frontend in main.py (chapter_09/in_progress_02/main.py in the GitHub repo):

```python
import streamlit as st
from game import Game

game = Game(st.secrets['llm_api_key'])

question = game.ask_llm_for_question()
st.container(border=True).write(question)

answer = st.text_input("Enter your answer")
if st.button("Submit"):
  evaluation = game.ask_llm_to_evaluate_answer(question, answer)
  if evaluation.is_correct:
    st.success("That's correct!")
  else:
    st.error("Sorry, that's incorrect.")
    st.info(f"The correct answer was: {evaluation.correct_answer}")
```

You should be able to understand what we're doing here pretty easily. Once we've posed the trivia question to the player, we display a text input for their answer, as well as a Submit button that, when clicked, triggers the ask_llm_to_evaluate_answer method in game.py.

The resulting value—stored in evaluation—is an instance of the AnswerEvaluation class. We use its is_correct attribute to display the appropriate correct/incorrect message, and evaluation.correct_answer for the real answer.

Try rerunning your app now and supplying an answer to the trivia question. Figure 9.5 shows what I got.

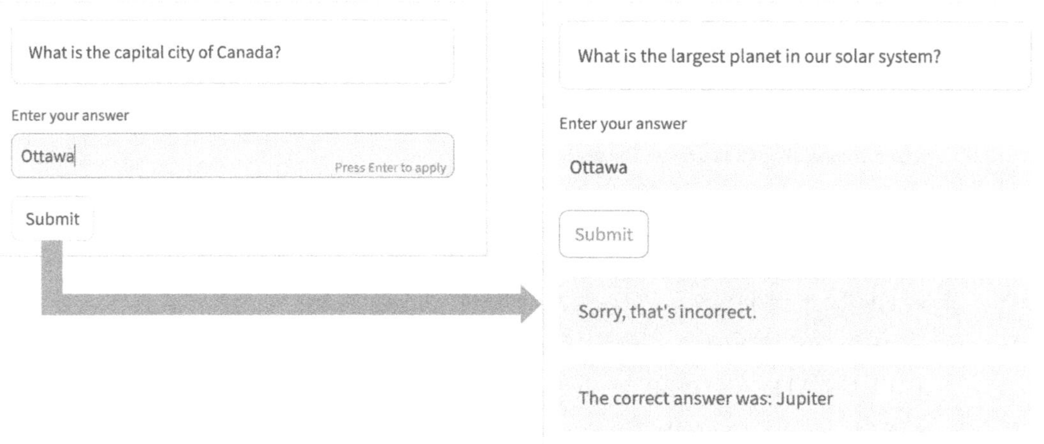

Figure 9.5 **A problem with session state causes our answer to be matched with the wrong question (see chapter_09/in_progress_02 in the GitHub repo for the full code).**

Oops! There are shenanigans afoot! The question I answered "Ottawa" to in the left part of figure 9.5 was "What is the capital of Canada?". But when I press the Submit button, the app displays a different question—"What is the largest planet in our solar system?"—and then has the nerve to tell me that Ottawa is, in fact, *not* the right answer to that. You'll notice a similar bait-and-switch in your testing. What's going on? Are our AI overlords toying with us?

As it turns out, the LLM is entirely innocent of this alleged mischief. The problem—as we've seen several times before in this book—is related to session state and Streamlit app reruns. In this particular instance, clicking the Submit button triggers a rerun from the *top*, meaning that before the code under `if st.button("Submit"):` can run, `game.ask_llm_for_question()` is called once again, resulting in a *new* question, which is what is passed as the first argument to `ask_llm_to_evaluate_answer`, along with "Ottawa" as the second argument pulled from the text input.

At the very least, the Structured Outputs part of our code appears to be working, as Jupiter is indeed the largest planet in the solar system, and Ottawa is incorrect. However, to get Fact Frenzy to exhibit the behavior we expect, we'll need to think through state management quite thoroughly in the next section.

9.4   *Moving through game states*

In previous chapters, Streamlit's rerun-the-whole-app-each-time model meant that we had to make extensive use of `st.session_state` to get the app to remember values. That holds true here as well.

Fact Frenzy, however, is *sequential* in a way that our previous apps weren't. You can think of the desired behavior of our game as moving between various *states*, taking a different set of actions, and displaying different widgets in each. Figure 9.6 illustrates this.

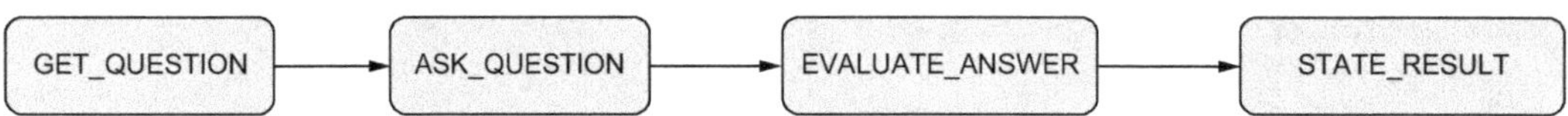

Figure 9.6   The game consists of four sequential states.

The diagram identifies four states the game can be in:

- GET_QUESTION retrieves a question from the LLM
- ASK_QUESTION poses a question to the player
- EVALUATE_ANSWER involves calling the LLM to evaluate the answer
- STATE_RESULT tells the player whether they were right

Each of these actions should only happen while the game is in the state that it corresponds to. Additionally, we need to ensure that each LLM request we're making only happens once per question, because the alternative messes up our logic *and* costs money.

A pattern that we'll find useful in sequential apps such as this one and others you may write in the future is to formally retain a state/status attribute in the app's central class (Game in our case) coupled with methods to modify it, and to use conditional logic based on this attribute in the frontend to display the right elements on the screen. Figure 9.7 should clarify what I'm talking about.

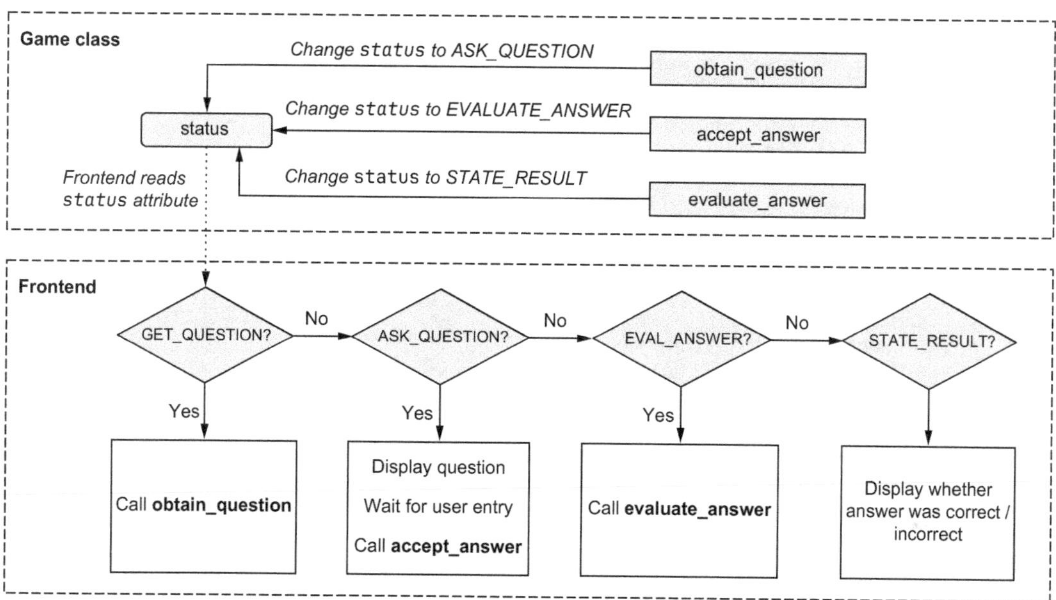

Figure 9.7 **Conditional branching in the frontend based on the game's state**

As you can see from our proposed logic in figure 9.7, the Game class will have a status attribute that indicates the state the game is in. We'll read this state in the frontend to branch between the various display elements—whether it's a text input for the answer in the ASK_QUESTION state, or simply a wait-during-the-LLM-request status element during the GET_QUESTION and EVALUATE_ANSWER states.

The Game class also has methods that change its status attribute, controlling all of this. obtain_question would presumably get the question from the LLM, but also change the status to ASK_QUESTION when it's done. accept_answer would take in the answer from the player and also switch the status to EVALUATE_ANSWER, and the evaluate_answer method, in addition to getting the LLM to give us the result, would shift the status to STATE_RESULT.

Let's put all this in action now, starting with the Game class, shown in listing 9.7 (chapter_09/in_progress_03/game.py in the GitHub repo).

Listing 9.7   **Moving through game states in a modified game.py**

```python
from llm import Llm
from prompts import QUESTION_PROMPT, ANSWER_PROMPT
from answer_evaluation import AnswerEvaluation

class Game:
  def __init__(self, llm_api_key):
    self.llm = Llm(llm_api_key)
    self.status = 'GET_QUESTION'

    self.curr_question = None
    self.curr_answer = None
    self.curr_eval = None

  def ask_llm_for_question(self):
    usr_msg, sys_msg = QUESTION_PROMPT['user'], QUESTION_PROMPT['system']
    return self.llm.ask(usr_msg, sys_msg)

  def ask_llm_to_evaluate_answer(self):
    sys_msg = ANSWER_PROMPT['system']
    user_msg = (
      ANSWER_PROMPT['user']
      .replace('{question}', self.curr_question)
      .replace('{answer}', self.curr_answer)
    )
    reply = self.llm.ask(user_msg, sys_msg, AnswerEvaluation)
    return reply

  def obtain_question(self):
    self.curr_question = self.ask_llm_for_question()
    self.status = 'ASK_QUESTION'
    return self.curr_question

  def accept_answer(self, answer):
    self.curr_answer = answer
    self.status = 'EVALUATE_ANSWER'

  def evaluate_answer(self):
    self.curr_eval = self.ask_llm_to_evaluate_answer()
    self.status = 'STATE_RESULT'
```

As discussed, the first big change here is the inclusion of a `self.status` attribute that formally indicates the state of the game. We initialize this to `GET_QUESTION` as that's the first sequential state we want.

You'll notice we also have three other attributes—`curr_question`, `curr_answer`, and `curr_eval`—to hold the current question, answer, and evaluation within the `Game` instance. This is a departure from the earlier version of game.py where we were handling `question` and `answer` as variables outside the class. Keeping track of these within the class is better suited to our new *stateful* approach.

You'll see this reflected in the `ask_llm_to_evaluate_answer` method, where we've dispensed with the `question` and `answer` parameters in favor of the `self.curr_question` and `self.curr_answer` attributes.

Additionally, we've introduced three new methods (also discussed earlier)—`obtain_question`, `accept_answer`, and `evaluate_answer`. `obtain_question` and `evaluate_answer` are wrappers around `ask_llm_for_question` and `ask_llm_to_evaluate_answer`, respectively, each merely assigning the result to its associated attribute—`self.curr_question` or `self.curr_answer`—before adding a line to move `self.status` to its next value.

`accept_answer` is even simpler; it just sets `self.answer` to an answer presumably provided by the player. The second half of the set of changes we need to implement—the state management approach we've envisioned—lies in main.py:

```python
import streamlit as st
from game import Game

if 'game' not in st.session_state:
  st.session_state.game = Game(st.secrets['llm_api_key'])
game = st.session_state.game

if game.status == 'GET_QUESTION':
  with st.spinner('Obtaining question...') as status:
    question = game.obtain_question()
    st.rerun()

elif game.status == 'ASK_QUESTION':
  st.container(border=True).write(game.curr_question)
  answer = st.text_input("Enter your answer")
  if st.button("Submit", type='primary'):
    game.accept_answer(answer)
    st.rerun()

elif game.status == 'EVALUATE_ANSWER':
  with st.spinner('Evaluating answer...') as status:
    game.evaluate_answer()
    st.rerun()

elif game.status == 'STATE_RESULT':
  if game.curr_eval.is_correct:
    st.success("That's correct!")
  else:
    st.error("Sorry, that's incorrect.")
    st.info(f"The correct answer was: {game.curr_eval.correct_answer}")
```

We start by placing our `Game` instance in `st.session_state`, ensuring that we'll be dealing with the same instance across reruns:

```python
if 'game' not in st.session_state:
  st.session_state.game = Game(st.secrets['llm_api_key'])
game = st.session_state.game
```

The last line here is for convenience, enabling us to refer to our `Game` instance simply as game, instead of spelling out `st.session_state.game` each time. The remaining code builds out conditional branching based on `game`'s `status` attribute. Let's briefly consider each such condition:

```
if game.status == 'GET_QUESTION':
  with st.spinner('Obtaining question...') as status:
    question = game.obtain_question()
    st.rerun()
```

The first branch deals with the `GET_QUESTION` state. The app handles this state without requiring user interaction, as it simply retrieves the question from the LLM. This can take a perceptible amount of time, however, so we display what's known as a *status element.*

A status element is a widget that gives some indication of what's going on to the user while a long-running operation happens in the background. Streamlit has several status elements—`st.spinner`, `st.status`, `st.toast`, `st.progress`—each with slightly different characteristics.

`st.spinner`, which we've used here, simply displays a spinning circle animation (the same one we saw in chapter 6 when we applied the `show_spinner` parameter to `@st.cache_data`) until the background operation has been completed.

Notice the `st.rerun()` after we've called `game.obtain_question()`. This exists because once `obtain_question` (from game.py) has changed the status to `ASK_QUESTION`, we need the code to run again, to enter the *next* conditional branch given by `elif game.status == 'ASK_QUESTION':`.

The remaining branches are quite similar. In each case, there is some kind of trigger causing the app to move to the next state, followed by a rerun. In the `ASK_QUESTION` state, clicking Submit calls `game.accept_answer(answer)`, which sets `game`'s `curr_answer` attribute and changes the state to `EVALUATE_ANSWER`. In `EVALUATE_ANSWER`, we call `game.evaluate_answer()` and display another `st.spinner` while we wait for it to return, eventually changing the status to `STATE_RESULT`.

After the rerun, we simply display the appropriate messages based on `game.curr_eval`, our `AnswerEvaluation` object. Check out the results now by rerunning the app (figure 9.8) This time, you'll see that the app correctly matches the question and answer, resolving the problem we encountered earlier.

9.5   *Game mechanics: Keeping score, a New Game button, and Game Over*

Fact Frenzy currently does the bare minimum we need it to do: it asks a player a question and evaluates the answer, all using AI. It isn't much of a *game,* though; there's no score, and no concept of when the game starts and ends. Let's tackle each of these problems in turn.

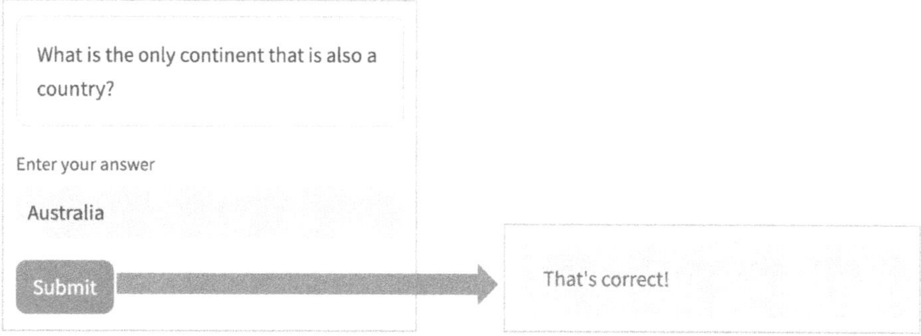

Figure 9.8   The question-answer mismatch problem has been resolved (see chapter_09/in_progress_03 in the GitHub repo for the full code).

9.5.1   *Keeping score*

We want Fact Frenzy to be easy to pick up, so we'll keep our scoring mechanism basic; each correct answer fetches one point. This should be fairly trivial to incorporate into the Game class (chapter_09/in_progress_04/game.py in the GitHub repo):

```python
...
class Game:
  def __init__(self, llm_api_key):
    self.llm = Llm(llm_api_key)
    ...

    self.score = 0

  ...
  def evaluate_answer(self):
    self.curr_eval = self.ask_llm_to_evaluate_answer()
    if self.curr_eval.is_correct:
      self.score += 1
    self.status = 'STATE_RESULT'
```

We simply add a new score attribute to the Game instance in __init__, setting it to 0 to start with. Later, in the evaluate_answer method, we increment this score by 1 if the LLM determines that the answer is correct.

GAME OVER

Our app doesn't yet have any concept of when the game is over, so let's define this. Again, we'll keep the logic simple: we'll ask a predefined number of questions, and the game is done when all of them have been asked and answered. This involves modifying the Game class again (chapter_09/in_progress_04/game.py in the GitHub repo):

```python
...
class Game:
  def __init__(self, llm_api_key):
    ...
```

```python
    self.score = 0
    self.num_questions_completed = 0
    self.max_questions = 1
  ...
  def evaluate_answer(self):
    self.curr_eval = self.ask_llm_to_evaluate_answer()
    self.num_questions_completed += 1
    if self.curr_eval.is_correct:
      self.score += 1
    self.status = 'STATE_RESULT'

  def is_over(self):
    return self.num_questions_completed >= self.max_questions
```

Again, this should be easy to follow. We add two more attributes to the instance in `__init__`: `num_questions_completed` and `max_questions` (set to 1 for now since we don't actually support multiple questions yet—that's coming up in the next section).

We increment `num_questions_completed` by 1 in `evaluate_answer`, and add a new method called `is_over` that returns `True` if the number of questions completed matches or exceeds `self.max_questions`.

A New Game button

At the moment, Fact Frenzy jumps straight into asking the LLM for a question as soon as the page loads. A New Game button would let users trigger the start of a game or take any other action we may want to add later before we engage the LLM. This will primarily affect our frontend code, so let's update main.py thus (chapter_09/in_progress_04/main.py in the GitHub repo):

```python
import streamlit as st
from game import Game

def start_new_game():
  st.session_state.game = Game(st.secrets['llm_api_key'])
  st.rerun()

def new_game_button(game):
  if game and not game.is_over():
    button_text, button_type = "Restart game", "secondary"
  else:
    button_text, button_type = "Start new game", "primary"
  if st.button(button_text, use_container_width=True, type=button_type):
    start_new_game()

game = st.session_state.game if 'game' in st.session_state else None
side_col, main_col = st.columns([2, 3])
with side_col:
  st.header("⚡ Fact Frenzy", divider='gray')
  new_game_button(game)

with main_col:
```

```python
if game:
  st.header("Question", divider='gray')
  if game.status == 'GET_QUESTION':
    ...


    ...
  elif game.status == 'STATE_RESULT':
    if game.curr_eval.is_correct:
      st.success("That's correct!")
    else:
      st.error("Sorry, that's incorrect.")
      st.info(f"The correct answer was: {game.curr_eval.correct_answer}")

  if game.is_over():
    with st.container(border=True):
      st.markdown(f"Game over! Your final score is: **{game.score}**")
```

There are several changes to highlight here. Firstly, there are two new functions: `start_new_game` and `new_game_button`, which we'll look into in a second. Since it's now possible for a game not to have started yet—before the New Game button is clicked, we allow for the game to be `None` if it hasn't been added to `st.session_state` yet:

```python
game = st.session_state.game if 'game' in st.session_state else None
```

We've also changed the layout of the app to have two columns: a side column (`side_col`) and a main one (`main_col`):

```python
side_col, main_col = st.columns([2, 3])
```

This side column could have simply been an `st.sidebar`, but in a later section, it'll turn out we need this column to have a higher width than `st.sidebar` offers by default.

Anyway, `side_col` contains a header introducing Fact Frenzy, and a call to `new_game_button`:

```python
with side_col:
  st.header("⚡ Fact Frenzy", divider='gray')
  new_game_button(game)
```

In chapter 8, we used the Material library to display icons. Here, we've given Fact Frenzy a lightning-bolt icon using a different approach: by pasting an emoji into our code. We're able to do this because emoji are part of the *Unicode* standard, which defines a consistent way to represent text and symbols across different systems and platforms. Whenever you want to add an emoji, you can search for it on a website like emojipedia .org and copy it.

The `new_game_button` function is defined like this:

```
def new_game_button(game):
  if game and not game.is_over():
    button_text, button_type = "Restart game", "secondary"
  else:
    button_text, button_type = "Start new game", "primary"
  if st.button(button_text, use_container_width=True, type=button_type):
    start_new_game()
```

In essence, we're checking if the game is already in progress—if game and not game.is_over() determines that game doesn't have the value None and that its is_over method returns False—and displaying a different button according to the result. We vary two characteristics of the button—its text and its type. The text says "Restart game" if the game is in progress, and "Start new game" if it's not.

How about the button's type parameter? We may have given it a value in previous chapters, but let's examine it more thoroughly now. The three values type can take are primary, secondary, and tertiary—each indicating how prominent the button should be. A button with type primary has a solid color (usually orange) with white text, a secondary button—the default if you don't specify a type—is white with solid-colored text, while a tertiary button is more subtle and appears as regular text without a border.

In UI design, it's a good practice to guide the user towards the "correct" or most likely action they might want to take at any given point—it makes for a more intuitive design. If the game hasn't started yet, the choice that makes the most sense is to click the Start New Game button, so we give it a type of primary. If the game is in progress, the default action should be to answer the question, not to restart the game. Therefore, while we make that possibility available, we don't overly emphasize it. These differences in the button are mostly cosmetic, however. In either case, a click issues a call to start_new_game, which has the following code:

```
def start_new_game():
  st.session_state.game = Game(st.secrets['llm_api_key'])
  st.rerun()
```

As before, we create a Game instance and assign it to st.session_state.game. Since the presence of game in st.session_state changes what should be displayed on the screen, we also issue an st.rerun().

By wrapping this logic in a function, we're preventing it from executing by default, instead requiring the New Game button to actually be clicked.

The main column of the game—main_col—is, of course, where the content is meant to be displayed. In this iteration of main.py, we've simply moved the widgets we had before into main_col. There are a few additions worth highlighting though.

If game is None—which means no game has started yet—we want the main column to be completely blank so the player's attention is focused on side_col. This explains why the code under with main_col starts with if game:

```
with main_col:
  if game:
    st.header("Question", divider='gray')
    if game.status == 'GET_QUESTION':
      ...
```

We've also added a header that just says Question. We'll update this later to show the question number. Finally, we've added some logic to handle the case of the game being over under the STATE_RESULT state:

```
elif game.status == 'STATE_RESULT':
    ...
    if game.is_over():
      with st.container(border=True):
        st.markdown(f"Game over! Your final score is: **{game.score}**")
```

This should be quite clear. We use the is_over method we defined earlier to check if the game is done, and show an appropriate message and the final score (game.score) if so. That concludes another iteration of our code. Go ahead and rerun your app to get figure 9.9.

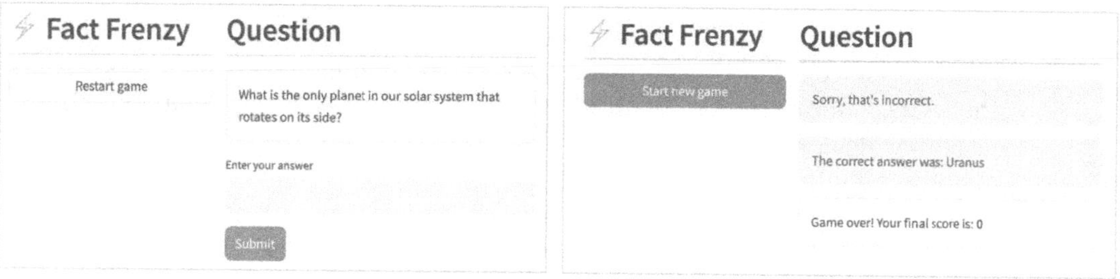

Figure 9.9 **Keeping score, a New Game button, and Game Over (see chapter_09/in_progress_04 in the GitHub repo for the full code).**

Sweet! Fact Frenzy is starting to look pretty slick. Adding support for multiple questions is next!

9.6 Including multiple questions

In the previous section, we introduced key game mechanics to our app—adding a score system and defining the game's start and end—to make it feel more like a real game. Fact Frenzy still only asks one question, though, so it's not much of one yet. It's time to change that. But before we do, let's explore an LLM-related challenge we'll face.

9.6.1   *Response variability, or lack thereof*

In many ways, an LLM is like a black box. Unlike a piece of "regular" code that tends to be deterministic—meaning that the same input always produces the same output—LLMs are *probabilistic*, which means you may get different responses for the same input (or similar inputs), based on a set of probabilities.

Depending on what you're trying to achieve, this variability can be a good or a bad thing. For example, if you're trying to get an LLM to generate poetry, you may want a fairly high amount of creativity or variability in the response, whereas if you're evaluating a mathematical equation, you want less. Vendors like OpenAI generally expose a few controls for this variability, making it easier to manage; however, we often need to engineer the prompt to extract the desired behavior from the model.

For our use case of generating questions, we want relatively high variability. If you've used our current app for a while, you may have noticed that the questions we receive from the LLM are often repeated. In my testing, for instance, the model had a particular fondness for asking about the only planet in the solar system that rotates on its side.

This won't work for us. For one thing, if a single game includes multiple questions, all of them *must* be unique. Secondly, even if a particular question isn't asked twice in the same game, we don't want it to repeat too often across *different* games either.

Let's take a look at a few ways in which we can control variability in the LLM's answer.

> **NOTE** One consequence of the fact that LLMs generate text based on probabilistic patterns (rather than an understanding of facts) is what we call *hallucinations*—instances where the model produces outputs that are plausible-sounding but factually incorrect or entirely fabricated. These hallucinations arise because LLMs rely on the statistical relationships in their training data, which can sometimes lead to confident but misleading responses. Strategies exist to reduce the likelihood of hallucinations, such as enabling LLMs to connect to external sources of information, but there's no way to guarantee they won't occur at all. Dealing with hallucinations is outside the scope of this chapter. We'll tackle supplementing an LLM's knowledge base with our own sources in the next one. Just be aware that our app may occasionally produce a question or answer that isn't factual. Fortunately, based on my testing, these occurrences tend to be infrequent.

VARYING TEMPERATURE AND TOP_P

The prompts we send to a large language model and the response we get back from it both consist of *tokens*. A token may be a single word, or only a part of it.

At its heart, an LLM constructs the response to a prompt step-by-step, or rather, token-by-token. In each step, it considers a wide range of possibilities for the next token to include in its response, assigning a *probability* of being picked (from high school math, a number between 0 and 1) to each token option.

These tokens form what's known as a *probability distribution*—think of it as a curve that represents the likelihood of each token being the next one, with the more likely tokens plotted at a higher place on the curve than the less likely ones.

OpenAI offers two parameters—`temperature` and `top_p`—that can adjust the composition of this curve. Figure 9.10 illustrates the effect of varying these parameters.

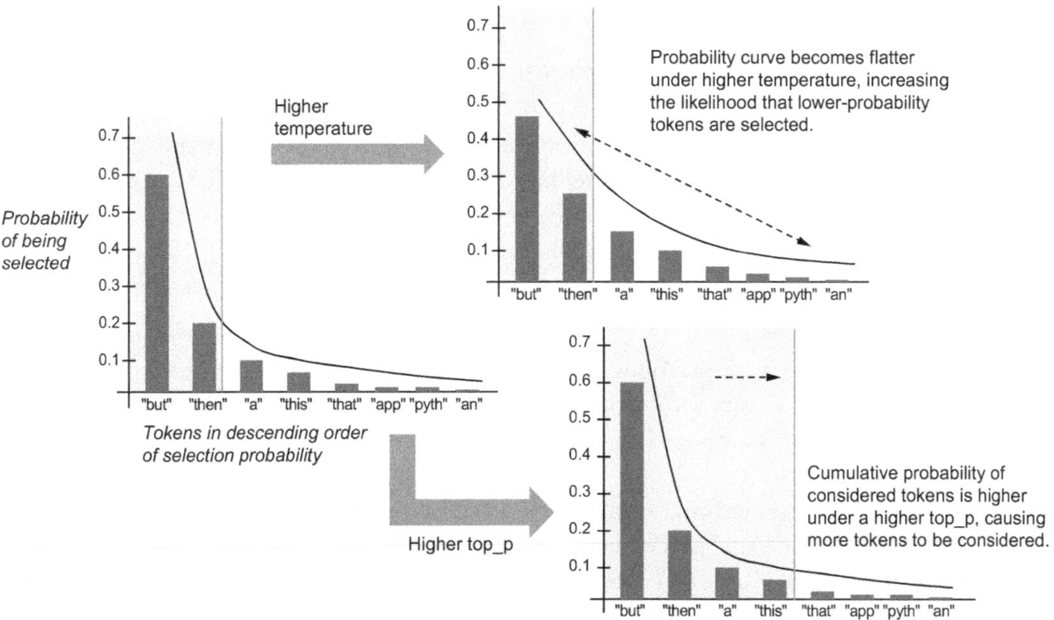

Figure 9.10 How `temperature` and `top_p` **affect the creativity and predictability of an LLM's output.**

`temperature` can take values from 0 to 2, with a higher value making the curve flatter, and a lower value making it more pronounced. A higher temperature thus tends to "even" out the curve, increasing the probability that some of the less likely token options may be picked, which makes the LLM take more "risks" and increases the overall creativity of its response.

`top_p` can go from 0 to 1. It represents a cutoff for the cumulative probability of the tokens that the model will choose from. To take an example, the LLM may determine that the five most likely next tokens in its response and their respective probabilities are: "but": 0.6, "then": 0.2, "a": 0.1, "this": 0.06, and "that": 0.02—with all other tokens having much lower probabilities.

A `top_p` of 0.8 would mean that the model should only choose between the most likely tokens with a combined probability of at least 0.8. In this case, since "but" and "then" together cover a probability of 0.6 + 0.2 >= 0.8, the model discards everything else.

A `top_p` of 0.95, on the other hand, would require the model to also consider "a" and "this" to cover the required cumulative probability (0.6 + 0.2 + 0.1 + 0.06 >= 0.95).

A higher `top_p`, therefore, means that the LLM will consider more token options, potentially reducing the predictability and coherence of the response, but increasing its diversity.

Getting back to our original goal of generating a variety of questions, we probably want a moderately high `temperature`—say 0.7 to 0.8—and a relatively high `top_p` of, say, 0.9.

INCLUDING PREVIOUS QUESTIONS IN THE PROMPT

As discussed, while it is ideal for questions not to repeat across different games, we must *guarantee* that the same question isn't asked twice in a *single* game. Fortunately, this is easily achieved by explicitly telling the LLM which questions have been asked so far in the game, so it knows to steer clear of those. For reinforcement, we could even tell the LLM to make sure never to ask the same question twice.

INJECTING RANDOMNESS

Another way to get a wider variety of questions back is to inject some structured randomness into the prompt. You may have heard of the word game Mad Libs, where players are provided a story with various parts of speech replaced with blanks. Each player then fills in a blank with a word of their choice, with the completed story often being hilarious.

We could do something similar here. We could change our prompt to something like "Generate a unique trivia question in the category ______ and a topic ______ within that category. The question should reference a person or thing whose name starts with the letter ______".

Within our code, we could then maintain lists of categories, topics, and letters, randomly picking one from each list to fill in the blanks before sending the prompt to the LLM. If we have, say, 10 categories, 10 topics within each category, we would have 26 (letters in the alphabet) × 10 × 10 = 2600 unique combinations, in addition to the variability that the LLM itself provides.

To save us the trouble of maintaining these lists, why not ask the LLM to pick a category and topic first? Interestingly, doing this increases the diversity of the responses generated.

Yet another way to inject randomness that seems to help is to explicitly provide a random *seed* in your prompt. In programming, a random seed is a value (generally an integer) that initializes a random number generator. While it's not very clear that adding one to the text of your prompt causes the LLM to generate a random number, in my testing, doing so did increase the variability of responses.

> **NOTE** It's important to note here that modifying your prompt to get the results you want is not pure science; often, you'll need to experiment with various techniques and prompts to identify the approach that works best. You may also see surprising results—for instance, AI researchers have found that asking

an LLM to think through its approach to solving a problem step-by-step often improves how well it performs the task.

9.6.2 *Implementing multiple questions*

Now that we've reviewed how variability works in LLMs and possible approaches to ensure we get different questions each time, let's modify Fact Frenzy so that it asks the user multiple questions during the game.

MODIFYING THE LLM PROMPT

Let's first make the requisite changes to our prompts to put into practice what we've learned. Before we do that, our `Llm` class doesn't currently offer a way to change the `temperature` and `top_p`, so we should modify its code (in llm.py) like this (chapter_09/in_progress_05/llm.py in the GitHub repo):

```python
from openai import OpenAI

class Llm:
  ...

  def ask(self, user_message, sys_message=None, schema=None,
          temperature=None, top_p=None):
    messages = self.construct_messages(user_message, sys_message)

    llm_args = {'model': 'gpt-5.1', 'messages': messages}
    if temperature:
      llm_args['temperature'] = temperature
    if top_p:
      llm_args['top_p'] = top_p

    if schema:
      completion = self.client.beta.chat.completions.parse(
        response_format=schema,
        **llm_args
      )
      return completion.choices[0].message.parsed
    else:
      completion = self.client.chat.completions.create(**llm_args)
      return completion.choices[0].message.content
```

As you can see above, we've refactored the `ask` method in the `Llm` class a fair bit. First, it accepts `temperature` and `top_p` as new arguments, both defaulting to `None`.

> **NOTE** OpenAI's "reasoning" models (such as `gpt-5-mini`) do not support configuring `temperature` and `top_p` explicitly, instead letting the model itself figure it out. Indeed, even `gpt-5.1` doesn't allow you to do it when its reasoning mode is turned on, which you can do by adding the key `reasoning_effort` to `llm_args` above and setting its value to `low`, `medium`, or `high`.

Instead of repeating the `model`, `messages`, `temperature`, and `top_p` arguments to the OpenAI client's `beta.chat.completions.parse` or `chat.completions.create`, we construct an `llm_args` dictionary that holds the right arguments and their values depending on whether each is provided.

We then use the `**` dictionary unpacking operator (which we encountered in chapter 7) to pass the arguments to the OpenAI methods. Note that we can combine this with the normal way of passing arguments:

```
completion = self.client.beta.chat.completions.parse(
  response_format=schema,
  **llm_args
)
```

Here we pass `response_format` in the regular way, but unpack `llm_args` for the remaining arguments.

Next, in prompts.py, edit our question-generation prompt so it now reads (chapter_09/in_progress_05/prompts.py in the GitHub repo):

```
QUESTION_PROMPT = {
    'system': 'You are a quizmaster who never asks the same question twice.',
    'user': '''
    First think of a unique category for a trivia question.
    Then think of a topic within that category.

    Finally, ask a unique trivia question, generated using the random seed
    {seed}, without revealing the category or topic.

    Do not provide choices, or reveal the answer.

    The following questions have already been asked:
    {already_asked}
    '''
}

ANSWER_PROMPT = {
  ...
```

You'll see that we've incorporated several of the techniques discussed in the last section:

- The system prompt requests the LLM to behave like a quizmaster who never asks the same question twice.
- We ask the LLM to think of a unique category and a topic within it.
- We add a "seed" variable and ask the LLM to generate the question using that seed.
- At the end of the prompt, for references, we provide the questions that have already been asked so that the LLM can avoid those.

We need to accompany these changes with additional ones in the `Game` class. Besides the LLM stuff, to enable asking multiple questions in a game, we need to be able to repeat the movement from the first game state to the last many times. In effect, our state diagram now becomes a *cycle* as opposed to a line, as shown in figure 9.11.

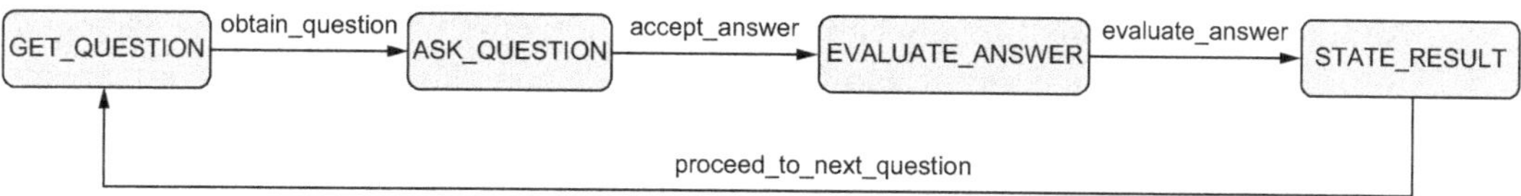

Figure 9.11 To implement multiple questions, we now cycle through the game states in a loop.

This means we also need another method to move from the `STATE_RESULT` state back to `GET_QUESTION`. Let's add this method along with the rest of the changes to game.py now (chapter_09/in_progress_05/game.py in the GitHub repo):

```
import time

from llm import Llm
...

class Game:
  def __init__(self, llm_api_key):
    ...
    self.max_questions = 5
    self.questions = []

  def ask_llm_for_question(self):
    seed = int(time.time())
    sys_msg = QUESTION_PROMPT['system']
    usr_msg = (
      QUESTION_PROMPT['user']
      .replace('{already_asked}', '\n'.join(self.questions))
      .replace('{seed}', str(seed))
    )
    return self.llm.ask(usr_msg, sys_msg, temperature=0.7, top_p=0.9)

  ...
  def obtain_question(self):
    self.curr_question = self.ask_llm_for_question()
    self.questions.append(self.curr_question)
    self.status = 'ASK_QUESTION'
    return self.curr_question

  ...
  def proceed_to_next_question(self):
    self.status = 'GET_QUESTION'

  ...
```

You'll see that we've added a new attribute, `self.questions`, within `__init__`, initializing it to an empty list. As you've likely guessed, this will hold all the questions we get from the LLM. We accomplish this through this addition in the `obtain_questions` method:

```
self.questions.append(self.curr_question)
```

Additionally, since we'll finally have more than one question to ask, we've changed the value of self.max_questions to 5. Feel free to change this to whatever number you like.

We've revamped the ask_llm_for_question method entirely, since our user message now has a couple of variables we need to provide values for. {already_asked} can simply be replaced by self.questions (with the individual list items separated by newlines).

For the random seed, we simply use the current timestamp converted to an integer:

```
seed = int(time.time())
```

Since timestamps always go up by definition, the current timestamp is guaranteed to be something the LLM has never gotten before from us. We also now pass temperature and top_p values to self.llm.ask in line with our exploration of these parameters.

To enable multiple questions, a newly added proceed_to_next_question sets the game's status back to GET_QUESTION, completing the state cycle in figure 9.11. The changes required to the frontend are relatively simple. Edit main.py like shown here (chapter_09/in_progress_05/main.py in the GitHub repo):

```
import streamlit as st
from game import Game


...
with main_col:
  if game:
    st.header(
      f"Question {len(game.questions)} / {game.max_questions}",
      divider='gray'
    )
    st.subheader(f"Score: {game.score}")

    if game.status == 'GET_QUESTION':
      ...


    ...
    elif game.status == 'STATE_RESULT':
      ...
      if game.is_over():
        with st.container(border=True):
          st.markdown(f"Game over! Your final score is: **{game.score}**")
      else:
        st.button(
          "Next question",
          type='primary',
          on_click=lambda: game.proceed_to_next_question()
        )
```

Firstly, we've modified the header of the main column to provide the question number (len(game.questions)) and the total number of questions (game.max_questions):

```
st.header(
  f"Question {len(game.questions)} / {game.max_questions}",
  divider='gray'
)
```

We've also added a subheader to display the score:

```
st.subheader(f"Score: {game.score}")
```

To facilitate the state change from `STATE_RESULT` to `GET_QUESTION`, we've added an `else` clause that will—if the game isn't over—display a Next Question button that triggers the game object's `proceed_to_next_question()` when clicked.

Notice the unfamiliar way in which we've written the `st.button` widget:

```
st.button(
  "Next question",
  type='primary',
  on_click=lambda: game.proceed_to_next_question()
)
```

`st.button`'s `on_click` parameter lets you specify a function to execute when the button is clicked. We *could* also have written this in the way we've done so far in this book, i.e. as:

```
if st.button("Next question", type='primary'):
  game.proceed_to_next_question()
  st.rerun()
```

The difference lies in when the triggered function is executed. Specifically:

- When we use the `if st.button` notation, the button click first triggers a rerun of the page, causing everything above the button to be re-rendered again before the code under the `if` executes, triggered by the fact that `st.button` evaluates to `True` in the rerun. After this code executes, we may need to manually trigger *another* rerun as shown above—and as we've been doing throughout this book, to see any changes in the page caused by it.

- With the `on_click` notation, the button click causes the function listed under `on_click` (called a *callback* by the way) to execute *before* the page is rerun and everything above the button is re-rendered. We don't need a manual `st.rerun()` in this case, because the rerun triggered by the button-click already takes into account the changes made by the callback since it has already executed.

So why haven't we been using this method all along? Well, the `if st.button` structure tends to be a little easier to grasp for simple apps. Besides, callbacks have some restrictions—you can't trigger an app rerun within a callback, for instance.

In any case, you should be able to rerun your app at this point to try out a working multi-question game (figure 9.12).

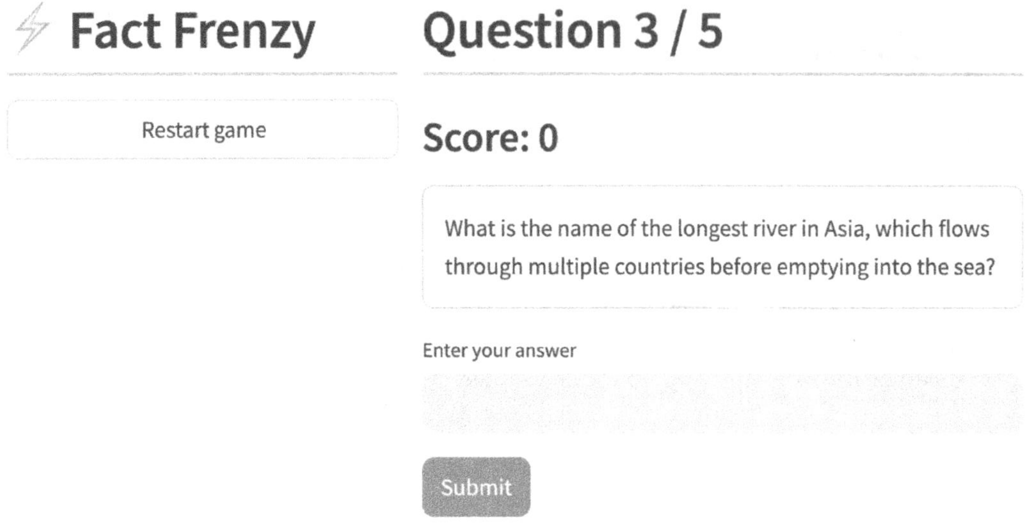

Figure 9.12   A working multi-question trivia game (see chapter_09/in_progress_05 in the GitHub repo for the full code).

Our trivia game is now technically complete, but let's see if we can make it more engaging in the next section.

Cost considerations

LLMs are an incredible general-purpose tool, but it is important to realize that using them in your app—especially in production where it may be accessed by hundreds of users—is not free. The last thing you want is to accidentally run up a huge bill.

Calculating the cost

When using an LLM, costs are typically calculated based on the number of *tokens* processed. As discussed in section 9.5.1, a *token* represents a chunk of text—a word or a part of a word—that the model reads (input) or generates (output).

OpenAI charges people based on the sum of the input and output tokens processed. This means that the size of the input prompt and the size of the output text *both* contribute to the cost. The pricing also differs by model. At the time of writing, the model we've been using in this chapter—gpt-5.1—costs $1.25 for every 1 million tokens processed.

You can use tools like https://platform.openai.com/tokenizer to count the tokens in a piece of text and determine costs.

Cost optimization strategies

There are several ways to optimize costs while working with LLMs. Here are a few ideas:

- Keep input prompts short and to the point to reduce costs associated with input tokens.
- Reduce the size of the output text, either by instructing the LLM to keep its response short or by explicitly restricting the number of tokens processed to a maximum value (e.g., by passing a value to the `max_tokens` argument while calling the OpenAI endpoint).
- Batch together multiple requests to reduce the total number of prompts sent to the LLM. For example, instead of providing a list of previously asked questions whenever we need a new question—as we're doing here—we could simply ask the LLM to generate the total number of questions we want in one go.
- Use less capable but cheaper models for some of your prompts. In our case, we're using gpt-5.1, but depending on your application, it may be possible to use cheaper models for less complex tasks. Familiarize yourself with OpenAI's pricing page.
- Avoid LLM costs altogether by asking the user to provide their *own* LLM API key. For our game, this involves a major hit to user experience as it requires players to create an OpenAI account before they can play, but you're guaranteed not to have to pay a dime in LLM-related costs.

9.7 Adding AI personalities

As an informative trivia game, Fact Frenzy works perfectly fine now. The end-to-end flow—from starting a new game to cycling through the questions and keeping score until the game ends—has been established. However, it still lacks a certain *je ne sais quoi*—it's rather dry and mechanical. Wouldn't it be cool if we could give our game a personality? Fortunately, this is precisely the kind of thing that LLMs excel at. We could, for instance, ask GPT-5.1 to mimic the style of various characters while asking questions.

In fact, we could let players choose what character they want their quizmaster to take. Sounds fun? Let's get to it!

9.7.1 Adding game settings

We don't currently have a page or place in the app where players can view or change any settings, so we'll tackle that first. What options do we want the user to be able to set? We've already talked about the quizmaster's speaking style, so that can be the first. We could also let the player pick a difficulty level that suits them.

We could use several designs for a "settings editor", but I want to use this opportunity to introduce a handy Streamlit widget we haven't encountered before: `st.data_editor`.

ST.DATA_EDITOR

In chapters 6 and 7, we learned about pandas dataframes, which make working with tabular data in Python easy. We discovered `st.dataframe`, used to render dataframes as a table in a Streamlit app for viewing.

`st.data_editor` displays dataframes too, but also makes them *editable*, providing users with an experience that you might expect in a spreadsheet. What does this have to do with adding settings to our app? Well, we could place the settings we want in a dataframe, and enable people to edit the dataframe to modify a setting. With the two settings we discussed a few paragraphs above, the settings dataframe might look like the following:

```
+----------------+------------+
|   Quizmaster   | Difficulty |
+----------------+------------+
| Alex Trebek    | Medium     |
+----------------+------------+
```

If this dataframe is stored in `default_settings`, we might write our `st.data_editor` widget like so:

```
settings = st.data_editor(default_settings, num_rows='fixed', key='settings_editor')
```

This would display the widget shown in figure 9.13.

The first argument here is the initial state of the data we want to edit—in this case, the default settings.

The `num_rows='fixed'` means that the data editor widget shouldn't allow users to add any new rows. This makes sense because we don't want to have multiple rows in the dataframe shown above—a single setting can only have one value.

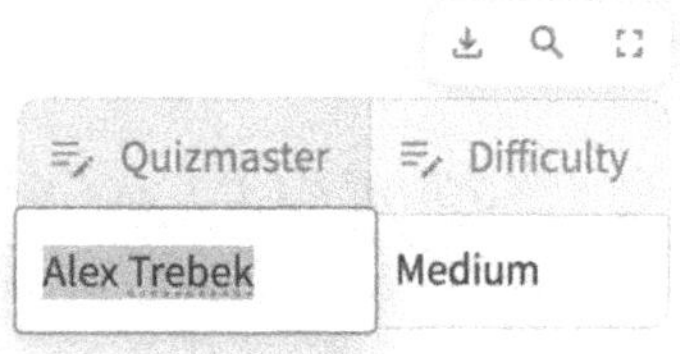

Figure 9.13   **A simple output of** `st.data_editor`

In any run of the app that happens before the user interacts with the data editor, `settings` will hold the same value as `default_settings`. Once the user changes a setting— for example, they might change Difficulty to `Easy`—`settings` will hold the edited dataframe across future reruns until the user edits it again.

> **NOTE**   The `key='settings_editor'` parameter adds a widget key to the session state for the data editor. While this isn't strictly required for the app to function correctly, it protects us from a certain quirk of Streamlit where it forgets the values of a widget without an explicit key between reruns if that widget isn't rendered for some reason in a particular run. Adding a widget key doesn't cost us anything, so it's safer to provide one to avoid unforeseen bugs.

Getting back to our example, we don't necessarily want users to have to type in the name of the quizmaster or a difficulty level; we'd rather have them select from a list of options. `st.data_editor` supports this in the form of *column configurations*:

```
st.data_editor(
  default_settings,
  column_config={
```

```
    'Quizmaster': st.column_config.SelectboxColumn(
        options=['Alex Trebek', 'Eminem', 'Gollum'],
        required=True
    ),
    'Difficulty': st.column_config.SelectboxColumn(
        options=['Easy', 'Medium', 'Hard'],
        required=True
    )
  },
  num_rows='fixed',
  key='settings_editor'
)
```

Here we exert more granular control over the editable data by configuring each column in the data through `st.column_config`.

For each of our columns, we use a `SelectBox-Column`, which lets us specify a list of options to choose from, and whether a value must be specified (the `required` parameter, set to `True` above). The results are shown in figure 9.14.

`st.column_config` supports many column types besides `SelectBoxColumn`, such as a `CheckboxColumn` for boolean values, a `DatetimeColumn` that displays a date/time picker, and a `LinkColumn` for clickable URLs.

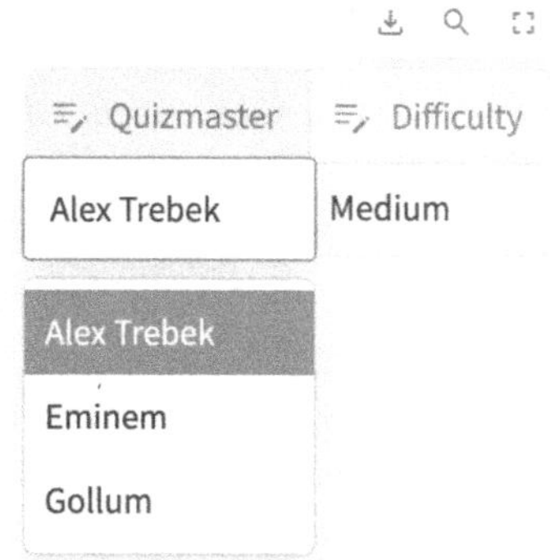

Figure 9.14 `st.data_editor` with one of the columns showing a `SelectBoxColumn`

It also supports non-editable types that can be used with `st.dataframe`, including `AreaChart-Column`, `BarChartColumn`, a `ListColumn` for lists, and even a `ProgressColumn` for numbers (displayed in a progress bar versus a target).

CREATING THE SETTINGS EDITOR

Now that we know how `st.data_editor` works, let's go ahead and create a settings editor UI. We'll put this in a new file called settings.py, as shown in listing 9.8 (chapter_09/in_progress_06/settings.py in the GitHub repo).

Listing 9.8 Placing game settings in settings.py

```python
import streamlit as st

QM_OPTIONS = ["Alex Trebek", "Eminem", "Gollum", "Gruk the Caveman"]
DIFFICULTY_OPTIONS = ["Easy", "Medium", "Hard"]

default_settings = {
  "Quizmaster": [QM_OPTIONS[0]],
  "Difficulty": [DIFFICULTY_OPTIONS[1]]
}

def settings_editor():
  with st.popover("Settings", use_container_width=True):
```

```python
return st.data_editor(
  default_settings,
  key='settings_editor',
  column_config={
    'Quizmaster': st.column_config.SelectboxColumn(
      options=QM_OPTIONS, required=True),
     'Difficulty': st.column_config.SelectboxColumn(
      options=DIFFICULTY_OPTIONS, required=True)
  },
  num_rows='fixed',
  use_container_width=True,
)
```

We place the options for the Quizmaster and Difficulty settings right at the top for easy access, listing them under `QM_OPTIONS` and `DIFFICULTY_OPTIONS`.

The Quizmaster options range from an actual quizmaster, the late Alex Trebek of *Jeopardy!* fame, to a range of fictional characters like Gollum from *The Lord of the Rings*, and Gruk the Caveman, an entirely made-up figure, to let the LLM go wild.

We've initialized `default_settings` as shown here:

```python
default_settings = {
  "Quizmaster": [QM_OPTIONS[0]],
  "Difficulty": [DIFFICULTY_OPTIONS[1]]
}
```

Note how this *isn't* a dataframe as we suggested initially—it's a dictionary with the name of each setting as a key, and a one-element list containing the default option for that setting as the corresponding value.

Interestingly, `st.data_editor` can display things that are not pandas dataframes. This includes native Python types such as dictionaries, lists, and sets. The quality of being able to display these types even applies to `st.dataframe`, despite the name. In this case, it means we don't have to maintain the settings as a dataframe; we can use the more readable dictionary form above.

The `settings_editor` function renders the actual settings editor UI. We place everything within yet another new Streamlit widget called `st.popover`:

```python
with st.popover("Settings", use_container_width=True):
  ...
```

`st.popover` displays a popover widget, which is a small pop-up screen that you can trigger by clicking an associated button—in a similar manner to `st.expander`. The first argument is the label for the button that triggers the `st.popover`.

The contents of the popover are written within the `with st.popover(...)` context manager. In this case, we're displaying the `st.data_editor` widget and returning its value, i.e. the edited `settings` dictionary:

```python
return st.data_editor(
  default_settings,
```

```python
    key='settings_editor',
    column_config={
      'Quizmaster': st.column_config.SelectboxColumn(
        options=QM_OPTIONS, required=True),
      'Difficulty': st.column_config.SelectboxColumn(
        options=DIFFICULTY_OPTIONS, required=True)
    },
    num_rows='fixed',
    use_container_width=True,
)
```

This is essentially the same code that we wrote in the previous section while discussing `st.data_editor`, though with the addition of a `use_container_width=True` argument, which adjusts the width of the popover.

APPLYING THE SETTINGS

How do we use these settings in Fact Frenzy? Both the Quizmaster and Difficulty settings relate to the question text generated by the LLM, so let's incorporate them in the question prompt in prompts.py (chapter_09/in_progress_06/prompts.py in the GitHub repo), which becomes

```python
QUESTION_PROMPT = {
    'system': '''
    You are a quizmaster who mimics the speaking style of {quizmaster} and
    never asks the same question twice.
    ''',
    'user': '''
    First think of a unique category for a trivia question.
    Then think of a topic within that category.

    Finally, ask a unique trivia question that has a difficulty rating of
    {difficulty} and is generated using the random seed {seed}, without
    revealing the category or topic.

    Do not provide choices, or reveal the answer.

    The following questions have already been asked:
    {already_asked}
    '''
}
...
```

Obviously, there are plenty of ways to work our two new variables into the prompt—the above is just one. We'll now modify game.py (chapter_09/in_progress_06/game.py in the GitHub repo):

```python
...
class Game:
  def __init__(self, llm_api_key, settings):
    self.llm = Llm(llm_api_key)
    self.settings = settings
```

```python
    self.status = 'GET_QUESTION'
    ...

  def get_setting(self, setting_name):
    return self.settings[setting_name][0]

  def modify_settings(self, new_settings):
    self.settings = new_settings

  def ask_llm_for_question(self):
    seed = int(time.time())
    sys_msg = (
      QUESTION_PROMPT['system']
      .replace('{quizmaster}', self.get_setting('Quizmaster'))
    )
    usr_msg = (
      QUESTION_PROMPT['user']
      .replace('{already_asked}', '\n'.join(self.questions))
      .replace('{seed}', str(seed))
      .replace('{difficulty}', self.get_setting('Difficulty'))
    )
    return self.llm.ask(usr_msg, sys_msg)

  def ask_llm_to_evaluate_answer(self):
    ...
  ...
```

Game's `__init__` now accepts a `settings` parameter, which—as you'd expect—is in the dictionary format we used in settings.py. This is assigned to `self.settings` so other methods can access it.

We've added two associated methods: `get_setting` and `modify_settings`. `get_setting` deals with getting the value of a given setting, which is slightly tricky because each dictionary value is a single-element list (designed that way so it works with `st.data_editor`). `get_setting` abstracts away this somewhat unsightly logic, so we restrict it to one place in the code.

`modify_settings` replaces `self.settings` with a given `new_settings` dictionary. This comes into play when the user changes a setting.

Turning to the `ask_llm_for_question` method, we replace the {quizmaster} and {difficulty} variables we added to the prompt with their corresponding values from the settings, obtained through `get_setting`.

The changes to main.py are all that remain now, so let's make those (chapter_09/in_progress_06/main.py in the GitHub repo):

```python
import streamlit as st
from game import Game
from settings import default_settings, settings_editor

def start_new_game():
  st.session_state.game = Game(st.secrets['llm_api_key'], default_settings)
  st.rerun()
```

```
...
with side_col:
  st.header("⚡ Fact Frenzy", divider='gray')
  settings = settings_editor()
  new_game_button(game)

with main_col:
  if game:
    game.modify_settings(settings)
    st.header(
      ...
    ...
```

In `start_new_game`, to obtain the initial `Game` instance, we now pass in `default_settings`, directly imported from settings.py. The actual settings editor is displayed within the side column (`side_col`), right above the New Game button. The return value—recall that this would be the `default_settings` dictionary before the user changes the value of any settings, and the modified dictionary afterward—is stored in the `settings` variable.

And, finally, in every rerun—provided that we're in a game—we run `game.modify_settings(settings)` to pick up any changes the user has made to the settings.

That should do it. Run your app again to see figure 9.15. Play around with the AI quizmaster options and difficulties; it's now more fun to read the questions!

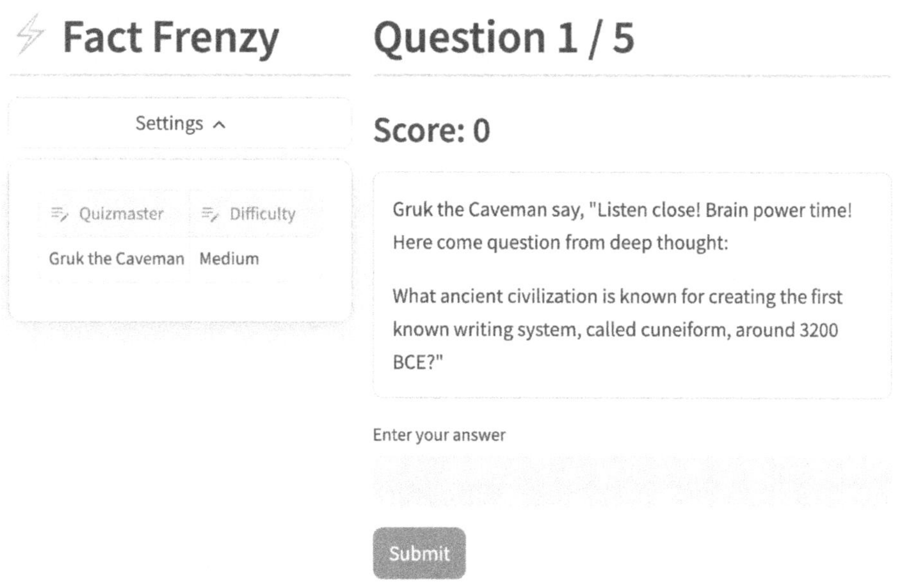

Figure 9.15 A final version of Fact Frenzy with editable settings (see chapter_09/in_progress_06 in the GitHub repo for the full code).

That concludes our development of Fact Frenzy, the first—and only—game we'll build in this book. In chapter 10, we'll continue our exploration of AI apps with a more practical application: a customer support chatbot.

Summary

- A Large Language Model (LLM) is an AI system designed to process and generate human-like text.
- LLMs can perform both creative and analytical tasks.
- OpenAI, one of the most popular LLM providers, lets developers access its GPT series through an API.
- The `openai` library provides a convenient way to call the OpenAI API in Python.
- You can pass a conversation to OpenAI API's chat completion endpoint with messages tagged as `system`, `assistant` or `user`, causing the model to complete the conversation in a logical way.
- Structured Outputs is a feature provided by OpenAI that ensures the model will generate a response that adheres to a given schema.
- A common pattern in linear Streamlit apps is to implement conditional branching logic based on a variable that's held in `st.session_state`.
- You can vary parameters such as `temperature` and `top_p` to affect the creativity and predictability of responses generated by an LLM.
- Injecting randomness into the prompt is a good way to ensure we get different responses to similar prompts.
- It's important to optimize cost in LLM-based applications. You can do this by having the LLM process fewer input and output tokens, reducing the number of prompts, using cheaper models, or even having users bear the cost by requiring them to supply their own API key.
- `st.data_editor` provides a way to create editable tables in Streamlit apps.
- `st.column_config` lets you configure columns to be of certain editable and non-editable types in `st.data_editor` and `st.dataframe`.
- `st.popover` displays a small pop-up screen triggered by clicking an associated button.

RAG and agentic apps with LangGraph and Streamlit

Creating a fun and engaging experience, like the trivia game we built in chapter 9, is exciting, but the true power of AI lies in its ability to drive real business value. AI isn't just about answering questions or generating text; it's about transforming industries, streamlining operations, and enabling entirely new business models.

But building AI applications that deliver economic value requires more than calling a pre-trained model. To be useful in real-world scenarios, AI must understand the context in which it operates, connect to external data sources, and take meaningful actions. Companies need AI to understand and respond to domain-specific queries, interact with business systems, and provide personalized assistance.

In this chapter, we'll build such an application: a customer service chatbot that retrieves real company data, helps customers track and cancel orders, and intelligently decides when to escalate problems to a human agent. By the end of the chapter, you'll know how to integrate LLMs with private knowledge bases, implement retrieval-augmented generation (RAG), and enable an AI agent to take action in the real world. Let's dive in.

NOTE The GitHub repository for this book is at https://github.com/ aneevdavis/streamlit-in-action. The chapter_10 folder includes the code for this chapter and a requirements.txt file that lists the exact versions of the required Python libraries.

10.1 *Nibby: A customer service bot*

Under the leadership of Note n' Nib's new CEO—renowned for his legendary decision-making prowess, aided by a certain dashboard revered across the company—the brand has flourished into a stationery powerhouse with rocketing sales.

But success brings its own challenges. The customer support department is swamped with calls from buyers who are impatient for their orders to arrive or seeking advice about fountain pen maintenance. After a month of complaints about long wait times, the CEO summons the one person known company-wide for reliable innovation.

And so it is that *you* are tasked with solving the support crisis. When you're not delivering seminars on Streamlit, you're reading up on the latest advances in AI; it is not long before an intriguing possibility hits you: might it be possible to *automate* customer support?

Over the course of a sleepless night, you sketch out plans for a Streamlit support bot named Nibby. Whispers of your project spread across the company. "We are saved!" some declare. "Nibby will not fail us!" Skeptics scoff: "'Tis folly! No *robot* can fix this."

Who will prove right? Let's find out.

10.1.1 *Stating the concept and requirements*

As always, we start with a distilled, short description of what we intend to build.

> *Nibby, a customer support chatbot that can help Note n' Nib's customers with information and basic service requests.*

Customer support obviously spans a lot of territory, so let's define the exact requirements more clearly.

REQUIREMENTS

In our vision of automating customer support, Nibby will be able to:

- Hold a human-like conversation with a customer
- Answer relevant questions about Note n' Nib and its products using a custom knowledge base
- Handle the following requests from the customer:

- Tracking an order
- Canceling an order

- Redirect to a human customer support agent if it cannot fulfill the request on its own

In essence, Nibby should take as much load off Note n' Nib's overworked human support agents as possible. Nibby should act as a frontline agent who can handle most basic requests, such as providing product information or canceling orders, and route customers to a human only when necessary.

WHAT'S OUT OF SCOPE

To keep this project manageable and small enough for this chapter, we won't implement the following:

- Storing or remembering prior conversations with users
- Any actions other than the two provided above (tracking and canceling orders)
- Practical logic for the two actions discussed, such as building an order-tracking or cancellation system

From a learning perspective, this book focuses on building a relatively complex AI system that can converse with users, understand a custom knowledge base, and take real-world actions.

The specific actions we enable the app to perform don't matter. For instance, the fact that our app can cancel an order, as opposed to replacing an item, is not of particular significance. Indeed, as implied by the third point above, the order cancellation we will implement is dummy "toy" logic. What *is* significant is that our bot should be able to intelligently choose to run that logic based on the free-form conversation the user is having with it.

10.1.2 Visualizing the user experience

The user interface for Nibby might be the most straightforward among all the apps in this book. Figure 10.1 shows a sketch of what we'll build.

Nibby's UI isn't significantly different from any chat or instant messaging app you may have used—from WhatsApp on your phone to Slack on your corporate laptop. You'll notice a familiar-looking text box at the bottom, where users can type messages. Each user message triggers an AI response, which is appended to the conversation view above.

10.1.3 Brainstorming the implementation

The difficult part of building this app will be the backend—specifically, getting the bot to answer questions correctly and connect to outside tools. Figure 10.2 shows the overall design.

While our trivia app from chapter 9 had an interesting design when it came to state management, its "intelligent" aspect was fairly simple—feed a prompt to an LLM and have it respond.

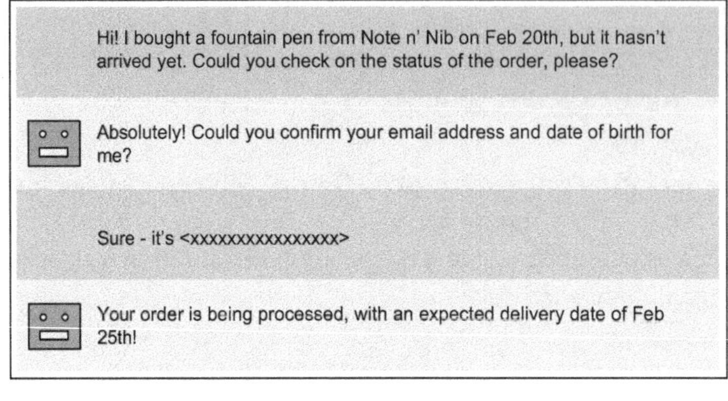

Figure 10.1   UI sketch for Nibby, a customer support chatbot

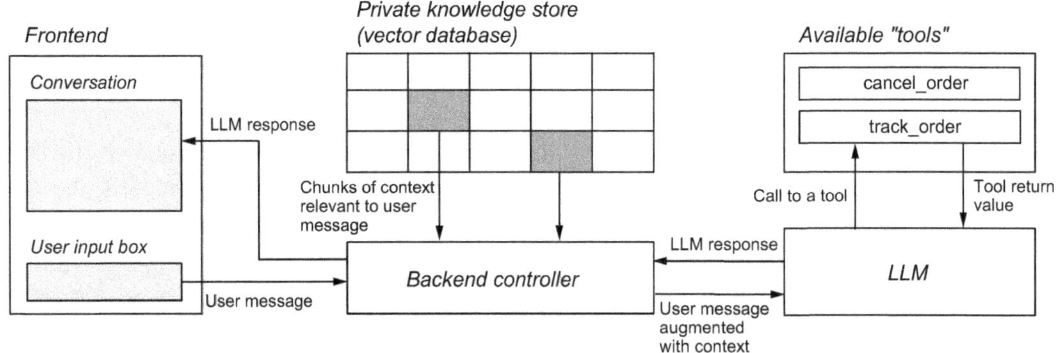

Figure 10.2   Nibby's overall design

On the other hand, a customer support app with the capabilities we're envisioning has a more involved design in at least two respects:

- It needs a way to augment a customer's query with private knowledge about the company that a human agent would possess.
- It needs to be able to execute code in the real world.

Figure 10.2 provides a basic overview of how we achieve these goals. When a user message comes in through our frontend, we retrieve context relevant to the message from a private knowledge store (a vector database, as we'll see later) and send that to the LLM.

We also organize the actions we want our bot to be able to take into so-called *tools* and make the LLM aware of their existence, what each tool does, and how to call them. For any given input, the LLM can either issue a call to a tool or respond to the user directly.

In the former case, we execute the tool as specified by the LLM and send the results for further processing, while in the latter case, we append the response to a conversation view on the frontend and await the user's next message.

10.1.4 Installing dependencies

We'll be using several Python libraries in this chapter. To get everything ready in advance, install them all at once by running the following command:

```
pip install langchain-community langchain-core langchain-openai
langchain-pinecone langgraph pinecone toml
```

10.2 Creating a basic chatbot

Chapter nine introduced LLMs and demonstrated how to use the OpenAI API for simple applications. While OpenAI's API is easy to integrate, developing more sophisticated AI-driven apps—such as those using Retrieval-Augmented Generation (RAG) or agent-based workflows, which we'll encounter soon—adds complexity.

A new ecosystem of libraries and tools has emerged to make creating complex AI apps as easy as possible. In this chapter, we'll explore LangGraph and LangChain, two libraries that work together to streamline the application creation process.

10.2.1 Introduction to LangGraph and LangChain

LLMs have undoubtedly been the most influential technological advance of the last decade. At their core, interacting with an LLM consists of providing a prompt that the LLM can complete. That's what everything else is built around.

Contrast this with the complexities that modern AI applications have to deal with:

- Handling multi-step workflows (e.g., retrieving information before responding)
- Integrating with external tools
- Retaining conversation context across multiple turns

Managing this complexity manually is difficult, which is where LangChain and LangGraph—both Python libraries—come in. LangChain provides building blocks for working with LLMs, including prompt management, memory, and tool integration. It also supports LLMs from many different providers (OpenAI, Anthropic, Google, etc.), with abstractions that make it easier to swap models in and out while minimizing code changes.

LangGraph—developed by the same company—extends LangChain by structuring AI workflows as *graphs*, allowing for decision-making, branching logic, and multi-step processing. By combining these, we can design structured, intelligent AI applications that go beyond simple chat responses, enabling Nibby to retrieve knowledge, call APIs, and make decisions dynamically.

In the rest of this chapter, we'll use these libraries extensively to achieve the functionality we want.

NOTE   Since we will model our chatbot as a *graph* in LangGraph, we'll primarily speak about and refer to LangGraph rather than LangChain. However, you'll notice that many of the underlying classes and functions we'll use are imported from LangChain.

10.2.2 *Graphs, nodes, edges, and state*

In LangGraph, you construct an AI application by building a *graph* of *nodes* that transform the application's *state*. If you don't have a background in computer science, that statement might trip you up, so let's break it down.

WHAT IS A GRAPH, EXACTLY?

In graph theory, a graph is a network of interconnected vertices (also known as nodes) and edges that connect vertices to each other. Software developers often use graphs to create conceptual models of real-world objects and their relationships. For instance, figure 10.3 shows a graph of people you might expect to find on a social media website.

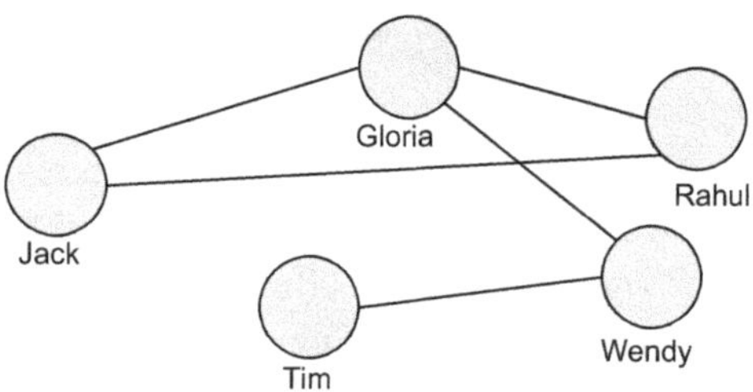

Figure 10.3   Using a graph to model friend relationships in a social network.

Here, each person is a vertex or node (shown by a circle), and the "friend" relationship between any two people is an edge (the lines between the circles).

By modeling relationships in this way, the social media website can apply various algorithms developed for graphs to do useful real-world things. For instance, there's an algorithm called breadth-first search (BFS) that finds the shortest path from one node to any other node. In this case, we could use it to find the fewest common friends required to connect two people.

In LangGraph, we model an application as a graph of *actions*, where a *node* signifies a single action that the application performs. A graph has a *state*, simply a collection of named attributes with values (similar to Streamit's concept of session state). Each node takes the current state of the graph as input, does something to modify the state, and returns the new state as its output (figure 10.4).

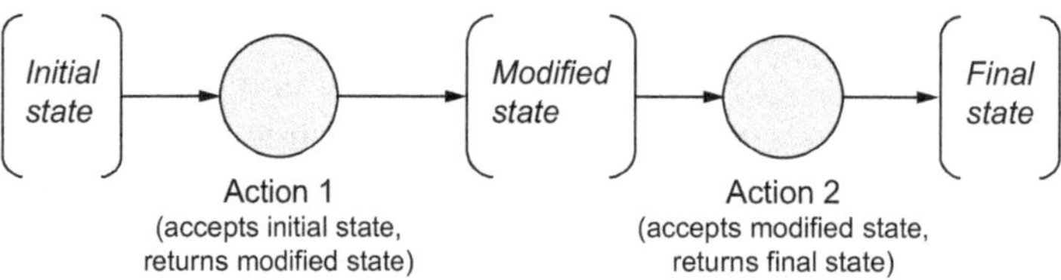

Figure 10.4   In LangGraph, nodes take in the graph state and modify it.

An edge in the graph represents a connection between two nodes, or in other words, the fact that the output of one node may be the input to another. Unlike in the case of a social media graph, where the edges had no direction (i.e., if two people are friends, each is a friend of the other), edges in LangGraph are *directed* because one node in the edge is executed *before* the other. Visually, we represent the direction as an arrow on the edge (as in figure 10.4). The input to the graph is its initial state, which is passed to the *first* node that's executed, while the output is the final state returned by the *last* node that's executed.

That was a fair bit of theory; let's now consider a toy example (figure 10.5) to make this all real.

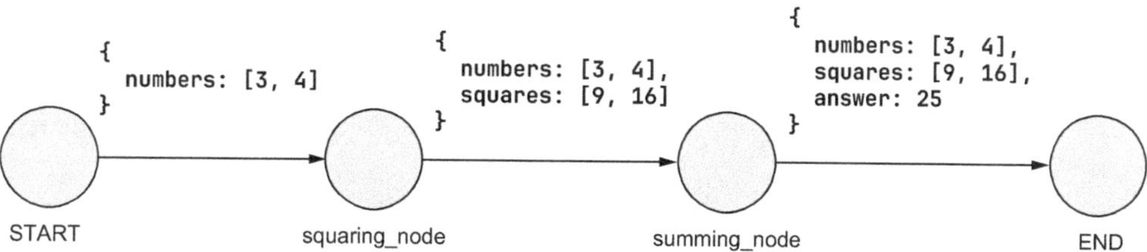

Figure 10.5   A graph in LangGraph that computes the sum of squares of numbers.

The application shown in figure 10.5 is a very simple one. There's no AI involved; it's just a program that takes a list of numbers and returns the sum of their squares—e.g., for the input [3, 4], the graph would calculate the output 25 (3^2 + 4^2 = 25).

The graph's state contains three values: numbers, squares, and answer. numbers holds the list of input values (e.g. [3, 4]), while squares and answer don't have a value to start with.

Each LangGraph graph has dummy nodes called START and END, which represent the start and end of execution. There are two other "real" nodes: squaring_node and summing_node.

Here's how the graph is executed:

1 The START node receives the initial state.

2 Since there's a directed edge from START to squaring_node, squaring_node is executed first.

3 squaring_node takes in the starting state, squares the numbers in the numbers list, and saves the new list ([9, 16]) under the variable squares in the state.

4 As there's an edge from squaring_node to summing_node, summing_node takes as input this modified state returned by squaring_node.

5 summing_node adds up the numbers in squares, and saves the result as answer.

6 summing_node has an edge to END, which means the end of execution. The final state returned will contain 25 under answer.

Of course, this is a simple graph with only one path the execution can take. In a later part of this chapter, you'll encounter a graph with multiple paths, where a single node may branch into multiple nodes based on the state at that point.

I hope this helped crystallize the concept of graphs and how LangGraph uses them to perform a task. It's now time to use what we've learned to start building our app.

10.2.3 A one-node LLM graph

The basic graph we built in the previous section had nothing to do with AI or LLMs. Indeed, you can use LangGraph to build anything you like, whether or not AI is involved, but in practice, the point of LangGraph is to make building AI applications easier.

CREATING AND RUNNING YOUR FIRST GRAPH

In chapter 9, we encountered the OpenAI API's chat completions endpoint. In this endpoint, we pass a list of messages to the API, which predicts the next message in the conversation. In LangGraph, such an application could be represented by a simple one-node graph, as shown in figure 10.6.

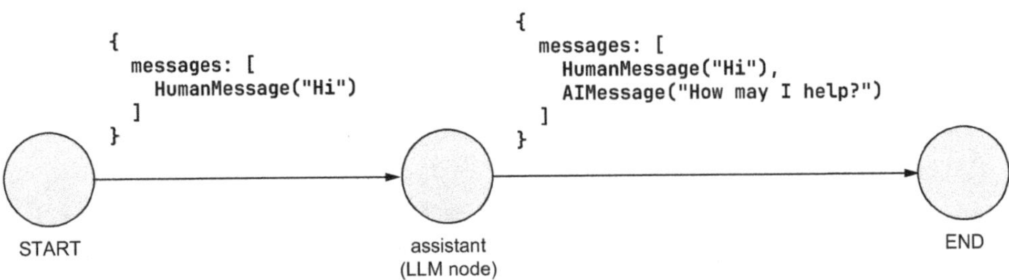

Figure 10.6   A basic single-node (apart from START and END) graph

The state of the graph consists of a single variable, messages, which is—as you might expect—a list of messages. The only node in the graph, assistant_node, passes messages to an LLM and returns the same list with an AI response message appended.

> **NOTE** This representation of an AI application as a graph may seem rather unintuitive right now, and you may question why we even bother with it. The true power of this approach becomes clearer when we have a *non-linear* graph, i.e., when the application may take multiple paths depending on the graph's state. I must ask for your patience here, as we only graduate to a non-linear graph at the very end of this chapter, where we introduce AI agents.

Listing 10.1 shows this graph translated to real (non-Streamlit) Python code (chapter_10/graph_example.py in the GitHub repo).

Listing 10.1   An example of a graph

```python
from langgraph.graph import START, END, StateGraph
from langchain_core.messages import AnyMessage, HumanMessage
from langchain_openai import ChatOpenAI
from typing import TypedDict

llm = ChatOpenAI(model_name="gpt-5.1", openai_api_key="sk-proj-...")

class MyGraphState(TypedDict):
  messages: list[AnyMessage]

builder = StateGraph(MyGraphState)

def assistant_node(state):
  messages = state["messages"]
  ai_response_message = llm.invoke(messages)
  return {"messages": messages + [ai_response_message]}

builder.add_node("assistant", assistant_node)
builder.add_edge(START, "assistant")
builder.add_edge("assistant", END)
graph = builder.compile()

input_message = input("Talk to the bot: ")
initial_state = {"messages": [HumanMessage(content=input_message)]}
final_state = graph.invoke(initial_state)

print("Bot:\n" + final_state["messages"][-1].content)
```

First, we initialize the LLM in this line:

```python
llm = ChatOpenAI(model_name="gpt-5.1", openai_api_key="sk-proj-...")
```

This is similar to what we did in chapter 9 when we created an OpenAI API client.
LangChain—a library closely related to LangGraph—provides a class called `ChatOpenAI`
that does essentially the same thing but is slightly easier to use. As before, don't forget
to replace `sk-proj...` with your actual OpenAI API key.

Consider the next part:

```python
class MyGraphState(TypedDict):
  messages: list[AnyMessage]
```

As we've discussed, a graph has a state. For each graph you define, you specify what
fields exist in the state by creating a class that contains those fields. In the above two
lines, we're creating `MyGraphState` to represent the state of the graph we're about to
define. In line with the example in figure 10.6, `MyGraphState` contains one field—
messages—which is a list of objects of the type `AnyMessage`.

In chapter 9, we saw that each message in an (OpenAI) LLM conversation has a *role*—
one of `user`, `assistant`, or `system`. In LangChain, the same concept is represented by

the `AnyMessage` superclass. `HumanMessage`, `AIMessage`, and `SystemMessage` are subclasses that inherit functionality from `AnyMessage`, and correspond to the `user`, `assistant`, and `system` roles, respectively.

`MyGraphState` itself is a subclass of `TypedDict`, a specialized dictionary type from Python's typing module that allows us to define a dictionary with a fixed set of keys and associated value types. Since it inherits all of `TypedDict`'s behaviors, we can treat instances of `TypedDict`—and therefore, `MyGraphState`— as regular dictionaries, using the same syntax for accessing their keys (i.e., the fields in the class) and values.

> **NOTE** We don't technically *have* to use a `TypedDict` to represent the state of the graph. We could also have used a regular class, a dataclass, or a Pydantic `BaseModel`, which we used in chapter 9. We've introduced and used `TypedDict` here because it plays well with `MessagesState`, a built-in LangGraph class that we'll discuss shortly.

The next line, `builder = StateGraph(MyGraphState)`, initializes the construction of our graph. Here we're telling LangGraph that we're building a `StateGraph`—the type of graph we've been talking about, where the nodes read from and write into a shared state—whose state is represented by a `MyGraphState` instance (which, as we've seen, will have a `messages` list).

We now define the only node in our graph like this:

```python
def assistant_node(state):
  messages = state["messages"]
  ai_response_message = llm.invoke(messages)
  return {"messages": messages + [ai_response_message]}
```

Each node in a LangGraph graph is a regular Python function that accepts the current state of the graph—a `MyGraphState` instance—as input, and returns the parts of the state it wants to modify.

The `assistant_node` we've defined above is quite minimal; it simply passes the `messages` list—accessed using square brackets as `state["messages"]` just like in a regular dictionary—to the `invoke` method of `llm`, obtaining the AI's response message. It then modifies the `messages` key of the state, adding `ai_response_message` to the end, and returns the result.

> **NOTE** In the preceding code, since `MyGraphState` has only one key, `messages`, it seems that `assistant_node` is simply returning the entirety of the modified state. That's not strictly true—it's actually only returning the keys it wants to modify, leaving any other keys untouched. This will become clear in later sections.

Now that we've created our only node, it's time to put it in our graph:

```python
builder.add_node("assistant", assistant_node)
builder.add_edge(START, "assistant")
builder.add_edge("assistant", END)
```

The first line adds a node called `assistant` to the graph, pointing to the `assistant_node` function we have just developed as the logic for the node.

As mentioned earlier, each graph has dummy `START` and `END` nodes. The remaining two lines create directed edges from `START` to our `assistant` node, and from our `assistant` node to `END`, thus completing the graph.

The immediately following line, `graph = builder.compile()`, *compiles* the graph, readying it for execution.

The last few lines of code in the file show how a graph can be invoked:

```
input_message = input("Talk to the bot: ")
initial_state = {"messages": [HumanMessage(content=input_message)]}
final_state = graph.invoke(initial_state)

print("The LLM responded with:\n" + final_state["messages"][-1].content)
```

We first use the `input()` function—which prompts the user to enter something in the terminal—to collect the user's input message.

We then construct the starting state of the graph as a dictionary with the key `messages`. The message itself is an instance of `HumanMessage` with its content attribute set to the `input_message` we just collected.

Passing `initial_state` to the graph's `invoke` method finally causes the graph to execute, effectively passing our user input to the LLM through `assistant_node`, returning the final state.

`final_state` contains all of the messages in the conversation so far (our user message and the LLM's response message), so we access the response message using `final_state["messages"][-1]` and print its content to the screen.

To see this in action, temporarily copy all the code to a new file called graph_example .py, and run your code in the terminal using the `python` command like this:

```
python graph_example.py
```

Enter a message when you see the `"Talk to the bot"` prompt. As an example output, here's what I got:

```
$ python graph_example.py
Talk to the bot: Howdy! Could you write a haiku about Note n' Nib for me?
Bot:
Ink and paper dance,
Whispers of thoughts intertwine—
Note n' Nib's embrace.
```

It looks like AI stole my dream haiku gig. Maybe I'll pivot to the performing arts—everyone loves a good mime.

TURNING THE GRAPH INTO A CLASS

We've run our first graph in the terminal, but what we really want is to use it to power a customer support bot. We'll organize the code using object-oriented principles, as we did in the last two chapters.

Let's start by converting the code from the prior section into a `SupportAgentGraph` class in graph.py, as shown in listing 10.2 (chapter_10/in_progress_01/graph.py in the GitHub repo).

Listing 10.2   The `SupportAgentGraph` class in graph.py

```python
from langgraph.graph import START, END, StateGraph, MessagesState
from langchain_core.messages import HumanMessage

class SupportAgentGraph:
  def __init__(self, llm):
    self.llm = llm
    self.graph = self.build_graph()

  def get_assistant_node(self):
    def assistant_node(state):
      ai_response_message = self.llm.invoke(state["messages"])
      return {"messages": [ai_response_message]}
    return assistant_node

  def build_graph(self):
    builder = StateGraph(MessagesState)
    builder.add_node("assistant", self.get_assistant_node())
    builder.add_edge(START, "assistant")
    builder.add_edge("assistant", END)
    return builder.compile()

  def invoke(self, human_message_text):
    human_msg = HumanMessage(content=human_message_text)
    state = {"messages": [human_msg]}
    return self.graph.invoke(state)
```

The code here is very similar to that in graph_example.py, but a few differences are worth highlighting. Most obviously, we're encapsulating our graph in a class—`SupportAgentGraph`—which has a method for building the actual graph (`build_graph`) and another (`invoke`) for invoking it by passing a human (user) message. Rather than creating the LLM object within the class, we accept it as a parameter in `SupportAgent-Graph`'s `__init__`, which builds the graph by calling `self.build_graph()` and saves it under `self.graph` for future invocations.

You'll notice that our `MyGraphState` class, which we defined earlier, is nowhere to be found. We've swapped it out for `MessagesState`, a built-in LangGraph class that does more or less the same thing. `MessagesState`, like `MyGraphState`, has a `messages` field, which is a list of `AnyMessage` objects. The big difference between `MyGraphState` and `MessagesState` is how the `messages` field can be modified in a node—more on that in a second.

Next, consider the `get_assistant_node` method:

```python
def get_assistant_node(self):
  def assistant_node(state):
    ai_response_message = self.llm.invoke(state["messages"])
    return {"messages": [ai_response_message]}
  return assistant_node
```

This method has a function definition for `assistant_node`, which we encountered in the previous section, nested under it. It seems to do nothing other than return the function. What's that about?

Well, since `assistant_node` needs to access the LLM object (`self.llm`), its code must live inside a method of the `SupportAgentGraph` class. But `assistant_node` can't *itself* be a method of the class, because the first argument passed to a method is `self`—the current instance of the class—while the first (and only) argument passed to a valid LangGraph node must be the graph state.

So instead, we define `assistant_node` as an inner function within an outer method called `get_assistant_node`—taking advantage of the outer method's scope to access `self.llm` within the inner function—and have the outer method *return* the inner function so we can plug it into the graph. This programming pattern is called a *closure* because the inner function retains access to variables from its *enclosing* scope, even after the outer function has returned. The aforementioned plugging-in of the node happens in the `build_graph` method in this line:

```python
builder.add_node("assistant", self.get_assistant_node())
```

Since `get_assistant_node()` *returns* the `assistant_node` function (as opposed to calling it), we can use the call to `get_assistant_node` to refer to the inner function. The `assistant_node` function differs from the one of the same name we defined in the prior section in one important way. Consider the return statement, which has changed from:

```python
return {"messages": messages + [ai_response_message]}
```

to:

```python
return {"messages": [ai_response_message]}
```

Why do we not return the other items in the `messages` list anymore? The answer has to do with our having replaced `MyGraphState` with `MessagesState`. You see, each node in LangGraph's `StateGraph` receives the complete state as input, but the value it returns is treated as a set of *updates* to each key in the state. How exactly these updates are merged with the existing values depends on how we've specified it in our state type.

In MyGraphState, we didn't mention any particular way of handling this, so the value associated with the key messages is simply replaced by whatever the node returns for that key. This is why we needed to return the entire list—because we would have lost the earlier messages otherwise.

On the other hand, MessagesState internally specifies that the value returned by a node should be appended to the existing list. So, ai_response_message is simply tacked on to the existing messages, and we don't have to return the older messages separately.

> **NOTE** MessagesState implements this append feature through a function called add_messages. In fact, the only difference between MyGraphState and MessagesState is that the messages field in MessagesState is defined (internally) like this: messages: Annotated[list[AnyMessage], add_messages]. I won't go into this in detail, but this is essentially saying that when updates occur, they should be handled by the add_messages function rather than by a simple replacement.

Whew! That was a lot of explanation, but hopefully, you now understand how graphs are modeled in LangGraph.

THE BOT CLASS

Let's set aside SupportAgentGraph now and pivot to our main backend class, which we'll call Bot. Bot will be the single point of entry to the backend for our Streamlit frontend, similar to the Game and Hub classes in earlier chapters.

Importantly, Bot will supply the LLM object that SupportAgentGraph needs and provide a user-friendly method that our frontend can call to chat with the bot.

To create it, copy the code in listing 10.3 to a new file, bot.py (chapter_10/in_progress_01/bot.py in the GitHub repo).

Listing 10.3   The Bot class in bot.py

```python
from langchain_openai import ChatOpenAI
from graph import SupportAgentGraph

class Bot:
  def __init__(self, api_keys):
    self.api_keys = api_keys
    self.llm = self.get_llm()
    self.graph = SupportAgentGraph(llm=self.llm)

  def get_llm(self):
    return ChatOpenAI(
      model_name="gpt-5.1",
      openai_api_key=self.api_keys["OPENAI_API_KEY"],
      max_tokens=2000
    )

  def chat(self, human_message_text):
    final_state = self.graph.invoke(human_message_text)
    return final_state["messages"][-1].content
```

Luckily, the Bot class is a lot more straightforward than SupportAgentGraph. __init__ accepts a dictionary of API keys—which, spoiler alert, we'll supply through st.secrets again—before setting up the LLM object with a call to the get_llm method, and passing it to the SupportAgentGraph instance, saved to self.graph.

get_llm simply uses LangChain's ChatOpenAI class to create the LLM object as discussed earlier. Notice that we've added a new parameter called max_tokens. As you may remember from the previous chapter, tokens are the basic units of text that language models process. By setting max_tokens=2000, we're telling OpenAI's API to limit responses to a maximum of 2000 tokens (about 1,500 words), which helps in both cost reduction and keeping responses (relatively) concise.

The chat method abstracts away the complexity of dealing with graphs and states. It has a simple contract—put a human message string in, and get an AI response string out. It fulfills this promise by calling the invoke method of our SupportAgentGraph's instance, and returning the content of the last message, which happens to be the AI message, as we saw earlier.

A CHATBOT FRONTEND IN STREAMLIT

Our app's backend is now ready, so let's focus on the frontend. Streamlit really shines when it comes to chatbot interfaces because of its native support for them.

This is evident in the fact that our first iteration of frontend.py—shown in listing 10.4 (chapter_10/in_progress_01/frontend.py in the GitHub repo)—is only 12 lines long.

Listing 10.4 A simple chatbot frontend in frontend.py

```python
import streamlit as st
from bot import Bot

if "bot" not in st.session_state:
  api_keys = st.secrets["api_keys"]
  st.session_state.bot = Bot(api_keys)
bot = st.session_state.bot

if human_message_text := st.chat_input("Chat with me!"):
  st.chat_message("human").markdown(human_message_text)
  ai_message_text = bot.chat(human_message_text)
  st.chat_message("ai").markdown(ai_message_text)
```

We start by putting a reference to our Bot instance—bot—in st.session_state, which is essentially the same pattern we've used in the last two chapters for the Hub and Game classes. To do so, we pass in the api_keys object from st.secrets to do so. We'll create secrets.toml in a bit.

The interesting part is in the last four lines. The first introduces a new Streamlit widget called st.chat_input:

```python
if human_message_text := st.chat_input("Chat with me!"):
  ...
```

`st.chat_input` creates a text input box with a Send icon, similar to what you're probably used to in various messaging apps. Besides the Send icon, it's different from `st.text_input` in a few noticeable ways:

- It's pinned to the *bottom* of the screen or the containing widget you put it in
- Unlike `st.text_input`, which returns a value once a user clicks out of the textbox, `st.chat_input` only returns a value once the user has clicked Send or pressed Enter.

Apart from `st.chat_input`, the code above may look unfamiliar for another reason; we're using the character sequence `:=`, which is called a *walrus operator* in Python (because if you tilt your head to the side, it kind of looks like a walrus).

The walrus operator is just a trick to make your code slightly more concise. It allows you to assign values to variables as part of a larger expression rather than requiring a separate line for assignment. In other words, instead of the line we're discussing, we could have written the following to obtain the same effect:

```
human_message_text = st.chat_input("Chat with Nibby!")
if human_message_text:
    ...
```

> **NOTE** Python developers are divided on whether the walrus operator increases or decreases the readability of your code. Regardless of whether you choose to use it, it's good to know what it is.

Once we have an input message from the user, we can display the conversation:

```
st.chat_message("human").markdown(human_message_text)
ai_message_text = bot.chat(human_message_text)
st.chat_message("ai").markdown(ai_message_text)
```

`st.chat_message` is a Streamlit display widget that accepts either of two strings—human or ai—and styles the container accordingly. This includes showing an avatar corresponding to a user or a robot.

In this case, we display `human_message_text` using `st.chat_message("human")`, call the `chat` method of our Bot instance, and display the response AI text with `st.chat_message("ai")`.

Just to be clear, `st.chat_message` is similar to other Streamlit elements like `st.column` in that we could also have written:

```
with st.chat_message("human"):
    st.markdown(human_message_text)
```

To complete the first version of Nibby, we need to create a secrets.toml file for our OpenAI API key, in a new .streamlit folder. The contents of this file are in listing 10.5.

```
[api_keys]
OPENAI_API_KEY = 'sk-proj-...'
```
Listing 10.5 The API key in .streamlit/secrets.toml

Replace sk-proj-... with your actual OpenAI API key.

Go ahead and run your app with `streamlit run frontend.py` to test it out. Figure 10.7 shows our chatbot in action.

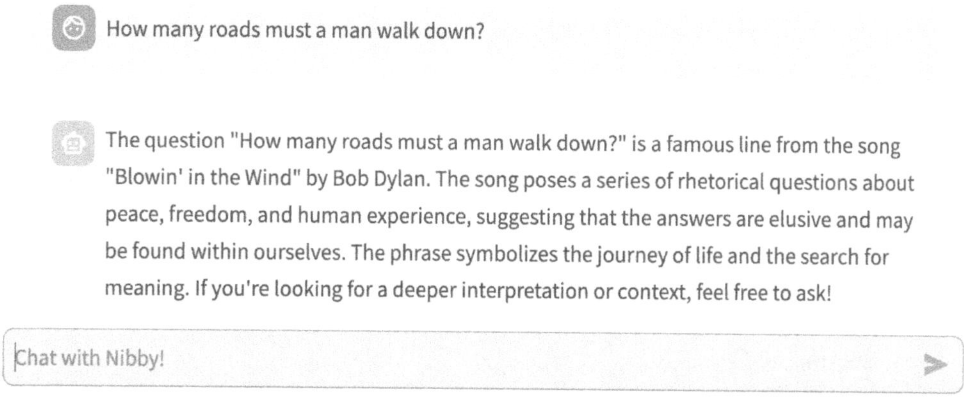

Figure 10.7 A single-prompt-single-response chatbot in Streamlit (see chapter_10/in_progress_01 in the GitHub repo for the full code).

Sweet! Notice the human and bot avatars, as well as the subtle background shading that distinguishes between the two types of displayed messages. If you experiment with the app, you'll notice that Nibby can't currently hold a conversation, but can only respond to individual messages. Next up, let's fix that!

10.3 Multi-turn conversations

It took some effort to get there, but we've built an initial version of Nibby. Unfortunately, at the moment, Nibby's idea of a conversation is a single response to a single message. For instance, consider the exchange in figure 10.8. Two things are wrong here:

- The bot didn't remember the information I gave it in the prior message.
- Our frontend treats the second message-response pair as a completely new conversation, removing all traces of the first.

In this section, we'll iterate on Nibby, solving both problems.

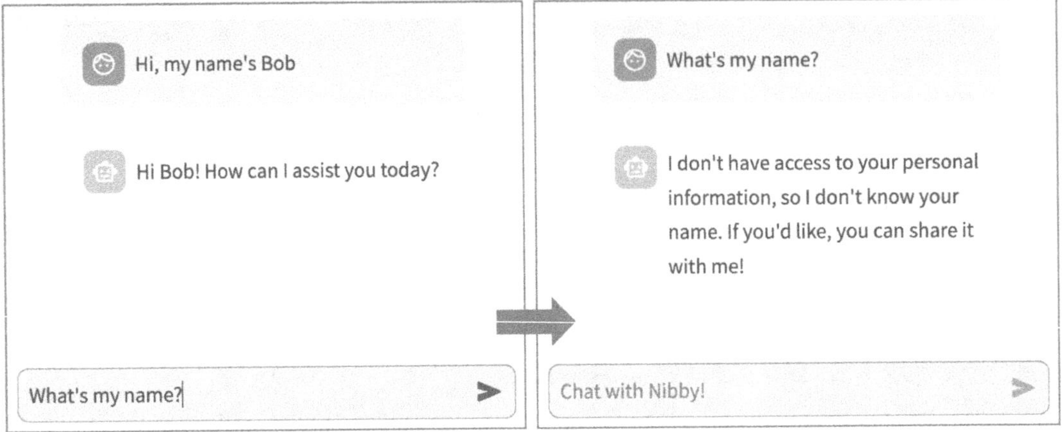

Figure 10.8   The chatbot doesn't remember previously shared information.

10.3.1 *Adding memory to the graph*

Recall the simple one-node graph: it starts with a state containing a human message, passes the message to an LLM, appends the AI's response to the state, and then returns the updated state.

What happens if you invoke the graph again with a follow-up message? Well, the process repeats—a *new* state containing *only* the follow-up message is created and passed to the graph, which treats this as a brand-new independent execution.

This is clearly a problem because conversations rarely consist exclusively of a single message and response. The user *will* want to follow up, and the chatbot needs to remember the previous conversation.

To enable our graph to remember prior executions, we need to *persist* the state, rather than start from scratch every time. Luckily, LangGraph makes this a snap through the concept of *checkpointers*, which can save the state of the graph at each step.

Specifically, we will use a checkpointer to enable our graph state to be stored in memory. We can then assign a *thread ID* to each invocation of the graph. Whenever we pass the same thread ID while invoking the graph, the graph will recall the state previously stored in memory for that thread ID and start from *there* rather than from a clean slate.

To implement this, make the changes shown below to graph.py (see chapter_10/in_progress_02/graph.py in the GitHub repo):

```python
from langgraph.checkpoint.memory import MemorySaver
from langgraph.graph import START, END, StateGraph, MessagesState
...

class SupportAgentGraph:
    def __init__(self, llm):
        self.llm = llm
```

```python
    self.config = {"configurable": {"thread_id": "1"}}...
...
  def build_graph(self):
    memory = MemorySaver()
    builder = StateGraph(MessagesState)
    ...
    return builder.compile(checkpointer=memory)

  def invoke(self, human_message_text):
    ...
    return self.graph.invoke(state, self.config)
```

Let's start our discussion of the code above with `build_graph`. We've added a line at the top of this method:

```python
memory = MemorySaver()
```

`MemorySaver` is a checkpointer built into LangGraph that can store graph states in memory. Various other kinds of checkpointers are available, depending on where you want to save your graph state. For instance, you could use different checkpointers to store conversations in a database like PostgreSQL or SQLite.

We pass this to our graph when we compile it at the end of the method:

```python
return builder.compile(checkpointer=memory)
```

This allows our graph to save its state, but that's not enough. If we don't make any more changes, each graph invocation would still be a new, independent one. We need a way to tell the graph that a particular invocation belongs to a *thread* it has seen before.

Direct your attention to `__init__`, where we've assigned a strange-looking value to a field called `self.config`:

```python
self.config = {"configurable": {"thread_id": "1"}}
```

The important part to notice here is `{"thread_id": "1"}`. Further down, in the `invoke` method, we pass this to the graph while invoking it:

```python
return self.graph.invoke(state, self.config)
```

We're essentially passing the thread ID 1 to the graph here so it knows that whenever we invoke it, we're always in the same conversation thread, which has an ID of 1. As a result of this change, the first invocation of the graph (`"Hi, my name's Bob"` in the example that prompted these changes) will be saved under the thread ID 1. At this point, the state will have two messages: the original human message and the AI response.

When the follow-up message (`"What's my name"`) arrives, since we already have an existing thread with ID 1, it will be *appended* to the existing state. The state that's passed to `assistant_node` (and therefore to the LLM) will have *three* messages, enabling it to respond correctly.

Additional questions you may have

Two natural questions may arise at this juncture:

- **Why is the thread ID always 1?**

  Recall that our Streamlit app session doesn't persist beyond a single browser refresh. So, each time the user accesses the app by opening it in a new tab or refreshing the browser, the `SupportAgentGraph` instance is rebuilt, and the graph is recompiled with a new `MemorySaver` object. Since `MemorySaver` stores graph states in memory instead of persisting them to an external data store like PostgreSQL, any thread from a different browser session—whatever the thread ID—is inaccessible, so we can safely use the same thread ID 1 for the new session.

  Long story short, how we've set things up guarantees that a single graph instance will see at most one conversation in its lifetime, so we only need to specify one thread ID.

- **Why is the value of self.config so convoluted?**

  Looking at our explanation of checkpointers and memory, it seems that all we need to pass the graph when we invoke it is the value 1. So why do we have this monstrosity: `{"configurable": {"thread_id": "1"}}`?

  Though they are beyond the scope of this book, LangGraph offers many options when you invoke a graph, such as the ability to specify metadata or the number of parallel calls it can make. The thread ID is the only configuration we're using here, but it's far from the only one available. The convoluted-seeming structure of `self.config` reflects this.

Try running Nibby again and entering the same messages as before. This time you should see something similar to figure 10.9.

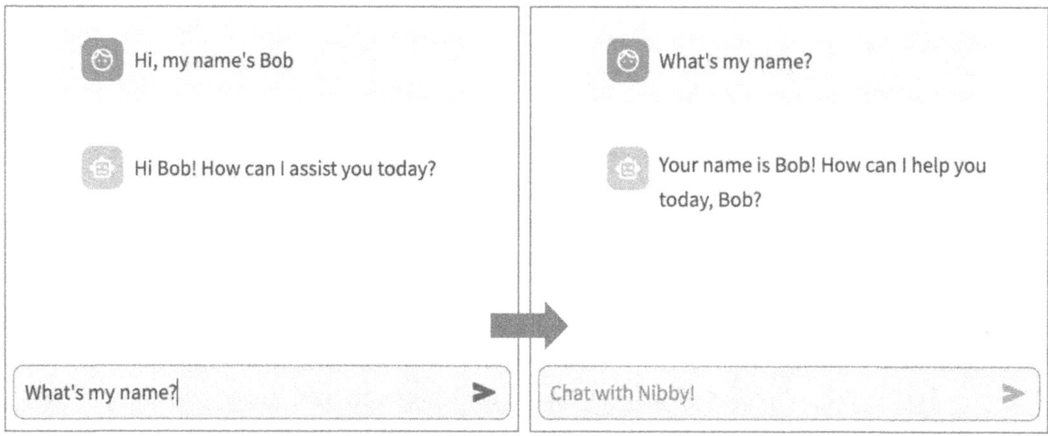

Figure 10.9   Nibby now remembers information we told it earlier in the conversation (see chapter_10/in_progress_02 in the GitHub repo for the full code).

As you can see, the app does remember the previous information we provided this time, but we still need to update the frontend to display the entire conversation.

10.3.2 *Displaying the conversation history*

Our Streamlit frontend is currently only set up to show the latest user-entered message and the AI's response. To display the full history, we need to first expose it in the backend. Let's start by adding a method to graph.py to get the entire conversation so far at any point (chapter_10/in_progress_03/graph.py in the GitHub repo):

```python
...
class SupportAgentGraph:

    ...
    def get_conversation(self):
        state = self.graph.get_state(self.config)
        if "messages" not in state.values:
            return []
        return state.values["messages"]
```

The `get_conversation` method in `SupportAgentGraph` simply returns the `messages` list in the graph's current state. To do this, it first gets a reference to the state (`self .graph.get_state(self.config)`), and then accesses the `messages` key using `state .values["messages"]`. Passing `self.config` to `get_state` is required to get us the correct conversation thread, though—as the sidebar in the previous section discusses—there's only one.

Next, let's expose the full `messages` list in bot.py (chapter_10/in_progress_03/bot .py in the GitHub repo):

```python
...
class Bot:

    ...
    def get_history(self):
        return self.graph.get_conversation()
```

All the `get_history` method does is to pass the result of the `get_conversation` method we just defined faithfully through to its caller.

We can now make the changes required in frontend.py (chapter_10/in_progress_03/frontend.py in the GitHub repo):

```python
...
bot = st.session_state.bot

for message in bot.get_history():
    st.chat_message(message.type).markdown(message.content)

if human_message_text := st.chat_input("Chat with Nibby!"):
    ...
```

We call `bot.get_history()` to get the list of messages and iterate through it, displaying each in its own `st.chat_message` container.

Recall that each message in the `messages` list is an instance of either `HumanMessage` or `AIMessage`. Either way, it also has a type field with a value of `human` in the case of `Human-Message` and `ai` for an `AIMessage`. This works perfectly as the type indicator argument in `st.chat_message`. `message.content` has the message's text, so we display that using `st.markdown`.

Rerun the app to see figure 10.10.

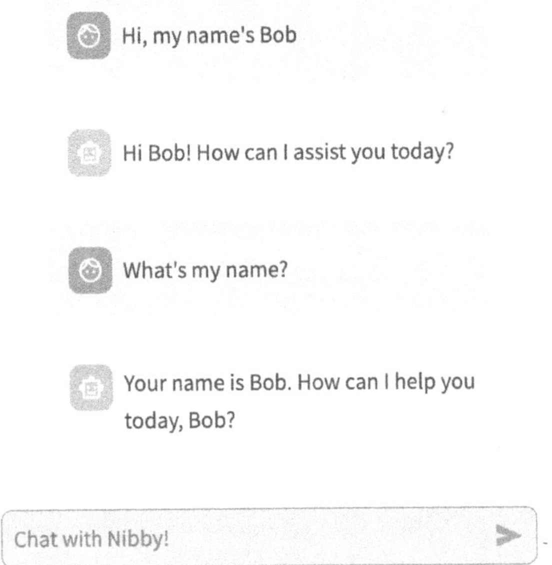

Figure 10.10   The frontend now displays the full conversation history (see chapter_10/in_progress_03 in the GitHub repo for the full code).

As expected, Nibby now shows the full conversation so we can keep track of what's going on.

10.4   Restricting the bot to customer support

Thus far, we've focused on getting Nibby's basic functionality right, including calling an LLM and handling a full conversation. The result is a *general* chatbot you can ask for pretty much anything. For example, consider what happens if we ask Nibby to sing a song (figure 10.11):

Nibby can sing a song all right. It can also help you solve math problems or write an essay about the fall of the Roman Empire. Unfortunately, it does all of that on the company's dime. Remember, interacting with a cloud-based LLM costs *money*.

Whenever someone makes a frivolous request to your customer support bot and the bot indulges the request with a long-winded response, it spends precious LLM tokens

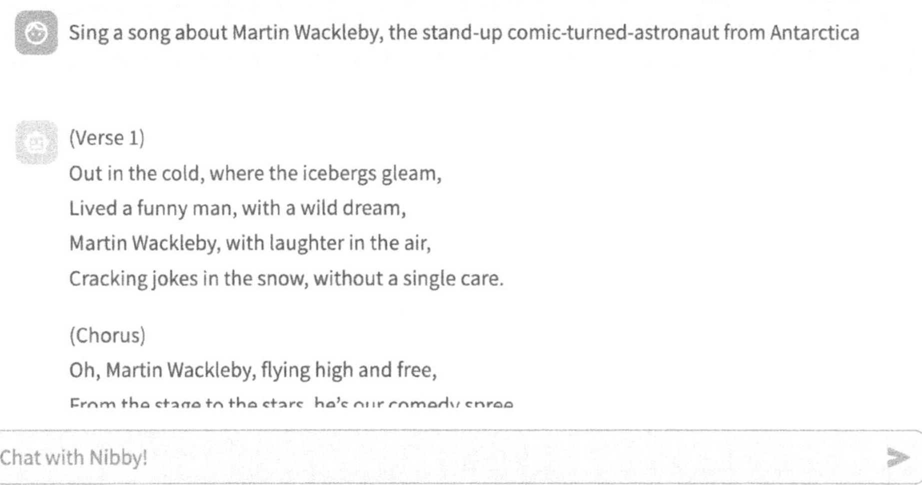

Figure 10.11   Nibby entertains frivolous requests, potentially costing money.

and costs you something. Sure, each message is only a fraction of a cent, but add up all the pleas for coding assistance or role-playing as a character from Battlestar Galactica, and suddenly your boss wants to know why there's a Nibby-shaped hole in the company's quarterly earnings report. Of course, I'm being hyperbolic, but the point stands: we want Nibby to be strictly business.

10.4.1 Creating a base prompt

As we did in chapter 9, we want to give the LLM some context about the use case we want it to serve. In that chapter, we did this by creating a message with the role `system`. That's essentially what we're going to do here, too, though the abstractions we'll use are slightly different.

Create a file called prompts.py with the content shown in listing 10.6 (chapter_10/in_progress_04/prompts.py in the GitHub repo).

Listing 10.6   Storing prompts in prompts.py

```
BASE_SYS_MSG = """
  You are a customer support agent for Note n' Nib, an online stationery
  retailer. You are tasked with providing customer support to customers who
  have questions or concerns about the products or services offered by the
  company.

  You must refuse to answer any questions or entertain any requests that
  are not related to Note n' Nib or its products and services.
"""
```

The prompt gives Nibby its first indication that Note n' Nib exists and that it's supposed to be providing customer support for the company. Importantly, `BASE_SYS_MSG` also has an instruction to refuse any requests that are unrelated to Note n' Nib. Next, let's incorporate this into our graph.

10.4.2 Inserting a base context node in the graph

As we learned in chapter 9, using OpenAI's chat completions endpoint involves passing a sequence of messages to the LLM. In our current graph, the list starts with the user's first instruction and contains only user messages and AI responses. To prevent Nibby from responding to frivolous requests, we just need to insert the system prompt we just created as the first message in the list we send to the LLM.

We'll do this by inserting a new node in the graph to add the system message to the graph state and modifying the existing `assistant_node` to pass this message to the LLM before anything else. Figure 10.12 shows the new graph.

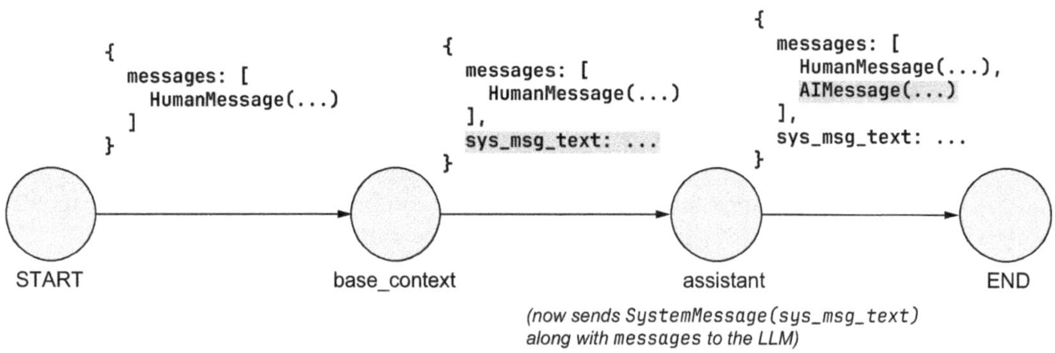

Figure 10.12   Adding a base context node in the graph

The changes required to graph.py are shown in listing 10.7 (chapter_10/in_progress_04/graph.py in the GitHub repo):

Listing 10.7   A modified graph.py

```
...
from langchain_core.messages import HumanMessage, SystemMessage
from prompts import *

class AgentState(MessagesState):
  sys_msg_text: str

class SupportAgentGraph:
  def __init__(self, llm):
    ...
```

```python
    @staticmethod
    def base_context_node(state):
      return {"sys_msg_text": BASE_SYS_MSG}

    def get_assistant_node(self):
      def assistant_node(state):
        sys_msg = SystemMessage(content=state["sys_msg_text"])
        messages_to_send = [sys_msg] + state["messages"]
        ai_response_message = self.llm.invoke(messages_to_send)
        return {"messages": [ai_response_message]}
      return assistant_node

    def build_graph(self):
      memory = MemorySaver()
      builder = StateGraph(AgentState)

      builder.add_node("base_context", self.base_context_node)
      builder.add_node("assistant", self.get_assistant_node())

      builder.add_edge(START, "base_context")
      builder.add_edge("base_context", "assistant")
      builder.add_edge("assistant", END)

      return builder.compile(checkpointer=memory)

    def invoke(self, human_message_text):
      ...
  ...
```

Starting from the top, we've added a couple of imports; we need the `SystemMessage` class in addition to `HumanMessage`, so that's one.

The statement `from prompts import *` allows us to access any prompt we may add to prompts.py using only its variable name, without a prefix like `prompt..` Since we're using the `*` wildcard here rather than importing specific objects, every object in prompts.py's global scope becomes part of graph.py's scope. In this case, it means we can refer to `BASE_SYS_MSG` directly, as we do later in the code.

We've defined a new `AgentState` class:

```python
class AgentState(MessagesState):
  sys_msg_text: str
```

`AgentState` inherits from `MessagesState`, so it also contains the `messages` field we've been using thus far. What we're effectively doing here is adding a new field to the state—called `sys_msg_text`—meant to hold the text of the system message.

Next, within the class, we added a new static method:

```python
@staticmethod
def base_context_node(state):
  return {"sys_msg_text": BASE_SYS_MSG}
```

This function represents the new node we're adding to the graph, called `base_context`. All this node does is to populate the `sys_msg_text` field we've added to the state. By returning `{"sys_msg_text": BASE_SYS_MSG}`, this node sets `sys_msg_text` to `BASE_SYS_MSG`—the context prompt we created a few minutes ago—in the graph's current state.

To understand how this works, it's helpful to remember that a graph node does not return the entirety of the state; rather, it only returns those keys in the state that need to be modified. Therefore, even though there's no mention of the `messages` field here, once this node has been executed, the state will continue to have that field—unmodified—in addition to `sys_msg_text`.

> **NOTE** Unlike in the case of `messages`, when we return a dictionary with a `sys_msg_text` key, it *replaces* the value of `sys_msg_text` in the state. This is because `sys_msg_text` uses the default update behavior, as opposed to the *append* behavior (enabled internally by the `add_messages` function) that `messages` uses.

Why have we made `base_context_node` a static method? Recall that each node in the graph needs to accept the graph state as its first argument. We would like to put `base_context_node` inside `SupportAgentGraph` for logical code organization purposes, but if we make it a regular method, it'll need to accept the class instance (`self`) as its first argument. Making it a static method removes that requirement and frees us to add a state argument.

Some of you might be asking, "Wait a minute, didn't we structure `assistant_node` as a nested function for the same reason? Why didn't we do *that* here?"

We could indeed have used a closure-based solution for `base_context_node` too, but we don't need to; unlike `assistant_node` which references `self.llm`, `base_context_node` doesn't need to access `self` at all. We therefore employ the more straightforward technique of applying the `@staticmethod` decorator to `base_context_node`.

Speaking of `assistant_node`, consider the changes we've made to its code above:

```
sys_msg = SystemMessage(content=state["sys_msg_text"])
messages_to_send = [sys_msg] + state["messages"]
ai_response_message = self.llm.invoke(messages_to_send)
```

Rather than invoking the LLM directly with `state["messages"]`, we now create a `SystemMessage` object with the `sys_msg_text` field we populated in `base_context_node` as the content and prepend it to `state["messages"]` to form the list we pass the LLM. This makes the system message available to the LLM.

Finally, note our updates to `build_graph`. Since we've extended `MessagesState` to include a `sys_msg_text` field, we use that to initialize the `StateGraph`:

```
builder = StateGraph(AgentState)
```

We add the base context node like this:

```
builder.add_node("base_context", self.base_context_node)
```

Notice how we're passing a reference to the `self.base_context_node` method itself here, as opposed to calling it with the double parentheses.

We also reorder the edges in the graph to insert the `base_context` node between `START` and `assistant`:

```
builder.add_edge(START, "base_context")
builder.add_edge("base_context", "assistant")
```

That should be all we need. Go ahead and rerun your app. Try requesting the bot to sing a song again to get a response similar to figure 10.13.

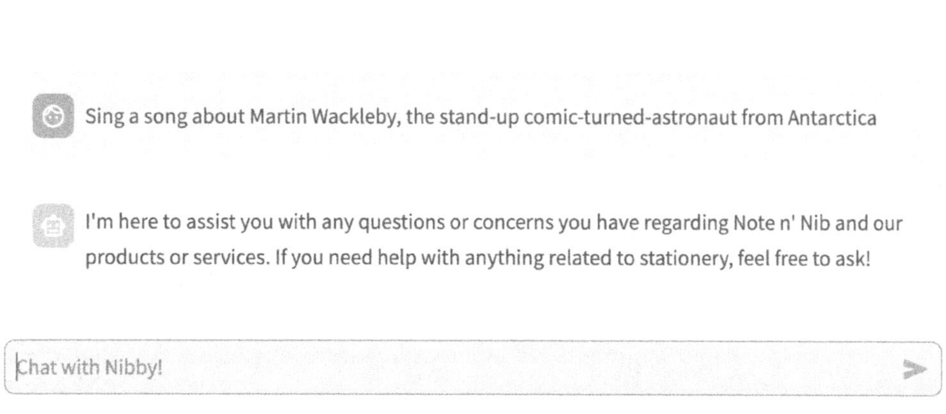

Figure 10.13   Nibby now refuses to entertain frivolous requests (see chapter_10/in_progress_04 in the GitHub repo for the full code).

It looks like Nibby got the memo! It won't help the user with irrelevant requests anymore. In the next section, we'll solve the opposite problem: getting it to help with *relevant* questions.

10.5   *Retrieval Augmented Generation*

Models like GPT-5.1 are so effective because they have been pre-trained on a huge corpus of publicly available information, such as books, magazines, and websites. It's why Fact Frenzy, our trivia app from chapter 9, was able to ask and answer questions on such a wide range of topics.

However, many of the more economically valuable use cases of generative AI require more than information in the public domain. Truly molding AI into something that fits your specific use case usually requires providing it with private information that only you possess.

Take Nibby, for instance, who is ultimately meant to assist customers of Note n' Nib with their queries. What happens if we pose a valid question about a stationery product to Nibby? Figure 10.14 shows such a conversation.

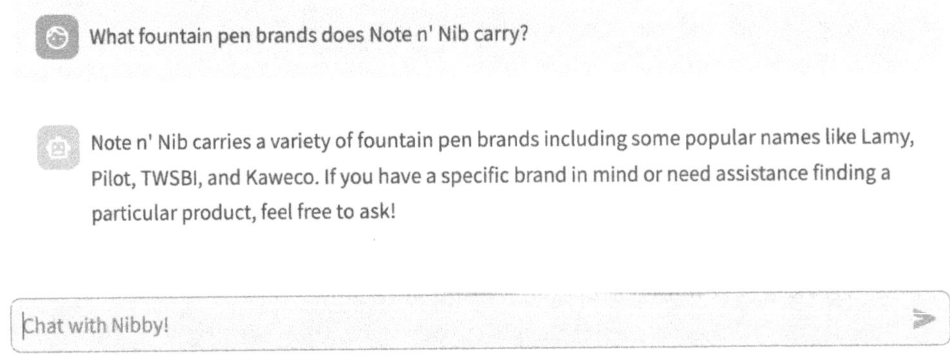

Figure 10.14   Nibby makes up information when it doesn't know the answer.

Seems like Nibby knocked that one out of the park, right? Not quite. We never told our bot what kinds of pens Note n' Nib carries, so where is it getting its information from? Additionally, where are the fictional brands—InkStream and RoyalQuill—that we encountered in chapter 6? As it turns out, Nibby had no information available about fountain pens and, therefore, simply hallucinated this response! In this section, we'll discover a way to augment Nibby's existing store of worldly knowledge with custom information that we provide.

10.5.1 *What is Retrieval Augmented Generation?*

So, how do we supplement all of the information an LLM has been trained on with our own? For relatively small pieces of information, it's trivially easy—in fact, we already know how! All we need to do is provide the info to the LLM as part of our prompt! We could get Nibby to get the question we posed in figure 10.14 right by listing the products Note n' Nib sells directly in the system message we send to the LLM.

What about other questions, though? Technically, we could give the model all of the contextual information it might realistically need to answer any question directly in the prompt. The maximum amount of such information we can provide is measured in tokens, called the model's *context window length.*

Recent models have a relatively large context window. For instance, GPT-5.1 can take up to 400,000 tokens (about 300,000 words, since, on average, a token is roughly three-quarters of a word). Models from other providers can take even more tokens in a single prompt. Google's Gemini 2.0 Pro has a context window that is a whopping *2 million* tokens long, enough to fit the entire *Harry Potter* series, with space left over for almost all of the *Lord of the Rings* trilogy.

Surely our problem is solved then? We can simply assemble all the information we possess about Note n' Nib and feed it to the LLM in each prompt, correct?

Certainly, we could, but we probably don't want to for a couple of reasons:

- LLMs are prone to information overload; we generally see degraded performance with extremely large prompts.
- Even if there were no such degradation, LLM providers usually charge by the token, so if we had to pass our entire custom knowledge base in every LLM call, the costs would go through the roof.

No, we need a different solution. If only we could read in a user's question and feed the LLM just the *relevant* parts of our knowledge base required to answer it. And that—in case you've somehow failed to realize where this spiel is going—is exactly what Retrieval Augmented Generation (RAG) is.

RAG has the following essential steps:

1 *Read* the user's question
2 *Retrieve* the context *relevant* to the question from the knowledge base
3 *Augment* the question with the context required to answer it
4 *Generate* the answer to the question by feeding the question and context to the LLM

The hard part of RAG is the *retrieve* step. Specifically, given a user question and a large custom knowledge base, how do you identify the parts of the knowledge base that are relevant to the question and extract only those parts from the base? The answer lies in the concept of *embeddings* and a piece of software known as a *vector database*.

EMBEDDINGS AND VECTOR DATABASES

While we don't—strictly speaking—need to learn how embeddings or even vector databases work under the hood to implement RAG, it would be a good idea to gain a basic understanding of these concepts.

Let's start with a simplified example to achieve this. Say you're known as something of a movie buff in your friend circle. Your buddy approaches you and says, "Hey, I watched *The Dark Knight* yesterday and loved it! Could you recommend another movie like it?"

You're in a fix because—though you have an encyclopedic knowledge of movies—you're not sure how exactly to measure the *similarity* between two movies, so you can recommend the one that's the *most* similar to *The Dark Knight*. Refusing to accept defeat, you flee to your underground lair and try to work it out in solitude.

Eventually, you come up with a system. You reckon that when people express their preference for various movies, they're subconsciously talking about two attributes: *comedic value* and *explosions per hour*. Therefore, you rate your entire catalog of movies against those two scales and plot the results in a chart (partially reproduced in figure 10.15).

As you can see, *The Dark Knight* has a comedic value of 1.2 but a relatively high explosions-per-hour of 6. We can represent it as a list of numbers: [1.2, 6], called a *vector*. We can call the vector [1.2, 6] the *embedding* of the movie *The Dark Knight* in the two-dimensional comedic-value/explosions-per-hour space.

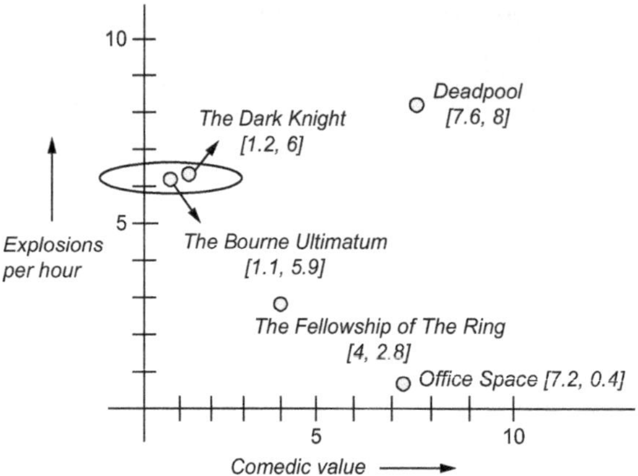

Figure 10.15   Converting movies into vectors and plotting them on a chart.

Converting movies into numbers in this way makes it possible to measure their similarity. For instance, *Office Space* is represented as [7.2, 0.4] in the same space. The similarity (or, rather, lack thereof) between *Office Space* and *The Dark Knight* can be calculated mathematically by considering their *geometric distance*. The closer the embeddings of two movies are geometrically—as measured by the length of a straight line drawn between them—the more similar the underlying movies are.

After several such calculations, you find that *The Bourne Ultimatum*, which has the vector [1.1, 5.9] is the closest to *The Dark Knight*. Having concluded your research, you get back to your friend and let them know (to which your friend responds, "Thank goodness you're alive! It's been two years, where have you *been?*").

The question we're facing with Nibby is analogous to the movie recommendation problem above. Given a user's message (the movie your friend liked), and a knowledge base (your catalog of movies), we have to find the paragraphs/chunks (movies) that are most relevant (most "similar") to the user's message.

To answer this efficiently, we need two things:

- A way to convert a given piece of text into embeddings that capture its meaning (or *semantics*)
- A way to store these embeddings and quickly calculate distances between them

Obviously, the movie example above is overly simplistic. Our "space" only had two dimensions: comedic value and explosions per hour. Encoding the meaning of a piece of text requires a lot more dimensions (like hundreds or thousands), and the dimensions themselves would not be human-understandable concepts like "comedic value." We'll use a text embedding model provided by OpenAI for our use case.

To store the embeddings, we'll use a program called a *vector database*. Vector databases make it easy to calculate the distance between embeddings or find the entries closest to a specific one. Rather than the "straight line" (or *Euclidean*) distance between vectors, we'll use a score called *cosine similarity*, which measures the *angle* between two vectors to determine their similarity. The vector database we'll use is Pinecone, a cloud-hosted service.

10.5.2 Implementing RAG in our app

Armed with a conceptual understanding of RAG, let's now focus on implementing it to assist Nibby in answering customer questions.

PREPARING THE KNOWLEDGE BASE

The GitHub folder for this chapter (https://github.com/aneevdavis/streamlit-in-action/tree/main/chapter_10) has a subdirectory called articles with a series of customer support articles for Note n' Nib. Each article is a text file containing information about Note n' Nib's products or how it conducts business. For instance, our_products.txt includes a list of product descriptions, while fountain_pen_maintenance.txt is about maintaining RoyalQuill and InkStream pens.

Here's an excerpt from the article that we'll reference later:

```
Proper care ensures your InkStream and RoyalQuill fountain pens write
smoothly for years.

- Cleaning: Flush the nib with warm water every few weeks.
- Refilling: Use high-quality ink to prevent clogging.
- Storage: Store pens upright to avoid leaks and ensure ink flow.
```

Copy the articles folder into your working directory now. This is the knowledge base that Nibby will have access to.

SETTING UP A VECTOR DATABASE

As mentioned briefly in the previous section, we will be using Pinecone, a managed vector database optimized for fast and scalable similarity search that's popular for AI applications. Pinecone's free "Starter" plan is more than enough for this chapter.

Go to https://www.pinecone.io/ and sign up for an account now. Once you've completed the setup, you'll be presented with an API key, which you should save immediately. Once that's done, create a new *index*. An index is analogous to a table in a traditional non-vector database, such as PostgreSQL. The index will store our support articles broken into parts, along with their embeddings.

You'll be asked to supply values for various options during the creation process:

- *Index name*—You can use whatever you like, but remember to save it since we'll use it in our code.
- *Model configuration*—Choose `text-embedding-3-small`, the OpenAI embedding model we'll use; set the dimension to 1536.
- *Metric*—Pick `cosine` to use the cosine similarity score we briefly discussed earlier.
- *Capacity mode*—Should be `Serverless`.
- *Cloud provider*—`AWS` is fine for this.
- *Region*—At the time of writing, only `us-east-1` is available in the free plan, so pick that.

NOTE   It's possible that you'll find entirely different model options by the time you read this. If so, just pick a cost-effective OpenAI model.

INGESTING THE KNOWLEDGE BASE

To incorporate the vector store into our chatbot app, we'll create a `VectorStore` class. Before doing so, add your Pinecone API key and the index name you just created to secrets.toml so it now looks like this:

```
[api_keys]
OPENAI_API_KEY = 'sk-proj-...'
VECTOR_STORE_API_KEY = 'pcsk_...'

[config]
VECTOR_STORE_INDEX_NAME = 'index_name_you_chose'
EMBEDDING_MODEL_NAME = 'text-embedding-3-small'
```


We've added a new key to `api_keys` and a new section called `config` to hold the index name and the name of the embedding model we chose.

Now on to the `VectorStore` class. Create a file named vector_store.py with the contents shown in listing 10.8 (chapter_10/in_progress_05/vector_store.py in the GitHub repo).

> **Listing 10.8   The `VectorStore` class in `vector_store.py`**

```python
from pinecone import Pinecone
from langchain_openai import OpenAIEmbeddings
from langchain_pinecone import PineconeVectorStore
from langchain_community.document_loaders import DirectoryLoader, TextLoader
from langchain.text_splitter import RecursiveCharacterTextSplitter

class VectorStore:
  def __init__(self, api_keys, index_name, model_name):
    pc = Pinecone(api_key=api_keys["VECTOR_STORE_API_KEY"])
    embeddings = OpenAIEmbeddings(
      api_key=api_keys["OPENAI_API_KEY"], model=model_name)
    index = pc.Index(index_name)
    self.store = PineconeVectorStore(index=index, embedding=embeddings)

  def ingest_folder(self, folder_path):
    loader = DirectoryLoader(
      folder_path,
      glob="**/*.txt",
      loader_cls=TextLoader
    )
    documents = loader.load()
    splitter = RecursiveCharacterTextSplitter(
      chunk_size=1000,
      chunk_overlap=200
    )
    texts = splitter.split_documents(documents)
    self.store.add_documents(texts)
```

```python
def retrieve(self, query):
    return self.store.similarity_search(query)
```

There's a fair amount going on here, so let's go through it step by step.

The `__init__` has the boilerplate code required to set up the vector store connection. It accepts three arguments: `api_keys` (the dictionary of API keys), `index_name` (the name of the Pinecone index), and `model_name` (the name of the embedding model).

`__init__` first creates the `Pinecone` object—`pc`—using the Pinecone API key we noted a minute ago, and then an `OpenAIEmbeddings` object by passing it the OpenAI key and the name of the model. `pc.Index(index_name)` refers to the index we created earlier. Finally, we obtain a vector store object from the index and embeddings and assign it to `self.store` so we can use it in other methods.

The `ingest_folder` method accepts the path to a folder and saves its contents to the Pinecone index. Consider the first part of this method:

```python
loader = DirectoryLoader(
  folder_path,
  glob="**/*.txt",
  loader_cls=TextLoader
)
```

LangChain provides various *document loaders* to help ingest and parse various types of data (text files, PDFs, web pages, databases, etc.) into a structured format suitable for processing. `DirectoryLoader` makes it easy to load files from a specified directory.

The `glob="**/*.txt"` ensures that all text files (.txt) in the folder (including subfolders) are included. `loader_cls=TextLoader` tells `DirectoryLoader` to use another loader class called `TextLoader`—also provided by LangChain—for loading individual text files. Once the `DirectoryLoader` is created, the next step is to load the documents:

```python
documents = loader.load()
```

This reads all .txt files in the directory and loads them into a list of `Document` objects, which LangChain uses to store the raw text and metadata.

At the moment, each `Document` consists of an entire article. While the articles in our folder are relatively small, one can easily imagine a support article being thousands of words long. The point of fetching just the relevant text from our knowledge base is to reduce the overall size of the prompt; simply fetching entire articles defeats this purpose.

Therefore, we want to divvy up the articles into manageable *chunks* of text that are roughly of equal size. That's what the next part of our code does:

```python
splitter = RecursiveCharacterTextSplitter(
  chunk_size=1000,
  chunk_overlap=200
)
texts = splitter.split_documents(documents)
```

RecursiveCharacterTextSplitter is a text-splitting utility from LangChain that can break documents into chunks while preserving meaningful context. chunk_size=1000 sets the length of each chunk to 1000 characters. chunk_overlap=200 means that chunks will have a 200-character overlap to maintain context.

After splitting the documents, the chunks—available in texts—are ready to be stored:

```
self.store.add_documents(texts)
```

add_documents takes the split text chunks and adds them to the Pinecone index, storing both the text and embeddings generated using the text-embedding-3-small model, making them searchable.

The retrieve method allows callers to query the vector store:

```
def retrieve(self, query):
  return self.store.similarity_search(query)
```

The similarity_search method of our PineconeVectorStore instance (self.store) searches the vector store for documents similar to query—the user's message—using the generated embeddings, returning a list of relevant Document objects based on the query.

At this point, we've coded up the vector store functionality into a handy little class; next, let's use the class to ingest our articles/ folder. This is an *offline* step that you only need to perform one time; once you've stored your articles in Pinecone, they'll remain there until you remove them.

Go ahead and create a file called ingest_to_vector_store.py, copying the contents from listing 10.9 (chapter_10/in_progress_05/ingest_to_vector_store.py in the GitHub repo).

> **Listing 10.9   Vector store ingestion in ingest_to_vector_store.py**

```
import toml
from vector_store import import VectorStore

secrets = toml.load(".streamlit/secrets.toml")
api_keys = secrets["api_keys"]
index_name = secrets["config"]["VECTOR_STORE_INDEX_NAME"]
model_name = secrets["config"]["EMBEDDING_MODEL_NAME"]
vector_store = VectorStore(api_keys, index_name, model_name)
vector_store.ingest_folder("articles/")
```

Since this isn't meant to be run using Streamlit, we use the toml module directly to read the secrets.toml file:

```
secrets = toml.load(".streamlit/secrets.toml")
```

At the end of this, `secrets` should be a dictionary that contains the `api_keys` and `config` keys we organized secrets.toml into earlier.

Next, we grab the values we need:

```
api_keys = secrets["api_keys"]
index_name = secrets["config"]["VECTOR_STORE_INDEX_NAME"]
model_name = secrets["config"]["EMBEDDING_MODEL_NAME"]
```

We can now instantiate the `VectorStore` class:

```
vector_store = VectorStore(api_keys, index_name, model_name)
```

Finally, we trigger the `ingest_folder` method:

```
vector_store.ingest_folder("articles/")
```

To perform the actual ingestion, run this file in a terminal with the `python` command:

```
python ingest_to_vector_store.py
```

Once it completes, you can go to the page corresponding to your index on the Pinecone website to see the newly ingested chunks, as shown in figure 10.16.

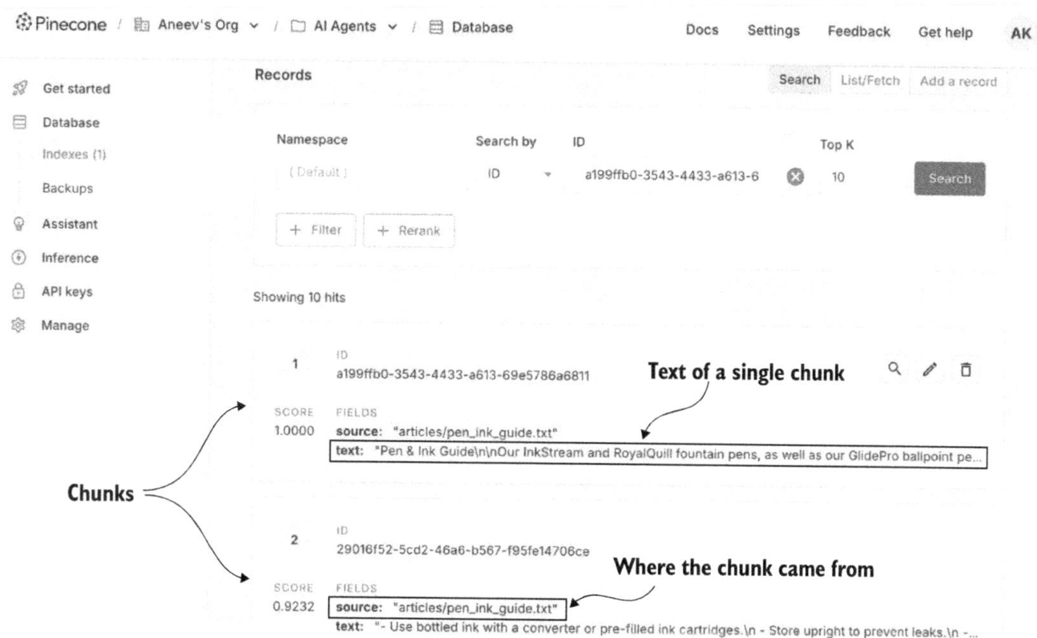

Figure 10.16 You can see the chunks in the index on the Pinecone website.

Notice the source field, which holds the file name each chunk came from. You can also click the Edit button on a record to add more metadata or to see its numeric vector values. If you were to count them, you'd find that there are 1536 of them, corresponding to the number of dimensions in the embedding model.

ADDING RAG TO THE GRAPH

The Pinecone index we need for RAG is ready to go, but we still need to incorporate the functionality in our chatbot. For this, let's first lay out the additional instructions Nibby needs to use the knowledge base. Append the following to prompts.py (chapter_10/in_progress_05/prompts.py in the GitHub repo):

```
SYS_MSG_AUGMENTATION = """
  You have the following excerpts from Note n' Nib's
  customer service manual:
  ```

  {docs_content}
  ```

  If you're unable to answer the customer's question confidently with the
  given information, please redirect the user to call a human customer
  service representative at 1-800-NOTENIB.
"""
```

In a moment, we'll write the logic to replace {docs_content} with the document chunks we retrieve from Pinecone. The idea here is to give Nibby the context it needs and to get it to stop fabricating an answer out of thin air if it's not confident.

Next, let's modify graph.py as shown in listing 10.10 (chapter_10/in_progress_05/graph.py in the GitHub repo) so that it implements RAG.

Listing 10.10   Adding RAG nodes to graph.py

```
...
from langchain_core.messages import HumanMessage, SystemMessage
from langchain_core.documents import Document
from prompts import *

class AgentState(MessagesState):
  sys_msg_text: str
  retrieved_docs: list[Document]

class SupportAgentGraph:
  def __init__(self, llm, vector_store):
    self.llm = llm
    self.vector_store = vector_store

    self.config = {"configurable": {"thread_id": "1"}}
    self.graph = self.build_graph()

  ...
  def get_retrieve_node(self):
    def retrieve_node(state: AgentState):
      messages = state["messages"]
```

```python
        message_contents = [message.content for message in messages]
        retrieval_query = "\n".join(message_contents)
        docs = self.vector_store.retrieve(retrieval_query)
        return {"retrieved_docs": docs}
    return retrieve_node

@staticmethod
def augment_node(state: AgentState):
    docs = state["retrieved_docs"]
    docs_content_list = [doc.page_content for doc in docs]
    content = "\n".join(docs_content_list)
    new_text = SYS_MSG_AUGMENTATION.replace("{docs_content}", content)
    return {"sys_msg_text": BASE_SYS_MSG + "\n\n" + new_text}


...
def build_graph(self):
    ...
    builder.add_node("base_context", self.base_context_node)
    builder.add_node("retrieve", self.get_retrieve_node())
    builder.add_node("augment", self.augment_node)
    builder.add_node("assistant", self.get_assistant_node())

    builder.add_edge(START, "base_context")
    builder.add_edge("base_context", "retrieve")
    builder.add_edge("retrieve", "augment")
    builder.add_edge("augment", "assistant")
    builder.add_edge("assistant", END)

    return builder.compile(checkpointer=memory)


...
```

The first change is to `AgentState`, which now looks like this:

```python
class AgentState(MessagesState):
    sys_msg_text: str
    retrieved_docs: list[Document]
```

We'll now store the list of chunks retrieved from Pinecone in the graph state in a variable called `retrieved_docs`.

`__init__` now accepts `vector_store`—an instance of our `VectorStore` class—as an argument and saves it to `self.vector_store`. Note that rather than create the `Vector-Store` instance *within* graph.py, we've chosen to have it be created elsewhere (bot.py, as we'll soon find out) and simply pass it to the `SupportAgentGraph` class. This is because we want graph.py to contain only the core logic of the graph. Objects that the graph *depends* on, such as `llm` and `vector_store` should be passed to it. This coding pattern is called *dependency injection,* and is helpful while writing automated tests.

Next, we need to introduce the process of retrieval-augmented generation to our graph. Figure 10.17 shows what the graph should look like by the end of this.

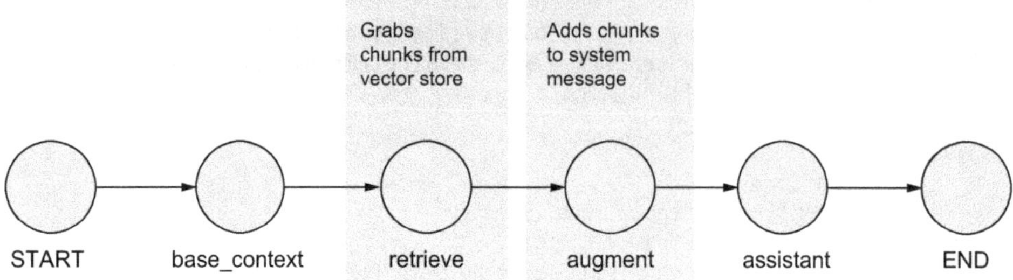

Figure 10.17   The graph now has retrieve and augment nodes for RAG.

We've inserted two nodes in between the `base_context` and `assistant` nodes: a `retrieve` node that grabs context from the knowledge base that's relevant to the user's query and an `augment` node that adds this info to the prompt.

Here's the code for the `retrieve` node:

```python
def get_retrieve_node(self):
    def retrieve_node(state: AgentState):
        messages = state["messages"]
        message_contents = [message.content for message in messages]
        retrieval_query = "\n".join(message_contents)
        docs = self.vector_store.retrieve(retrieval_query)
        return {"retrieved_docs": docs}
    return retrieve_node
```

As with `assistant_node`, `retrieve_node` is structured as a nested function within a class method. It extracts the content of all the messages in the conversation and puts them in a single string to form the query that we'll pass to the vector store.

The idea here is to find the chunks most relevant to the conversation. Since we're measuring relevance against the query, it makes sense that this is simply the text of the conversation.

Once we have the query, we can call the `retrieve` method we defined earlier and return the list of retrieved documents in a dictionary, thereby updating the `retrieved_docs` key of the graph state.

> **NOTE**   While we've kept things simple here by including the text of the entire conversation in the retrieval query, you'll likely run into challenges as the conversation gets longer and longer. For any particular AI response, the most *recent* messages in the conversation are probably more contextually relevant, so it might be a good idea to form the retrieval query from just the last, say, five or six messages in the conversation.

The following snippet shows the augmentation node:

```python
@staticmethod
def augment_node(state: AgentState):
```

```
docs = state["retrieved_docs"]
docs_content_list = [doc.page_content for doc in docs]
content = "\n".join(docs_content_list)
new_text = SYS_MSG_AUGMENTATION.replace("{docs_content}", content)
return {"sys_msg_text": BASE_SYS_MSG + "\n\n" + new_text}
```

This one doesn't need to access anything from `SupportAgentGraph`, so we structure it as a static method, as we did for `base_context_node`.

`augment_node` mostly does the tedious work of wrangling and inserting the retrieved chunks into the system message. Once it has formed a string by concatenating the contents of the retrieved `Document` chunks, it simply plugs it into the text of the `SYS_MSG_AUGMENTATION` value we added to prompts.py, replacing `{docs_content}`.

At the end of this node, `sys_msg_text` has the full system message—the earlier base message warning Nibby not to entertain frivolous questions, as well as the retrieved context. The edits to `build_graph` should be fairly obvious given figure 10.17; we officially add the `retrieve` and `augment` nodes, and attach them to the right edges.

The next file to edit is bot.py (chapter_10/in_progress_05/bot.py in the GitHub repo). Make the changes shown here:

```
...
from vector_store import VectorStore

class Bot:
  def __init__(self, api_keys, config):
    self.api_keys = api_keys
    self.config = config

    self.llm = self.get_llm()
    self.vector_store = self.get_vector_store()

    self.graph = SupportAgentGraph(
      llm=self.llm, vector_store=self.vector_store)

 def get_vector_store(self):
    index_name = self.config["VECTOR_STORE_INDEX_NAME"]
    model_name = self.config["EMBEDDING_MODEL_NAME"]
    return VectorStore(
      api_keys=self.api_keys, index_name=index_name, model_name=model_name)...
```

`get_vector_store` has the code required to complete the loop. It obtains the Pinecone index name from `self.config` and passes `self.api_keys`, `index_name`, and `model_name` to create an instance of `VectorStore` before returning it.

The last change we need to make is a pretty small one in frontend.py (chapter_10/in_progress_05/frontend.py in the GitHub repo):

```
...
if "bot" not in st.session_state:
  api_keys = st.secrets["api_keys"]
  config = st.secrets["config"]
```

```
    st.session_state.bot = Bot(api_keys, config)
bot = st.session_state.bot
...
```

Since the `Bot` class now accepts a `config` parameter, we get its value from `st.secrets` and pass it in while instantiating the class.

Let's try asking Nibby what products Note n' Nib sells again. Rerun the app and talk to it. Figure 10.18 shows an example of the new interaction.

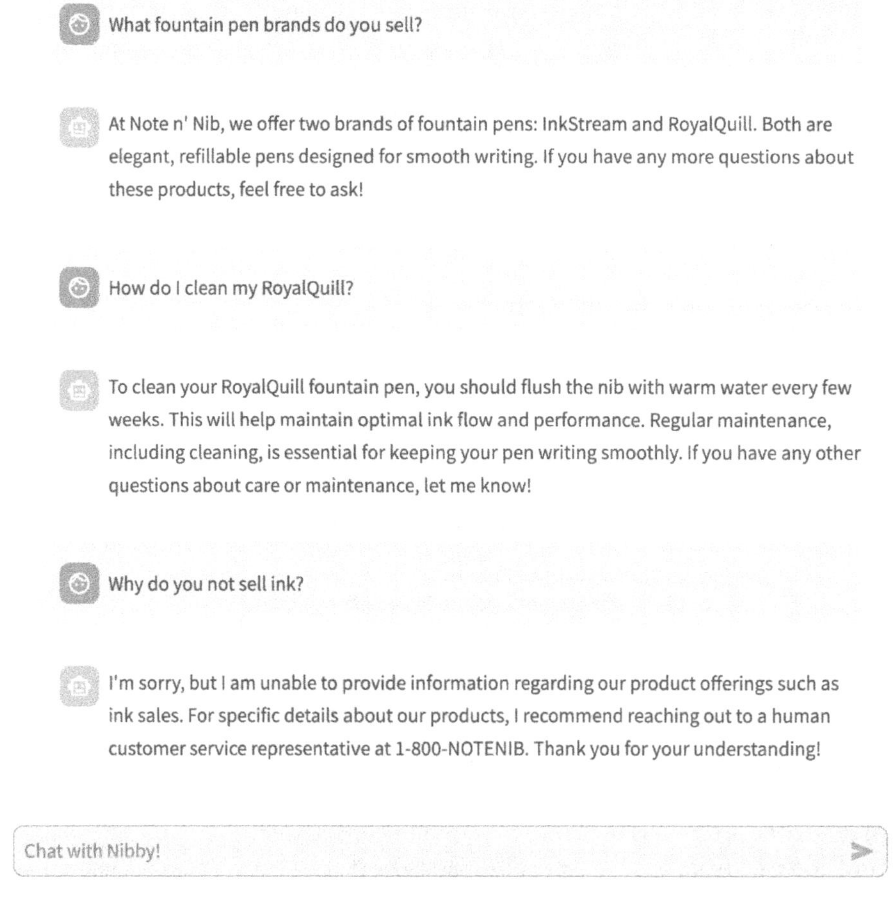

Figure 10.18   Nibby can now access and use information from the knowledge base (see chapter_10/ in_progress_05 in the GitHub repo for the full code).

Notice how Nibby answers our questions using information from our knowledge base and redirects to a 1-800 number when it encounters a question it doesn't know how to answer.

10.6 Turning the bot into an agent

Giving Nibby access to Note n' Nib's customer support knowledge base has turned Nibby into a capable assistant, but it's still a purely informational bot. When customers call a support number or chat with a service representative, they're more often than not looking for help with their specific situation or order.

For instance, a customer might wonder why their placed order is taking so long to arrive and want to check on the status, or they might want to simply cancel it. To resolve such issues, Nibby can't just rely on static textual articles; it needs to connect to Note n' Nib's systems and retrieve the right information or take the appropriate action. AI applications that can interact with the real world in this way have a special name: agents.

10.6.1 What are agents?

Traditional AI chatbots follow a question-answer pattern, providing helpful but static responses. However, when users need personalized assistance—such as checking an order status, updating an address, or canceling an order—an informational bot falls short.

This is where *agents* come in. Unlike passive chatbots, AI agents—also called *agentic apps*—can reason, plan, and interact with external systems to complete tasks. They don't just retrieve knowledge; they take actions based on it. These agents often rely on *tool use*, meaning they can call APIs, run database queries, and even trigger workflows in real-world applications.

For example, instead of telling a customer to reach out to a customer care number for an order tracking number, an agent can fetch the tracking details and provide an update directly. Instead of directing a user to a cancellation policy page, it can process a cancellation request on their behalf.

In short, agents make AI practical by allowing it to interact with the systems people already use. The key to making an agent work effectively is a framework that enables it to reason and decide the next steps dynamically. One such popular framework is called *ReAct*, short for *Reasoning + Acting*.

10.6.2 The ReAct framework

To function as a true agent, an AI system must do more than just retrieve facts—it needs to reason about a situation, determine the right action, execute that action, and then incorporate the result into its next steps. The ReAct framework is designed to facilitate this process.

> **NOTE** The ReAct AI framework is not to be confused with React, a JavaScript toolkit for building web apps.

Figure 10.19 is a visual representation of the ReAct framework.

ReAct structures an AI agent's behavior as an interleaving of reasoning steps and actions:

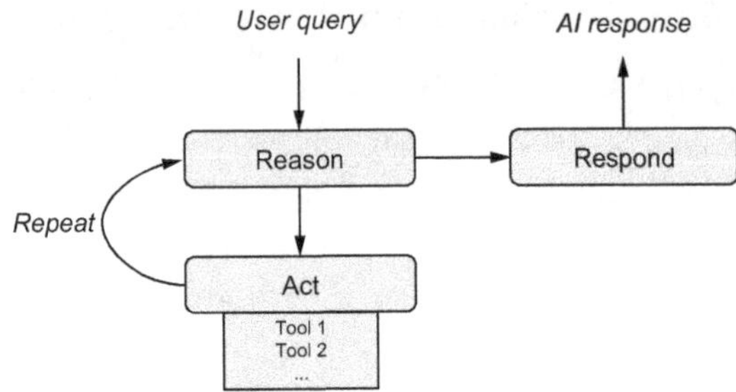

Figure 10.19   The ReAct framework

1 *Reason*—The agent analyzes the user's query, breaks it down into logical steps, and determines what needs to be done.

2 *Act*—The agent takes a concrete action, such as calling an API or querying a database, to retrieve relevant data or execute a task.

3 *Reason*—The agent incorporates the action's results into its reasoning and decides whether further steps are necessary.

4 *Repeat*—If further steps are needed, the cycle repeats.

5 *Respond*—If no further steps are needed, respond to the user.

For example, consider a customer asking Nibby: "What's the status of my order?" Using the ReAct framework, the bot might follow these steps:

1 *Reason*—"The customer wants to check their order status. I need to fetch order details from the order database."

2 *Act*—Call Note n' Nib's order management system to retrieve the order status.

3 *Reason*—"The system shows the order has shipped and is in transit. I should provide the expected delivery date."

4 *Respond*—Respond to the customer with the latest tracking details and estimated delivery date.

10.6.3 Creating tools an agent can use

The concept of *tools* is central to the process of developing a ReAct AI agent. In AI parlance, a tool is a function or API that an AI agent can call to perform real-world actions.

Referring back to the requirements we drafted, we want our bot to be able to track and cancel orders on behalf of Note n' Nib's customers. Of course, Note n' Nib is a fictional company with no real orders or customers.

This means we need some example data to work with. You can find this in the database.py file in the GitHub repository (https://github.com/aneevdavis/streamlit -in-action/tree/main/chapter_10/in_progress_06/). Copy the file to your working directory. Listing 10.11 shows a couple of excerpts from it.

Listing 10.11   Example data in database.py

```
users = {
    1: {
        "first_name": "Alice",
```

```
        "last_name": "Johnson",
        "date_of_birth": "1990-05-14",
        "email_address": "alice.johnson@example.com"
    },
    ...
}

orders = {
    101: {
        "user_id": 1,
        "order_placed_date": "2025-02-10",
        "order_status": "Shipped",
        "tracking_number": "TRK123456789",
        "items_purchased": ["RoyalQuill", "RedPinner"],
        "quantity": [1, 1],
        "shipping_address": "123 Main St, Springfield, IL, 62701",
        "expected_delivery_date": "2025-02-18"
    },
    ...
}
```

The file has two dictionaries—users and orders—keyed on user ID and order ID, respectively. Highlighted in the listing is user ID 1 (Alice Johnson) and a corresponding order the user placed on 2025-02-10.

In a real application, this information would be stored in a database like PostgreSQL. Still, since our focus is on the mechanics of building an AI agent, the static data in database.py will suffice for our purposes.

There's another file in the repo called tools.py. Copy that one over, too. tools.py contains all the functions or tools that Nibby will be able to call. The file defines four such functions:

- retrieve_user_id looks up a user's user ID, given their email address and date of birth.

- get_order_id returns the ID of a particular order, given the user ID of the user who placed the order, and the date they placed it. For simplicity, we assume that a user can only place one order on a particular day.

- get_order_status accepts an order ID and returns its order status, tracking number, and expected delivery date.

- cancel_order cancels an order, given an order ID.

We're not interested in the actual implementations of these functions, though you can read through them in tools.py. What matters is that Nibby needs to be able to call and use them correctly.

For this, we'll rely on type hints and docstrings. For instance, consider the definition of one of these functions in tools.py (chapter_10/in_progress_06/tools.py in the GitHub repo):

```python
def retrieve_user_id(email: str, dob: str) -> int:
    """
    Look up a user's user ID, given their email address and date of birth.
```

```
If the user is not found, return None.

Args:
  email (str): The email address of the user.
  dob (str): The date of birth of the user in the format "YYYY-MM-DD".

Returns:
  int: The user ID of the user, or None if the user is not found.
  """
for user_id, user_info in users.items():
  if (user_info["email_address"] == email and
      user_info["date_of_birth"] == dob):
    return user_id
```

Notice how we're using type hints in the function signature ((email: str, dob: str) -> str), and explaining in detail what the function does in a docstring (the multi-line string after the signature), along with details about the arguments and return value. These auxiliary items are what the AI model will use to determine which tool to call. At the bottom of tools.py, there's this line that exports all the functions in the file as a list named tools:

```
tools = [retrieve_user_id, get_order_id, get_order_status, cancel_order]
```

We'll use the tools variable in our graph in a bit.

10.6.4 *Making our graph agentic*

Consider an example of how Nibby might use the four tools we've made available to help a customer. Let's say the customer in the example data, Alice Johnson, wants to know the status of their order (order 101 shown in the excerpt from database.py). Here's how the interaction might proceed:

- **User:** "Hi, my name's Alice! I placed an order on Feb 10, 2025. Could you check on its status, please?"
- **Nibby (reasoning to itself):** "I have a tool called get_order_status that will give me the status of an order. To call it, I need an order_id. I don't have one, but I can get one by calling the get_order_id tool, which needs a user_id and an order_placed_date. The user says the order_placed_date is Feb 10, 2025, so I have that. I still need a user_id. To obtain *that*, I can call the retrieve_user_id tool, which requires an email and a date of birth. Therefore, I should ask the customer for this info."
- **Nibby:** "Could you give me your email address and date of birth?"
- **User:** "Sure, my email is alice.johnson@example.com and my date of birth is May 14, 1990."
- **Nibby (tool call):** Call the tool retrieve_user_id with the parameters email=alice.johnson@example.com and dob=1990-05-14

- `retrieve_user_id('alice.johnson@example.com', '1990-05-14')`: <returns the value 1, which is Alice's `user_id`>
- **Nibby (tool call):** Call the tool `get_order_id` with the parameters `user_id=1` and `order_placed_date=2025-02-10`
- `get_order_id(1, 2025-02-10)`: <returns the value 101, the correct order ID>
- **Nibby (tool call):** Call the tool `get_order_status` with the parameter `order_id=101`
- `get_order_status(101)`: <returns a dictionary: {'order_status': 'Shipped', 'tracking_number': 'TRK123456789', 'expected_delivery_date': '2025-02-18'}>
- **Nibby:** "Your order has been shipped and should arrive on Feb 18, 2025. You can use the tracking number TRK123456789 to track it."

Note how the bot needs to alternate between conversing with the user, reasoning about what needs to be done next, and issuing a call to a tool. How do we code all of this up? LangGraph actually makes this surprisingly easy.

First, let's modify bot.py to make our LLM aware of the tools available to it:

```python
...
from vector_store import VectorStore
from tools import tools

class Bot:
  def __init__(self, api_keys, config):
    ...
    self.llm = self.get_llm().bind_tools(tools)...
  ...
```

Here we're *binding* the tools we defined earlier—imported from tools.py—to our LLM object so that it knows they exist. As a result, if the LLM thinks it's appropriate, it can respond with a *tool call*.

In the previous example, the tool calls are marked with "Nibby (tool call)". In practical terms, these are `AIMessages` produced by the LLM that have a property called `tool_calls`, which contains information about any tools that the LLM wants us to call on its behalf and the parameters to call them with. The binding logic uses the docstrings and type hints we specified in tools.py to explain to the LLM what each tool does and how to use it.

What about the graph itself? Listing 10.12 shows the changes required to graph.py to turn our bot into an agent (chapter_10/in_progress_06/graph.py in the GitHub repo).

Listing 10.12　An agentic graph.py

```python
from langgraph.checkpoint.memory import MemorySaver
from langgraph.graph import START, StateGraph, MessagesState
from langgraph.prebuilt import tools_condition, ToolNode
from langchain_core.documents import Document
from langchain_core.messages import HumanMessage, SystemMessage
from prompts import *
```

```python
from tools import tools

...
class SupportAgentGraph:
  ...
  def build_graph(self):
    ...
    builder.add_node("tools", ToolNode(tools))...
    builder.add_edge("augment", "assistant")
    builder.add_conditional_edges("assistant", tools_condition)
    builder.add_edge("tools", "assistant")

    return builder.compile(checkpointer=memory)
  ...
```

Incredibly, all we needed to do was add three lines to the `build_graph` method and import a few extra items! Let's go through the line additions, starting with the first one:

```python
builder.add_node("tools", ToolNode(tools))
```

This adds a node named tools to our graph. `ToolNode` is a node already built into Lang-Graph, so we don't have to define it ourselves. It essentially does the following:

1 Takes the last message in the messages list (from the graph state) and executes any tool calls in it based on the list of tools we pass it.

2 Appends the value returned by the tool(s) as a `ToolMessage`—like `HumanMessage` and `AIMessage`—to the messages list.

At the end of a `ToolNode`, the last message in the messages variable is a `ToolMessage` representing the output of calling a tool. We now have all the *pieces* we need, but how do we orchestrate the kind of thinking process outlined in the example interaction at the beginning of this section?

Before we get into that, turn your attention to figure 10.20, which is what our graph will look like at the end of these changes:

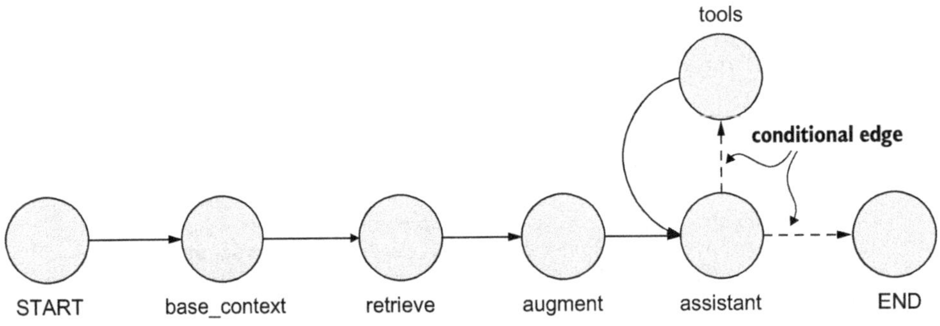

Figure 10.20   Our graph now has a tools node and a conditional edge.

Notice that there are now *two* lines flowing out from the assistant node—one goes to
END as before, while the other goes to our newly added `tools` node.

In LangGraph, this is known as a *conditional edge*. We can choose the next node to
execute from multiple option, depending on a specified condition. A conditional edge
is implemented as a function that takes the following form:

```python
def some_condition(state):
  # Branching
  if <something is true>:
    return "name_of_node_1"
  elif <something else is true>:
    return "name_of_node_2"
  ...
```

In our case, we don't actually need to build our own conditional edge because Lang-
Graph already has exactly what we want:

```python
builder.add_conditional_edges("assistant", tools_condition)
```

`tools_condition`—imported from `langgraph.prebuilt`—simply routes to our `ToolNode`
(named `tools`) if the last message in the conversation—i.e., the LLM's response—
contains any tool calls, or to END otherwise.

Since `tools_condition` already has the logic to route to END, we can remove the earlier line that created a direct (non-conditional) edge between `assistant` and END.

Once the `ToolNode` executes, we need the LLM to read the return value and
decide what to do with it—whether it's calling *another* tool or responding to the
user. Therefore, we create a *loop* in the graph by connecting the tools node *back* to
`assistant`:

```python
builder.add_edge("tools", "assistant")
```

And that's all it takes! Now, when a request comes in, the LLM will reason about what
to do. If it decides to call a tool, it'll put a tool call in its response, causing `tools_`
`condition` to route to the `ToolNode`, which executes the call. Since `ToolNode` has a direct
edge to the assistant, the LLM will get the updated list of messages with the appended
`ToolMessage` and can again reason about what to do with the response.

If the LLM decides it doesn't need to call any more tools—or that the next step in
the process is to get some information from the user—it won't include any tool calls in
its response, which means that `tools_condition` will route to END, and the final message
will be displayed to the user.

While that's all that's required to get the bot to work correctly, we need to
make a last change in graph.py related to what gets shown to the customer in the
frontend.

As the above paragraphs hopefully make clear, the communication between the `assistant` and `tools` nodes happens through the `messages` variable in the graph state, and consists of internal messages of two types: `AIMessages` containing tool calls, and `ToolMessages` containing tool return values.

Since we don't want to expose these internal messages to the user of our Streamlit app, we need to hide them when we pass the conversation history back. Recall that this history is relayed through the `get_history` method in bot.py, which calls the `get_conversation` method in graph.py.

Let's make the appropriate changes in graph.py to remove these messages (chapter_10/in_progress_06/graph.py in the GitHub repo):

```python
...
@staticmethod
def is_internal_message(msg):
  return msg.type == "tool" or "tool_calls" in msg.additional_kwargs

def get_conversation(self):
  state = self.graph.get_state(self.config)
  if "messages" not in state.values:
    return []
  messages = state.values["messages"]
  return [msg for msg in messages if not self.is_internal_message(msg)]
```

First, we define `is_internal_message`, a static method that determines whether a message that we pass is an "internal" one, i.e., one that's not fit to show the user. Above, we're defining an internal message as one that either has the type "tool"—which is true of `ToolMessages`—or has a "tool_calls" property (within `additional_kwargs`, a property that the LLM will use to set metadata within a message).

Then, rather than returning all the messages from the state in `get_conversation`, we now filter for the non-internal messages and only return those. With that out of the way, rerun the app and test out its new capabilities! Figure 10.21 shows an example. By allowing Nibby to access external tools, we've given it superpowers and saved Note n' Nib's customer support division some serious time!

This has been our most advanced app yet. If you've been following along and working on these projects yourself, you probably appreciate that the more complex an app becomes, the more things can go wrong in the real world when users actually start interacting with it. In the next chapter, we'll explore how to catch these problems beforehand and test your app to make it as robust as possible.

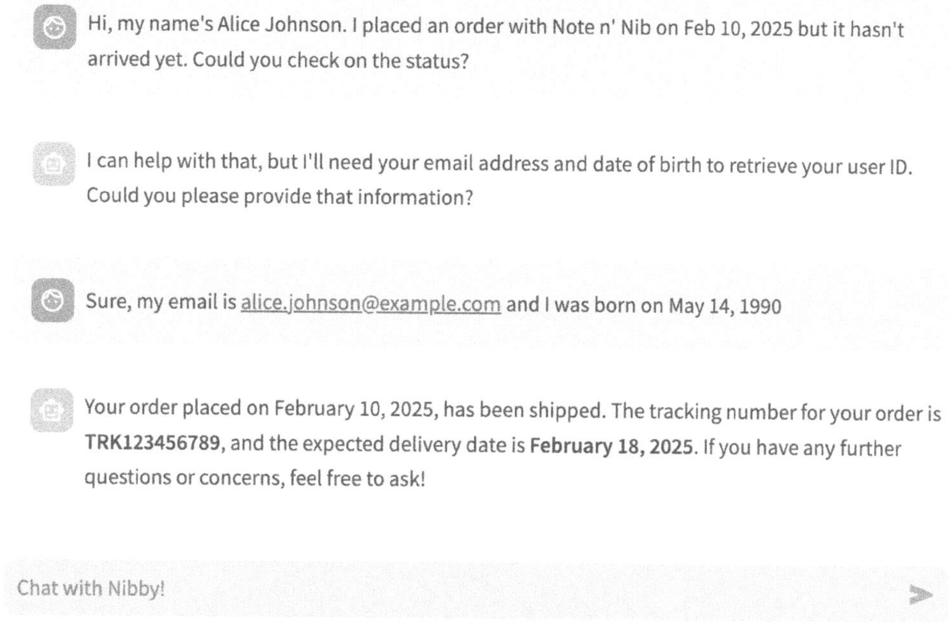

Figure 10.21 Nibby can handle real-world actions like tracking and canceling orders (see chapter_10/in_progress_06 in the GitHub repo for the full code).

Summary

- Real-world AI applications require advanced capabilities, such as knowledge retrieval and action execution.
- LangGraph structures AI workflows as graphs. Nodes represent steps in the process, and edges define the flow of execution between them.
- Each node in LangGraph takes the graph state and modifies it.
- `st.chat_input` renders a textbox where users can type messages.
- `st.chat_message` displays human and AI messages appropriately.
- LangGraph uses checkpointers to persist information across multiple graph executions.
- It's important to explicitly instruct the LLM to stay on-topic and ignore irrelevant requests. The system message is a good place to do that.
- Embeddings involve converting an object, such as a piece of text, into a list of numbers called vectors to find relevant content using similarity search.
- Retrieval Augmented Generation (RAG) is a technique for providing custom knowledge to a pre-trained LLM by retrieving chunks of context relevant to the user query from a vector database like Pinecone.

- A *tool* is simply a well-documented function that an LLM can choose to call in response to a user query.
- An agentic app—or simply an *agent*—can use tools to interact with the real world.
- LangGraph makes it extremely easy to write agentic apps through its `ToolNode` and `tools_condition` abstractions.

Testing and deploying apps

You've built your app and even given it smarts. Now comes the final step: making it robust. In this part, we'll show you what it takes to produce a Streamlit app by testing it thoroughly and deploying it professionally.

Chapter 11 focuses on testing: you'll use pytest to write unit tests, test different parts of your app in combination, and test entire flows from end to end. You'll also explore Streamlit's testing utilities to validate frontend interactions. Chapter 12 moves to deployment beyond the free Streamlit Community Cloud: you'll learn how to package your app with Docker, deploy it to AWS, and secure it with a custom domain and HTTPS.

These final chapters are about long-term success. They'll help ensure that your app works today and will continue to work tomorrow.

Testing Streamlit apps

This chapter covers

- Developing a testing strategy for an application
- Differences between unit, integration, and end-to-end tests
- Writing and running automated tests with pytest
- Using Streamlit's AppTest to create a live app with simulated user interactions
- Evolving your tests alongside your code

You've spent hours building your Streamlit app. The UI looks great, the code runs smoothly, and you're ready to share it with the world. But what happens when a user suddenly enters unexpected data? Or when the API you're calling changes its response format? Or when you deploy an update that inadvertently breaks existing functionality?

Without proper testing, your elegant application can quickly transform into a frustrating experience for your users. As the saying goes, "Untested code is broken code"—a sentiment that applies as much to Streamlit apps as to any other piece of software.

In this chapter, we'll demystify the process of testing Streamlit applications. You'll learn how to verify the behavior of the different parts of your app—whether it's the frontend, the backend, or an external dependency—and how to validate that your app behaves correctly under various conditions. You'll catch bugs before your users do, and ensure that code changes don't break existing features. We'll explore different types of tests—from unit tests that focus on individual components to end-to-end tests that validate the entire application flow, understanding how each forms a vital piece of your larger testing strategy.

The techniques you'll learn aren't just academic exercises—they are *necessary* for any application beyond a certain size that is meant to be used in a professional environment. So let's get to it and make our apps bullet-proof!

NOTE   The GitHub repo for this book is at https://github.com/aneevdavis/ streamlit-in-action. The chapter_11 folder has this chapter's code and a requirements.txt file with exact versions of all the required Python libraries.

11.1   *MovieScout: An app to test*

Before we get to the good stuff, we need a Streamlit app that we can test—something that's simple enough not to take the focus away from the testing, but complex enough that writing tests for it will teach us something meaningful. Enter MovieScout, a search tool for movies. MovieScout is going to be quite simple: enter a search query, and receive a set of matching movies.

At this point in the book, you should be well-placed to build this yourself. Since this chapter is concerned more with *learning to test* the app than with *building* it, we're going to speed through the implementation, only pointing out a few aspects that will be important for the subsequent testing.

First, figure 11.1 shows the app design. A search term entered on the Streamlit frontend is used in the backend to call an external movie search API, which returns an API response object with search results and information about each movie, like its release date and an overview. The backend then parses the API response into a more convenient format and returns the results to the frontend, which renders the search results in a user-friendly way.

11.1.1   *Using the TMDB API to pull movie info*

We'll outsource the actual mechanics of searching for and obtaining information about movies to a third-party API, allowing us to keep our logic simple.

TMDB, or The Movie Database, is an online platform that hosts a film database, providing access to movie synopses, user ratings, posters, and more. Of interest to us is the free TMDB API that can programmatically fetch data and images about movies.

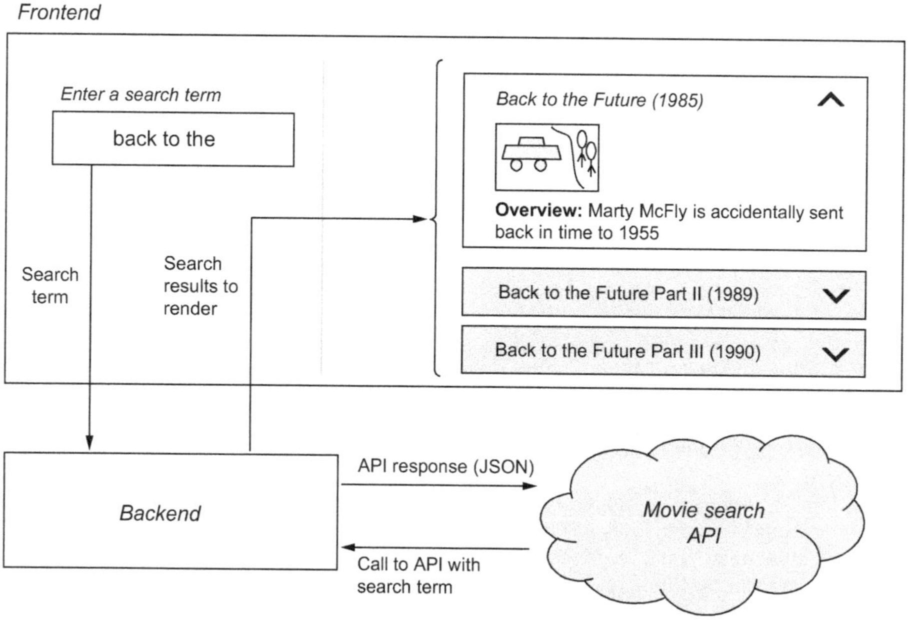

Figure 11.1 The design for the MovieScout app

OBTAINING AN API KEY

Sign up for a TMDB account at https://www.themoviedb.org/signup. Then log in, open the API registration page (at the time of writing, https://www.themoviedb.org/settings/api), and register for a key.

The process requires you to enter quite a few bits of information, such as your address, contact details, and details of the application you're going to be building. Pick Personal as the Type of Use. For the application URL, you can enter something like `https://your-app-name.streamlit.app/` (after replacing your-app-name with something more meaningful). Don't worry; the URL doesn't really matter or need to actually exist.

Anyway, when you've submitted your info, you should get your API key straight away with no further hoops to jump through. Note that the value you're interested in is the `API Key`, and *not* the `API Read Access Token`. Write the key down somewhere.

QUERYING THE API

To pull information using the TMDB API, we'll use the `requests` library, just as we did in chapter 5. To test this out quickly, open a Python shell in your terminal by typing `python`, and enter the following:

```
>>> import requests
>>> params = {'api_key': 'Replace with your API key', 'query': 'ferris bueller'}
>>> response = requests.get('https://api.themoviedb.org/3/search/movie',
params=params)
>>> response.json()
```

Here, we're searching the TMDB API by sending an HTTP GET request to the URL
https://api.themoviedb.org/3/search/movie with a params dictionary containing the
API key—which you'll obviously need to replace with your real key—and a search term.

Here's an example output, formatted for readability, with only the stuff we care about:

```
{
  ...
  "results": [
    {
      ...
      "id": 9377,
      ...
      "overview": "After high school slacker Ferris Bueller successfully
fakes an illness in order to skip school for the day, he goes on a series
of adventures throughout Chicago with his girlfriend Sloane and best friend
Cameron, all the while trying to outwit his wily school principal and fed-up
sister.",
      "popularity": 26.269,
      "poster_path": "/w7gDfRXdK8S8GKLvpVepFSLxVZv.jpg",
      "release_date": "1986-06-11",
      "title": "Ferris Bueller's Day Off",
      ...
      "vote_average": 7.6,
      "vote_count": 4966
    },
    { ... },
    { ... }
  ],
  ...
}
```

As you can see, `response.json()` returns a dictionary that contains a `results` key
(among others) with a list of movies. Each movie has an ID, an overview, and so on.

11.1.2 *The backend*

Armed with this knowledge, you're ready to create the backend. Create a file called
backend.py with the contents shown in listing 11.1 (chapter_11/in_progress_01/
backend.py in the GitHub repo).

> **Listing 11.1   The Backend class**

```
import requests

SEARCH_URL = "https://api.themoviedb.org/3/search/movie"
POSTER_URL_PREFIX = "https://image.tmdb.org/t/p/w500"

class Backend:
  def __init__(self, api_key):
    self.api_key = api_key

  def search_movies(self, query):
```

```
    params = {"api_key": self.api_key, "query": query}
    response = requests.get(SEARCH_URL, params=params)
    response.raise_for_status()
    results = response.json().get('results', [])
    return {movie["id"]: movie for movie in results}

@staticmethod
def get_poster_url(poster_path):
    return f"{POSTER_URL_PREFIX}{poster_path if poster_path else ''}"
```

The `Backend` class has two methods. `search_movies` accepts a search query from the
caller and queries the API. It converts the results list from the API response to a dictionary keyed on the movie ID. For instance, the result we obtained above would become:

```
{
  9377: {"title": "Ferris Bueller's ...", "popularity": ...},
  ...
}
```

`get_poster_url`—a static method—takes the `poster_path` (which we'll get from the
`poster_path` field in the API response, e.g. `/w7gDfRXdK8S8GKLvpVepFSLxVZv.jpg`) and
converts it to a full URL containing the poster image: https://image.tmdb.org/t/p/
w500/w7gDfRXdK8S8GKLvpVepFSLxVZv.jpg

11.1.3 *The frontend*

We'll keep our frontend similarly uncomplicated. Begin by placing your API key in a
secrets.toml file, as shown in listing 11.2.

Listing 11.2 Putting the API key in .streamlit/secrets.toml

```
api_key = "187..."          ◄————┐
                                  │ Replace with your actual TMDB API key.
```

Next, create frontend.py using the code in listing 11.3 (chapter_11/in_progress_01/
frontend.py in the GitHub repo).

Listing 11.3 The frontend

```
import streamlit as st
from backend import Backend

backend = Backend(st.secrets["api_key"])

with st.sidebar:
  movie_query = st.text_input("Search for a movie")
  if st.button("Search", type="primary"):
    st.session_state.results = backend.search_movies(movie_query)

if "results" in st.session_state:
  for _, movie in st.session_state.results.items():
```

```
title, date = movie["title"], movie["release_date"]
year = date.split("-")[0] if date else "N/A"
with st.expander(f"{title} ({year})"):
  poster_url = Backend.get_poster_url(movie.get('poster_path', None))
  st.image(poster_url, width=250)
  st.markdown(f"**Overview:** {movie.get('overview', 'N/A')}")
  st.markdown(f"**Rating:** {movie.get('rating', 'N/A')}")
```

On startup, the app displays a sidebar with a textbox and a Search button that triggers the `search_movies` method from backend.py, storing the results as `results` in `st.session_state`.

Once the results are available, we loop through them, displaying an `st.expander` for each movie—labeled with its title and year of release. Within the expander, we grab the full URL of the movie's poster (if it exists) using the `Backend` class' `get_poster_url`.

The next line uses an element we haven't seen before:

```
st.image(poster_url, width=250)
```

You can probably guess what this does; it takes the poster URL and renders it to the screen with a fixed width of 250 pixels. Optionally, `st.image` can display a caption below the image—using the `caption` argument—or even show a series of images in a row—unlocked by passing a *list* of URLs as the first argument instead of a single one.

Finally, we use `st.markdown` elements to provide the overview and rating of each movie (figure 11.2).

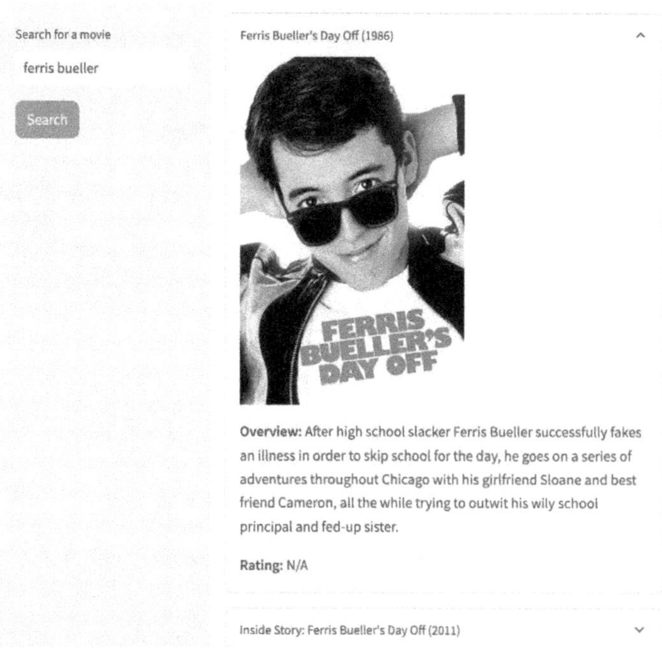

Figure 11.2 Screenshot of the working MovieScout app (see chapter_11/in_progress_01 in the GitHub repo for the full code).

Fantastic! No more scrolling through Netflix aimlessly for an hour only to give up and go to bed; with MovieScout, you can now waste time with *purpose—searching* for movies you'll never watch!

With the app built and ready to go, we can now turn our attention to the real point of this chapter—testing.

11.2 Testing the application

Testing is the cornerstone of reliable software development. While building features can be exciting, thorough testing ensures your application works as intended, not just under ideal conditions but also when faced with unexpected inputs or when components change over time.

In this section, we'll lay the groundwork for testing your Streamlit applications effectively. First, we'll explore the various categories of tests you can perform, with each type serving a specific purpose in your overall strategy. We'll then outline our specific test approach for MovieScout, and introduce `pytest`, a powerful Python testing framework that will power our test suite.

11.2.1 Different kinds of tests

We can broadly categorize testing into manual and automated testing:

- *Manual testing*—Involves a developer or tester running the app and manually verifying expected behaviors. While useful during early development, it is time-consuming and prone to human error.
- *Automated Testing*—Consists of writing code to automatically check if various components work correctly. Automated testing includes:
  - *Unit tests*—Focus on individual functions or methods, ensuring they work in isolation.
  - *Integration tests*—Validate the interaction between different components, such as verifying that the frontend and backend work together as expected.
  - *End-to-end (E2E) tests*—Verify the entire application's workflow under real-world conditions.

In this chapter, we'll focus on unit, integration, and end-to-end tests, as they provide a solid foundation for catching errors early and maintaining code quality.

11.2.2 Our testing approach

For our MovieScout app, we'll take a bottom-up testing approach, where we start with the smallest testable components and gradually integrate them into larger tests.

START WITH UNIT TESTS FOR THE BACKEND

We'll begin by testing the backend (the `Backend` class) in isolation, ensuring that it correctly sends requests and processes responses, without actually calling the TMDB API, which, as we'll see, is an external dependency that needs to be *mocked*.

MOVE ON TO FRONTEND UNIT TESTS

Next, we test the frontend logic independently. Since our app involves user interaction, we'll use Streamlit's `AppTest` class to simulate user actions, such as entering a search term and clicking buttons. These tests ensure that UI elements update correctly without requiring a real backend.

WRITE INTEGRATION TESTS THAT COMBINE COMPONENTS

Once the individual components are verified, we test the interaction between the frontend and the backend. We'll also write our first test that calls TMDB, testing the integration between the backend and the external API.

FINISH WITH AN END-TO-END TEST

Finally, we run a true end-to-end test, where the entire app (frontend, backend, and API) is tested without mocks. This test simulates a real user search and verifies that results appear correctly using live API data.

11.2.3 *A quick introduction to pytest*

Throughout this chapter, we'll be using the `pytest` library to write and execute automated tests. `pytest` is a flexible and widely used testing framework for Python that offers powerful features such as concise syntax, automatic test discovery, and rich debugging information.

To get started, install `pytest` using `pip`:

```
pip install pytest
```

A MINIMAL EXAMPLE

Let's look at a simple piece of Python code and write a test for it to understand how pytest works. Create a file called test_example.py with the following:

```
def add(x, y):
    return x + y

def test_add():
    assert add(2, 3) == 5
    assert add(-1, 1) == 0
```

Here, the `add` function—which returns the sum of two numbers, obviously—is the function we're testing, while `test_add` is the test itself. `test_add` runs add for various inputs and checks that the results are as expected through Python's `assert` keyword (which we'll learn more about soon).

To run the test, run `pytest -v` in your terminal from the folder where you saved test_example.py. You should get output similar to:

```
collected 1 item

test_example.py::test_add PASSED                                      [100%]
================================ 1 passed in 0.02s ================================
```

indicating that the test passed and that your code is working correctly.

Now that we understand the basics, we can apply `pytest` to our MovieScout app, starting with unit tests for the backend. We'll learn more about `pytest` along the way.

11.3 Unit testing the backend

We'll test the backend part of our app first. As we've seen, the `Backend` class is responsible for communicating with the TMDB API, fetching results for a search query, and converting the results into the dictionary format that we return to the frontend.

In this part, we're going to write *unit tests* for the backend. You know that unit testing is a software engineering technique where individual components of our code are tested in isolation. But what does that truly *mean*?

11.3.1 How unit testing works

Consider diagram in figure 11.3, which illustrates what the `Backend` class does (it mostly consists of the `search_movies` method).

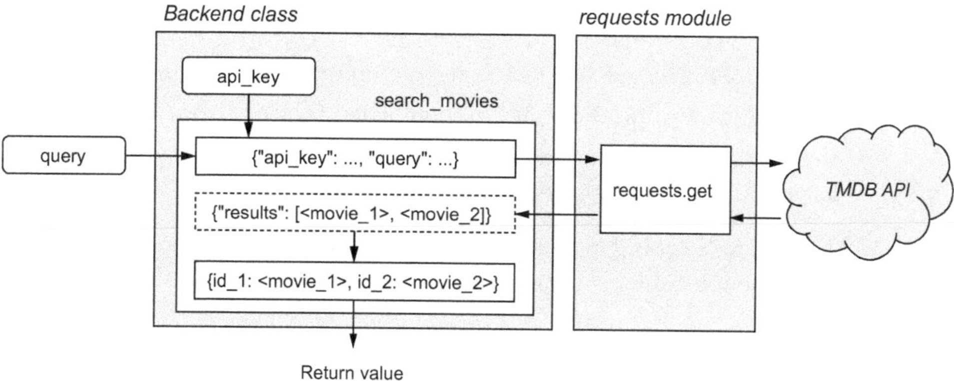

Figure 11.3   The requests module and the TMDB API are external dependencies of `Backend`.

`Backend`'s `search_movies` method accepts a search term, calls the TMDB API with it, turns the results into a dictionary, and returns it. No surprises here, right? We know all of this already.

A more interesting question is this: what does this method *not* do, or—more specifically—what does it not do *by itself?* In figure 11.3, this is represented by the things that lie outside of the box labeled Backend Class:

- `search_movies` does not send the HTTP `GET` request to the TMDB API's URL; sure, it makes the *call* to `requests.get`, but the actual code that sends the `GET` request lies in the `requests` module.

- `search_movies` does not execute the search to construct the JSON response; the TMDB API does that once it gets the request.

We did not write the requests library, and we do not control the TMDB API. Therefore, from the perspective of the Backend class, these are *external dependencies.*

When unit testing a component, we want to:

- Isolate the component we're testing from any external dependencies, and
- Ensure that nothing outside of the component influences the tests.

Put simply, we're interested solely in whether our *own* code is correct. For instance, let's say the TMDB API is currently experiencing high traffic and isn't returning anything. That's not our fault, and the Backend class' unit tests shouldn't fail because of it.

> **NOTE**   This doesn't mean we don't care about external components failing. We absolutely do care; it's just that these failures are in the realm of integration tests or end-to-end tests, rather than unit tests. We'll explore those later.

So, how do we isolate code from external dependencies during testing? By *mocking* them.

MOCKING DEPENDENCIES

Mocking is the process of replacing real dependencies with fake, controlled versions during testing. Mocking has several benefits, including the ability to:

- Control the behavior of external dependencies (e.g., simulate API responses)
- Prevent any unpredictability in their actual behavior from affecting unit tests
- Ensure that tests run independently of network conditions
- Prevent real API calls (they can be slow or unreliable)

In our case, we're going to create mock versions of any functions we're using from the requests module and any results we get from the API. We'll discover shortly how this works in code.

A MENTAL MODEL OF UNIT TESTS

Before we write any test code, I want you to have a clear mental picture of unit testing. A single unit test checks one method or piece of functionality. There may be many different tests that check the behavior of the same method under various conditions. Generally speaking, a test has the following structure:

- *A setup phase,* where we set up the environment for each of our tests to run. In our case, we'll create an instance of the Backend class in this phase so we can test its methods.
- *A testing phase,* where we:
  - Set up the conditions required for the individual test to run; this includes swapping out any external dependencies (such as the results from the API or methods from the requests module) for fake mock versions.
  - Set up the inputs to the method or function we're about to test.
  - Define the expected output of the method or function.
  - Run the method or function for those inputs.

- – Compare the actual output obtained by running the method with the expected output, making various assertions about what we expect.
  - – Mark the test as "failed" if any of the assertions we make turn out to be false, or "passed" if they are all true.
- A *teardown phase*, where we clean up the environment so the next test can run. In our particular case, there isn't really anything to clean up, so we won't have this phase, though `pytest` will handle some of this in the background.

Figure 11.4 illustrates this model.

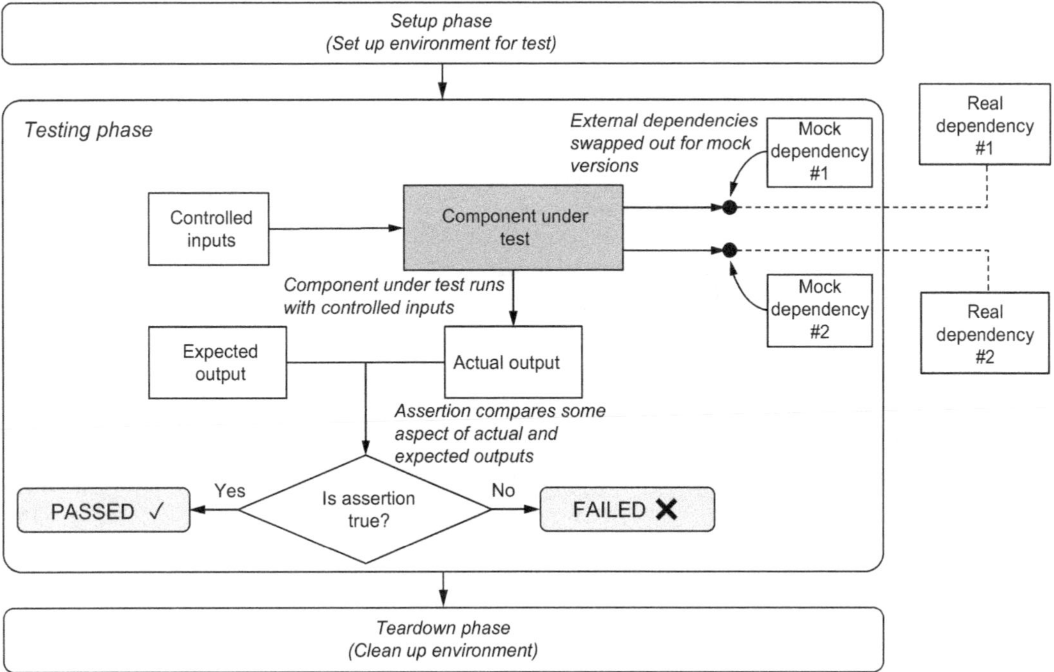

Figure 11.4 How a unit test works.

We can—and ideally, should—write as many tests as required to convince ourselves that a given piece of code has no defects. With this theoretical knowledge attained, let's write some real tests.

11.3.2 Writing unit tests for the backend

In this section, we'll use `pytest` to write and run tests for the backend in accordance with the mental model just described. Before writing the actual tests, let's set up some of the mock data we'll need. Create a new file called mock_data.py with the content from listing 11.4 (chapter_11/in_progress_02/mock_data.py in the GitHub repo).

Listing 11.4   Mock data in mock_data.py

```
MOCK_MOVIE_1 = {
  "id": "123",
  "title": "Test Movie 1",
  "overview": "This is a test movie",
  "vote_average": 8.5,
  "release_date": "2023-01-01",
  "poster_path": "/test_poster1.jpg"
}

MOCK_MOVIE_2 = {
  "id": "456",
  "title": "Test Movie 2",
  "overview": "Another test movie",
  "vote_average": 7.0,
  "release_date": "2022-05-15",
  "poster_path": "/test_poster2.jpg"
}

MOCK_MOVIES = [MOCK_MOVIE_1, MOCK_MOVIE_2]
MOCK_RESULTS = {"123": MOCK_MOVIE_1, "456": MOCK_MOVIE_2}
```

mock_data.py contains two mock movies—MOCK_MOVIE_1 and MOCK_MOVIE_2—with dummy data. You'll notice that each movie is structured as a dictionary that matches the format we obtain from the TMDB API, though it only contains the fields we actually use.

We also have a MOCK_MOVIES variable, which is a list that contains the two movies; we'll use this as a stand-in for the value of the results key we get from the API, which, as you'll recall, is also a list.

Finally, there's a MOCK_RESULTS, which is the MOCK_MOVIES list as a dictionary keyed on the movie ID, matching the structure we're expecting to get from the search_movies method. Next, we'll build the unit tests one by one. Add a file named test_backend.py with the initial code shown in listing 11.5 (chapter_11/in_progress_02/test_backend .py in the GitHub repo).

Listing 11.5   Backend unit tests

```
import pytest
from unittest.mock import patch, Mock
from backend import Backend, SEARCH_URL
from mock_data import MOCK_MOVIES, MOCK_RESULTS

@pytest.fixture
def backend():
    api_key = "test_api_key"
    return Backend(api_key)

@patch('requests.get')
def test_search_movies_success(mock_get, backend):
    mock_response = Mock()
    mock_response.json.return_value = {'results': MOCK_MOVIES}
    mock_get.return_value = mock_response
```

```python
    results = backend.search_movies("test query")

    mock_get.assert_called_once_with(
        SEARCH_URL,
        params={"api_key": backend.api_key, "query": "test query"}
    )
    assert len(results) == len(MOCK_MOVIES)
    for _id, movie in MOCK_RESULTS.items():
        assert _id in results
        assert results[_id]["title"] == movie["title"]
```

Let's start with the first few lines after the imports:

```python
@pytest.fixture
def backend():
    api_key = "test_api_key"
    return Backend(api_key)
```

The backend function creates an instance of the Backend class with a dummy API key, which is appropriate since our unit tests won't make any real API calls. This corresponds to the setup phase in our mental model of testing.

When decorated with @pytest.fixture, this function becomes, well, a pytest *fixture*— a reusable component that provides specific features to tests. By defining the backend fixture once, it becomes available to any test function that includes it as a parameter, as we'll see in a minute. This pattern is particularly useful since all our tests require a Backend instance.

Now look at the actual test:

```python
@patch('requests.get')
def test_search_movies_success(mock_get, backend):
    mock_response = Mock()
    mock_response.json.return_value = {'results': MOCK_MOVIES}
    mock_get.return_value = mock_response

    results = backend.search_movies("test query")

    mock_get.assert_called_once_with(
        SEARCH_URL,
        params={"api_key": backend.api_key, "query": "test query"}
    )
    assert len(results) == len(MOCK_MOVIES)
    for _id, movie in MOCK_RESULTS.items():
        assert _id in results
        assert results[_id]["title"] == movie["title"]
```

The name of the function—test_search_movies_success—starts with test_ so that pytest can easily identify it as a test.

The test accepts two parameters: mock_get and backend. Notice that the second of these—backend—has the same name as the fixture function we defined. As a result, when we run this test, pytest will *automatically call the fixture and pass its return value as the value of the* backend *argument.*

What about the first argument, mock_get? What does it do? Recall that the original method we're testing—search_movies from backend.py—contains a call to requests .get, which we determined earlier to be an external dependency that needs to be *mocked.* mock_get is the mocked version of this dependency. It acts as a function, so it can be *called* (like this: mock_get()), but it also gives us special characteristics that make controlling and observing its behavior easy, such as the ability to set its return value manually, or check whether it was called during a test—both of which we'll encounter shortly. But how do we obtain such an object?

Consider the decorator over our test function: @patch('requests.get'). This decorator—which we imported from unittest.mock—is what temporarily replaces requests.get with our special mock object during the execution of the test function. The mock object is then passed as the value of mock_get, the first parameter to our test function.

By patching requests.get, we prevent our test from making actual HTTP requests and instead give ourselves complete control over what "response" is returned. This is crucial for creating reliable, deterministic tests that don't depend on external services.

In the first few lines of the test function, we configure the mock:

```
mock_response = Mock()
mock_response.json.return_value = {'results': MOCK_MOVIES}
mock_get.return_value = mock_response
```

Here, we're creating a fake response object with a json method that returns our test data (from mock_data.py), and then telling our mock_get to return this response when called. This effectively simulates a successful API call returning our predefined movie data.

> **NOTE** You may find the expression mock_response.json.return_value interesting here because we haven't explicitly defined a .json method in mock_response. It works because mock_response is an object of the Mock class, which creates the .json method on the fly when we refer to it in the expression above. We could have used this approach to define any mock method on mock_response. For instance, mock_response.pokemon.return_value = 'pikachu' would have caused a call to mock_response.pokemon() to return the string 'pikachu'.

After setting up our mocks, we call the actual method we're testing with a dummy query:

```
results = backend.search_movies("test query")
```

Finally, we verify both the function's behavior and its results, by making a series of *assertions*:

```
mock_get.assert_called_once_with(
  SEARCH_URL,
  params={"api_key": backend.api_key, "query": "test query"}
```

```
)
assert len(results) == len(MOCK_MOVIES)
for _id, movie in MOCK_RESULTS.items():
  assert _id in results
  assert results[_id]["title"] == movie["title"]
```

An *assertion* is essentially a condition that must evaluate to `True` for the test to pass. If any assertion fails, `pytest` will mark the test as failed and report which assertion failed and why. For example, if we had an assertion comparing an expected movie title with the actual title in the results, and they didn't match, `pytest` would fail the test and show a detailed error message highlighting the difference between the expected and actual values. This clear reporting helps developers quickly identify and fix problems in their code.

The first assertion checks the behavior of `search_movies`:

```
mock_get.assert_called_once_with(
  SEARCH_URL,
  params={"api_key": backend.api_key, "query": "test query"}
)
```

This checks if `requests.get` (or its mocked version, `mock_get`) was called exactly once with the correct URL and parameters, ensuring that our function is interacting correctly with the external API.

These assertions verify the results:

```
assert len(results) == len(MOCK_MOVIES)
for _id, movie in MOCK_RESULTS.items():
  assert _id in results
  assert results[_id]["title"] == movie["title"]
```

They check that the number of movies returned matches our mock data, and then iterate through each expected movie to ensure it exists in our results with the correct title. These assertions confirm that our function is correctly processing the API response and transforming it into the expected format.

Next, add a few more tests to the same file, as in the following listing (chapter_11/in_progress_03/test_backend.py in the GitHub repo):

Listing 11.6 Adding the remaining tests

```
...
from backend import Backend, SEARCH_URL, POSTER_URL_PREFIX...

...
@patch('requests.get')
def test_search_movies_success(mock_get, backend):
  ...


@patch('requests.get')
```

```python
def test_search_movies_no_results(mock_get, backend):
  mock_response = Mock()
  mock_response.json.return_value = {'results': []}
  mock_get.return_value = mock_response

  result = backend.search_movies("query with no matching results")
  assert result == {}

def test_get_poster_url():
  poster_path = "/test_path.jpg"
  expected_url = f"{POSTER_URL_PREFIX}{poster_path}"
  result_url = Backend.get_poster_url(poster_path)
  assert result_url == expected_url

def test_get_nonexistent_poster_url():
  poster_path = None
  expected_url = POSTER_URL_PREFIX
  result_url = Backend.get_poster_url(poster_path)
  assert result_url == expected_url
```

The first new test, `test_search_movies_no_results`, checks the behavior of `search_mov-ies` when the search query doesn't return any results. It's structured quite similarly to `test_search_movies_success` in that it first mocks the API response (with an empty result set in this case), runs `search_movies`, and then asserts something about the output. The assertion here, `assert result == {}`, is that the method should return an empty dictionary.

The other two tests—`test_get_poster_url` and `test_get_nonexistent_poster_url`—pertain to the Backend class' `get_poster_url` static method. These tests don't need to be decorated with `@patch` because `get_poster_url` doesn't call any external functions. They also don't need the backend fixture since we can call `get_poster_url` directly without an instance of Backend—using `Backend.get_poster_url`—as it's a static method.

These tests are pretty simple; in each case, we pass a pre-defined poster path (`/test_path.jpg` for the first test and `None` for the second) to `get_poster_url` and check that the returned URL is what we expect.

11.3.3 *Running the tests*

With the unit tests for the Backend class in place, let's go ahead and run them to make sure everything's good with our code. You can do this by going to the directory that contains test_backend.py in your terminal window and running:

```
pytest -v
```

The `-v` stands for "verbose", meaning that `pytest` will provide more information about our tests than it otherwise would. You should get something like the following:

```
collected 4 items

test_backend.py::test_search_movies_success PASSED  [ 25%]
```

```
test_backend.py::test_search_movies_no_results PASSED [ 50%]
test_backend.py::test_get_poster_url PASSED           [ 75%]
test_backend.py::test_get_nonexistent_poster_url PASSED [100%]


==================== 4 passed in 0.08s ======================
```

Looks like all the tests passed, so good job!

What would it look like if one of our tests were to fail? To answer this, let's intention-ally introduce a bug in a test. Modify the last line of the test_search_movies_no_results function like this:

```
@patch('requests.get')
def test_search_movies_no_results(mock_get, backend):
  mock_response = Mock()
  mock_response.json.return_value = {'results': []}
  mock_get.return_value = mock_response

  result = backend.search_movies("query with no matching results")
  assert result == []
```

We've replaced {} with [] here.

If you now run pytest -v, you should get:

```
collected 4 items

test_backend.py::test_search_movies_success PASSED     [ 25%]
test_backend.py::test_search_movies_no_results FAILED  [ 50%]
test_backend.py::test_get_poster_url PASSED            [ 75%]
test_backend.py::test_get_nonexistent_poster_url PASSED [100%]


========================= FAILURES ==========================
________________ test_search_movies_no_results ________________

mock_get = <MagicMock name='get' id='4532345824'>
backend = <backend.Backend object at 0x10f1f9880>

    @patch('requests.get')
    def test_search_movies_no_results(mock_get, backend):
      mock_response = Mock()
      mock_response.json.return_value = {'results': []}
      mock_get.return_value = mock_response

      result = backend.search_movies("query with no matching results")
>     assert result == []
E     assert {} == []
E
E       Full diff:
E       - []
E       + {}

test_backend.py:35: AssertionError
==================== short test summary info ====================
FAILED test_backend.py::test_search_movies_no_results - assert {} == []
```

Note how `test_search_movies_no_results` now fails. pytest shows us the "diff" between what the test expected to see as the return value of the function (`[]`) and what it actually saw (`{}`). Undo the change you just made, and let's move on to frontend testing.

11.4 *Unit testing the Streamlit frontend*

The foundations of unit testing remain the same whether we're dealing with the frontend or backend of your application. We still need to set up the testing environment before each test and tear it down afterwards. We also need to isolate the component we're testing from all external dependencies by patching or mocking them.

Testing the frontend introduces a new wrinkle, though; while the execution of the backend is entirely defined by the input values we provide it, the behavior of the frontend depends on how the *user* interacts with it. We therefore need a way to simulate user interaction, such as clicking a button or entering text in an input box.

As usual, Streamlit offers a simple way to accomplish this, in the form of the `AppTest` class. `AppTest` simulates a running Streamlit app built from your code. It has methods to mimic user interaction and inspect the rendered output. We'll demonstrate how `AppTest` works as we go along.

11.4.1 *Writing unit tests for the frontend*

Let's now jump to writing our frontend tests. You'll encounter several of the same constructs you first saw in the previous section—fixtures, mocks, and so on—but we'll also introduce a few new twists.

Create a file called test_frontend.py and copy the contents of listing 11.7 into it (chapter_11/in_progress_05/test_frontend.py in the GitHub repo).

Listing 11.7   Testing the frontend

```python
import pytest
from unittest.mock import patch
from streamlit.testing.v1 import AppTest
from mock_data import MOCK_RESULTS

class MockBackend:
    @staticmethod
    def get_poster_url(path):
        return "https://mock-image-server.com/poster.jpg"

    def __init__(self, api_key):
        self.api_key = api_key

    def search_movies(self, query):
        return MOCK_RESULTS

@pytest.fixture
def setup_app():
    at = AppTest.from_file("frontend.py")
```

```
  at.secrets["api_key"] = "test_api_key"
  return at

@patch("backend.Backend", MockBackend)
def test_initial_state(setup_app):
  at = setup_app
  at.run()

  # Check if sidebar has search input field and button
  assert len(at.sidebar.text_input) == 1
  assert len(at.sidebar.button) == 1
  assert "Search" in at.sidebar.button[0].label

  # Check that results are not visible initially
  assert "results" not in at.session_state
  assert len(at.expander) == 0
```

This section shows a single test function and the pieces required to get the test ready. Let's focus on the latter first.

MOCKING THE BACKEND

Recall from the prior sections in this chapter that unit testing involves isolating the specific component we're testing from any external dependencies, requiring us to mock stuff the backend depends on, such as `requests.get` and the API response.

Well, from the perspective of the frontend, the *backend* is an external dependency. Unit tests for the frontend should be unaffected by backend failures. Therefore, we need to treat the Backend class the same way we treated the other external dependencies earlier; in other words, we need to *mock* it.

That's what the `MockBackend` class from listing 11.7 does:

```
class MockBackend:
  @staticmethod
  def get_poster_url(path):
    return "https://mock-image-server.com/poster.jpg"

  def __init__(self, api_key):
    self.api_key = api_key

  def search_movies(self, query):
    return MOCK_RESULTS
```

Notice that `MockBackend` has the same methods as the `Backend` class—a `__init__` that accepts an `api_key` parameter, a `search_movies` method, and a static `get_poster_url` method. However, it doesn't have any of the logic for these methods. Instead, it returns mock values, such as a dummy URL in the case of `get_poster_url` and the `MOCK_RESULTS` we defined in mock_data.py in the case of `search_movies`.

SETTING UP THE APP FOR EACH TEST

The next piece sets up the running Streamlit app for each test:

```
@pytest.fixture
def setup_app():
  at = AppTest.from_file("frontend.py")
  at.secrets["api_key"] = "test_api_key"
  return at
```

This function is decorated with `@pytest.fixture`, which means that pytest will automatically run it and pass its return value to any subsequent test function we add that has a `setup_app` parameter. Within the function, we create an `AppTest` instance by calling `AppTest.from_file("frontend.py")`. This creates a runnable Streamlit app from frontend.py.

The next line, `at.secrets["api_key"] = "test_api_key"` adds a mock API key to the app's `st.secrets`. This is particularly useful because if we didn't have the option to set values in the `secrets` dictionary directly like this—something we *can't* do from the actual Streamlit app code, by the way—we might have had to set up a mock secrets .toml and things would have been more complicated.

Anyway, with that done, we can return the runnable app. Note that we're not actually *running* the app here; we're merely setting it up so that the actual tests can run it.

A FRONTEND TEST FOR THE INITIAL STATE

Consider our first frontend test function next:

```
@patch("backend.Backend", MockBackend)
def test_initial_state(setup_app):
  at = setup_app
  at.run()

  # Check if sidebar has search input field and button
  assert len(at.sidebar.text_input) == 1
  assert len(at.sidebar.button) == 1
  assert "Search" in at.sidebar.button[0].label

  # Check that results are not visible initially
  assert "results" not in at.session_state
  assert len(at.expander) == 0
```

This test checks the starting state of the app before any user interactions. As in the case of the backend tests, we've decorated the test with the `@patch` decorator from `unittest.mock`, but the format we're using is different:

```
@patch("backend.Backend", MockBackend)
def test_initial_state(setup_app):
```

Rather than passing the patched object as an argument to the function—like we did with `mock_get` in the backend tests—we're passing `MockBackend` directly to the decorator. This is because we're not actually going to be referencing or modifying the `MockBackend` object within the test (unlike in the case of `mock_get` where we modified its return value). We just need any references to the Backend class that are executed within the test to be replaced correctly with MockBackend.

As before, pytest will recognize setup_app as a fixture and pass its return value correctly at run time. The first two lines of the function run a simulated version of the app:

```
at = setup_app
at.run()
```

At this point, we have a running app; it's as though we've started the app using streamlit run frontend.py, and a browser window has opened up—except we can't actually *see* the browser window, only interact with the app using code. The rest of the test checks various things about the initial state of the app. Let's focus on the first two of these:

```
assert len(at.sidebar.text_input) == 1
assert len(at.sidebar.button) == 1
```

Here, we've obtained references to the various Streamlit elements on the page using dot notation. For instance, at.sidebar is a reference to the sidebar element within our running app.

What about at.sidebar.text_input? Well, when we access a Streamlit UI element type through AppTest, we get a list of all elements of that type that appear in our app. So at.sidebar.text_input is a list of all text input elements that appear in the sidebar.

The assertions len(at.sidebar.text_input) == 1 and len(at.sidebar.button) == 1 are checking that our app has exactly one text input and one button in the sidebar, which is what we'd expect based on our frontend code. The next assertion checks the button text:

```
assert "Search" in at.sidebar.button[0].label
```

This verifies that the label of the first (and only) button in our sidebar contains the text Search. It's important to test not just that elements exist, but that they have the correct content, as this example highlights. The final assertions check that no results are being displayed yet, since the user hasn't performed any searches:

```
assert "results" not in at.session_state
assert len(at.expander) == 0
```

The first of these checks that there's no results key in the app's session_state, while the second verifies that there are no expander elements on the page (which would be used to display movie details).

TESTING USER INTERACTIONS

So far we've created a test for the starting state of the app, but we haven't simulated any user interactions. That's up next.

Update test_frontend.py as shown in listing 11.8 to add a couple more tests (chapter_11/in_progress_06/test_frontend.py in the GitHub repo).

Listing 11.8   A couple more frontend tests

```
...
from mock_data import MOCK_MOVIES, MOCK_RESULTS

...
@patch("backend.Backend", MockBackend)
def test_initial_state(setup_app):
  ...

@patch("backend.Backend", MockBackend)
def test_search_functionality(setup_app):
  at = setup_app
  at.run()

  # Enter search query and click button
  at.sidebar.text_input[0].set_value("test movie").run()
  at.sidebar.button[0].click().run()

  # Verify results are in session_state
  assert "results" in at.session_state
  assert at.session_state["results"] == MOCK_RESULTS

  # Verify expanders are displayed
  expected_expanders = len(MOCK_MOVIES)
  actual_expanders = len(at.expander)
  assert actual_expanders == expected_expanders, \
    f"Expected {expected_expanders} expanders, found {actual_expanders}"

@patch("backend.Backend", MockBackend)
def test_movie_details_display(setup_app):
  at = setup_app

  # Set up session state with search results
  at.session_state["results"] = MOCK_RESULTS
  at.run()

  # Verify expanders are created
  assert len(at.expander) == 2

  # Verify both movies' details are in the markdown elements
  markdown_texts = [m.value for m in at.markdown]
  for movie in MOCK_MOVIES:
    overview_text = f"**Overview:** {movie['overview']}"
    rating_text = f"**Rating:** {movie['vote_average']}"

    assert any(overview_text in text for text in
               markdown_texts), f"Overview for {movie['title']} not found"
    assert any(rating_text in text for text in
               markdown_texts), f"Rating for {movie['title']} not found"
```

True to its name, the first newly added test function—test_search_functionality—
checks the search function. It starts out the same way as test_initial_state, by running the app that was set up in the fixture. The interesting part comes after this:

```
at.sidebar.text_input[0].set_value("test movie").run()
at.sidebar.button[0].click().run()
```

The first line programmatically enters the value test movie in our search box, while
the second simulates clicking the button using .click(). Notice how after each of
these interactions, we chain on a call to .run(), thereby *manually* triggering the rerun
that would have happened in the app if a user had taken these actions.

The next couple of assertions verify the presence of search results by checking for
their presence in session_state:

```
assert "results" in at.session_state
assert at.session_state["results"] == MOCK_RESULTS
```

The last line also checks if the returned results are the same as MOCK_RESULTS from
mock_data.py. We also check if the expanders are displayed correctly:

```
expected_expanders = len(MOCK_MOVIES)
actual_expanders = len(at.expander)
assert actual_expanders == expected_expanders, \
  f"Expected {expected_expanders} expanders, found {actual_expanders}"
```

We expect two st.expanders (since we have two mock movies). The above makes sure
that's true. Notice the string message that we've added to the assert statement here.
This is an error message that pytest will display should our test fail. Adding detailed
error messages to your assertions is a good practice that makes debugging much
easier.

The last test—test_movie_details_display—adds further assertions to ensure the
results display is as expected. Rather than simulate the user interactions again, this test
takes a shortcut:

```
at = setup_app
at.session_state["results"] = MOCK_RESULTS
at.run()
```

Before running the app for the first time, populate the results key in session_state
with MOCK_RESULTS.

Recall that in our actual frontend code, the button click ultimately causes session_
state["results"] to contain the search results object, and that the rest of the app uses
the condition if "results" in st.session_state: to display the results.

Thus, by assigning a value to session_state["results"] directly, we can bypass the
button click that's required in the real app. As before, we check the number of expanders with assert len(at.expander) == len(MOCK_MOVIES).

The most complex part is verifying the content of the markdown elements, showing the details of each movie:

```python
markdown_texts = [m.value for m in at.markdown]
for movie in MOCK_MOVIES:
  overview_text = f"**Overview:** {movie['overview']}"
  rating_text = f"**Rating:** {movie['vote_average']}"

  assert any(overview_text in text for text in
          markdown_texts), f"Overview for {movie['title']} not found"
  assert any(rating_text in text for text in
          markdown_texts), f"Rating for {movie['title']} not found"
```

This approach is more sophisticated than just checking element counts—we're actually examining the content of the UI elements to verify that the correct information is being displayed for each movie.

The expression any(overview_text in text for text in markdown_texts) checks that markdown_texts—the list of st.markdown elements in the running app—contains the overview_text for the mock movie we're currently considering in the code.

> **NOTE** Though we've aimed for brevity here—all code needs to be printed on the page, after all—and only created two tests, you should feel free to create as many tests as are required to check your code completely. This might involve considering how your app handles edge cases or various types of failures, such as when the API returns an unexpected response.

11.4.2 *Running frontend tests*

You can run the frontend unit tests the same way we ran the backend ones: by running pytest -v from the directory containing them. Do so now to get the following (shortened) output:

```
test_backend.py::test_search_movies_success PASSED                      [ 14%]
test_backend.py::test_search_movies_no_results PASSED                   [ 28%]
test_backend.py::test_get_poster_url PASSED                             [ 42%]
test_backend.py::test_get_nonexistent_poster_url PASSED                 [ 57%]
test_frontend.py::test_initial_state PASSED                             [ 71%]
test_frontend.py::test_search_functionality PASSED                      [ 85%]
test_frontend.py::test_movie_details_display FAILED                     [100%]


==================================== FAILURES ====================================
______________________________ test_movie_details_display ______________________________

setup_app = AppTest(
    _script_path='frontend.py',
    ...
)

    @patch("backend.Backend", MockBackend)
```

```
def test_movie_details_display(setup_app):
    ...

    # Verify both movies' details are in the markdown elements
    markdown_texts = [m.value for m in at.markdown]
    for movie in MOCK_MOVIES:
        overview_text = f"**Overview:** {movie['overview']}"
        rating_text = f"**Rating:** {movie['vote_average']}"

        assert any(overview_text in text for text in
                   markdown_texts), f"Overview for {movie['title']} not found"
>       assert any(rating_text in text for text in
                   markdown_texts), f"Rating for {movie['title']} not found"
E       AssertionError: Rating for Test Movie 1 not found
E       assert False
E        +  where False = any(<generator object test_movie_details_
display.<locals>.<genexpr> at 0x1144a42b0>)

test_frontend.py:76: AssertionError
...
=========================== short test summary info ===========================
FAILED test_frontend.py::test_movie_details_display - AssertionError: Rating
for Test Movie 1 not found
========================= 1 failed, 6 passed in 0.65s =========================
```

pytest tells us that the test failed on the last assertion, which checks for the presence of each movie's rating (`rating_text`) in the markdown elements.

```
>       assert any(rating_text in text for text in
                   markdown_texts), f"Rating for {movie['title']} not found"
E       AssertionError: Rating for Test Movie 1 not found
```

Specifically, it can't find the rating for Test Movie 1. Tracing this through our code, we can see that `rating_text` is defined as:

```
rating_text = f"**Rating:** {movie['vote_average']}"
```

So we need to figure out the reason our first mock movie's `vote_average` field isn't showing up in the markdown elements. Let's revisit the portion of our original frontend code (from frontend.py) that's responsible for populating these elements:

```
if "results" in st.session_state:
    for _, movie in st.session_state.results.items():
        title, date = movie["title"], movie["release_date"]
        year = date.split("-")[0] if date else "N/A"
        with st.expander(f"{title} ({year})"):
            poster_url = Backend.get_poster_url(movie.get('poster_path', None))
            st.image(poster_url, width=250)
            st.markdown(f"**Overview:** {movie.get('overview', 'N/A')}")
            st.markdown(f"**Rating:** {movie.get('rating', 'N/A')}")
```

Ah! Do you see the problem? Look at the last line! We're mistakenly looking for a non-existent `rating` key in the movie dictionary instead of `vote_average`! But why didn't we catch this earlier?

Well, since we're supplying a default value of `N/A` in case the `rating` key is not found, Python doesn't raise an exception, and instead fails silently. But if you run the app, you'll find that the rating for every movie is always `N/A`! This is an example of how writing tests can alert us of problems we might otherwise have missed. Make the appropriate correction in the last line of frontend.py and save it:

Run the tests again with `pytest -v`. This time, you should get:

```
test_backend.py::test_search_movies_success PASSED                    [ 14%]
test_backend.py::test_search_movies_no_results PASSED                 [ 28%]
test_backend.py::test_get_poster_url PASSED                           [ 42%]
test_backend.py::test_get_nonexistent_poster_url PASSED              [ 57%]
test_frontend.py::test_initial_state PASSED                           [ 71%]
test_frontend.py::test_search_functionality PASSED                    [ 85%]
test_frontend.py::test_movie_details_display PASSED                  [100%]

=============================== 7 passed in 1.25s ===============================
```

Perfect! As far as we can tell, when taken in isolation, both our frontend and our backend are now doing what they're supposed to. But that doesn't necessarily tell us whether they work correctly when combined. For that, we need integration tests.

11.5 Testing the integration between components

So far in our testing, we've placed a lot of emphasis on isolating the various components we're testing from any external influence. When a test fails, this helps us pinpoint exactly *where* the problem lies.

However, the mere fact that our components work correctly in isolation does not guarantee they'll work correctly when they come *together*. Additionally, while we've taken pains to test our code separately from its external dependencies, these dependencies remain critical for the app's functionality. For instance, if the TMDB API isn't returning the right results, that means our app isn't working as intended either. All of this implies that we need a different kind of test—an integration test—to verify that the interactions between the various parts of our app work well.

11.5.1 Writing integration tests

We can think of our app as consisting of three components—the frontend, the backend, and the external API—connected in a chain. Therefore, we might write two different types of integration tests: tests that check the behavior of the frontend and the backend taken together, and those that check the integration of the backend with the API.

Let's try this out. Copy the code shown in listing 11.9 to a new file called test_integration.py (chapter_11/in_progress_08/test_integration.py in the GitHub repo).

Listing 11.9 Integration test

```python
import pytest
from unittest.mock import patch, Mock
from mock_data import MOCK_MOVIES, MOCK_RESULTS
from streamlit.testing.v1 import AppTest

@pytest.fixture
def setup_app():
  at = AppTest.from_file("frontend.py")
  at.secrets["api_key"] = "test_api_key"
  return at

@patch('requests.get')
def test_frontend_backend_integration(mock_get, setup_app):
  mock_response = Mock()
  mock_response.json.return_value = {'results': MOCK_MOVIES}
  mock_get.return_value = mock_response

  at = setup_app
  at.run()

  # Enter search query and click button
  at.sidebar.text_input[0].set_value("test movie").run()
  at.sidebar.button[0].click().run()

  # Verify results are in session_state
  assert "results" in at.session_state
  assert at.session_state["results"] == MOCK_RESULTS

  # Verify expanders are displayed
  expected_expanders = len(MOCK_MOVIES)
  actual_expanders = len(at.expander)
  assert actual_expanders == expected_expanders, \
    f"Expected {expected_expanders} expanders, found {actual_expanders}"

  # Add more assertions as required
```

Let's start with a test that checks the integration of the frontend and the backend. Hopefully, this code doesn't require much explanation—it's simply constructed from the pieces of our existing unit tests!

What's going on here is that we're testing the frontend as we did in test_frontend .py—creating a `setup_app` fixture and simulating user interactions—but instead of mocking the entire Backend class, we're only patching `requests.get`, just as we did in `test_backend.py`. The result is that we're able to verify the frontend and backend work together in harmony when taken together, without the external influence of the API.

How about the other kind of test—one that tests the backend and the API? Let's add another test in the same file, as shown in listing 11.10 (chapter_11/in_progress_09/ test_integration.py in the GitHub repo).

Listing 11.10   Another integration test

```python
import pytest
import toml
from backend import Backend
from unittest.mock import patch, Mock
...


@patch('requests.get')
def test_frontend_backend_integration(mock_get, setup_app):
  ...


def test_backend_api_integration():
  secrets = toml.load(".streamlit/secrets.toml")
  backend = Backend(secrets["api_key"])
  results = backend.search_movies("ferris bueller")

  # Assert that there's at least one result
  assert len(results.keys()) > 0, "No results returned from backend API"

  # Assert that 1986 classic "Ferris Bueller's Day Off" is in the results
  has_fbdo_movie = any(
    movie["title"] == "Ferris Bueller's Day Off"
      and movie["release_date"].startswith("1986")
    for _id, movie in results.items()
  )
  assert has_fbdo_movie, "Ferris Bueller's Day Off not found in results"
```

The `test_backend_api_integration` tests the Backend class without mocking the API, but also without the influence of the frontend. To achieve this, we instantiate the Backend class directly, taking advantage of our existing secrets.toml file to supply the API key:

```python
secrets = toml.load(".streamlit/secrets.toml")
backend = Backend(secrets["api_key"])
```

Since we're going to be hitting the real API, we search for a term that's likely to yield real results:

```python
results = backend.search_movies("ferris bueller")
```

As we don't control the TMDB API, we can't be entirely sure what it will return for this search term, but we *can* make a couple of reasonable assumptions: that there will be at least one result, and that at least one of those results will be the movie we're looking for, i.e. the 1986 cult classic *Ferris Bueller's Day Off*. The last few lines in the file make these assertions.

Let's see if our tests still pass. You know the drill—run `pytest -v` to get:

```
test_backend.py::test_search_movies_success PASSED                        [ 11%]
test_backend.py::test_search_movies_no_results PASSED                     [ 22%]
```

```
test_backend.py::test_get_poster_url PASSED                              [ 33%]
test_backend.py::test_get_nonexistent_poster_url PASSED                  [ 44%]
test_frontend.py::test_initial_state PASSED                              [ 55%]
test_frontend.py::test_search_functionality PASSED                       [ 66%]
test_frontend.py::test_movie_details_display PASSED                      [ 77%]
test_integration.py::test_frontend_backend_integration PASSED           [ 88%]
test_integration.py::test_backend_api_integration PASSED                 [100%]


================================= 9 passed in 1.05s =================================
```

Awesome! The building blocks of our app—the frontend, backend, and API—all work correctly when taken two at a time. All that remains is to test the entire app in one shot.

11.6 *Testing the end-to-end flow*

In contrast to unit and integration tests that isolate certain parts or part combinations of our app from external influences, end-to-end tests check the behavior of the whole app under real-world conditions. As it turns out, writing end-to-end tests can actually be a whole lot easier than writing unit or integration tests. The thing that makes unit testing tricky is the "purity" requirement of making sure that we're truly only checking the behavior of the component under test, as opposed to that of its subcomponents or external dependencies.

With an end-to-end test, we don't care about any of that—what we want to know is: "taken as a whole, does this system do what it's supposed to?" Let's make this real by actually writing an end-to-end test for MovieScout. Create a file named test_e2e.py with the code in listing 11.11 (chapter_11/in_progress_10/test_e2e.py in the GitHub repo).

Listing 11.11   End-to-end test

```python
from streamlit.testing.v1 import AppTest

def test_movie_search_end_to_end():
  at = AppTest.from_file("frontend.py")
  at.run()

  # Verify initial state has search components
  assert len(at.sidebar.text_input) == 1
  assert len(at.sidebar.button) == 1

  # Enter search query and click button
  at.sidebar.text_input[0].set_value("Inception").run()
  at.sidebar.button[0].click().run()

  # Verify results are in session_state
  assert "results" in at.session_state
  results = at.session_state["results"]

  # Verify there's at least one result
  assert len(results) > 0
```

```python
# Verify there's an expander for each result
assert len(at.expander) == len(results)

for idx, movie in enumerate(results.values()):
  title = movie["title"]
  assert title in at.expander[idx].label

  # Verify overview is in markdown elements
  overview_text = f"**Overview:** {movie.get('overview', 'N/A')}"
  assert any(overview_text in m.value for m in at.markdown), \
    f"Overview for {title} not found"
```

One thing you'll likely notice straight away about test_e2e.py in comparison to our earlier tests is its relative simplicity. There's no mocking or patching going on here. The test simply creates a running instance of the app using `AppTest` just as in the frontend tests, but without bothering to patch the `Backend` class or set up any mock data.

You'll find most of the test code familiar as it checks more or less the same things that the frontend tests looked for. As in the API integration test, we use a real search term that's likely to fetch results because we expect the real TMDB API to be called:

```python
at.sidebar.text_input[0].set_value("Inception").run()
```

We then simply assert that there's at least one result—something we can reasonably be sure of, as *Inception* is a real movie that's unlikely to be removed from the database.

```python
assert len(results) > 0
```

The rest of the code proceeds as before, checking that there's a Streamlit expander for each returned result, and so on. Let's now run our end-to-end test along with all the others! Run `pytest -v` to get something similar to the following:

```
collected 10 items

test_backend.py::test_search_movies_success PASSED                  [ 10%]
test_backend.py::test_search_movies_no_results PASSED               [ 20%]
test_backend.py::test_get_poster_url PASSED                         [ 30%]
test_backend.py::test_get_nonexistent_poster_url PASSED             [ 40%]
test_e2e.py::test_movie_search_end_to_end PASSED                    [ 50%]
test_frontend.py::test_initial_state PASSED                         [ 60%]
test_frontend.py::test_search_functionality PASSED                  [ 70%]
test_frontend.py::test_movie_details_display PASSED                 [ 80%]
test_integration.py::test_frontend_backend_integration PASSED      [ 90%]
test_integration.py::test_backend_api_integration PASSED            [100%]

========================== 10 passed in 0.63s ==========================
```

All of our tests passed, which gives us confidence that our app is working as expected.

11.7　*Evolving code and tests*

We now have a decent suite of unit, integration, and end-to-end tests for our app. It's not necessarily *comprehensive*, since there are plenty of conditions it doesn't check for, but it'll do for the instructive purposes of this chapter.

What do we now *do* with the tests? Why did we bother to write automated tests rather than checking the output manually with, say, `print` statements temporarily inserted into the code? Our automated tests are meant to be run repeatedly to alert us of problems at any point in the development process. Figure 11.5 illustrates how this should happen.

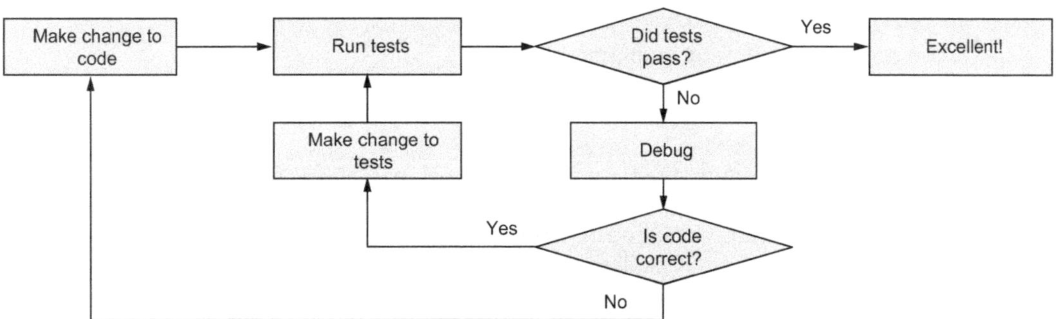

Figure 11.5　Flowchart showing how the app code and test code evolve.

You should run the tests you've written whenever you update your code in some way. If you find that a test fails after you've changed your code, it can mean one of two things:

- The change you made inadvertently broke some existing functionality, in which case, you need to fix your code.

- As a result of your change, your tests no longer check your app's functionality correctly, in which case you need to update your tests.

Of course, you may also need to add entirely *new* tests to cover any net new functionality that isn't checked by existing tests. In this way, your application code and your test code evolve alongside each other, each acting as a check against the other. Think of them as two halves of the same code contributing to the same "whole" that is a robust, error-free production application.

> **NOTE**　Unit tests tend to be fast and help pinpoint problems, so they should be run frequently. Integration and end-to-end tests simulate real-world behavior, but can be slower or rely on external services, which may have usage limits, introduce delays, or incur costs. To save time and money during development, it's useful to avoid running all the tests every time. `pytest` lets you tag and filter tests so you can run only what you need. Refer to the `pytest` docs for how to set this up.

Automating test runs

Rather than having to remember to run your tests whenever you make a change to your code, you can automate the process. If you're using Git for version control, a simple way to automate tests is through Git *hooks*. For example, to create a pre-commit hook that runs tests before each commit:

1   Create a file named pre-commit in the .git/hooks/ directory (from the root of the repository).
2   Add the following lines to the file:

```
#!/bin/bash
pytest -v || exit 1
```

3   Make the file executable by running:

```
chmod +x .git/hooks/pre-commit
```

This creates a script that automatically runs your non-API tests before each commit, preventing the commit if tests fail. You could also create a pre-push hook to run tests before pushing your code to a remote repo. For larger teams or projects, *continuous integration* (CI) services like GitHub Actions can run tests automatically on code pushes and notify teams of failures. Whichever method you choose, automated testing helps catch problems early and ensures your test suite remains a valuable guardian of code quality rather than an afterthought.

You now have the skills to build not just engaging and powerful Streamlit apps, but also rock-solid ones hardened against errors. With a robust testing strategy in place, you can catch issues early and ensure your app delivers a polished experience.

In the next chapter, you'll learn how to deploy your apps to a production-grade cloud environment, moving beyond the free Streamlit Community Cloud and setting up your app on platforms like AWS or GCP, ensuring it scales efficiently and runs seamlessly in a professional setting.

Summary

- Testing your code can help you catch bugs before they reach your users and harden your application against failures.
- Use `st.image` to render images in a Streamlit app.
- Automated testing consists of writing test code to check if your app code works correctly.
- Automated tests include unit tests, integration tests, and end-to-end tests.
- `pytest` is a popular framework for testing Python scripts and apps.
- Unit testing requires isolating the component under test from any dependency external to it, controlling its behavior by *mocking* it—i.e., swapping it out for a fake version.

- A test function runs the component under test—with mocked dependencies—and compares the actual results with the expected ones.
- Write as many tests as needed to check each component.
- A fixture is a reusable component that provides specific features to tests. `pytest` provides the `@pytest.fixture` decorator to mark a function as a fixture.
- Use the `@patch` decorator from `unittest.mock` to mock a real dependency and replace it with a fake.
- An assertion is a condition that is evaluated during a test; for a test to pass, all assertions must be true.
- You can run tests in `pytest` using the `pytest` command, adding the `-v` flag for verbose output.
- Streamlit's `AppTest` class simulates a running Streamlit app built from your code and has methods to mimic user interaction and inspect the rendered output.
- `AppTest.from_file(...)` creates a runnable instance of your Streamlit app, which can be started by calling its `run()` method.
- You can use dot notation on the `AppTest` instance to access lists of Streamlit elements of a particular type—for instance, `at.button` returns a list of buttons.
- You can simulate a user interaction on an element with methods such as `set_value(...)` and `click()`, chaining a call to `run()` to manually trigger an app rerun.
- Integration tests check how components behave when they are used together.
- An end-to-end test verifies an app's entire flow under real-world conditions, with no mocking.
- As an app evolves, update tests to match.
- You can automate test runs with a Git pre-commit hook; you can even set up CI tools like GitHub Actions to run tests automatically when code is pushed.

Packaging and deploying Streamlit apps

This chapter covers

- Paid deployment options without Streamlit Community Cloud limitations
- Packaging a Streamlit app using a Dockerfile and Docker Compose
- Creating and configuring an AWS account for deployment
- Deploying a Dockerized app to AWS Elastic Beanstalk
- Adding a custom domain and HTTPS to an app

By now, you've deployed more than one Streamlit app to the internet. You've pushed your code to GitHub and shared `.streamlit.app` links with the confident swagger of someone who knows their app runs in the cloud.

So far, however, the training wheels have stayed on. You haven't had to think too much about how your app handles traffic, how to port your app to a different platform, or what happens when it needs more memory. And that's been great for prototypes, demos, and quick wins.

But at some point, you'll want more. Maybe your app goes to sleep because of Streamlit Community Cloud's policy of killing apps that haven't been accessed in a while, embarrassing you in the middle of a demo. Maybe you want a proper domain so people don't think your labor of love is a half-baked side project. Or maybe you just want to have more control over the environment your app runs in.

This chapter is about what comes next. We'll take your app and package it like *real* software using Docker. Then we'll deploy it to AWS—a cloud provider that gives you as much flexibility as you need. We'll set up a custom domain, add HTTPS, and walk through what happens when your app executes in the cloud. Before long, you'll have an app that feels like it belongs in production.

NOTE   The GitHub repo for this book is https://github.com/aneevdavis/streamlit-in-action. The chapter_12 folder has this chapter's code and a requirements.txt file with exact versions of all the required Python libraries.

12.1   *Deployment considerations*

Until this chapter, we've been deploying our apps using Streamlit Community Cloud—a free, beginner-friendly hosting service provided by the creators of Streamlit themselves. It's been perfect for testing and sharing small projects, and we've used it throughout the book for exactly that purpose.

However, as we approach the final stretch, we will aim higher. If you want to deploy your Streamlit app professionally—say, for a startup, internal company tool, or relatively high-traffic product—Streamlit Community Cloud may not cut it.

This section will explore some of the limitations of Streamlit Community Cloud, give you a tour of possible deployment alternatives—ranging from simple to advanced—and explain why we're choosing the approach we'll implement in this chapter.

12.1.1   *Why Streamlit Community Cloud may not work for some users*

Streamlit Community Cloud is a fantastic place to deploy your Streamlit apps in many ways. It's dead simple, custom-built for Streamlit, and tightly integrated with GitHub. You push a commit, and your app goes live. What's not to love?

Well, eventually, quite a few things:

- *No custom domain support*—Your app will always live at a .streamlit.app URL. If you're building something professional or customer-facing, this doesn't exactly scream polish.

- *Resource limits*—Streamlit Community Cloud is not designed for heavy traffic and/or computation. If your app uses too much memory or CPU, it may be throttled or killed.

- *Apps sleep when idle*—If your app hasn't been accessed in a while—typically 12 hours or so—it shuts down; this can be especially frustrating if you're aiming for high availability.

- *Limited customizability*—You don't have a lot of control over the server environment that Streamlit runs in. For instance, if you want to install some non-Python software in production (like a database), you can't do that—you have to host it outside of Community Cloud.

Streamlit Community Cloud is great for learning and lightweight apps, but once you want more control, performance, or professionalism, you'll need to look elsewhere.

> **NOTE** Most of these limitations exist because Streamlit Community Cloud is free, and Snowflake—the company that owns Streamlit—doesn't make any money off it. This brings us to an important point to note about this chapter: getting rid of these limitations usually costs money. The deployment approach we'll describe here may require you to spend *some* money because the services we'll use aren't always free. Luckily, if you only care about *learning* how to deploy an app, you can keep these costs to just a few cents by shutting things down as soon as you're done. That said, towards the end of the chapter, we'll register a custom domain, which can cost $10+ to acquire for a year.

12.1.2 *Deployment alternatives*

Fortunately, there's no shortage of alternatives. Here's a quick overview of just *some* of what's out there. This is by no means an exhaustive list.

FULLY MANAGED PLATFORMS

For most simple apps that aren't expecting a lot of traffic and don't require a high degree of control and customization, Streamlit Community Cloud is great, *except* for the fact that it doesn't—as of the time of writing—have an option to *pay* to simply remove the resource limits and idle-app-killing. If it had one, I'd have no difficulty recommending it for most users.

Instead, here are what I think are the closest alternatives that retain most of Community Cloud's simplicity when it comes to deploying Streamlit apps, but will also take your money to do away with some of its limits:

- *Render*—(https://www.render.com) Offers deployment functionality that's quite similar to Streamlit Community Cloud, where you can link a GitHub repository and get going straight away. The paid tiers give you scaling and stop shutting down your apps when they're idle for too long.
- *Heroku*—(https://www.heroku.com) Another developer-friendly platform that abstracts away much of the deployment complexity. Like Render, you can connect your app to a GitHub repo and deploy with minimal setup.
- *Streamlit in Snowflake*—Technically, the Streamlit website (https://streamlit.io) does advertise a "Pro" option for deployment. However, this option currently requires you to sign up for the Snowflake data warehouse. This can be a great option if you're building internal apps for your workplace and your company already uses Snowflake.

NOTE While services like Render and Heroku are quite easy to set up, they do tend to become expensive as your app scales up.

INFRASTRUCTURE-AS-A-SERVICE (IaaS)

On the other end of the spectrum, if you want the ultimate flexibility, you may choose to run your app on the raw infrastructure services provided by the leading public cloud providers:

- *Amazon Web Services (AWS)*—If you were to go full DIY on AWS, you might spin up EC2 instances to run your app, use S3 for storage, and set up a load balancer and security groups manually.
- *Microsoft Azure*—You could use Azure Virtual Machines to host your app, Azure Blob Storage for file storage, Azure DNS for domain management, and Azure Application Gateway as your load balancer and SSL terminator—piecing together the infrastructure using Azure's equivalents.
- *Google Cloud Platform (GCP)*—On GCP, you'd likely use Google Compute Engine to run your app, Cloud Storage for static files, Cloud DNS for routing, and set up a firewall, load balancer, and optionally a managed SSL certificate through Google-managed services.

If you're comfortable with containerized apps and want fine-grained control over how they're scheduled, scaled, and managed, Kubernetes offers a powerful abstraction layer on top of raw infrastructure. AWS, GCP, and Azure all offer managed Kubernetes services.

NOTE Don't worry if you don't know what some or most of the terms above mean. Deploying an app entirely on your own using raw cloud services can get quite complicated, and is probably overkill for most Streamlit apps anyway. Besides, you'll understand the basics of most of these—at least the AWS stuff— by the end of this chapter.

PLATFORM-AS-A-SERVICE (PaaS)

In the happy middle, for apps that require some more customizability but where you still want a relatively straightforward deployment process, the top cloud providers offer their own *platform-as-a-service* (PaaS) solutions that strike a balance between convenience and control:

- *AWS Elastic Beanstalk*—This is what we'll use in this chapter. It uses a variety of AWS services under the hood, but handles provisioning, scaling, and deployment without you having to wire them all up manually.
- *Google App Engine (Flexible)*—Probably the closest GCP alternative to Elastic Beanstalk that offers similar functionality.

NOTE While evaluating a cloud hosting platform, one important thing to consider is whether it supports a technology called WebSockets. That's because

Streamlit relies on WebSockets, and your app won't work on a platform that doesn't support it. In fact, that's why I've listed Google App Engine (Flexible) as an option above, as opposed to Google App Engine (Standard), which does *not* currently support WebSockets.

12.1.3 Our approach

As you can see, there are a lot of ways to deploy your app to the cloud without Community Cloud's limitations, and we couldn't possibly cover all of them in detail here. Instead, in this chapter, we'll pick *one* approach and explain it fully.

The path we'll choose is *not* the easiest way to do this—that would probably involve a platform like Render or Heroku—but it does offer the most potential for learning. I want to take you a level deeper than the simple-yet-opaque abstraction of "a web app running on the cloud", and give you a taste of what goes into making that abstraction possible.

Specifically, we'll package the app with a tool called *Docker*, deploy it to *AWS Elastic Beanstalk*, and then add a custom domain (for professionalism) and HTTPS (for security). Here are the reasons we're taking this route:

- *You'll gain real-world skills.* Docker and AWS are industry standards. Knowing how to work with them is valuable regardless of where your career takes you.
- *Docker makes your app portable.* Docker enables you to package the app and all of its dependencies into a single, reproducible image, which ensures your app runs the same way everywhere—on your machine, on someone else's, or in the cloud.
- *Elastic Beanstalk gives you cloud power with manageable complexity.* It handles provisioning and scaling infrastructure under the hood, but still exposes enough of the internals—like EC2, load balancers, and S3—that you get a realistic sense of what modern cloud deployments involve. You don't need to hook everything up together manually, but you can see and understand what's happening.
- *Custom domains and HTTPS make your app production-ready.* A memorable, branded URL and encrypted connections aren't just nice-to-haves—they're essential for user trust, security, and professionalism. Whether you're sharing your app with colleagues, clients, or customers, this step makes it feel real.

By the end, you'll not only have a live, production-ready Streamlit app—you'll also have a solid grasp of what it takes to deploy a containerized app to a real cloud provider.

12.2 Packaging the app using Docker

Deploying a Streamlit app to the cloud means running it in an environment that may be very different from a local machine. A common way to make sure everything works smoothly is to bundle it into a portable, self-contained unit, something that behaves the same regardless of where it runs. That's exactly what *Docker* is for.

In this section, we'll use Docker to package our app along with everything it needs to run: Python, the required libraries, and the app code itself. Once packaged, the app can run inside a container—the portable unit we were referring to.

We'll begin with a quick introduction to what Docker is and how it works, then take a look at what it means for our app to run inside a container. After that, we'll create a Dockerfile that specifies exactly how to build this container and use it to run our app locally. This containerized version of our app will be the basis for deployment to the cloud later in the chapter.

12.2.1 *Intro to Docker*

Imagine you've built a Streamlit app that works perfectly on your machine. But when you send it to a colleague or a friend to test, they get an error about missing dependencies. Or one that says that they're using a different version of Python. Or their OS doesn't support a package you're using. You could easily spend hours debugging these types of environment issues instead of building features.

Docker is a piece of software that solves this problem by creating a consistent environment that travels with your application. It lets you define your app's environment—operating system, installed packages, configurations, and more—in a file called a *Dockerfile*. Docker then uses this file to create a Docker *image*, which serves as a blueprint for running your app. Once you have an image, you can run it in a *container*—an environment that behaves like a mini-computer inside your computer.

Docker images are built layer by layer. Each instruction in your Dockerfile adds a new layer that prepares the environment for your running app: installing a base operating system, installing Python, copying files, installing packages, and so on. The result is a versioned, reusable image that can be shared or deployed anywhere.

For instance, the Dockerfile we'll write starts with a minimal Python 3.12 image, installs your app's dependencies, copies over your code, and finally runs the app. That image can be built once and run wherever Docker is installed—on your laptop, on a server, or in the cloud.

INSTALLING DOCKER

Time to get your hands dirty by installing Docker. Head to the Docker website at https://www.docker.com, download Docker Desktop (as of the time of writing, it's listed under "Products"), and run the executable.

There really isn't much to the installation process. When prompted, choose to use the "recommended settings", which will work just fine. You don't have to create an account, though you can if you like. When you're done, you should see the Docker Desktop UI in figure 12.1.

When you eventually run a container, it'll show up here. Although we won't use this UI in our practical demo, you can return to it to view the containers you have running and to pause or stop them.

12.2.2 *The app in a container*

Before we dive into the technical details of creating a Dockerfile, let's understand how our Streamlit app will operate within a Docker container. Turn your attention to

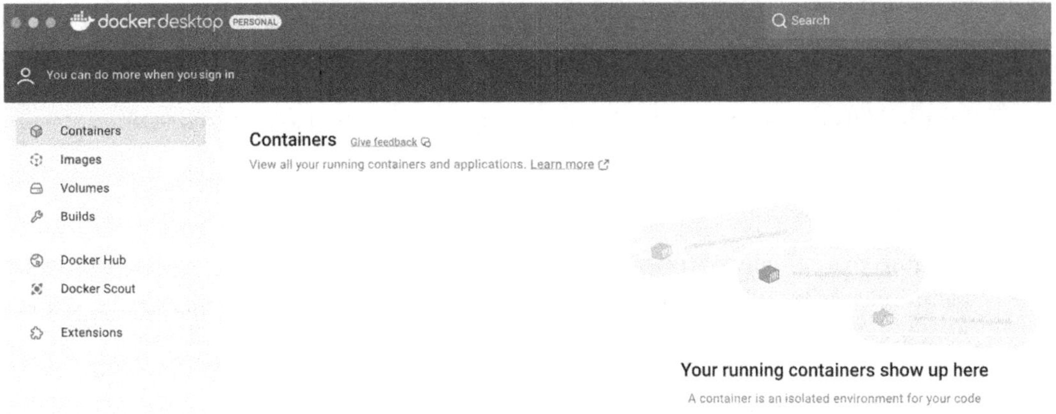

Figure 12.1   The Docker Desktop interface

figure 12.2, which illustrates this. The figure shows how Docker creates layers of abstraction between your application and the host computer.

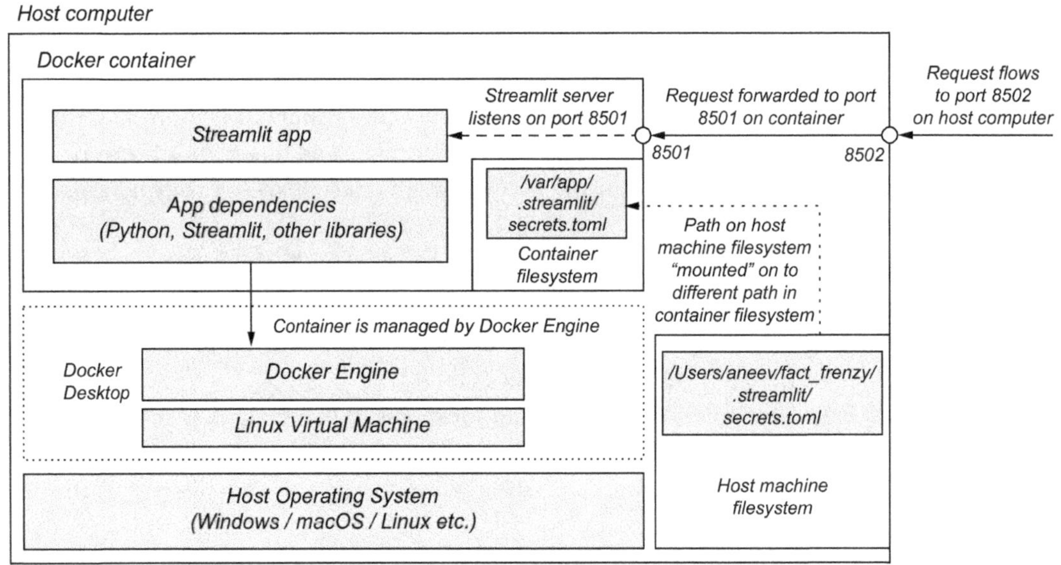

Figure 12.2   Docker runs the Streamlit app in a container.

Our app runs within a Docker container, which is managed by Docker Engine, the core technology that creates and runs containers. Docker Engine requires a Linux kernel, provided by a Linux *virtual machine* within Docker Desktop, which we just installed.

NOTE If you're running Docker on a computer that's already using a Linux operating system, you actually don't need Docker Desktop to provide a separate Linux virtual machine. In this scenario, Docker Engine can directly use the host machine's Linux kernel.

The container includes a minimal Linux distribution (all the files, utilities, etc. that make up Linux apart from the kernel), Python, Streamlit, our application code, and all of its dependencies. This self-contained unit has everything our app needs to run consistently. Notice the two key interactions between the container and host illustrated in the diagram:

1 *Port forwarding*—The arrow connecting port 8502 on the host to port 8501 in the container shows how user requests are directed. When someone accesses http://localhost:8502 on the host machine, Docker forwards that traffic to port 8501 inside the container where our Streamlit server is listening.

NOTE We don't *have* to use the 8502/8501 setup described here; it's just an example that helps make things clear.

2 *Volume mounting*—The host and the container can share files through a mounted volume, something we'll explore in more detail later. This is crucial for managing secrets and configuration files without embedding them in the container itself.

This architecture ensures the Streamlit app runs in a consistent environment anywhere Docker is installed, while still allowing the necessary connections to the outside world.

12.2.3 Creating a Dockerfile

As we've established, a Docker container is essentially an instance of a Docker image. A Docker image is created from a *Dockerfile*, which is where we'll start our practical deployment journey.

To begin, choose any one of the applications we've developed in the course of this book. For the purposes of demonstration, I'm going to pick Fact Frenzy—the trivia game we put together in chapter 9—but really, the steps described in this chapter should work for any of the apps we've created together.

NOTE If you're deploying Haiku Haven (our CRUD app from Chapter 8), you'll need to continue to use Neon as a managed PostgreSQL service to follow the steps in this chapter without modification. Managing PostgreSQL yourself will require a multi-container setup that we won't cover here.

ADDING A REQUIREMENTS.TXT

If you don't already have one, add a requirements.txt to the root directory of your app. For the app from chapter 9, listing 12.1 shows what this would look like (chapter_12/in_progress_01/requirements.txt in the GitHub repo).

```
openai==1.58.1
pydantic==2.10.4
streamlit==1.40.2
```

NOTE   The requirements.txt in the root of the chapter_12 directory (as opposed to the in_progress_ folders) has one additional library (`awsebcli`) that's not in listing 12.1. That's because `awsebcli` is something that we use later in the chapter to deploy to Elastic Beanstalk. Your Docker container doesn't need it.

CREATING A DOCKERFILE

Now, create a new file named Dockerfile (with no extension) and copy over the contents of listing 12.2 (chapter_12/in_progress_01/Dockerfile in the GitHub repo).


```
# Start with Python 3.12 as base image
FROM python:3.12-slim

# Set working directory in the container
WORKDIR /app

# Copy requirements file and install dependencies
# (We do this first to use Docker's layer caching)
COPY requirements.txt .
RUN pip install --no-cache-dir -r requirements.txt

# Copy the rest of the application
COPY . .

# Expose the port Streamlit runs on
EXPOSE 8501

# Set Streamlit to run in headless mode
ENV STREAMLIT_SERVER_PORT=8501
ENV STREAMLIT_SERVER_HEADLESS=true
ENV STREAMLIT_SERVER_ADDRESS=0.0.0.0

# Command to run when the container starts
CMD ["streamlit", "run", "main.py"]
```

A Dockerfile is a recipe used to create a Docker image. It consists of a series of *instructions* to build the image. Each instruction creates a new *layer* in the resulting image, essentially a snapshot of the file system changes made by that instruction. Let's go through each of the instructions in the listing to understand what's going on here.

```
# Start with Python 3.12 as base image
FROM python:3.12-slim
```

This is the foundation of our image. It specifies that we're starting with the official Python 3.12 image, specifically the "slim" variant. When Docker sees this during the build process, it will first check your local image cache to see if you already have this base image downloaded. If not, it will pull the image from Docker Hub—Docker's official public registry.

The `python:3.12-slim` image was itself created by its own Dockerfile, maintained by the Docker community. If you went into *this* Dockerfile, you'd see that it is, in turn, built on a Debian image—Debian being a flavor of the Linux operating system. Our Docker image thus depends on more foundational images. Our Streamlit app will thus run on Python 3.12 installed on the Debian OS when we spin up a container.

NOTE The Debian Docker image doesn't include the Linux kernel. As discussed previously, Docker containers rely on the kernel of the host system— either directly (on Linux) or via a Linux virtual machine (on macOS or Windows).

```
# Set working directory in the container
WORKDIR /app
```

This instruction sets the working directory for any subsequent instructions in the Dockerfile and for the running container. It's similar to entering a directory called app in the root of your file system. When the container starts, this will be the directory from which commands are executed. If the directory doesn't exist, Docker will create it.

```
# Copy requirements file and install dependencies
# (We do this first to use Docker's layer caching)
COPY requirements.txt .
RUN pip install --no-cache-dir -r requirements.txt
```

This code does two things:

- First, we copy just the requirements.txt file from our host machine (where we're building the Docker image) to the current working directory in the container (which is /app as we set earlier).
- Then we run the `pip install` command to install all the Python dependencies listed in the requirements.txt file.

The comment about "layer caching" is interesting: Docker caches each layer (instruction) in the build process. By copying and installing dependencies before copying the rest of the application code, we ensure that if only our application code changes but the dependencies remain the same, Docker can reuse the cached dependency layer, making subsequent builds much faster.

The `--no-cache-dir` flag tells `pip` not to cache downloaded packages, helping keep the image smaller.

```
# Copy the rest of the application
COPY . .
```

This copies all files and directories from the current directory on the host—where the Dockerfile is located—to the working directory in the container (/app). The first dot represents the source (current directory on host) and the second dot represents the destination (current working directory in the container). In our case, this means that everything within the app's directory (i.e. the files game.py, llm.py, main.py etc. if you're working with our Chapter 9 app) will be copied to the container's /app.

```
# Expose the port Streamlit runs on
EXPOSE 8501
```

This instruction informs Docker that the container will listen on port 8501 at runtime. Recall that this is the default port that Streamlit uses. Note that this doesn't actually expose the port—it's more like documentation.

```
# Set Streamlit to run in headless mode
ENV STREAMLIT_SERVER_PORT=8501
ENV STREAMLIT_SERVER_HEADLESS=true
ENV STREAMLIT_SERVER_ADDRESS=0.0.0.0
```

The ENV instruction sets an *environment variable* in the container. You can think of an environment variable as a named value stored within the operating system that a program can read to adjust how it behaves.

STREAMLIT_SERVER_PORT=8501 sets the port Streamlit will use, the same one we were planning to expose above.

STREAMLIT_SERVER_HEADLESS=true tells Streamlit to run in "headless" mode, which means that no browser will be opened when we start the server.

STREAMLIT_SERVER_ADDRESS=0.0.0.0 tells Streamlit to listen on all *network interfaces*, making it accessible from outside the container. Network interfaces are essentially connection points between a computer and a network, sort of like different doors allowing entry into a house from various directions. A single computer has different "doors" or network interfaces for the different ways another computer might connect to it, like Wifi or a wired Ethernet connection. There's also a so-called "loopback" interface—with the address 127.0.0.1 or simply "localhost"—which is like an internal door that only allows communication from within the same computer.

The special IP address we're using—0.0.0.0—means "accept connections coming in through *any* network interface, whether internal or external".

```
# Command to run when the container starts
CMD ["streamlit", "run", "main.py"]
```

Once we've set everything up, the last instruction is to start the Streamlit server, just as we've been doing throughout this book, with the streamlit run command followed by the name of our entrypoint file. This is main.py in the case of Fact Frenzy, but you should replace it with the path to your entrypoint if you're trying to deploy a different app.

> ### Streamlit configuration options
>
> The three `STREAMLIT_` environment variables we set above are *configuration options* that Streamlit understands. There are many more such options which can be used for things like increasing the level of logging that your Streamlit server does, changing the theme colors used in the UI, etc.
>
> You can see a list of all available configurations using the command `streamlit config show` in your terminal.
>
> There are also multiple ways to specify these configuration options:
> - You can set environment variables that begin with `STREAMLIT_`, as shown above.
> - You can use a special config.toml file in the .streamlit folder.
> - You can pass them as flags with the `streamlit run` command.
>
> For example, let's say that you want your app to produce more detailed logging messages in the terminal window when you start the server. You could achieve this with any of the following methods:
> - Set the environment variable `STREAMLIT_LOGGER_LEVEL` to `debug`
> - Create a .streamlit/config.toml file with the following content:
>
>   ```
>   [logger]
>   level = "debug"
>   ```
>
> - Run `streamlit run <path to .py file> --logger.level debug`

12.2.4 Excluding files from an image

We have a bit of a security problem at this stage. If you're deploying one of the apps from this book that—like Fact Frenzy from chapter 9—has a secrets.toml, our Dockerfile will include that file in our Docker image as part of the `COPY . .` instruction.

Docker images are meant to be shareable artifacts that can be distributed to run your application in different environments. Including secrets directly in these images creates a security vulnerability, as anyone who obtains the image can extract those secrets. Even if you don't intentionally share the image, secrets remain embedded in the image layers and can be exposed through various means. To avoid this, we need a way to exclude our secrets.toml file—or indeed our entire .streamlit folder—from the image when running the `COPY . .` instruction.

The answer is a file called .dockerignore, which lets you list files and directories that should be excluded when copying files into the Docker image. It works similarly to

.gitignore files, using pattern matching to specify which files should be ignored during the build process.

Create .dockerignore in the same folder as the contents shown in listing 12.3 (chapter_12/in_progress_01/.dockerignore in the GitHub repo).

> **Listing 12.3   The .dockerignore file**

```
__pycache__/
.git/
.gitignore
.streamlit/
```

Now, when we get around to building our image, Docker will ignore the .streamlit/ folder, along with other files and folders with metadata like .git and .gitignore.

12.2.5 *Building an image and running a container*

As discussed previously, a Dockerfile is a recipe used to build a Docker image, which in turn is a blueprint from which a running Docker container can be spun up. With our Dockerfile and .dockerignore in place, let's build an image. You can do this with the following command issued from your terminal in the root directory of your app (which should also contain the Dockerfile):

```
docker build -t fact-frenzy .
```

This causes Docker to go through your Dockerfile and run the instructions. This includes downloading the `python:3.12-slim` from Docker Hub, copying your working directory, pip-installing your requirements, etc.

Vitally, this does *not* include actually *running* the command in our final instruction—`CMD ["streamlit", "run", "main.py"]`. CMD simply specifies the command that *should be* run when the *container starts*. Contrast this with most of the other instructions like FROM, WORKDIR, COPY, and RUN, which specify things to be executed when we *build the image*.

Once the command is done, we should have a newly built Docker image with the name `fact-frenzy`. To verify this, type:

```
docker images
```

This should give you a list of the images you've built, including the `fact-frenzy` one:

```
REPOSITORY                  TAG       IMAGE ID       CREATED          SIZE
fact-frenzy                 latest    9861d6d3340d   21 minutes ago   764MB
...
docker/welcome-to-docker    latest    eedaff45e3c7   16 months ago    29.5MB
```

Next, enter the following command to spin up a container from the image:

```
docker run -p 8502:8501 fact-frenzy
```

This should give you:

```
You can now view your Streamlit app in your browser.
  URL: http://0.0.0.0:8501
```

which should seem quite familiar to you by now. It signals that the `streamlit` run command has been executed within the container. However, if you now access the given URL— http://0.0.0.0:8501—it won't work.

Recall that a Docker container is like a computer-within-a-computer. When you start a container from our image, the Streamlit server is started within the *inner* computer, or the "container machine." On the other hand, the web browser you're going to use to access the app is installed on the *outer* computer—the one you're operating, called the *host machine.*

The `-p <port-on-host>:<port-on-container>` option is used to map a port on the host with a port on the container. So `-p 8502:8501` would forward traffic from the host machine's port 8502 to the container's port 8501. The correct way to access our running app, then, is to navigate to http://localhost:8502, which would route the request to the container's 8501, thus reaching the Streamlit server listening there. Sure enough, if you now go to http://localhost:8502 on your browser, you should be able to see and interact with the app.

Unfortunately, since we made Docker ignore our secrets.toml, you'll probably see something like figure 12.3 when you try to start a new game.

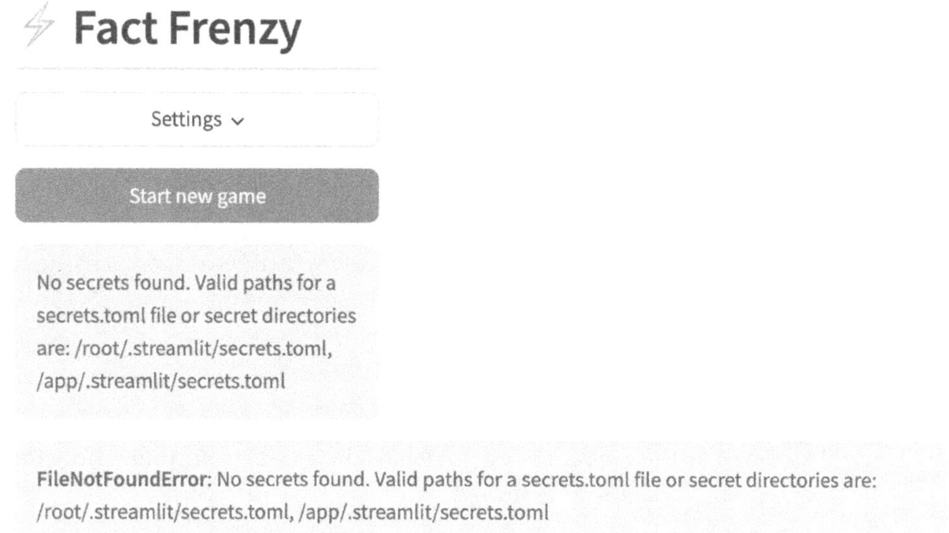

Figure 12.3 Since we added secrets.toml to .dockerignore, we need another way to make it available to our app at runtime (see chapter_12/in_progress_01 in the GitHub repo for the full code).

So if putting our secrets directly in the Docker image is insecure, how *do* we feed them to our app? One way is to use the -v flag with docker run to *mount* our .streamlit folder into the container at runtime:

```
docker run -p 8502:8501 -v ./.streamlit/:/app/.streamlit fact-frenzy
```

What we've done here is keep our .streamlit folder on our host machine and only mount it—or copy it to the container—when we start the container, rather than building it into the image itself.

The -v flag takes an argument of the form <path-on-host>:<path-on-container>. So -v ./.streamlit/:/app/.streamlit is saying "Take .streamlit from the current working directory—or '.'—on the host, and put it in the path /app/.streamlit within the container".

If you *now* visit http://localhost:8502, the app should work just fine.

12.2.6 *Adding a Docker Compose configuration*

So far, we've been using Docker commands directly in the terminal to build our image and run our container. This works, but presents a challenge: to run our app correctly, we need to remember and type in complex commands with multiple options.

To address this, we'll introduce Docker Compose, a separate tool that comes with Docker. Think of it as a configuration manager for Docker. Instead of typing out long commands each time, you write down your instructions once in a special file, and Docker Compose reads this file to set everything up for you.

This special file is called docker-compose.yml. It's a text file written in a format called YAML, which uses indentation and simple syntax to organize information in a way that's both human-readable and machine-parseable.

Listing 12.4 shows the docker-compose.yml file we'll use (chapter_12/in_progress_02/docker-compose.yml in the GitHub repo).

> **Listing 12.4   The docker-compose.yml file**

```yaml
services:
  fact-frenzy-app:
    build: .
    ports:
      - "8502:8501"
    volumes:
      - ./.streamlit/:/app/.streamlit
```

You'll notice that the listing closely matches our docker run command from earlier. This configuration does several things:

- It defines a *service* named fact-frenzy-app (feel free to rename this)
- The build: . directive tells Docker Compose to build an image using the Dockerfile in the current directory, just like our docker build command did.

- The `ports` section maps port 8502 on the host to port 8501 in the container, exactly like our `-p 8502:8501` flag did when using `docker run`.

- The `volumes` section mirrors the `-v` flag we used in the previous section, mounting the .streamlit directory in our host machine's working directory to /app/.streamlit directory inside the container.

We can now start the application using a different command:

```
docker-compose up
```

This command will build the image if it doesn't exist yet and then start a container with the proper port mappings and volume mounts. Your Streamlit app should now be accessible at http://localhost:8502 with the secrets properly configured.

12.3 Deploying to AWS Elastic Beanstalk

In the last section, we Dockerized our Streamlit app, got it running locally, and then simplified our setup with Docker Compose. But our ultimate goal in this chapter isn't just to run the app on our own machine—it's to host it online so anyone can access it from anywhere.

While we've been using Streamlit Community Cloud for this purpose throughout this book, it's time to level up! This section will walk you through how to deploy your Dockerized app to AWS, the market leader in cloud computing services—used prolifically by companies, websites and apps across the world. We'll specifically use AWS Elastic Beanstalk, a service that offers a great balance between convenience and control.

If you've never worked with AWS before, don't worry! I don't assume any prior knowledge; this section will go through everything you need—from signing up for AWS for the first time to setting your app live.

We'll start with a high-level overview of AWS and Elastic Beanstalk, and then build an intuitive mental model of what's happening under the hood when you deploy. That way, the commands you run and the configuration files you write won't feel like magic—they'll make sense.

12.3.1 An overview of AWS

Amazon Web Services, or AWS for short, is Amazon's cloud computing platform that powers all shapes and sizes of websites—from your neighborhood bakery's online ordering system to Netflix and Reddit. You can think of it as a massive online toolbox full of digital infrastructure that you can rent by the hour or minute.

Instead of buying and maintaining servers (which is expensive, time-consuming, and hard to scale), AWS lets you rent computing power, storage, databases, and more on demand. This means you can:

- Run the application on a virtual computer in the cloud
- Store files in a cloud-based "drive"
- Automatically scale an app up or down depending on traffic

All of this is provided through an enormous catalog of services. Here are a few of the ones we'll encounter in this chapter:

- EC2 or Elastic Cloud Compute provides virtual machines to host our Dockerized Streamlit app; these are like computers in the cloud.
- S3 or Simple Storage Service gives us cloud storage to temporarily hold our app code during deployment.
- IAM or Identity and Access Management lets us authenticate ourselves to AWS, and control which AWS services can talk to each other securely.
- AWS Certificate Manager helps to secure the app with HTTPS when we use a custom domain.

Imagine AWS as a cloud-based lego set that developers can play with. Each service is a building block, and you can mix and match them to build whatever kind of infrastructure your app needs. However, this flexibility comes with a lot of associated complexity. Deploying an application using the "raw" AWS services mentioned above can be a challenging undertaking. Enter Elastic Beanstalk.

12.3.2 *Introducing Elastic Beanstalk*

The whimsically named *Elastic Beanstalk* is a platform that helps you deploy and manage web apps on AWS without needing to configure all the underlying infrastructure yourself.

Normally, if you wanted to host your app on AWS, you'd have to manually:

- Spin up virtual machines (EC2 *instances*)
- Install Docker and other system dependencies
- Configure networking rules to allow traffic
- Set up a load balancer to distribute traffic
- Monitor performance and handle scaling

Elastic Beanstalk bundles all of this into a single tool. Think of it as a deployment concierge that takes Streamlit app code and sets up the servers, networking, monitoring, and scaling behind the scenes.

Here's what makes Elastic Beanstalk especially helpful:

- It supports Docker, which means we can just hand it a Dockerfile.
- It abstracts away infrastructure, so you still get the power of EC2, S3, and other AWS services, but you don't need to configure them individually.
- It's CLI-friendly. You can manage deployments entirely from the terminal using the EB CLI (which we'll install shortly).
- It's customizable if you need it; if you decide later that you want to tweak how things work, you're free to do so.

12.3.3 A mental model of the deployed app

Our deployment is going to rely upon a variety of AWS services, many of which are highly complex and might merit their own chapters or books if we were to attempt to cover them fully, which we won't, of course.

Instead, we're merely going to touch upon each of them briefly in the context of our app. To avoid overwhelming you, it would be useful to establish a clear mental model of the end result: our deployed app running on AWS. Figure 12.4 gives you a detailed look at the architecture of this end state.

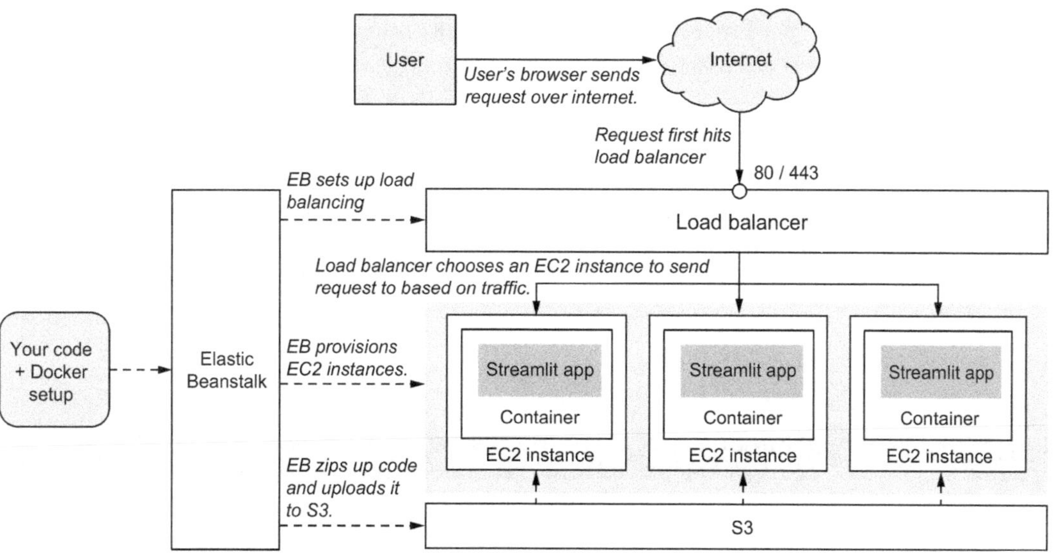

Figure 12.4   The end state of the deployed Streamlit app on AWS

Let's walk through what happens in a typical request, say when a user opens an app in their browser:

1 The user enters the URL, something like http://fact-frenzy.us-east-2 .elasticbeanstalk.com (though it will eventually have a more professional-looking custom domain by the end of this chapter)

2 The request first hits the load balancer, which is listening on port 80 (or eventually 443, when we enable HTTPS later)

3 The load balancer forwards the request to one of the EC2 instances running your app. If you have multiple instances running, it balances traffic between them.

4 Each EC2 instance has a Docker container instantiated from the image built from your Dockerfile. When an instance receives the request from the load balancer, it passes it to the container on the port it's listening on.

  5 Inside the container, the Streamlit app runs just as it did locally. It receives the request, processes it, and generates a response.

  6 The load balancer sends the response back to the user's browser.

To set all of this up, Elastic Beanstalk provisions and configures the necessary components automatically: the EC2 instances, S3 storage, the Docker environment, the load balancer, and the networking rules that allow everything to talk to each other securely. It even monitors the health of your app and replaces instances if they fail.

12.3.4 Creating and preparing an AWS account

Before we're ready to implement our mental deployment model in the real world, there are quite a few setup steps to perform, including signing up for AWS and enabling various services to talk to each other.

CREATING AN AWS ACCOUNT

To create an AWS account, go to https://aws.amazon.com/ and sign up. The account creation flow is straightforward: enter contact details, verify an email address and phone number, create a root user password for administrator access, and so on. You'll also need to enter payment method details.

Once you've created an account, you can access Elastic Beanstalk, EC2, and all the other services we talked about from the AWS Management Console, which—in my case—looks like figure 12.5.

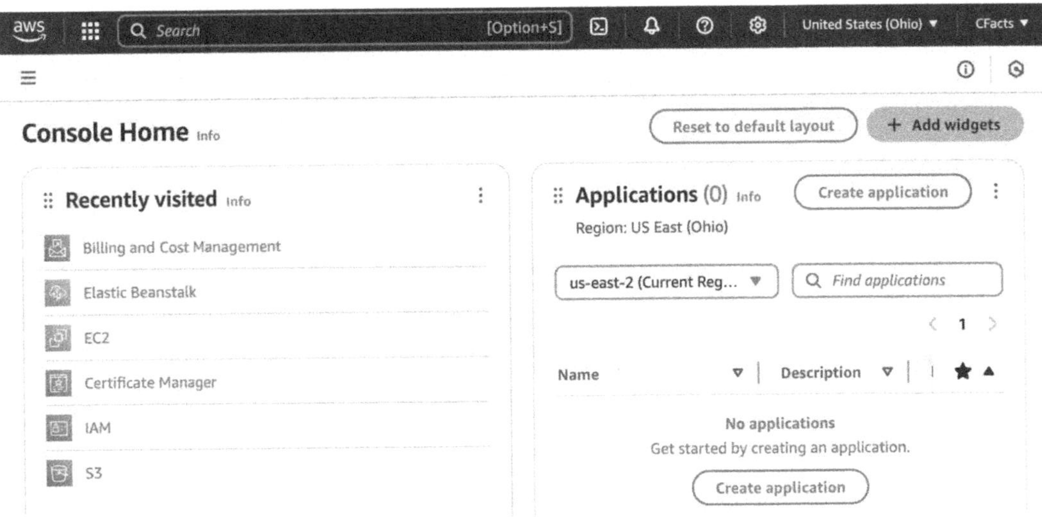

Figure 12.5   **The AWS Management Console**

Generally speaking, the easiest way to navigate to a particular service is to search for it in the search bar at the top.

NOTE AWS does offer a 12-month or so free tier for many services. For example, you can get a free low-resource EC2 instance that runs continuously for free this way, along with some S3 storage. AWS doesn't charge for Elastic Beanstalk per se—only for the underlying raw services it orchestrates. The part of the chapter that *will* actually require us to spend money is adding a load balancer and auto-scaling (through multiple EC2 instances) to our app, which is not covered by the free tier. Again, you can minimize these costs to a few pennies if you turn everything off immediately after you're done. To see and keep track of costs, navigate to Billing and Cost Management from the AWS Management Console.

SETTING UP ACCESS AND PERMISSIONS

As we've discussed at some length, AWS is like an interconnected web of services, many of which we'll utilize in deploying and running our app. For instance, here are a few interactions that will take place when we use Elastic Beanstalk to deploy our app:

- Elastic Beanstalk will upload the code to S3
- Elastic Beanstalk will spin up EC2 instances to run the Docker container
- The EC2 instances will download the application's code from S3
- The EC2 instances will report their health to Elastic Beanstalk

While these different services—Elastic Beanstalk, EC2, and S3—are all part of AWS, they can't freely interact with each other unless *you* allow them to. To fulfill the above actions, that means:

- Elastic Beanstalk needs permission to access S3 and EC2
- EC2 needs permission to access S3 and Elastic Beanstalk (in a limited way)

If this weren't enough, there's the question of how we'll authenticate *ourselves* to AWS when we want to interact with these services, since we mostly *won't* be using the AWS website to do so. Much of the remaining setup we need to perform involves configuring the appropriate access and permissions.

CREATING AN ACCESS KEY FOR ELASTIC BEANSTALK

Though we'll use the AWS Management Console a lot for other purposes, we're primarily going to be interacting with Elastic Beanstalk through the command line rather than through the web console. To do this, we need a way to authenticate ourselves on the command line—that's where *access keys* come in.

In AWS, an access key consists of two parts—an access key ID and a secret access key. Together, they serve as long-term credentials for programmatic access to your account, such as through the AWS CLI or SDKs. They're essentially the username and password for your scripts and tools.

Now, while your root user has full access to everything in your AWS account, it's strongly discouraged to create access keys for it. Root access combined with long-term credentials like access keys poses a major security risk, especially if those keys are ever exposed, since they can be used without multi-factor authentication.

Instead, the recommended best practice is to create an IAM (Identity and Access Management) user with the necessary permissions and generate access keys for that user. This approach limits the scope of access, supports more robust security controls, and protects your account from potentially catastrophic misuse.

You can do this on AWS' IAM page (which you can get to by searching for IAM in the search bar). The exact steps here are prone to change as the AWS UI evolves, but as of the time of writing, clicking Users under Access Management should show you a list of the IAM users that exist and offer up an option to create a new one.

During the user creation process, you'll be prompted to set permissions. When you reach this step, choose the option to attach policies directly. The specific policies (see figure 12.6) you need are:

- `AdministratorAccess-AWSElasticBeanstalk`
- `AmazonEC2FullAccess`
- `AmazonS3FullAccess`

which grant access to ElasticBeanstalk, EC2, and S3, respectively.

Permissions policies (3/1336)

Choose one or more policies to attach to your new user.

	Policy name [↗]		Type
☑	⊞ AmazonEC2FullAccess		AWS managed
☑	⊞ AmazonS3FullAccess		AWS managed
☐	⊞ AWSElasticBeanstalkWebTier		AWS managed
☐	⊞ AWSElasticBeanstalkWorkerTier		AWS managed
☐	⊞ AWSElasticBeanstalkMulticontainerDocker		AWS managed
☐	⊞ AWSElasticBeanstalkEnhancedHealth		AWS managed
☐	⊞ AWSElasticLoadBalancingServiceRolePo...		AWS managed
☐	⊞ AutoScalingServiceRolePolicy		AWS managed
☐	⊞ AWSTrustedAdvisorServiceRolePolicy		AWS managed
☐	⊞ AWSSupportServiceRolePolicy		AWS managed
☑	⊞ AdministratorAccess-AWSElasticBeanstalk		AWS managed

Figure 12.6   Adding the appropriate permissions for an IAM user

Once you've created an IAM user, it should be visible in the Users page. To create an access key for it, click into the user and look for an option to create one. Figure 12.7 shows this option as of the time of writing, and a few other screenshots from this flow.

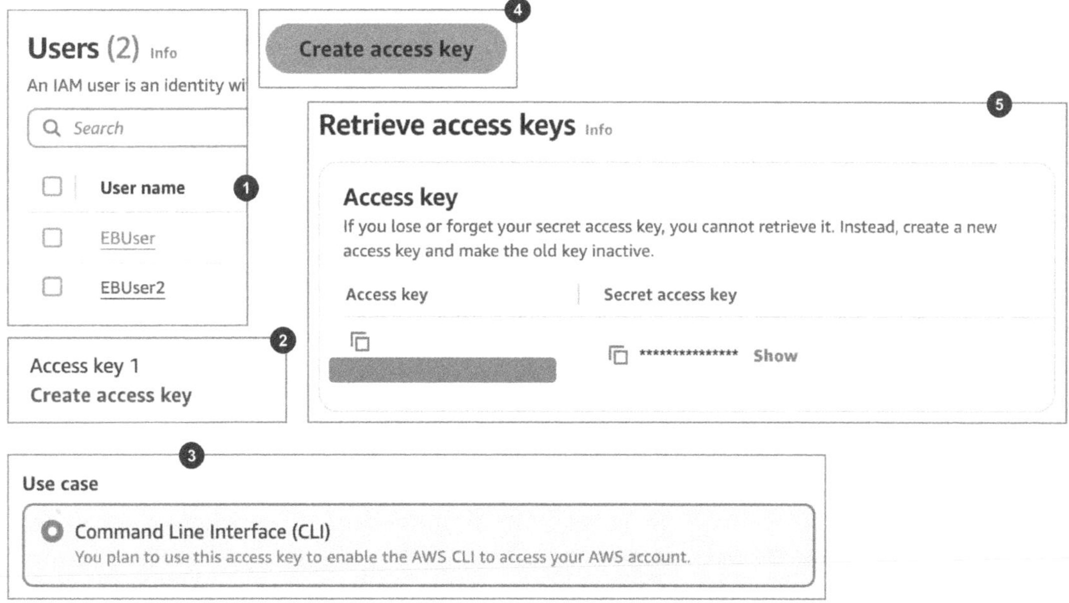

Figure 12.7   Generating an access key and secret pair for an IAM user

When you're done, note down the access-key/secret-access-key pair somewhere safe—you won't be able to access it from AWS again.

CREATING AN EC2 INSTANCE PROFILE

Up next is creating an *instance profile*—a kind of role that we can attach to an EC2 instance to allow it to access various AWS services. As mentioned earlier, we're going to use this to let EC2 interact with S3 and report to Elastic Beanstalk.

Head back to your IAM dashboard, and look for an option to create a new role (you should be able to find Roles under Access Management and then click Create Role). Make the following selections while you're setting up the role:

- Trusted Entity Type: AWS service (since we're creating this on behalf of EC2, which is an AWS service)
- Service or Use Ccase: EC2
- Use Case: EC2

- Permission Policies: `AWSElasticBeanstalkWebTier`
- Role Name: `aws-elasticbeanstalk-ec2-role`

Once this is done, the role you just created should appear under IAM > Roles.

That concludes the AWS setup we need to do on the UI before we can deploy. Let's now shift our attention back to the app for the actual deployment!

> **NOTE** The eagle-eyed reader will notice that though we described *two* sets of required permissions earlier—one for EC2 and another for Elastic Beanstalk—we've only issued permissions for EC2 above. That's because the permissions for Elastic Beanstalk will be created automatically later on when we run the `eb create` command.

12.3.5 *Modifying your app setup for Elastic Beanstalk*

We've already Dockerized our Streamlit app and run it locally within a container using the `docker run` and/or `docker-compose up` commands. However, having the app run in Elastic Beanstalk requires making a few changes.

REPLACING SECRETS.TOML

When we created a Docker Compose configuration (docker-compose.yml) for our app several pages ago, we included the following lines:

```
volumes:
  - ./.streamlit/:/app/.streamlit
```

The point of this was to keep the .streamlit folder outside of our Docker image and mount it into the container at runtime instead. While running `docker-compose up` locally, we could simply keep the .streamlit folder in our current working directory, and Docker could pick it up from there.

However, this approach won't work in Elastic Beanstalk because we won't have direct access to the filesystem to place our .streamlit directory. We need a different way to provide our secrets.toml file to the container.

Elastic Beanstalk provides a solution through a special configuration mechanism called `.ebextensions`. This is a powerful feature that allows us to customize the hosting environment before our application starts. Think of `.ebextensions` as a set of instructions that tell Elastic Beanstalk how to prepare this environment.

To use this feature, we'll create a new directory in our app's root folder called .ebextensions and place configuration files inside it. These files will be automatically processed when we deploy our application to Elastic Beanstalk.

For our specific need of handling secrets, we'll create a configuration file that tells Elastic Beanstalk to create our secrets.toml file at a specific location on the server. Go ahead and make the .ebextensions folder now, and add a file called secrets_file .config with the contents of listing 12.5.

Listing 12.5 .ebextensions/secrets_file.config

```
files:
  "/var/app/secrets/.streamlit/secrets.toml":
    mode: "000644"
    owner: webapp
    group: webapp
    content: |
      llm_api_key = "sk-proj-..."
```

This should be replaced with the content of your actual secrets.toml.

This configuration instructs Elastic Beanstalk to:

- Create a directory path /var/app/secrets/.streamlit/ on the EC2 instance.
- Create a secrets.toml file inside that directory with the exact contents of your existing secrets.toml file; note how we've copied its full text into the content field.
- Set appropriate permissions (644 means the file is readable by all users that have access to the EC2 instance, but only writable by the owner).
- Set the file's owner and group to webapp (the default user Elastic Beanstalk uses).

NOTE Notice the format of the content field. As its value, it requires a pipe (|) symbol followed by the copied contents of the file in the subsequent lines. Indentation is important here; if your secrets.toml has multiple lines, each line needs to have the same level of indentation.

If you like, you can now go ahead and delete the actual .streamlit folder from the app's root folder, though you may want to retain it so you can run your app locally.

EDITING DOCKER-COMPOSE.YML

Now that we have a way to create our secrets file on the server, we need to update our docker-compose.yml to use this new location instead of our local .streamlit directory, as shown in listing 12.6 (chapter_12/in_progress_03/docker-compose.yml in the GitHub repo).

Listing 12.6 An edited docker-compose.yml

```
services:
  fact-frenzy-app:
    build: .
    ports:
      - "80:8501"
    volumes:
      - /var/app/secrets/.streamlit:/app/.streamlit
```

There are two important changes here:

- We've changed the port mapping from 8502:8501 to 80:8501. Elastic Beanstalk expects the application to be accessible on port 80, which is the standard HTTP port.

- We've updated the volume mount to point to the absolute path /var/app/secrets/.streamlit on the server, where the .ebextensions configuration creates the secrets.toml file.

When your application deploys to Elastic Beanstalk, it will first process the `.ebextensions` configurations to set up the environment, then start your containers using the docker-compose.yml file, which will correctly mount the secrets from the location we've prepared (/var/app/secrets/.streamlit).

KEEPING SECRETS_FILE.CONFIG SAFE

Since the configuration file we created in .ebextensions includes everything in our original .streamlit/secrets.toml, we should afford it the same protections we give secrets.toml. This implies the following:

- We should never commit this file to version control. In fact, it's a good idea to add .ebextensions/ to your .gitignore file if you're using Git.
- We should add .ebextensions/ to .dockerignore so it doesn't accidentally get included in your Docker image.

NOTE While you're at it, you should also add .elasticbeanstalk/ to .dockerignore and .gitignore. Though we don't have this directory yet—and won't really refer to it at all in this chapter— running `eb init` in the next section will generate it, so it's best to add the entry now.

12.3.6 *Creating an Elastic Beanstalk app*

The moment we've been waiting for is finally here: the actual deployment to AWS! The EB CLI exposes much of the functionality of Elastic Beanstalk through the terminal, so you don't have to visit the AWS console repeatedly to deploy your app. The `eb init` command that we'll use shortly has an interactive guided flow that takes you through the various options available while creating an application, while `eb create` will perform the actual deployment of your code to an environment within the application.

STAGE 1: INITIALIZATION

To begin, simply go to the root directory of the app and type:

```
eb init
```

This launches an interactive setup wizard to configure your app. This is how Elastic Beanstalk learns what kind of application you're deploying, where you want to host it, what credentials to use, and how to connect to your instance securely. Let's walk through the process step by step, so you understand what's happening and why it matters.

CHOOSING AN AWS REGION

```
Select a default region
1) us-east-1 : US East (N. Virginia)
2) us-west-1 : US West (N. California)
```

```
3) us-west-2 : US West (Oregon)
...
14) us-east-2 : US East (Ohio)
...
(default is 3): 14
```

Elastic Beanstalk asks you to choose a *region*, which is just AWS-speak for a physical data center location. Every AWS service you use lives in one of these regions. Why does this matter? Well, the latency of your app—the time it takes to respond to a user's request— is partly determined by geography.

If you or your users are mostly based in the eastern U.S., then `us-east-2` (Ohio)— the option I've selected above—is a solid choice. If you're targeting users in India, you might pick `ap-south-1` (Mumbai).

ENTERING THE ACCESS KEY

The next step is about authentication:

```
You have not yet set up your credentials or your credentials are incorrect
You must provide your credentials.
(aws-access-id): <enter access ID>
(aws-secret-key): <enter secret key>
```

This is where you establish your identity as an authorized AWS user so the CLI can do things on your behalf. To do this, you provide the AWS access key ID and secret access key you created some time ago for your IAM user. You only need to do this the first time you set up the EB CLI, or if your credentials have changed.

NAMING YOUR APPLICATION

```
Enter Application Name
(default is "<name of folder>"): fact-frenzy
Application fact-frenzy has been created.
```

Every Elastic Beanstalk deployment lives inside an *application*, which contains one or more *environments*. The application name is really just a label to help you group environments that belong together. For instance, you might later create a "production" and a "staging" environment under the same application.

Here, we override the default name (usually the name of the folder you're running `eb init` from) and instead type `fact-frenzy`, which becomes our application name.

IDENTIFYING DOCKER AS THE APP'S PLATFORM

```
It appears you are using Docker. Is this correct?
(Y/n): Y
```

Elastic Beanstalk supports a range of platforms—Node.js, Python, Java, Go, and so on. But in our case, we're deploying a Dockerized app, which means the environment will be created with Docker support.

The EB CLI is smart enough to detect that the project has a Dockerfile and offers to use the Docker platform. We confirm with Y:

```
Select a platform branch.
1) Docker running on 64bit Amazon Linux 2023
2) ECS running on 64bit Amazon Linux 2023
3) Docker running on 64bit Amazon Linux 2
4) ECS running on 64bit Amazon Linux 2
(default is 1): 1
```

Here, you're choosing the specific flavor of Docker you want to run. Option 1 is the latest standard platform as of the time of writing: Docker on Amazon Linux 2023. Let's just go with the default.

SETTING UP SSH

```
Cannot setup CodeCommit because there is no Source Control setup, continuing
with initialization
Do you want to set up SSH for your instances?
(Y/n): Y
```

The line about CodeCommit is just a heads-up. AWS CodeCommit is AWS's own Git hosting service. If you're using Git, you may be prompted to complete this setup, but we'll ignore it here since we want to focus on the deployment.

The next line asks you if you want to set up SSH—Secure Shell—so you can later connect to the EC2 instance that Elastic Beanstalk will create under the hood. While we won't technically need to connect directly to the instance in this chapter, I *strongly* recommend you set this up. Without this, you'll have no direct access to the EC2 instances actually running your app, and will therefore be unable to diagnose and troubleshoot certain problems that may occur.

SSH is essentially a way for you to open a terminal session in a different "remote" computer from your "local" computer so you can enter commands in the remote machine. Doing this securely requires setting up *public key cryptography*, where you have a *private key* on your machine and the corresponding *public key* on the remote machine. The theory behind public key cryptography is beyond the scope of this chapter; suffice it to say that it lets the server verify your identity without ever seeing your private key, which must be kept secret as the name suggests. This keeps your connection both authenticated and encrypted, so only you can log in, and your session stays secure.

Once you enter Y, the CLI will prompt you to create a key pair:

```
Type a keypair name.
(Default is aws-eb):
Generating public/private rsa key pair.
Enter passphrase (empty for no passphrase):
...
WARNING: Uploaded SSH public key for "aws-eb" into EC2 for region us-east-2.
```

This is just the EB CLI setting up the key pair locally and uploading the public part to AWS. When you try to SSH into your instance, AWS will check that you have the private key before letting you in.

With that, you're done with initialization. But to complete the deployment, you need to create an environment within the app.

> **NOTE** This book does not actually cover connecting to your EC2 instance via SSH. If you run into trouble here, refer to the AWS docs at https://docs.aws .amazon.com/ (search for something like "connect to ec2 instance via ssh")

STAGE 2: ENVIRONMENT CREATION AND DEPLOYMENT

Now that your application is initialized, go ahead and run:

```
eb create
```

This command spins up a wizard that puts together everything needed to serve the app: EC2 instances, a load balancer, networking rules, monitoring, and more.

As before, let's go through what's asked.

> **NOTE** By default, the `eb create` will create a load-balanced app which distributes traffic between multiple EC2 instances. Load balancers are not covered by the AWS free tier, so if you're anxious about staying within the free tier, you could opt for a single-instance deployment without a load balancer. To do so, you would use the command `eb create --single --instance-type t2.micro`. Note that you should still check AWS' Billing and Cost Management page to keep an eye on your true costs.

NAMING THE ENVIRONMENT

```
Enter Environment Name
(default is fact-frenzy-dev): fact-frenzy-prod
```

Elastic Beanstalk environments represent live instances of an app. For example, you might choose one environment for development, one for staging, and another for production. Here, we go with `fact-frenzy-prod`. Choose whatever makes sense for your workflow.

CHOOSING A DNS NAME

```
Enter DNS CNAME prefix
(default is fact-frenzy-env-1): fact-frenzy
```

Elastic Beanstalk gives your app a public URL. The DNS prefix you choose here becomes the subdomain. So if you enter `fact-frenzy`, and the region you chose when you ran `eb init` is `us-east-2`, your app will be reachable at:

```
http://fact-frenzy.us-east-2.elasticbeanstalk.com
```

This is great for testing and demos. Later in the chapter, we'll also attach a custom domain.

PICKING A LOAD BALANCER TYPE

```
Select a load balancer type
1) classic
2) application
3) network
(default is 2): 2
```

Elastic Beanstalk uses *load balancers* to distribute traffic across multiple instances of your app. Stick with the default, i.e., application. This will create an *application load balancer* that supports modern features like *SSL termination*, which we'll explore soon.

FINALIZING THE DEPLOYMENT

```
Would you like to enable Spot Fleet requests for this environment? (y/N): N
```

Spot instances are cheaper EC2 instances that AWS can reclaim at any time. They're great for batch jobs or non-critical environments, but for a web app that needs to stay online, it's safer to say N.

```
2.0+ Platforms require a service role. We will attempt to create one for you.
You can specify your own role using the --service-role option.
Type "view" to see the policy, or just press ENTER to continue:
```

Remember, earlier in this chapter, when we created an EC2 instance profile but *didn't* create a service role for Elastic Beanstalk? The reason we didn't bother with it *then* is that the eb create wizard can do it for us automatically *now*. Simply press Enter as suggested, and the CLI will take care of it.

Elastic Beanstalk now has everything it needs to set our app live, which it will now proceed to do.

```
Creating application version archive "app-250323_164015228511".
Uploading fact-frenzy/app-250323_164015228511.zip to S3. This may take a while.
Upload Complete.
...
Printing Status:
2025-03-23 23:40:17    INFO    createEnvironment is starting.
...
Application available at fact-frenzy.us-east-2.elasticbeanstalk.com
Successfully launched environment: fact-frenzy-prod
```

This part can take a few minutes. Behind the scenes, Elastic Beanstalk will:

- Package the app into a zip file
- Upload it to an S3 bucket

- Create EC2 instances and set up the app using a Dockerfile
- Configure the load balancer
- Set up a security group, essentially a virtual firewall that controls traffic to and from EC2 instances
- Set up an auto-scaling group—a collection of EC2 instances that work to scale your app automatically based on utilization
- Wire up CloudWatch—an AWS service that monitors your app
- And finally, launch the app!

When it's done, you'll see the URL where the app is now available:

```
Application available at fact-frenzy.us-east-2.elasticbeanstalk.com
```

You can now either visit the URL in your browser or simply issue the command `eb open` to view your newly deployed app.

Your application and environment should now also be visible on the Elastic Beanstalk site in the AWS Management Console (see figure 12.8). As always, you can get to the right page by searching for it in the console search bar.

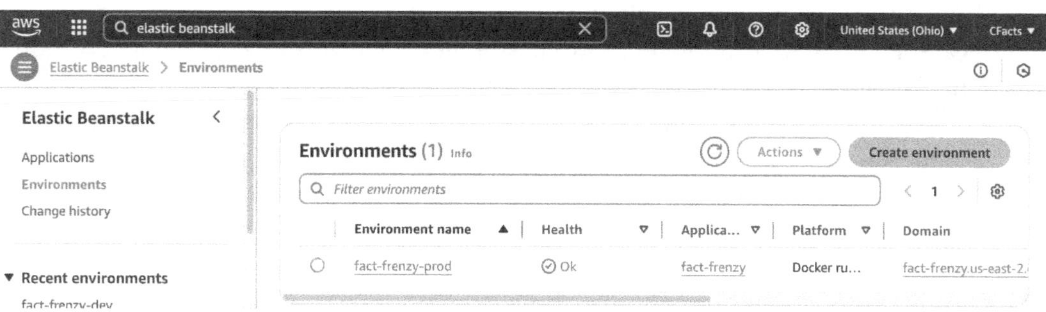

Figure 12.8 Our application and environment within the Elastic Beanstalk UI on the AWS console

MAKING CHANGES

One of the reasons we chose to use the CLI instead of the web UI for deploying your app is that this approach makes it quite easy to redeploy your app when you make code changes. Whenever you update your app, all you need to do to reflect the changes in Elastic Beanstalk is to enter the following command from your app's directory.

```
eb deploy
```

Try it out now! Make any small change to your Streamlit app and issue the above command. You should see a few status messages like:

```
Creating application version archive "app-250323_164631566504".
Uploading fact-frenzy/app-250323_164631566504.zip to S3. This may take a while.
Upload Complete.
2025-03-23 23:46:33    INFO    Environment update is starting.
2025-03-23 23:46:36    INFO    Deploying new version to instance(s).
2025-03-23 23:46:50    INFO    Instance deployment completed successfully.
2025-03-23 23:46:54    INFO    New application version was deployed to
running EC2 instances.
2025-03-23 23:46:54    INFO    Environment update completed successfully.
```

And that's all! The re-deployment process should be done in a couple of minutes, and
your app should then show the changes.

12.4   Adding a custom domain and HTTPS

Now that your app is live on Elastic Beanstalk, you can share the link with friends, colleagues, or the world! But let's be honest—http://fact-frenzy.us-east-2.elasticbeanstalk
.com isn't exactly the most memorable or professional-looking URL.

Another problem is that, by default, your app is only served over HTTP. That
means data sent between your users and your app isn't *encrypted,* which is a security
risk, especially if you ever plan to handle logins or sensitive data. For example, if
a user signs in by typing their email and password into a login form, those details
could be intercepted by someone snooping on the network, like on public Wi-Fi at a
cafe. Without HTTPS, there's nothing stopping an attacker from seeing that traffic
in plain text.

Modern browsers will often flag HTTP sites as Not Secure, and some may even block
them altogether. In this section, you'll learn how to give your app a "real" web address
like www.factfrenzyapp.com and secure it with HTTPS so visitors can interact with your
app *without* their identities being stolen and sold on the dark web, which is always a nice
bonus.

12.4.1   Adding a domain

Before we can enable HTTPS and give our app a more polished, professional presence, we need a custom domain—something that's short, memorable, and easy to
share. If you already own a domain, great, you can use it. If not, this is a good time to
register one.

> **NOTE** You could technically add HTTPS to your Elastic Beanstalk app *with-
> out* getting a custom domain, but that comes with major caveats. To add
> HTTPS, you need an SSL certificate for your app's domain signed by a Cer-
> tificate Authority—as we'll see in a bit. CAs won't issue an SSL certificate for
> the default .elasticbeanstalk.com domain since Amazon owns it and you can't
> prove you control it. You could get around this with a self-signed certificate,
> but most modern browsers will then flag your site as insecure and try to warn
> people away from it.

BUYING A DOMAIN

To buy a domain, you need to pick a *domain registrar* that can check if your chosen name is available, handle the purchase process, and set up your web address so it works properly on the internet.

There are many such registrars to choose from—GoDaddy, Namecheap, Squarespace Domains (formerly Google Domains), and Cloudflare, to name a few. You could also register a domain with AWS' own Route 53 service. I personally like Cloudflare since, at the time of writing, they offer new domain registration at-cost with (reportedly) no markup or hidden costs, but the process is largely the same regardless of which one you go with:

- Search for the domain name you want
- Provide payment information to register it

NOTE You should be able to get a domain for less than $20 a year. If you choose a domain that ends in something niche like .online, it can be cheaper, while something that ends in .io or .ai would be more expensive. Cloudflare charged me about $11 for a .com domain.

Once the purchase is complete, your registrar should give you access to a DNS (Domain Name System) management dashboard, where you can configure how your chosen domain behaves.

POINTING A DOMAIN TO ELASTIC BEANSTALK

Now that you have a domain, the next step is to configure it so that when people visit the address, it'll take them to your Elastic Beanstalk app. To do this, you'll need to update your domain's *DNS* settings.

DNS—short for Domain Name System—is like a phone book for the internet. It's what helps browsers figure out which server to contact when someone types in a web address. Within your DNS settings, you'll add a *CNAME record*, which is basically a type of *DNS entry* that says, "When someone goes to this domain, redirect them to this *other* address". In this case, we want the following redirection to take place:

```
www.factfrenzyapp.com -> fact-frenzy.us-east-2.elasticbeanstalk.com
```

You can usually do this by going to your domain's DNS settings (in your Cloudflare—or other DNS provider—account), and adding a new record with the following options:

- Type / DNS Record Type: `CNAME`
- Name / Host: `www`
- Target / Value: `fact-frenzy.us-east-2.elasticbeanstalk.com`

Obviously, you'll need to change this based on your own Elastic Beanstalk URL. Figure 12.9 shows this in Cloudflare's UI. The path to accomplish this for your chosen provider may vary, of course.

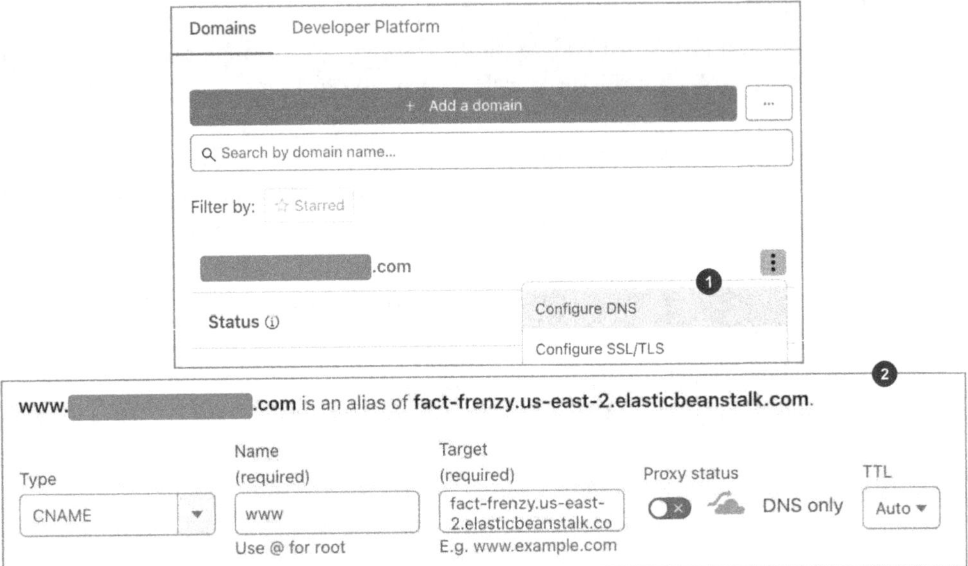

Figure 12.9   Adding a CNAME record to point your custom domain to your app.

If there's a proxying or forwarding option (e.g., see Proxy Status in figure 12.9), turn it off for now so as not to complicate things.

Once this is done, requests to www.factfrenzyapp.com—or whatever your domain is—will be redirected to your Streamlit app running on AWS. Try visiting it now.

NOTE   Don't panic if the domain doesn't direct you to your app immediately after you add the CNAME record. It could take a few minutes to an hour for DNS changes to propagate through the system.

12.4.2 Creating a certificate

With your custom domain now pointing to your app, there's one more important step before it's ready for the real world: making sure it's secure. Right now, if someone visits your app using a browser, they're using the HTTP protocol, which means their connection is not encrypted. Any communication sent between your users and your app is vulnerable to prying eyes. To fix this, we want to enable something called HTTPS. The "S" stands for secure, and it means that all communication is encrypted.

WHAT IS A CERTIFICATE?

To allow a secure HTTPS connection, a browser needs to see proof that the server it's communicating with really does belong to your domain—the alternative being that someone is intercepting your connection in a *man-in-the-middle* attack, redirecting traffic to their servers where they can view or modify all data being exchanged between your users and what they think is your website.

This proof comes in the form of a *digital certificate*, which serves as an identity document for your website. Without this certificate, the browser can't establish a secure connection, and users will either see a warning or be blocked from visiting your site.

A browser will only fully trust a certificate if it is issued by a trusted *Certificate Authority* (CA)—which will only do so once it has verified that you actually control the domain.

REQUESTING A CERTIFICATE WITH AWS CERTIFICATE MANAGER

Fortunately, AWS provides a free tool called AWS Certificate Manager (ACM) that can talk to a CA on your behalf, generate a certificate for you, and auto-renew it periodically so you don't have to think about it.

Go to the AWS Management Console now and navigate to Certificate Manager. As always, you can find it quickly by searching for it in the top bar. Once there, look for an option to request a certificate (like a Request Certificate button), and follow the instructions. You'll need to make the following choices along the way (figure 12.10):

- Certificate Type: Request a public certificate, not a private one
- Fully Qualified Domain Name: Enter your app's custom domain, e.g., www .factfrenzyapp.com (feel free to also include just the domain name—without the www—to cover them both under the same certificate)
- Validation Method: DNS validation
- Key Algorithm: RSA 2048

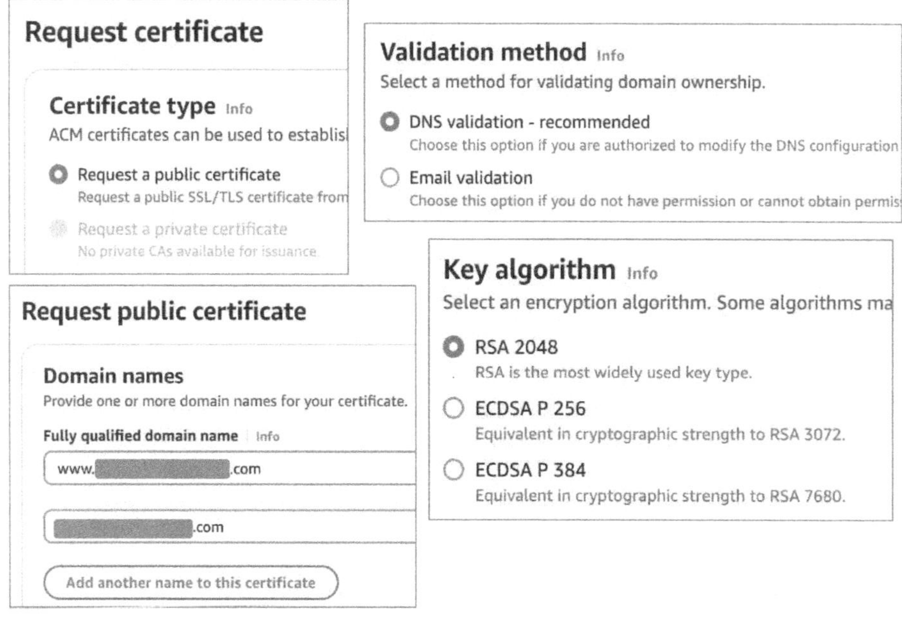

Figure 12.10 Options to choose while requesting a certificate in ACM.

On the next screen, you should see that a certificate has been issued, but that it's "pending validation."

PROVING YOU OWN THE DOMAIN

To complete the certificate issuance, you need to prove to AWS that you actually own the domain you've requested a certificate for—this is the validation that's "pending."

On the same page (see figure 12.11), you should see the domain you've requested and a couple of CNAME entries.

Figure 12.11   ACM shows CNAME records to add to your domain's DNS to prove ownership.

The way you provide proof of domain ownership is by adding these CNAME entries to your domain's DNS configuration in the same way that you created the www entry when you pointed your domain to the app in a prior section.

For example, the CNAME record suggested by AWS might be:

- CNAME name: `_60be6cf64d...www.factfrenzyapp.com`
- CNAME value: `_23eb2...xlfg...acm-validations.aws.`

You would add another entry into your DNS provider's website (e.g., Cloudflare) for your domain like this:

- Type / DNS Record Type: CNAME
- Name / Host: `_60be6cf64d...www.factfrenzyapp.com`
- Target / Value: `_23eb2...xlfg...acm-validations.aws`

Once you've done this, in a few minutes to an hour, AWS will hit the validation record and confirm that you control the domain, at which point your certificate's status will change from Pending Validation to Issued.

12.4.3 Adding the certificate to your load balancer

At this point, your domain points to your Elastic Beanstalk app, and AWS has issued a certificate that proves your app is allowed to use HTTPS. Now, we need to actually *attach* that certificate to your app's infrastructure—specifically to the load balancer that Elastic Beanstalk created for you behind the scenes when you ran the `eb create` command.

WHAT'S A LOAD BALANCER, AGAIN?

A load balancer is a piece of infrastructure that sits between your users and your app. It distributes incoming traffic between the EC2 instances serving the app, which helps keep things scalable and reliable. For instance, if one instance becomes overloaded or fails, the load balancer automatically redirects traffic to healthy instances, preventing downtime and ensuring that users experience consistent performance.

The load balancer is also the perfect place to handle HTTPS connections. Instead of making your app deal with encryption directly, we'll configure the load balancer to handle secure connections and then forward the traffic to your app.

NOTE If you created a single-instance non-load-balanced environment to save on costs earlier in the chapter, you can still technically enable HTTPS on your app, but the process is fairly complicated and out of the scope of this chapter.

ATTACHING THE CERTIFICATE

To add the certificate to your app, we'll use Elastic Beanstalk's web UI. Go to the AWS Management Console and search for Elastic Beanstalk. Once there, click into your application and the `fact-frenzy-prod` environment you created. Find the Configuration page (which should be on the left bar under your environment).

Next, go to the Instance Traffic and Scaling section and click the Edit button. If you scroll down, you should see a sub-section called Listeners where you can specify the ports the load balancer will listen on. At the moment, there should be just one listener port—80, for regular unencrypted HTTP traffic. Add a new listener to this list with the following configuration (figure 12.12):

- Listener Port: 443, which is the default port for HTTPS
- Listener Protocol: HTTPS
- SSL Certificate: Choose the certificate you just created in ACM from the dropdown
- SSL Policy: `ELBSecurityPolicy-2016-08`; this setting specifies things like what versions of SSL (Secure Sockets Layer) and what encryption algorithms are allowed—you could also choose a later policy with the caveat that some older browsers may not be supported.
- Default Process: default

Once you save the listener and apply your settings (click Apply at the bottom), your environment will update—you can watch the process in the environment's page in Elastic Beanstalk.

When it's done, head over to https://www.factfrenzyapp.com (or whatever your domain actually is)—notice the "s" in https://. As in the example shown in figure 12.13, you should see some indication in your browser that the connection is now secure.

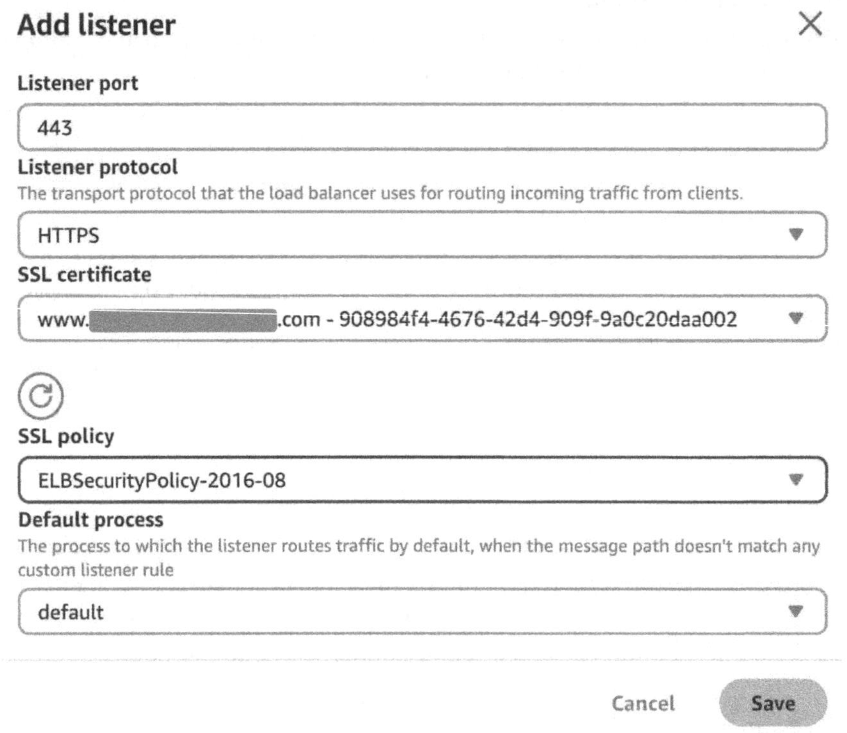

Add listener
Listener port
443
Listener protocol
The transport protocol that the load balancer uses for routing incoming traffic from clients.
HTTPS
SSL certificate
www.[redacted].com - 908984f4-4676-42d4-909f-9a0c20daa002
SSL policy
ELBSecurityPolicy-2016-08
Default process
The process to which the listener routes traffic by default, when the message path doesn't match any custom listener rule
default
Cancel
Save

Figure 12.12 Adding an HTTPS listener and a certificate to the load balancer

[redacted].com
Davis7_Streamlit i...
SIA review feedback
[redacted].com
Connection is secure
Cookies and site data
Site settings
About this page
Learn about its source and topic
Fact Frenzy
Settings
Start new game

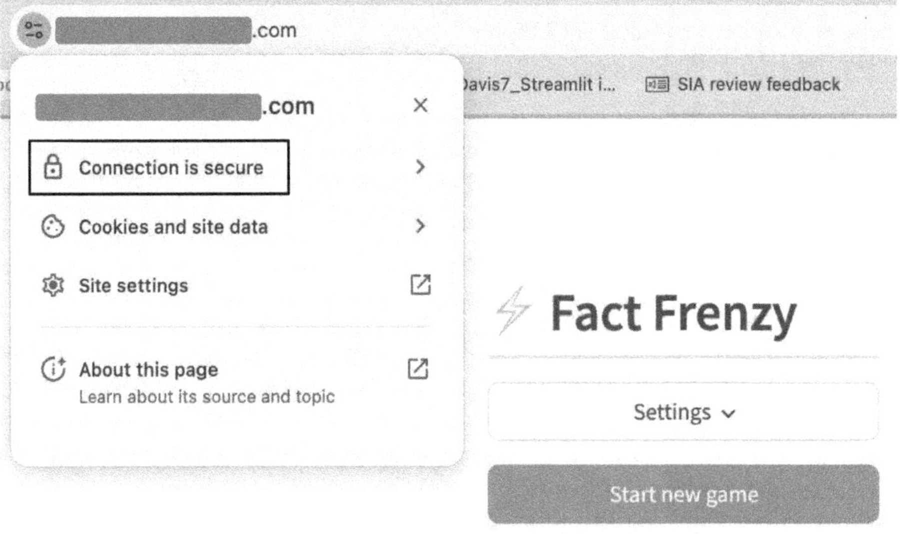

Figure 12.13 The browser now confirms that HTTPS is enabled and the connection is secure.

You're now serving a Streamlit app over HTTPS on a custom domain. It not only looks more professional, but it also gives users confidence that their data is protected.

12.5 Go forth and develop!

We began this journey with a simple but powerful idea: pure-Python web apps in minutes. If you know Python, you should be able to build and share interactive applications—quickly, intuitively, and beautifully. Streamlit makes that possible.

Throughout this book, we've seen how Streamlit transforms what Python developers can make. Instead of static notebooks or opaque command-line tools, you now have the ability to create engaging, responsive web apps. From to-do list apps to data dashboards, from CRUD interfaces to trivia games and AI-powered support bots, we've built real, working projects that go far beyond toy examples.

Along the way, we didn't just focus on walking through the features of Streamlit—we focused on *good software*. You've learned how to design with users in mind, how to separate concerns for maintainability, and how to test and deploy your work. We've talked about practical trade-offs—from cost optimization to scalability concerns. We even saw how Streamlit can tap into the wondrous world of generative AI to build experiences that wouldn't have been possible a few years ago.

But now it's up to you to take what you've learned and run with it. You might use Streamlit to make life easier for your coworkers, replacing spreadsheet hell with a sleek internal tool. Or maybe you'll use it to whip up a quick prototype for a startup idea, explore a data set that's been puzzling you, or present insights to an executive team in a compelling way. Or maybe you'll build something the rest of us haven't even imagined yet.

If you're hungry to keep learning, there's a wide world waiting for you beyond Streamlit. You might deepen your Python skills by diving deeper into data visualization libraries or writing your own packages. If you enjoyed building apps, you could explore software design patterns and architecture principles that are essential to developing robust, collaborative projects. Curious about the frontend? Maybe it's time to take the leap into full frontend development after all—picking up HTML, CSS, and JavaScript, or modern frameworks like React to gain full control over the client side of your apps.

Where you go next depends on your goals—but one thing is clear: in Streamlit, you have a powerful launchpad, a tool that can help you build faster, share better, and iterate more boldly. So go forth and develop. You're just getting started!

Summary

- Streamlit Community Cloud, though free, comes with several limitations, such as resource limits, lack of support for a custom domain, and idle app shutdowns.
- There is a wide range of alternatives to choose from: low-complexity platforms like Render, medium-complexity options like Elastic Beanstalk, and even high-complexity ones like hand-configuring raw AWS services like EC2.
- Docker is a tool that makes it possible to package your app so it runs anywhere.

- To use Docker, you write a Dockerfile, build a Docker image from it, and spin up Docker containers from the image.
- A Dockerfile has instructions to build an image layer by layer.
- Streamlit offers configuration options that can be set using environment variables, a special config.toml file, or as flags in the `streamlit run` command.
- The `docker build` command builds an image, while `docker run` spins up a container.
- Docker Compose is a configuration manager for Docker, where you define the runtime instructions in a docker-compose.yml file.
- AWS is the world's leading cloud provider, offering services like EC2 for virtual machines and S3 for storage.
- Elastic Beanstalk is a layer on top of raw AWS services like EC2 and S3 that automatically configures these services, making app deployment easy.
- You can use Identity and Access Management within AWS to set up permissions for services like EC2 and Elastic Beanstalk to perform various tasks.
- While preparing a Streamlit app for Elastic Beanstalk, specify the content of secrets.toml in a file within the .ebextensions folder rather than placing it with the code.
- You can use the EB CLI to interact with Elastic Beanstalk in a terminal.
- The `eb init` command sets up an EB application; `eb create` creates an environment under it.
- Use the `eb deploy` command to redeploy the app when making changes.
- To add HTTPS to an EB app (without browser warnings), get a custom domain from a domain registrar.
- AWS Certificate Manager will issue an SSL certificate for the domain once you verify ownership.
- To complete the process of enabling HTTPS, add a listener to the load balancer on port 443 and attach the issued certificate.

appendix
Installing Python
and Streamlit

This appendix covers

- How to check the iinstalled Python version (if any)
- Installing Python on macOS and Windows
- Using `pip` to install Streamlit

Depending on the operating system, you may need to follow slightly different steps to get Streamlit working. This guide covers these steps for the two dominant desktop operating systems—macOS and Windows.

A.1   *Checking the current Python version*

Streamlit supports Python versions 3.10 and above, so if you have an older version, you need to install a newer one. To check the Python version installed on your system, or whether Python is installed at all, open a terminal window (Terminal on macOS and Command Prompt or, better yet, PowerShell on Windows) and enter:

```
python --version
```

or

```
python -V
```

NOTE   The -V is case-sensitive (it's a capital V, not a small v).

If you don't have Python installed, this will give you some kind of error, like:

```
'python': command not found
```

or

```
'python' is not recognized as an internal or external command, operable
program or batch file.
```

or

```
'Python' was not found; run without arguments to install from the Microsoft
Store
```

If you *do* have Python installed, the command returns a version number like this:

```
Python 3.7.3
```

If this version number is 3.10 or above (e.g., 3.10.0 or 3.12.2), you're good. If it's lower than 3.10 (as shown here), install a later version.

A.2   *Installing the right Python version*

This section provides instructions on how to install the right version of Python on Windows and macOS.

A.2.1   *Windows*

If you're using Windows, you can install Python from the Microsoft Store. To do this, open the Microsoft Store and search for "python." As shown in figure A.1, the search

Figure A.1   A search for "python" in the Microsoft Store offers an easy way to install the latest Python.

returns several versions of Python. Select the latest version available (in this case, Python 3.12) and click Get.

Once the process finishes, enter `python -V` in the Command Prompt again to see whether the command now reports the version you have just installed as the default Python version. If it does, great! If it gives you an older version, the easiest way to proceed is to uninstall that version. You can do this in the Settings app by going to Apps & Features. If you type `python -V` now, you should be able to see the newer version.

A.2.2 *macOS*

Python comes pre-installed on macOS, so if you're here, you probably need to install a newer version.

You can do this in severel ways, but one of the easiest is to visit https://www.python.org/downloads/macos/ and download an installer. On that page, pick the installer for the latest version listed under Stable Releases. For instance, in figure A.2, you would click "Download macOS 64-bit universal2 installer" under Python 3.12.4.

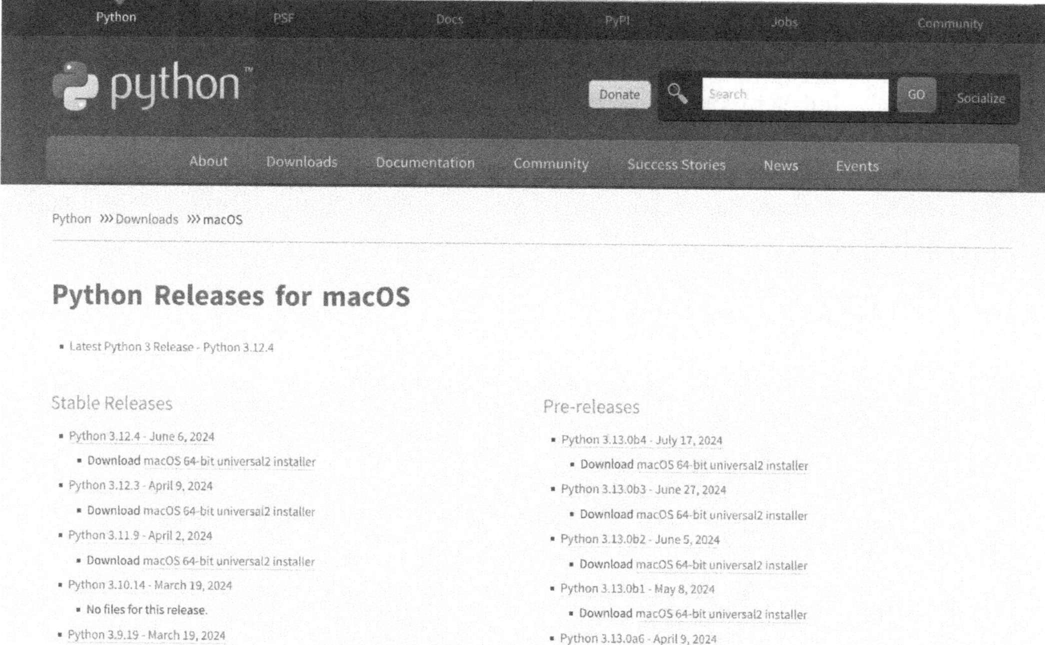

Figure A.2 The URL https://www.python.org/downloads/macos/ gives you a link to download Python on macOS.

Once the download is done, open the installer and follow the on-screen instructions.

When the installation is complete, open Terminal and type `python -V` again. If the command displays the version you installed, you're done. Otherwise, you'll need to perform a few extra steps to ensure that typing `python` or `pip` in the command line calls the correct version. Again, there are multiple ways to do this, but here's an easy one:

1 Type `nano ~/.bash_profile` to open the text file .bash_profile in a text editor.

2 At the bottom, append the lines shown here:

```
alias python=python3.12
alias pip=pip3.12
```

NOTE   Replace the version numbers in these lines with the version you actually installed. For example, if you installed Python 3.11, write `python3.11` and `pip3.11`.

3 Restart the terminal

When you type `python -V`, you should see the right version.

A.2.3   *What if I want multiple Python versions on my system?*

It's quite common for Python developers to install more than one version of Python, especially when working on multiple projects. Managing this can be painful, so if you're on this path, I recommend the tool `pyenv` (or `pyenv-win` for Windows). Detailed installation instructions are out of the scope of this appendix, but you can find them at https://github.com/pyenv/pyenv (and https://github.com/pyenv-win/pyenv-win for `pyenv-win`).

Once you have `pyenv`, it's really easy to install, manage, and switch between different versions of Python. For instance, to see which versions of Python are currently installed, you could type

```
pyenv versions
```

To install Python 3.12.2, type:

```
pyenv install 3.12.2
```

To switch to that version of Python, run:

```
pyenv global 3.12.2
```

And to switch back:

```
pyenv global system
```

Easy peasy.

A.3   *Installing Streamlit*

Once you have Python installed, you can use `pip` to install Streamlit. `pip` (a recursive acronym for Pip Installs Packages) is a package manager for Python, used to install and manage Python libraries. It comes bundled with Python starting with version 3.4, so as long as you've followed the Python installation instructions above, you don't have to install `pip` separately.

Once you have `pip`, adding popular third-party libraries (like Streamlit) to your Python installation becomes simple; you just have to type the following in your terminal:

```
pip install <package_name>
```

So, to install Streamlit, you would type:

```
pip install streamlit
```

To execute this command, `pip` will find the latest version of the Streamlit library compatible with your version of Python and install it, along with its dependencies.

You may also sometimes want to install a *specific* version of a library. In such cases, you can add that condition to your command. For example, to install version 1.23.0 of Streamlit:

```
pip install streamlit==1.23.0
```

Perhaps more commonly, you may want to specify a *minimum* version of the library to install, for instance, if you are relying on a feature that was introduced in that version. This is as simple as: `pip install streamlit>=1.32.0` (to install a version of Streamlit that's at least 1.32.0).

Once this is done, try the following if you're on macOS to see what version of Streamlit you have installed:

```
pip list | grep streamlit
```

or the following if you're on Windows:

```
pip list | findstr streamlit
```

This should give you output similar to the following:

```
streamlit                1.33.0
```

This signals that Streamlit has been installed correctly as a Python module. However, one more step is needed before we can effortlessly run Streamlit apps.

A.4 Getting the streamlit command to work

When you start creating Streamlit apps, you'll be running them using the `streamlit run` command in a terminal window, like this:

```
streamlit run <path to filename.py>
```

The `streamlit` module may already be installed correctly, but you *may* need to perform additional steps to get this command to work. First, type the following to check if it's already working:

```
streamlit --version
```

You should see something similar to the following:

```
Streamlit, version 1.33.0
```

If you see this (or a different version number), the `streamlit` command is already working, and you can skip the rest of this section.

If instead you see a message that "streamlit" is not recognized as a command, you'll need to take further steps. The problem is that your computer doesn't know the command "streamlit" yet. You need to tell it where to find it by adding the path to the command in an *environment variable*. The steps to do this differ by operating system.

A.4.1   *Editing environment variables on Windows*

To start, figure out where the `streamlit` executable is installed on the computer. For this, open a new Python shell by typing `python` at the command line. Then enter the following:

```
>>> import os
>>> import streamlit
>>> print(os.path.dirname(streamlit.__file__))
```

The last command should give you a path to a file on your computer. For example, when I typed it, I got:

```
C:\Users\Aneev Kochakadan\AppData\Local\Packages\PythonSoftwareFoundation
.Python.3.12_qbz5n2kfra8p0\LocalCache\local-packages\Python312\site-packages\
streamlit
```

This is the path where the `streamlit` module is installed, which is not quite what we're looking for. What we need is the path to the directory that contains the `streamlit` *executable*, which we can derive by replacing the ending `site-packages\streamlit` from the path above with `Scripts`. In my case, the path to the executable was:

```
C:\Users\Aneev Kochakadan\AppData\Local\Packages\PythonSoftwareFoundation
.Python.3.12_qbz5n2kfra8p0\LocalCache\local-packages\Python312\Scripts
```

We now need to add this path to the `Path` environment variable. To do this, first open the Start menu and search for Environment Variables. Then select Edit the System

Environment Variables. This should open up the Advanced tab in the System Properties dialog, as shown in figure A.3.

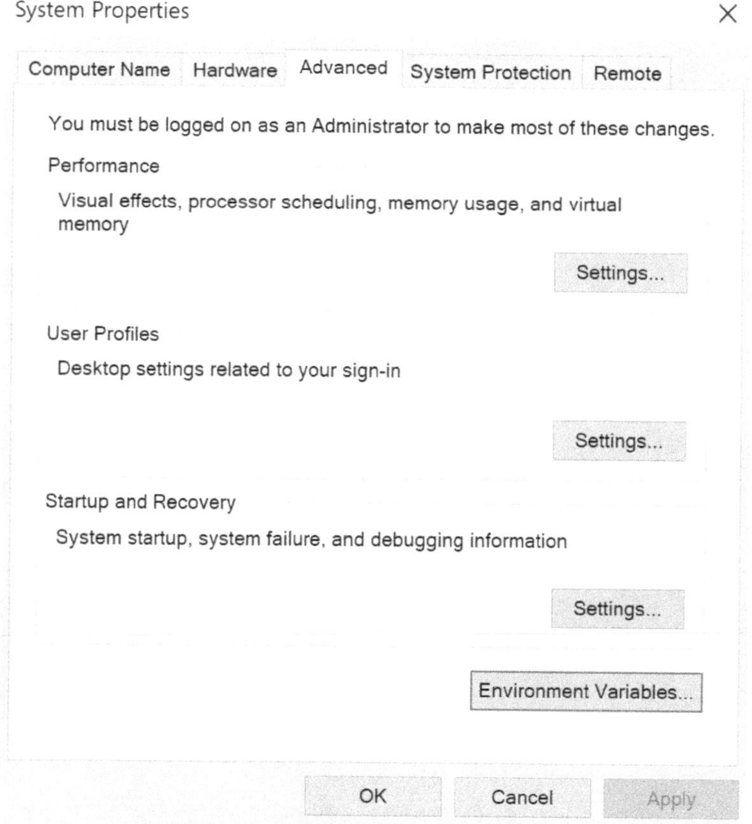

Figure A.3   The Advanced tab in the System Properties dialog has a button at the bottom to manage your environment variables.

Click Environment Variables… at the bottom to see a list of your current environment variables. The one we care about is the `Path` variable under your User Variables (the top box), so go ahead and select that one and click Edit… (figure A.4).

In the dialog that now opens up, click New and enter the path you noted earlier (in my case, it was `C:\Users\Aneev Kochakadan\AppData\Local\Packages\PythonSoftware-Foundation.Python.3.12_qbz5n2kfra8p0\LocalCache\local-packages\Python312\Scripts`), as shown in figure A.5.

Click OK to apply the changes and close the window. Restart your terminal and try entering `streamlit --version` again. This time, it should give you a version number, which means that the `streamlit` command is now working.

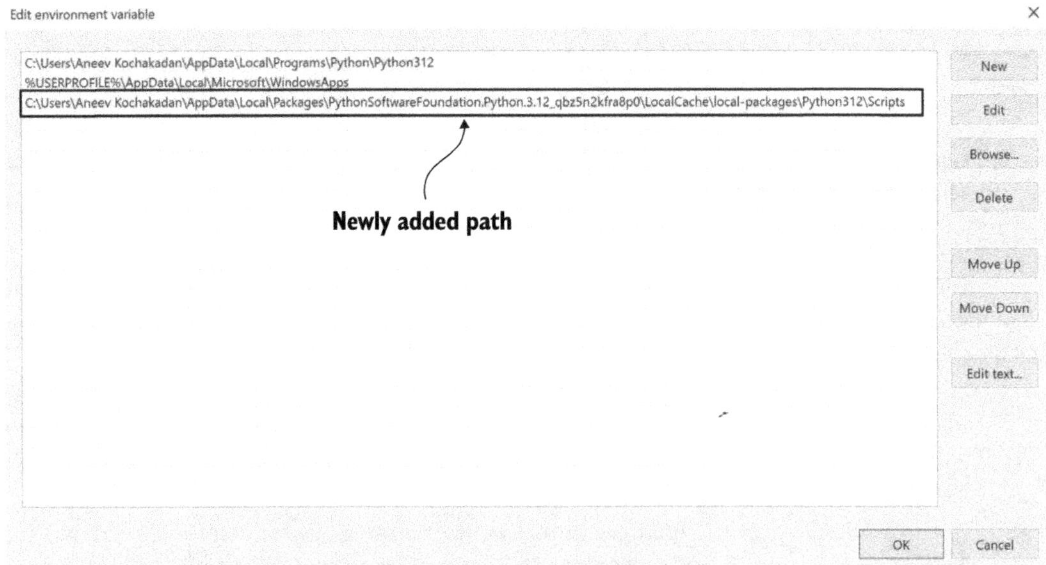

Figure A.4   The `Path` **environment variable is the one we need to edit.**

Figure A.5   You can add a new path to the `Path` **environment variable by clicking New.**

A.4.2 *Editing environment variables on macOS*

On macOS, just as in Windows, we first need to find where the `streamlit` executable is, so go ahead and open a Python shell by typing `python` in a terminal, and then enter the following commands:

```
>>> import os
>>> import streamlit
>>> print(os.path.dirname(streamlit.__file__))
```

This should print a path to where the `streamlit` module is installed. For example, on my computer, I saw:

```
/Library/Frameworks/Python.framework/Versions/3.12/lib/python3.12/site
-packages/streamlit
```

This is the path to where the `streamlit` module is installed. The path we really need, however, is the path to the `streamlit` executable, which we can get by replacing `lib/python3.12/site-packages/streamlit` at the end of the above path with `bin`. In my case, this works out to be:

```
/Library/Frameworks/Python.framework/Versions/3.12/bin
```

To wrap up, add this path to the `PATH` environment variable by following these steps:

1 Type `nano ~/.bash_profile` to open the file .bash_profile in a text editor.
2 At the bottom, append the following lines:

```
PATH="/Library/Frameworks/Python.framework/Versions/3.12/bin:${PATH}"
export PATH
```

Restart your terminal window and enter `streamlit --version`. It should work this time and give the version number you installed.

B

backend
  implementing 51, 55, 57
  unit converter app 60
  unit testing 373–382
BaseModel class 282
bcrypt library 244
BFS (breadth-first search) 318
BigQuery, supercharging dashboards with 212–220
  creating service account 216
  deployment to Streamlit Community Cloud 219
  enabling BigQuery and BigQuery Storage APIs 216
  generating secrets.toml 217
  getting data into BigQuery 213
  setting up Python-BigQuery connection 216–217
  updating dashboard to load data from BigQuery 217–219
boolean indexing 154
brainstorming, implementation 36

C

CA (Certificate Authority) 431
caching data, st.cache_data 146–148
callables, defined 160
CEO dashboards
  calculating and displaying metrics 158–164
  metrics dashboards 136–140
  prepping and filtering data 148–158
certificates 430–432
chatbots, creating 317–329
  graphs, nodes, edges, and state 318–329
  one-node LLM graph 320–329
chat completions endpoint 277
chat method 327
checkboxes, for tasks 78
checkpointers 330
chunks of text 345
CI (continuous integration) 396
closures, defined 325
code
  editors 22
  reusability 54
  writing 36

columns 225
  configurations 306
  selection 149
  specifications 230
Community Cloud, deploying to 267
concepts
  requirements 38–39
  stating 36
conditional edge 359
conditional formatting 201
configuration file 43
containers, defined 403
context window length 340
conversations, multi-turn 329–334
  adding memory to graph 330–333
  displaying conversation history 333
conversion factors 43
converting units 41–42
cosine similarity 343
cost considerations 304
CRUD (create, read, update, and delete) apps 221
  building with Streamlit 257–266
  creating, reading, updating, and deleting haikus 257
  creating user accounts 242–248
  deploying 267
  Haiku Haven 222–225
  multi-page login flow 249–257
  setting up multi-page login flow 249
  setting up persistent storage 225–241
CSS (Cascading Style Sheets) 6, 17
CSV (Comma-Separated Values) 137
custom domains 428–430
  adding 428–430
  adding certificate to load balancer 432
  buying 429
  creating certificate 430–432
  pointing to Elastic Beanstalk 429
customer service bots 314–317
  brainstorming implementation 315
  installing dependencies 317
  stating concept and requirements 314–315
  visualizing user experience 315
customer support, restricting bots to 334–339
  creating base prompt 335
  inserting base context node in graph 336–339

D